Magone's book is a splendid and extremely welcome contribution to our knowledge of how democracies operate. Earlier statistical research had already suggested that consensus democracies showed superior policy performance as well as democratic quality. Because Magone's work is an in-depth comparative analysis of relatively few key cases, it presents a particularly powerful reinforcement of this proposition. These five democracies have been admirably resilient in spite of the impact of Europeanization and globalization. The evidence favoring consensus democracy is now overwhelming. It contains crucially important lessons for political engineers who write constitutions for new democracies or try to improve existing democratic systems. Consensus democracy is also the most attractive model for the European Union as it moves toward becoming a true federation. I recommend Magone's book with great enthusiasm to both scholars and practical decision-makers.

Professor Arend Lijphart, *University of California San Diego, USA*

The Statecraft of Consensus Democracies in a Turbulent World

Drawing on the work of Arend Lijphart, this book focuses on consensus democracies. These democracies entail a complex set of democratic institutional and conventional arrangements and can be regarded as a product of path-dependent development towards a national culture of compromise and bargaining.

Taking a multi-dimensional and multi-spatial approach, this book examines the West central European consensus democracies of Austria, Belgium, Luxembourg, Netherlands and Switzerland, over the past 40 years. Magone examines how these democracies have been transformed by Europeanization thrusts and global turbulence yet are able to maintain political stability. It provides historical context including the different phases of transformation: the golden period (1945–1979); disorganised capitalism (1979–1993); and re-equilibration (1993–). It includes chapters on political culture, government, parliament, the rise of populism and political parties, subnational government, and the political economy and concludes deliberating on the relevance of consensus democracies' experiences for the future of European and global governance.

Based on original research, this book will be of strong interest to students and scholars of comparative politics, European government, West European politics, the politics of small states in Europe, and those with a particular interest in the politics of Austria, Belgium, the Netherlands, Luxembourg and Switzerland.

José M. Magone is Professor of Regional and Global Governance at the Berlin School of Economics and Law, Germany.

Routledge Research in Comparative Politics

58 **Government Accountability and Legislative Oversight**
Riccardo Pelizzo and Frederick Stapenhurst

59 **Corruption and Legislatures**
Riccardo Pelizzo and Frederick Stapenhurst

60 **Global Perspectives on the Politics of Multiculturalism in the 21st Century**
A case study analysis
Edited by Fethi Mansouri and Boulou Ebanda de B'béri

61 **Party Organization and Electoral Volatility in Central and Eastern Europe**
Enhancing voter loyalty
Sergiu Gherghina

62 **Politics of Religion and Nationalism**
Federalism, consociationalism and seccession
Edited by Ferran Requejo and Klaus-Jürgen Nagel

63 **Deficits and Debt in Industrialized Democracies**
Edited by Gene Park and Eisaku Ide

64 **Citizenship and Democracy in an Era of Crisis**
Edited by Thomas Poguntke, Sigrid Roßteutscher, Rüdiger Schmitt-Beck and Sonja Zmerli

65 **Drivers of Integration and Regionalism in Europe and Asia**
Comparative perspectives
Edited by Louis Brennan and Philomena Murray

66 **Generations, Political Participation and Social Change in Western Europe**
Maria T. Grasso

67 **The Politics of Think Tanks in Europe**
Jesper Dahl Kelstrup

68 **The Statecraft of Consensus Democracies in a Turbulent World**
A comparative study of Austria, Belgium, Luxembourg, the Netherlands and Switzerland
José M. Magone

69 **Policy Change under New Democratic Capitalism**
Edited by Hideko Magara

The Statecraft of Consensus Democracies in a Turbulent World

A comparative study of Austria, Belgium, Luxembourg, the Netherlands and Switzerland

José M. Magone

LONDON AND NEW YORK

First published 2017
by Routledge
2 Park Square, Milton Park, Abingdon, Oxon OX14 4RN

and by Routledge
711 Third Avenue, New York, NY 10017

Routledge is an imprint of the Taylor & Francis Group, an informa business

© 2017 José M. Magone

The right of José M. Magone to be identified as author of this work has been asserted by him in accordance with sections 77 and 78 of the Copyright, Designs and Patents Act 1988.

All rights reserved. No part of this book may be reprinted or reproduced or utilised in any form or by any electronic, mechanical, or other means, now known or hereafter invented, including photocopying and recording, or in any information storage or retrieval system, without permission in writing from the publishers.

Trademark notice: Product or corporate names may be trademarks or registered trademarks, and are used only for identification and explanation without intent to infringe.

British Library Cataloguing in Publication Data
A catalogue record for this book is available from the British Library

Library of Congress Cataloging in Publication Data
Names: Magone, Josâe M. (Josâe Marâia), 1962– author.
Title: The statecraft of consensus democracies in a turbulent world: a comparative study of Austria, Belgium, Luxembourg, the Netherlands and Switzerland / Josâe M. Magone.
Description: Abingdon, Oxon; New York, NY: Routledge is an imprint of the Taylor & Francis Group, an Informa Business, [2017] | Series: Routledge research in comparative politics | Includes bibliographical references and index.Identifiers: LCCN 2016032528| ISBN 9780415502788 (hbk) | ISBN 9781315407869 (ebk)
Subjects: LCSH: Democracy–Austria. | Democracy–Benelux countries. | Democracy–Switzerland. | Consensus (Social sciences)–Austria. | Consensus (Social sciences)–Benelux countries. | Consensus (Social sciences)–Switzerland. | Austria–Politics and government. | Benelux countries–Politics and government. | Switzerland–Politics and government.
Classification: LCC JN2026.M34 2017 | DDC 320.3094–dc23
LC record available at https://lccn.loc.gov/2016032528

ISBN: 978-0-415-50278-8 (hbk)
ISBN: 978-1-315-40786-9 (ebk)

Typeset in Times New Roman
by Wearset Ltd, Boldon, Tyne and Wear

Printed and bound in Great Britain by
TJ International Ltd, Padstow, Cornwall

Dedicated to Teresa, Peter and Leo

Il y a souvent bien la différence entre la volonté de tous et la volonté générale; celle-ci ne regard qu'a l'intérêt commun; l'autre regard l'intérêt privé, et n'est qu'une somme de volontés particuliéres: mais ôtez de ces mêmes volontés les plus et les moins qui s'entredétruisent, reste pour somme des différences la volonté générale.

(Jean-Jacques Rousseau, *Le contrat social ou Principles du Droit Politique.* Amsterdam: Marc Michel 1762, Book II, ch. 3)

Contents

List of figures	x
List of tables	xii
Preface	xiv
List of abbreviations	xvi

1	The statecraft of consensus democracies	1
2	The creation and development of consensus democracies	32
3	Constitutional change in consensus democracies	63
4	Society and civic culture	86
5	The Americanisation of electoral and party politics	106
6	Patterns of government in consensus democracies	144
7	The institutional performance of parliaments in consensus democracies	176
8	Regional and local patterns in consensus democracies	211
9	The changing political economy of consensus democracies	243
10	Consensus democracies as the model for European and global governance	273

List of interviews and written testimonies	284
References	287
Index	333

Figures

1.1	Consensus and majoritarian democracies in the European Union	6
1.2	Map of West Central Europe	14
1.3	The great transformation in post-1979 European politics	20
1.4	The multi-dimensional institutional foundations of consensus	27
1.5	Re-equilibration of consensus democracies since 1979	28
1.6	Consensus democracies and their relations to the European Union	29
3.1	The core political system of Belgium: a federal state	75
3.2	The core political system of Luxembourg	76
3.3	The core political system of the Netherlands: a unitary decentralised state	77
3.4	The core political system of Switzerland: a federal state	78
3.5	The core political system of Austria: a federal state	80
4.1	Social expenditure in consensus democracies as percentage of GDP, 1990 to 2014	87
4.2	Social benefits per capita in € in power purchasing parity (PPS), 2013	89
4.3	Satisfaction with performance of national democracy, 1974 to 2015	94
4.4	Trust in main political institutions, 2000 to 2015	95
4.5	Support for different state models in Belgium, 2014	96
4.6	Use of direct democracy votes in Switzerland, 1848 to 2016	104
5.1	Legislative elections in the Netherlands, 1982 to 2012	131
5.2	Legislative elections in Belgium, 1981 to 2014	133
5.3	Legislative elections in Austria, 1983 to 2013	134
5.4	Legislative elections in Luxembourg, 1979 to 2013	135
5.5	Legislative elections in Switzerland, 1983 to 2015	137
5.6	Total volatility in consensus democracies of West Central Europe, 1947 to 2014	138
5.7	Fragmentation of parties according to Effective Number of Electoral Parties (ENEP) and Effective Number of Parliamentary Parties (ENPP), 1950 to 2014	141

Figures xi

6.1	The chancellery of the prime minister in Belgium in 2015	152
6.2	Core executive in the Netherlands	153
6.3	Prime minister's office in Luxembourg in 2016	154
6.4	Chancellor's office in Austria in 2015	155
6.5	Chancellery of federal council in Switzerland in 2015	157
6.6	Types of government in consensus democracies according to years between 1945 and 2015	158
6.7	Composition of the federal council, 1848 to 2016	168
9.1	Government budget deficit, 2004 to 2015	263
9.2	Public debt, 2004 to 2015	264

Tables

1.1	Majoritarian vs. consensus democracy	5
1.2	Mapping consensus and majoritarian democracies in Europe, 2016	7
1.3	Quality of democracy, governance and policy performance according to the Sustainable Governance Indicators (SGI) of the Bertelsmann Foundation, 2015	12
1.4	West Central Europe: basic data	15
1.5	From the industrial to the information age	22
3.1	Reforming the Belgian Constitution, 1970 to 2011	68
4.1	Foreign-born population in consensus democracies, 2014	92
4.2	Income distribution in selected European democracies, 2005 and 2014	93
5.1	Political parties in West Central European democracies, 2016	108
5.2	Public funding to political parties in the Netherlands, 2014	125
5.3	Party public funding and membership in Belgium	126
5.4	Membership and public funding of political parties in Austria, 2012 to 2015	128
5.5	Membership and public funding of parliamentary parties in Luxembourg, 2012 to 2013	129
6.1	Coalition government in Belgium, 1981 to 2016	160
6.2	Coalition government in the Netherlands, 1982 to 2016	161
6.3	Coalition government in Luxembourg	163
6.4	Coalition government in Austria, 1983 to 2016	165
6.5	Longevity of government	174
7.1	Parliamentary groups in Swiss Parliament in 49th legislature period (2011–2015) and 50th legislature period (2015–)	178
7.2	Parliamentary groups in the Belgian House of Representatives in 2014	179
7.3	Parliamentary groups in the lower house (*Tweede Kamer*) and upper house (*Eerste Kamer*), 2015	180
7.4	Parliamentary groups in Lower (*Nationalrat*) and Upper (*Bundesrat*) Chambers in legislature period, 2016	181
7.5	Parliamentary groups in Luxembourg Chamber of Deputies in the legislature period since 2013	182

7.6	Average time spent by MPs in plenary sessions per year, lower house	189
7.7	Adopted governmental and parliamentary bills in Switzerland, 2003 to 2015	196
7.8	Success rate of government and private bills in Belgium Chamber of Representatives, 1991 to 2014	197
7.9	Submitted government and private bills in Dutch *Tweede Kamer*, 2001 to 2013	198
7.10	Bills adopted in *Nationalrat* (lower house) of the Austrian Parliament, 1971 to 2013	200
7.11	Government bills and private bills submitted and adopted in the Chamber of Deputies in Luxembourg, 2009 to 2013	201
7.12	Committees of EU affairs in consensus democracies, 2015	205
7.13	Strength of consensus democracies parliaments in EU multi-level governance before and after Lisbon, 2001 and 2014	209
8.1	Number of civil servants at different government levels, 2003 and 2012	214
8.2	Expenditure at different levels of government in selected OECD countries, 1995 to 2013	215
8.3	Public expenditure according to subnational structures, 2005 and 2011	216
8.4	The 26 cantons in Switzerland, 2015	223
8.5	The nine provinces (*Bundesländer*) of Austria	229
8.6	Type of provincial government in Austria, 1945 to 2015	231
8.7	Ten provinces in Belgium in 2016	236
8.8	The regions and communities of the Belgium Federation	237
8.9	Budgets of federal, regions and communities in Belgium, 2015	239

Preface

It was a great pleasure to do research on these countries and to discover the pressures on consensus democracy. I was lucky enough to be able to conduct over 50 qualitative interviews as well as written testimonies divided among the five countries; this resource contributed to the understanding of politics in each polity. I anonymised all quotations from and references to the interviews by adding the abbreviation for the country (e.g. Interview A = Interviewee from Austria; B = Belgium; CH = Switzerland; LU = Luxembourg; NL = Netherlands).

In terms of academic influence on the book, I would also like to thank my past teachers at the University of Vienna, including Hans-Georg Heinrich, Charlotte Teuber-Weckersdorf, Wolfgang C. Müller, Peter Gerlich, Karl Ucakar and Emmerich Talós, for their excellent instruction and voluminous research. Moreover, I want to express my gratitude to certain colleagues whom I have always admired as representatives of the countries analysed in this book: Gerda Falkner, Peter Mair, Ingrid van Biezen, Rudy Andeweg, Lieven de Winter, Régis Dandoy, Kris Deschouwer, Allison Woodward, Karen Célis, Bart Kerremans, Paul Pennings, Hans Keman, Frank Hendriks, Arco Timmermans, Catherine Moury, Yannis Papadopoulos, Klaus Armingeon, Adrian Vatter, Fritz Saager, Daniele Caramani, and of course Ulrich Klöti.

I am also grateful to Luxembourg for its generosity in providing me with a visiting professorship in the Department of Political Science at the University of Luxembourg during the summer semester of 2012. In particular I wish to thank Robert Harmsen, Patrick Dumont, Philippe Poirier and Astrid Spreitzer for their hospitality. Robert was instrumental in organising the fellowship of the Fondation National de Recherche of Luxembourg that allowed me to stay in (jaw-droppingly expensive) Luxembourg and travel back and forth to Belgium. The greatest moments in Luxembourg were when our small group went to the restaurant around the corner from the department, where a Portuguese woman worked. It was there that most of the department's meetings seemingly took place, just as informal as Luxembourg politics. The company and the food were certainly outstanding.

I also need to thank my former home, the Department of Politics and International Studies at the University of Hull, which awarded me a small grant in the summer semester of 2005 which I spent on a first round of preliminary research trips during that same year. In addition, the Faculty of the Berlin School of Economics and Law was very kind in approving my sabbatical during the summer semester of 2012 to complete the project. This is when I conducted most of the interviews in Luxembourg and Belgium.

As is evident, this project has had a long period of gestation. I started it in 2005, and it has taken over ten years (with interruptions) to complete it. One of the referees of the book proposal suggested that I should allow myself enough time to write the manuscript – I took his or her advice seriously! Due to the nature of the project – a qualitative comparison of five countries – mistakes may emerge, for which, of course, I take the blame. It may be far from perfect, but I wanted to produce a book that will be useful for a wider community; I therefore included a wealth of data and facts to facilitate access.

In a nutshell, this book is a comparative study of the five classical consensus democracies and how they have fared in an increasingly turbulent world. The main thesis is that their political institutions have thus far survived, partly via a 'muddling-through' strategy, but also as a result of innovative approaches. Each country developed different strategies. Due to the amount of information involved, I concentrated on four main aspects: government, parliament, subnational government and the political economy. All this is framed by descriptions of both historical legacies and political cultures. A general conclusion is that the future of these like-minded consensus democracies will require them to work closely together and to invest in European integration so that they can upload their values and patterns of behaviour to the European and global levels. This is the challenge they will face in the coming decades.

I would like to thank Heidi Bagatzo and Craig Fowlie, who commissioned the book, and Andrew Taylor, who later took over as Senior Editor at Routledge, for believing in this project and supporting it despite the extension of deadlines. Their patience in waiting for the manuscript knew no bounds. Former editorial assistants Alex Quayle and Charlotte Endersby, and now Sophie Iddamalgoda, have offered invaluable and kind support in the queries they had about the manuscript, and also in overseeing my progress.

I am very lucky to rely on the excellent editing skills of Claire Bacher, who has contributed considerably to the improvement of the text. I want to thank her for her insightful review of and comments on the manuscript. I take the opportunity to express my gratitude to the production team of the book, project managers Matt Deacon, Phillippa Clubbs and Hannah Riley, as well as copy editor Ann King. Without their input the magic transformation of a manuscript into an excellent book would not have been possible.

Last but not least, it is always a joy to share the development of my work with my beautiful Mum, whose significant contributions of encouragement, patience and love enabled this book to be completed.

Abbreviations

ABBL	Association des Banques et Banquiers de Luxembourg – Association of Banks and Bankers of Luxembourg (L)
AdR	Alternative Democratësch Reformpartei-Parti Democratique Reformateur – Alternative Democratic Reform Party (L)
AGALEV/Groen!	Anders Gaan Leven – To Start Living Differently (Name until 2003, afterwards Green) (B)
AK	Arbeiterkammer Österreichs – Labour Chamber of Austria (A)
ALEBA	Association Luxembourgeoise des Employés de Banque et Assurance – Luxembourg Association of Bank and Insurance Employees (L)
ALDE	Alliance of Liberal and Democrats in Europe (EU)
ARP	Anti-Revolutionaire Partij – Anti-Revolutionary Party (NL)
ASTI	Association pour le Soutien de Travailleurs Immigrés – Association for the Support of Immigrant Workers (L)
Atlas of EVS	Atlas of European Values Survey
AUNS	Aktion für ein Unabhängiges und Neutrales Schweiz-Action for an independent and neutral Switzerland (CH)
AWVN	Algemene Werkgevers Vereiniging Nederlands – General Association of Employers of the Netherlands (NL)
B	Belgium
BB	Boerenbond (B)
BDP	Bürgerliche Demokratische Partei – Citizens' Democratic Party (CH)
BFP-FPB	Bureau federal du Plan-Federal Planbureau (B)
BGB	Bauern, Gewerbe und Bürger Partei – Farmers, Small trade, Citizens' Party (CH)
BZÖ	Bündnis Zukunft Österreichs – Alliance Future of Austria (A)
CCE-CCB	Conseil Central de l' Economie-Centrale Raad voor het Bedrijfsleven – Central Council of the Economy (B)
CDA	Christlich-Democratische Appél – Christian Democratic Appeal (NL)

Abbreviations xvii

CDH	Centre democrátique humaniste – Democratic Humanist Centre (B)
CD&V	Christiaan Democratisch en Vlaams – Christian Democratic and Flemish (B)
CES	Conseil Economique et Social – Economic and Social Council (L)
CGSLB/ACLVB	Centrale Générale des Syndicats Libéraux de Belgique/ Algemene Centrale der Liberale Vakbonden van België – General Confederation of Liberal Trade Unions of Belgium (B)
CGFB	Confédération Générale de la Fonction Publique – General Confederation of Civil Service (L)
CH	Switzerland
CHF	Schweizer Franken – Swiss Francs (CH)
CHU	Christelijke Historische Unie – Christian Historical Union (NL)
CLAE	Comité de liaison des associations d'étrangers – Committee of Liaison with Foreigners Associations (L)
CLC	Confederation Luxembourgeois du Commerce (L)
CME	Coordinated Market Economy
CNE	Conseil National d' Ètrangers – National Council of Foreigners (L)
CNT-NAR	Conseil National du Travail-Nationale Arbeidsraad – National Council of Labour (B)
CNV	Christenlijk Nationaal Vakverbond – Christian National Trade Union Confederation (NL)
COSAC	Comité des organs specialisés en Affaires communautaires – Committee of bodies specialised in European Affairs (EU)
CPB	Centraal Planbureau – Central Planning Bureau (NL)
CPL	Central Paysanne Luxembourgeois – Luxembourg Farmers' Confederation (L)
CSC-ACV	Confédération des Syndicats Chrétiens/Algemeen Christelijk Vakverbond – Confederation of Christian Trade Unions (B)
CSV	Chreschtlesch-Sozial Vollekpartei – Christian Social People's party (L)
CVP	Christliche Volkspartei – Christian People's Party (CH)
CVP/PSC	Christiaan Volkspartij/Parti Social Chrétien – Christian People's Party (B)
DP	Democratesch Partei – Democratic Party (DP)
EC	European Community
EEA	European Economic Area
EEC	European Economic Community
Ecolo	Ecologistes confederés pour le organisation des luttes

xviii *Abbreviations*

	originales – Confederated Ecologists for the organisation of original struggles (B)
ECSC	European Community of Steel and Coal (EU)
EFTA	European Free Trade Area
EIGE	European Institute of Gender Equality (EU)
EMU	Economic and Monetary Union (EU)
ENEP	Effective number of electoral parties
ENPP	Effective number of parliamentary parties
EPP	European People's Party (EU)
ESM	European Stability Mechanism (EU)
ESP	European Socialist Party (EU)
ESS	European Social Survey
EU	European Union
FDA	Fédération des Artisans – Federation of Artisans (L)
FDP/PLR	Freisinnige Demokratische Partei der Schweiz/Parti Liberal Radical Suisse – Liberal Democratic Party of Switzerland (CH)
FEDIL	Federation des Industriels de Luxembourg – Federation of Industrialists of Luxembourg (L)
FLB	Fräie Lëtzebuerger Bauernverband – Free Luxembourg Association of Farmers (L)
FGFC	Fédération générale de la fonction communale – General Federation of Local Civil Servants (L)
FGTB-ABVV	Federation General de Travail de Belgique/Algemeen Belgische Vakverbond – General Confederation of Labour of Belgium (B)
FNCTTFEL	Landesverband Fédération nationale des cheminots, travailleurs du transport, fonctionnaires et employés de Luxembourg (L)
FNO-NCW	Federatie Nederlandse Ondernemer/Nederlandse Christelijk Werkgeversverbond – Federation of Dutch Enterpreneurs/ Dutch Christian Association of Employers (NL)
FNV	Federatie Nationaal van Vakverbond – National Trade Union Confederation (NL)
FPÖ	Freiheitliche Partei Österreichs – Freedom Party of Austria (A)
FWA	Fédération Wallone Agriculture – Wallon Federation of Agriculture (B)
GDP	Gross Domestic Product
GLP	Grüne-Liberale Partei – Green Liberal Party (CH)
GPS	Grüne Partei der Schweiz – Green Party of Switzerland (CH)
GRECO	Groupe d' États contre la corruption – Group of States against Corruption
GsOA	Gruppe für eine Schweiz ohne Armee – Group for a Switzerland without Army (CH)

Abbreviations xix

Horesca	Federation Nationale des Hoteliers, Restaurateurs et Cafetiers – National Federation of Hotel, Restaurant and Coffeeshop Owners (L)
ICANN	The Internet Corporation for Assigned Names and Numbers
IGC	Inter-governmental Conferences (EU)
IMF	International Monetary Fund
IPU	Interparliamentary Union
IV	Industrielle Vereinigung (A)
KVP	Katholieke Volkspartij – Catholic People's Party (NL)
LCGB	Lëtzebuerger Chrëschtleche Gewerkschafts-Bond (L)
LKÖ	Landwirtschaftskammer Österreichs – Chamber of Agriculture in Austria (A)
LME	Liberal Market Economy
LPF	Lijst Pim Fortujn – Pim Fortuyn list (NL)
LSAP	Lëtzebuerger Sozialistesch Aarbechterpartei – Luxembourg Socialist Workers' Party (L)
LTO	Land en Tuibouworganisation – Land and Gardening Organisation (NL)
MEP	Members of European Parliament (EU)
MKB Nederland	Koninglijke Vereiniging Midden en Kleinbedrijfen Nederland – Royal Association of Small and Medium Sized Entreprises (NL)
MP	Member of Parliament
MR	Mouvement reformateur – Reform movement (B)
NEOS	Neues Österreich und Liberales Forum – New Austria and Liberal Forum (A)
NKV	Nationaal Katholieke Verbond – National Confederation of Catholic Trade Unions (NL)
NL	The Netherlands
NPM	New Public Management
NSB	Nationaal Socialist Beweging – National socialist movement (NL)
N-VA	Nieuw Vlaamse Alliantie – New Flemish Alliance (B)
NVV	Nationaal Verbond Vakvereinigingen – National Trade Union Confederation (NL)
OECD	Organization for Economic Cooperation and Development
OEEC	Organization for European Economic Cooperation
ÖGB	Österreichischer Gewerkschaftsbund – Austrian Trade Union Confederation (A)
OGB-L	Onofhängege Gewerkschaftsbond Lëtzebuerg – Independent Trade Confederation of Luxembourg (L)
ONEM/SA	Office national d'emploi/Rijksdienst voor Arbeidsvorziening (BE)
Open VLD	Open Vlaamse Liberalen en Democraten – Open Flemish Liberals and Democrats (B)

xx *Abbreviations*

ÖVP	Österreichische Volkspartei – Austrian People's Party (B)
PBOs	Publiekrechtlike Bedrijfsorganisatie – Public Enterprise Organisation (NL)
PdA	Partei der Arbeit – Labour Party (CH)
PdR	Partei der Rechten (L)
PEGIDA	Patriotische Europäer gegen die Islamisierung des Abendlandes – Patriotic European against the Islamisation of the Occident (D)
PLP/PVV	Parti pour Liberté et Progrés/Partij voor Vrijheid en Voruitgang – Party for Freedom and Progress (B)
POB	Parti Ouvriére de Belgique – Workers' Party of Belgium (B)
PPS	Power Purchasing Standard
PR	Proportional Representation
PS	Parti Socialiste (de Wallonie) – Sozialistische Partei (der Wallonie) (B)
PvdA	Partij van der Arbeid – Labour Party (NL)
PvdD	Partij voor de Dieren – Animals Party (NL)
PVV	Partij voor Vrijheid – Party for Freedom (NL)
RCO	Raad van de Centrale Ondernemensorganisationen – Council of Central Enterpreneurs' Organisations (NL)
RSVP	Roomsch-Katholieke Staatspartij – Roman Catholic State Party (NL)
RTL	Radio Television Luxembourg (NL)
SAV-USP	Schweizerischer Arbeitgeberverband-Union Suisse Patronal – Swiss Confederation of Employers (CH)
SBV-USP	Schweizerischer Bauernverband-Union swiss des paysans – Swiss Farners' Union (CH)
SCP	Sociaal en Culturel Planbureau – Social and Culture Planning Bureau (NL)
SDAP	Sociaal Democratische Arbeiderpartij – Social Democratic Workers' Party (NL)
SEA	Single European Act (EU)
SEM	Single European Market (EU)
SER	Sociaal Economische Raad – Social and Economic Council (NL)
SGB-USS	Schweizerischer Gewerkschaftsbund/Union des Syndicats Suisse – Swiss Trade Union Confederation (CH)
SGP	Staatskundig Gereformeerde Partij – Reformed Political Party (NL)
SGP	Stability and Growth Pact (EU)
SGV-USAM	Schweizerischer Gewerbeverband-Union Suisse des arts et métiers – Swiss association of small trade and artisans (NL)
SP.a	Sozialistische Partij.Anders-Sociaalprogressief.alternatif – Socialist Party.Different.Socialprogressive.alternative (NL)

Abbreviations xxi

SPÖ	Sozialdemokratische Partei Österreichs – Socialdemocratic Party of Austria (NL)
SPS	Sozialdemokratische Partei der Schweiz – Socialdemocratic Party of Switzerland (CH)
STAR	Stichting van der Arbeid (NL)
SVO	Shareholder Value Orientation
SVP/UDC	Schweizerische Volkspartei/Union Democratique du Centre – Swiss People's Party/Democratic Centre Party (CH)
TEU	Treaty of the European Union (EU)
UCM	Union des Classes Moyennes (B)
UEL	Union des Enterprises Luxembourgeois – Union Luxembourg Enterprises (L)
UELB	Union Economique Luxembourg et Belgique – Economic Union of Luxembourg and Belgium (L)
UNISOC	Organisation patronale du secteur à profit social de Belgique – Employers organisation of the social profit sector in Belgium (B)
UNIZO	Unie van Zelfstandige Ondernemers – Union of Independent Enterprises (B)
VB	Vlaams Belang/Vlaams Blok (Name until 2004) – Flemish Interest/Flemish Block (B)
VCP	Vakcentrale voor Professionals – Central Trade Union for Executive Professionals (NL)
VdU	Verband der Unabhängige – Association of Independents (A)
VNG	Vereiniging van Nederlandse Gemeenten – National Association of Local Authorities (NL)
VNV	Verbond Nationaal de Vlanders – National Association of Flanders (B)
VU	Volksunie – People's Union (B)
VUB	Vrije Universiteit Brussel – Free University Brussel (B)
VVD	Volkspartij voor Vrijheid en Democratie – People's Party for Freedom and Democracy (NL)
WEF	World Economic Forum
WKÖ	Wirtschaftskammer Österreichs (A) – Chamber of Economy in Austria
WRR	Wetenschappelijke Raad voor regeringsbeleid – Scientific Council for Government Policy (NL)
ZBO	Zelf-bestuursorganisatie – Independent Administrative Organisation (NL)

1 The statecraft of consensus democracies

Introduction: political change in consensus democracies

In the turbulent modern world, the statecraft required to achieve political, economic, social and cultural stability within democracies has become an indispensable aspect of politics (Rosenau 1990). Beginning in the sixteenth century, polities have increasingly operated in a global capitalist world economy. This is highly significant: modern capitalism must be regarded as a civilisation and, as such, as a unique form of political, social and economic organisation. Consensus democracies are a product of this civilisation, arising from the importance of economic rationality in the way in which politics is framed (Braudel 1979). Since the 1980s, but particularly following the fall of the Berlin Wall in 1989, no country in the world – even closed political systems such as North Korea and Iran – has been able to escape the impact of systems that combine a liberal market economy with a liberal democracy. Such polities represent outcomes of this capitalist civilisation as well as the influence of a highly interdependent world system. Financial capitalism and new technologies have contributed substantially to these changes (the best studies on this latest trend are Castells 1996, 1997, 1998). In this context of a globalised world economy and a widespread model of liberal democracy, the small European democracies of West Central Europe and the Nordic countries have been remarkable examples of success in reconciling the two phenomena. These states are all characterised by a consensus approach to democracy, which is distinct from the Anglo-Saxon model of majoritarian democracy. The peak of this consensual style of politics was in the 1950s and 1960s, when these small democracies managed to achieve both a strong economy and a strong democracy. Through an unconscious (or, more likely, conscious) strategic choice resulting from alliances between political parties, this balance between economy and democracy allowed the creation of relatively egalitarian societies by means of strong welfare states. There was also a process by which politics acted against the markets in order to tame capitalism, as seen in the Nordic countries (Esping-Andersen 1985).

However, in the 1970s and 1980s, domestic social changes and new forces of globalisation led to major challenges for consensus democracies. Internally, demographic changes bringing about an ageing society paired with the emergence of a

2 Statecraft of consensus democracies

more heterogeneous and multicultural population contributed to the emergence of new political parties and social movements that advocated either greater inclusion and internationalisation (mainly Green parties) or the exclusion of immigrants and the protection of nationals (mainly new or extreme Right parties). Externally, globalisation increased pressures on national political and economic systems. The political statecraft required to strategically manage these small European democracies became more complex. Since the 1980s, Europeanisation has become an important strategic element utilised by small European democracies to protect themselves from the more challenging pressures of globalisation.

This book seeks to analyse these processes of what I call the political craft of 're-equilibration' in small European democracies in the context of a turbulent world (for a similar argument based on the Netherlands, see Touwen 2014). Although the political economy of small democracies is a crucial variable, we are primarily interested in the political restructuring and re-equilibration of consensus democracies between the oil crisis of 1973 and the present. This longitudinal approach is conducive to developing a better understanding of continuity and change over time in the consensual style of politics in Austria, Belgium, Luxembourg, the Netherlands and Switzerland. We argue that democratic consensus politics (including consultation, cooperation and compromise) is a way of life in these countries, such that conflict is resolved through these mechanisms. Although these countries are losing their consociational character (Lijphart 1977, 2008: ch. 2), they have internalised many of the devices created during the golden age of consensus democracies, when they were divided and segmented societies.

This chapter starts with an exploration of the concept of consensus democracy. Subsequently, we discuss the political craft of 're-equilibration' exercised by political elites in the context of a chaotic world. We allude here to the concept of strategic management, a term that is quite common in business studies, vesting it with a political character. After all, strategy is a key element of political manoeuvring. The third section addresses the dimensions of political change over the past 40 years. We refer to this as the 'great transformation of the late twentieth century', a hypothesis influenced by Karl Polanyi's masterpiece *The Great Transformation* (1944). Finally, some conclusions will be drawn.

Conceptualising consensus democracies

The concept of consensus democracy was developed by the Dutch-American scholar Arend Lijphart. Lijphart's cogent analysis of the Dutch political system in the 1960s and 1970s led him to regard consensus democracies as a type or vision of democracy. Taking the Netherlands as an example, Lijphart was interested in determining how political stability could remain sustainable despite the considerable erosion of traditional subcultures. The success of the Dutch democratic political system was heavily dependent on the joint efforts of political leaders in peace-keeping and ensuring peaceful change (Lijphart 1975: 112). Moreover, in the case of the Netherlands, there was great pride in what the

Dutch call consultation democracy (*overlegdemocratie*), which is institutionalised at the highest level in the Social and Economic Council (*Sociaal-Economische* Raad, SER), founded in 1950. The SER became the model for similar institutions at various levels of politics, economy and society (Lijphart 1975: 113–114; Hendriks 2012; SER 2014b, 2015). Moreover, policy issues were depoliticised by the creation of neutral research institutions in which all political parties participate, such as the Central Planning Bureau (*Centraal Planbureau*, CPB) founded in 1945, the Social and Cultural Planning Bureau (*Sociaal en Cultureel Planbureau*, SCP) founded in 1973 and the Scientific Council for Government Policy (*Wetenschappelijke Raad voor Regeringsbeleid*, WRR) founded in 1972.

Consensus democracies are particularly relevant in divided consociational societies such as Austria, the Netherlands, Switzerland, Belgium and (to a lesser extent) Luxembourg. The number of cleavages (state vs. church, workers vs. capital, centre vs. periphery, ethnolinguistic cleavages) existing in these societies has resulted in a continuing search for consensus in many areas, in particular in the field of public policy.

There is always a danger of conflating the concepts of consensus and consociationalism. In fact, the two are interlinked, but historically speaking consociationalism emerged earlier, leading to the development of consensus patterns of behaviour. Although consociationalism is an important aspect of divided societies, consensus democracies may also emerge in homogeneous states.

Lijphart asserted that consociationalism and consensus democracies are two different concepts and that they must be separated analytically. Consociationalism represents more of a categorisation of political culture, whereas consensus democracy denotes a set of features with regard to how a political system is organised; the former is a political-sociological term, whereas the latter is a political-scientific ideal type (Lijphart 2002a: 14). Consociationalism refers to a segmented society in which politics attempts to achieve consensus among subcultural interests at the level of political elites; in contrast, consensus democracy may also emerge in more homogeneous nations such as the Nordic countries. The peak of consociationalism in West Central European countries was the period between the end of the nineteenth century and the 1960s. Since then, these countries have become less consociational, although they remain consensual in their approach to politics. Welfare policies and consumer society (through the expansion of national markets) have significantly contributed to the erosion of the once rigid subcultures in these countries (on consociationalism, see a special issue by Steiner and Ertman 2002; Daalder 2011: 193–206, 207–222).

Lijphart envisioned his ideal type of the consensus democracy as a contrast to the ideal type of the majoritarian democracy as practised in the UK, many Commonwealth countries and the USA. In two books, *Democracies* and *Patterns of Democracies*, he developed a typology contrasting these two ideal types of democracies (Lijphart 1984, 1999, 2012). To this end, he identified several features that could be mapped along two main dimensions.

4   Statecraft of consensus democracies

1   *The executive–parties dimension:* reflects the way in which parties form governments and which kinds of governments they form.
2   *The federal–unitary dimension:* reflects the way in which power is distributed over the territory (Lijphart 1999: 3–4).

On the executive–parties dimension, consensus democracies are characterised by five features, including a highly fragmented party system, an electoral system of proportional representation that ensures the representation of all relevant groups in society, the predominance of coalition government, and some form of neo-corporatist system of interest intermediation through which the relevant social partners agree on short-, medium- and long-term policies for the benefit of the entire society. Moreover, although Lijphart does not specifically mention this point, consensus democracies are arguably based on strong, comprehensive welfare states as a consequence of the trade-off between capital and labour in building a social market economy (Esping-Andersen 1985, 1990).

The five features of majoritarian democracies are the concentration of executive power in a single actor (party), the dominance of the executive over the legislature, a two-party system, a majoritarian electoral system and a pluralist system of interest intermediation.

On the federal–unitary dimension, the five features of consensus democracies are federalism, decentralisation, a bicameral parliamentary system, a constitution that is rigid or difficult to amend and constitutional review by a constitutional court. In contrast, the features of majoritarian democracies are a unitary state, a unicameral system, a flexible constitution that is easy to amend, judicial review by Parliament and central banks that are dependent on the executive (see Table 1.1).

Lijphart's statistical comparative study allows us to map most countries in Europe. As a starting point, we can use the categorisation developed by Manfred G. Schmidt based on the calculations of Lijphart's consensus democracy index in his second edition of *Patterns of Democracy* (2012).

In order to also include Central and Eastern European countries, I have tentatively created certain additional categories (see Figure 1.1 and Table 1.2).

Although the British Westminster model and the Dutch consensus democracy are used as templates for the pure types, no country in Europe or the wider world is an exact match for either type. It must also be acknowledged that the UK has changed considerably since 1997; in fact, it is currently engaged in a major constitutional reform that entails the convergence of many majoritarian features towards the consensus democracy model. Andrew Gamble regarded the efforts of the New Labour government (1997–2010) in this regard as an attempt to achieve a shift in British politics towards continental Europe, which is dominated by the consensus democracy ideal type. Due to a hung Parliament, Britain had a coalition government between 2010 and 2015, and the proportional representation electoral systems in Scotland, Wales and Northern Ireland have contributed to more frequent coalition governments in recent years (Laws 2016; Seyd 2004). The 2015 general elections produced one of the most disproportional

Statecraft of consensus democracies 5

Table 1.1 Majoritarian vs. consensus democracy

Categories	Majoritarian democracy	Consensus democracy
	Executive–party dimension	
Nature of executive power	Concentration of executive power in single party	Executive power-sharing in broad multi-party coalitions
Executive–legislative relations	Dominant executive	Balance between executive and legislative
Party system	Two-party system	Multi-party system
Electoral system	Majoritarian, disproportional electoral system	Proportional representation electoral system
System of interest intermediation	Pluralism	Neo-corporatism
	Federal–unitary dimension	
Nature of territorial organisation	Unitary centralised	Federal, decentralised
Organisation of legislative power	Unicameral system	Bicameral balanced system
Constitutions	Flexible constitution, easy to amend	Rigid constitution, difficult to amend
Judicial review	Judicial review lies in Parliament	Judicial review lies in constitutional court or supreme court
Central Bank	Central banks that are dependent on executive	Central banks that are independent of the executive

Source: own compilation based on Lijphart (1999: 31–47).

parliaments in terms of representation in the history of the UK, reviving the debate on the fairness of the electoral system (Garland and Terry 2015).

For many Central and Eastern European countries, the cleavage between representatives of the old communist regime (now part of the Social-Democratic family) and more liberal anti-communist forces is the most salient (for more details, see the case of Hungary in Ágh 2001).

The Southern European democracies have already undergone 40 years or more of continuous democratisation. Lijphart's statistical calculations categorise only Portugal and Italy as unitary consensus democracies; however, whereas Italy had a long tradition of consensus democracy until 1992, Portugal is still working towards it (Magone 2014; Köppl 2012).

In contrast, Greece and Spain are identified as majoritarian democracies; this is also part of the ingrained political cultures of these countries. It is therefore highly problematic when no bloc is able to achieve an absolute majority, as occurred in Spain following the general elections of 20 December 2015. The outcome was a hung Parliament in which new parties emerged and successfully challenged the old party system. The inability to build bridges and common

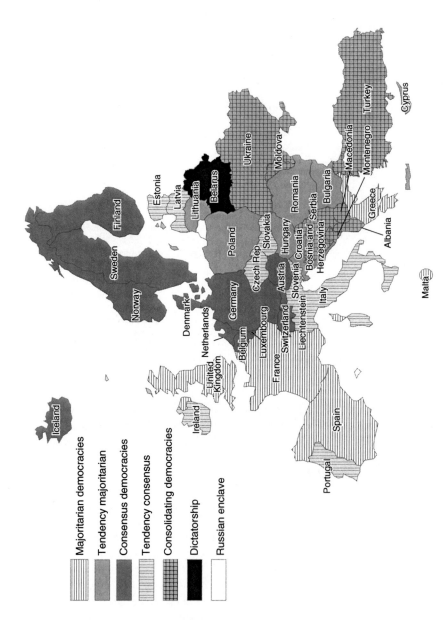

Figure 1.1 Consensus and majoritarian democracies in the European Union.

Statecraft of consensus democracies 7

Table 1.2 Mapping consensus and majoritarian democracies in Europe, 2016

Federal–unitary dimension	*Executive–parties dimension*	
	Federal or regionalised majoritarian democracies	*Federal or regionalised consensus democracies*
	USA UK Spain France	Germany *Switzerland* *Belgium* *Austria* *Netherlands*
	Tendency federal or regionalised majoritarian	*Tendency federal or regionalised consensus*
	Poland Hungary	Italy Czech Republic Slovakia
	Unitary majoritarian democracies	*Unitary consensus democracies*
	Greece Malta Cyprus	*Luxembourg* Denmark Sweden Norway Finland Iceland
	Tendency unitary majoritarian	*Tendency unitary consensus*
	Bulgaria Romania Lithuania	Ireland Portugal Latvia Estonia Slovenia

Sources: influenced by Lijphart (1999, 2012); Norris (2001: 989); Schmidt (2013: 7). Own judgement based on reports of the *European Political Data Yearbook* (EPDY).

Note
A quantitative approach gives the sense of a false reliability; it needs always to be improved by a qualitative knowledge-based approach. The non-EU Balkan countries – Turkey, Ukraine and Moldova – are still consolidating democracies. Highlighted countries are part of this study.

ground between political parties led to an impasse and new elections following five months of negotiations which took place on 26 June 2016, reproducing a similar hung Parliament (*El Pais*, 26 April 2016, 28 June 2016).

The most interesting case in Western Europe is probably Ireland. According to Hament Bulsara and Bill Kissane, over the past century Ireland has moved from a majoritarian system to a consensus democracy. The country's electoral

8 *Statecraft of consensus democracies*

system is certainly a factor, but it is also significant that the number of parties has increased over time; this has made single-party governments more difficult to achieve and thus coalition governments have become increasingly common. Another related outcome is a definite increase in socio-economic cooperation between the social partners, specifically in social pacts between the government and the social partners as well as among the social partners themselves, in contrast to the situation in the UK. This has contributed considerably to the emergence of the economically successful 'Celtic tiger'. The global financial crisis represented a painful interruption in this trend, but Ireland is already back on the path to economic growth (Bulsara and Kissane 2009; for a comparison between Ireland and the UK on the subject of industrial relations, see Hamann and Kelly 2010: ch. 5).

In his typology, Lijphart also assigns the European Union to the category of consensus democracies on the basis of practices within the institutions of the European Union, namely the European Commission, the Council of the European Union, the European Council and the European Parliament. Consensus tends to prevail in any decision-making in these institutions, even though it may take quite a long time to achieve a compromise. The best examples are, of course, the Intergovernmental Conferences (IGC) leading up to reforms of the European treaties. The introduction of the European Convention to draft Constitutional Treaties is a further example of this dominance of the consensus mode in European Union politics. Similarly, the College of Commissioners must achieve consensus in all legislative proposals (Lijphart 1999: 42–47; Schmidt 2002; Costa and Magnette 2003; Kalina 2012). In the European elections in 2014, the European political parties fielded candidates (*Spitzenkandidaten*) for the presidency of the European Commission for the first time – a position that may be regarded as the equivalent of a prime minister at the European level. Despite a veto threat from British Prime Minister David Cameron following these elections, this new method of nominating the president of the European Commission has prevailed. Jean Claude Juncker, a former prime minister of Luxembourg, thus became President of the European Commission. Although it won the greatest share of the vote in the elections, the European People's Party (EPP) did not have enough seats in the European Parliament to form the government on its own. Juncker was consequently forced to form a government with members of other political parties, namely the Socialists (ESP), the Liberals (ALDE) and the Greens. Since the Juncker European Commission consists of members coming from various political parties in the European Parliament, it may be called a coalition government (for a detailed description of this process, see Peñalver Nereo and Priestley 2015).

Globally speaking, consensus democracies are most likely to be found among the members of the Organisation of Economic Cooperation and Development (OECD). The OECD was created in 1961 as a successor to the Organisation for European Economic Cooperation (OEEC), which had been established by the USA primarily in order to administer the European Recovery Programme (ERP Marshall Plan). The OECD, which is based in Paris, has contributed to

Statecraft of consensus democracies 9

benchmarking and best practices in the political economies of its members. The 'OECDisation' of these countries has also been a major factor in improving performance efficiency. Among OECD countries, only the West Central European countries of Austria, Belgium, Luxembourg, the Netherlands, Switzerland and Germany, as well as the Nordic countries of Sweden, Denmark, Finland, Norway and Iceland, may truly be considered consensus democracies. Although Germany belongs to this group of consensus democracies it was not included in this book due to its sheer size, which puts the country in a different situation. We focus on how small consensus democracies of West Central Europe develop around Germany.

Many other European and non-European member countries exhibit tendencies of consensual politics, but they clearly lag far behind the countries listed above. Thus, only 11 countries of about 202 states worldwide may be characterised as advanced consensus democracies. Lijphart's pioneering work identifies more states than the 11 (out of 36 states examined), but this is largely due to the fact that his level of analysis is quantitative and not qualitative; it also results from the nature of the comparative method. As one analyses at a deeper level and the numbers of case studies are reduced, fewer and fewer countries may be counted as consensus democracies. Lijphart himself has recognised this dilemma on several occasions, and he is well aware of the simplification that his comparative statistical method entails in terms of the definition and operationalisation of the variables involved (Lijphart 1971, 2008: 19–20). In this book, we do not seek to challenge the innovative findings of Lijphart, who has done an excellent job of finding a way to operationalise his two types. Nevertheless, there is also an inherent agenda in his work of presenting consensus democracies as superior to majoritarian systems. This claim has been criticised by several authors who have shown that consensus democracies can lead to so-called 'blockades', or inertia in decision-making processes, which Fritz Scharpf refers to as the 'joint decision-making trap' (*Politikverflechtungsfalle*; Scharpf 1988; see also Schmidt 2011: 12–14; Armingeon 2002: 89–92; and the response by Lijphart 2002b). Another major issue involves the labelling of what Lijphart calls consensus democracies. Scholars from Switzerland, the Netherlands, Belgium, Austria and Luxembourg tend to emphasise the uniqueness of their respective countries. The best examples of this are Jürg Steiner's characterisation of Switzerland as an 'amicable agreement' (1971), Gerhard Lehmbruch's discussion of Austria and Switzerland as *Proporzdemokratie* (i.e. referring to the proportional distribution of political power and spoils between the main parties and interest groups) and the introduction of concepts such as 'concordance democracy' (*Konkordanzdemokratie*) and even 'negotiation democracy' (*Verhandlungsdemokratie*; Lehmbruch 1967, 1991, 1996; for a detailed historical review of the concept, see Lehmbruch 2012; also Krannenpohl 2012). Gerhard Lehmbruch has contributed immensely to the historical aspects of consensus democracy in West Central Europe, particularly in the Drei-Sat countries (Austria, Switzerland and especially Germany). The consociational democracy theme has been particularly highlighted by the Dutch scholar Hans Daalder, and by Lijphart himself (Daalder 2011: 193–206, 206–221;

10 *Statecraft of consensus democracies*

Lijphart 1975, 1977, 2008). For more pragmatic reasons, when speaking with policy-makers, Lijphart also uses the label 'power-sharing democracy' rather than the difficult-to-spell 'consociational democracy' (Lijphart 2008: 6). The concept of 'democratic corporatism', which was brought to the fore by Peter Katzenstein (1984, 1985) in connection with the political economies of consensus democracies, is also important in this context; Katzenstein was clearly influenced by the previous work of Gerhard Lehmbruch and Philippe Schmitter (1979, 1982).

Among these myriad labels, concepts and definitions, 'consensus democracies' is probably the best term to ensure a broader understanding of a type of democracy that prioritises cooperation over conflict, compromise over majority decisions, the integration of minority positions through consultation procedures and a system in which there are (at least psychologically) no losers. Such consensus democracies are most well suited to political systems with fragmented party structures in which the constitutional engineers have a genuine interest in preserving diversity in the polity, either for reasons of social pacification (due to divisions in the wider society) or as a general way of life. Consensus democracies are difficult to establish because they rely on the self-limitation of political actors, a trusting political environment and highly sophisticated skills of political bargaining. One of the main arguments of this study is that consensus democracies are even more difficult to maintain due to the fact that such consensual political-cultural skills must be passed on from one generation to the next in the context of a competitive capitalist world economy. Consensus democracies entail a highly complex set of democratic institutional and conventional arrangements. Indeed, consensus democracy may be regarded as a product of path-dependent development towards a national culture of compromise and bargaining. The system entails different dimensions, of which the political is the most visible. The complexity of such consensus democracies arises from the kinds of arrangements and consensual pacts that have been agreed upon over time in order to ensure a peaceful polity. This means that, in addition to all the institutional features that Lijphart identifies, one must also take into account the political culture and civil society of the country in question (as acknowledged by Lijphart 1999, 2012: ch. 16). Like Lijphart, we regard antagonistic majoritarian politics as rather negative in the long run, and assert that the cultural and structural proprieties of consensus democracies make them the most appropriate type of democracy for twenty-first-century European and global governance. Consensus democracies require an inclusive spirit and cooperative civic behaviour in which there are no losers and no winners. We argue that this is the ideal model for the European Union as well. However, majoritarian democracies such as the UK, France, Spain, Poland and Hungary may be at odds with this emerging model of the European Union.

Consensus democracies in Europe are overwhelmingly 'kinder and gentler' and perform better in terms of the even redistribution of national wealth among their respective populations, which is itself an important motivational element in achieving higher levels of productivity in the economy. Lijphart's attempts to measure the performance of these economies were innovative and pioneering.

Statecraft of consensus democracies 11

However, since 2009, the Bertelsmann Foundation has been evaluating the performance and quality of democracy of all OECD countries, including many Central and Eastern European countries, allowing us to more precisely specify the differences between consensus and majoritarian democracies. The Bertelsmann Foundation has developed three important indices that consist of further subindices: the democracy, governance and policy performance indices. The democracy index takes into account the quality of democracy (electoral processes, access to information, civil rights and political liberties and the rule of law). The governance index examines executive capacity (strategic capacity, interministerial coordination, evidence-based instruments, societal consultation, policy communication, implementation, adaptability and accountability, which includes citizens' participatory competences, legislative actors' resources, the media, parties and interest groups). The index of policy performance addresses economic policies (the economy, labour markets, taxes, budgets, research and innovation, the global financial system), social policies (education, social inclusion, health, families, pensions, integration, safe living, global inequalities) and environmental policies (the environment, global environmental protection). These indices, which are produced by three expert panels made up of specialists on the respective countries, also employ international standards and data.

Table 1.3 allows us to make further differentiations. First of all, one can distinguish between democracies that are relatively substantive, with strong civil societies and strong welfare states, and more procedural systems that have a high-functioning democratic institutional framework but in which civil society and political culture are still weak and therefore unsettled in terms of consensual politics. In this context, it is evident that most substantive consensus democracies have a higher democratic sustainable governance level than substantive majoritarian democracies. The United Kingdom, as the prototype for majoritarian democracies, is only ranked eleventh overall. The excellent ranking of Estonia is intriguing, since it must be characterised as a procedural consensus democracy, as is that of Lithuania, which is still evolving towards a procedural majoritarian type. Substantive consensus democracies such as the Netherlands, Belgium and Austria fare better in terms of democratic sustainable governance than substantive majoritarian states like France and Spain. It is interesting that Slovakia is the only procedural consensus democracy in the mid-range category; at this level, the majority of countries are majoritarian democracies (Magone 2014).

Although it is important to differentiate between historically well-established substantive consensus democracies and those that emerged from the third or fourth wave of democratisation (and therefore need more time to further strengthen their democratic cultures), in this work we will focus exclusively on the former category.

The main focus of this book is an analysis of how economically advanced substantive consensus democracies have been able to re-invent themselves in the context of internal and external forces of change. We are particularly interested

Table 1.3 Quality of democracy, governance and policy performance according to the Sustainable Governance Indicators (SGI) of the Bertelsmann Foundation, 2015

	Country	Democracy	Governance	Policy performance	SGI Index	Type of democracy
Very high level of democratic sustainable governance (10–17)						
1	Sweden	9.11	8.42	7.83	8.45	Consensus
2	Norway	9.01	8.37	7.74	8.37	Consensus
3	Denmark	8.9	8.27	7.72	8.30	Consensus
4	Finland	9.15	8.38	7.52	7.89	Consensus
5	Germany	8,7	7.25	7.19	7.71	Consensus
6	*Switzerland*	*8.7*	*6.85*	*7.67*	*7.7*	*Consensus*
7	*Luxembourg*	*7.87*	*7.45*	*6.88*	*7.4*	*Consensus*
8	Estonia	8.36	6.31	7.15	7.27	Procedural consensus
9	Lithuania	8.12	6.38	6.65	7.05	Procedural majoritarian
10	Ireland	8.28	6.64	6.14	7.02	Consensus
11	United Kingdom	7.22	7.02	6.79	7.01	Majoritarian
High level of democratic sustainable governance (7–6)						
12	Poland	8.37	6.73	5.85	6.98	Procedural Majoritarian
13	*Netherlands*	*7.7*	*6.4*	*6.77*	*6.96*	*Consensus*
14	Iceland	7.21	6.84	6.31	6.83	Consensus
15	Latvia	8.07	6.2	6.21	6.79	Procedural consensus
16	*Austria*	*7.46*	*6.64*	*6.11*	*6.73*	*Consensus*
17	*Belgium*	*7.43*	*6.38*	*6.06*	*6.62*	*Consensus*
18	Czech Republic	7.36	6.05	6.11	6.51	Procedural consensus
19	France	7.01	5.7	6	6.57	Majoritarian
20	Slovenia	7.55	5.32	5.90	6.26	Procedural consensus
21	Spain	6.84	6.43	5.27	6.18	Majoritarian
22	Italy	7.2	6.05	5.11	6.12	Procedural consensus
23	Portugal	7.38	5.54	5.3	6.07	Procedural consensus

Medium level of democratic sustainable governance (6–5)

24	Slovakia	7.02	5.4	5.54	5.99	Procedural consensus
25	Malta	5,47	5.59	5.23	5.43	Majoritarian
26	Greece	6.9	5.02	4.40	5.4	Majoritarian
27	Bulgaria	5.75	5.01	5.02	5.26	Procedural majoritarian
28	Croatia	5.92	4.82	5.01	5.25	Procedural majoritarian
29	Cyprus	6.2	4.30	4.73	5.08	Procedural majoritarian
30	Romania	5.05	4.48	5.23	5.02	Procedural majoritarian

Low level of democratic sustainable governance (5–0)

31	Turkey	4.42	5.55	4.81	4.93	Consolidating
32	Hungary	4.11	4.99	5.03	4.71	Procedural majoritarian

Source: Bertelsmann Foundation (2015: 16–17).

Note

Author's classification on level of democratic sustainable governance. Total SGI Index as the average of the sum of all three indices. Procedural majoritarian and procedural consensus are third- and fourth-wave democratisation democracies which have well-functioning institutions, but not as yet strong civic cultures or civil society.

14 *Statecraft of consensus democracies*

Figure 1.2 Map of West Central Europe.

in five classic examples of consensus democracies: Austria, Belgium, Luxembourg, the Netherlands and Switzerland. There are several reasons for this choice.

First, they all belong to a geographical area with a common culture (following Gerhard Lehmbruch's characterisation of West Central Europe), and they are cited in the literature as the best examples of the consensus democracy type. The histories of these five countries are highly intertwined; the role of Germany should not be underestimated in this context. There has also been a considerable

Table 1.4 West Central Europe: basic data

Countries	Area in thousand square km	Population in millions	Gross domestic product				Unemployment rate in percentage		Income distribution 2014 lower 20/top 20 per cent quintiles	Global competitiveness index 2015 ranking out of 144 countries	Perceived corruption index 2015 100 = no corruption	
			In billion € 2013	Per capita in € 2013	Growth rate average 2010–2015 %	Growth rate 2015 %	Average 2009–2015	2015			Ranking	Value
Austria	83.9	8.43	313.1	32,200	0.5	0.8	5.1	5.7	4.1	23	16	76
Belgium	32.6	11.1	382.7	30,500	0.7	1.3	7.9	8.5	3.8	19	15	77
Luxembourg	2.6	0.525	45.5	67,900	1.9	3	5.1	6.4	4.4	20	10	81
Netherlands	41.5	16.7	602.7	32,600	0.1	2.2	5.5	6.9	3.8	5	5	87
Switzerland	41.3	8.2	490	61,100	1.2	0.7	4.4	4.5	4	1	7	81

Sources: Eurostat (2016d, h, i); OECD (2016g, h); WEF (2015: 7–8); TI (2016).

16 *Statecraft of consensus democracies*

institutional transfer among these countries, particularly among the Benelux countries (Lehmbruch 1996: 4; see Chapter 2, this volume).

Second, our objective is not merely to analyse their similarities but, more importantly, to depart from the bird's-eye view that characterises Lijphart's statistical method in *Patterns of Democracy*, zooming in to identify the specific varieties of consensus democracies. We are interested in the particularities and path-dependent developments of these countries and how they have played out in the past, present and tentatively in the future. In this regard, we are influenced by Adrian Vatter's excellent work on Switzerland; his pioneering comparative study on the 26 cantonal political systems in Switzerland is a major source of inspiration for this work (Vatter 2002, 2007, 2012, 2014).

Third, these are the five countries that considerably influenced Lijphart's work. Consciously or subconsciously, all his theoretical work can be traced back to his case study on the politics of accommodation in the Netherlands. With all due respect for Lijphart's groundbreaking work, he has consistently promoted the Dutch model of democracy (see the cogent critique of Lijphart's work by Bormann 2010). The five democracies analysed here are regarded as the classic consociational democracies; as such, they deserve a closer look than the indiscriminate picture offered by the statistical method.

Fourth, Germany is a consensus democracy, but does not fit into the category of small consensus democracies analysed here. All these five democracies are dependent on the democratic and economic performance of Germany; however, they themselves built consensus democracies much earlier than Germany. In particular, Benelux and Switzerland have a lengthier history of path-dependent consensual politics. Austria, like Germany, moved towards consensus democracies following the Second World War. Moreover, Germany would require a book on its own which would undermine a more consistent and deeper look at these small democracies.

Strategic management in consensus democracies: a permanent process of re-equilibration

Between 1970 and the present day, consensus democracies have had to deal with processes of change and to move towards a new equilibrium in terms of political status quo. Such 're-equilibration' has been essential for the survival of these small democracies as they compete in an increasingly globalised world.

Our main research question is how the classic consensus democracies – Austria, Belgium, Luxembourg, the Netherlands and Switzerland – have restructured and adjusted their institutions to the changing global capitalist environment. The role of political and economic elites is acknowledged, albeit in the context of the institutional framework. In this sense, political and socio-economic institutions are our main unit of analysis.

We assume that, in comparison to the successful golden 30 years (*trentes glorieuses*) between 1945 and 1975, the past four-and-a-half decades have not offered much stability. Instead, they have required structural changes as countries adapt from welfare states to 'competition' states that are better adjusted to the globalised world economy (Cerny 1990: ch. 8, 1997).

Consequently, political elites have had to develop political-strategic management skills in order to deal with the 'turbulence' of transition from a state-centric system to a new architecture based on a global governance that, according to Rosenau, is split into state-centric and multi-centric systems that coexist with one another. States are operating in a disorderly transition to the new equilibrium emerging in the post-Cold War era. The difference is that this equilibrium is no longer dominated by states, but instead is shared with non-governmental organisations, economic actors such as multinationals and enterprises, and private governance actors such as rating agencies and the private internet governance enterprise (Internet Corporation for Assigned Names and Numbers (ICANN); Rosenau 1990; Rosenau and Czempiel 2000).

In the process of this highly turbulent global transition from the bipolar Cold War period to a (still emerging) global governance regime, the assumption of political stability has necessarily been replaced by the principle of constant change. As political elites deal with the unrelenting contingency of options stemming from a globalised economy and politics, they have had to adopt political 'strategic management' tools and skills. Moreover, a sense of powerlessness has become widespread in politics, the economy and society (see Naim 2013).

'Strategic management', a concept borrowed from business studies, essentially refers to the development of strategies intended to ensure the long-term survival of an organisation – in our case the nation-state – in an increasingly chaotic world (for more details, see Mintzberg et al. 2009).

The term will be used here in a more flexible way to characterise long-term structural processes of change in the political field. High levels of contingency and contextual variables such as elections do not allow us to use the concept as it is applied in business studies. Here, it is merely a heuristic, empirical, theoretical concept that allows us to better understand long-term change in consensus democracies. One particular question involves to what extent processes of change are intentional or unintentional, taking into account the pressures arising from various contexts. In many cases, strategic management may simply be actors 'muddling through' in a crisis situation, clumsily reacting to an ongoing long-term predicament. Moreover, structural processes in an open environment may lead to unintended outcomes that radically diverge from the intended effects. Jan-Erik Lane is highly critical of the analysis of public administration under the prism of strategic management, pointing out that in the political field, strategic management has a different meaning than in the business context. Lane evidently welcomes strategic management at the macro (or rather governmental) level as an important tool transition to the new equilibrium emerging in the post-Cold War era (Lane 2009: 166–177).

A country cannot be run like an enterprise, not even an enormous enterprise such as a multinational corporation. In an enterprise, success is measured in terms of profit in the marketplace. Naturally, other side effects related to corporate social responsibility may enhance the quality of this success; however, they

18 *Statecraft of consensus democracies*

are of secondary priority. In contrast, a government in a substantive democracy is evaluated according to the quality of life of its citizens in political, economical and social terms. Although adequate management of the economy in a globalised world has become a constraining reality of governments, their main task is to maximise the quality of life of their citizens in all these dimensions. A culture of social partnership between employers, employees and civil society organisations is central to the preservation of citizens' quality of life in the context of turbulent global change. Thus, a high level of democratisation in economic life is an important element of consensus democracies.

Strategy is a political concept frequently used in war studies; nevertheless, we argue here that an increasingly difficult global political and economic environment has led to the strategicisation of thinking in most European governments, in particular in small European democracies with fewer resources (for an excellent account of the history of strategy, see Freedman 2013). Therefore, we assert that political strategic management is an indispensable methodology used by political elites to navigate their polities through the turbulent processes of globalisation (see Raschke and Tils 2007).

Multi-dimensional (political, social, economic, cultural), multi-spatial (regional, national, EU, global) and multi-temporal (different time frames between and within dimensions and spatial levels) perspectives are the foundations necessary to understand how consensus democracies have been able to maintain political stability despite domestic changes, global turbulence and Europeanisation trends. This book examines comparatively how political and socio-economic institutions in Austria, Belgium, Luxembourg, the Netherlands and Switzerland have adjusted to the new global reality of permanent change. The time frame will be what we call the 'great transformation of the late twentieth century': the period between 1973 and the present day. One particular focus will be the loss of political stability and the process of re-equilibrating a democratic polity to achieve a new equilibrium in consensus politics. The theoretical basis for this process of 're-equilibration' was developed by Juan Linz and Alfred Stepan, who define it as follows:

> Re-equilibration of a democracy is a political process that, after a crisis that has seriously threatened the continuity and stability of the basic democratic political mechanisms, results in their continued existence at the same or higher levels of democratic legitimacy, efficacy, and effectiveness. It assumes a severe jolting of those institutions, a loss of either effectiveness or efficacy, and probably legitimacy, that produces a temporary breakdown of the authority of the regime.
>
> (Linz and Stepan 1978: 87)

Juan J. Linz and Alfred Stepan's 're-equilibration' concept was intended to characterise democratisation processes and the danger of the reversal of such processes; here, however, we transfer the concept to more 'mature' established democracies and explore whether, in a turbulent, constantly changing world,

Statecraft of consensus democracies 19

such re-equilibration is an inherent feature of postmodern democracies of which political elites must always be aware. We also use the terms 're-equilibration' and political 'strategic management' interchangeably to describe the attempts of political elites to ensure political stability and economic competitiveness in the long term.

What we refer to as the 'statecraft' of consensus democracies has been influenced by Giuseppe Di Palma's study on democratic transitions, in which the author discusses the skills political actors require to deal with all possible challenges in the establishment of a new political regime during democratic transition. Di Palma defines 'political crafting' as follows:

> By 'crafting', I mean to describe chiefly four aspects of democratization: (1) the quality of the finished product (the particular rules and institutions that are chosen among the many available); (2) the mode of decision making leading to the selection of rules and institutions (pacts and negotiations versus unilateral action); (3) the type of 'craftsmen' involved (the alliances and coalitions forged in the transition); and (4) the timing imposed on the various tasks and stages of the transition. Naturally, political actors in the transition may or may not have the objective opportunity – or the subjective ability that transcends opportunities – to make the correct choices. Nonetheless, it is these four aspects that ultimately influence the success of transitions.
>
> (Di Palma 1990: 8–9)

We argue in *Statecraft of Consensus Democracies* that 'political crafting' is not limited to the skills employed by political leaders during democratic transitions; rather, it is a permanent practice that may also be found in strong, advanced democracies in general, due in particular to the modern simultaneous processes of political, economic, social and cultural change.

The concept of political 'crafting' is used in reference to the processes of adjustment to turbulent global changes. We argue that a constant process of 're-equilibration' is undertaken so that national political and economic institutions will be compatible with internal and external political, social and economic changes.

The great transformation of the late twentieth century and consensus democracies

Since the 1970s, a worldwide transformation has been taking place that has substantially affected the way in which politics is conducted in most countries. In particular, small consensus democracies in the European Union have been subject to major social, economic, political and cultural changes. These changes have been profound across all these dimensions, gradually creating new societies and, in part, new political systems. In this book, we refer to this worldwide transformation of politics, economies, societies and cultures as the 'great transformation of the late twentieth century' (Magone 2006: 51–55; 2011: 11–16, 95–135; 2015: 8–14).

Karl Polanyi's seminal work *The Great Transformation* (1944), which describes and analyses the impact of industrial capitalism on society and politics from the nineteenth century to the first half of the twentieth century, is a key reference for understanding change in consensus democracies. This unstable period, with its shifts towards democratisation and industrialisation, also triggered reactive side effects such as the emergence of totalitarian movements (National Socialism, Communism, Fascism) that offered alternative solutions to the impact of change (Polanyi 1944, 1957: ch. 20; see Figure 1.3).

The consensus democracies analysed in this book are particularly vulnerable to this cluster of simultaneous change at different levels of the world system. For one thing, all these consensus democracies opted for a liberal democratic regime embedded in a global capitalist economy. In this sense, many pressures of

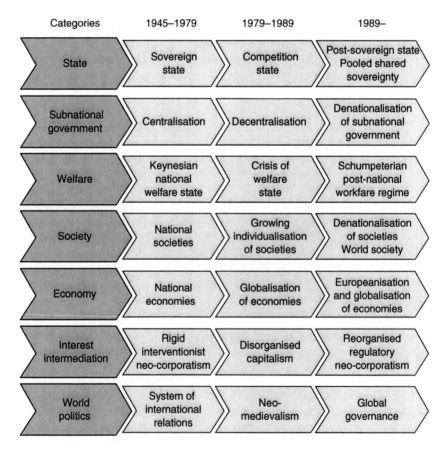

Figure 1.3 The great transformation in post-1979 European politics.
Source: Magone (2011: 13).

Statecraft of consensus democracies 21

change have been external rather than domestic. This vulnerability requires political and economic elites to make choices that preserve the competitiveness of their economies in the context of political stability. The balance between politics, economy and society must be just right to enable responses to external change. Finally, these circumstances also require political elites to think ahead in order to deal with the increasing turbulence of the external world.

Figure 1.3 shows how political elites must understand change in different dimensions and adjust institutions accordingly. In the following pages, I delineate some of the issues that will be discussed in this book in a comparative perspective. Table 1.5 may help contextualise these processes of simultaneous change within European democracies in general and in consensus democracies in particular.

Our main approach will be neo-institutionalist, which signifies that the book will refer extensively to the literature on historical institutionalism and emphasise path-dependent changes in institutions (Pierson 1998; Thelen and Steinmo 1992).

Sociological institutionalism/social constructivism will also be important approaches in this work. We are interested in the continuity of and change in norms, values and worldviews within institutions over time. As a result, our study focuses on the core institutions of the consensus democracies: political parties, governments, parliaments, subnational governments and neocorporatist structures. Although socio-economic change is discussed throughout the book, our primary interest is how such change has affected the institutional settings and political cultures of the specific countries. We also assume that there are processes of deconstruction and reconstruction within institutions as they attempt to adjust to new realities. The case of Belgium quite clearly illustrates a reconstructive process (moving from a unitary state to a federal state) framed by the rules of consensual politics.

Table 1.2 provides a summary of the cluster of simultaneous changes in politics, economy and society that are shaped by political and economic leaders as well as by civil society actors, also in the more advanced European democracies. This important element of Anthony Giddens' structuration theory is a central argument of the book. There is an ongoing and constant political crafting of change by political leaders, but ultimately political leaders are embedded in specific changing socio-economic frames that also change them (Giddens 1984, 1985). This is also a central thesis of social phenomenology, a field associated with Alfred Schütz. The social construction of reality becomes highly relevant in the way in which consensus democracies emerge (Schütz 1932; Berger and Luckmann 1966, 1991). Many rules and symbols of consensus democracies have been taken for granted as a reality that frames how politicians and the population shape politics. In this sense, this book takes into account the fact that past patterns of behaviour and political-cultural reified institutions reach into the present and allow for adjustments to changing conditions. Thus, democracy is not regarded as a static polity that achieves a peak and then remains forever at that level, but rather as a dynamic process of permanent

Table 1.5 From the industrial to the information age

	Dimensions	Industrial age (1945–1979)	Information age (1980s–)
Politics	**State**	Government, welfare state	Governance, workfare state
	Parties	Catch-all parties and mass parties	Cartel party
	Participation	Monopoly of political parties through encapsulation of cleavages	Pluralisation of participation forms, conventional and unconventional
	Territorial structure	Tendency towards centralised, hierarchical structures	Tendency towards decentralisation and subnationalisation of politics
Economy	**Economy**	Economy centred around industrial sector	Economy centred around tertiary sector
	Structure of economy	• Fordism; • dominance of huge factories; • synchronisation of national space and time due to dominance of industrial sector	• Post-Fordism; • lean production; • decentralisation and relocation of production to labour-intensive countries; • erosion of national space and time in detriment to global space and time
	Labour market objective	Full employment	Employability
	Interest intermediation	Interventionist social democratic neo-corporatism	Regulatory liberal neo-corporatism
Society	**Nature of society**	Homogeneous national society	Heterogeneous multicultural society
	Social structure	Class-based society Dominant working class	Knowledge-based society New middle classes dominant
	Social mobility	Increase of upward mobility through redistributive de-commodifying welfare policies	Increase of both upward and downward mobility due to re-commodified workfare policies
	Civil society	Emergence of civil society organised within collective official organisations	• Increase in complexity of civil society; • non-governmental organisations

Source: Magone (2011: 97).

Statecraft of consensus democracies 23

re-equilibration in order to maintain a high level of quality in the context of a system of competitive capitalism.

In this book, we are unable to address all aspects of these processes of change. Our focus is the impact of internal and external change on primary political institutions. What are the levels of continuity and change in political and economic institutions? Can we identify re-equilibration processes that attempt to cope with the pressures of change? How does consensual politics contribute to and facilitate this statecraft in a turbulent world?

In the following section, we delineate some of the transformations that have taken place over the past five decades in Europe in general and in consensus democracies in particular.

From international to global politics and governance

There is a tendency to refer to globalisation as an economic process, but in reality it is also a political, social and cultural one. The world economy is not a power-free system of market interactions; rather, it is clearly dominated by certain hegemonic designs. The most attractive hegemonic design of the world economy remains US-style neoliberalism, elements of which are created and disseminated by the USA in conjunction with the United Kingdom, Ireland, Canada, New Zealand and Australia. These countries all represent very strong economies that work to sustain this hegemonic design of neoliberalism (for two critical views, see Agnew 1993; Gindin and Panitch 2013). The opposing model of Chinese state capitalism is not as attractive due to its lack of liberal democratic foundations. Issues related to the nation's underdeveloped rule of law, accountability and transparency further undermine the appeal of the Chinese model (McNally 2013). The European Union project aims to shape globalisation, not only politically but also economically. However, internal dissent and national resistance on the part of some member-states have thus far prevented the EU from becoming a political superpower (see Magone *et al.* 2016; Telò 2006). According to the political scientist George Modelski, since the end of the Cold War we have been experiencing a major transition towards a new, stable hegemonic world system in which the USA and China are the main competitors. It is expected that struggles over the world economy and the political-economic categories of the world economy will continue up until 2025 or 2030. Small states with open economies will have to deal with the insecurity created by the struggles between the major superpowers. Trade (and the lack of it) will increasingly be used as a political weapon against countries that challenge the hegemonic political and economic design (Modelski 2000; Attinà 2003, 2011). Despite attempts by neo-conservatives in the USA to return to power politics (see the insightful critique of American foreign policy by the former 'neo-con' Fukuyama 2006) and China's neo-imperialist tendencies, the overall trend seems to be towards a multi-level global governance system with coordinating structures at the top and regional counterparts (such as the European Union and Mercosur) as intermediate structures. The power of the nation-states will be

24 *Statecraft of consensus democracies*

constrained; nevertheless, the pooling of resources will enhance international and global stability and provide more security. It is in this context of transformation that we seek to analyse the ability of nation-states to achieve the best deals for their countries (Magone 2006; Kennedy *et al.* 2002; Attinà 2011).

George Modelski's long-cycle model may be compared to what the French historian Fernand Braudel referred to as *la longue durée*. According to Braudel, there are three time dimensions that coexist with one another but have different spans. The dimension of everyday life (*temps evenementiel*) focuses on day-to-day events and occurrences, on our everyday world and all its facets. Structural or civilisational time (*temps structurel ou civilisationel*) frames an almost immutable period that may comprise centuries. Finally, *la longue durée* represents a timespan between everyday time and immutable time, usually between 40 and 50 years (Braudel 1993: 34–35). This timespan helps us to understand the great transformation that the world (and particularly the small democracies of West Central Europe) has been experiencing. Over this time interval, one may expect to observe simultaneous change at global, European, national and local levels. New information technologies have created the conditions for a 'flat world' with a more dynamic spatio-temporal world geography (Friedman 2007). As Manuel Castells argues, we are now in a different stage of capitalism as a civilisation: specifically, the 'informational age' in which time and space are converging (see Castells 1996, 1998). So-called 'glocalisation' (the merging of the global and local) is affecting our way of life and changing our behaviour on a daily basis (Robertson 1992: 173–174).

The Europeanisation of national politics: from governments to multi-level governance

Thatcherism and Reaganomics both played a major role in shifting the global economy towards neoliberalism, which had a definite impact on the open economies of West Central Europe.

Up until 1985, political elites in consensus democracies had to develop their own national strategies with regard to the processes of change; subsequently, European integration based on shared sovereignty between the member-states became an important strategic management process to respond to the growing pressures of globalisation. Although the strategy was devised at the European level (Cecchini Report 1988, Lisbon Strategy 2000 and Europe 2020), it was negotiated between the member-states. In this context, it is important to differentiate between the globalisation and the Europeanisation of national strategies (for more detail on the concept of Europeanisation see Ladrech 2010). Whereas globalisation represents a general pressure on all countries worldwide, Europeanisation stems from the accelerated European integration project to create a Single European Market, which makes it easier for EU member-states to strategically protect themselves to some degree from the pressures of the global economy and politics. The European Community/European Union is a project that entails a shift from national to shared pooled sovereignty in part in order to reduce exposure to the pressures of globalisation. As William Wallace has long recognised, this process of shared pooled sovereignty is untidy, uneven across policies and incomplete. It is a process in the making, one that requires a change of mentality from a one-dimensional national level to a multi-level perspective (Wallace 1999, 2005). The innovations introduced by former president of the European Commission Jacques Delors between 1985 and 1995 were instrumental in accelerating the process of European integration. Over the course of a decade, Delors transformed the European Community from a system in which nation-states dominated despite its supranational nature into what we know today as the European Union, using a 'Russian dolls' approach to expand the EU's competences (for more details see Ross 1995). Since the beginning of his tenure, in addition to substantially increasing its budget, the EU has become responsible for new areas, such as coordinating foreign and security policies towards a common policy and, especially following the refugee crisis of 2015, securing the external borders of the European Union. These trends fall under what Stefano Bartolini refers to as 'restructuring Europe'. The EU's external borders have become 'hard', whereas the internal borders between the member-states have grown softer (Bartolini 2005: ch. 4; Magone 2006; on Delors' creeping competences, see Pollack 1994, 2000). Since Delors' presidency, the European Union has been engaged in a global transition, becoming the most important partner of the United Nations as the primary agent of global governance, at least in funding terms; however, there has also been a transition from a mentality based on methodological nationalism to a perspective of methodological Europeanism (Callaghan 2010; Vauchez 2015; Wimmer and Schiller 2002). This has been quite an arduous process, especially after more than two centuries of deeply ingrained visions of national communities. In terms of population, due to negative demographic changes, the EU and more so individual countries in Europe will become increasingly irrelevant in the world over the coming decades as larger countries such as China, India, Brazil and potentially Russia will gain in importance. Consequently, a united European Union is the only way to maintain a degree of relevance in the world economy and politics (see Magone *et al.* 2016; Rüger 2016).

A good example of acting together in a highly turbulent world on behalf of all of its members is the response of the EU to the financial and Eurocrisis between 2008 and 2013, a catastrophe triggered by the collapse of Lehmann Brothers and other banks in the USA due to exposure to toxic assets from the subprime mortgage market. After a period of confusion and panic, European political leaders were forced to devise a strategy to overcome the Eurocrisis. Cooperation between Germany and France (specifically, between German Chancellor Angela Merkel and French President Nicolas Sarkozy; the so-called 'Merkozy' duo was instrumental in creating political and economic defences against speculative markets; Crespy and Schmidt 2014). The establishment of a temporary bailout fund in 2010 and a permanent fund in October 2012, the European Stability Mechanism (ESM), may be regarded as one of the most important measures implemented to protect the Eurozone countries. For small European states in a

26 *Statecraft of consensus democracies*

turbulent global economy, the European integration process is an extremely important project due to its protective nature. Further reforms to the Economic and Monetary Union (EMU) and economic governance were introduced and signed by almost all member-states (with the exception of the UK and the Czech Republic, both of which are outside the Eurozone; Schweiger 2014; Laffan 2014, 2016; Verdun 2013b). However, there is still considerable work to be done. Major issues include not only the still looming sovereign debt crisis in Southern European member-states but also the postponement of joining the Eurozone on the part of many Central and Eastern European countries, either because they do not meet the criteria or because they do not want to. Nevertheless, a positive note is that the three Baltic states regard being part of the EMU as an asset, particularly in light of deteriorating relations with Russia. As a result, a system of differentiated integration has prevailed (see Schweiger 2014). In this context, Austria, the Netherlands, Belgium and Luxembourg are net payers to the EU budget and therefore also part of the club of rule-makers (see Magone *et al.* 2016).

Despite all the problems of the Eurozone, EU membership is more or less accepted in Austria, Belgium, Luxembourg and the Netherlands. Critical voices are strongest in Austria and the Netherlands, especially among the nationalist populist forces of the Freedom parties in each country (see Chapter 5). The mainstream political and economic elites, together with civil society, have been actively constructive in shaping European political and economic governance institutions towards a culture of stability. The high level of integration of Switzerland has also exposed the Swiss Franc in relation to the Euro, in particular when a major devaluation of the latter took place and the Swiss National Bank could no longer artificially maintain a stable exchange rate. The Swiss economy is currently struggling with the strong Swiss Franc (*Handelsblatt*, 28 February 2016, Interview CH). The Euro offers considerable stability to the business communities in all Eurozone member-states, as it is the second most important currency in the world after the US dollar. Following the Eurocrisis, it may even gain in importance in a long-term perspective.

Politics: political change, insecurity and the rise of populism

Both globalisation and Europeanisation are reinforcing factors for trends in many European societies. The decline of the nation-state as a 'bordered power container' (Giddens 1985: 13, 120) defining insiders and outsiders, citizens and non-citizens is being challenged domestically by the individualisation of societies and globally by global processes of immigration from poorer to richer regions. The European Union countries are a target area for these processes of immigration, and the refugee crisis has shown just how vulnerable the EU (like the USA, Australia, and other rich parts of the world) has become as a target of mass immigration. Consequently, the nation-state is being restructured as a larger 'bordered power container' at the European level in order to better manage immigration flows. This is probably one of the main lessons emerging from the refugee crisis. Our five consensus democracies are among the richest in the world and have been targeted by such immigration; however, this has led to major resistance in these societies. The emergence of populist political parties reflects both a nationalist populist backlash against the established elites and the dwindling steering capacity of the nation-state.

National political economy: adjusting to globalisation

Over the past 40 years, the five consensus democracies of West Central Europe have been engaged in redesigning their national political economies, moving towards globalisation and European integration. These nations are among the most competitive economies in the world: in the Global Competitiveness Index (see Table 1.4), they regularly occupy top positions in the global ranking, indicating that the reform processes of the past four decades have been successful. The European integration process further erodes national economies, as its objective is to create a single European market that will be able to maintain a degree of market power in a world economy (Figure 1.4).

The Benelux countries are among the founders of the European Union. Austria joined in 1995 and Switzerland, although a non-member, is strongly integrated. Thus, it is evident that all of these countries regard the EU as an important supporting factor in their future economic success. Today, all Eurozone member-states in general, and Austria, Belgium, Luxembourg and the Netherlands in particular, enforce strict economic policies in order to meet the agreed-upon targets outlined in national growth and stability pacts. The finance crisis of 2008 to 2013 has weakened their overall budgetary positions, and all four countries have struggled to re-equilibrate their finances. However, here we can already see some patterns. The expensive political systems of Austria and Belgium have had more difficulties in re-equilibrating their finances than Luxembourg and the Netherlands, but all four nations experienced significant deterioration in their public

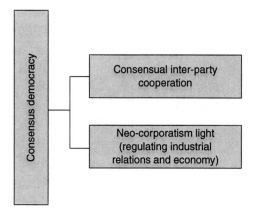

Figure 1.4 The multi-dimensional institutional foundations of consensus.

debt ratio. The European semester introduced as a consequence of the financial and Euro sovereign debt crises requires member-states to submit their budget outlines to peer review under the leadership of the European Commission before approval by national parliaments. This hollows out and constrains the choices of governments at the national level; instead, decisions are increasingly taken at the European level, following a rationale of methodological Europeanism (see Figure 1.5).

One of the major challenges for consensus democracies in the future will be preserving their social market economies as well as their robust systems of industrial relations and generous welfare states. As we will argue in Chapter 9, all five consensus democracies have become more liberal in their versions of coordinated market economies over the past 40 years as a kind of hybridisation has taken place. This has had clear consequences for these advanced consensus democracies, which rely on a highly coordinated market economy based on some form of neo-corporatist permanent arrangement between labour and capital. Social partnerships between employers' and employees' organisations have been weakened, especially due to the significant erosion of the influence of trade unions. We argue in this book that the advanced consensus democracies of West Central Europe will only be able to survive if they can keep alive the traditions of economic democracy established over decades. If the socio-economic dimension begins to resemble US-style capitalism, then there is a danger that alliances at the political level will erode in the long term.

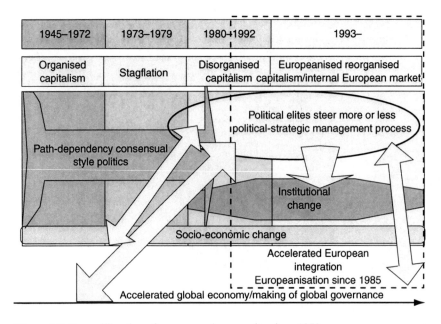

Figure 1.5 Re-equilibration of consensus democracies since 1979.

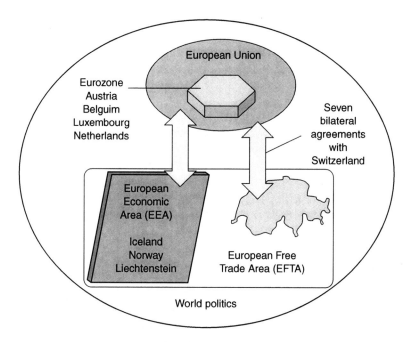

Figure 1.6 Consensus democracies and their relations to the European Union.

In this context, in light of attempts to reorganise national capitalism towards a European capitalist system, European integration framed by ideas related to the 'European social model' will become more important in the future. The role of the consensus democracies in this reorganisation will be crucial (Figure 1.6).

Society: denationalisation and social investment

According to Michael Zürn, a denationalisation process is taking place due to the increase in interactions across borders in contrast to those within nation-states. Globalisation is hollowing out the previous dominance of nationally bordered systems (Zürn 1998).

We argue that we are already living in a global society that is producing a new social stratification. Middle classes in all countries have become more mobile, and they are actively challenging nationally organised societies (for an excellent study on this subject see Münch 2011: 167–168). The management of societal heterogeneity and integration policies will become even more important in the future. The consensus democracies of West Central Europe are at the forefront of this shifting social stratification. Poorly educated natives in any given country will be less well equipped to succeed in the information age, and they will be the ones who will be left behind. This accelerated social mobility, both downward and upward, has similarities to the American model. Consequently, it

30 *Statecraft of consensus democracies*

will be critical for the consensus democracies to determine the appropriate policies of social cohesion and also competitiveness in order to bolster the stability of their eroding national societies. Investing in European but also national solutions may be the best way to control the acceleration of global social stratification. Failure to do so will result in an increase in nationalist populist resentments. The refugee crisis has ably demonstrated how uncontrolled mass immigration can lead to the rise of populist parties.

Through its widely promoted 'flexicurity' model (flexible labour markets sustained by strong social welfare systems), the employment strategy of the European Union is re-commodifying labour at all levels of society in order to achieve higher productivity. The principle of 'social investment' in people (specifically, activation policies seeking to integrate as many people as possible into the labour market) has become central to the policies of all West Central European nations (Hemerijck 2013). This is a vital element in developing a more efficient 'competition state'.

The structure of the book

In the context outlined above, our focus will be on how political and economic institutions have dealt with change. To this end, Chapter 2 reconstructs the political histories of our five countries, examining the historical junctures of consensus democracies. This review is necessary in order for us to understand all that has taken place over the past five decades. Chapter 3 presents an outline of the political systems as they are constitutionally enshrined; Chapter 4 then offers an overview of the societies and civic cultures of the five countries analysed. This is followed by Chapter 5 on the changing party systems and the rise of populist parties in these countries, with the exception of Luxembourg. The subsequent Chapter 6 investigates how the fragmentation of party systems has affected the national governments. Chapter 7 then analyses how parliamentarianism has been impacted by this party fragmentation and the growing importance of European integration. In Chapter 8, the subnational governments of these five consensus democracies are thoroughly explored. In Chapter 9, neo-corporatism and a social market economy are highlighted as intrinsic to the model of advanced consensus democracy. Finally, Chapter 10 provides a reflection on the five consensus democracies, questioning whether their experiences are in fact the model towards which the European Union is moving.

Conclusions: the consensus democracies of West Central Europe

In this chapter, the research question and the basic theoretical assumptions of the book have been presented. This book focuses on the question of how the core political and economic institutions of the consensus democracies of West Central Europe have managed to adjust to societal, global and European change. Here, we borrow the concept of 're-equilibration' developed by Juan J. Linz in his democratisation studies to develop an understanding of the process of transitioning from difficult socio-economic and political circumstances to a better situation in the context of a quickly changing global capitalist economy. Moreover, we assume that in a liberal democracy in the context of a global capitalist economy, political and economic elites are under considerable pressure to use their 'craft' to strategically steer the polity from troubled waters to more peaceful ones. As a result, political actors in advanced substantive democracies must be constantly on alert in order not to fall behind economically, thereby endangering the foundations of democracy. We also argue that political and economic elites work closely together to preserve a holistic model of democracy that comprises both the political and socio-economic standards. The five countries of West Central Europe – Austria, Belgium, Luxembourg, the Netherlands and Switzerland – are regarded as classical examples of consensus democracies; they also share a common history and geographical context. In the next chapter, we seek to provide a comparative account of their successes and failures in crafting their democracies over the past five decades of the great transformation of the late twentieth century.

2 The creation and development of consensus democracies

The creation of national political cultures is a long process of collective historical experiences that are framed and selected in order to provide a sense of belonging to a particular community. Eric Voegelin describes this process as political religions replacing the dominance of the Catholic and later Protestant churches since the nineteenth and twentieth centuries (Voegelin 1938). The French Revolution was the innovative element in the rise of civil or political religion, which Benedict Anderson refers to as the taken-for-granted 'imagined community' that in reality is made and invented by political elites in a context of advancing capitalism. The nation-state is based on ideology, and it is merely a historical phenomenon (Anderson 1991: 6–7). The West Central European democracies are no exception to the rule in this regard. None of the countries existed before the Vienna Congress of 1815, and it was the French Revolution and the Napoleonic invasion of these territories that contributed to the rise of nationalism (Hobsbawn 2000).

In this chapter, we seek first to briefly delineate the development of these political spaces prior to the nineteenth and twentieth centuries. The subsequent period from the modern foundation of the West Central European nation-states up until 1945 is discussed in a comparative perspective. The third section concentrates on the golden age of the welfare state, which lasted until the end of the 1970s. This is followed by a description of the transformation of this golden age welfare state to the present competition state in the context of global and European governance.

The three main spaces of West Central Europe prior to the early nineteenth century

It was in particular the work of Gerhard Lehmbruch that introduced West Central Europe as a distinct cultural area that contributed to the emergence of what he calls 'negotiated democracy' (*Verhandlungsdemokratie*). All of the countries studied in this book were strongly connected to the breakdown of the Empire of the Franks in the ninth and tenth centuries and the establishment of the German-Roman Holy Empire after the Middle Ages, and they clearly influenced one another in terms of politics and culture (Lehmbruch 1996, 2012). We can

Creation and development of democracies 33

roughly differentiate between three spaces in West Central Europe that in terms of political jurisdiction may be overlapping: the Austrian territories and adjacent regions in East Central and Southeastern Europe, the Lowlands in the north comprising the Benelux countries, and Switzerland. Although none of the countries in this study existed in the ninth and tenth centuries, these three political-geographical spaces and their peoples serve as the foundations for the new nations in the nineteenth and twentieth centuries.

Rise and decline of the Habsburg Empire, 1273 to 1866

The first political-geographical space we examine is the modern Austrian territory and the regions around it. The main actors are the monarchs of the Habsburg monarchy, who became the new rulers of Austria in 1273. The Habsburg Empire expanded up until the nineteenth century to form a huge contiguous space. One important strategy of the Habsburgs was its successful matrimonial policy: a primary motto of the Austrian Habsburg dynasty was 'Bella gerant alii, tu felix Austria nube, Nam que Mars aliis, dat tibi regna Venus' (Let others wage war, but thou, O happy Austria, marry, for those kingdoms which Mars gives to others, Venus gives to thee). By the sixteenth century, through this matrimonial policy, Charles V (1500–1580) had control or influence over other territories as well, such as the wealthy Duchy of Burgundy, Spain, Bohemia and Moravia, in addition to a small western part of Hungary. He split the administration of the Empire with his brother Ferdinand I, who had to deal with the Reformation and Counter-reformation – movements that led to important understandings of tolerance in consensus democracies. The Augsburger religious peace in 1555 introduced the principle 'cuius regio, eius religio', which became a formula for coexistence among the states with different confessions in the Holy Roman Empire of the German Nation. This allowed the prince of each individual state to choose the religion of his territory. This principle was confirmed after the Thirty Years' War (1618–1648) in the Westphalia Peace Treaty in Münster and Osnabrück in 1648. The consolidation of the Austrian territories continued throughout the seventeenth and eighteenth centuries. By the time of Maria Theresia (1740–1770) and Josef II (1770–1790), monarchs could rely on a modern centralised state to implement surprisingly modern policies influenced by enlightened absolutism. These were particularly important for the education of the largely illiterate population and the establishment of a modern economic policy based primarily on mercantilism (Williams 1999: 403–406). This was complemented by a continuous programme of centralisation which reduced the power of the regional princes, but also that of the Church (Williams 1999: 406–412).

The French Revolution of 1789 would become a major juncture in European history. Austria was one of the few monarchies that managed to resist the Napoleonic invasions. Following the defeat of Napoleon and his 100-day return, the Vienna Congress of 1815 finally created a contiguous Austrian Empire reaching from Bukovina in the southeast to Galicia, including western Poland, northern

34   *Creation and development of democracies*

Italy and the northern Balkans. The new Austrian Empire was dominated by the conservative Francis II and Prince Metternich.

Between 1815 and 1848, Metternich became the architect of an extremely conservative regime in Austria, but also the leader of the conservative Holy Alliance with Russia, Prussia and France, which acted against democratic revolutionary movements (Höbelt 1998: 19).

Despite a revolutionary movement in 1848, the Austrian Emperor maintained the old autocratic order up until 1866. Only the defeat against the alliance of northern German states led by Prussia in Königgrätz in 1866 put an end to this period of absolutism, as well as any ambitions to play a role in Germany. This led to a new constitutional structure, the Austro-Hungarian Monarchy, which was adopted after the compromise (*Ausgleich*) of 1867.

The difficult road to internal statehood: the case of Switzerland, 1291 to 1848

The second political-geographical space in West Central Europe is Switzerland. This region was able to preserve its freedoms and independence from outside powers (Swabia, Savoyen, Upper Burgundy, the German Empire) by creating a system of collective security. This facilitated a freer 'Alpine' society due to the fact that feudalist structures were only superficially imposed. Instead, a society of farmers and shepherds in the mountains and valleys worked together to resist outside influences (Marchal 2004: 155–165). The system of collective security, a medieval network of short-term overlapping authorities and alliances, originated among the rich cities of Bern, Zurich and Solothurn to protect their trade routes and interests. The first such alliance was in 1243 between Bern and Freiburg, but probably the first core alliance leading to modern Switzerland took place in 1291 between three small territories in the central Alpine area: Uri, Nidwalden and Schwyz. From that point on, a network of variable alliances spread across the territories of Switzerland. In 1370, the core alliance issued a 'parson's letter' (*Pfaffenbrief*) introducing a common law for all members. This was the first time the words 'unser Eydgnossenschaft' (our confederation) were used in written documents (Marchal 2004: 202). Several wars (such as the Battle of Sempach in 1386) had to be fought against the German Empire before their independence as a loose collective of free entities was acknowledged. The Peace of Westphalia in 1648 confirmed *de jure* the independence of the territory. This victory over the German Empire was a major milestone in establishing an independent political entity in the emerging European system of states.

Constitutional elements in the confederation could be found already during this period. There was an assembly that functioned as a conference of delegates as well as a federal government. Each member, known as a canton or state, would send two delegates who shared one vote. Decision-making was unanimous, meaning that the minority group would simply join the majority group, especially if the issues debated were not of great significance. At the end of the fifteenth century, Zurich became the permanent seat of the assembly. Over

Creation and development of democracies 35

more than two centuries, the confederation had accumulated several federal letters (*Bundesbriefe* or *Pfaffenbrief*) with detailed rules on how to deal with conflict and war. The customs law was also used to resolve major issues, and a system of arbitration was developed that issued binding decisions. In the case of conflict in a particular region, a more specialised assembly of stakeholder members would be established to solve the problem (Körner 2004: 387–388). Wars between the cantons were also frequent; the Reformation and Counter-reformation in particular triggered religious wars. The first and second Peace of Kappel in 1529 and 1531, respectively, settled these disputes by introducing the principle of 'cuius regio, eius religio' (Körner 2004: 419–425; de Capitani 2004: 477–478).

In the eighteenth century, a growing centralisation and oligarchisation of decision-making may be observed in the cities, as well as a tendency to expand power over the surrounding rural areas. The ancient democratic decision-making structures competed with attempts in some member-states to establish absolutist regimes, and the resulting conflict was a major impediment to the creation of modern states in rural member-states of the confederation. Many of these old democratic structures still exist today in Appenzell-Innerrhoden, Aargau, Glarus, Nidwalden and Obwalden (de Capitani 2004: 482–487). Culturally, a national Swiss consciousness began to emerge in the eighteenth century. Both the American Revolution in 1776 and the French Revolution in 1789 were major influences for the transformation of the loose confederation into a modern state. In addition to the idea of national constitutionalism, the centralising tendencies of the French had a particular impact. After three years of war, France controlled Switzerland and enforced a centralising constitution in 1798. This Helvetic Republic eliminated the independence of the cantons and concentrated all power in the centre. However, the new constitution was only barely accepted by the cantons; also in the centre, several *coups d'états* prior to 1802 prevented the establishment of a stable government. Finally, in 1803, following the mediation of Emperor Napoleon Bonaparte, a new constitution restored the rights of the cantons. The Helvetic Republic then consisted of 19 cantons. The assembly of the Republic met once a year in a rotating scheme in Freiburg, Bern, Solothurn, Basel, Zürich and Luzern. The *Schultheiß* or mayor of the city of the assembly was called the *Landammann* of Switzerland, and he represented Switzerland to the outside world. Moreover, a chancellery of the confederation was established as a new institution that would move each year to the new assembly place.

The defeat of Napoleon in 1814 also marked the end of the Helvetic Republic and a return to the old system. In 1815, the Vienna Congress confirmed the recaptured independence of the confederation, which increased in size to 22 cantons. Independence was confirmed, but only under the condition of permanent neutrality (de Capitani 2004: 514–522). The federal treaty (*Bundesvertrag*) of 1815 abolished the few structures that the constitution of 1803 had created. This fragmented web of interests was tolerated without major conflict until 1844, but subsequently led frequently to military conflict (Andrey 2004: 621–628). Liberal political elites tried to achieve the unification of the country; however,

36   *Creation and development of democracies*

this was resisted by the more conservative cantons. The internal conflicts within the confederation led to a civil war between the Catholic *Sonderbund* and the confederation, in part because the constitution had been accepted by majority voting, which had only recently been introduced to the decision-making process. The civil war lasted for 26 days in November 1847 (Andrey 2004: 629–630). The constitution of 1848 represented the culmination of a process of nation-state building that lasted for over 560 years, if we consider the alliance of Schwyz of 1291 to be the historical origin of Switzerland.

Between autonomy and centralisation: the origins of the Netherlands, Belgium and Luxembourg, 1300 to 1848

The third political-geographical space with a common history comprises the Lowlands (the Benelux countries). This history dates back to the emergence and then division of Lotharingia (840–873), a kingdom between France and Germany. It is a rich region, particularly in the northwest, in which city-states gained strategic importance. Prior to the French Revolution, two important major entities emerged: the Duchy of Burgundy (1384–1477) and the Dutch Republic (1581–1795).

The Duchy of Burgundy is an interesting larger entity that tried to structure a space dominated by powerful and rich cities. Since the thirteenth century, these cities had worked together and formed alliances in order to create collective security systems against outside forces. The main cities (Bruges, Ghent and Ypres) established a basic coordinating and administrative structure in order to maintain peace and stability in the country that was later expanded to include other cities.

The marriage policies of the Burgundy dukedom altered the autonomous positions of these cities. A marriage between Philip the Bold of Burgundy and Margarethe of Flanders led to the expansion of Burgundy to the north. Between 1384 and 1477, most of the space that is now Benelux was united under the Burgundy dynasty. This is significant because tendencies towards centralisation of the territory were resisted by the cities and the local population. The rich cities were important for the funding of the new Burgundy state, which was emulating the French model. New institutions were created in order to integrate the local population, such as the States-General in 1477, and symbols such as the Order of Golden Vlies in 1429 helped co-opt the nobility (Blockmans 2014: 96).

The matrimonial policies of the Habsburgs enabled them to inherit Burgundy in the sixteenth century, and the rich cities became an important source of income for the huge Empire. The Habsburg Empire consisted not only of Austria, but also Spain and its colonies, and it was expensive to maintain such a huge territory. The wealthy cities of the Lowlands were used as a source of financing, but the centralised administration became more oppressive over time (Israel 1998: 35–40).

In addition, Philip II of Spain introduced major changes to the political system through centralisation. Already in 1549, Charles V had adopted the

Creation and development of democracies 37

'Pragmatic Sanction'; this introduced one law system for all 17 provinces, which became an indivisible entity (Rietbergen 2014: 69–71).

Moreover, the religious wars in Germany led to the Augsburger peace of 1555, which followed the rule of 'eius regio, cuius religio' (the religion of the prince is also the religion of the people). In the case of the Netherlands, this meant that the largely Protestant Dutch had to accept Catholicism as their religion. The Spanish Inquisition was extremely brutal in enforcing Catholicism as the main religious confession. The resistance of minor magnates and the population further exacerbated the situation. The crumbling authority of the Habsburgs in the Netherlands prompted a harsh response by Philip II, who sent 10,000 troops under the Duke of Alba, who was to become the empire's new representative in the Netherlands (Israel 1998: 154). The magnates were generally inclined to accept peaceful settlements; however, the brutal response of Philip II to the revolt of 1566/1567 increased their commitment to resistance, and ultimately freedom was won after 80 years of conflict. The beheading of two of the most important magnates in the northern Netherlands, Count Egmont and Count Horn, at the Grand Place in Brussels was a crucial turning point (Israel 1998: 156).

The 80-year war lasted with interruptions from 1568 to 1648, the year of the Peace of Westfalia. In the act of abjuration issued in 1581, the seven northern provinces (Holland, Zeeland, Gelderland, Friesland, Utrecht, Overijssel, and Groningen and Ommerland) declared their independence and seceded from the Habsburg Netherlands.

The breakaway of the northern provinces from the Habsburg Empire created two different entities that evolved related political cultures. One was the Dutch Republic, which became a world power between 1581 and 1795, and the other was the southern Spanish Netherlands, comprising most of modern Belgium and Luxembourg. These different political cultures still play a major role in the way politics is conducted in these countries.

The constitution of the Dutch Republic, comprising the seven northern provinces, avoided the concentration of power in one hand. The most important institution was the States-General, which made all the decisions for the confederation. A State Council (*Raad van de Staate*) was the executive of the new political system. The *primus inter pares* of the executive was a civil servant called the Grand Pensionary (*raadspensioneer*), who was usually an individual with extensive experience in administrative matters recruited from the nobility (Israel 1998: 223). Hierarchically, the Grand Pensionary was the number two figure in the government, after the elected Stadtholder (*Stadhouder*), usually the Prince of Orange. The role of the Grand Pensionary became particularly important during periods in which there was no Stadtholder. For example, during 'stadtholderless' periods in 1650 to 1675 and 1702 to 1722, the position of the Grand Pensionary was strengthened. Such periods occurred due to a general antagonistic atmosphere between several provinces and the States-General concerning the focus on foreign policy of the Princes of Orange; the Grand Pensionary was regarded as focusing on the more important field of domestic policy.

38   *Creation and development of democracies*

The success of the Dutch Republic was based on the expansion of trade and innovation in industries, the freedom of religion and a high level of organisation in the sixteenth century. These principles did not do as well in eighteenth-century society, which led to a decline in the economy, particularly after 1770. As Jonathan Israel asserts, the Netherlands was then a society of rentier capitalists who lived off of their investments; this permitted the gap between rich and poor to increase considerably (Israel 1998: 1016–1017). Revolts influenced by the French and American Revolutions became commonplace (Rietbergen 2014: 127, 133). Finally, with the backing of the French, the Dutch Republic became the Batavian Republic between 1795 and 1806, and after 1806 it was annexed by France.

Following the breakaway of the northern provinces and the establishment of the Dutch Republic, the southern territory remained under the control of the Spanish branch of the Habsburgs. Catholicism dominated political and cultural life. In the second half of the eighteenth century, this region became part of Habsburg Austria. The enlightened absolutism of Charles VI, Maria Theresia and Joseph II adhered to centralising policies similar to those applied to Austria. Under Joseph II, Ostend and Ghent became important trade centres. The expansion of the city of Ostend was also aided by the new Ostend company, founded in 1722 in Vienna, which intended to compete with the British and Dutch East Asian companies (Vander Linden 1920: 180–181).

However, centralisation remained a major issue of contestation. On the eve of the French Revolution, in 1788/1789, a major revolt took place, leading for a brief period in early 1790 to the establishment of a United States of Belgium that included Luxembourg.

In the seventeenth and eighteenth centuries, Fortress Luxembourg, a major strategic location, was heavily contested (Trausch 2003: 185).

Famine, disease and war prevented Luxembourg from flourishing like the northern part of the Spanish Netherlands. However, reforms under Austrian rule (Maria Theresia and Joseph II) considerably altered this situation (Trausch 2003: 188–191, 194–200).

In 1792, the Austrian Lowlands became an integral part of revolutionary France, leading to centralisation. French rule lasted up until 1814, and the French Revolution has had an enduring administrative legacy in all three countries.

The Congress of Vienna in 1815 created the Kingdom of the Netherlands, which consisted of the territory of all three modern Benelux countries.

The creation of consensus democracies, 1815 to 1945: the nationalisation of politics

Between 1815 and 1945, our five consensus democracies were engaged in nation-state building. As Daniele Caramani has reconstructed in his study, this period was marked by the nationalisation of politics.

Caramani identifies two processes of structuring that became important for the creation of nation-states in the nineteenth century: on the one hand, external structuring through territorial boundary building (defining the borders of the new

Creation and development of democracies 39

polity) and functional socio-cultural boundary building (defining who belongs to the new polity), and on the other, internal structuring through democratisation allowing for a 'voice' through representation and nation building mainly due to the structuring of major cleavages (Caramani 2004: 18). The author lists three main phases since the 1830s. The first phase lasted from 1830 up until 1910 and was characterised by limited suffrage. The second phase was basically the inter-war period (1920–1939), and was characterised by the establishment of mass democracy. The third phase of this nationalisation of politics began after 1945 and lasts until the present day (Caramani 2004: 77).

The nationalisation of politics in Austria: the difficult change in mentality from empire to small state

Even today, the Austro-Hungarian monarchy exerts major influence on post-1918 Austria, and one can identify continuities in public administration and the political culture of the country. The expansion of suffrage in 1918 was a crucial turning point. In 1861, there were only indirect elections through the regional parliaments (*Landtage*) in which just 5.4 per cent of the country's 19.8 million inhabitants participated; this figure steadily increased following the introduction of restrictive suffrage in the direct elections of 1873, a system that was substantially expanded in 1892 and 1896. Finally, in 1907, male universal suffrage was introduced (Ucakar 1985: 132). Moreover, the roots of the traditional political parties – the Social Democrats, the Christian Socials and the German Nationals (*deutschnationale*) – can be traced back to the late nineteenth century.

The Social Democrats founded their party in 1888/1889 in Hainfeld, reliant on a rising working class. They opted for an 'Austro-Marxism' perspective that advocated an evolutionary process towards socialism through peaceful participation in institutions (Maderthaner 1996: 67, 69; Hanisch 2005: 123–126).

The Christian Socials had their stronghold in the conservative Catholic rural population and the lower middle classes. The Catholic Church was an important pillar of support. Karl Lueger, the charismatic first leader of the party, tended to employ populist and anti-Semitic language to mobilise the electorate (Hanisch 2005: 118–120). Georg Schönerer also used anti-Semitic discourse. After 1918, calls for unification with Germany were common (Hanisch 2005: 120–123).

Although the Habsburg emperor never resigned, a new 'Deutsch-Österreich' (German-Austrian) Republic was proclaimed on 12 November 1918. Following the collapse of the monarchy, the electoral system shifted from a majoritarian model to a system of proportional representation. Moreover, women were granted the right to vote in 1919. Austria thus became one of the first countries in Europe to introduce universal suffrage and proportional representation (Vocelka 2003: 272; Ucakar 1985: 385–403). The main winners of these developments were the three mass parties, in particular the Social Democrats and the Christian Socials.

Despite a relatively progressive constitution that was influenced strongly by the jurist Hans Kelsen (adopted in 1920 and revised in 1929: Ucakar 1985: 411), in the constitutional reality, violence dominated the political arena.

40   *Creation and development of democracies*

The First Republic may be characterised as a failed state, as the political elites were oriented more towards Germany than towards state and nation building. The Christian Socials worked closely with the moderate German Nationals to prevent the Social Democrats from coming to power. Political parties had paramilitary armies, resulting in constant conflict and violence (Vocelka 2003: 287). The catastrophic economic situation in the 1920s and 1930s further exacerbated the crisis of the new nation (Simon 1994: 98–99).

In the 1930s, the external environment was an additional factor affecting politics in Austria, with both German National Socialism and Italian Fascism attempting to influence the situation in the country. Following a three-day civil war between the Socialists and the Christian Socials in February 1934, Austria became a Fascist state under the leadership of Engelbert Dollfuss and later Kurt Schuschnigg. These men established what has become known as Austrofascism in the constitution of May 1934. Pressure from Nazi Germany ultimately led to the end of Austrofascism in 1938 and the annexation of Austria by Hitler. There was strong domestic support for the *Anschluss*, even among the political elites; the general idea was that Austria would be a member of a confederation or even part of a federation. However, the centralistic streamlining policies of Germany soon led to dissatisfaction with the manner of integration.

Switzerland: from civil war to a virtuous evolution towards inclusive democracy

The federal constitution of 1848 was a key turning point for the model of consensus and consociational democracy that we know today as Switzerland. Drafted by 14 politicians, it is still (in revised form) the constitution of the country, 168 years on. On 12 September 1848, a referendum resulted in a majority of 15.5 cantons comprising 1,897,887 votes supporting the new constitution, to 6.5 cantons comprising 292,171 votes against it (Brooks 1920: 45). In 1874, a revision of the constitution was confirmed by an overwhelming victory of 14.5 to 7.5 cantons, with 340,199 and 198,013 votes, respectively (Brooks 1920: 46).

Between 1848 and 1891, a liberal elite (*radikal Freisinnige*) focused on nation-state building. Even today, the Liberal Party of Switzerland (*Freisinnige Demokratische* Partei, FDP, Die Liberalen) remains central to the political system (Gruner 1981: 615).

Although a Catholic subculture existed, it was quite fragmented. In the 1890s, the emergence of early party structures consisting of notables may be observed, and it was only in 1891 that a Catholic conservative won a seat in the Federal Council (Gruner 1981: 600). Finally, in 1912, the Swiss Conservative People's Party (*Konservative Volkspartei der* Schweiz, KVPS) was founded (Gruner 1981: 604; 1969).

Up until 1918 democracy was dominated by a majority system based on male universal suffrage. On 13 October 1918, this was changed to proportional representation (Ruffieux 2004: 702). In the 1919 parliamentary elections, the Radical

Creation and development of democracies 41

Liberals lost their considerable majority, and an additional seat in the Federal Council was allocated to the Catholic conservatives. In 1929, the Farmers', Small Trade and Citizens' Party (BGB) won another seat, and in 1943, the Social Democrats joined the institution. Until that point, the Swiss government had been quite anti-socialist and anti-communist, excluding the SPS from the political system. Thus, at the end of the interwar period, the Federal Council consisted of three Liberals, two Christian Democrats, one Social Democrat and one representative of the BGB (Gruner 1981: 602; 1969).

A major national strike (*Landesstreik*) went into effect in November 1918; however, after the Federal Council threatened to break it up with violence, the SPS and its affiliated trade union (SGB) interrupted it. The parliamentary elections of 1919 based on proportional representation were an important factor in integrating the SPS. However, due to its radicalism, the party was excluded from power during the interwar period; consequently, it made extensive use of the instrument of direct democracy to influence the Federal Council. The Lucerne party programme of 1935 was more moderate, leading to a significant increase in support for the party in the 1943 elections (Gruner 1981: 625; 1969). The peace agreement of 19 July 1937, which established an ordered system of industrial relations in the metallurgy and machine-building industries, was crucial for the integration of the SPS and its trade union confederation (SGB). This agreement ensured wages and working condition rights for workers in exchange for social peace. The model was later expanded to other areas of the economy (Jost 2004: 794).

Of the four main parties, the BGB was the last to establish its party organisation, in 1936. It viewed itself as a highly conservative party of the people, directed against the larger interest groups. The party changed its name to the Swiss People's Party (*Schweizerische Volkspartei*, SVP) in Bern in September 1971 (Gruner 1981: 619–621; 1969).

The First World War expanded the competences and centralisation of the political system. An economisation of politics (*Verwirtschaftlichung der Politik*) took place in the 1930s. This pre-parliamentary process of consultation of interest groups has become an inherent part of the Swiss policy-making process. This permitted the cartelisation of politics by powerful industrial sectors as well as protectionism in the agricultural sector, particularly among the disadvantaged farmers in the mountainous rural areas (Jost 2004: 774–776).

The emergence of Fascist organisations at cantonal and national levels in the early 1930s was quite problematic. However, at the end of the decade, cooperation between the main parties (including the Social Democrats after 1943) prevailed.

At the end of the Second World War, the only major deficit of Swiss democracy was its inability to win approval for women's suffrage, which was only to be achieved in 1971. Until then, as Brigitte Studer cogently observes, 'L'Etat c'est l'homme' (The state is man: Studer 1996).

42 *Creation and development of democracies*

The Netherlands: evolutionary democracy in a centralised state

Between 1815 and 1830, the Kingdom of the Netherlands consisted of all three Benelux countries. However, opposition to centralising tendencies and the imposition of Dutch as the main language of the kingdom led to a revolution in Belgium demanding independence. The Netherlands was unable to reintegrate Belgium, even through war. Luxembourg became *de jure* independent in 1839, but remained de facto in personal union under the Dutch king until 1890. The secession of Belgium from the Kingdom of the Netherlands in 1830 had major democratic repercussions for the country.

The original autocratic constitution of 1814 was revised and democratised in 1848. The liberal political elites under the leadership of Johan Rudolf Thorbecke were an important factor in democratising the system. Thorbecke is considered the founding father of the democratic Netherlands. Among his reforms, one should not overlook several laws in both the central and local administrations that he designed and implemented in his first Cabinet between 1849 and 1853 (Kickert 2004: 84–86).

Successive reforms enabled the continuous expansion of universal suffrage. In 1917, compulsory universal male suffrage finally extended the vote to 70 per cent of the male population. Finally, as in Austria, universal suffrage was granted to women in 1919 (Secker 2000: 273).

Between 1848 and 1890, two main groupings dominated politics: the Liberals and the Conservatives, who worked closely with the Catholics. The main issue of the Catholics was the protection of confessional schools against liberal policies. After 1879, the conservative Protestant Anti-Revolutionary Party (ARP) under the leadership of the charismatic Abraham Kuypers changed the game, introducing a shift towards mass parties. As a consequence, other parties emerged. After a long process, a new Roman Catholic State Party (*Roomsch-Katholieke Staatspartij*, RKSP) was founded in 1926. A more radical confessional party was the Christian Historical Union (*Christelijk-Historische Unie*, CHU), founded in 1908. This was a splinter party from the ARP that was against cooperation with the Catholics. In 1885, the Liberal Union was founded.

In 1888, the Social Democratic Workers' Party (*Sociaal Democratische Arbeiderspartij*, SDAP) was established, clearly affected by ideological divisions with regard to the way to shape politics. Moreover, in 1920, the Communist Party of Netherlands was founded as a splinter party from the SDAP (Van Dooren 2000: 59). Also in the nineteenth century, the first trade union confederations emerged, promoting the social question in the context of accelerated industrialisation.

These political parties were a political representation of social pillarisation (*verzuiling*), which reached its peak in the interwar period. Different subcultures with their own organisations and cultural rituals lived parallel to one another (see de Rooy 2014: 197–203).

A crucial turning point towards a consensual and consociational democracy was the Pacification (*Pacificatie*) of 1917, which led to a compromise on the

Creation and development of democracies 43

funding of confessional schools and also later on the social question (Bloom 2014: 391, 406).

Three factors contributed to the stability of consensual politics during the interwar period. First, monarchs had long periods of incumbency – William III (1848–1890) and Wilhelmina (1890–1948) – and kept themselves out of politics. Second, this was complemented by a stable political class that alternated in power. Between 1922 and 1940, the Catholic Charles Ruijs Beerenbrouck (1918–1925, 1929–1935), the anti-revolutionary Hendrikus Colijn (1925–1926, 1937–1939) and the Christian-historical Dirk Jan Geer (1926–1929, 1939) basically took turns leading the government. In addition, the Social Democrats were included in government shortly before the war in 1939. Third, also during the depression years, Dutch capitalism profited from political stability and the governmental social programmes of the 1930s (Rietbergen 2014: 159; North 2003: 98–100).

According to J.C.H. Blom, Dutch society of the interwar period was a pillarised society with a bourgeois pattern of values. These values were order and authority, love for the fatherland, a work ethic, thrift and control (self-control preferred) – clearly, ideal values for a successful capitalist society (Blom 2014: 420).

The rise of National Socialism also had an impact on the Netherlands. The National Socialist Movement (NSB) was led by Anton Mussert, who profited from the developments in Nazi Germany as well as the economic crisis. The party had barely 1000 members in 1933, but by 1936 membership had increased to 52,000. The peak of support was 8 per cent in provincial assembly elections in 1935; however, thereafter it lost importance, largely due to its exaggerated radicalisation and overt anti-Semitism (North 2003: 96).

Between 10 May 1940 and the end of the war in 1945, the Netherlands became an integral part of the Third Reich, especially after 1943. Queen Wilhelmina and her government went into exile in London (North 2003: 101–108; Bloom 2014: 423–427).

Belgium: from a model constitution to a consensual democracy

The independence of Belgium in 1830 was due to a revolutionary coalition of upwardly mobile middle classes, including a heterogeneous group of intellectuals, teachers, wealthy craftsmen, journalists, civil servants and traders (Witte *et al.* 2009: 22). A moderate but highly modern constitution was adopted by a national constituent assembly elected by a census electoral system on 7 February 1831. Overall, just 1 per cent (46,000 people) of the population was eligible to vote in the early 1830s. The country had a unitary centralised state based on the French *departement* structure (Bitsch 2004: 65). The main language was French, despite the fact that a large part of the population also spoke Flemish. Leopold Saxe-Coburg, who had close ties to the British royal family, became the new king with 152 out of 196 votes in Parliament on 4 June 1831 (Bitsch 2004: 83–85).

Although the Belgian Revolution of 1830 was staged by a coalition between Liberals and Catholics, such unionism had vanished by 1847. Liberal governments

44 *Creation and development of democracies*

were instrumental in nation-state and market building. Belgian capitalism was quite dynamic in the context of early industrialisation. The country's economic stability lasted for more than 80 years between 1830 and 1914, due in large part to the dominance of the Liberals and later the Catholic party. The Liberals governed between 1847 and 1888 with minor interruptions, and the Catholics held power between 1888 and 1918. Also after the First World War, the Catholic party was the dominant party in coalition governments until 1945, with just a few exceptions between 1937 and 1939.

Similar to the Netherlands, funding for confessional schools and social legislation were the most salient questions. Catholic governments introduced state funding for faith-based schools, which was quite controversial (Vander Linden 1920: 329). Due to the appalling social conditions of Belgian capitalism, social legislation was expanded considerably at the end of the nineteenth and early twentieth centuries (Vander Linden 1920: 327, 328–330).

The expansion of suffrage became an important issue in the 1880s. Proportional representation based on plural voting was introduced in 1899 based on the innovative Victor D'Hondt method (Caramani 2000: 151). Universal male suffrage based on proportional representation was enacted in 1919, a long-standing demand of the Socialists and Liberals. However, universal female suffrage was only introduced in 1948 (Mabille 1997: 225–226; Caramani 2000: 151).

As mentioned above, three main parties emerged as central to the new political system of Belgium: the Liberals, the Catholics and the Socialists. All three parties are still central to the Belgian party system today. The Liberals founded the General Confederation of Liberalism in Belgium on 14 June 1846. In 1900, restructuring led to the establishment of the Liberal Union. This party was instrumental to the political system due to the antagonism between the Catholics and the Socialists, particularly in the interwar period, during which it participated in 17 out of 20 governments (De Winter 2000: 145–150; Wende 1981: 23–26).

The Catholic movement could rely on the vast network of organisations created by the Church, and so a proper party organisation was only established in 1879. However, the party basically consisted of a network of loose Catholic organisations that were unable to achieve cohesion before the Second World War, and it was refounded several times (De Winter 1992: 31–32; Wende 1981: 20–22).

In addition to its deep Catholic and Liberal traditions, Belgium also has one of the richest traditions of Socialism. The Labour Party of Belgium (*Parti Ouvriére de Belgique*, POB) was founded in 1885. The reform of the electoral system contributed to the advancement of the POB as a parliamentary party. During the interwar period they were sporadically in power.

A third linguistic cleavage began to emerge after 1860. French was the only official language according to the constitution; consequently, the Flemish population felt disadvantaged. Over the last quarter of the nineteenth century, new legislation was introduced that allowed Dutch to be spoken in courts and in the public administration in Flanders.

After the war, on 11 November 1918, in the royal residence of Loppem, King Albert I managed to achieve an important compromise on a reform package

Creation and development of democracies   45

between the three main party leaders – the Liberal Paul Janson, the Catholic Paul Anseele and the Socialist Henri Jaspar – the equivalent of *Pacificatie* in the Netherlands. The compromise package introduced pure and simple proportional representation for the entire male population, a solution to the school question and the resolution of issues related to the linguistic conflict (including the establishment of a Dutch-speaking University in Ghent, which took place in 1930). Furthermore, Article 310 of the criminal code, which made strikes illegal, was repealed (Mabille 1997: 224–225; Witte *et al.* 2009: 146–148). A revision of the constitution in 1921 addressed these issues.

Between 1918 and 1939 there were 18 governments, almost one per year (Mabille 1997: 204). One major difficulty was the antagonism between the Catholics and the Socialists. Anti-communist sentiment dominated politics in the 1920s, creating tensions between Catholics and Socialists, even though the Labour Party was moderate; however, in the 1930s, the economic crisis was a major factor in bringing the parties together, particularly after 1935. The Socialists Henri de Man and Paul Henri Spaak presented their 'Work Plan' (*Plan de Travail*) in 1835, and it became part of government policy between 1935 and 1939 (Mabille 1997: 239).

New populist parties emerged, such as the Flemish National Association (*Verbond Nationaal de Vlanders*, VNV) in 1933, a group that was supported by the rural masses and was quite sympathetic to Nazi Germany, and Léon Degrelle's Rex Party, influenced by Fascist ideology, which achieved sudden success in the elections in 1936 only to collapse in 1939. On the radical left, the Communist Party was quite active in strikes and extra-parliamentary activities.

Following the German invasion during the Second World War, Nazi Germany installed a military administration, again dividing Belgium into Walloon and Flemish regions. King Leopold III remained in the country, but under the control of the Germans; meanwhile, the government went into exile.

Luxembourg: re-inventing identity through democratisation

The birth of a Luxembourg state was quite a difficult process. After the independence of Belgium in 1830, Luxembourg remained in personal union with the Netherlands. This was reconfirmed in 1839. The constitution of 1841 was crucial but still very autocratic, influenced by the Dutch constitution. In 1848, a new democratic constitution influenced by the Belgian model was adopted. However, the new King William III reintroduced a more autocratic style. The culmination of this trend was the *coup d'état* of 1856, which led to a new restrictive constitution (Bumb 2011: 63–69). In 1868, a compromise constitution again upgraded the Chamber of Deputies to the Parliament of the country, reduced the power of the king, strengthened the government and linked it to majorities in Parliament (Bumb 2011: 74–75).

Between 1868 and 1918, liberalism dominated government policy despite Catholic opposition. Three prime ministers remained in power for lengthy periods, contributing to the stability of the political system: Emmanuel Servais

46 Creation and development of democracies

(1867–1874), Baron de Blochhausen (1874–1885) and Paul Eyschen (1888–1915). As in the Netherlands and Belgium, social legislation and the question of state-funded confessional schools were the main issues dealt with by Luxembourg governments. Membership in the German *Zollverein* since 1842 and substantial German investment contributed to the establishment of a modern metal industry, enabling the funding of large infrastructure projects.

In 1890, the Dutch King William III died without leaving a male heir; his brother Adolphe Nassau-Weillbourg thus became the new king. This broke off Luxembourg's personal union with the Netherlands, and the country became de facto independent, with its own royal dynasty (Thewes 2011b: 56).

As was seen in the other countries, modern political parties also emerged in Luxembourg during this period. The first party to create a modern party organisation was the Luxembourg Socialist Workers' Party (LSAP) in 1902. The progressive Liberals created the loosely organised Liberal League in 1904, the precursor of today's Democratic Party. The most important party in Luxembourg was without a doubt the Christian Social People's Party, which in the interwar period was known as the Party of the Right (*Partei der* Rechten, PdR), founded in 1914. Like most Christian Democratic parties, it consisted of a variety of currents, including working-class and farmers' movements, and was supported logistically by the Church (Trausch 1981: 389–393).

Following German occupation during the First World War, there was growing opposition to Grand Duchess Marie Adelaide due to her strong sympathies for Germany before and during the occupation period. On 15 January 1919, she decided to abdicate in favour of her younger sister Charlotte. The decision by the government with the support of Parliament to conduct a referendum on 28 September 1919 on the monarchy as a state form was a critical development; however, 80 per cent of the population supported the monarchy and Grand Duchess Charlotte. In a second referendum on the same day, the people voted for economic union with France, but this was thwarted by the Allied powers. In the end, the Economic Union of Luxembourg and Belgium (*Union Economique Luxembourg et Belgique*, UELB) was established.

A revised constitution was adopted on 15 May 1919. This constitution introduced male and female universal suffrage based on proportional representation (Thewes 2011b: 76). During the interwar period, only four prime ministers ruled the country: Emile Reuter (1918–1925), Pierre Prüm (1925–1926), Joseph Bech (1926–1937) and Pierre Dupong (1937–1944). This enhanced political stability in the country.

Despite the commemorations of the centenary of independence in 1939 and its declaration of neutrality during the war, Luxembourg was occupied by Nazi Germany on 10 May 1940. The government under Prime Minister Pierre Dupong as well as Grand Duchess Charlotte went into exile to London, returning on 23 September 1944.

The glorious 30 years: national capitalism in consensus democracies

Following the Second World War, our five consensus democracies enjoyed a peak in their national systems based on a long period of sustainable growth between 1945 and 1975. In addition to political stability and booming economies, the five small consensus democracies could rely on a stable international environment created by the Cold War and a long period of peaceful coexistence after 1953. The Marshall Plan and the Organisation for Economic Co-operation and Development (OECD) played a major role in transforming Western European economies. European integration created a stable political and economic environment of peace for the Benelux countries. All five countries developed strong consensus democracies based on pillarised segmented societies and neo-corporatist arrangements between political and economic actors. Demand-oriented Keynesianism was the major economic policy during this period (for an excellent comparative European overview see Therborn 1995).

Austria: consensus politics as a new-found political culture of national unity

Austria emerged without national sovereignty following the Second World War. The ambiguous relationship between the Austrian population and Nazi Germany and the fact that the Soviet Union controlled part of eastern Austria were major factors in the delayed return of national sovereignty. It took a decade for Austria to regain its sovereignty through the State Treaty of 25 May 1955. The new Second Republic emerged from the country's negative experience with the failed First Republic (1918–1938). An important mythos of the new Austrian political culture was that Christian Social and Social Democratic prisoners started the process of reconciliation in the Nazi concentration camps (the 'Myth of the *Lagerstrasse*'), a conceit that survived until the 1980s (Rathkolb 2005: 165–166). The political elites decided to keep the old constitution of 1919/1929 to emphasise continuity to the previous turbulent democratic period (Rathkolb 2005: 88–90). Austria remained a federal state; however, the centralistic tendencies of executive federalism tended to dominate. Between 1945 and 1966, Austria was governed by a grand coalition between the newly founded Austrian People's Party (*Österreichische Volkspartei*, ÖVP), which replaced the Christian Socials of the First Republic, and the Socialist Party of Austria (*Sozialistische Partei Österreichs*, SPÖ). The two political parties established a consensus democracy, dividing all the important positions in the Republic between themselves according to an agreed-upon formula. This became known as *Proporzdemokratie* (distributive system of spoils and party patronage), a system that was subsequently practised in politics, the economy and society in a federal multi-level setting (see Lehmbruch 1967: 6–8). Between 1945 and 1983, 21 out of the 38 years (55.3 per cent of the total) saw grand coalition governments in power in Austria. These administrations featured a relatively stable political personnel that was densely networked with the economic elites of the nationalised

48 Creation and development of democracies

and private sectors, sometimes with overlapping positions (Müller *et al*. 1996; Treib 2012).

One factor sustaining the grip of the ÖVP and the SPÖ on power involved the two main subcultures of Catholics and Socialists, respectively. Between 1945 and 1979, between 80 and 95 per cent of voters supported the two main parties which were equal in terms of strength.

In 1954, 73 per cent identified with a political party; in 1969, this figure was still 75 per cent, but by 1976 to 1979 it had declined to 63 per cent, a considerable drop in only a decade. In 1994, just 44 per cent identified with a party; however, just 12 per cent were considerably attached to the existing political groups. In contrast, 57 per cent did not identify with any party (Plasser and Ulram 1995: 344).

Initially, the third party, the Freedom Party (*Freiheitliche Partei Österreichs*, FPÖ) founded in 1956, was too small to make a difference (about 5 per cent support). Many of its members had been involved in the former Nazi regime and continued to advocate a strong connection to Germany. Only in the 1970s did a new generation with liberal values emerge, making the party suitable for coalition government (*koalitionsfähig*).

Another factor in Austria's political stability was the fact that there were only five chancellors up until 1983, four of whom were from the ÖVP: Leopold Figl (1945–1953), Julius Raab (1953–1961), Alfons Gorbach (1961–1963), Josef Klaus (1963–1970) and the Social Democrat Bruno Kreisky (1970–1983). Figl was instrumental in negotiating the State Treaty (*Staatsvertrag*) with the Allies on 25 May 1955 that established the independence of Austria. Notably, this treaty characterised Austria as the first victim of Hitler's policies (Rathkolb 2005: 168). Raab was one of the architects of the informal Austrian social partnership, of which the main institution is the parity commission (*paritätische Kommission*) founded in 1957. This became the strategic instrument established with the social partners to shape macro-economic policies in the country's coordinated market economy. Together with Finance Minister Reinhard Kamnitz, he developed the 'Raab-Kamnitz Kurs' based on ordoliberalism similar to Germany's. This meant an efficient macro-economic policy combined with a restricted monetarist policy in order to reduce inflation. The general theme was that the best social policy was a well-run economic policy (Chorherr 2005: 26–27).

Between 1945 and 1970, Austria not only reconstructed its country but also created a relatively competitive economy based on a strong nationalised economic sector, including steel industries (e.g. the VOEST AG Conglomerate).

Between 1970 and 1983, successive Socialist governments under Chancellor Bruno Kreisky focused on improving the conditions of the working population through the expansion of the welfare state. Despite these socially expansive policies, the 'Raab-Kamnitz Kurs', based on ordoliberal philosophy, remained central to economic and monetary policy.

However, longevity in power also led to many scandals and instances of political corruption. Among these were the 'pharaonic' project of the central hospital in Vienna (*Allgemeine Krankenhaus*, AKH), the mismanagement of the steel

Creation and development of democracies 49

industry conglomerate VOEST AG, illegal weapons exports by the public firm Noricum and the insurance fraud related to the ship *Lucona*, which led to the death of six people (Kriechbaumer 2004: 67–86).

Switzerland: the 'magic formula' and the continuity of consensus politics

Similar to the case of Austria, the politics of *Proporzdemokratie* (also known as the 'amicable agreement') was a major feature of Swiss politics (see Lehmbruch 1967; Steiner 1971).

A crucial factor for Swiss stability was the successive integration of the most relevant parties into the Federal Council (*Bundesrat*), leading to the implementation of the 'magic' formula' in 1959. Since then, the federal council has consisted of two Liberals, two Social Democrats, two Christian Democrats and one BGB member. Switzerland has been a country of small parties ever since the introduction of proportional representation, and thus the magic formula institutionalised a permanent system of coalition government. Postwar Switzerland was basically a male-dominated world, due in part to the fact that women lacked voting rights. Women's suffrage was only achieved in a referendum on 7 February 1971; the final result was 66 per cent for female universal suffrage and 33 per cent against, with a participation rate of 58 per cent (Ziegler 1996; Studer 1996). Despite this milestone achievement, it took several years before all the cantons finally introduced female universal suffrage in their respective political systems.

During the interwar period, the Federal Council gained special powers in many policy areas in a context of either economic crisis or war, but these powers were revoked in 1952. The strong cooperation between the state and private interest groups is specific to Switzerland; however, it was initially an informal arrangement. Finally, in 1947, Article 32 (Article 147 in the 1999 constitution), the so-called 'economic article', was upgraded to require that interest groups and cantons be consulted before any legislative proposals of the Federal Council are submitted to the national Parliament. Thus, this informal practice became enshrined in the constitution, and it has become the normal procedure for decision-making in the legislative process (Linder 2005: 197–198). This has facilitated the establishment of a liberal democratic neo-corporatism in which the social partners (namely business organisations in industry, agriculture and services and workers' organisations) are able to co-shape the economic structures and regulatory framework of the country. The system relies heavily on a 'private interest government' dominated by the main socio-economic interest groups and cartels, meaning that the state delegates socio-economic tasks to the main interest groups (Katzenstein 1985: 112, 118; on private interest government see Streeck and Schmitter 1985; for Switzerland see Kriesi 1980, 1982). In the postwar period, Switzerland was one of the most cartelised countries in the world (Katzenstein 1985: 91–92). Also during this period, Switzerland started building the structures of a welfare state; however, these were modest and were dominated by the private sector until the 1980s.

50 *Creation and development of democracies*

The Netherlands: consensus democracy and the scientification of policy-making

Despite the conflicts between the Benelux countries in the nineteenth century, in the second half of the twentieth century they established robust cooperation through the Benelux organisation and later through European integration. Key politicians, including the Dutch Johan Beyen and the Belgian Paul Henri Spaak, are the founding fathers of this new peaceful Europe. Nevertheless, each country had its own trajectory towards consensual politics.

Between 1946 and 1982 there were 18 governments in the Netherlands, meaning that on average a government lasted for two years. However, in reality, there was a high level of continuity among the personnel representing the different parties in the coalition, particularly if one discounts interim governments (Thomassen *et al.* 2014: 192).

The successive governments of Prime Minister Willem Drees from the Labour Party (*Partij van der Arbeid*, PvDA) between 1948 and 1958 were instrumental in achieving a stable government and creating the beginnings of a welfare state. Drees had been engaged in politics in the interwar period. After the war, he was the minister for social policy between 1945 and 1948 before becoming prime minister. He is known as the father of the Dutch welfare state, mainly due to the adoption of the General Old Age Law (*Algemene Ouderdomswet*) in 1957. In other parties, one can also observe the longevity of participation in successive governments. In this way, a very compact political elite was able to consensually establish the foundations of a strong Dutch democracy. Up until 1958, Dutch politics exhibited many elements of continuity, as well as elements of change. In particular, the cooperation between Labour and the Catholic People's Party (*Katholiek Volkspartij*, KVP) represented a major change that contributed to social peace in the country. Although the pillarisation structure continued to be quite strong, the country's economic success (due in part to the Marshall Plan, but also to Dutch ingenuity and innovation) facilitated its modernisation. The Dutch tendency towards the scientification of information through long-term planning has been crucial in this regard. The Central Planning Bureau (*Centraal Planbureau*, CPB) was founded in 1945 and has significantly contributed to the gradual depoliticisation of policy-making.

The broad consensus among the three main parties underwent a substantial shift in 1958. After this point, consensus among the political elites was replaced by increased competition between the left and the right. A growing tension between the KVP and the Labour party in the late 1950s had at its roots the excommunication of Catholic Socialists by the Church. The process of secularisation was impacting upon the religious pillars, and this was regarded as a threat to the cohesion of the Church's subcultures.

Throughout the 1960s, the booming economy enabled the considerable expansion of the welfare state. The discovery of natural gas in Slochteren further contributed to the country's wealth. In the 1960s and 1970s, new social movements consisting of young people, such as the provos, a movement against the

Creation and development of democracies 51

establishment, played a major role in challenging the establishment and changing society.

One of the reasons behind the economic success of the Netherlands was the establishment of neo-corporatist structures to integrate economic interest groups. These institutions, such as the Economic and Social Committee (*Sociaal en Economische Raad*, SER) and the Labour Foundation (*Stichting van der Arbeit*, STAR) were instrumental in fostering a culture of dialogue and pragmatism.

In the 1970s, everything suddenly came to a halt. Economically, this was a period of stagflation and declining economic development. In addition, the Lockheed scandal affecting the husband of Queen Beatrix represented a further problem for the government. Internationally, the Joop den Uyl (1973–1977) government had to deal with the oil crisis of 1973 that emerged out of the Six-day War between Israel and the Arab states. Due to the Netherlands' support of Israel, the Organization of the Petroleum Exporting Countries (OPEC) boycotted the country. The Dries van Agt governments between 1977 and 1982 were also unable to improve the economic situation of the country, and the budget deficit and public debt increased significantly.

Belgium: consensus and conflict in a divided country

As was the case for all Benelux countries, occupation by Nazi Germany was a major traumatic experience for Belgium. The main difference between Belgium and the Netherlands and Luxembourg is that King Leopold III decided to remain in the country and work with the Nazi occupiers. According to his version of events, he wanted to stay with his people and protect them as much as possible from the arbitrary rule of the occupants. This possibility was severely diminished when the King was sent to Germany and detained there, far away from his subjects. This behaviour was criticised by the government in exile in London. The question of the Monarch returning to Belgium remained a major issue. In the meantime, his brother Charles served as Regent. This dilemma was only resolved by a referendum in 1950 in which the vast majority voted for King Leopold III to return. In particular, the newly founded Social Catholic Party (*Parti Social Chrétien*, PSC) supported his return, whereas the Socialists, Liberals and Communists were against it. The result of the referendum was 57.68 per cent in favour of the return of the King; however, support for his return was much stronger in Flanders, at 72.2 per cent, and much weaker in Brussels and Wallonia, at 48.16 per cent and 42.2 per cent, respectively. Despite the result, opposition to Leopold III continued, and within the year the King decided to abdicate on behalf of his son Baudoin, on the condition that the divided political forces would rally around him (Mabille 1997: 310–311; Witte *et al.* 2009: 139–145). In 1951, Baudouin became the new King of Belgium and was able to overcome the crisis in the monarchy through his conciliatory and low-profile style.

In 1958/1959, after continuing conflict, a school pact between the main parties restored consensus in education policy. Catholic schools were quite

52   Creation and development of democracies

popular in Flanders, but less so in Wallonia. In 1972, 66.7 per cent of Flemish pupils attended Catholic schools and just 17.6 per cent attended public schools; in the Francophone territory, 42.4 per cent went to public schools and 20.9 per cent went to Catholic schools. The rest of pupils would choose other private schools (Witte *et al.* 2009: 251–255).

The third major issue in Belgian politics concerned the tensions between Flanders and Wallonia. A new Flemish nationalist political party called the People's Union (*Volksunie*) emerged in 1954, just one element of a growing Flemish movement that included students. In 1961, a new law introduced an official language based on census data in order to better recognise the borders between Francophones and Flemish-speaking areas.

Tensions between Wallonia and Flanders flared up over the issue of expanding the Francophone part of the Catholic University of Leuven in 1968/1969. Since 1962, both parts were autonomous but belonged to the same university located in Leuven, in the bilingual province of Brabant. The north of the province is predominantly Flemish, the south francophone. The bishops wanted to expand the Francophone university section; however, this proposal met with considerable opposition on the part of students and Flemish political parties. In the end, the Gaston Eyskens government provided a substantial amount of funding so that the francophone part of the university could move southward to a green field called Louvain la Neuve. Since then, Louvain-la-Neuve, founded in 1971, has become a city of 29,000 inhabitants. The Dutch Free University Brussel (*Vrije Universiteit* Brussel, VUB) was created during the same year (Witte *et al.* 2009: 374–376; Léton and Miroir 1999: 87–88).

In 1970 and 1980, revisions to the constitution took place in response to the demands of the Flemish nationalists (see Chapter 3, this volume; Teggelbekkers 1974: 64–65; Molitor 1980).

Postwar Belgium may be regarded as a successful example of social market economy. The cooperation between the social partners was embryonic in the interwar period. After the Second World War, there was a widespread ambition to create a more peaceful pattern of industrial relations. Similar to the Netherlands, neo-corporatist institutions were created, including the Central Council of the Economy (*Conseil Central de l'Economie/Centrale Raad voor het Bedrijfsleven*, CCE/CRB) founded in 1948, which advises the government on economic issues, and the National Labour Council (*Conseil National du Travail/Nationale Arbeidsraad*, CNT/NAR) founded in 1952, which is an advisory forum for socio-economic issues, but is also responsible for national collective agreements.

Luxembourg: the creation of a national model

In the elections in Luxembourg on 21 October 1945, the old party system of the interwar period was more or less reinstated. The Christian Democrats, now under the label of the Christian Democratic People's Party (*Chrëschtlech-Sozial Vollekpartei*, CSV) continued to be the strongest party. The second largest party

Creation and development of democracies   53

was the renamed Luxembourg Socialist Workers' Party (*Lëtzebuerger Sozialistesch Arbechter Partei*, LSAP). The Liberals refounded themselves as the Liberal Group, later called the Democratic Party (*Demokratesch Partei*, DP). The dominance of the CSV remained a major aspect of the Luxembourg party system.

The first postwar government (1945–1947) chaired by Pierre Dupong was one of national unity, comprising the Christian Democrats, the Socialists, the Liberals and the Communists. Quite salient in the case of Luxembourg is the longevity of prime ministers and ministers in office, such as Pierre Dupong (1937–1944, 1954–1957), Joseph Bech (1926–1937, 1953–1958) and Pierre Werner (1959–1974); this has contributed significantly to the stability of the political system (Thewes 2011a: 142–147, 153–184).

The postwar period was characterised by substantial economic growth centred on the steel industry. One major concern for Luxembourg policy-makers was to make the country an attractive place for investment; consequently, the state invested heavily in infrastructure and modernisation. A policy of economic diversification was an important aspect in this respect (Trausch 2003: 254–256). In addition, the welfare state was considerably expanded during this period.

Historically speaking, the creation of the Luxembourg social model took a long time to become a reality. After several institutional attempts, an Economic and Social Council (*Conseil Economique et Social*, CES) similar to the Dutch example was finally established in 1966, quickly becoming the core institution of the emerging Luxembourg social model (Trausch 2006: 13–36). In the 1970s, due to the steel crisis, other bodies such as the Committee of Conjuncture, the Committee of Tripartite Coordination and the Tripartite Steel Industry Conference emerged. Several social programmes such as early retirement and relocation to other industries were devised to help unemployed workers (Hirsch 2010a, 2010b).

The turbulent world since 1980: re-equilibrating consensus democracies

Following three decades of growth, the economies of the West Central European countries began to falter. Their expensive welfare states and continuing demands from trade union confederations started to affect the ability of key enterprises to remain competitive in an increasingly globalised world. In particular, the Asian tigers of Hong Kong, Taiwan, Singapore and South Korea joined Japan as major competitors in Asia. Later, the rise of China had a considerable impact. Moreover, following the fall of the Berlin Wall in 1989, the globalised world economy changed the context in which consensus democracies had to restructure themselves, shifting from welfare states to competition states (Cerny 1990; Jessop 2002; Leibfried and Zürn 2005). European integration after 1985 played a major role in gradually transforming national economies into European ones. Such processes of change have led to the emergence of populist movements opposing the established elites.

54 *Creation and development of democracies*

Austria: the politics of memory and European integration

After expanding the welfare state during the absolute majority Socialist Bruno Kreisky governments (1970–1983), the Socialist Party found itself unable to rule alone; it had to find a coalition partner. Consequently, for the first time, a FPÖ–SPÖ coalition (1983–1986) was formed.

In 1986, the politics of memory began to shatter Austria's image of itself as Hitler's 'first victim'. In the presidential elections, Kurt Waldheim, the distinguished former Secretary-General of the United Nations, was one of the candidates. However, it was discovered that he had been economical with the truth in his biography, leaving out his military service in the German army during the Second World War. Although he was elected on 8 June 1986, he was ostracised by the international community. The USA declared him a 'persona non grata', and most governments boycotted him (Tóth and Czernin 2006; Uhl 1992: 16, 375).

The rise of the populist Jörg Haider in the FPÖ led to the end of the SPÖ–FPÖ coalition. Between 1986 and 1997, the SPÖ's new leader Franz Vranitzky was prime minister of five coalition governments and managed to keep Austria on the path of economic growth and low unemployment. On 8 July 1991, Vranitzky apologised in Parliament for the part played by citizens of his country between 1938 and 1945, thereby destroying the myth of Austria as the first victim of Hitler's policies (Gehler 2012: 163–165). The main task of Vranitzky's grand coalition governments was to restructure and privatise the large public sector, which was incurring considerable losses (Kriechbaumer 2004: 259).

In 1985, Mikhail Gorbachev's *Glasnost* and *Perestroika* policies gave hope to Austrian leaders that they could finally join the European Community. After reassurances by the Austrian government that it would uphold permanent neutrality, the Soviets gave the green light to the accession process (Gehler 2012: 175). A letter was attached to the application sent on 14 July 1989, in which the Austrian government presented its explicit reservations about neutrality (Gehler 2012: 167).

Following the fall of the Berlin Wall in 1989, France under President François Mitterrand expressed worries about the potential 'cold' *Anschluss* of a so-called 'third German state'. For the Austrian government under Franz Vranitzky, this remark was offensive. Austria had its own identity and, despite being heavily dependent on the German market, the nation had learned to appreciate its own distinctive culture and statehood (Gehler 2012: 169, 173). Austria therefore avoided seeking support from Germany's Helmut Kohl, and instead looked for support from other, smaller member-states such as the Netherlands. The country was also part of a wave of membership candidates, including Finland, Sweden and Norway. Moreover, Austria assured Switzerland that it would not change its status of permanent neutrality (Gehler 2012: 166–167, 173). The negotiations were concluded relatively quickly, but two issues stood out as problematic: the agricultural sector, which was stringently protected in Austria, and the issue of traffic through Austria, one of the most travelled routes from north to south, and

Creation and development of democracies 55

later east to west as well. After marathon meetings of the Austrian delegations, these two dossiers were closed. The Vranitzky government was quite successful in rallying the ÖVP, the SPÖ, the new pro-European Liberal Forum (LF) and the social partners to support European integration. The groups against membership included Haider's FPÖ and the Greens. Total mobilisation of the main parties and social partners led to an overwhelming 'yes' vote of 66.6 per cent (Gehler 2012: 176; Gehler 2009). Austria joined the European Union on 1 January 1995 and became one of the first members of the third stage of EMU in 1999. Vranitzky, who resigned from office in January 1997, was succeeded by Viktor Klima, who formed a cabinet until the end of the legislature period one year later.

The permanent grand coalition between the two parties bolstered the rise of the opposition. The FPÖ under Jörg Haider was able to increase the party's share of the vote from election to election. In addition, the Green Party remained an important critical voice of the grand coalition.

In the general elections of 3 October 1999, the FPÖ became the second largest party, surpassing the ÖVP by a whisker. Both parties won 26.9 per cent of the vote, but the FPÖ received more votes. The two groups formed a coalition government that lasted until 2006. The international response was quite negative, particularly in Israel, and demonstrations took place against the new government. On 4 February 2000, President Thomas Klestil swore in the new ÖVP–FPÖ government. The FPÖ had to declare that it would respect the constitution and the rule of law, as well as not allow its leader, Jörg Haider, to participate in the government. European Union leaders decided to ostracise the Austrian government as a result, and several measures were adopted in order to isolate the country. Finally, in June, a commission of three wisemen wrote a positive report about the developments in Austria in the hopes of ending the crisis (Kopeinig and Kotango 2000: 7; Merlingen *et al.* 2001: 72–73).

The ÖVP–FPÖ government under Chancellor Wolfgang Schüssel lasted for six years. The main aim of the coalition government was to dismantle the old *Proporzdemokratie* structures and introduce a more market-friendly environment in Austria. However, in 2005, the FPÖ split into two parties, and most members of the government joined the new party: the Alliance for the Future of Austria (*Bündnis für die Zukunft Österreichs*, BZÖ) led by Jörg Haider.

Since 2007, Austria has again been ruled by a grand coalition government. Following the legislative elections on 1 October 2006, a grand coalition with the ÖVP under Chancellor Alfred Gusenbauer was formed. In early elections in 2008 he was replaced by Werner Faymann, who also formed a grand coalition. In the 2013 elections, the grand coalition's hold on power was reconfirmed. Consequently, Faymann had to deal with the Eurocrisis and the banking crisis. One bank based in Carinthia became a particular headache for the government. The speculations of the Hypo Alpe Adria bank in the tourism industry in Croatia, investments that had been supported by the Regional President Jörg Haider, led to major losses. Due to the high level of debt, the Austrian state had to intervene, settling a dispute with the Bavarian government which held a stake in the bank

56   *Creation and development of democracies*

and asked for compensation (*Der Spiegel*, 8 May 2016). Moreover, in the summer of 2015, Austria was at the front line of the refugee crisis. Its original liberal approach towards the wave of refugees was soon shattered by the fact that this contributed to the rise of the anti-immigration FPÖ. This reinforced a certain bunker mentality among the grand coalition parties. Between 1983 and 2016, the grand coalition has been in power for 22 out of the past 33 years, representing two-thirds of the total time. This definitely says something about the political culture of the country.

Switzerland: consensus and populism in turbulent times

Although the Federal Council was keen on strategically integrating Switzerland into the international community, direct democracy through referenda and popular initiatives impeded this process. The best example is the negative result in the referendum on the accession of Switzerland to the United Nations in 1986: over three-quarters of the population rejected the proposed accession. Only in 2002 did a new referendum demonstrate the populace's consent to the idea of Switzerland becoming a member of the United Nations.

Socially, since 1968, Switzerland has been confronted with a generational change. The younger generation opposed the conservative bunker mindset of the Federal Council, which during the interwar period became known as the 'mental defence of the country' (*geistige Landesverteidigung*) against an increasingly globalised world. In 1980, there was a major riot in Zürich that led to the burning down of the opera house, which was regarded as a symbol of the establishment.

One particular problem for the Swiss Federal Council was the growing importance of the European integration process. The EC started negotiations with all European Free Trade Association (EFTA) members in 1989. As an interim stage, the EEC offered Switzerland the chance to join the European Economic Area (EEA); however, this was rejected by 50.3 per cent of the population in a referendum on 6 December 1992, and also by the Council of States (*Ständerat*) by 16 votes out of 23. This was a vote against the preferred option of the established parties, which clearly favoured accession to the European Union. In Parliament, all political parties apart from the SVP and the Greens voted for accession. The 'no' vote relied on the support of the SVP and an association called Action for an Independent and Neutral Switzerland (*Aktion für eine Unabhängige und Neutrale Schweiz*, AUNS), which had been quite successful six years earlier in preventing Swiss membership in the United Nations (Linder 2011: 44–45; on AUNS, see Chapter 4, this volume). According to Wolf Linder, most of the 'no' voters came from the German-speaking part of Switzerland, from the traditional rural areas, and disadvantaged socio-economic areas (Linder 2011: 44). The French-speaking areas voted predominantly for the EEA Treaty.

Switzerland had already had a bilateral free trade agreement with the EEC since 1972, and in the 1980s it began to adjust its legislation to the supranational organisation through its Eurolex programme. As an alternative, the Federal Council had to develop a different approach towards integration. A package of

Creation and development of democracies 57

seven bilateral agreements was negotiated with the European Union. The negotiations were started in 1994 and concluded in 1999. Bilateral agreements in seven key areas were reached, but the EU clearly viewed them as a package, and so Switzerland had to ratify all of them. The 800-page agreement included legislation in the areas of research, air and road transportation, public procurement, the freedom of movement of persons, and technical barriers to trade and agriculture (Linder 2011: 46). On 21 May 2000, the complete package was accepted in a referendum by the population, with three-quarters of voters supporting it. After securing the ratification of the 'Bilaterals I' package, a new round was started in 2002 to cover even more areas. In 2007, in two referendums, the Swiss agreed to join Schengen/Dublin and extended the freedom of movement to include the ten new member-states. Two years later, an extension to include Bulgaria and Romania was also approved (Linder 2011: 47).

The exponential rise of the SVP under Christopher Blocher in the 1990s and the first decade of the new millennium contributed to radical changes in the party system. In the October 2015 general elections the SVP became the largest party, with about 30 per cent of the vote. In a country of small parties this is a major achievement. Finally, in 2003, the 'magic formula' had to be changed: the Christian Democrats lost one seat on the Federal Council and the SVP received one more. Blocher became one of the new federal councillors; however, he played a double game, being part of the government but also the main leader of the opposition. In this sense, he countervened one of the most important rules of the Federal Council: the collegiality principle. Despite increasing his party's share of the vote in 2007, Blocher was not re-elected to the Federal Council by Parliament. Instead, Eveline Widmer-Schlumpf was elected. She was then excluded from the party, and went on to found a new political party, the Citizen's Democratic Party (*Bürgerliche Demokratische Partei*, BDP). Widmer-Schlumpf's re-election to the Federal Council in 2011 meant that the SVP was unable to get its second seat according to the magic formula. At one stage the SVP lost their other seat as well, as Ueli Müller joined the BDP. However, soon thereafter he resigned, and was replaced by a SVP representative. Widmer-Schlumpf retired in 2015 and Guy Parmelin from the SVP was elected, thereby restoring the balance in the Federal Council.

In addition to these troubles, the image of the Swiss banking sector was shattered by historical evidence that Swiss banks amassed a considerable amount of money from Jews who were fleeing from the Nazis between 1938 and the end of the war. In 1997, a compensation fund was established. In 2014, according to statistics from the Swiss Banks Settlement Fund, over US$1.23 billion was set aside for 457,100 claimants, with the vast majority of the funding representing a return of assets deposited in Swiss banks and compensation for the harsher cases of slave labour (Swiss Banks Settlement 2014).

The other problem that Swiss banks have had to deal with is the growing international criticism of their upholding of account secrecy in the context of rampant money laundering and illicit money transfers. The USA initiated several processes against Swiss banks that had branches in the country. More than 100

58   Creation and development of democracies

banks complied with the rulings and paid heavy fines. Moreover, the German tax authorities were able to get whistleblowers to provide information about German citizens who had Swiss bank accounts and had not paid their taxes, further undermining the secrecy of deposits (*Süddeutsche Zeitung*, 16 April 2013). All this led to the decision by the Banking Association to no longer to keep its accounts secret. Switzerland also joined all the relevant international initiatives to reduce money laundering and illicit money transfers.

The Netherlands: reviving the Polder model

In the three Lubbers governments between 1982 and 1994, a complete reform of the state and economy was undertaken in order to restore the competitiveness of the Dutch economy (Touwen 2008: 451, 453; 2014; Wolinetz 1989: 91).

The foundation of this new-found consensus for reform was the Wassenaar Agreement (*Wassenaar Akkoord*). The social partners were under considerable pressure from the government to support this agreement. Overall, the Dutch government introduced a three-policy track (*Driesporenbeleid*) that entailed a reduction in the budget deficit by getting rid of loss-making public enterprises, the restructuring of the welfare state and a reduction in unemployment through job redistribution (Touwen 2008: 447; 2014). The Dutch government also introduced a major privatisation programme for the national post and telephone companies in 1989. Wage moderation was ensured by the main trade union confederation FNV, and reduced working hours, early retirement and flexible labour contracts for hiring younger workers were introduced. Of course, the reduced working hours also meant wage cuts.

The Lubbers government relied on the depoliticised scientific Central Planning Bureau, whose figures and studies are trusted by the political parties, institutions and social partners (van Dyk 2006: 415–416). Moreover, the Labour Foundation (STAR) and the Economic and Social Committee (SER) facilitated the negotiation of more concrete agreements (see Hendriks 2012). Taking this path-dependent legacy into account, one of the strengths of the Dutch model has been its ability to learn by overcoming the immobile neo-corporatism of the 1970s, as well as the development of a more responsive system in the 1980s (Hemerijck 1995; Touwen 2008: 441; 2014). In 1984 unemployment was still 9 per cent, but in 1990 it had decreased to 6 per cent, and in 1998 it was as low as 4 per cent (Touwen 2008: 442).

In 1993, an additional pact called 'A New Direction' (*Een nieuwe koers*) was approved; this further liberalised the labour market, but at the same time reinforced the activation of employment policies (Touwen 2008: 442; 2014).

Between 1994 and 1998, a new Liberal–Labour government came to power under the Social Democratic Prime Minister Wim Kok, who continued on the path of socio-economic reform established by the previous governments. The Jan Peter Balkenende governments (2002–2010) also remained on the path of reform. His first government was quite controversial, as it included the populist List Pim Fortuyn (LPF), which had won 17 per cent of the vote in the elections

Creation and development of democracies 59

of 2002. After one year the government collapsed, and from then on coalition governments of established parties dominated. Since 2010, Balkenende's successor Mark Rutte from the Liberal Party has continued to make the state and economy more competitive (Otjes and Voerman 2013: 164–165, 229, 232–233; Interview NL).

However, a major fragmentation of the party system took place. The vote share of the three established parties (Liberals, Social Democrats and Christian Democrats) declined from 80 to 85 per cent in the 1980s, to 60 per cent in the new millennium. Since 2002, Eurosceptic, anti-immigration and anti-Islam parties have emerged, increasing the tensions in the public debate. In addition to the Pim Fortuyn List (LPF) in 2002/2003, Geert Wilders' Freedom Party has also played a major role in shaping the debate in this direction since 2006. The murder of Pim Fortuyn by an animal activist shortly before the elections and the murder of film-maker Theo van Gogh by a fanatic Islamist on 2 November 2004 further exacerbated the political conflict (van Holsteyn *et al.* 2003; *Deutsche Welle*, 13 April 2015). On 1 June 2005 the constitutional treaty was rejected, and in 2016 the free trade agreement with Ukraine was rejected by more than two-thirds of voters; however, turnout was just 32 per cent (BBC News, 7 April 2016). Nevertheless, this rejection had a major impact on Mark Rutte's government, which wishes to renegotiate the agreement with other European leaders.

According to an exit opinion poll conducted during the constitutional treaty referendum, among the reasons for 'no' votes were as follows: 'The Netherlands pays too much to the EU' (62%), 'The Netherlands will have less control over its internal affairs' (56%), 'Too little influence in comparison with other countries' (55%) and 'The Netherlands will lose its own identity' (53%; Harmsen 2005: 10–11). The loss of identity in a growing European Union seems to be a major factor in the increase in Euroscepticism. All this demonstrates that the political culture in the Netherlands is increasingly dominated by insecurity and erosion of the 'heartland' of Dutch consensus democracy (SCB 2015: 8–9).

Belgium: from a unitary state to a federal state

The federalisation of Belgium reached its peak with the adoption of the federal constitution of 1993 (see Chapter 3, this volume; Hecking 2003: 45–64; Reuchamps 2014; Government of Belgium 2015a).

In terms of government stability, Prime Minister Wilfried Martens presided over nine different coalition governments between 1981 and 1992; however, the personnel remained more or less the same. In the 1980s it became clear that the Belgian concordance system was too expensive: the Martens government struggled with a soaring budget deficit and increasing public debt (Jones 2008: 176–177). Major painful reforms therefore had to be carried out with the support of the social partners (Jones 2008: 185–190).

As a consequence, the Martens and Dehaene governments in the 1980s and 1990s, respectively, contributed to the hollowing-out of the state. It was in particular the European integration process through the introduction of Economic and

60 Creation and development of democracies

Monetary Union (EMU) that forced the Dehaene governments between 1992 and 1998 to maintain rigid austerity policies and to reduce the role of public administration in the political system in the context of economic crisis. It was a matter of pride that the Dehaene government was able to take part in the third phase of the euro after 1998, despite the country's public debt being above 100 per cent of GDP (it should be below 60 per cent; Witte *et al.* 2009: 319–323, 326).

Several political corruption scandals that emerged were quite damaging for the Martens and Dehaene governments (e.g. the Agusta–Dassault scandal involving a number of politicians; Witte *et al.* 2009: 422–423). Probably the most odious scandal was the Marc Dutroux affair, which uncovered a series of child murders linked to a paedophile network. The sloppy criminal and judiciary work in the Dutroux case undermined the confidence of the public in its institutions. Conspiracy theories about a network of paedophiles undermining the police and the judiciary were quite widespread at the time (Witte *et al.* 2009: 440–442).

On 20 October 1996, the White March of about 300,000 people demonstrated popular indignation with the moral situation of the country after the Dutroux affair was publicised in the press. The White March became a White Movement that sought to clean up the negative effects of the 'old' political culture and replace it with a 'new' one (Witte *et al.* 2009: 323–326).

Between 12 July 1999 and 20 March 2008, Guy Verhofstadt from the Flemish Liberal Party served as the Belgian Prime Minister. He chaired three governments, although the last one was only a caretaker administration. Verhofstadt attracted attention as a dynamic young politician who symbolised the 'new' political culture, in contrast to previous governments. He also represented a break with the dominance of the Christian Democrats in government. After 115 years, this was the first time that a Liberal politician became prime minister. The main aim of the Verhofstadt governments was to make Belgium more competitive by improving the budgetary and public debt situation, and to privatise sacred cows such as the national postal service and Sabena. Unfortunately, Sabena collapsed and went into bankruptcy before the government could reach an agreement with Swissair. Another important issue was the phasing-out of nuclear energy in Belgium between 2015 and 2025. This was clearly an important topic for the Green parties in the first Verhofstadt government; however, this paradigmatic change was fiercely contested by the energy lobbies. In the second half of 2001, in the Belgian EU presidency, Verhofstadt contributed to the revival of the European integration process through the Laeken declaration, which established a roadmap for a European constitution (Bunse 2009: 139–140).

Since the 1990s, the established political parties have built a *cordon sanitaire* against the xenophobic right-wing Flemish Block/Flemish Interest (*Vlaams Blok/ Vlaams Belang*, VB). Although the VB is a separatist party, it is simultaneously xenophobic against Muslim immigrants.

Between 2008 and 2015, the linguistic conflicts made it quite difficult to achieve compromises. Since 20 March 2008 there have been five prime ministers: Yves Leterme (2008, 2009–2011), Herman van Rompuy (2008–2009), Elio

Creation and development of democracies 61

di Rupio (2010–2014) and Charles Michel (2014–). This means that every 1.4 years there has been a new government. In 2011, the Walloon Socialist leader Elio di Rupio managed to create a stable coalition government consisting of the traditional party families. The emergence of a new party called the New Flemish Alliance (*Nieuw Vlaamse Alliantie*, N-VA), which promoted a non-violent path towards Flemish independence, created major problems for the traditional parties in their attempts to create stable coalitions. The N-VA refused to be part of the coalition government in 2010. The Di Rupio coalition government mainly concentrated on getting the sixth state reform – which increases devolution – approved. Economically, the government was operating under significant constraints due to the need to keep the budget deficit within the Maastricht criteria of 3 per cent of GDP. In 2012, the government had to announce cuts of over €811 million in the budget in order to keep the budget deficit at 2.8 per cent. Subsequently, the economic situation remained poor.

In the 2014 general elections, the share of the vote won by the N-VA increased even further, to 20.3 per cent. A new government under Prime Minister Charles Michel from the Liberal Francophone Reformist Movement (*Movement Reformateur*, MR) formed a coalition, including the N-VA and the Flemish Christian Democrats. This was quite innovative, since the Francophone Prime Minister is working with a Flemish-dominated cabinet. It will be interesting to see whether this new constellation will lead to greater stability (Teffer 2014). In 2015–2016, the Michel government continued the policies of budget consolidation. However, after the November 2015 Islamist terrorist attacks, Belgium came under international scrutiny, as many of the terrorists had come from the Brussels city district of Molenbeek. On 22 March 2016, Brussels itself became the target of three coordinated attacks (in the Zaventem airport and in the underground station of Maelbeek near the European Parliament) carried out by Islamist terrorists, increasing fears of further terrorism in the country (BBC News, 22 March 2016).

Luxembourg: consensus as a way of life

Between 1979 and 2013, there were three prime ministers in Luxembourg who enjoyed lengthy tenures: Pierre Werner (1979–1984), Jacques Santer (1984–1995) and Jean-Claude Juncker (1995–2013). The Liberal Gaston Thorn (1974–1979), the only prime minister with a shorter incumbency, left office to become president of the European Commission (1980–1985).

In the 1980s, the Pierre Werner government had to deal with the permanent crisis related to the decline in the steel industry. The 'anti-crisis division' (*division anti-crise*-DAC) played a major role in mitigating the consequences of this crisis (Thewes 2011b: 198). The grand coalition governments of Prime Minister Jacques Santer between 1984 and 1995 may be regarded as quite successful due to his policies of economic diversification and the attractive taxation policy for large enterprises (Thewes 2011b: 201; Hirsch 1994: 362). After Santer became President of the European Commission in 1995, he was replaced by one of his

62 Creation and development of democracies

former ministers, Jean-Claude Juncker. Juncker wanted to be more proactive in tackling problems such as the pension system (which would go bankrupt in the new millennium if there were no reforms), the education sector and immigration (Thewes 2011b: 238). The financial crisis in 2008 affected Luxembourg as well. The Fortis Bank was bailed out to the tune of €2.5 billion, with the state getting a 49.9 per cent share in the institution. This crisis contributed to an increase in unemployment beyond 6 per cent, which is high by Luxembourg standards; in addition, the public debt rose to 21 per cent in 2012. All these were signs of the weakening of the Luxembourg economy.

At the European level, Luxembourg's red lines are any legislation undermining the country as a financial centre. This policy became more difficult to defend in the new millennium as the OECD and the Council of Europe began to flag internationally non-conforming financial legislation that provided loopholes for potential tax evasion, bribery and corruption (Thewes 2011b: 248). This also seems to have had implications for European appointments. In 2009, there was the possibility that Prime Minister Jean-Claude Juncker could become the new president of the European Council, but the damaged image of Luxembourg (from being on the 'grey' list) prevented this, and the Belgian Herman van Rompuy was chosen instead. In 2014, the whistleblower Antoine Deltour illegally disclosed a large number of documents related to the alleged organisation of tax evasion for 300 corporations by the Luxembourg tax authorities, a scandal that became known as Luxleaks (*Süddeutsche Zeitung*, 7 November 2014, 26 April 2016).

Juncker's government concluded with an electoral defeat on 20 October 2013. Several scandals have severely damaged the reputation of the former prime minister, including the disclosure of illegal activities by the Luxembourg Secret Service with his knowledge and the intervention in judiciary processes by Justice Minister Luc Frieden. Xavier Bettel (DP), who was Mayor of Luxembourg, became the new prime minister, forming a coalition with the Socialists and the Greens, who were included in government for the first time.

Conclusions: crafting consensus democracies in turbulent times

In this chapter it was important to outline the main historical junctures in the development of West Central European small democracies. The main aim was to show that these consensus democracies have a long history of interaction throughout the course of their development. Due to the intertwined nature of their histories in the West Central European space they clearly show many commonalities, but there are also significant differences. In the next chapter, we will focus on how political institutions have evolved in this new turbulent world.

3 Constitutional change in consensus democracies

Introduction

Following the historical contextualisation of our five consensus democracies in the previous chapter, we now turn to a brief examination of constitutional change in these countries. In addition, we seek to provide an overview of the current political structure in each country. The chapter is divided into three sections. First, reference is made to the longevity of the constitutions of these West Central European countries and any major changes in the documents. This is followed by a section on the core institutional frameworks in the respective countries. The chapter ends with some conclusions.

Longevity of and changes in the constitutions of consensus democracies

In times of rapid change and constant global turbulence, political constitutions represent an important element of stability in democratic polities. Two major developments have impacted upon the national uniqueness of these documents over the past 71 years (1945–2016). First, a steadily increasing amount of international rights legislation has become part of domestic legal *acquis* due to membership in myriad organisations such as the United Nations and the Council of Europe. This has facilitated convergence among the most advanced democracies, with peer group pressure from like-minded countries accelerating processes of homogenisation and internationalisation. Second, Europeanisation has led to top-down changes in national constitutions. The primacy of European law over national law, a doctrine established in 1964 by the Costa/ENEL case, has seen national constitutions evolve into something like US state constitutions in a multi-level constitutional space (Kruis 2011; see also the daring thesis by Stone Sweet 2000). However, the constitutional reality reflects the almost parallel coexistence of national and European courts. Ingolf Pernice refers to this as a less hierarchical but more flexible constitutional space of cooperation (Pernice 2015). In this context, it is worthwhile to recall Robert Ladrech's very simple definition of Europeanisation:

64 *Constitutional change in democracies*

> Europeanization is an incremental process reorienting the direction and shape of politics to the degree that EC political and economic dynamics become part of the organizational logic of national politics and policy-making.
>
> (Ladrech 1994: 69–70)

Ladrech's article is crucial for this chapter, as he dedicated one of his case studies to the French constitution, which was being changed in order to adapt to the Treaty of the European Union (Maastricht) adopted in 1993. National parliaments' powers of scrutiny were upgraded through the protocol attached to the Treaty (see Chapter 7, this volume; Ladrech 1994: 76–79; 2010; the most accepted definition is by Radaelli 2003, influenced by Ladrech 1994).

The adoption of the Treaty of the European Union in 1993 transformed the former European Community dominated by nation-states into an integrated polity. Some authors refer to the EU as an integrated multi-level governance system; more scholars, however, call it a political system (Hix and Hoyland 2011; Wessels 2008). According to William Wallace, member-states are no longer nationally sovereign, but share sovereignty interdependently. This process of shared sovereignty has been expanding over time (Wallace 1999, 2005). The basic problem of politicians and populations is that they still think in terms of the nation-state framework, even as EU structures move more towards a European approach to problem resolution.

Ever since the Treaty of the European Union was ratified, it has been difficult to convince the European populations of the need for further Treaty reform towards the development of a constitution. Although bottom-up democratisation of the European Union has slowly taken place through the emergence of critical social and political movements, the process has remained elitist. A major blow towards a constitutionalisation of the EU was the rejection of the Constitutional Treaty by France and the Netherlands in May and June 2005. After a phase of reflection, political elites simply returned to the old elitist and technocratic intergovernmental system and approved a document that was almost identical to the Lisbon Treaty in 2009 (Christiansen and Reh 2009; Verdun 2013a).

In terms of constitutional reform, the Dutch constitution has been quite moderate over time. According to Leonard Besselink, the major transformations of the Dutch constitution occurred before 1922. The constitution of 1815, known as the Basic Law (*Grondwet*) of the Kingdom of the Netherlands, was drafted in the period before the restoration of the monarchy as therefore absolutist in nature. Changes in 1841 and 1848 allowed for the democratisation of the constitution. Finally, in 1917 and 1922, universal male and female suffrage, respectively, was introduced through Acts of Parliament. In 1983, there was a major modernisation of the constitution (Besselink 2008). Decolonisation redefined the relationship between the European Netherlands and its remaining territories through the Charter for the United Kingdom of the Netherlands (*Statuut voor het Koninkrijk der Nederlanden*) in 1956 and 1963.

The *Statuut* outranks than the Dutch constitution due to its 'imperial' tendencies (Besselink 2008: 17). The Kingdom of the Netherlands is now a complex network of dependent overseas territories with the status of municipalities (the tiny Caribbean islands of Bonaire, St. Eustatius and Saba) linked to the European Netherlands and the independent states (the islands of Aruba, Curaçao and Sint Maarten). Due to these new constellations, the Dutch Antilles ceased to exist in 2010. All these polities share a common foreign policy.

A particular feature of the Dutch constitution is that it is extremely open to international society and international law (Besselink 2008: 49, 51). Article 90 of the present Dutch constitution specifically states that the 'Government shall promote the development of the international legal order', one of only a few ideological assertions in the document. Moreover, following the 2000 revision, which sought to adjust the constitution to the new realities of the post-Cold War era, paragraph 1 of Article 97 asserts that 'there shall be armed forces for the defence and protection of the interests of the Kingdom, and in order to maintain and promote the international legal order' (Besselink 2008: 17). Karin Van Leeuwen argues that Dutch constitutional changes between 1953 and 1956 represent a milestone for the European integration process, influencing the landmark decisions of the European Court of Justice in the 1960s. The Dutch constitution was pioneering in opening up the national political system to European and international law (Van Leeuwen 2012).

One of the Dutch interviewees describes quite well the powerlessness dilemmas of the internationally and European open-minded Dutch constitutional law. He asserts as follows:

> Now in our constitution we have ruled that all international law has direct effect in our Dutch legal system, we are not unique in that a lot of other countries have that too.
>
> Second we have ruled in our own constitution, that the whole body of international law is of higher order as preference over Dutch law, we are still not unique in that, however that group of countries that have the same starting point is already like getting smaller.
>
> Where we are unique in, is that in our same constitution, we do not only rule that international law has direct effect in the Netherlands, is of a higher order and standard than Dutch legislation, but it is even of a higher order than our own constitution. That makes in effect that we gave away our legal sovereignty.
>
> (Interview NL)

In the Netherlands, one of the reasons for the relatively low level of major constitutional change has been the difficulty of winning support in both houses for such an endeavour. First, the constitutional amendment must be discussed and adopted in a first reading by both houses. Parliament is then dissolved, and new elections take place. The new Parliament starts the process towards a second reading; subsequently, the constitutional amendment must be approved by two-thirds of both houses. In Luxembourg, changes were made to allow the population to support or reject amendments by a two-thirds majority in a referendum

66 Constitutional change in democracies

following approval in Parliament, but otherwise the Dutch model of constitutional amendment has been influential in the other Benelux countries. In all three countries, a parliamentary majority of two-thirds is required; this is only possible through significant compromises among the political parties. Consequently, in the Netherlands, the constitution was amended just 23 times between 1814 and 2012, a stark contrast to the Austrian case described below. As Wim Voermans asserts, a great deal of *polderen* (negotiation of package deals) must take place to achieve a compromise. A mechanism similar to the popular referendum enacted by Luxembourg was proposed by the National Convention in the Netherlands in 2006 but was ultimately rejected. Referendums have also been rejected in Belgium due to the uneven population size of the two linguistic-ethnic groups. In this case the rigidity of the constitution is welcome, as it blocks any constitutional route to Flemish independence (for the Netherlands, see Voermans 2013: 261–266; for Belgium, see Behrendt 2013: 51–52, 55–56; for Luxembourg, see Gerkrath 2013b: 241–245).

Although Luxembourg's constitutional history starts in 1841, followed by new constitutions in 1848 and 1856, it was only in 1868 that Luxembourg devised a more liberal constitution that has lasted until the present day. In 1890, Luxembourg established its own royal dynasty (the Nassau-Weillbourg dynasty) and became completely independent of the Dutch monarchy. The subsequent constitutional revision of 1919 was quite important, as it enshrined universal suffrage in the document. The constitution has been amended several times since. Possibly the most important amendment came about very recently (2008–2009), when Grand Duke Henri informally told the government that he would have to reject the law on euthanasia because it was against his conscience to promulgate it. This led Prime Minister Jean-Claude Juncker to initiate a constitutional revision that resulted in the abolition of the right of sanction by the Grand Duke; afterwards, the law on euthanasia was successfully passed. Between 1868 and 2009 there were 34 amendments to the constitution, 26 of which were ratified after 1972 (Gerkrath 2013b: 234–235).

Since 2004, the national Parliament, in cooperation with the Council of State (an advisory forum to both the government and Parliament), has been engaged in a major reform of the constitution, a process that accelerated in 2009 and is scheduled to be completed by 2017. One element of this reform will add an article to the constitution on the rights of citizens, incorporating the best aspects of international legislation on the matter. In addition, the role of the Grand Duke in the political system must be properly defined – specifically, the role must be reduced to that of a formal head of state. The conventions and procedures of parliamentary work must also be enshrined in the constitution, and a major reform of the judiciary is to take place, in particular the creation of a Supreme Court and improvements in judicial management through the creation of a National Council of the Judiciary (*Conseil National de la Justice*) as is the case in many other countries (e.g. France, Spain; Gerkrath 2013a: 454, 455–459; Forum 2015). Thus far, over 70 amendments have been made to the constitution. The population has also been able to make proposals for consideration through the parliamentary website. In a referendum on 7 June 2015, Luxembourgers rejected three constitutional proposals in a major blow to the Bettel government. These three proposals would have lowered the voting age to 16 (81%), extended the vote to foreigners (78%) and limited government offices to two terms (two years (70%); *L'essentiel*, 7 June 2015). It is expected that the new constitution will be put to a referendum in June or July 2017, but a potential delay may mean postponement to early 2018. A group of citizens will have the opportunity to express their opinions on the new constitution, as will the University of Luxembourg (*Luxemburg Wort*, 11 June 2015; a first draft of the constitution is available at Chambre des Deputés 2015a).

Among the three Benelux consensus democracies, Belgium has experienced the most revolutionary changes to its constitution. The constitution of 1831 borrowed heavily from the contemporary French and Dutch constitutions (Behrendt 2013: 52). The 1831 constitution was reviewed only twice, in 1899 and 1919, in order to change the country's electoral system. Minor alterations to the constitution were made throughout the nineteenth century and the first half of the twentieth century. Many of these accommodations helped reduce tensions between the two main cleavages in Belgian politics based on religion and class. In the 1960s, these two cleavages were practically resolved by the political elites through constitutional amendments and additional legislation, such as the Social Pact of 1945 and the School Pact of 1958. However, subsequently, the subaltern third cleavage came to the fore with renewed emphasis. This third cleavage is based on language, reflecting a tension that has existed since the nineteenth century between the French and Dutch (Flemish) linguistic communities. The revival of the Flemish political movement through its political party, the People's Union (*Volksunie*), triggered considerable conflict between the two linguistic communities in the 1960s (for more details see Léton and Miroir 1999: 78–83, 87–88). Since 1970, there have been six state reforms leading up to the transformation of the unitary constitution into a federal one, and this process is still ongoing.

Table 3.1 shows the basic steps towards the substantially revised Belgian constitution ratified on 5 July 1993 and beyond. In the case of Belgium, the easiest way to resolve tensions was to agree on the establishment of cultural communities, which were originally a parallel structure co-opted by Parliament: the members of each linguistic community from both Houses of Parliament met separately to discuss issues related to their responsibilities. Up until 1980 there were no regional governments, and so, for each community, the members of the national government were responsible for implementing what was agreed (Molitor 1980: 142–146). Finally, in the second state reform in 1980, the cultural communities were granted more competences that went beyond merely cultural matters. Moreover, it was agreed that regional institutions separate from the national structures be established; these would be directly elected by the respective subnational electorates. The regions were also established in this second state reform, albeit only Wallonia and Flanders. The Flemish region and the Dutch-speaking community merged, for a total of five subnational units (Molitor

68 *Constitutional change in democracies*

Table 3.1 Reforming the Belgian Constitution, 1970 to 2011

Reform	Year	Undertaken changes
First State Reform	1970	• Legal setting up of cultural communities • Agreement of establishment of two regions in Wallonia and Flanders
Second State Reform	1980	• Implementation of institutions (council and government of communities) • Implementation of two regions of Wallonia and Flanders and their institutions • Merging of Flemish region and Dutch-speaking region
Third State Reform	1988–1989	• Implementation of region Brussels-Capital
Fourth State Reform	5 July 1993	• Substantially revised constitution reflecting new federal nature of the constitution
Fifth State Reform	2001	• *Lambermont Agreement*: Devolution of further powers to the regions, local and provincial authorities assigned to respective regions • *Lombard Agreement*: Further fine-tuning of the institutions and electoral process of Brussels-Capital representatives
Sixth State Reform	2012–2014	• Further fine-tuning of separation of linguistic communities • Division of Brussels-Halle-Vilvoorde (BHV) district • Legal division of BHV, particularly in the judiciary sector and public prosecutor's office • Split of electoral districts in BHV • Flemish region can appoint its own judges • Metropolitan community of Brussels for better governance between levels • Voting rights for Belgians living abroad • Elected Members of Parliament have to take their seat and candidacy in different lists (e.g. legislative and European elections) at the same time for main and alternate candidates.

Source: Government of Belgium (2015a).

1980: 148–149; Van Den Wijngaert 2011: 26–30). Finally, in 1988/1989, agreement was achieved on the linguistically mixed region of Brussels-Capital. The manner by which Francophone and Dutch-speaking representatives would be elected to the community parliaments (in the Flemish case, just to the common Parliament) was also determined (Van Den Wijngaert 2011: 30–33). In the

Constitutional change in democracies 69

fourth state reform in 1993, a major revision of the constitution led to the federal state that we know today; the subsequent fifth state reform in 2001 devolved even more powers to the communities, increased their financial autonomy and allocated local and provincial authorities to the respective regions (Van Den Wijngaert 2011: 34–37). Finally, in 2011/2012, further agreements were made to fine-tune the territorial division of Brussels-Halle-Vilvoorde, especially the outskirts of the Dutch-speaking part of the city (Van Wynsberghe 2014: 75–78). The process is far from complete, and in the long run, centrifugal tendencies may result in a confederal organisation of the state or even independence of its parts.

Following the collapse of the Austro-Hungarian Empire, the new small state of Austria adopted a constitution in 1919 that was revised in 1929. The role of the constitutional law expert Hans Kelsen in drafting this quite sophisticated constitution cannot be overstated (Ucakar 2006: 130). After 1945, Austria was divided into four sectors by the Allies and had to wait a decade, until 1955, to become an independent country again. The price of independence was everlasting (*immerwährender*) neutrality, like in Switzerland. Instead of adopting a new constitution, the old one, revised in 1929, was reinstated after 1945 (Ucakar 2006: 123–128). The constitution is now almost 100 years old (the centenary is in 2019).

The current constitution or constitutional order in Austria is based on the constitution as the highest ranking document in the country, but also on many other documents that were adopted during the Austro-Hungarian Empire. According to a study by Karl Ucakar, in 2006 there were 1300 laws at the same level of the constitution that were created over a period of about 150 years (Ucakar 2006: 130). This highlights why it is important for researchers to consider the Austro-Hungarian era: despite discontinuities in regime since 1918, there are also many continuities in terms of constitutional law and political culture dating back to the nineteenth century.

According to the constitutional law expert Manfred Stelzer, there have been over 100 amendments to the constitution since the 1920s. Most of them occurred after 1945, during the peak period of *Proporzdemokratie* that was dominated by the grand coalition between the two main parties: the People's Party (ÖVP) and the Social Democrats (SPÖ). Even the directly elected president and the Constitutional Court were unable to undermine this *Proporzdemokratie*; in fact, in both cases, representatives from the institutions were carefully selected in order to avoid an upset of the system. The president of the Republic has some powers of appointment and dismissal as well as veto powers, suggesting a kind of semi-presidential system; however, in the constitutional reality, most representatives have thus far refrained from being too active, serving as more of a formal head of state with symbolic and representative duties. The Constitutional Court must be regarded as the most innovative element of the 1920 constitution; actually adopted from the former constitutional monarchy, it has thus far seldom rejected bills on substantial constitutional grounds. In a rare example in 2008, a public procurement law related to the *Bundesländer* was rescinded because it contravened the principle of the rule of law (*Rechtsstaatsprinzip*) (Stelzer 2013: 27).

70 *Constitutional change in democracies*

Since 2007, constitutional amendments have become more difficult: the two main parties no longer command a two-thirds majority, and the FPÖ has emerged as an anti-establishment populist party with strong support of between 20 and 30 per cent in recent decades. In addition, it is no longer possible to adopt international law treaties in so-called 'parallel constitutional laws'. Since 2008, these treaties must be included in the constitution, probably leading to a total revision due to changes in constitutional principles. Moreover, a subsequent referendum in which the population approves the change is a requirement. Although Austria has several instruments of direct democracy such as the referendum, popular initiatives (*Volksbegehren*) and public consultation (*Volksbefragung*), they have been used only sparsely. For example, there have been only two referendums. One, on the establishment of a nuclear power plant in Zwentendorf in 1978, had a negative outcome despite the support of the political and economic elites. This also marked the beginning of the Green movement in Austria. The second referendum was in 1994 on Austrian accession to the EU; it had a positive outcome, with 66.6 per cent of the population approving membership. Popular initiatives have been the most frequently used instrument, particularly by the Freedom Party. There have been no public consultations thus far (Stelzer 2013: 19–21).

In comparison to the cases of the Benelux countries, membership in the European Union had a major impact on the Austrian constitution. This has been the only time that a referendum was organised in connection with a total revision of the constitution. The main reason for this total revision was that accession affected the three core constitutional principles: democracy, federalism and the *Rechtsstaat* (national rule of law). All the criticism of the European Union notwithstanding, the national democratic order is only partially affected by membership; the core democratic structure and culture remain in place. This is also the case for federalist Austria, although the addition of the supranational level has substantially reduced the ability of the nine *Bundesländer* to influence European policy. However, the written provisions of federalism allocating specific competences to the federal national level and the *Bundesländer* have always been dominated by a tendency towards a centralising 'executive federalism', such that most areas are competences of the federal government delegated only for purposes of implementation. Finally, the rule of law (*Rechtsstaat*), which is mainly based on the provisions of legal certainty (*Rechtssicherheit*) and legal protection (*Rechtsschutz*), does not differ very much from European views on the matter (Stelzer 2013: 17–18). In addition to these three core principles of the Austrian constitution, the principles of republicanism and the separation of powers should also be mentioned. The republican principle is a rejection of the monarchy as a state form, but also of any person belonging to previous dynasties that ruled the country, such as the Habsburgs. The separation of powers refers to the mutual independence of the government, Parliament and the judiciary. However, modern representative democracy has created a great number of interdependencies between the government and Parliament. The dominance of government over Parliament, particularly in a *Proporzdemokratie*, has been a major

Constitutional change in democracies 71

feature of the Austrian system (Ucakar 2006: 132–133). Moreover, there are some state objectives that form part of the constitutional order in Austria. These include a commitment to anti-fascism, permanent neutrality, comprehensive defence of the country, equal treatment of disabled people, equality between women and men, the protection of ethnic minorities, the independence of the broadcasting sector and total economic balance (Ucakar 2006: 133).

The acknowledgement that European law supersedes national law may be regarded as a highly significant aspect of this change following accession to the EU. According to Theo Öhlinger, Kelsen's original idea of the national constitution as the highest legal stratum in a hierarchy of norms has been downgraded to just one of many national constitutions in a supranational setting. The national constitution thus becomes similar to a subnational constitution in a 'federal' state (Öhlinger 2002: 93–94; Ucakar 2006: 130). Another consequence of this relationship between European law and Austrian federalism is that the existing highly centralised implementation federalism (*Vollzugsföderalismus*) may actually be reinforced by the pressure upon governments to implement directives from Brussels. It also means that the provinces (*Bundesländer*) will have fewer opportunities for influencing EU and national legislation (Öhlinger 2002: 92–93). According to one interviewee, the upper chamber of Parliament has become a kind of Europakammer (European chamber) for the provincial parliaments. Most implications on subsidiarity of EU legislation is discussed in the *Bundesrat* (federal council, upper chamber) in cooperation with the *Nationalrat* (national council, lower chamber). Due to the lack of resources at subnational level, these discussions at national level in the upper chamber are extremely useful (Interview A). Another interviewee made aware that in some provincial parliaments, such as the case of Vienna, there is a European committee which deals with European issues related to the province, including cross-border cooperation (Interview A).

Moreover, the Common Foreign and Security Policy (CFSP) may lead to some tensions with Austria's principle of permanent neutrality, especially if the country takes part in the Petersberg tasks of the European Union (Öhlinger 2002: 82). One Interviewee made aware that neutral countries are under considerable pressure in a EU dominated by NATO countries, leading sometimes to a naming-and-shaming pressure to follow their lead. The sanctions against Russia due to the Ukraine crisis after 2014 are a good example in this respect (Interview A).

Over the past two decades of membership, further amendments have been made to the constitution in order to include many provisions of European integration, such as the role of national parliaments in the European policy-making process (in Articles 23b to 23h) and the inclusion of the Maastricht criteria and provisions of Economic and Monetary Union in the federal budget law (Stelzer 2013: 23).

In 2003, in parallel with the European Convent, Austria organised a similar national process that led to the drafting of a new constitution. However, this was not taken on board by the political elites (Ucakar 2006: 134–135; for more details see Pollack and Slominski 2005).

72   Constitutional change in democracies

In Switzerland, after a 27-day civil war between the confederation troops and the Catholic cantons, a modern constitution influenced by the American and French constitutions was adopted in 1848. In 1874, certain changes to the constitution were made to adapt it to historical developments. Finally, in 1999, a major revision of the constitution was undertaken in order to bring it into line with the requirements of the twenty-first century. These have been the only total revisions of the constitution, which still closely follows elements of the more progressive cantonal constitutions that existed at the time of its creation. All of these were considerably influenced by the French Revolution, and so the role of the people is emphasised in the national constitution through the direct democracy instruments of the referendum and the people's initiative (Fleiner 2013: 337–340). Kayser and Richter also point out that a total revision of the constitution was long overdue: over 140 partial revisions had taken place over the decades, making the document less transparent and more confusing (Kayser and Richter 1999: 987–989). Any major constitutional amendment requires a double majority of the people and the cantons (at least 17.5 per cent of votes, meaning 17 cantons and one half canton; Fleiner 2013: 338).

Significant attempts have been made to modernise the constitution since the 1960s. Finally, an initiative by Parliament resulted in the pre-draft of 1977 undertaken by the Federal Council (*Bundesrat*). However, in 1983, a report issued on the latest status of the total revision of the federal constitution asked whether the work should be continued. Finally, in 1986, efforts led to fruition. Beyond a mere revision, a virtually new document was created based on the principle of adjustment to the constitutional reality (*Nachführung*). The objectives of this endeavour were that the document should include the written and unwritten constitutional law, be easily understandable and be organised systematically as well as with unified language. The Federal Council was in charge of undertaking this task (Kayser and Richter 1999: 988). In 1995, a proposal for a new constitution was presented to the cantons, interest groups and other stakeholders. One year later, the Federal Council submitted a slightly revised draft to Parliament for further deliberations. Finally, in 1998/1999, the constitution was approved (Kayser and Richter 1999: 988–989).

As with the Benelux countries, one of the main reasons for the most recent constitutional reform was the introduction of a charter of fundamental rights. This was an adjustment to the European Convention of Human Rights, the Universal Declaration of Human Rights and the International Covenant on Civil and Political Rights. The systematisation of such rights in Title Two represents a major contribution to the modernisation and Europeanisation of the Swiss constitution.

This total revision of the constitution was part of a larger reform of the country's political system. This broader agenda of state reform that identified the main building blocks of the constitution and the relationships among them was a key factor in achieving a broader consensus (the so-called *Baukastensystem*; see Kayser and Richter 1999: 991). However, in the process of decision-making, the individual building blocks were separated from one another; as a result, it was much easier to achieve consensus on the more concrete steps towards reform.

Constitutional change in democracies 73

It took quite a long time for all of the building blocks to be approved in Parliament and then in several referendums by the population. In this sense, taking time is another lesson that may be learned from the Swiss experience (Behnke 2009: 6). The whole process started in 1989 and was completed as the Swiss Federation was celebrating the 950th anniversary of the Swiss Federation in 1999 (Behnke 2009: 10).

Subsequently, however, additional building blocks were taken into account. A successful parliamentary reform took place in 2002, and a judicial reform between 2004 and 2008. The largest building block was the major reform of Swiss federalism. In the 1990s, it was largely acknowledged by most actors that federalism was no longer working. Specifically, it was creating significant differences in welfare between the richer and poorer cantons. The high level of decentralisation was also problematic for policy areas such as education and social policy. To remedy these deficits, an overhaul of the relationship between the central government and the cantons was undertaken (Behnke 2009: 6). For example, in the case of education, which was usually a highly decentralised competence belonging to the cantons, there was a move towards centralisation in order to achieve a level playing field, at least in the higher education sector (Fischer *et al.* 2010: 766). Taking time and informal structures were certainly important factors in achieving an agreement (Fischer *et al.* 2010: 764; see also Quesel 2012).

According to Behnke, leadership was another central element in this successful completion of the constitutional process, particularly with regard to financial compensation among the cantons. The role of the Federal Department of Finances (*Eidgenössisches Finanzdepartement*) in formulating guidelines and proposals that could be easily understood by all the cantons was crucial. These guidelines emphasised 'enhancing efficiency, strengthening subsidiarity and promoting New Public Management'. Experts helped prevent the politicisation of the process so that in the end a consensual agreement could be achieved (Behnke 2009: 9). In terms of actors, it was vital to have the cantons on board with the process from the very beginning, as they can mobilise the population for particular initiatives. For their part, the cantons saw an opportunity to obtain a fairer federal structure to replace the 'muddling through' of the previous decades. For the federal players, it was important to have as many potential veto players as possible included in the process in order to ensure success (Behnke 2009: 11).

A more critical view is presented by Martin Kayser and Dagmar Richter, who describe a process characterised by divisions among the cantons and lack of interest on the part of the population. Only 35.3 per cent of citizens participated in the referendum on the main constitutional change in 2000; of that number, 59.2 per cent voted for the revisions. In addition, the majority in Parliament through the canton-plus (*Ständemehr*) procedure required in Parliament was slim: 12 cantons and two half cantons voted yes, but eight cantons and four half cantons voted no. Kayser and Richter cite the divisions between German and French Switzerland, between the mountains and the valleys, but also between rural and urban centres. Whereas the German-speaking population and the rural

74 *Constitutional change in democracies*

areas tended towards a no vote, the Romandie and the cities voted yes (Kayser and Richter 1999: 987).

Outlining the institutional political framework of consensus democracies

Before we turn to an analysis of the political institutions of consensus democracies in subsequent chapters, it is important to provide a brief overview of the core political institutional frameworks of these countries. This will serve as an orientation map to develop an understanding of the various aspects of the West Central European democracies.

The head of state and the government

Over time, the Benelux core political systems have become very similar, emulating one another's good practices (see Figures 3.1, 3.2 and 3.3). In contrast to the republics of Austria and Switzerland, all three Benelux countries are constitutional monarchies, and therefore the head of state is the monarch: a king or queen in the case of the Netherlands and Belgium, and a grand duke in Luxembourg. Nevertheless, all three are also categorised as parliamentary democracies, but explicitly only in the Luxembourg constitution (Article 51; see Government of Luxembourg 2013b). The Dutch constitution does not define who the sovereign is (the people or the monarch), but the constitution of Luxembourg states that the monarch is merely a representative of the will of the nation, not above it. In both the Belgian and Luxembourg constitutions, all powers emanate from the nation (Constitution du Luxembourg: Article 32.1; see Government of Luxembourg 2013b; Constitution of Belgium: Article 33.1; see also Senat de Belgique 2016b).

In the Benelux countries, the monarch remains an important symbolic figure with formal duties of representation. However, it has also become an important moderating power in the triangle between monarch, government and parliament.

In the case of the Netherlands, the king and his ministers form the government, but only the ministers are part of the Cabinet, which is chaired by the prime minister, who is in charge of government policy (Constitution of the Netherlands: Articles 42.1, 45; see Government of the Netherlands 2008). In this sense, there is some ambiguity in the separation between the head of state and the government. Clearly, this is due to the fact that the constitution dates back to the nineteenth century, when governments would simply follow the instructions of the monarch. However, only the ministers are responsible for the acts that they undertake during their term in office (Constitution of the Netherlands: Article 42.2; see Government of the Netherlands 2008). Probably the strongest role assigned to the monarch may be found in the 1994 constitution of Belgium, which states that federal legislative power is exercised jointly by the king, the House of Representatives and the Senate, and that the federal executive power, as regulated by the constitution, belongs to the king (Constitution of Belgium: Articles 36 and 37; see Senat de Belgique 2016b). Similar to the Dutch case, the

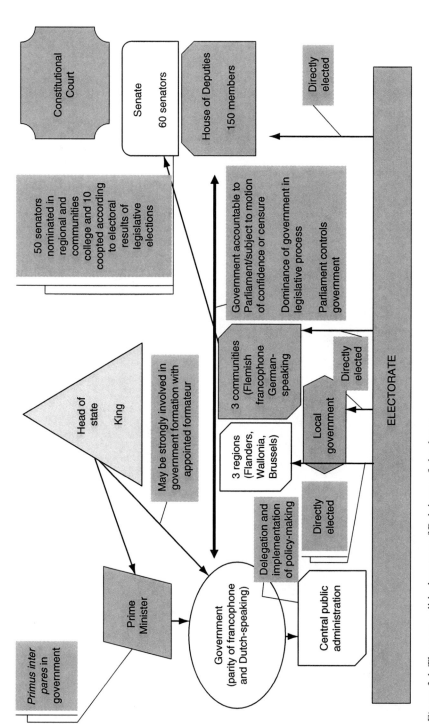

Figure 3.1 The core political system of Belgium: a federal state.

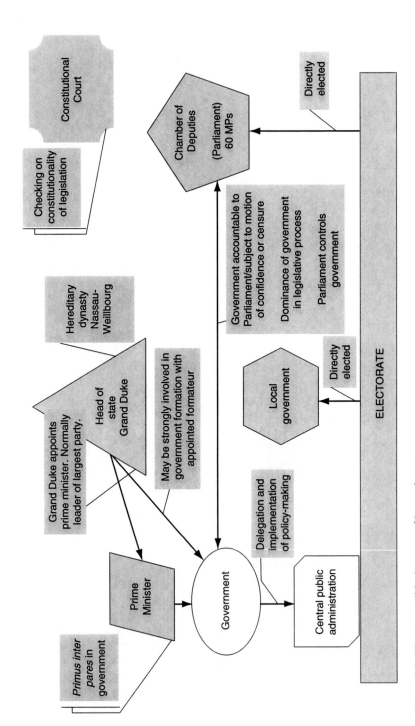

Figure 3.2 The core political system of Luxembourg.

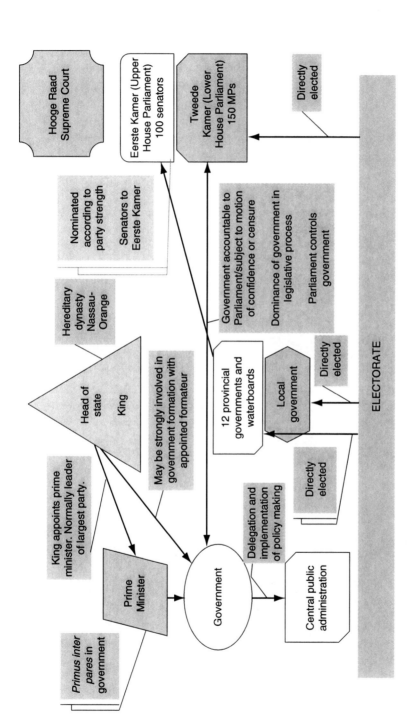

Figure 3.3 The core political system of the Netherlands: a unitary decentralised state.

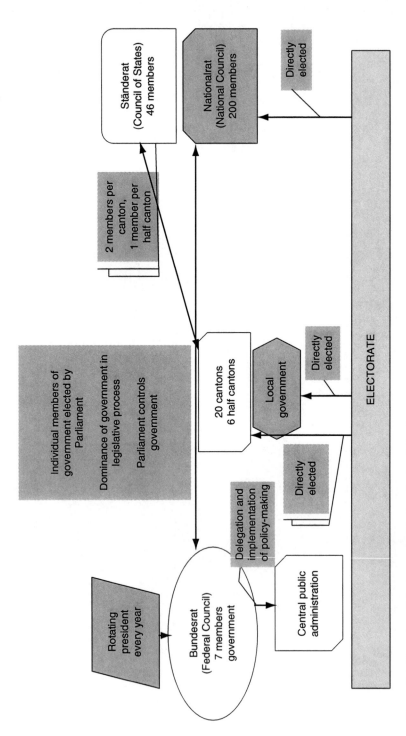

Figure 3.4 The core political system of Switzerland: a federal state.

Belgian constitution locates the section on the parliament before the sections on the king and the government, implying that the parliament is the centre of the national political system, at least in symbolic written terms.

In the case of all three constitutions, the appointment or dismissal of ministers or state secretaries must be countersigned by the prime minister (Constitution du Luxembourg: Article 77; see Government of Luxembourg 2013b; Constitution of the Netherlands: Article 48; see Government of the Netherlands 2008; Constitution of Belgium: Article 96; see Senat de Belgique 2016b). However, the Belgian constitution is quite explicit with regard to the procedure for dismissal: following the German, Spanish and Polish examples, a constructive motion of censure was introduced. This means that governments can only be forced to resign if there is an absolute majority in the House of Representatives in this respect and the opposition can find a successor to the prime minister within three days (Article 96). This is an important device to safeguard the stability of the government, as it indicates that the Belgian monarch is constrained by the parliamentary constructive motion of censure if he or she wants to dismiss a government.

The highly fragmented party systems in the Benelux countries have contributed to a stronger role for the monarch as a facilitator of government formation. Due to their complexity, negotiations may take a long time; particularly in the cases of the Netherlands and Belgium, the monarch may appoint an *informateur* to determine which personalities and parties are willing to form a government together. However, in none of the three constitutions is there any explicit reference to this role of the monarch (see Chapter 6).

The republican constitution of Austria gives the president a merely symbolic role; it is Parliament that is at the core of the political system (Constitution of Austria: Articles 60–68; Figure 3.5; see Government of Austria 2013). The Swiss Federal Council, the country's government, elects one of its seven members as president for a one-year non-renewable term, but his or her powers are extremely limited to symbolic duties of representation (Constitution of Switzerland: Article 156; Figure 3.4; see Government of Switzerland 2015). There is no clear division between the head of state and the actual government. However, the Federal Council is explicitly described in terms of organisation, procedure and powers in Title 5, Chapter 3, almost at the end of the constitution (Constitution of Switzerland: Articles 174–187; see Government of Switzerland 2015).

The Austrian president, who is elected for a seven-year term, has the right to appoint and dismiss governments and ministers, although these powers are constrained by parliamentary procedure. The Austrian president is a rather symbolic and merely formal head of state. In the presidential elections of 24 April/22 June 2016, the candidate from the FPÖ, Norbert Hofer, advocated a more semi-presidential approach to the office, asserting that he would dismiss the government. Although this power is enshrined in the constitution, doing so would go against constitutional convention and practice (*Die Presse*, 3 March 2016). The formation of a government is left to negotiation processes among the main political parties, and it is the recommendation of the prospective prime minister that

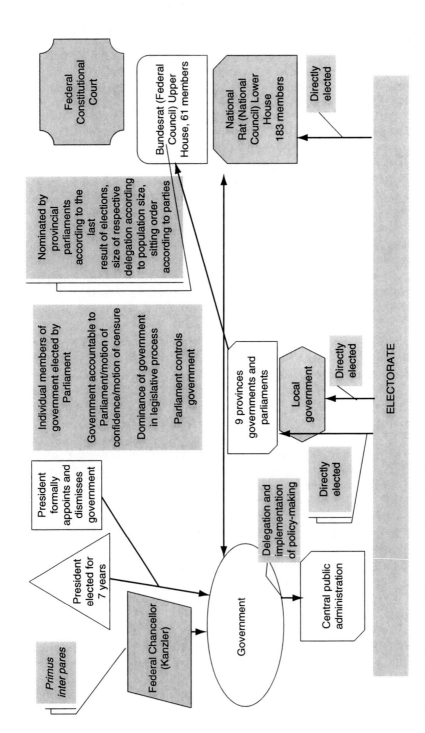

Figure 3.5 The core political system of Austria: a federal state.

leads to the appointment of the government by the federal president; therefore, a countersignature of the new prime minister is required. For dismissal of the government, there is no need for the countersignature of the outgoing prime minister (Constitution of Austria: Article 70; see Government of Austria 2013).

The Swiss Federal Council remains a unique form of government. It was influenced by the French Revolution and emulates the Executive Directory of 1795. As such, it may be antiquated due to the increased complexity of government affairs, but it has provided the political system with a high level of political stability, due to the low rate of turnover among its members (Fleiner 2013: 350, 356). After each general election, the seven members of the Federal Council are elected by the Federal Assembly, consisting of both houses. If a member resigns before the end of the term, a new election takes place. Those who wish to continue in office are usually re-elected. Since 1959, the so-called 'magic formula' has informally determined the composition of the Federal Council in terms of the main parties. However, in recent decades, the rise of the Swiss People's Party to become the largest party has created intra- and interparty tensions that raise questions about the validity of the 'magic formula'.

The structure and procedures of Parliament

In all five constitutions, the role of Parliament is defined in specific sections. However, in the Dutch and Luxembourg constitutions, the procedures of government accountability and control are not described; they are regulated elsewhere in the standing orders of the respective parliaments. Despite this, in both cases, the incompatibility of office is enshrined. What seems to be lacking is the definition of procedures governing executive–legislative relationships, even the way in which legislation is enacted. In the Luxembourg constitution, there is a very brief subsection in Chapter 3 on the sovereign power, which includes three vague articles on legislation. These sections merely state that bills must be approved and proposed by the Chamber of Deputies (Constitution du Luxembourg: Articles 46 and 47; see Government of Luxembourg 2013). A slightly more detailed section may be found in the Dutch constitution, in Chapter 5 on administration and legislation (Constitution of the Netherlands: Articles 81–89; see Government of the Netherlands 2008). In contrast, the Belgian constitution is more concrete with regard to the procedure of the legislative process in Chapter 2 on federal legislative power (Constitution of Belgium: Articles 74–84; see Senat de Belgique 2016b). The Austrian constitution also has a lengthy Chapter 2 on the two Houses of Parliament and their proceedings and on the provisions of legislative procedure (Constitution of Austria: Articles 54–59; see Government of Austria 2013). The new Swiss constitution places the section on the national federal institutions at the end of the document. The section on Parliament is quite well organised, including details on the structure, the procedure and the powers of the two houses (Constitution of Switzerland: Articles 148–173; see Government of Switzerland 2015). In all five countries, the lower houses are regularly directly elected. The members of the lower house in the

82   *Constitutional change in democracies*

Netherlands, Austria and Switzerland are elected every four years by a proportional representation system, but Luxembourg and Belgium have adjusted their national cycle to that of the European Parliament elections, which is every five years. The upper Houses of Parliament in Austria and the Netherlands are indirectly elected. In Austria, the Federal Council (*Bundesrat*) consists of appointed members from the respective provincial parliaments (*Landtage*); in the Netherlands, the *Eerste Kamer* consists of members appointed by the political parties according to their share of the vote in the respective provincial elections. These representatives are not members of the provincial assemblies; rather, they are politicians selected by the parties for positions in the *Eerste Kamer*.

Since the sixth state reform of 2014, the Belgian Senate has consisted of 50 members appointed by the respective subnational parliaments, as well as ten members who are directly elected in the legislative elections according to the share of the vote in each linguistic constituency. Of these ten, six are elected from Flanders and four from Wallonia. In Switzerland, the Council of States (*Ständerat*) is directly elected through a majoritarian electoral system. Each canton elects two members and each half canton one member (for a total of 46) through a majoritarian first-past-the-post system. Only Luxembourg has a unicameral Parliament.

In the case of the Netherlands, we can identify elements of the ancient constitution similar to the British case – for example, in the annual procedure whereby the monarch opens the new legislative session with a speech detailing the intentions of the government for the next year in a joint session of the two Houses of Parliament on the third Tuesday in September (Constitution of the Netherlands: Article 65; see Government of the Netherlands 2008). Moreover, in the same Chapter 2 on the States General, the relationship between the two chambers in the legislative process is briefly mentioned. All legislation must be approved by both houses, sometimes in joint sessions (Constitution of the Netherlands: Article 67; see Government of the Netherlands 2008). The right to exercise controlling mechanisms such as oral or written questioning of government members or the establishment of committees of enquiry is enshrined in the Dutch constitution, but absent in the case of Luxembourg (Constitution of the Netherlands 2008: Articles 68–71; see Government of the Netherlands 2008). The Belgian constitution is once again the most expansive on the procedure of both chambers, to which separate sections are dedicated. The 1994 constitution goes into particular detail on the representation of the linguistic communities in the two houses (Constitution of Belgium: Articles 42–73; see Senat de Belgique 2016b).

The Dutch constitution also includes specific articles on the Audit Court (Articles 76–78) and the National Ombudsman (Article 78a). Moreover, other permanent and advisory bodies may be created and assigned public tasks (Article 79). This latter provision refers to many bodies such as the Economic and Social Council that were created over time and have become part of the constitutional reality of the country.

Constitutional change in democracies 83

The constitutional and administrative court system

In terms of constitutional review, Austria, Belgium and Luxembourg have constitutional courts to determine the constitutionality of Acts of Parliament. Possibly the oldest and most experienced constitutional court is found in Austria, whereas in Belgium and Luxembourg they are new institutions, established in 1994 and 1997, respectively (Constitution of Austria: Articles 137–148; see Government of Austria 2013; Constitution of Belgium: Articles 142 and 143; see Senat du Belgique 2016; Constitution du Luxembourg: Article 95; see Government of Luxembourg 2013b). Neither the Netherlands nor Switzerland has a constitutional court; their highest courts are the High Court (*Hooge Raad*) and the Supreme Court, respectively. These institutions also fulfil the role of constitutional review in the last instance.

In the Benelux countries, the Council of State is assigned particular importance in the constitution. This is an advisory council to the government comprising former policy-makers, politicians and constitutional experts who help the Cabinet formulate good legislation. In all three countries, the Council of State also has a division dealing with administrative issues and specialised in administrative law. However, this is not explicitly formulated in the constitution of Luxembourg, which introduced these competences in the Council in 1997, but it is found in the Dutch and Belgian documents (Constitution of the Netherlands: Articles 73–75; see Government of the Netherlands 2008; Constitution of Belgium 2015: Article 160; see Senat du Belgique 2016).

In contrast, Austria has quite a sophisticated multi-level system of administrative courts topped by a federal administrative court. Moreover, a federal financial court very similar to that of Germany is enshrined in the constitution (Constitution of Austria: Articles 130–136; see Government of Austria 2013b). Switzerland introduced a major reform following the approval of the country's new constitution that led to the creation of a Federal Administrative Court in 2007. This institution replaced 36 federal appeals commissions that had about 7500 cases pending at the time of the change. The new court was designed to increase efficiency and improve the quality of judgments, but also to relieve the Federal Supreme Court (at that point the only high-level court in the country) of the increasing burden of case law which at that point was the only higher level court in the country. Since 2012, the Federal Administrative Court, which is based in St Gallen, has simplified processes and improved access to administrative justice (Bundesverwaltungsgericht 2016; Rothmayr Allison and Varone 2014: 222–224). In addition to these courts, a Federal Criminal Court was created in 2004, and a Federal Patent Court in 2012. The Federal Supreme Court remains the court of last instance for any complaints and also functions as a constitutional court for any disputes between cantons and the federal level and on issues related to human and civil rights linked to international law. Although the Federal Supreme Court dates back to the constitution of 1848, it became a permanent institution only with the revision of 1874. Whereas Austria, Belgium and Luxembourg have moved towards a European model involving the separation of

84 *Constitutional change in democracies*

specialised law branches, in Switzerland, the court is an institutionally diffuse entity similar to the US Supreme Court. Even today, the Federal Supreme Court is forbidden (or at least limited in its powers) to decide on major constitutional issues; this power is reserved for the two chambers of Parliament (Schweizerisches Bundesgericht 2016; Rothmayr Allison and Varone 2014: 220–221; Fleiner 2013: 343, 345).

The subnational structure

Having analysed the constitutional provisions related to the core national parliaments, it is important to briefly examine the subnational level. In our study, three countries are federal systems (Switzerland, Belgium and Austria), and two are unitary states (the Netherlands, Luxembourg). Switzerland, with its 26 cantons, has the highest level of decentralisation at the subnational level, followed by Belgium and then Austria. Although the Netherlands and Luxembourg are unitary decentralised countries, their levels of devolution are far from those observed in the three federal countries. The federal constitutions of Switzerland, Belgium and Austria include large sections defining the competences of the federal institutions and those of the subnational units. In particular, following a catalogue of human, civil and political rights, the constitution of Switzerland dedicates a very lengthy Title Three to the federal governance of the country (Constitution of Switzerland: Articles 42–135; see Government of Switzerland 2015). In addition, Title Four is dedicated to the people and the cantons (Constitution of Switzerland: Articles 136–142; see Government of Switzerland 2015). However, the constitution does not expound in detail on the communes, which are the third tier of government. The cantonal governments take care of the communes within their territories (Constitution of Switzerland: Article 50; see Government of Switzerland 2015). In Belgium, the redesigning of the state led to the establishment of six subnational units: three regions (Wallonia, Flanders and Brussels-Capital) and three linguistic communities (French-speaking, Dutch-speaking and German-speaking). The merger of the Flemish region and the Dutch-speaking community reduced the number of subnational units to five. A similar merging process, at least in terms of political personnel, between the French-speaking community and the region of Wallonia is currently taking place, although the institutional settings are still separate. Thus, there are currently five subnational units, but more synergies may evolve in the future. According to an interviewee, the merger between the Flemish region and the Dutch-speaking community was much easier, because the number of Dutch living in Brussels is about 130,000 (10%), and more on the periphery towards Flanders; this is more difficult for the French-speaking population in Brussels which is clearly about one million (90%). This makes it difficult to negotiate a merger deal between the region and French-speaking community (Interview B). In the Belgian constitution, the section on the regions and communities is quite lengthy and seemingly central to the new political system (Constitution of Belgium: Articles 115–138; see Senat de Belgique 2016b). The regions are in charge of the communes within their territories (Articles 162–166). Austria has a similar structure, with the nine *Bundesländer* responsible for the communes within their territories. Of the two unitary countries, Luxembourg is probably simpler due to the fact that there is no tier between the national and local levels (Constitution du Luxembourg: Articles 107–108; see Government of Luxembourg 2013). The Dutch system of 12 provinces is more complex: officers are directly elected, but basically have only coordinating and some financial governance powers in relation to the communes. The executive body of each province is chaired by a King's Commissioner appointed by the monarch following consultation with the prime minister (Constitution of the Netherlands: Articles 123–133; see Government of the Netherlands 2008).

This brief summary of the core institutions of the five national constitutions will help us understand and better analyse each of the parts of their political systems.

Conclusions: constitutions and political practice

There are many constitutional similarities between the five consensus democracies. Apart from the principle of parliamentary democracy, they all have proportional representation systems that create fragmented party systems. This clearly contributes to shared governments and thereby cooperation in Parliament. Following this analysis of the constitutions of our five countries, it is important to examine the reality in detail. The following chapters will deal with the core institutions, the governments and the parliaments of these consensus democracies.

4 Society and civic culture

Introduction: the complexity of consensus democracies

Following the historical overview and explanation of the constitutional orders of our five countries, it is important to briefly review the socio-political and cultural foundations of these consensus democracies. A short description of their welfare states, political cultures and civil societies should be sufficient in this regard.

The West Central European democracies are highly complex societies that are heavily reliant on the population's strong social trust. Although we lack the space required to fully discuss the theoretical aspects of a postmodern society, it may suffice to characterise such an entity as a 'society of organisations' due to the fact that the welfare state contributes to the socialisation and structuring of individuals into a collective from 'cradle to grave' (for more on this concept, see Ahrne 1990; on structuration theory, see Giddens 1984, 1985).

This chapter will focus first on the structuring aspects of the welfare state in consensus democracies. Subsequently, the systemic political cultures of these countries will be analysed. Finally, some references will be made to the strong civil societies that exist in these countries.

From the welfare state to the social investment state: recommodifying labour

The main foundation of social capitalism, or rather 'coordinated market economies' (Hall and Soskice 2001; see also Chapter 9, this volume) relies on a balance between the competitiveness of business organisations and social justice in terms of redistribution. The social market economies of consensus democracies have been successful largely because they are based on these sound socio-economic foundations.

Welfare states emerged in the nineteenth and early twentieth centuries as a consequence of social struggles and evolutionary reform in an attempt to improve the living and working conditions of the populace. In this context, the West Central European countries evolved towards very advanced comprehensive welfare states. If we compare the level of social expenditure in terms of GDP in our five consensus democracies to the average for Organisation for Economic

Cooperation and Development (OECD) countries they can clearly be characterised as generous and consistent over time (see Figure 4.1).

In all five consensus democracies, the development of the welfare state was a combination of bottom-up and top-down approaches. Many of the structures were built from the bottom up throughout the nineteenth and early twentieth centuries; however, in the second half of the twentieth century, due in part to the influence of the OECD, the state became a very important actor. In all five consensus democracies, the state currently funds about one-third of all social expenditures, with the remainder coming from employees' and employers' contributions to social insurance funds.

One problem for all consensus democracies involves their generous pension systems, which are heavily supported by the state budget, leading to a constant question about the sustainability of the welfare system as a whole in the long run.

The importance of welfare policies for the stability of consensus democracies cannot be overestimated. For the sake of simplicity, all West Central European countries may be categorised as part of the continental-conservative model of welfare regimes. The major exception, Switzerland, could earlier be described as a liberal regime in terms of public expenditures; however, in recent decades it has become increasingly similar to other continental-conservative welfare states (Wicki 2001: 266–267; Bonoli and Häusermann 2011: 196–197). Nonetheless, it still spends less in relation to GDP than the other countries in the same group. This is somewhat misleading, as Swiss federalisation allows many welfare policies to be implemented by the cantonal governments, and there is strong

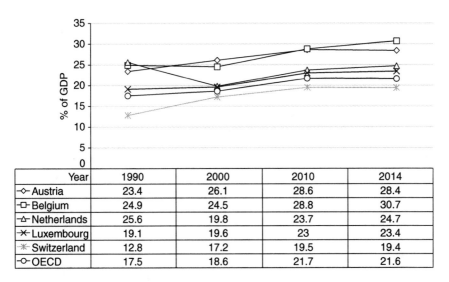

Figure 4.1 Social expenditure in consensus democracies as percentage of GDP, 1990 to 2014.

Source: author's graph based on data in OECD (2014c, 2016a).

88 Society and civic culture

participation on the part of the private sector in the private–public mix. Originally, welfare policies were implemented solely at the cantonal level, but policy areas have been transferred to the federal level over time. According to a study in 1998, 58.4 per cent of welfare policy expenditure was spent at the federal level, 27.3 per cent at the cantonal level and 14.3 per cent at the local level (Armingeon *et al.* 2004: 22). We can also identify differences in welfare provision in a more moderate form in the two federal states of Belgium and Austria. In Belgium, the federalisation process has led to a significant transfer of competences to the subnational level. However, the social insurance system remains at the national level, despite attempts by the Flemish government to gradually transfer it to the regional governments. Thus far these attempts have largely failed, although some policy aspects are now managed at the regional level (Houwing and Vandaele 2011: 128). Employment services have already been regionalised, resulting in certain differences in employment policies. This raises the unwelcome possibility of a complete division of the Belgian labour market into two regional markets due to linguistic and cultural reasons. Currently, Wallonia and Brussels are profiting considerably from a social security system that it is still federal in nature. In the context of fiscal federalism, Flanders is supporting the rest of the country through financial transfers of equalisation that come in large part from its budget, but also from the social insurance system (Cantillon *et al.* 2006: 1041).

Although the nation is highly centralised, until 2010 the nine Austrian provinces enjoyed some autonomy in terms of social assistance, leading to differences in provision across the territory (Österle and Heitzmann 2009: 40). However, since 1 January 2010, these differences have been eliminated through a national system of minimum income that is closely linked to labour market participation: anyone who receives the minimum wage must take any job offered by the employment services; otherwise, sanctions will follow. Luxembourg employs a similar national system without local differences, whereas the Netherlands has introduced major changes in its welfare system, particularly at the local level. Local governments now have more leeway to administer funding related to social and work assistance, which are linked to participation in the labour market, thus creating differences across the territory. The Dutch welfare state is increasingly becoming a social investment state, meaning that collective responsibility is being replaced by individual responsibility. The main goal is to ensure that the greatest number of people possible participate in the labour market (Delsen 2012: 14–19; Oorschot 2009: 364–365; a detailed discussion of the concept of social investment may be found in Hemerijck 2013).

Changes and reforms over recent decades notwithstanding, these countries still provide some of the highest levels of benefits: above €8800 per capita in all five countries in 2013; this is substantially more than the benefits found in liberal welfare regimes, and similar to those in the Scandinavian social democratic systems. Luxembourg is an outlier, with an average of €14,230 per capita; however, this may be explained by inclusion of the foreign workers who cross the border from neighbouring countries every day. When such individuals are excluded, the average figure is significantly lower (see Figure 4.2).

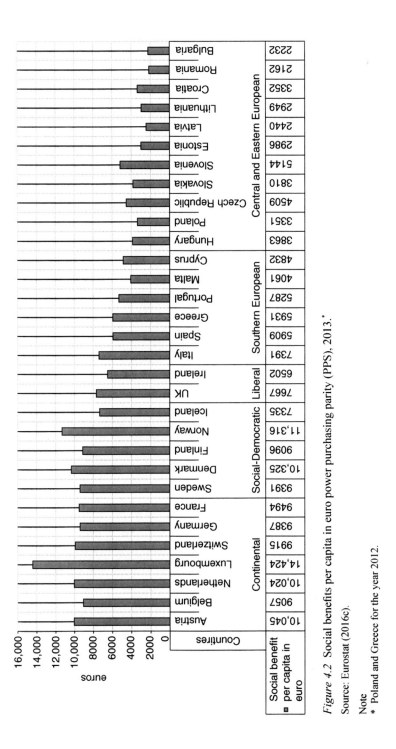

Figure 4.2 Social benefits per capita in euro power purchasing parity (PPS), 2013.*

Source: Eurostat (2016c).

Note
* Poland and Greece for the year 2012.

90   *Society and civic culture*

The main problem over the next 20 to 30 years will be the need to maintain or even increase the rate of employment in order to sustain the welfare state. This has been a vexing issue for most European countries, as fertility rates are quite low on average and immigration is also below necessary levels. Although the EU population has been increasing over recent years, the figures for our five consensus countries have been rather mixed. It seems that the Netherlands is the only country among the five that is still capable of natural population increase. Belgium, Luxembourg, Austria and Switzerland are heavily dependent on continuing immigration at even higher levels than the current rate in order to reduce the old-age dependency ratio (European Commission 2013: 6).

A crucial variable in this quest for a sustainable welfare state is the potential increase in the employment rate in the national labour market through extending the age of retirement from 65 and 67, or by equalising the age for men and women. Alternatively, older people could be allowed to work longer in currently age-restricted positions if they so wished. The original concept of the welfare state entailed social protection and redistribution, but its core objectives are shifting towards the Anglo-Saxon workfare model. The European euphemism for this workfare model is 'flexicurity', meaning that the flexibility of the labour markets should be accompanied by strong welfare and activation policies (for a critical view of the concept see Burroni and Keune 2011; for the emergence of the concept see Antoniades 2008). Although Denmark is regarded as the prototype for this model, the recent difficulties experienced by Danish employment services due to a substantial increase in unemployment have illustrated some of its limitations (Andersen *et al.* 2011). The Netherlands is also sometimes cited as an example of the ideal type of flexicurity; however, the Dutch enjoy a higher level of protection for jobs than the Danish. Thanks to its booming economy, the Netherlands can rely on a permanent workforce, but the consequence is that long-term unemployment is much higher in comparison to Denmark (Andersen *et al.* 2011). In terms of employment legislation (namely how difficult it is to fire workers), the Netherlands, together with Austria, appears to be the strictest. Switzerland and Belgium are at the opposite extreme, and Luxembourg has an intermediate level of protection for workers (OECD 2016b). Despite the transition to greater flexicurity and social investment policies, a large part of the labour market enjoys good job quality. Although there was a decline in job quality during the financial crisis, the five consensus democracies all have robust systems of industrial relations protecting their advanced labour standards (OECD 2016c: 2; Leschke *et al.* 2012: 17).

The labour market is dominated by a growing tertiarisation, and the industrial and agricultural sectors are declining steadily. Moreover, in the context of the Lisbon Strategy (2000–2010) and now the Europe 2020 Strategy (2010–2020), these societies are obliged to increase their employment rates and upgrade their workforces with the necessary skills for the knowledge economy.

Up until the 1970s, Belgium was a very successful industrial nation; however, the successive oil crises dramatically affected the nation's industrial sector, which represented 40 per cent of employment. Over recent decades, Belgium has had substantial losses in this sector, particularly in Wallonia, and it now accounts for just

Society and civic culture 91

18.9 per cent of employment. Notably, government policies have failed to create enough jobs to compensate for this shortfall. One major problem seems to be an inability to integrate the nation's youth and older workers into the labour market, especially in Wallonia. As a result, long-term unemployment rates are much higher in Belgium than in the other four countries. Due to decentralisation from the centre to the regions, there are also differences between Wallonia and Flanders in terms of labour market activation policies. The latter appears to be more successful and has evidently learned a great deal from the Dutch experience. Nevertheless, the overall Belgian labour market may be characterised as 'welfare without work' (Marx 2009: 50). The region of Wallonia has introduced a so-called 'Marshall plan' to remedy the situation in Wallonia (the new wave since 2014 is called 'Marshall Plan 4.0'), but improvements have been very gradual (Interview B).

One problem affecting all five countries is the integration of the young migrant community, the vast majority of whom were born in these countries but cannot find work due to poor educational qualifications, their social background and/or discrimination. These individuals represent the third or fourth generation of immigrants, descendants of workers who arrived in the 1960s when these economies were booming and decided to stay and build new lives. An integration crisis began to emerge in the 1980s when the five economies slipped into recession. In Switzerland, immigrants were laid off and unemployment was thereby exported (Katzenstein 1984: 104), but in the other four countries this remained a major issue. Nonetheless, these five consensus democracies continued to be attractive countries for immigrants, such that immigration was fairly constant. During the refugee crisis in the summer of 2015, most refugees wanted to go to either Germany or Sweden; however, many also stayed in Austria (in transit to Germany), the Netherlands, Belgium and Luxembourg. Integration policies have thus far been only partially successful. Among the many associated problems are poor educational qualifications (or none whatsoever), educational systems unprepared to handle the needs of immigrant children, poor quality of life, lack of motivation and guidance within families, and latent discrimination in the labour market despite highly developed equal rights legislation. In 2014, the largest number of foreigners could be found in Luxembourg (43.7%) and in Switzerland (28.3%); in Austria (16.7%), Belgium (15.5%) and the Netherlands (11.7%), the numbers are slightly lower. Labour market activation policies are therefore of the utmost importance (see Table 4.1), in particular because unemployment is much higher among immigrant communities than among the native population. In addition, the proper integration of young immigrants would contribute to the sustainability of welfare systems in the future. It would also be a sign that these societies are interested in fostering a socially sustainable multicultural society based on language skills and knowledge of the country. In this context there are major differences in terms of integration. Luxembourg and Switzerland seem to be countries into which immigrants can integrate themselves more easily: they have the largest foreign populations, but they also have the lowest unemployment figures among these groups. Belgium would appear to be more difficult in terms of integration, largely due to the permanently high level of long-term

92 Society and civic culture

unemployment among the native population and the very low employment rate. Despite a national culture that declares violence to be unacceptable in any form, many Belgian (but also Dutch and Austrian) Muslim youths are being successfully recruited by the Islamic State (ISIS)/Daesh, which is currently terrorising the populations of Syria and Iraq, in addition to fomenting domestic terrorism in Europe (BBC News, 2 December 2015).

The district of Molenbeek in Brussels has been cited as one of the ghettos in which poor immigrant communities can live parallel lives. Lack of perspective seems to be one reason for the radicalisation of some young people. However, more significantly, there is a widespread identity crisis occurring among young Muslim men and women in Western European societies that have become more repressive with regard to expression of the Islamic way of life. France and Belgium introduced legislation against the wearing of burkas in 2010 and 2011, respectively (*Euractiv*, 14 July 2011; King 2015; on repressive liberalism, see Gustavsson 2015: 80–83). In this climate, IS recruiters can manipulate young people who have become insecure in their identity (*Die Welt*, 22 November 2015). Similar ghettos enabling parallel lives have been identified in Rotterdam and Amsterdam, the two largest cities in the Netherlands (De Wijk 2006). According to a report by the Soufan Group, at the end of 2015 ISIS/Daesh had 27,000 to 30,000 fighters in Syria and Iraq, of which 5000 came from Western Europe. This group comprised 470 Belgians, 300 Austrians, 220 Dutchmen and 57 Swiss, but no Luxembourg nationals. The largest groups came from France (1700), Germany (760) and the UK (760; Soufan Group 2015: 8–9; see also Neumann 2015: 152–154).

This major issue affecting the social cohesion of all five consensus democracies notwithstanding, these societies are overall extremely happy. They are characterised by high levels of equality in terms of income distribution and, above all, the highest levels of gender equality, despite the persistent pay gap between men and women (see the *World Happiness Report*; Helliwell *et al.* 2016: 20). The national gaps in income distribution are fairly low in comparison to other European countries. However, Luxembourg's ratio is deteriorating rapidly, as is Austria's, albeit more moderately (see Table 4.2). In terms of

Table 4.1 Foreign-born population in consensus democracies in 2014

	Foreign-born population		Percentage of population	Unemployment among foreign population
	2000	2014	2014	2014
Austria	843,000	1,215,695	16.7	10.8
Belgium	1,058,797	1,414,624	15.5	18.7
Luxembourg	144,844	205,262	43.7	7.1
Netherlands	1,615,317	1,953,576	11.6	12.2
Switzerland	1,570,576	2,289,560	28.3	7.1

Source: OECD (2016e).

Table 4.2 Income distribution in selected European democracies, 2005 and 2014

	Income distribution		Gini coefficient	
	Top S20 quintile in relation to bottom S20 quintile			
	2005	*2014*	*2005*	*2014*
Austria	3.8	4.1	26.3	27.6
Belgium	4.0	3.8	28	25.9
Luxembourg	3.9	4.4	26.5	28,7
Netherlands	4.0	3.8	26.2	26.7
Switzerland	4.7	4.2	30.4	28.5
Denmark	3.5	4.1	23.9	27.7
Sweden	3.3	3.7	23.4	25.4
Finland	3.6	3.6	26	25.6
UK	5,9	5.1	34.6	31.6
Germany	3.8	5.1	26.1	30.7
France	4.0	4.5	27.7	29.2
Italy	5.6	5.6	32.7	32.4
Spain	5.5	6.5	32.2	34.7
Poland	5.6	4.9	35.6	30.8
EU 28	4.9	5.2	30.4	31

Sources: Eurostat (2016e, f).

gender equality, there is a major cleavage between Switzerland, the Netherlands and Belgium, which are among the leaders internationally, and Luxembourg and Austria as reactive followers (EIGE 2015: 75; WEF 2016).

The civic culture: attitudes towards politics, democracy and the political system

Consensus democracies are characterised by what Gabriel A. Almond and Sidney Verba refer to as a strong civic culture: despite the fact that a large segment of the population exhibits a subject, deferential or parochial behaviour towards politics and the political system, the number of participants in political life is relatively high (Almond and Verba 1963: 29–30). In 2014, 50.3 per cent of Austrians, 47.6 per cent of Belgians, 61.3 per cent of Swiss and 65.3 per cent of Dutch were very or fairly interested in politics (ESS 2014). Luxembourg fits this pattern as well: 55 per cent of inhabitants were interested in politics, according to the 2008 European Values Survey (EVS) (Atlas of European Values Survey 2016). The same study found that 60 per cent of Austrians and Dutch and 47 per cent of Swiss were likewise interested in politics, but only 34 per cent of Belgians were interested, probably due to the end of the Verhofstadt government and the difficulties in forming a new one.

The longevity of these democracies has created strong civil societies that, in turn, work to shape the democracies according to their desires. Democracy is the form of government accepted by the overwhelming majority of all five national

94 *Society and civic culture*

populations (ESS 2012; Atlas of EVS 2016; for Austria, see Ulram 2006: 518). The system of direct democracy is much more strongly ingrained in the mentality of the Swiss than in citizens of the other countries. This may be related to their constant mobilisation in elections and instruments of direct democracy, and also to the design of a militia democracy. Democracy is both a way of life and a mentality in Switzerland. It is completely integrated into the daily lives of citizens – politics is always present, particularly at the commune level (Interviews CH). This evidently leads to a different understanding of democracy. In the ESS in 2012, 87.4 per cent of Swiss agreed that citizens should have a final say through referendums, whereas just 36.4 per cent of Belgians and 44 percent of Dutch felt the same way. All three of these democracies seem to emphasise the importance of coalition governments for democracy, but in Switzerland (99.7%) and the Netherlands (97.2%), this concept is much more strongly anchored in the mentality of the population. However, 93 per cent of Belgians also regard coalitions as important (ESS 2012; unfortunately, there are no data for Luxembourg and Austria).

The political and financial crises notwithstanding, the majority of the population is satisfied with the performance of the national democracies and trust in their institutions in our five countries (see Figures 4.3 and 4.4).

The past 25 years have been quite difficult for Belgium. The quasi-collapse of traditional Belgian politics in the 1990s, constitutional changes resulting in a federal state (although this process started in the 1960s and 1970s), the political scandals of the 1990s (especially the Dutroux affair) and the government formation crisis after

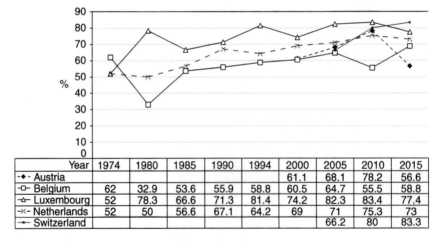

Figure 4.3 Satisfaction with performance of national democracy, 1974 to 2015.

Sources: author's graph based on Eurobarometer Interactive (2016); for Switzerland years ESS 2004 for 2005, ESS 2010 for year 2010 and ESS 2014 for year 2015.

Note

Similarly, there is considerably high trust in political institutions. However, there are fluctuations due to specific conjunctural bad performance or instability.

Society and civic culture 95

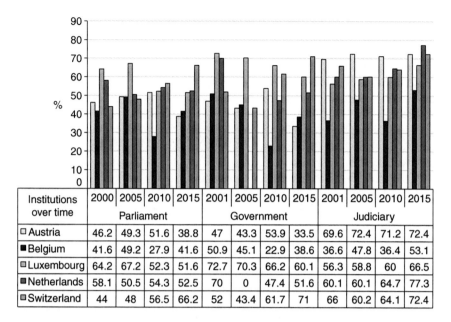

Figure 4.4 Trust in main political institutions, 2000 to 2015.

Sources: author's graph based on Eurobarometer Interactive (2016); for Switzerland: ESS 2002 for 2000 or 2001; ESS 2004 for 2005 value; ESS 2010 for 2010 value and ESS 2014 for 2015 value.

the successful Verhofstadt era (1999–2008) precluded any feelings of stability. In addition, the rise of Islamic terrorism in Belgium related to the Paris bombings on 13 November 2015 and the bombings in Brussels on 9 April 2016 further ravaged the country's self-image (BBC News, 9 December 2015, 22 March 2016). Possibly the greatest damage to Belgium has resulted from the hollowing-out of the Belgian central state and the transfer of most powers to the regions and municipalities. Jaak Billiet, Bart Maddens and André Paul Frognier have shown us that the two Belgian communities have separate party systems, educational systems and cultural policies, as well as different languages. Moreover, the media are divided linguistically. This clearly contributes to the erosion of the national culture; two separate cultures are emerging in its place as Belgium de facto becomes a confederation. As discussed above, this has repercussions for the economy, which is increasingly segmented along linguistic lines, thereby limiting mobility and efficient job allocation (Billiet et al. 2006: 913–915). In spite of this, most citizens still regard their primary identity to be 'Belgian', a sentiment fostered by the role of the monarchy – in particular, King Baldouin, who died in 1993, but also the current King Philippe and the royal family – and the recent success of the national team (the 'Red Devils') in the European and World Championships (Billiet et al. 2006: 918–919; Maddens and Billiet 2002). Research on the 2014 general elections has confirmed that most Belgians remain primarily attached to the nation-state of Belgium, and that they seem to be tired of so much change (Swyngedouw et al. 2015; see Figure 4.5). The heartland of Flemish independence seekers (representing about 20 per cent of the nation) is located in the north of the country; about 80 per cent are instead supporters of a federal but united Belgium. In times of crisis there is an increase of support for Flemish independence to about 30 per cent (Lefévre 2014). A major intergenerational study suggests that the younger generation are less inclined to support separatism as a political solution, and that they seem to strongly endorse the federal state (Rimé et al. 2015).

In the Netherlands, the Pim Fortuyn electoral revolution of 2002 led to a decline in support for major institutions, although this so-called 'Dutch drop' was reversed in 2005. The Dutch drop is a major topic of discussion among Dutch political scientists. Dutch political culture is changing radically, and the Pim Fortuyn phenomenon in the 2002 elections may have been a catalyst for a more long-term trend (see Thomassen et al. 2014; Bovens and Wille 2008). Dutch people are rather quiet and unused to expressing their feelings in public, but Fortuyn created the conditions for a more expressive political culture going beyond the rational consensus democracy of the three traditional parties (Liberals, Social Democrats and Christian Democrats). The electoral strength of these three parties has been declining steadily as the fragmentation of the party system increases (Hendriks 2012: 112). Frank Hendriks has described this development as a new politics of feelings that is influenced by the media, in particular by television shows that choose the best singer or other talented individual through a live voting process. In some ways, a referendum culture about everything seems

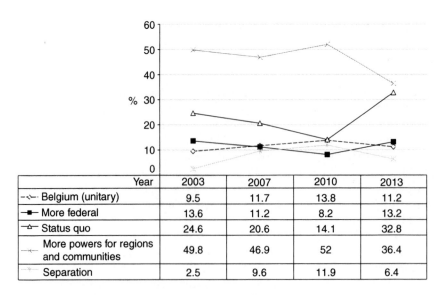

Year	2003	2007	2010	2013
Belgium (unitary)	9.5	11.7	13.8	11.2
More federal	13.6	11.2	8.2	13.2
Status quo	24.6	20.6	14.1	32.8
More powers for regions and communities	49.8	46.9	52	36.4
Separation	2.5	9.6	11.9	6.4

Figure 4.5 Support for different state models in Belgium, 2014.

Source: author's graph based on Swyngedouw et al. (2015: 15); permission kindly granted by the authors upon request.

Society and civic culture 97

to be slowly emerging (Hendriks 2012: 89–90). Pim Fortuyn voiced harsh criticism of the establishment and the cartelisation of the political system by the main traditional political parties. He also appears to have evoked among a segment of Dutch people the need to overcome the negative aspects of consensus democracies and to encourage strong leadership and strong action (Hendriks 2012: 104). The case of the constitutional treaty referendum in 2005 and that of the consultative referendum on Ukraine in 2016 are good examples of this renewed engagement of citizens in Dutch politics. Despite all these changes in the public space, support for the main institutions has remained relatively stable.

Probably the least polarised or fragmented political culture in Benelux is that of Luxembourg. This small country has had the highest approval ratings for its institutions throughout the first years of the new millennium. Luxembourg's population tends to follow a political culture emphasising stability. This is sustained by the longevity of prime ministers in power, as well as strong continuity in electoral behaviour (Lorig 2009: 34–36).

The citizens of Luxembourg are heavily dependent on a large foreign labour force to sustain their way of life, such that openness and internationalisation have become important values. The core of the Luxembourg identity is its language. In Luxembourg, students must learn French (which dominates the public administration), German (a major language in the country) and above all Luxembourgish (*Letzebürgisch*). Some consider Luxembourgish to be a German dialect of the Rhein-Mosel region, but in Luxembourg it is the most important language in terms of identity. Many foreign students have difficulties in school due to this trilingualism. For native Luxembourgers Luxembourgish is not a problem, as it is spoken at home; in this sense there is a 'hidden reality' that differentiates native citizens of Luxembourg from new ones. Luxembourgish is a springboard to the mastery of German, and French is normally learned in school. Citizenship is dependent on learning the language; however, in the school curriculum, not enough time is devoted to Luxembourgish in comparison to German and French. Consequently, children from Portugal, the former Yugoslavia and Italy struggle to be admitted to the higher levels of education. The school system is evidently a selection machine for success in the Grand Duchy (Forum Luxembourg 2012). According to an interviewee, during the financial crisis Luxembourg schools became under more pressure due to an increased inflow of immigrant children from Portugal and the Balkans (Interview LU).

In Austria, the refugee crisis of 2015 considerably affected support for Parliament and the government. There was widespread rejection of the established parties (ÖVP and SPÖ) as representatives of the old political culture of *Proporzdemokratie*. The dominance of grand coalition governments led by the SPÖ and the ÖVP and the associated *Proporzdemokratie* has resulted in protest votes for the populist, xenophobic FPÖ. The turning point for this change of political culture was the Waldheim affair in 1986, which opened up a Pandora's box that destroyed Austria's self-image as a victim of National Socialism (*Opfertheorie*; for a detailed discussion see Tóth and Czernin 2006; Uhl 1992: 84–90; Fröhlich-Steffen 2003: 115–156). This scandal triggered an extensive discussion in politics

98   *Society and civic culture*

and society about the real role of Austrians during the Third Reich, revealing that some segments of the population had ambiguous feelings about the period of Nazi occupation (1938–1945). This context related to the 'politics of memory' (*Vergangenheitsbewältigung* or *Vergangenheitspolitik*) – or, as Josef Haslinger characterised it, 'the politics of feelings' (*Politik der Gefühle*) – has shaped a remarkable stable political culture (Manoschek and Geldmacher 2006; Uhl 1992: 30–31; Haslinger 1987). Despite this discussion, the strength of Austrian identity has only increased over time. In 1956, 46 per cent of Austrians characterised Austria as a nation; in the 1990s and at the beginning of the millennium, this figure reached 76 per cent (Ulram 2006: 519; on changing identity see Fröhlich-Steffen 2003).

With regard to Switzerland, Wolf Linder has identified four cleavages in the country's political culture. First, there is a cleavage between confessional and lay cultures. Secularisation has been advancing rapidly in Switzerland, substantially reducing the power of the Christian Democrats. Second, the cleavage between urban and rural areas is still very important. Switzerland is very much a bottom-up democracy, with rural areas and the more rural and traditional cantons at the centre of the Swiss model (one could say ideology). Taxation begins at the local level, so that the level of responsibility for its commune is quite high (Interview CH). However, the cities have become quite large, leading to individualisation and secularisation, and the rural areas have lost influence as a result. Nevertheless, it should be noted that the SVP receives considerable support from rural areas, as does the CVP. Third, in the highly liberal Swiss economy there is a permanent cleavage between labour and capital. One of the reasons for labour's relative weakness is that industrialisation was a decentralised process that prevented large proletarian agglomerations from uniting (as seen in the larger countries of Germany, the UK and France). These old cleavages still play a role; however, since the 1970s, new social movements have been shaping Switzerland, such as those advocating women's rights, the environment and pacifism (Linder 2003: 18–22; for more detail on the urban–rural cleavage see Kreis 2015).

One very important event that dramatically impacted upon the political culture of the country was women's suffrage, which was accomplished in 1971. Previously, all decisions were taken by men. This late integration of women into politics is related to the negative aspects of the instrument of direct democracy. In a fairly conservative country it was difficult for women to gain access to labour markets and public life. The high point of this development thus far was in 2010/2011, when women held a four-to-three majority in the Federal Council (*Bundesrat*). However, in the National Council (*Nationalrat*) and the Council of States (*Ständerat*), women have played a secondary role, supporting the work of their male colleagues (*Neue Zürcher Zeitung*, 14 August 2015).

The Swiss population has always been critical of its own national democracy, but it exhibits very strong support for its institutions. The Swiss political labyrinth brings to the fore the interaction of three key aspects of the country's political system: consensus, federalism and direct democracy. These three elements make Swiss democracy unique in the world, a fact that is acknowledged and appreciated by the population. As a result, the rights of the people (*Volksrechte*) at the cantonal and national levels are particularly important for the Swiss population and represent a crucial part of their identity (Linder 2003: 23–28; Freitag 2014: 78–79; Interviews CH). One significant aspect of this identity is the linguistic and regional diversity of the 20 cantons and six half cantons (for more details see the excellent studies conducted by Vatter 2002, 2007, 2014) that basically created 26 different subcultures (see Chapter 8).

The high levels of trust in the police and army are vital for the stability of the five consensus democracies. The monopoly on violence is one of the most important achievements of a democratic state, and thus trust in these institutions enhances a culture of peaceful conflict resolution (Atlas of EVS 2016; Tresch *et al.* 2015: 93).

The low values for trust in religious institutions across all countries are related to two issues. This sentiment may be linked to the scandals involving child abuse in the Catholic Church. Most of these countries are Catholic or have large Catholic populations. The values also reflect a growing level of secularisation and the emergence of post-materialist values that are more critical of traditional institutions. Religious sentiment and spirituality remain strong, but they are expressed in non-traditional ways outside the established religious institutions (i.e. Catholic or Protestant churches; see Inglehart and Welzel 2005: 22, 31). Although support for political parties and trade unions is also low, these figures are still higher than the EU average, except in the case of Switzerland.

The low level of support for political parties is related to dissatisfaction with the behaviour of politicians. One important way to gauge the political cynicism of a population is to measure their trust in politicians. In 2014, just 18.8 per cent of Austrians and 29.5 per cent of Belgians, but 44.9 per cent of Dutch and 47.5 percent of Swiss trusted politicians (ESS 2014). Luxembourgers also exhibit strong support for politicians and politics (ESS 2004; RTL Letzebuerg, 13 November 2015a, b; Zahlen 2016: 2). The refugee crisis of 2015 and its management by politicians are major issues in Luxembourg and Austria. At present, this negatively influences the ratings of government and politicians. The increasing complexity of Belgian politics in a highly dynamic federation may be one of the reasons for the low level of trust in Belgian politicians. Notably, data from 2013 reveal considerable differences in terms of trust in the political system across our five West Central European consensus democracies. On a scale of 0 to 10, Switzerland has the highest score among 33 European countries in terms of trust in the political system, with 6.6. In seventh place, behind the Scandinavian countries, we find the Netherlands with 5.5, followed by Luxembourg with 5.0; some places below, behind Germany and Romania, are Belgium (11) with 4.6 and Austria (14) with 4.4. This seems to confirm the values for trust in politicians. There is definitely less trust in the political system and politicians in Austria and Belgium, whereas citizens of Switzerland, the Netherlands and Luxembourg tend to have a lower level of political cynicism (Zahlen 2016).

100 *Society and civic culture*

From pillarisation to a new, strong civil society

Now that we have discussed attitudes towards politics and political institutions in these countries, it is important to dedicate this final section of the chapter to political and social participation in civil society. Civil society may be defined as the dynamic group of political, social, cultural and economic associations and non-governmental organisations that act independently of state institutions but within the context of the democratic order (Keane 2010: 461). Levels of engagement in civil society provide a measure of the quality and sustainability of a democracy. Ultimately, critical citizens represent an important element in the prevention of an opaque and less democratic government.

First of all, the five consensus democracies have relatively high values in terms of inter-personal trust, which facilitates more extensive cooperation in associations. However, there are substantial differences among the countries: Austria, Belgium and Luxembourg have a more divided society in terms of social trust, whereas the Netherlands and Switzerland are very similar to the Nordic countries. With regard to social trust and associationism, they are rated behind the highly active Nordic civil societies.

William Maloney and Jan Van Deth carried out one of the most comprehensive analyses of civil societies in Europe in their project 'Citizenship, Involvement and Democracy' (CID), which was conducted over the first decade of the new millennium. The Netherlands and Switzerland were included in the study, and the authors seem to suggest the existence of strong associationism in these countries. A summary of all relevant European surveys between 1990 and 2010 tends to confirm the high level of participation in associations in West Central Europe, a rate just below that of the Nordic countries. For the Netherlands, the average value for the period is 82 per cent (ranking of 4), for Switzerland 68 per cent (6), for Luxembourg 66 per cent (7), for Austria 66 per cent (9) and for Belgium 62 per cent (10). This pattern in relation to the Nordic countries seems to be a West Central European phenomenon, as Germany, with 65 per cent (8), also belongs to this cluster (Van Deth and Maloney 2015: 833).

In the West Central European consensus democracies (including Germany), one-quarter to one-third of the population regularly participate in associations. Among our five small democracies, the Netherlands, Luxembourg and Switzerland show a higher level of social engagement than Belgium and Austria. Signing petitions and boycotting products are evidently the most frequent forms of social engagement across all countries. West Central European democracies have a relatively dense and intensive civil society committed to voluntary service and based on networked social capital (see the special Eurobarometer on social capital, Eurobarometer 2005: 66). We may therefore assert that all these consensus democracies have a strong civic culture.

As noted in Chapter 2, these five consensus democracies emerged out of segmented and fragmented pillarised societies. Today, they are still characterised by a transition from the old pillarised civil society to a new, more market-like, American-style civil society. This erosion process has been more rapid in the

Society and civic culture 101

Netherlands and Switzerland than in Austria and Belgium, and Luxembourg is more of an intermediary case.

One reliable indicator of the level of importance of the old pillarised civil society is the party patronage index developed by Peter Mair, Petr Kopécky and Maria Spirova, which is based on expert interviews. The researchers analysed 15 countries, among them the Netherlands and Austria, which may be situated at the two poles of the process of erosion of the old pillarised civil society. On a scale from 0 to 1, the Netherlands (0.12) emerges as one of the countries with the lowest levels of party patronage, along with the UK (0.09) and Denmark (0.16). At the other end of the spectrum are Austria (0.49) along with Greece (0.62), Italy (0.47) and Germany (0.43; Kopécky and Mair 2012: 370; see also Jalali and Silva 2015: 567). One can then identify Austria and Belgium as having a high level of party patronage, while the Netherlands would be located at the other end of the spectrum. Luxembourg would be closer to Belgium and Austria, while Switzerland would be closer to the Netherlands (Müller 2006).

This is clearly only a snapshot that provides an orientation regarding the levels of party patronage; it does not tell us a great deal about the role of civil society organisations. In particular, Belgium, Austria and Luxembourg are known for their partyocracies. In these three countries, political parties have dominated all aspects of political life for almost a century. Political parties in Switzerland and the associated ideological subcultures are weaker than in the other countries; apart from the SVP, parties do not have many resources, and they are heavily regionalised. Each of the 20 cantons and six half cantons has its own distinctive subcultural composition.

The principle of *Proporzdemokratie* remains important in Belgium, as well as in Austria, Luxembourg and, to a lesser extent, Switzerland. Tim King characterises Belgium as a 'failed state' due to its high level of inefficiency, with specific reference to the Marc Dutroux affair and Molenbeek's connection to the bombings in Paris on 13 November 2015 (see De Winter 1996, 2008; King 2015).

As Marc Hooghe asserts, de-pillarisation has been taking place over the past four decades. The regionalisation process has certainly contributed to the fragmentation of the 'national pillars'; however, they are also reconstituting themselves at the regional level. Despite this development, health insurance is still provided through national organisations with close ties to political parties or organisations that have emerged from this tradition. For example, Belgians must become members of one of the country's health insurance organisations, which obtain their funding from the national government (Hooghe 2012: 61). There are five such *mutualités* organised according to the pillars (Christian, Socialist, Liberal, independent workers and neutral; Weyrauch 2012: 205). Hooghe estimates that the Christian and Socialist *mutualités* have four million and two million members, respectively, in a country with 11 million inhabitants. The Christian Democratic and Socialist pillars are also the best organised among the pillars; however, the Christian Democratic pillar is the densest, and it can rely on the structures of the Catholic Church as well as on those of the state. It is strongest in Flanders (Hooghe 2012: 67). Although a decline in the party's share of the

102 *Society and civic culture*

vote may further decrease the influence of the Christian Democrats, the Catholic Church remains a very important player in Belgian society. There is a constitutionally enshrined separation between the state and religion, and all five main faiths (Catholicism, Protestantism, Judaism, Islam, Christian Orthodox) are supported with subsidies from the state; however, 90 per cent of funding is allocated to the Catholic Church. Personnel and material costs also are paid by the state (Hooghe 2012: 62).

The Socialists are quite strong in southern Wallonia, relying on a working-class culture that persists despite de-industrialisation (Hooghe 2012: 67). Liége is regarded as the centre of this subculture in Wallonia. In many ways, it is a culture of resistance. Party representatives and their associations permeate the dense system of parity consultation and decision-making committees in all policy areas (Hooghe 2012: 62; see also Chapter 5, this volume).

According to Hooghe, new social movements and interest groups have few opportunities to become dominant in this partyocratic system that controls part of civil society through its organisations. Consequently, they must hope for selective co-optation into the system by the established parties and organisations (Hoeghe 2012: 70–72; Hooghe 1999).

Austria exhibits a similar trend involving the erosion of pillarisation. The two so-called *Lager* (camps) together now hold about a 50 per cent share of the vote. This is highly problematic, as the main challenger, FPÖ, currently holds about 30 per cent. Nevertheless, in addition to socio-economic organisations and the social partnership (see Chapter 9), sports leagues, pensioners, young people and drivers are all organised by groups with close ties to political parties. This is reminiscent of the heyday of the encapsulation of the electorate within the subcultures. Social charity organisations are also dominated in part by the political parties. Through its organisations, the Catholic Church is still a major player in Austria. Importantly, it is entitled to receive funding from a compulsory church tax on the salaries of all Catholics (Karlhofer 2012: 537–538, 541–542). However, also in Austria, one can find new civil society organisations in the areas of the environment, human rights and support for refugees. Karlhofer identifies two important events that became catalysts for the country's 'new' independent civil society. One was the protest movement that prevented the opening of the Zwentendorf nuclear plant in 1978; the other was the intention to construct a hydroelectric power station in the environmentally protected area of Hainburger Au in the province of Lower Austria in 1984 (Karlhofer 2012: 539). The Austrian environmental movement also led to the emergence of two Green parties that later merged into one and eventually became an important political force in Austrian politics. The increase in civil society associations since the 1970s has been quite positive for the country. In 1962, the number of civil associations was 42,269; this increased to 78,835 in 1990, 104,203 in 2000 and 120,861 in 2014 (Karlhofer 2012: 527; Statistik Austria 2016: 198).

An intermediate case in terms of the old pillarised civil society is Luxembourg. The three main political parties are still dominant, but their associated organisations have suffered erosion. Among the important new civil society

Society and civic culture 103

organisations dealing with immigrants, we should mention the Committee of Liaison of Foreigners' Associations (*Comité de liaison des associations d'étrangers*-CLAE), founded in 1985, and the Association for the Support of Foreign Workers (*Association pour le Soutien de Travailleurs Immigrés*-ASTI), founded in 1979 (Schroen 2012: 429; CLAE 2016).

Due to the importance of foreigners' organisations in Luxembourg, a parity National Council of Foreigners (*Conseil National d'Étrangers*-CNE) was established in 2008 in order to advise the government on policy-making and monitor the integration process in Luxembourg. The Council's members are both foreigners and native citizens in equal numbers (CNE 2016).

The fragmentation of the Dutch party system has contributed to the more rapid erosion of pillarisation. The three traditional parties (Liberals, Socialists and Christian Democrats) have all been declining in terms of electoral strength. In comparison to the situations in Austria and Belgium, ideological aspects have lost significance. The merger of the Christian Democratic and the Socialist trade union confederations was an important event that facilitated the revival of the Polder model. The principles of consultation democracy (*overlegdemocratie*) have influenced the pragmatic, solution-oriented Dutch approach to politics, and the professionalisation of trade unionism has contributed to the separation of political and socio-economic issues. Both the Social and Economic Committee (*Sociaal en Economische Raad*, SER) and the Foundation of Labour (*Stichting van der Arbeit*, STAR) serve as templates for several such deliberative fora that may be found throughout the Dutch political system. All relevant interest groups are included in order to ensure the broadest approval for long-term policies (see Chapter 9; see also Hendriks 2012). Moreover, the new social movements since the 1960s have radically altered civil society. In addition to the Provos movement in the late 1970s based on an anti-establishment and anti-capitalist approach, there have been a number of other emancipatory social movements that have changed the civic culture of the country. In particular, environmental and women's movements have played a role in the transformation of civil society. In the process, however, both old and new interest groups must take into account the laws of the market (Kleinfeld 2012: 485).

Although direct democracy is one of the most salient strengths of the consensual political system in Switzerland, it can also act as a constraint on the further political and economic development of the country. According to Hans-Peter Kriesi and Alexander Trechsel (2008: 57), there were 543 direct democracy national votes between 1848 and 2008. Direct democracy has been a major factor in keeping Swiss civil society alive and vital. Although the number of referendums at the national, cantonal and local levels has increased significantly, turnout has been low on average, as well as in regular elections; only for very important initiatives does the turnout increase considerably. At the national level, the number of referendums has been increasing since the 1950s: between 1951 and 1980 there were 35 referendums, rising to 125 referendums between 1981 and 2015 (see Figure 4.6). This may also be an indication of a stronger civil society that challenges the decisions taken by the

104 *Society and civic culture*

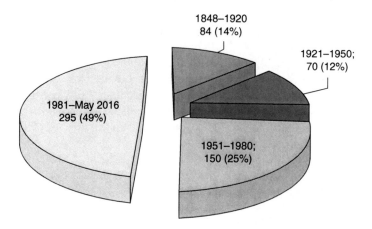

Figure 4.6 Use of direct democracy votes in Switzerland, 1848 to 2016.
Source: author's graph based on data from website of Federal Chancellery of Switzerland (2016a).

political elite (*Handelsblatt*, 28 February 2016; for more details on direct democracy see Linder and Wirz 2014; Kreis 2016).

One of the most controversial referendums, initiated by Christoph Blocher's SVP, sought to halt the construction of minarets in mosques in Switzerland in 2009. This was clearly a xenophobic referendum that symbolically linked expansion of mosques with an increase of power for a minority in the country. The referendum was definitely influenced by anti-Islamic sentiment, which is widespread in many extreme and radical right-wing parties. Even though planning permissions are granted at the cantonal level and are therefore not a federal matter, on 29 November 2009, 57.5 per cent of voters and 19.5 cantons out of 23 approved the initiative, ignoring the fact that it likely contravened international law and that the legal argumentation of the Federal Council was probably flawed (Fleiner 2013: 347). Some civil society associations have specialised in initiating referendums on problematic issues. For example, pro-neutrality activists fear that the neutral identity of Switzerland is being eroded. This is the position represented by the Action for an Independent and Neutral Switzerland (*Aktion für eine unabhängige und neutrale Schweiz*, AUNS), founded in Geneva in 1986 after a successful referendum was staged against membership in the United Nations. AUNS has very close ties to Christoph Blocher and the SVP (AUNS 2015: 21, 28). Its successful referendums include the rejection of European Economic Area (EEA) membership in 1992 and the mass immigration initiative in 2014. This system thereby entails a major problem for the country's relationship with the EU. Due to a so-called 'guillotine clause', if one agreement is suspended or not implemented, all the others are no longer valid (*Der Spiegel*, 20 June 2014; *Neue Zürcher Zeitung*, 4 December 2015). However, the SVP and AUNS lost their latest referendum on the implementation of a previous successful referendum on the expulsion of criminal foreigners from Switzerland. The new initiative sought more drastic measures in relation to foreigners. However, Operation Libero (a civil society group of young people and over 100 university professors), the other parties in the *Bundesrat* and the trade union confederations united in a common campaign for a 'no' vote, which was successful on 28 February 2016. Operation Libero was established after the 2014 referendum approving the mass immigration initiative, one of a series of referendums organised by AUNS and the SVP whose outcomes disappointed young people and intellectuals in particular. The group's charismatic leader is Flavia Kleiner, who seems to have the ability to mobilise what Operation Libero calls *Mutbürger* (courageous citizens). The movement started with an appeal on the group's website for a 'Switzerland of opportunities, not an open-air museum Switzerland' (*Für Chancenland Schweiz, anstatt Freilichtmuseum Schweiz*; *Tagesanzeiger*, 12 September 2014; *20 Minuten*, 29 February 2016; Operation Libero 2016). This seems to have been a major turning point for such right-wing populist referendums. Christoph Blocher has already advised AUNS and the SVP to use direct democracy instruments more sparingly. However, the main reason behind this restraint is that the SVP again holds two seats in the Federal Council, and therefore it no longer needs to use instruments of the opposition (*Tagesanzeiger*, 1 March 2016).

Another important social movement is the Group for a Switzerland without an Army (*Gruppe für eine Schweiz ohne Armee*, GsOA), founded in 1982. The GsOA has submitted several popular initiatives, including proposals to abolish the army and establish a peace corps (1999 and 2001), to prohibit Swiss international arms sales (29 November 2009) and to eliminate compulsory military service (22 September 2013). However, thus far it has not been very successful (see GsOA 2016).

Conclusions: strong civil societies as a foundation of consensus democracies

Consensus democracies in West Central Europe were built over more than a century. Welfare states, political cultures and civil societies emerged as by-products to the core political system. Democracy is not only a way of life for the political elite working in the political institutions of these nations; rather, it is to a great extent widespread throughout the societies. In this context we may describe these countries as strong democracies embedded within strong participatory civil societies.

5 The Americanisation of electoral and party politics

Introduction: the rise of populism in Americanised electoral markets

The rise of populism in most consensus democracies may be regarded as a sign of the increasing gap between society and the established political elites. At the centre of this argument is the increasing erosion of encapsulated subcultures and the emergence of an electoral market of individualised voters. Here, we refer to this as the Americanisation of electoral and party politics. In this chapter, following a short theoretical section, we present a brief review of the main political party families in our five countries. The subsequent section discusses electoral systems and opportunities for public funding. This is followed by a section on the broad trends of change in the respective party systems. Finally, some conclusions on the party systems are drawn.

From pillarisation to Americanisation

In 1956, Gabriel A. Almond wrote a seminal article in the *Journal of Politics* comparing different political systems. His starting point was the American political system, which he regarded as characterised by a 'homogeneous secular culture'. By secular, he meant a 'multi-valued', 'rational-calculating, bargaining and experimental' political culture; it was homogeneous because there was a 'sharing of political ends and means'. Almond went on to describe how values such as freedom, mass welfare and security were shared, but some groups might emphasise one value in relation to the others in the marketplace. In the view of continental Europeans, this is a sloppy kind of political culture. The complex system of balancing different values and arguments based on those values is not as logically simple as the ideologically segmented subcultures of Western Europe. For this complex American market to function, there is a need for individuation and autonomy in the roles of citizens. The political system is dominated by 'an atmosphere of the market', and the votes of citizens are available in exchange for policies. The brokers of this exchange are officeholders and politicians. The outcome is generally uncertain, and therefore American politics is as experimental as a laboratory, acting in an 'atmosphere of the game' (Almond

1970: 37–38). According to Almond, it is exactly this lack of individuation and autonomous roles that has prevented West European democracies from adopting similar market behaviours and developing strategies in an 'atmosphere of the game'. Roles have been assigned within the various subcultures, and thus they are not dynamic but 'frozen' within the subculture. In short, the political market behaviour of Europeans has been thwarted (Almond 1970: 46).

In Western Europe, such an Americanised electoral market began to emerge in the 1960s in the form of what Otto Kirchheimer called *Volksparteien* (people's parties), the main characteristics of which were limited ideology and an emphasis on pragmatism, inter-class vote seeking and the use of new media, especially television. These groups became known as 'catch-all parties' (Kirchheimer 1965; Mair 1997: 37–38).

Since then, electoral markets have become far more complex, such that the logics of political marketing and professional electoral campaigning are increasingly important issues (Deschouwer 2009a: 102; 2004; Mair *et al.* 2004). The problem with this is that such complexity is fairly expensive, conflict-oriented and polarising, all qualities that politicians in consensus democracies attempt to avoid (Plasser and Lengauer 2009: 335–342). Nevertheless, since the emergence of television as a political tool in the 1960s, all five consensus democracies have seen a stronger emphasis on the personalisation of politics. Hans Daalder has shown how the main newspapers associated with the pillars began to have difficulties maintaining their readerships as television grew in relevance. In Switzerland the process was slower, but in the same direction (Dewaechter 1987: 306–307; Daalder 1987: 247–248; Gerlich 1987: 86–88; Kerr 1987: 170–171).

As a result, political parties in consensus democracies are increasingly operating in an electoral market environment. After losing their encapsulated constituencies, the traditional parties have become what Peter Mair and Richard Katz call 'cartel parties': apart from being vote-seeking parties, they are above all office-seeking parties. Catastrophic electoral results may jeopardise the very survival of such organisations. In countries such as Belgium, Austria and Luxembourg, electoral losses mean the loss of considerable public funding. Cartel parties are interested in the oligarchisation of politics; they also seek to encapsulate power structures and potentially use them to remain in government. Therefore, parties seek to avoid a return to the opposition at all costs by minimising losses in elections. The alternative may be successive austerity plans within the party in order to save money (Katz and Mair 1995: 18).

The political families in the twenty-first century

West Central European democracies feature quite similar parties that have common historical roots. This section will provide an overview of the main parties in the consensus democracies examined in this study. On the left there are the radical left parties and the Communists; on the centre-left, the Socialists; on the centre right, Christian Democrats and Liberals; and on the right, the new right and extreme right (see Table 5.1).

Table 5.1 Political parties in West Central European democracies, 2016

	Radical left	Communists	Greens	Socialists	Christian Democrats	Liberals	Right	New right	Extreme right	Other parties
Netherlands	SP		Groen-links	**PvdA**	**CDA**, CU, SGP	**VVD**, D'66		PVV		
Belgium		PTB-PvdA	De Vlaamse Groen, Ecolo	**SP.A, PS**	**CD&V, CDH**	**Open VLD, MR**, LDD,* PP*			VB	N-VA
Switzerland		PdA	Grüne, GLP	**SP**	**CVP**, EVP, CSPOW	**FDP**	**BDP**	**SVP**, Lega dei Ticinesi MCG		
Austria			Grüne	**SPÖ**	**ÖVP**	NEOS*		**FPÖ**		Team Stronach
Luxembourg	Dei Lénk		Dei Gréng	**LSAP**	**CSV**	**DP**	ADR			

Source: author, based on the database of Parties and Election in Europe (2016).

Note
* Represented in Parliament for the first time. **Bold:** core parties.

The Socialist family

The largest Social Democratic party among the five consensus democracies is the Social Democratic Party of Austria (*Sozialdemokratische Partei Österreichs*, SPÖ), which carries about 26 to 30 per cent of the vote in regular elections. The SPÖ has a long tradition dating back to 1884. Between 1945 and 2016 it was in power for 60 years (84.5 per cent of the time; Müller 1996). A recent leader, Werner Faymann, found it difficult to rally the party's troops. In the last party conference on 29 April 2014, Faymann was only able to win 83.9 per cent of votes. This was a major blow, as he had hoped for more than a 90 per cent rate of support (*Kurier*, 29 November 2014). He later resigned as chancellor after the debacle of the first round of the presidential elections in April 2016; he was replaced by Christian Kern, a renowned crisis manager who was CEO of the former Austrian railway company (ÖBB; *Der Spiegel*, 17 May 2016).

In the Netherlands, the Labour Party (*Partij van der Arbeid*, PvdA) was refounded in 1945. Like the SPÖ, it has a long tradition that dates back to 1894. It is largely a pragmatic party that became bourgeoisified (Van Kersbergen 1999: 159). As Frans Becker and René Cuperus argue, the Social Democrats are losing votes among the cosmopolitan, international-oriented new middle classes and in their traditional heartland, which has been neglected. The impossible balancing act between being a responsible government party that takes on global and European challenges and being an activist party that thrives on the growing alienation of the eroded subculture has contributed to the decline of the party (Becker and Cuperus 2010: 8–9).

In Luxembourg, the Luxembourg Socialist Workers' Party (*Lëtztebuergesch Sozialistesch Arbechterpartei*, LSAP) was founded in 1902 as the country's Social Democratic party. In recent years trade unions generally associated with the party staged protests against it. Due to the country's stagnating economy, the Luxembourg social model is badly in need of reform (*Luxemburger Wort*, 15 March 2012). LSAP Member of Parliament Vera Spautz resigned from her seat due to the planned changes in the indexation of wages (*L'essentiel*, 14 November 2012). Party president Claude Haagen has initiated a process of renewal in the LSAP, with the Party Congress in 2014 publicised as the beginning of an adjustment to the new reality (for more details on the party see Fitzmaurice 1999; Dumont *et al*. 2009: 180–184).

In Switzerland, the Social Democratic Party (*Sozialdemokratische Partei der Schweiz*, SPS), founded in 1888, is the only left-wing party in the Federal Council. It is also the second largest party after the SVP. Originally a working-class party, the SPS now has a different electoral profile: it is the party of well-educated new middle classes in the urban centres, and its traditional blue-collar supporters have migrated to the SVP in recent decades. It shares some of its electorate with the liberal party (FDP) (Ladner 2001: 138; see also Bühlmann and Gerber 2015).

In Belgium, the linguistic divide led to a split of Social Democrats into a Wallonian and a Flemish party. The Socialist Party (*Parti Socialiste*, PS) in Wallonia

110 *Americanisation of electoral politics*

is the stronger of the two. The Workers Party of Belgium (*Parti Ouvrier de Belgique/Partij van der Arbeid België*, POB/PAB) was founded in 1888 and was the last of the larger parties to split in 1978. Wallonia is also the heartland of the Belgian Socialist movement, despite the fact that the working-class subculture is eroding quickly. One interesting point is that the PS is quite successful in winning supporters from the Muslim population: according to Pascal Delwit, it has a 43 per cent penetration among Belgian Muslims (Delwit 2011b: 122). Moreover, the party remains well organised at the local level. In Wallonia, the party won about 38 per cent of the vote, which is quite remarkable (Delwit 2011b: 107; 1999).

The Flemish counterpart to the PS is much weaker. In 2001, the group changed its name to the Socialist Party Different/Social Progressive Alternative (*Socialist Partij Anders/Sociaal Progressief Alternatif*, sp.a). The party was initially able to win about 20 per cent of the vote in Flanders, but since the turn of the millennium it has been losing votes. In the general elections of 2013 it won only 8.8 per cent of the vote (Dandoy 2011a: 90).

The Communist family

Between 1919 and 1921, the Communist parties in all five countries split from their Social Democratic rivals. In the Netherlands, the CPN lost representation in 1981 and 1986, respectively, despite being one of the strongest parties in Western Europe in 1946. In Switzerland, the Labour Party (*Partei der Arbeit*, PdA) still maintains representation of one seat, and in Luxembourg there is the Left Party (*Dei Lenk*), which is a coalition of various groups with Communist and radical-left tendencies. Interestingly, there is an even more radical and orthodox Communist Party of Luxembourg still competing at the national and local level (Dumont *et al.* 2009: 184–186). In the Netherlands, the Socialist Party (*Socialistisch Partij*, PS), founded in 1971–1972, is part of the country's radical-left tradition, as symbolised in particular in the small Communist Party of the Netherlands (Marxist–Leninist) supporting Maoist China, and fiercely opposed to the CPN. One such group based on Maoist grass roots democratic ideology was the SP. Over the past 20 years, the party's radical policies have gradually become more moderate and therefore electable. The SP has exhibited left-wing populist tendencies, particularly during the financial crisis, but it has ambitions of being an established party. Over the decades, the party has nurtured subcultural grass-roots support, and the party now wins about 9 to 10 per cent of the votes. In a country of small parties, this is a considerable success: it is now the fourth largest party after the Liberals, Social Democrats and the new-right populists of the Party of Freedom.

The Christian Democratic family

For Dutch social democracy, the bourgeoisification of the working class has been a major factor eroding the social basis of parties; in the case of Christian

Americanisation of electoral politics   111

democracy the problem has been secularisation. The Dutch Christian Democratic Appeal (*Christen-Demokratisch Appél*, CDA) was founded in 1980 as a merger between the Catholic People's Party (*Katholieke Volkspartij*, KVP) and two small Protestant parties, the Anti-Revolutionary Party (*Anti-Revolutionaire Partij*, ARP) and the Christian Historical Union (*Christen-Historische Unie*, CHU), in a reaction to declining electoral opportunities. In terms of ideology, its programme centres on the responsibility of the individual in the social context, such as family and work. This so-called 'social personalism', namely individualism embedded in social contexts, remains the party's main approach to politics, albeit in a watered-down form. After 2000, an ideology of 'social conservatism' integrating law and order and a tough stand on immigration and integration developed (Lucardie 2004: 167–170).

In Belgium, the Christian People's Party/Christian Social Party (*Christene Volkspartij/Parti Social Chrétien*, CVP/PSC) was the dominant party in the political system until the 1990s, although, like its counterparts, it split in 1972 (the first party to do so; Van Haute 2011a: 38–39). Due to its longevity in power, the CVP/PSC became embroiled in political scandals and came to symbolise the old political culture based on patronage and clientelism, as represented by *éminence grise* such as Winfried Martens and Jean Luc Dehaene. In the 1999 elections the Christian Democrats suffered a major defeat, which was repeated in 2003 (Van Haute 2011a: 39–40). This led to a major renewal of the two Christian Democratic parties. One of these signs of reform was the change in party names, a move that was part of a general reordering of political parties in the respective regions. The Flemish party became more regionally oriented, although it still advocated Belgian unity and the continuing evolution of federalism; this organisation was renamed the Christian Democratic and Flemish party (*Christen-Demokratisch en Vlaams*, CD&V) in 2001 (Beke 2004: 143). According to Wouter Beke, the CD&V still exhibits a strong tendency to follow the patterns of a mass party rather than a cartel party (Beke 2004: 156). Nevertheless, in terms of elections, CD&V has not had much luck in finding charismatic leaders. A good example of the new generation is Yves Leterme, who found it difficult to form a government in both 2007 and 2010 (*Der Spiegel Online International*, 22 December 2008; BBC News, 26 April 2010). A major rival for the party is the New Flemish Alliance (N-VA), a party with a similar Christian Democratic profile but that advocates independence for Flanders.

The Christian Democrats in Wallonia have been called the Democratic Humanist Centre (*Centre Democratique Humaniste*, CDH) since 2002. Due to the growing secularisation in Wallonia and the dominance of the secular parties, the CDH choose its new name to attract voters beyond the traditional Catholic core who may be interested in religious and moral-ethical issues (Pilet 2011: 68–69). A new Charter of Humanism marked the party's attempt to redefine itself in a secularised, changing society (Beke 2004: 145). Ideologically, the party moved to the centre, seeking to become a moderate actor in the fragile party system. It may be categorised as a *belgicain parti* (a pro-Belgian unity party) supporting federalism.

112   *Americanisation of electoral politics*

On the moral-ethical dimension, CDH and also CD&V have been fierce opponents of euthanasia and gay marriage, both of which were supported by the Socialists and Liberals (Pilet 2011: 68–71; Beke 2004: 149).

The trajectory of the Christian Social Party (*Chrëschtlech-Soziaal Vollekpartei*, CSV) in Luxembourg has been more straightforward. The CSV can trace its history back to 1903, when various Catholic associations formed a political group. It became a *staatstragende partei* (state party) during the interwar period (then called the Party of the Right; Poirier 2004: 179). After 1945, it renamed itself the CSV. The social basis of the party is the rural, poorly educated and ageing Catholic population, the middle classes in the capital and immigrants, particularly Portuguese immigrants (Poirier 2004: 183, 186–187; see also Dumont *et al.* 2009: 169–274).

The Austrian People's Party (*Österreichische Volkspartei*, ÖVP) is a successor to the Christian Socials of the First Republic (see Chapter 2). It was originally founded in 1945 as a Christian Democratic party, but it also served for a long time as the representative of the right in Austria. Until 1970, it was the dominant party in the political system, working closely with the SPÖ (Gottweis 1983: 55–66). However, between 1970 and 1999 and after 2007, it consistently came in at a poor second. Chancellor Wolfgang Schüssel's coalition government between the ÖVP and the SPÖ changed this situation, allowing for a more pro-business policy between 2000 and 2007. Between 2007 and the present day, the ÖVP has again been a junior partner of the SPÖ. Ideologically, the ÖVP has evolved into a socially conservative party that emphasises the cultural identity of the country. It has also promoted a more neo-liberal policy concentrating on welfare reform (Fallend 2004: 104; 2005: 13–14).

In Switzerland, the Christian People's Party (*Christliche Volkspartei*, CVP) was founded in 1912. It was once the second strongest party, after the Liberals. In recent decades, the CVP's share of the vote has been declining due to secularisation and aggressive competition from the SVP in the party's former strongholds (Ladner 2004: 325–328). In both Houses of Parliament, the CVP tends to work together with other religion-based cantonal parties.

The Liberal family

According to Ruud Koole, one problem experienced by observers of Dutch politics is the fact that the major parties are all partially liberal in nature. Koole characterised the Netherlands as a paradise for Francis Fukuyama, who predicted a 'liberal world' following the fall of the Berlin Wall in his book *The End of History and the Last Man* (Koole 2000: 121; Fukuyama 1992).

The People's Party for Freedom and Democracy (*Volkspartij voor Vrijheid en Democratie*, VVD) was founded in 1948, although historically it dates back to the early nineteenth century. The VVD has always been liberal-conservative with a definite market orientation. Over the past four decades, VVD has become a pivotal party engaged in reforming the welfare state through neo-liberal policies (Koole 2000: 132–133).

Americanisation of electoral politics 113

Belgium also has a fairly liberal political culture due to its history. After the Second World War, the Liberal party was able to remain one of the most important members of the party system. In 1961, it changed its name to the People's Party for Freedom and Progress (*Parti pour Liberté et Progrés*, PLP/*Partij voor Vrijheid en Voruitgang*, PVV). In the 1965 general elections, it increased its electoral share from 12.3 per cent to 21.6 per cent (De Winter 2000: 151). However, the linguistic conflict considerably affected the Liberals, who were committed to the Belgian state. In 1972, they split into a Wallonian and a Flemish party. The PVV in particular was targeted by the regionalist Brussels party, the Democratic Front of Francophones (*Front Democratique des Francophones*, FDF; Delwit 2002).

Both parties remained at the centre of power in several coalition governments between 1980 and 1987. The rise of the charismatic young leader Guy Verhofstadt for the Flemish liberals led to major reforms within the party, and in 1992 the party changed its name to the Flemish Liberals and Democrats (*Vlaamse Liberalen en Democraten*, VLD; Dedecker 2011a: 129–130). Verhofstadt represented a change of guard from the 'old' political culture to the 'new' system of transparency and accountability. Between 1999 and 2008, his party led three governments that introduced sweeping reforms in the political economy. The party changed its name again, this time to Open VLD; this name acknowledged its cooperation with VIVANT, a radical democratic party (Dedecker 2011a: 135). Ideologically, the party moved to the right by advocating neo-liberalism as well as law-and-order issues. The party also became quite sensitive towards immigration issues. Overall, its ideology may be categorised as socially liberal (Dedecker 2011a: 140–143).

On the francophone side, the former PLP transformed itself into the Reformist Movement (*Mouvement Reformateur*, MR) in 2002 (for a detailed history see Delwit 2002). This also marked its merger with several smaller liberal parties. Party leaders Didier Reynders and Louis Michel may be regarded as the main actors in shaping the new party up until 2011 (Dedecker 2011b: 153). Subsequently, Charles Michel, the son of Louis Michel, took over the leadership and became prime minister after the 2014 general elections. A predominantly male party (Dedecker 2011b: 153), it is particularly strong in Hainaut, Liège and Brabant Wallon (Dedecker 2011b: 155). It also numbers among the pro-Belgian unity parties, resisting separatism and blackmail by Flemish politicians (Dedecker 2011b: 162–163).

The Democratic Party (*Demokratesch Partei*, DP) in Luxembourg has had a long historical trajectory going back to the early twentieth century. According to Philippe Poirier, the DP combines two different ideological positions, namely that of social liberals supportive of the welfare state, and economic liberals supportive of small and medium-sized entrepreneurs keen on reductions in red tape and taxation (Poirier 2002: 252). The DP's most important stronghold was in Luxembourg City, particularly among public servants (Poirier 2002: 256). Prime Minister Xavier Bettel, a DP leader, was previously the Mayor of Luxembourg (see also Dumont *et al.* 2009: 174–177).

114   *Americanisation of electoral politics*

In Switzerland, the Liberal Democratic Party (*Freisinnige Demokratische Partei-Parti radical democratique Suisse*, FDP/PLR) was established in 1894 and may be considered to be the founding party of the Swiss political system. Like other West European countries such as the Netherlands and Belgium, politically radical liberalism played a major role in achieving a viable law-and-order state in the nineteenth century. The FDP/PLR is a right-centre party advocating law-and-order issues. In addition, neo-liberalism and the freedom of the individual remain central to its agenda. It is the third largest party after the SVP and the Social Democrats (for a historical review until the end of the 1960s, see Gruner 1969: 77–100).

Traditionally, the Freedom Party (*Freiheitliche Partei Österreichs*, FPÖ) represented the liberal tradition; however, this was always overshadowed by the national (or German) tradition. In 1986, it became a right-wing populist party with positions against continuing immigration and the *Proporzdemokratie* (see below). In 1997, remnants of the liberal tradition in the party formed the Liberal Forum (*Liberales Forum*, LiF), which won 6 and 5.5 per cent of the vote in 1994 and 1995, respectively. Subsequently, it has been unable to achieve significant representation; in 2006, it won one seat as part of a joint candidacy with the SPÖ. However, in 2013 it experienced something of a comeback as the new political formation New Austria and the Liberal Forum (*Neues Österreich und Liberales Forum*, NEOS), winning 5 per cent of the vote and nine seats (see the section below on populist parties).

The Greens

Green parties emerged in the 1980s in our five countries as a response to the growing concern over limited energy resources, as well as the consequences of climate change.

In the Netherlands, the Green Left (*Groenlinks*, GL) is the main representative. The GL was founded in 1989 as a merger of several pacifist parties, including the Communist Party. It is quite a small party, fluctuating between 2 and 7 per cent of the electorate. This presents a stark contrast to the Belgian Green parties Ecolo (*Ecologistes confederés pour le organisation des lutes originales*) in Wallonia and Groen! in Flanders, which became coalition partners in the Verhofstadt government between 1999 and 2003, albeit with catastrophic electoral consequences (for a more detailed account of the parties before their term in government see Pilet and Schrobiltgen 2011; Dandoy 2011b). Green parties in Luxembourg, Austria and Switzerland have been more successful. The Greens (*Dei Gréng*), founded in 1983 but united only in 1989, are currently part of the coalition government with the DP and the LSAP (Dumont *et al.* 2009: 177–179). A similar history of division and unification may be found in Austria in the conservative and progressive wings, resulting in the Green–Green Alternative (*Die Grüne–Die Grüne Alternative*), whose merger took place in 1986. In Switzerland, two Green parties compete with each other: the Greens (*Grüne Partei der Schweiz*, GPS) and the Green Liberals (*Grüne Liberale Partei*, GLP). These parties are supported by the well-educated segment of the population that is worried about the environment but also interested in democratic reform. The GPS tends to win about 7 to 9 per cent of the vote, whereas the GLP wins about 4 to 5 per cent (for the GLP see Stadelmann-Steffen and Ingold 2015).

Other parties

The volatility of the national party systems in our five countries has led to the emergence of other, smaller parties that gain representation in Parliament from time to time. In the Netherlands, the Party of Animals (*Partij van der Dieren*, PvdD) and the Union 50+ (Unie 50+), the latter representing the interests of pensioners and the elderly, are examples of this fragmentation. In Austria, Team Stronach was established by Frank Stronach, an Austrian-Canadian billionaire, in September 2012 to promote more market-oriented policies based on economic liberalism and less state interference in the economy; it also opposes the 'old' political culture of *Proporzdemokratie* (*Süddeutsche Zeitung*, 27 September 2012; *Der Standard*, 23 October 2015).

A new, more moderate populist-independentist movement, the New Flemish Alliance (*Nieuw-Vlaamse Alliantie*, N-VA), founded in 2001, has become the strongest party in Flanders since 2010, profiting from the collapse of support for the VB. The N-VA is a centre-right party with strong links to the CD&V, but it advocates a more nationalist Flemish position, proposing the peaceful division of Belgium. The party follows in the tradition of the People's Union (*Volksunie*, VU), a Flemish party that has contributed to the federalisation of Belgium since the 1960s (Van Haute 2011b: 204–205). The N-VA's leader, Geert Bourgeois, is now the first minister of the Flemish regional government; Jan Jambon, another high-ranking party official, is now a vice-president in the national government. Some politicians even refer to the party as the new VB, in part due to some xenophobic comments by N-VA leader Bart van der Wever (*De Redactie*, 25 March 2015).

Populist challengers

Following an era of considerable political and economic stability that lasted until the 1960s, the growing insecurity due to global change and turbulence has contributed to the emergence of both right-wing and left-wing populist parties in recent decades. In this context, populist challengers often present easy solutions for a return to an imaginary 'heartland' of the past.

Paul Taggart defines populism as 'an episodic, anti-political, empty-hearted, chameleonic celebration of the heartland in the face of crisis' (Taggart 2000: 5). 'New populism' interprets the 'heartland in the face of crisis' in relation to the transformations of the late twentieth century. Such reactions may come from either the right or the left, but they are particularly widespread among the more conservative groups (Mudde 2004: 549–550).

In another article, Taggart outlines five key features of the 'new populism', which is merely a new version of previous forms of the same phenomenon.

116   Americanisation of electoral politics

1   *Hostile to representative politics*: Instead, the new populism tends to use representative democracy as a structure of opportunities to promote the cultural leitmotiv of direct democracy in order to mobilise 'the people'.
2   *Identification with an 'idealised' heartland*: That is, the unitary and simplistic idea that in the past everything was better, and globalisation and Europeanisation are destroying our world. The true people of the 'heartland' are native citizens.
3   *There are no core values attached to the heartland*: Values, issues and themes change according to the public debate. Parties exhibit a chameleonic nature.
4   *Reaction to a sense of extreme crisis*: These parties emerge in times of instability, change and crises of legitimacy (*Parteienverdrossenheit*), and also after political scandals involving the established elites.
5   *Limited quality and long-term prospects*: The parties can be very successful in the short term due to their dependency on charismatic leadership; however, it is difficult to remain radical for a long time. Fast growth may undermine the institutionalisation of the party (Taggart 2004: 273–276).

In the Netherlands, the Pim Fortuyn List (*Lijst Pim Fortuyn*, LPF) was an important populist movement that was established in 2001 and managed to survive until 2007. Its founder was Pim Fortuyn, a professor of sociology at the Erasmus Rotterdam University. He declared himself to be homosexual, and expressed his condemnation of how homosexuality and homosexuals are treated in Islam. He also made generalised references to the way women are mistreated by the religion. Pim Fortuyn did not consider his party to be xenophobic or Islamophobic, but viewed it as contributing to the debate by raising taboo topics. The 'heartland' of the LPF was the Dutch way of life; the party fed on the growing alienation created by the lack of integration of the immigrant community, especially the Muslim parallel societies in the large cities (Van Holsteyn *et al.* 2003: 74, 76–84; Van der Brug 2003: 97, 102). According to Paul Pennings and Hans Keman, the LPF sought the 'restoration of a community spirit within small-scale communities' (Pennings and Keman 2003: 63). Fortuyn was assassinated by an animal rights activist nine days before the 2002 elections, prompting a sympathetic 'condolence vote' for the party. The LPF won 17 per cent of the vote and a place in the government with the CDA. By 2007, the party had disbanded (Van Holsteyn *et al.* 2003).

A more extreme successor to Fortuyn is Geert Wilders' Party of Freedom (*Partij voor de Vrijheid*, PVV), founded in 2006 before the general elections of that year. Wilders emerged as a new leader of an even more Islamophobic and xenophobic party. It seems he spent about two years in Israel and became sympathetic to the struggle of the small country against a hostile environment (Pauwels 2014: 114). At first, Wilders made his career in the conservative-liberal VVD; however, his positions against radical Islam soon became more aggressive. He demanded that radical mosques be banned and radical Muslims deported. Ignoring a request from the VVD to distance himself from these positions, he stuck to his

Americanisation of electoral politics 117

guns, resulting in his exclusion from the party in September 2004. Wilders then created his own 'Group Wilders' in Parliament. On 22 February 2006, he established the Freedom Party and won 6 per cent of the vote in the national elections later that year (Pauwels 2014: 115–116). In 2010, he almost trebled his result, increasing the party's share to 15.4 per cent, but in 2012, support declined to 10.4 per cent. Over the past decade, Wilders has shown a definite affinity towards conspiracy theories, such as the purported plot by Islam to colonise Europe. The danger of the 'Islamisation' of Dutch society is one of the trademarks of the PVV, which regards Islam as a totalitarian ideology (PVV 2012: 35). This has led to links with the extreme right-wing Patriotic Europeans against the Islamisation of the Occident (*Patriotische Europäer gegen die Islamisierung des Abendlandes*, PEGIDA) movement in Germany (*Der Spiegel*, 14 April 2015). Moreover, Wilders promotes a hard Eurosceptic line, rejecting the euro and embracing only the establishment of a Free Trade Area (PVV 2012: 17). The party's literature frequently compares the EU to the Soviet Union, referring to it as a EUSSR that seeks to undermine national governments (PVV 2012: 26).

In Belgium, the Flemish Interest (*Vlaamse Belang*, VB, until 2004 *Vlaams Blok*) emerged in the early 1980s and has been gaining electoral support from election to election. Its charismatic leader, Felip De Winter, has been an important factor contributing to the rise of the party. In Belgium, the imagined 'heartland' of the VB is an independent Flanders. Naturally, visions of this independent Flanders are accompanied by a xenophobic discourse against the Muslim population. A new position shared with the Austrian FPÖ and PVV is the rejection of Turkey's accession to the European Union and the Islamisation of the country (Pauwels 2011: 225–226). Gerolf Annemans and Steven Utsi, two VB members, wrote a book based on party research entitled *After Belgium: The Orderly Split-up* (Dutch version: *De Ordelijke Opdeling van België – Zuurstof voor Flanderen*), analysing the implications of possible peaceful independence for Flanders and the break-up of Belgium following the model of the Velvet divorce between the Czech Republic and Slovakia in 1992/1993. Most issues in such a division seem to be unproblematic due to the consensual linguistic cleansing that has been taking place over recent decades; nonetheless, two major problems are still unresolved and must be negotiated. One involves the question of Brussels, which is the capital of Belgium but also of Flanders, despite the fact that it has a French-speaking majority. The authors claim that Brussels is in Flemish territory and is therefore an integral part of Flanders. The best solution, they suggest, would be for Brussels to become the capital of Flanders; however, this would be opposed by the French-speaking population. A second option would be to make Brussels autonomous within Flanders, and a third option entails a confederation of two independent states (Flanders and Brussels; Annemans and Utsi 2011: 186–195). The second problem is the status of an independent Flanders in relation to the European Union. This is a highly significant problem, as many enterprises in Flanders want to be reassured that the business environment will remain the same. The authors cite the cases of Scotland and Catalonia, but they do not provide a final resolution (Annemans and Utsi 2011: 122–129). One important aspect of

118   Americanisation of electoral politics

this 'orderly splitting up' of Belgium is that it must be accomplished consensually and peacefully in the Belgian tradition (see also Karim Overmeire's similar ideas in *The Flemish Republic* (2008: 2)).

The other parties ostracised the VB at federal and regional levels through the *cordon sanitaire*; however, their actions merely strengthened the party, at least until 2010 (Pauwels 2011: 221). This strategy is regarded as an undemocratic act by the VB, which launched the campaign 'SOS Democracy' to alert people to the situation (*Vlaamse Belang* magazine 2007a: 15, 2007b: 10–11).

The stronghold of the VB was Antwerpen, which it held control of until the latest elections. It has recently been replaced by a coalition between the established parties and the moderate regionalist party N-VA under the leadership of Bart de Wever, whose challenges to the VB have led to a decrease in its vote share.

In Luxembourg, the Alternative Democratic Reform (*Alternative Demo-cratësch Reform/Parti Democratique Reformateur*, ADR/PDR), founded in 1987, originally focused on the interests of pensioners but evolved towards a broader agenda; it now regards itself as the defender of the country's native citizens. The party highlights in particular the importance of the Luxembourgish language and the need for all foreigners to learn it. Local politics is another major aspect of the ADR/PDR. An anti-establishment party, it works closely with local celebrities to get its message across (Dumont *et al.* 2009: 168–169; Van Kessel 2015: 59).

In Austria, the 'heartland' for the FPÖ was a German national identity, a desire to become part of Germany and a hatred of the new Austrian republic. After its founding in 1956, the party relied on the support of a large number of people who had been active in the Third Reich and were in search of a political party. The FPÖ thus became the main vehicle for about 750,000 people who had collaborated with the Nazi regime. However, in the late 1970s, a younger generation committed to liberalism attempted to shift the party towards the centre-right (Perchinig 1983: 78–89). Internal tensions within the party led to the rise of a charismatic leader, Jörg Haider, who had an at best ambiguous relationship with the Third Reich and Austria's wartime role. Certain older FPÖ politicians also had connections to the former Nazi regime. Haider's moment came in the general elections of 1999, when the party managed to match the support of the ÖVP and to become part of the coalition government between 2000 and 2006 (Kopeinig and Kotanko 2000; Falkner 2005).

These developments led to considerable party infighting due to ongoing criticisms of Jörg Haider, then the president of the province of Carinthia. In the end, the party split into two in 2005: the old party was taken over by Heinz-Christian Strache, and the new Alliance for the Future of Austria (*Bündnis für die Zukunft Österreichs*, BZÖ) was led by Haider. After Haider's death in a car accident in December 2008, Strache tried to reunite the party. Currently, the heartland of both the FPÖ and the BZÖ is the Austrian way of life established after 1945. As a result, excessive interference by the European Union in domestic affairs is regarded as negative. Both parties have also advocated a restrictive immigration policy and promote anti-Islamic positions. The mismanagement of the refugee crisis by the grand coalition in 2015 contributed further to the rise of the FPÖ, which was able to foment fears about the Islamisation of the country, the threat to Austria's national identity and ultimately the loss of the 'Austrian heartland' (*Der Standard*, 27 March 2015; *Kleine Zeitung*, 24 April 2015). The *Proporzwirtschaft* (distribution of spoils between the two main parties) is an additional major topic of interest.

In Switzerland, the rise of the Swiss People's Party (*Schweizerische Volkspartei*, SVP) started with the 1992 referendum, when it was the main vocal opposition to the accession of Switzerland to the European Economic Area (EEA), despite support by all major parties.

The SVP has been characterised by Daniele Caramani and Yves Meny as 'Alpine populism' that attempts to defend an 'idealised heartland' of Switzerland against the winds of change, in particular immigration. The party family of 'Alpine populism' includes not only the SVP but also the FPÖ, La Lega Ticinese and arguably the German Christian Social Union (CSU; Caramani and Meny 2005: 33–34).

The SVP evolved as a merger between the Farmers, Small Trade and Citizens' Party (*Bauern, Gewerbe- und Bürgerpartei*, BGB) and the Democratic parties of the cantons of Glarus and Graubünden in 1971. It has taken the organisation 20 years to achieve its current prominence. In the 1990s, the SVP leader Christoph Blocher was instrumental in improving the position of the party. The SVP is well entrenched in German-speaking Switzerland, but has also expanded to francophone Switzerland under the name of the Democratic Union of the Centre (*Union Democratique du Centre*, UDC). The party's main targets are the discontented middle classes and the small business community (the *Mittelstand*), but it is also making inroads into the traditional constituencies of the CVP and the SPS. The SVP has won support among blue-collar workers, traditional backers of the SPS, as their insecurity grows in the context of Europeanisation and globalisation (Ladner 2001: 138; Manatschal and Rapp 2015: 190). The preservation of Switzerland's independence and the defence of Swiss neutrality as part of the national identity, as well as the implementation of a restrictive immigration policy, are key issues for the SVP, accompanied by liberal economic policies such as lowering taxes, reducing state spending, limiting the size of the administration and ensuring good conditions for the economy. Naturally, the party is also against membership in the European Union (SVP 2007: 5). The fear of Islamisation is a major trait of the SVP (SVP 2007: 26–30, 42–46; 2015: 29–32, 47–51, 121–123); it also reflects a rural movement in opposition to the larger cities that are engines of change and transformation of the Swiss way of life (Hermann and Leuthold 2004, 2005; on the rural–urban cleavage see Kreis 2015).

The contextual variables of the party system

There are two main contextual variables that must be taken into account when analysing the party systems of the consensus democracies included in our study: the electoral system and the system of party funding.

120   *Americanisation of electoral politics*

The electoral system: the importance of proportional representation

All five countries have proportional representation (PR) systems. However, they are quite diverse and use different electoral methods.

The Netherlands is certainly the most accessible PR system in the European context. Party candidates formally compete in one large constituency, but in practice this constituency is divided into 19 districts. The electoral quota is calculated by dividing the number of voters by the seats. The Hare electoral system is used in all 19 districts; remainders are then allocated through the D'Hondt system also at the district level, except that national political parties tend to link the remainders from all 19 districts for the respective party to increase its changes of receiving extra seats (Andeweg 2008: 493–497). There is preferential voting, but it is strictly controlled by the political parties. Generally, the first places are reserved for the most important party politicians; other candidates are only found lower down on the list. In order to be directly elected, one must win 25 per cent of a party's vote. This requirement seems high, but prior to 1998 the threshold was 50 per cent. Political parties thus control the selection process, and preferential voting is still peripheral (Andeweg 2008: 506).

In Belgium, a D'Hondt electoral system was introduced as early as 1892; however, universal suffrage for men was enacted in 1919, and for women only in 1948. The regionalisation process that led to a new federal constitution in 1994 divided the national constituency into two regional groups, Flemish and Walloon, and two distinct party systems were de facto created. Until 2003, there was a similar two-tier system for the allocation of seats in the 11 constituencies (five provinces in each region and Brussels, the capital). A reform of the electoral system that same year led to the elimination of the second tier of allocation. Now, all MPs are elected at the provincial level through a D'Hondt electoral system, with a 5 per cent threshold at this level replacing the second tier. As a result, in 2003, many small parties (such as the Greens) lost much of their representation (De Winter 2008: 421). Constituency representation can range from four to 28 MPs, with the number regularly reviewed following a ten-year census. The allocation of seats to constituencies is based on the number of legal residents who live in the constituency – including foreigners. Of course, this leads disproportionately to an advantage in Wallonia (De Winter 2008: 420). Although political parties dominate the selectorate and the recruitment process, preferential voting has been increasing over recent past decades. In addition, more women have been recruited thanks to laws compelling party lists to be at least one-third women, with the first two names on the list of opposite genders. On 1 December 2015, according to the database of the Inter-parliamentary Union, women made up 39.2 per cent of the lower House of Parliament and 50 per cent of the upper House (IPU 2016; De Winter 2008: 428; on the evolution of preferential voting, see Dewaechter 1989: 307–310).

The Austrian electoral system based on proportional representation was established in 1920 following the proclamation of the First Republic. A first electoral law was valid from 1920 to 1971, when it was reformed. A second reform took

Americanisation of electoral politics 121

place in 1992. Since then, the electoral system has consisted of three tiers: the third tier is the national level and the last to be scrutinised, the second tier is the nine *Bundesländer* (*Landeswahlkreise*) and at the core is the first tier of 43 regional electoral districts (*Regionalwahlkreise*). Each *Bundesland* is allocated two to eight regional electoral districts. On average, each regional district consists of four or five seats. The electoral quota is calculated based on the size of the population in each *Bundesland*, including Austrians living abroad. The electoral process involves all three tiers. First, the seats at the first tier are allocated; to be eligible, a party has to win at least one seat (*Grundmandat*). The provincial second tier allocates seats to all parties that either won one seat in the first regional tier or 4 per cent of the vote nationwide. Finally, the rest of the seats are allocated in the national third tier for parties winning one seat in the regional tier or 4 per cent of the vote nationwide. In the first two tiers, the Hare electoral system is used, which is highly proportional, whereas the D'Hondt electoral system used in the national tier tends to be more disproportional and to favour the larger parties (Müller 2008: 401–402). According to calculations by Wolfgang C. Müller for the general elections of 2002, 54 per cent of seats were allocated at the first tier, 32.9 per cent at the second tier and 13.1 per cent at the third tier. The three larger parties, the ÖVP, the SPÖ and the FPÖ, won 65.7, 61.1 and 46.3 per cent of the seats allocated at the first tier, respectively; the Greens and the Liberal Forum won zero seats at the first tier and had to rely on overcoming the 4 per cent threshold to ensure representation (Müller 2008: 405). Interestingly, Müller finds that MPs elected at the first tier have stronger relations to their constituency than those elected at the second and third tiers (Müller 2001: 185).

Preferential voting has become quite important within political parties. There is a general trend to allow popular candidates to be higher on the party's list in order to avoid political upsets (Müller 2008: 409).

Luxembourg's electoral system, a proportional representation system based on the Hagenbach-Bischoff system, has been relatively stable since 1919, despite featuring a rather high level of built-in disproportionality. The novelty of the system relates to the level of choice in selecting candidates: each voter can either vote for one party list of all the potential candidates for the constituency or vote across different lists for individual candidates (but not more than the number allocated to the constituency). If a party list does not have enough candidates to fill the allocated seats, then the voter may still choose additional MPs. This is a panachage system, a method seldom used in Europe. There are four constituencies: the North with nine seats, the Centre with 21 seats, the East with seven seats and the South with 23 seats (Dumont *et al.* 2009: 158–162).

Switzerland operates under a similar system. The Swiss also use the Hagenbach-Bischoff system with the same disproportional effects favouring larger parties; however, as in Luxembourg, voters have considerable freedom to individualise the lists. Voters may select their preferred candidates, remove the name of one candidate in a list or even give two votes to one candidate. According to Georg Lutz and Peter Selb, these options are employed by half of Swiss

122 *Americanisation of electoral politics*

voters, while the other half simply votes for a list (Lutz and Selb 2014: 467–468). The 26 cantons are the constituencies in Switzerland. The number of MPs can vary, from one in the Alpine cantons with very small populations to 34 in Zurich. Thus, in reality, there is no national party system, but 26 different ones. The presence of the main national parties in all constituencies effectively makes them national (for an excellent study, see Bernauer and Mueller 2015). Moreover, the PR system is not applicable in all cantons, since some of them elect one or only a very few MPs. In some cases, such as Uri, Oberwalden, Niederwalden, Glarus and Appenzell Innerrhoden, a majoritarian plurality system is used instead (Wernli 2002: 514–515). The elections for the Council of the States are also based on a majoritarian system, with the exception of canton Jura (Lutz and Selb 2014: 468).

The party funding system in consensus democracies

The Council of Europe, through its Groups of States against Corruption (GRECO), has been instrumental in highlighting the problems of the private and public funding of political parties. In this regard, these five consensus democracies employ very different approaches; this has led to criticisms of GRECO.

Switzerland has the lowest level of party funding. Electoral campaigns are not funded by the public purse; as a result, the funding raised for elections is relatively opaque and not very transparent. There are no upper limits, although in some cantons such as Ticino and Geneva parties are obligated to declare any private donations over a certain amount.

The structures of Swiss parties also diverge significantly from those of countries in which the nationalisation of parties has been more successful. Switzerland's multi-level party system follows a similar pattern to that of the USA. The national parties are merely coordinating structures of essentially cantonal parties from the same party families. The primary funding is at the cantonal level. It is also the cantonal party that campaigns in national and cantonal elections. Consequently, proposals for national party funding have thus far encountered opposition. Moreover, the political system of Switzerland is based on a militia, or voluntary people working within the institutions. This also applies to the MPs in the National Council and the Council of States. In both cases, politicians only receive (rather generous) lump sums for per diem expenses and time spent in the four sessions of Parliament as well as annual committee meetings, in addition to a lump sum for an assistant; MPs with more responsibility, such as the president or vice-presidents, receive additional public funding support. However, thus far the Swiss political system has not been very charitable towards its organisational representatives. According to a GRECO report in 2011, the only funding that political parties receive is an annual lump sum of CHF94,500 (€85,185) for each parliamentary group and an additional CHF17,500 (€15,775) per MP of the respective party. This amounts to an average payment of CHF4.5 million (€4.1 million) per year. In 2015, this figure increased to CHF144,500 (€130,256) and CHF26,800 (€24,158) per MP. In total, CHF6.2 million (€5.6 million) was allocated

Americanisation of electoral politics 123

for this public party funding. The cantonal parliaments also allocate similar amounts to parliamentary groups (GRECO 2011: 9; Frey 2015).

In the 2015 national elections, the four main parliamentary parties spent CHF28.2 million (€25.5 million), but there was no transparency with regard to their fundraising. Interestingly, the SVP spent 37.5 per cent of this sum, followed by the FDP at 32.2 per cent and the CVP at 11.6 per cent; the second largest party, the SP, accounted for just 8.8 per cent (Statista 2015).

In GRECO's third evaluation round, the lack of transparency in party funding was highlighted as a major concern and a possible avenue for political corruption. The group expressed its disappointment that Switzerland had chosen not to adopt the legislation necessary to remedy the situation. Following the implementation of such legislation in Sweden, Switzerland remains the only European country that lacks transparency in party funding (GRECO 2015: 6).

Party funding is highly dependent on membership fees. In February 2015, the FDP had about 120,000 members, the CVP 100,000, the SVP 90,000, the SP 30,000, the Greens 7500, the EVP 4500, the GLP 3800, La Lega Ticinesi 1500 and the Geneva Movement of French-speaking Citizens (*Mouvement des Citoyens Romands*, MCR) 1500 (Statista 2016a; Federal Chancellery of Switzerland 2015). In total, there are 358,800 party members, although according to the studies conducted by Andreas Ladner, these figures may be inflated and inaccurate. There is no tradition of compiling and maintaining records of party members, particularly in the local party branches. The only major exception is the SP which reports a relatively small membership but imposes stricter requirements; the party also has a history of better record keeping than the other groups (Ladner 2014: 378–379). Overall, about 6.8 per cent of the population of voting age are party members, which is a fairly healthy membership figure in European terms.

The other four countries have moved to more transparent party funding systems. The Netherlands previously lacked public funding for political parties as well; however, this changed in 1998 when a law on modest public funding for political parties was adopted. Before this law, funding was only available to research institutes and youth organisations, but since its adoption the amount of funding for parliamentary parties has been steadily increasing over time (Daalder 1987: 239). The public funding is intended for the operation of the parliamentary groups, but not for electoral campaigns, such that a grey area similar to that in Switzerland persists. In 2013, new legislation was put in place to reduce the loopholes in private funding; specifically, any donations above €4500 must be declared in the party's financial report. Although membership has declined considerably since the days of pillarisation, membership fees still represent 50 per cent of all party funding. Moreover, fundraising activities are regularly undertaken, and some parties collect a tax on the salaries of representatives (the exceptions being the VVD and the CDA). SP MPs give their pay cheques directly to the party, which then provides all representatives with a basic income; the remainder is used to finance party functionaries (Interview NL). One very positive aspect of the public funding of parties is that the basis for allocation of

124   *Americanisation of electoral politics*

the funds is not the number of voters in the previous election, but the number of party members. This sends a clear message to political parties that they must support their constituents and to be active also between elections. Overall, Dutch political parties receive four kinds of subsidies: the party subsidy and funds for the party's youth organisation, the party research organisation and international work (Ministry of the Interior Netherlands 2016; Algemen Rekenkamer 2011: 5).

In 2014, a total of €15.5 million in subsidies were allocated to political parties by the state (Minister of the Interior Netherlands 2016). Table 5.2 summarises the distribution between the various political parties.

Although the Dutch public funding model seems to be quite generous, in reality the other three consensus democracies have devised even more generous systems.

In Belgium, state funding was allocated for the first time in 1974, and the amount provided has been increasing considerably ever since. Electoral processes are quite expensive in Belgium (Dewaechter 1987: 328). According to a study by Jef Smulders and Bart Maddens, political parties have approved a reform of the public funding system for political parties as part of the package of the sixth state reform (Smulders and Madden 2014a: 1). This reform will apparently lead to an increase in the total funding for political parties from €33 million to €38 million (Smulders and Madden 2014a: 5; see also Table 5.3). At the national level, political parties receive two kinds of public grants: a general grant for parliamentary parties and a grant for the parliamentary group.

Public funding also applies at the regional level. In the legislative elections in 2014, the N-VA, which won the greatest support, was granted €8.1 million at the federal level and an additional €4.1 million at the regional level through the Flemish Parliament and the Brussels Parliament for a total of over €12.2 million (Smulders and Maddens 2014b: 1). This allowed the party to employ about 160 people supporting the parliamentary groups at the federal and regional levels (Smulders and Maddens 2014b: 9). Similarly, the PS received €12.11 million in 2014 (*Le Vif*, 17 February 2015: Smulders 2014a). Some parties are heavily dependent on this public funding, which accounts for 94.6 per cent of the budget of the CDH, 90.5 per cent for Ecolo, 87.9 per cent for the PS and 81.5 per cent for the MR (*Le Vif*, 17 February 2015; *Le Soir*, 17 February 2015; reports based on Smulders 2014a, 2014b). Smulders calculated that in total political parties received €73 million in 2013, of which €32.2 million went to the francophone parties and €40.8 million to the Flemish parties (*Le Vif*, 17 February 2015; *Le Soir*, 17 February 2013; reports based on Smulders 2014a, 2014b). It should also be noted that political parties can advertise for free on public television during electoral campaigns.

In Austria, public subsidies for political parties were introduced in 1972, and the amount allocated to parties has been growing ever since (Gerlich 1987: 84–85). Criticism by GRECO led to the adoption of new legislation in 2012 intended to overcome the deficits highlighted by the Council of Europe (Federal Law on Financing of Political Parties, BGBL I 56/2012-RIS; see Bundeskanzleramt 2016a);

Table 5.2 Public funding to political parties in the Netherlands, 2014 (without donations and public subsidies to research institutes and youth organisations)

	Election results 2012 in %	Membership 2009	Percentage	Membership fees 2014	Direct party subsidy 2014
VVD	26.5	36,678		2,002,000	2,086,044
PvdA	24.7	55,471		5,051,430	3,592,977
PVV	10.1			150	0
SP	9.6	43,856		1,007,722	1,239,833
CDA	8.5	54,548		3,378,350	1,138,079
D66	8	11,604		2,515,000	920,000
CU	3.1	25,378		1,105,754	560,383
Groenlinks	2.3	16,847		1,699,000	698,000
SGP	2.1	28,874		507,383	517,693
50+	1.9			120,000	345,590
PvdD	1.9	7649		210,000	360,000
Total		**280,905**	**2.2**	**17,596,789**	**11,458,599**

Sources: author's compilation based on annual reports of parliamentary political parties and available on website of the Ministry of the Interior of the Netherlands (2016). Membership taken from Algemen Rekenkamer (2011: 6).

Table 5.3 Party public funding and membership in Belgium

Political parties	2010 elections (%)	Membership 2010	Percentage of voters	Funding 2014	Funding after elections of 2014 under new system***
N-VA	20.3	15,799		6,422,259	6,893,045
PS	11.7	81,491		5,341,750	5,802,122
CD&V	11.6	71,287		3,710,052	4,367,096
MR	9.6	33,056		3,522,907	3,900,472
SP.A	8.8	49,345		3,292,882	3,685,442
Open VLD	9.8	66,662		3,026,959	3,500,280
VB	3.7	22,500		2,597,779	3,118,085
CdH	5.0	26,069		2,035,558	2,363,285
Ecolo	3.3	6029		2,032,119	2,126,612
Groen	5.3	4997		1,397,677	1,782,895
LDD	0.4	6248*		595,338	624,914
Total		**377,235****	**4.85**	**33,975,280**	**38,164,248**

Sources: Smulder and Maddens (2014b: 5); Van Haute *et al.* (2013: 75).

Notes
* Figure for 2007.
** Without LDD.
*** Extrapolated calculations by authors.

Federal Law on Federal Subsidies for Political Parties, BGBL I 57/2012-RIS; see Bundeskanzleramt 2016b). The revised legislation on party financing resulted in a significant increase in funding for political parties after 2012. A great deal of relevant information is posted on the website of the Chancellor's Office, allowing us to assess the amount of money political parties receive from the state at the federal level. Similar to Belgium, the federalised districts (the nine *Bundesländer*) also offer substantial public funding for the regional branches of political parties. Apart from this parliamentary public funding for parties and parliamentary groups, Austrian political parties represented in Parliament are also entitled to reimbursement for their electoral campaigns in accordance with the results obtained in legislative and European Parliament elections. In addition, there is also considerable funding for research, training and political education academies (Federal Law on federal subsidies of political education and journalism, BGBL I 369/1984-RIS; see Bundeskanzleramt 2016c; for details see Sickinger 2009: 252–253). Each political party has established such an academy (see Table 5.4).

According to an excellent study by Hubert Sickinger, the bulk of funding comes from the regional budgets of the *Bundesländer*, as in Belgium. For a long time this fact was not well known. Much of the party financing came directly from the regional budget, but in ways that were not clearly regulated through law. According to the figures provided by Sickinger for 2009, political parties received a total of €119 million from the nine provinces (calculated from data provided by Sickinger 2009: 288–238). Moreover, public party funding is also common at the local level, particularly in the larger regional capitals, but also in smaller communities (Sickinger 2009: 339–341). *Proporzdemokratie* is still evident in how interest groups finance political parties. Just before the legislative elections of 2008, the interest groups in the Economy chamber spent €15.7 million on donations to political parties (mainly to the ÖVP, but also to the SPÖ); the Labour chamber also contributed to electoral campaigns to the tune of €6.5 million (mainly to the SPÖ). These donations do not come directly from the chambers, but rather from the main political groups within them, which are basically offshoots of the political parties (Sickinger 2009: 180).

Despite the de-pillarisation process in Austria, political parties can still rely on large memberships. In comparison to other consensus democracies, the ratio of party members to voters is quite high, at 15.8 per cent (2013); Luxembourg is slightly lower, at 11 per cent, followed by Switzerland at 6.8 per cent, the Netherlands at 2.2 per cent and Belgium at 4.8 per cent (Table 5.5).

The extremely generous Belgian public funding system for political parties is topped only by Luxembourg, if calculated in terms of public money spent per capita. In 2012, the parliamentary parties in Luxembourg received about €2.5 million from the public purse. Political parties are also reimbursed for electoral campaigns in accordance with the electoral results. In the legislative elections in 2013, annual payments rose to €3.9 million. Political parties are allowed to receive public funding amounting to up to 75 per cent of their total budget. In 2012, the CSV's budget was 66 per cent public funding, whereas the LSAP and the DP had 56 per cent and 74.7 per cent public support, respectively. The

Table 5.4 Membership and public funding of political parties in Austria, 2012 to 2015

Parties	Elections		Membership		Party funding			
	2008	2013	2014	% voters	2012	2013 election year	2014 EP election year	2015
SPÖ	29.3	26.8	205,224		4,633,388	11,117,609	11,493,926	8,188,124
ÖVP	26	24	700,000		4,137,734	9,894,056	11,049,443	7,347,617
FPÖ	17.5	20.5	50,000		2,863,861	6,749,424	9,017,349	6,311,853
BZÖ	10.7				1,832,431	4,203,276	414,365	
Greens	10.4	12.4	6500		1,792,306	4,104,226	5,900,179	3,907,679
Team Stronach		5.7					1,919,411	1,919,411
LIF/NEOS	2.1	5.0	2200				2,809,570	1,693,132
KPÖ			350				102,438	
Other			12,042					
Total			**976,316**	**15.3**	**15,259,720**	**36,068,591**	**42,706,681**	**29,367,816**

Sources: Bundeskanzleramt (2016d); Statista (2016b); Zirnig (2014).

Table 5.5 Membership and public funding of parliamentary parties in Luxembourg, 2012 to 2013

Parties	Legislative elections		Membership	Public funding	
	2009	2013	2013	2012	2013
CSV	38	33.7	10,363	851,985	1,323,554
LSAP	21.6	20.3	6000	525,845	777,653
DP	15	18.3	6000	440,860	778,696
Dei Greing	11.7	10.1	1500 (est.)	363,695	570,595
ADR	8.1	6.6	270 (est.)	232,626	340,638
Dei Lenk	3.3	4.9	1000 (est.)	214,626	130,472
			25,133	11% **2,629,637**	**3,921,608**

Sources: membership taken from CSV (2014: 16); LSAP (2015); DP (2014). Estimate based on members' contribution figures in party accounts for the year 2013 posted at Chambre des Deputés (2015b). Public funding compiled from party accounts for the year 2013 posted at Chambre des Deputés (2015).

smaller parties – the Greens, the ADR and the Left – are funded publicly at rates of 64 per cent, 70 per cent and 60 per cent, respectively. The DP thus seems to be the party that is most dependent on public funding. Membership fees represent a small part of the party's budget; the second most important item after public funding appears to be the contributions (party tax) that Members of Parliament make from their wages (calculations based on *L'Essentiel*, 30 July 2014). If we consider such donations as part of the public purse, then public funding increases to 88 per cent for the CSV, 82 per cent for the LSAP, 92 per cent for the DP, 89 per cent for the Greens, 90.4 per cent for the ADR and 85 per cent for the Left Party (author's calculations based on *L'Essentiel*, 30 July 2014, as well as party accounts from 2012 posted in Chambre des Deputés 2015b). This illustrates that, as in Belgium and Austria, the parties in Luxemburg would not survive without state funding. It also seems that the allocation of public funding for electoral campaign expenses is based on something of a gentleman's agreement signed by the parties six months before elections. In this sense, there is still a grey area in public party funding in Luxembourg (Dumont *et al.* 2009: 165–166). These parties are the best examples of cartel parties, in particular the CSV, the LSAP and the DP, and more recently the Greens, all of which have participated or are participating in coalition governments.

Party system change in consensus democracies

Following this discussion of the main actors and the contextual aspects of electoral politics in the five consensus democracies of West Central Europe, it is important to provide a brief analysis of how party systems have changed over the past four decades in order to develop an understanding of political change in these countries. We concentrate on three main aspects:

130 *Americanisation of electoral politics*

1 The decline of traditional parties and vote concentration.
2 The increase in total volatility over the past 40 years.
3 The increase in the fragmentation of the party system over the past 40 years.

Party system change and the decline of established parties

One clear feature in all five countries is the erosion of the dominance of the traditional parties (Christian Democrats, Socialists and Liberals). Figures 5.1 to 5.5 depict the losses of these three party families in terms of their share of the vote over the past 40 years.

Changes in the party system in the Netherlands since the 1970s have been quite drastic. One of the major aspects in this regard is the rapid decline of the traditional socio-economic cleavages based on religion and class. Both the Christian Democrats as well as the Labour party have seen their shares of the vote decline substantially. In 1980, due to widespread secularisation and declines in membership, the various Christian parties (KVP, ARP, CHU) had to merge into a single unit in order to maintain their leading role in the political system. Nonetheless, in the 1990s, the electoral results of the three traditional parties (Christian Democrats, Social Democrats and Liberals) began to balance out. The high level of volatility also led to the first coalition government between the Social Democrats and the Liberals – without the Christian Democrats – between 1994 and 2002. The victories of Jan Peter Balkenende in the 2002, 2003 and 2007 elections brought the Christian Democrats back to power, allowing the party to build governments with the Liberals and later with Labour, but afterwards there was a substantial decline in the Christian Democratic vote. In parallel with these dynamics among the three main parties, new parties are beginning to emerge to challenge their dominance. The rise of the SP since the 1990s and the right-wing populist PVV since 2006 has further fragmented the vote; as a result, the two main parties are no longer able to win an absolute majority to build a government. The two Mark Rutte administrations have been minority governments, lacking majorities in one or (as in 2010) both of the two houses (Daalder 1987; Ten Napel 1999; Lucardie 2006; Wilp 2012).

In the Netherlands, support for the traditional parties declined, from over 82.8 per cent in 1982 to 59.7 per cent in 2013. As a result, the two main parties can no longer form governments by themselves, as they do not have the absolute majority necessary. Martien Ten Napel regards this as a transition from a de-pillarised society towards a society of individuals (Ten Napel 1999: 179). Paul Lucardie highlights the declining ability of political parties to mobilise the traditional electorate, in part because of generational change, but also due to the declining numbers of people joining political parties (Lucardie 2006: 345–346).

Changes in the Belgian party system have been taking place since the 1970s. The ethnolinguistic cleavage between French-speaking and Dutch-speaking populations led at first to the informal division of the party system into two distinctive electoral spaces based on the respective languages. This was due to the splitting of political parties into two different linguistic groups that competed

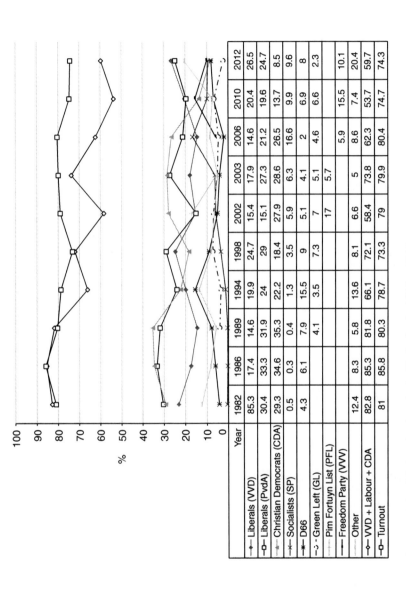

Figure 5.1 Legislative elections in the Netherlands, 1982 to 2012.
Source: author's graph based on Parties and Elections in Europe (2016).

132   *Americanisation of electoral politics*

only in French-speaking or Dutch-speaking constituencies. The dual-party system that led to the duplication of party families along territorial-linguistic lines began to emerge in the 1980s. The first time that parties began to compete along these lines was in the European Parliament elections of 1979; however, at that time there were three constituencies: Brussels as well as Wallonia and Flanders. The dual national electoral markets were gradually established in the 1980s. Amendments to the federal constitution in 1995 introduced three electoral spaces for the Senate and regional elections. Formally, parties were still competing in one electoral market, but the split of the party families into Wallonian and Flemish parties competing only in Wallonian or Flemish constituencies created a de facto division. Only the Communist Party maintained a united party faction in this dual electoral market (information provided by Patrick Dumont via email on 4 January 2016). Nonetheless, the Christian Democrats still dominated the party system until 1999, when a government was formed without them for the first time. In 2008, the Christian Democrats returned to power, but in the new reality they must compete with other parties in a field of small parties. In particular, the moderate Flemish separatist N-VA has been the largest party in Flanders since 2010. Before that point, they had participated in an electoral coalition with the CD&V that damaged their electoral chances. The N-VA became part of the national government following the 2014 elections (see Dewaechter 1987; Delwit 2006a, 2011a).

Ignoring the divisions in parties along linguistic-territorial lines, the three main party families in Belgium (Christian Democrats, Socialists and Liberals) together have declined in terms of electoral share, from 73.1 per cent to 56.5 per cent between 1981 and 2014. The fragmentation of the party system now requires coalitions of five or more parties in order to achieve an absolute majority.

The Austrian party system was characterised by a two-and-a-half party system until the 1980s. The elections in 1986 created a two-and-two-halves system, with the Greens becoming a force in Parliament. During the 1990s, the high level of volatility impacted upon the party system, facilitating the rise of the populist FPÖ, whose support soon equalled that of the SPÖ and the ÖVP. However, the FPÖ's vote collapsed to about 10 per cent after its coalition government with the ÖVP, and the splinter party BZÖ managed to do well in the 2006 elections, and thus a two-and-three-halves party system emerged. Over the past decade, the FPÖ has been able to regain its electoral strength, and now the party might surpass the traditional parties in terms of its share of the vote (30 per cent or more). Other parties have also emerged, such as the NEOS and Team Stronach in 2013, indicating an increase in volatility and fragmentation (Gerlich 1987; Luther 1992, 1999; Plasser and Ulram 2006). Overall, between 1986 and 2013, the vote concentration of the two main parties (SPÖ and ÖVP) declined, from 84.4 per cent to 50.8 per cent.

According to Kurt Richard Luther, during election campaigns the two main parties wage a fierce battle leading to a polarised pluralism in the party system. The roles of political marketing and spin doctors have become increasingly

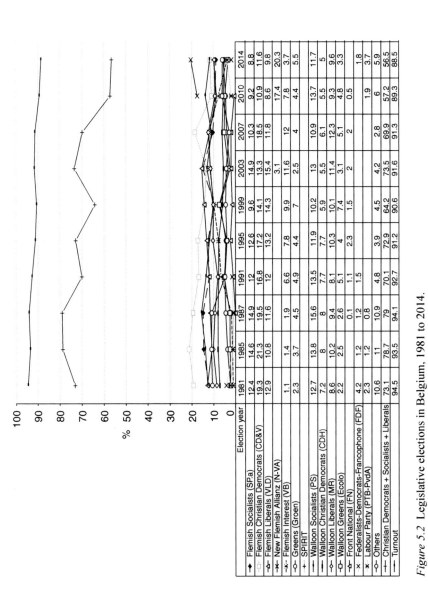

Figure 5.2 Legislative elections in Belgium, 1981 to 2014.

Source: author's graph based on Parties and Elections in Europe (2016).

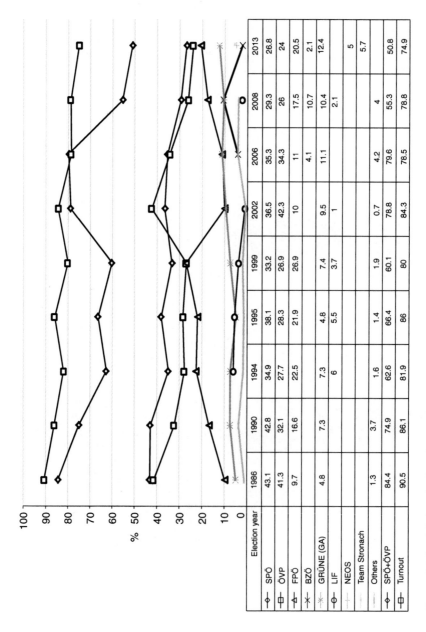

Figure 5.3 Legislative elections in Austria, 1983 to 2013.
Source: author's graph based on Parties and Elections in Europe (2016).

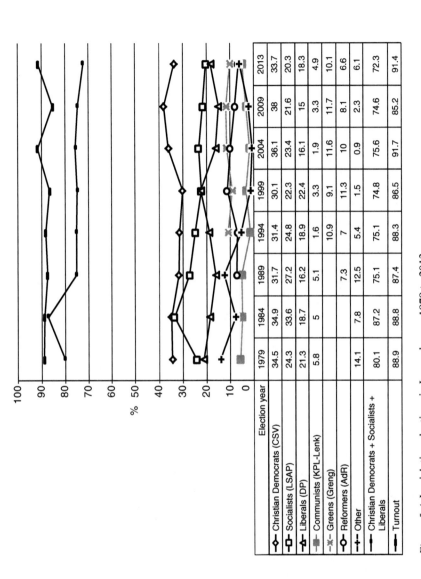

Figure 5.4 Legislative elections in Luxembourg, 1979 to 2013.
Source: author's graph based on Parties and Elections in Europe (2016).

136   *Americanisation of electoral politics*

important. Changes in political communication have compensated for the loss of encapsulated subcultures, including a substantial decline in party identification. In 1954, 73 per cent of voters identified with a political party, but in 1994 this figure was just 44 per cent (Luther 1999: 131–133; see also Gerlich 1987: 80; Hofer 2005). In 1987 to 1990, opposition parties won 14.7 per cent of the vote; this rose to 32.2 per cent in 1999 and even 35.8 per cent in 1994 (Plasser and Ulram 2006a: 361). In the elections of 2013, opposition support was as high as 43.6 per cent.

The established parties are more resilient in Switzerland and Luxembourg. In Luxembourg, the decline of the traditional parties has been less dramatic. In 1979, they won an electoral share of 81.4 per cent, a figure that declined in 2013 to 72.1 per cent. The main party, the CSV, managed to win all of the elections during this period with over 30 per cent of the vote; in 2009, its support peaked at 38 per cent. This gives the CSV a comfortable lead with regard to the two other main parties. Support for the LSAP has been fluctuating between 20 and 30 per cent, reaching a high of 33 per cent in 1984. The Liberals have found it difficult to overcome their electoral ceiling of 20 per cent (Janssen 2006; Dumont *et al.* 2009).

Switzerland's traditional parties have also been resilient on the whole, resisting losses in electoral shares. Over the past 30 to 40 years, the magical formula parties (SVP, CVP, SPS and FDP) have successfully maintained an electoral share of around 72 per cent. However, changes in the party system took place in terms of the electoral share of each party within the group. The major winner has been the populist SVP, which is now the largest party in Switzerland; the major loser within the group is the CVP, once the most important party. The FDP has also been steadily declining in terms of its share of the vote. Only the SP seems to be able to maintain a stable electorate. According to Andreas Ladner, after the 1995 elections the Swiss party spectrum may be described as ranging from a right-wing pole with the SVP and the FDP to the CVP at the centre and then the SP at the left-wing pole (Ladner 2006: 408–409; see also Kerr 1987; Armingeon and Engler 2015).

Turnout at general elections has been quite high in four of the five consensus democracies, with Austria and the Netherlands around 70 per cent and Luxembourg and Belgium (two countries with compulsory voting) around 80 per cent. Switzerland is an exception in this regard, with turnout of about 50 per cent.

The rise of total volatility in consensus democracies

The social basis of these pillarised societies has eroded during the period from the late 1960s up until the present day. Mogens Pedersen sought to demonstrate how volatility has increased over time, defining total volatility as 'the net change within the electoral party system resulting from individual vote transfers' (Pedersen 1979). The Pedersen index measures the level of party system change in a long-term perspective.

Our intention is to describe the overall trends in the five party systems. In general, an increase in total volatility may be identified, particularly in the

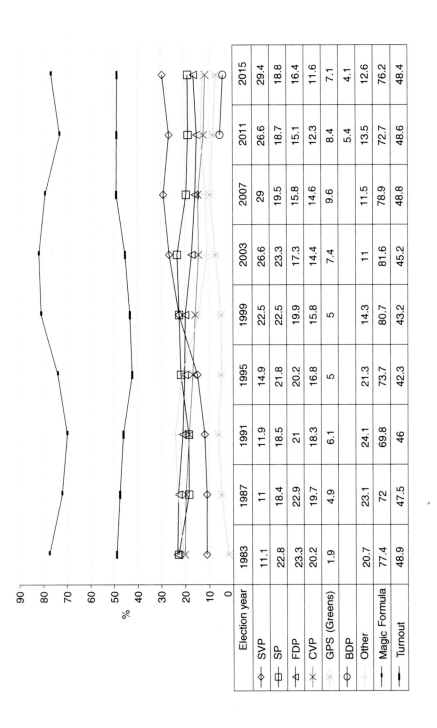

Election year	1983	1987	1991	1995	1999	2003	2007	2011	2015
SVP	11.1	11	11.9	14.9	22.5	26.6	29	26.6	29.4
SP	22.8	18.4	18.5	21.8	22.5	23.3	19.5	18.7	18.8
FDP	23.3	22.9	21	20.2	19.9	17.3	15.8	15.1	16.4
CVP	20.2	19.7	18.3	16.8	15.8	14.4	14.6	12.3	11.6
GPS (Greens)	1.9	4.9	6.1	5	5	7.4	9.6	8.4	7.1
BDP								5.4	4.1
Other	20.7	23.1	24.1	21.3	14.3	11	11.5	13.5	12.6
Magic Formula	77.4	72	69.8	73.7	80.7	81.6	78.9	72.7	76.2
Turnout	48.9	47.5	46	42.3	43.2	45.2	48.8	48.6	48.4

Figure 5.5 Legislative elections in Switzerland, 1983 to 2015.
Source: author's graph based on Parties and Elections in Europe (2016).

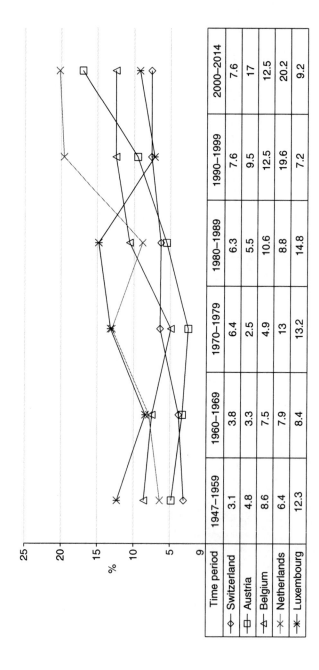

Figure 5.6 Total volatility in consensus democracies of West Central Europe, 1947 to 2014.

Source: author's calculations based on Emanuele (2015).

Note
The median of total volatility was calculated for each decade.

Americanisation of electoral politics 139

Netherlands, Austria and Belgium. Volatility in Switzerland has also increased, but more moderately than in the other countries. Andreas Ladner argues that the Pedersen index is not appropriate to measure party system change in Switzerland, as the rise of the SVP has been very gradual, taking place over the course of two decades; the Pedersen index is more suited to measuring sudden changes from one election to the next (Ladner 2014: 370–372) (see Figure 5.6).

In the 1980s, the Austrian party system was still characterised by a relatively low volatility, but this figure has risen considerably in the 1990s and in the new millennium. The introduction of the Green Party has moderately affected the party system; however, it was the rise of the FPÖ that brought significant changes. As the FPÖ grew in influence in the 1990s, the two main parties (the SPÖ and ÖVP) lost a large share of the vote, dropping from their traditionally 40 per cent shares to slightly above 30 per cent. Much of this share was picked up by the FPÖ, which now attracts the traditional electorate of both the SPÖ (unskilled workers) and the ÖVP (employees, independents; Plasser and Ulram 1995: 377–378). In the 1999 elections, the FPÖ managed to surpass the ÖVP in votes and won an identical number of seats. In addition, the Liberal Forum, a splinter party from the FPÖ, emerged in the late 1990s. As a result, volatility rose to 15.95 per cent in the 1994 elections. An excellent study by Fritz Plasser and Peter Ulram determined that between 1979 and 1994 the percentage of independent voters increased from 27 per cent to 62 per cent. It also seems that disappointment with the major parties is a major factor encouraging defection to the smaller parties (Plasser and Ulram 1995: 351–352). The next peak in volatility came with the elections of 2002 and 2006, when the FPÖ's support collapsed due to the party's weak performance in the coalition government with the ÖVP and internal divisions within the party. The FPÖ's vote declined from 26.9 per cent to 10 per cent in 2002, and, with the emergence of the BZÖ in 2005, it was split between two parties in the 2006 general elections. This indicates a clear tendency towards electoral markets, primarily induced by the FPÖ as a major actor in the process of party system realignment. It would seem that the presidential elections in 2016 reflect a further increase in volatility.

In Belgium, the dual party system has created a highly fragmented Parliament, with considerable implications for overall volatility. The doubling of political parties aside, the VB and the N-VA have played the most important roles in shaping this volatility. The volatility from election to election has been quite high since the early 1990s. After 2010, the N-VA became a major rival of the C&DV. The emergence of the N-VA had radical effects on the more xenophobic and Flemish nationalist VB; after a soaring rise until 2010, the party's support declined considerably in 2014. Generally speaking, there has been an increase in volatility, from 7 per cent to 11.8 per cent from the period between 1948 and 1979 to the period between 1980 and 2014.

This presents a stark contrast with the situation in Luxembourg, where there was a decline in total volatility in the latter period, from 11.3 per cent to 10.8 per cent. In the 1980s and 1990s, new parties were able to enter Parliament: the Pensioners' party (ADR) and the Greens in 1989, and the Left party in 1994. The year 1989 thus represents a peak in the volatility of the party system, at 15.45 per cent. Since that

140 *Americanisation of electoral politics*

time, volatility has been below the 10 per cent mark; in 2009, the figure was only 4.5 per cent. However, in recent elections, volatility has risen to 9.5 per cent due to the decline in support for the CSV and the increase in the share won by the DP.

Currently, the most volatile of the party systems is found in the Netherlands. Dutch voters make more individualised choices, and ideology has become increasingly irrelevant. Parties in power may suffer considerably as their tenure drags on. Since 1994, total volatility has been above 15 per cent, with a peak of 31.3 per cent in 2002, when the Pim Fortuyn list won 17 per cent of the vote. The 2010 elections, marking the end of the Balkenende era, led to the second highest peak in terms of volatility, at 23.6 per cent, primarily due to the collapse of the CDA's vote. Other contributing factors include the significantly increased support for the SP in 2006, as well as support for the right-wing, populist Party of Freedom, which managed to increase its vote share and enter Parliament in 2010. The main institutional factor leading to this high volatility is the structure of opportunities for political parties provided by a low threshold in the electoral system. For Peter Mair, in a comparative European perspective, the Netherlands is a case of exceptionalism. De-pillarisation has allowed for the emergence of an unstructured, open space in which new parties can easily rise. This is confirmed by Mair's ranking of the most volatile elections in Western Europe since 1945. Of the 11 most volatile elections, three were in the Netherlands, namely the elections of 2002 (Fortuyn revolution), 1994 (new Social Democratic-Liberal 'Paars' coalition) and 2006 (the rise of the SP and the Freedom Party; Mair 2008b: 239). According to Mair, this easy access to electoral markets is reflected in easy access to government. The Dutch aversion to minority governments results in a merry-go-round of innovative coalition governments in which a variety of parties are included. The Dutch do not elect government alternatives, but rather different party compositions within the coalition government. The nation therefore appears to be the champion of innovative government composition (Mair 2008b: 243–248). Relatively new parties such as the SP, Groenlinks and, more recently, the PVV that have built an electorate over a fairly lengthy period of time can reasonably hope to be co-opted into the coalition government. In this context there are no losers, only winners.

The fragmentation of the party system

All of the consensus democracies in West Central Europe have shown signs of party system fragmentation. The traditional parties are being challenged by new political parties. Some of these parties have already established themselves, such as the Greens and new left-wing groups.

This fragmentation of the party system will force political parties to be more pragmatic and to seek coalition partners in an unbiased fashion. In this regard, if we exclude the case of Switzerland, two main patterns may be identified. On the one hand, there is Belgium and the Netherlands, where it has become more difficult to form small coalitions that surpass the absolute majority threshold; on the other hand, in Austria and Luxembourg, fragmentation has been more moderate (see Figure 5.7).

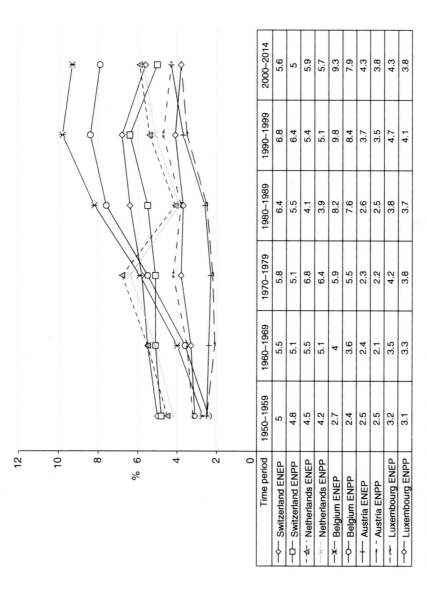

Figure 5.7 Fragmentation of parties according to Effective Number of Electoral Parties (ENEP) and Effective Number of Parliamentary Parties (ENPP), 1950 to 2014.

Source: author's calculations based on Dassoneville (2015).

142 *Americanisation of electoral politics*

The Netherlands must form governments of two parties or even three; otherwise it has no majority. Belgium in particular must now form coalitions of more than five parties in order to achieve absolute majorities in Parliament. According to the fragmentation index developed by Laakso and Taagepera (1979), which measures the effective number of electoral parties (ENEP) and also the effective number of parliamentary parties (ENPP), Belgium had 9.62 effective electoral parties and 7.48 effective parliamentary parties following the 2014 elections. Originally, the Belgian party system had about 2.7 effective electoral parties and 2.1 effective parliamentary parties; however, the reforms of the 1960s and 1970s led to an increase in the respective values to 6.4 and 5.9, and between 1980 and 2014 the values rose to 9.1 and 8, respectively (see Delwit 2003, 2011a).

Overall, the Netherlands had 4.5 effective electoral parties and 4.2 effective parliamentary parties in 1950, but fragmentation in the 1970s increased these figures to 6.8 effective electoral parties and 6.4 in Parliament. The period between 1951 and 1979 had an average ENEP of 5.6 and an ENPP of 5.2; however, between 1980 and 2012 there was a slight decrease in the respective values to 5.4 and 5.1. Therefore, superficially, one could say that there has been no significant change in the national party system. However, when volatility figures are taken into account, we can identify structural party changes stemming from the rise of new parties with parliamentary representation such as the SP, Groenlinks and the PVV.

The multi-level nature of the Swiss party system shows high levels of fragmentation both before and after 1980 (Kerr 1987: 116). There was a slight increase in ENEP and ENPP, from 5.4 and 5.0 to 6.3 and 5.6 per cent; however, this does not seem to indicate any major changes. As in the other countries, apart from the traditional magic formula parties, the newcomers are the two Green parties, the GPS (which achieved representation in 1979 and increased its vote share to between 7 and 9 per cent) and the Green Liberals (GLP) that emerged only in 2004 as a splinter of the Green Party.

The second pattern is illustrated by the case of Austria, which now features three major parties (the SPÖ, ÖVP and FPÖ), all with a potential share of 30 per cent, but also two smaller parties, the Greens and the Liberals (LIF/NEOS). In comparison to Belgium, the Netherlands and Switzerland, the fragmentation of the Austrian party system has been moderate, although it has definitely increased over the past 20 years. During the period from 1950 to 1979, the two-and-a-half model was the main configuration of the party system; however, between 1979 and 2013, ENEP and ENPP values increased from 2.2 and 2.3 to 3.5 and 3.3 per cent, respectively. Notable changes are due in part to the rise of the FPÖ, which has become a serious challenger to the traditional parties with a potential share of up to 30 per cent; the Greens have also become an important established party (on the Green Party see Dachs 2006b; Luther 1999).

Similar conclusions regarding the fragmentation of the party system may be drawn for the party system in Luxembourg. During the period from 1950 to 1979, ENEP and ENPP values for the country were about 3.6 and 3.4 per cent, respectively; there was a slight increase in the period from 1980 to 2013, to 4.3

and 3.9 per cent, respectively. The CSV continues to be the dominant party, although it needs either the cooperation of the LSAP or the DP to form a government. The Greens became an alternative coalition partner (together with the LSAP and the DP) in the Xavier Bettel government formed in 2013. This confirms the development towards four effective parliamentary parties, due to the fact that the ADR and Dei Lenk tend to adhere to anti-establishment positions.

Conclusions: the Americanisation of party systems in consensus democracies

The encapsulation of the electorate by traditional political parties such as the Christian Democrats, Social Democrats and Liberals was the precondition for the establishment of consensus democracies by their respective political elites. Secularisation, modernisation, de-industrialisation, the policies of the welfare state and eventually shifts in values from materialism (survival values) to post-materialism (self-expressive values) have eroded these subcultural and segmented encapsulated electorates, thereby facilitating the rise of volatility in the party system. In recent years, electoral markets have become Americanised, leading to cartel parties that require considerable funding to survive in the volatile electoral markets.

6 Patterns of government in consensus democracies

Introduction

Arend Lijphart's simple differentiation between majoritarian and consensus democracies remains a valid method of creating a typology of governments. On the one hand, there is the Westminster majoritarian winner-takes-all principle of electoral competition, and, on the other, minority or coalition governments based on compromise and consensus.

In this chapter, we examine government in the strictest sense of the word, looking for variations among our five consensus democracies. Wolfgang C. Müller and Kaare Strøm's pioneering study on coalition government in Western Europe will be an important basis for this analysis, due to its scholarly quality and encyclopaedic collection of data through the year 2000 (Müller and Strøm 2000; I had the great privilege to be part of their research group). Switzerland also has coalition governments of the four parties in the 'magic formula' (*Zauberformel*); however, as this chapter will describe, it diverges considerably from the other countries in several ways.

The chapter starts with a comparison of government structures (i.e. prime minister and Cabinet). The second section deals with patterns of government formation in the five countries. The third section discusses the rules of the game within coalition governments and how party discipline is enforced inside and outside the Cabinet. Finally, some information is provided on how governments are terminated.

Comparing government structure

In terms of government structures, there are no major differences in our consensus democracies. This has a great deal to do with European patterns of convergence that have allowed for institutional transfer over the past two centuries. However, the inner lives of the five governments reveal different political cultures, although all are based on a technology of consensual politics acquired over a long period of time. Here, we may refer to a sociology of knowledge with regard to institution building in the sense of historical institutionalism (Thelen and Steinmo 1992). The council of ministers, chaired by the prime minister and consisting of senior ministers, is the highest-ranking decision-making body in four of our consensus governments. The exception is Switzerland, which has a rotating president.

The Cabinet: collegiality and ministerial autonomy

Each of the consensus democracies has a Cabinet of a different size. In 2013, Luxembourg, the smallest of our consensus democracies, had 15 ministers in its Cabinet, whereas Austria had 14 senior ministers, Belgium had a total of 19 (12 senior and six junior ministers), the Netherlands had 12 senior ministers and Switzerland had seven federal councillors. In comparison, majoritarian democracies such as the UK had 23 ministers, and the USA had 22 secretaries (ministers). The case of Luxembourg shows that policy-making in the country has become so complex that the number of ministers had to increase over time (see below). Switzerland, with just seven federal councillors, is struggling to cope with the ever-growing complexity. However, reform attempts focused on the Cabinet have thus far failed (Klötli *et al.* 2014: 210–214). In 2013, the average for the 21 countries of Western Europe was about 17 members, ranging from nine and seven in Iceland and Switzerland to 23 and 38 in the UK and France. In 11 Central and Eastern European countries, the average figure is slightly lower, at 16. Here, the number ranges from ten in Hungary to 25 in Romania. For the 32 countries of Europe, the average number of Cabinet members is 16.7 (Bågenholm *et al.* 2014: 8–9). In this sense, the consensus democracies on West Central Europe, perhaps with the exception of Belgium, have Cabinets of a moderate size, below any European average.

All Cabinets in consensus democracies follow the same principles as other core executives in Europe, specifically collegiality, departmental autonomy and collective responsibility. This final principle does not apply to Switzerland (see below).

The principle of collegiality implies that members of the Cabinet should not express dissenting views against a fellow colleague in the public sphere once a decision has been taken. This ensures that the government can speak with one voice and maintain an image of cohesion to the outside world. This is particularly important in coalition governments, which consist of different parties with varying points of view that are bound by the coalition agreement. As discussed below, many informal devices within and outside the government are used to ensure that everybody presents a cohesive image of the Cabinet.

This collegiality notwithstanding, ministers traditionally have autonomy over the management of their particular department. Autonomy does not mean complete sovereignty over the policy area; rather, there is some leeway with regard to how agreed-upon policies should be implemented. In the case of coalition governments, the coalition agreement sets out the policy programme and the mechanisms to avoid or resolve conflicts, and to prevent ministers from having initiatives of their own that were not set out in the coalition agreement. The third principle is that of collective responsibility, which means that any decision taken

146   *Patterns of government in democracies*

in the council of ministers has to be accepted by all ministers, even if they are in a minority position. This is especially important in a coalition government due to its heterogeneity in terms of party composition.

All five consensus democracies have a relatively long Cabinet tradition. Here, we will only briefly describe the main features of this tradition. According to Rudy Andeweg, in the Netherlands, a Cabinet or council of ministers did not constitutionally exist until the modernisation of the constitution in 1983. Before that point there were merely individual ministers, and a prime minister existed in name only. It took a long time to create the position of prime minister. During the Second World War, the prime minister was chosen from among the ministers, but only for a short term of three months. Ministers tended to protect their autonomy at all costs and found it difficult to adhere to collective responsibility. Individual responsibility for ministerial acts was the principle preferred by Parliament as well, as this gave the legislative more power over the ministers. Already during the interwar period, but particularly after the Second World War, the dominance of coalition governments led to a growing need to structure Cabinet governance. In the end, the only way to keep coalition governments together was to emphasise the principles of collegiality and collective responsibility over ministerial departmental autonomy (Andeweg 1988: 50–51).

While the government was in exile in London, it learned a great deal from the British model, especially the position of prime minister. Although a small Department of General Affairs had been established in 1937, after the war, a new Standing Order of the government introduced the figure of a permanent prime minister with his or her own Department of General Affairs. Any accumulation of offices was regarded with suspicion by the other ministers and other parties that were in the coalition government (Andeweg 1988: 51–52).

The Belgian and Luxembourg experiences show similarities to the Dutch case. Also in the Belgian constitution, there was no such thing as a Cabinet until the constitutional revision of the 1970s, and the position of prime minister was not enshrined in the constitution. However, the informal convention was that ministers would meet regularly, and prime ministers had existed since 1890 (officially recognised in 1918). Finally, in the constitutional revision of 1970, the prime minister was mentioned as part of a Cabinet consisting of an equal number of Flemish- and French-speaking ministers (Article 36b; Frognier 1988: 68).

In Luxembourg, ministerial responsibility was introduced in the very liberal constitution of 1848, and the principle remained important after the constitutions of 1856 and 1868 were adopted. Therefore, in 1848, the monarch chose a Minister of State (*Ministre d'État*; Thewes 2011a: 8), who would then form the government of the monarch. Senior government officials were called general administrators (*administrateurs*) or directors-general; in 1936, they received the title of minister (Thewes 2011a: 9). The number of ministers was quite small up until the Second World War; however, the complexity of modern government affairs has altered this situation. Between 1848 and 1945, the Cabinet had four to six members; between 1945 and 1964, six to eight members; between 1964 and 1979, eight to ten members; between 1979 and 1994, 12 members; and between

Patterns of government in democracies 147

1994 and 2013, 14 to 16 members (author's calculations based on Thewes 2011a). Even today, prime ministers may accumulate more than one department, similar to the case in Switzerland (see below).

The original Austrian constitution of 1920 was quite terse in defining the structures of government, and a Cabinet or council of ministers is barely mentioned. Most of the structuring of the government in Austria has been done by informal convention. One important element of the Austrian governmental system is the figure of the chancellor (*Kanzler*), who enjoys considerable in-house resources through the chancellery. Nevertheless, this power may be curtailed by coalition governments. According to Peter Gerlich and Wolfgang C. Müller, three aspects shape government work. First, there is the role of the chancellor as *primus inter pares*, but there is always the possibility to enhance the role if the chancellor has a charismatic personality and uses resources skilfully (e.g. Bruno Kreisky, Franz Vranitzky). The second aspect is the importance of the unanimity rule in the decisions of the council of ministers, which reinforces a consensual approach in all matters. This also strengthens the collective responsibility principle. Finally, parliamentary supremacy requires the government to have a working majority in the legislature and to be accountable to it. Although the Austrian political system has features of a semi-presidential system due to the direct election of the president, in reality, presidential power is significantly constrained (Gerlich and Müller 1988: 140–142). As mentioned above, the presidential elections of April/May 2016 (meanwhile nullified by the Federal Constitutional Court due to electoral management mistakes) led to a heated discussion on the competences of the president, who has the power to dismiss governments de jure. The FPÖ candidate stated that he would use this power if the grand coalition government was not functioning, contravening the de facto convention of a president with a purely representative role (*Die Presse*, 3 March 2016).

Although Switzerland is the exception in terms of government structures, the Federal Council has some similarities to a Cabinet. As already mentioned, the responsibility principle does not apply. However, there is another principle: that of non-hierarchy between members. As a result, the president is *primus inter pares* for a very limited term of one year. The main reason for this is to prevent the abuse of power by dictators, similar to the motives of the Directory of five people established in 1795 following the *terreur* of Maximilien Robespierre during the French Revolution. The Federal Council is elected by Parliament but subsequently maintains its independence. Members of Parliament are elected every four years, and then the Federal Assembly of both houses elects the seven members of the Federal Council. Kriesi and Trechsel therefore believe that this system may represent a third model of government, or rather a fourth model if we take into account presidential, semi-presidential and parliamentary systems, the so-called directory model as mentioned above (Kriesi and Trechsel 2008: 75; Fleiner 2013: 350). In contrast to the other four cases of consensus democracies, Switzerland deviates because the Federal Council is not responsible to Parliament (Kriesi and Trechsel 2008: 76; Vatter 2014: 224). The collective body was

148 *Patterns of government in democracies*

established by the 1848 constitution and has not been altered since. What have changed are the structures of governance. As in the other consensus democracies, there is a thorough negotiation process between members of the Federal Council as well as with external stakeholders. This makes the process quite lengthy, but, in the end, policy-making exhibits a higher level of continuity (Kriesi and Trechsel 2008: 76). Although the Federal Council is independent and has the power of asymmetrical information in relation to the two-chamber Parliament, direct democracy can play an important role as a veto player of last resort.

The prime minister: primus inter pares

Mediatisation has transformed the role of government into a 'permanent electoral campaign'. Prime ministers and their parties want to be re-elected in order to maintain their grip on power. Modern political parties are fairly poor in terms of financial resources, in particular because party memberships are declining in most countries. The media, including social networks and the internet, have thus become substitute methods of control over the eroding traditional electorates. However, the use of media is quite an expensive undertaking. In this sense, being in government provides a great deal of visibility for prime ministers and political parties.

Prime ministers must therefore have strong charismatic personalities in order to mobilise traditional and new electorates. However, 'charisma' has different meanings in different societies. Thomas Poguntke and Paul Webb have identified a trend towards the presidentialisation of prime ministers in most Western European countries (e.g. Tony Blair (1997–2007), Silvio Berlusconi (1994–2011), Gerhard Schröder (1998–2005)), including Belgium and the Netherlands (Poguntke and Webb 2005: 1). In general, the prime minister is officially president of the Council of Ministers, but 'presidentialisation' refers to the tendency towards the American way of politics.

Despite this overall trend, the process of 'presidentialisation' has been quite difficult in most small consensus democracies. First of all, prime ministers in consensus democracies are constrained by the other parties, which also have vice-prime ministers in the coalition government, limiting the space for individual action. Second, the negotiation process for policies is extremely time-consuming, such that prime ministers must dedicate considerable time to coordination and persuasion. Third, in fragmented party systems absolute majorities become impossible, and thus the 'permanent electoral campaigns' seen in majoritarian countries are either very moderate or even non-existent. Such complex systems, particularly when they are federal and multi-level (Germany, Austria, Switzerland and Belgium), may be characterised by many veto players and blockades: the so-called 'decision-making trap' (*Politikverflechtungsfalle*; Scharpf 1988; Benz 2009). Consultation and negotiation skills are therefore vital for prime ministers. In Belgium, it is an advantage if a prime minister speaks both of the country's main languages, namely French and Dutch. Prime Minister

Patterns of government in democracies 149

Elio di Rupio obviously found it difficult to speak Dutch; however, his willingness to speak the language enhanced the cohesion of the coalition government and the country (BBC News, 5 December 2011).

According to Poguntke and Webb, the causes of presidentialisation are the internationalisation of politics, the growth in government complexity, the changing structure of mass communication and the erosion of traditional social cleavages (Poguntke and Webb 2005: 13–17).

First, the internationalisation of politics – particularly European integration, but also the growing importance of global governance in issues such as environment, humanitarian aid, humanitarian intervention and other matters – forces governments to look for collective solutions. A positive international role on the part of the prime minister may result in more autonomy of leadership.

Second, as noted above, Switzerland's small executive struggles to coordinate the ever-increasing number and scope of policy areas. The same may be said for countries that traditionally have coalition governments. Prime ministers in these settings must play a leading role in the coordination of individual departments.

Third, modern politics is heavily influenced by the 24/7 media coverage, now including aggressive social networks that respond in real time to events; this requires that leaders have strong communication management skills to enhance both their position in government as well as in ongoing or future election campaigns (Mair *et al.* 2004).

Fourth, the mediatisation of politics is a consequence of the decline of consociationalism based on social cleavages. The erosion of social cleavages has created political market behaviour dominated by competition for individual voters. According to Peter Mair, the number of people who identify with particular parties has decreased considerably over recent decades; in addition, bipolar competition is now observable in more European countries, including Austria, although it is still only a minor factor in the other consensus democracies (Mair 2008b: 220–221; see Chapter 5, this volume).

It seems that prime ministers in the Netherlands, Belgium and Luxembourg still maintain a low profile; the position is more hierarchical in Luxembourg and Belgium, and less so in the Netherlands. The European integration process has not significantly affected this aspect (Dumont *et al.* 2015).

According to Stefaan Fiers and André Krouwel, at least some moderate tendencies towards the presidentialisation of the prime ministerial office may be identified in the Netherlands and Belgium. This phenomenon may be observed since the 1970s in the Netherlands and since the 1980s in Belgium. One influential factor is the longevity in power of many leaders in both countries. In the case of the Netherlands the obvious example is Ruud Lubbers, who increased his autonomy on the basis of the policy performance of his Cabinet in the 1980s. Wim Kok in the 1990s was at times more popular than his party. Jan-Peter Balkenende also enhanced his reputation over time, and may be credited with emulating the Blairite model of leadership. In the case of Belgium, Wilfried Martens in the 1980s, Jean-Luc Dehaene in the 1990s and Guy Verhofstadt between 1999 and 2007 represent examples of this moderate presidentialisation

150 *Patterns of government in democracies*

of the office. Longevity is an important factor in terms of political experience, negotiation and consultation skills. The international stage is also critical, particularly with regard to the European Union. Such longevity and executive resources have implications for both control over party resources and electoral success (Fiers and Krouwel 2005).

Prime ministers in both the Netherlands and Belgium are supported by a general affairs department that assists them in coordination, as well as their international role.

Luxembourg and Austria are also characterised by prime ministers with long incumbencies. In the case of Luxembourg, this has been a long-standing tradition. Between 1945 and 2015, Luxembourg had only eight prime ministers. Pierre Werner (1959–1974, 1979–1984), Jacques Santer (1984–1994) and Jean-Claude Juncker (1994–2013) were all in power for more than ten years – 19 years for Juncker. Luxembourg also exemplifies the fact that the European stage is an important additional factor in increasing a prime minister's autonomy. Pierre Werner was highly engaged in the European integration process. The Werner Plan on the establishment of a single European currency in the 1970s may certainly be cited here as contributing to the enhancement of the office of the prime minister. Jacques Santer and Jean-Claude Juncker were also heavily involved with the European arena while they were prime ministers; subsequently, both men were appointed to the presidency of the European Commission by the European Council, in 1994 and 2014, respectively. This is an indication of the international credibility that these moderate consensual prime ministers enjoy on the European scene. Jean-Claude Juncker was not only prime minister but also finance minister, establishing an excellent reputation as the first president of the informal Eurogroup and chair of the finance ministers of the Eurozone, a role that has gained crucial importance over time (as the bailouts to Greece, Ireland, Portugal, Cyprus and Spain between 2010 and 2012 have shown; for more details see Magone *et al.* 2016a). The dominance of the Christian Democrats since 1945 has also created conditions conducive to strong control over party resources. Another feature of the Luxembourg core executive is that ministers are also characterised by long periods of incumbency. Both Jacques Santer and Jean-Claude Juncker were ministers for a long time before being promoted to the position of prime minister. Jacques Santer became state secretary in 1972 and then minister of Social and Labour Affairs in the 1980s before becoming prime minister in 1984. Jean-Claude Juncker, who became state secretary in 1982, became minister of Finance and Labour Affairs in 1989 and then prime minister in 1994 after Santer was appointed president of the European Commission. The political culture of Luxembourg seems to emphasise political stability, and so these well-known leaders were re-elected several times.

Similarly, Austrian politics is characterised by the longevity of leaders, with some interruptions. Between 1970 and 2015 – a period of 45 years – there were seven prime ministers, but two of them, Bruno Kreisky and Franz Vranitzky, account for 24 of these years: more than half of the entire period. Wolfgang Schüssel was in power for six years and Werner Faymann for eight years; in

Patterns of government in democracies 151

contrast, the terms of the uncharismatic Fred Sinowatz (1983–1986), Viktor Klima (1997–1999) and Alfred Gusenbauer (2007–2008) ended abruptly. Probably the most charismatic leader of the Austrian Second Republic was Chancellor Bruno Kreisky, who managed to govern the country for a period of 13 years, much of it with an absolute majority government (for an in-depth discussion of the Kreisky government see Kriechbaumer 2004). However, one should not underestimate the five Franz Vranitzky grand coalition governments (1986–1997). Vranitzky played an important management role in resolving the major economic crisis affecting in particular the *Proporzdemokratie* system in the public economic sector of the state through reorganisation and privatisation. Vranitzky also became known for adopting a more honest approach towards Austrian history, related to the international ostracising of the federal President Kurt Waldheim due to his involvement in military operations during the Second World War; Vranitzky informally became the substitute head of state. Despite all the constraints of a coalition government, he cleverly used the chancellor's office as well as party resources to remain in power for a long time, contributing to the economic and also political renewal of the country. Since he was a rather modest and reserved person, his achievements have been neglected in comparison to those of Bruno Kreisky (for a review on Vranitzky see Gehler 2012). Kreisky's era and that of his predecessor Josef Klaus may be regarded as the closest that Austria has come to a chancellor democracy (*Kanzlerdemokratie*) similar to Konrad Adenauer's incumbency at the beginning of the Bonner Republic (1949–1966; for a historical review of this concept see Nicklauss 2014).

Chancellor Wolfgang Schüssel (2000–2007) tried hard to be a strong leader in the coalition government between the ÖVP and the Freedom Party (FPÖ). The latter group had gained a bad reputation as a xenophobic, anti-immigration party, and thus the coalition government was rejected by large segments of society, including federal President Thomas Klestil. However, in the end, the federal president had to swear in the new coalition government. Wolfgang Schüssel adhered closely to the Blair model of presidentialisation. The main problem was that the junior partner, the FPÖ, was very inexperienced, and tensions within the party tended to affect the cohesion and work of the coalition government (Pelinka and Rosenberger 2003; Luther 2005; Wineroither 2009: 282, 296–297; 2012).

Among the five consensus democracies Belgium seems to have the most politicised infrastructure, in which political and administrative structures support the government. The Copernicus reform undertaken in the new millennium attempted to increase transparency and accountability at the highest levels by introducing New Public Management innovations (for a summary see Thijs 2008). Nevertheless, the vast powers of patronage in the prime minister's office and those of the individual ministers remain important. Each minister has a secretariat and a policy cell that are political in nature. The policy cell is used to employ a large research and support staff from the political parties. According to Lieven de Winter and Patrick Dumont, the size of this staff varies between 12 and 200 people, but as a rule of thumb there are about 60 staff members. The

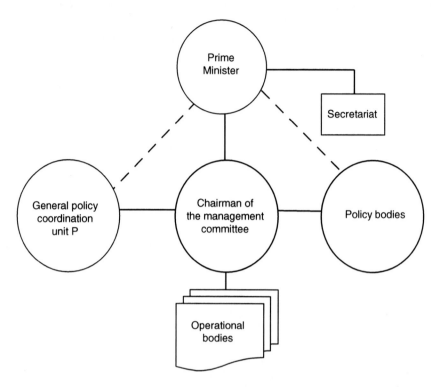

Figure 6.1 The chancellery of the prime minister in Belgium in 2015.
Source: author's graph based on Chancellerie du Premier Ministre (2016).

policy cell is also called the 'Cabinet of the minister' and is headed by a chief of staff. These Cabinets or policy cells are paid for by the state and represent an important source of patronage for ministers (De Winter and Dumont 2006: 963; Moury 2013: 58). Since 2001, there has been a stricter separation between the political and operational-administrative aspects of policy-making. There is a small secretariat for direct logistical issues supporting the prime minister, a general policy coordination unit and a policy-coordinating cell in charge of creating some cohesion in the work of the government (Government of Belgium 2015; see also Figure 6.1). These Cabinet political advisers (*kabinetmedewerkers*) play an important role in maintaining a vast network within the bureaucracy, Parliament and society at large; they are the spindles of policy networks (*beleidsnetwerkspil*) and thereby marginalise the neutral civil servants (Vancoppenolle and Brans 2010: 510; Interviews B). In 2014, the chancellery of the prime minister comprised 151 people, of which 60 had fixed-term contracts; most of these probably belong to the group of political advisers on his team (Chancellerie du Premier Ministre 2015: 9). Such ministerial Cabinets also exist in regional and community governments; they are important pacifiers and are in

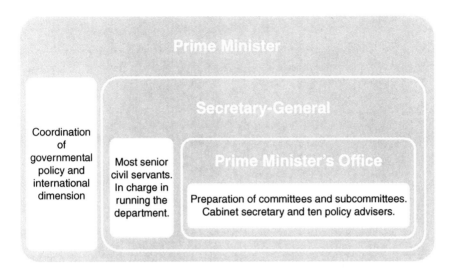

Figure 6.2 Core executive in the Netherlands.
Source: author's graph based on Government of the Netherlands (2015).

charge of consensus-seeking in the highly complex multi-level system. In this regard, a certain politicisation of the civil service is a side effect.

In the case of the Netherlands, the prime minister is supported by a lean but quite efficient structure. A secretary-general assists the prime minister; this is the most senior civil servant in the ministry and heads the prime minister's office. He or she is responsible for the coordination of security and the secret service. A senior management board is at the top of the ministry hierarchy and takes decisions on everything related to the ministry. The prime minister's office consists of ten advisers to the prime minister. A secretary to the Cabinet prepares its meetings. The secretaries of the subcommittees are normally political advisers. There are three other departments in the ministry: the Government Information Service deals with press relations and also information for the Royal House, the Public and Communications Office focuses on providing information to the population at large and the Office of the Scientific Council for Government Policy is an important resource for scientific support in the preparation and drafting of reports, and in the commission of external reports (Government of the Netherlands 2015; see also Figure 6.2).

In Luxembourg, the prime minister tends to head several ministries. Prime Minister Xavier Bettel is also Minister for Communication and Religious Affairs and therefore wears three hats. Thus far, his main position of prime minister is supported by the ministry of the presidency. This is clearly a highly important resource for the coordination of government work. The presidency includes several research institutes that support the work of the government. Probably the

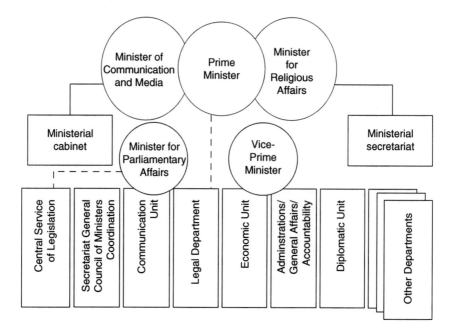

Figure 6.3 Prime minister's office in Luxembourg in 2016.
Sources: author's graph based on Government of Luxembourg (2016a, 2016b).

most important body within the ministry is the Central Service of Legislation (*Service Central de Legislation*) attached to the Department of Parliamentary Relations, as it is the most salient transmission system between the government and Parliament. It collects all the correspondence between these actors and provides a real-time picture via the internet of the state of legislative bills (Schroen 2009b: 114). In 2013, there were 17 members of staff working for the Central Service of Legislation (Government of Luxembourg 2014: 5; see also Figure 6.3).

In all three Benelux countries, there is a state council with an advisory function consisting of renowned former politicians and legal experts that examines the quality of legislation. In the case of Luxembourg, it has informally acquired the role of a second deliberative chamber. Both government and private bills must be submitted to this Council of State so that it can scrutinise them in terms of legality and constitutionality. According to the 2013 report, 95 government and nine private bills were submitted to Parliament after the Council of State gave its opinion (Government of Luxembourg 2014: 10, 13–14).

Overall, the Austrian model of chancellor (*Kanzler*) has strong similarities to the German model. Despite the many veto players in the system (coalition partners, *Bundesrat*, federal constitutional court, federalised units), the position of the chancellor is quite strong. The chancellor's office (*Bundeskanzleramt*), the

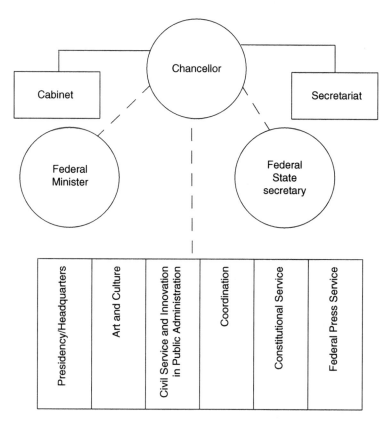

Figure 6.4 Chancellor's office in Austria in 2015.
Source: author's graph based on Bundeskanzleramt (2016f).

constitutional information office (*Verfassungsdienst*) and also the power of appointment of federal personnel offer some power of information asymmetry in relation to the other Cabinet members (see Figure 6.4). Moreover, in 2000 these structures were upgraded; the chancellery now also has a service informing the prime minister about policy-making in each department (Müller 2006b: 174–175). There are about 400 employees in the chancellery, of which 15 are politically appointed by the chancellor; they play a major role in policy formulation, whereas implementation is carried out by the administrative services (SAFEGE Baltija 2015: 26).

In contrast to the other four countries, Switzerland has no dual executive; the Federal Council is the government, but it also has presidential tasks. A president is elected by the Federal Assembly on an annual basis. The president of the Federal Council is not hierarchically above the other six members, but merely *primus inter pares*. It seems that the original constitution of 1848 regarded the president as more important and allocated the position more competences, but

156 *Patterns of government in democracies*

since 1913 it has become an informal convention that the president is first among equals (Brühl-Moser 2007: 685–686). The selection of the president is based on the principle of seniority in terms of election to the Federal Council; each member is elected president or vice-president according to an informal list (Brühl-Moser 2007: 689).

As discussed above, the Swiss executive is relatively small and over-burdened by the growing number of policy areas. This is even more problem-atic for the president, who must wear two hats: one as president and the other as a normal member of the Federal Council. Although it is supported by the federal chancellery, the agenda of the president is dominated by a large number of international and national representation engagements, making it difficult to schedule meetings with other councillors on the Federal Council. This clearly has implications for long-term relationships with international figures (Brühl-Moser 2007: 688). The Swiss president is in charge of preparing and chairing the meetings of the Federal Council. He or she also has responsibility over the entire federal administration; moreover, the president must maintain close contact with Parliament (Brühl-Moser 2007: 691–693). The limitations on the presidential office are designed to avoid the accumulation of power within the Federal Council, thus preventing the phenomenon of presidentialisation. The most important structure supporting the president and the other members of the Council is the federal chancellery (*Bundeskanzlei*; see Figure 6.5), which consists of 270 employees, mainly civil servants. The chancellor is generally a high-ranking civil servant with an excellent knowledge of the Swiss political system and is elected by the Federal Assembly (like the federal councillors). The federal chancellery prepares the legislative programme for the council and functions as the institution's memory. The departments of planning and strategy are tasked with preparing the legislative programme that is politically approved by the Federal Council. This programme represents a process negotiated between the political parties in Parliament and the Federal Council; it is a substitute for a coalition agreement and in this sense is less politicised (Schweizerische Bundeskanzlei 2016; Interview CH).

Patterns of government formation

With the exception of Switzerland, government formation in consensus demo-cracies is a complex process of negotiation. Three aspects are particularly important in such negotiations: the party composition, the coalition agreement and the allocation of portfolios.

Although the Benelux countries have fairly sophisticated systems of coalition government formation, there are definite differences among the countries. All three countries use so-called informateurs and formateurs to conduct exploratory discussions with the political parties and then to form a government. The infor-mateur is generally a senior politician who has been in government before and has accummulated considerable experience; this politician determines the best possible coalition government after talking to all the political parties. The electoral

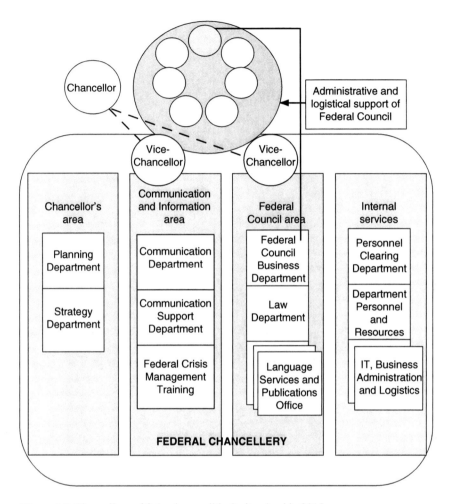

Figure 6.5 Chancellery of federal council in Switzerland in 2015.
Source: author's graph based on Schweizerische Bundeskanzlei (2016).

results can be an important guide for the formation of a government, but according to studies of the period between 1945 and 2000, the political parties in the three countries are not very responsive to electoral defeat. In some cases, it may be that the losers of elections return to government.

The fragmentation of the party systems in Belgium and the Netherlands has created many possibilities for coalition formation; consequently, in these countries, it takes a long time to create a government. Several rounds of negotiations with several parties must take place before a government is finally formed. Figure 6.6 offers an overall impression of how coalition government has become the main type of government in all four countries.

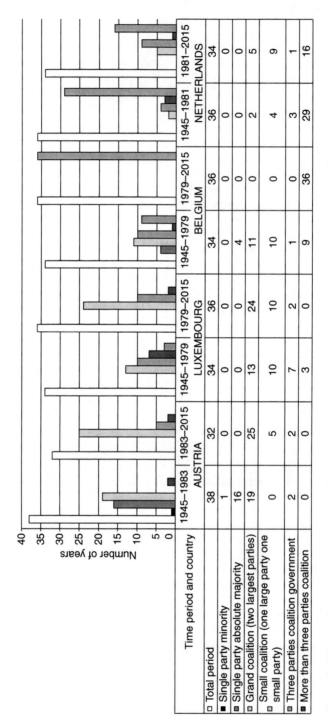

Figure 6.6 Types of government in consensus democracies according to years between 1945 and 2015.
Source: author's calculations.

Patterns of government in democracies 159

In Belgium between 1945 and 2000, government formation lasted for about a month; however, since then, it has become more difficult to form coalitions. Belgium clearly finds it difficult to create small coalition governments; in all instances since 1979, at least four parties have been involved in coalition government (see Table 6.1). This is a major factor leading to long periods of government formation. The socio-linguistic cleavage complicates the negotiation process further. This was particularly evident in the government formation process of the first Yves Leterme government between 2007 and 2009: it took 197 days to form a government that collapsed six months later. In contrast to Austria and Luxembourg, coalition governments may involve more than two parties. The federalisation of the country and the duplication of political parties along the linguistic cleavage have created a highly complex system of multi-level coalition governance. Directly after the establishment of the new federal state, there were attempts to replicate the complex multi-party coalition government at the national level in the different subnational units. However, despite major efforts, this has become more problematic over time, as parties that belong to the same ideological family have developed independently in different directions. As we can see, the fragmentation of the party system leads to the inclusion of a considerable number of parties in coalitions. Since 1981, there have only been coalition governments consisting of more than four parties. This results in lengthy coalition negotiations and difficult coalition governance. For example, it took 541 days to form a government following the June 2010 elections. The main issue was the increase in support for the moderate Flemish pro-independence party, the New Flemish Alliance (N-VA), which put considerable pressure on the other political parties in issues related to the linguistic conflict. One important milestone in creating the government was the agreement on splitting the Brussels-Halle-Vilvorde (BHV) district along linguistic borders leading up to the sixth state reform agreed in 2012, and in force since 2014. Constitutionally, the government is limited to 15 ministers: the president and seven ministers from each of the two main regions.

Coalition government is also quite complex in the case of the Netherlands. Thus far, the vast majority of Dutch governments have been minimal winning coalitions: one of the three main parties forms a coalition, usually the winner of the elections with one of the other parties. According to Arco Timmermans and Rudy Andeweg, between 1945 and 1999, government formation took from 31 to 208 days: 68 days on average (Dumont *et al.* 2015). Following the 1994 elections, the purple coalition between the PvdA and the VVD required 111 days to be formed (Timmermans and Andeweg 2000: 369–370). This was an innovative kind of coalition, attempted for the first time. The past two Mark Rutte governments have been minority governments, at least in one of the houses. The Mark Rutte II (2012–) government between the VVD and the PvdA took 43 days to form. Due to the lack of a majority in the upper house, the government had to sign agreements with several additional parties in the upper house, the *Eerste Kamer* and interest groups outside Parliament (see Table 6.2; Otjes and Voerman 2013: 168; 2014: 232–233; Interviews NL).

Table 6.1 Coalition government in Belgium, 1981 to 2016

Prime Minister Start Date-End Date	Christian Democrats		Social Democrats		Liberals		Greens			Flemish Regionalists		Number of parties	Percentage total	Percentage of seats Lower Chamber (212 until 1995/150 after 1995)	Coalition type
	CVP/ CD&V	PSC/ CDH	PS	SP/SP.A	PVV/VLD	PLR/MR	ECOLO	AGALEV/ GROEN!		VU	N-VA				
Wilfried Martens V 17.12.1981–14.10.1985												4	49.5	51.8	MW
Wilfried Martens VI 28.11.1985–14.12.1987												4	51.3	54.2	MW
Wilfried Martens VII 9.05.1988–29.09.1991												4	56	66	OW
Wilfried Martens VIII 29.09.1991–25.11.1991												5	50	63.7	MW
Jean Luc Dehaene I 7.03.1992–21.05.1995												4	50	63.7	MW
Jean Luc Dehaene II 23.06.1995–13.07.1999												4	49.4	57.1	MW
Guy Verhofstadt I 12.07.1999–12.07.2003												6	64.7	60	O
Guy Verhofstadt II 12.07.2003–21.12.2007												4	54.7	64.7	O
Guy Verhofstadt III 21.12.2007–20.03.2008												5	49.6	67.3	O
Yves Leterme I 20.03.2008–30.12.2008												5	49.6	67.3	MW
Herman van Rompuy 30.12.2008–31.12.2009												5	49.6	67.3	MW
Yves Leterme II 25.11.2009–6.12.2011												5	49.6	67.3	MW
Elio di Rupio 6.12.2011–11.10.2014												6	57.2	64	GC
Charles Michel 11.10.2014–												4	51.3	56,7	MW

Table 6.2 Coalition government in the Netherlands, 1982 to 2016

Prime Minister Start date–end date	CDA	PVdA	VVD	D66	CU	LPF; PVV after 2006	Number of parties	Percentage elections total	Percentage of seats Lower Chamber (150 seats)	Coalition type
Ruud Lubbers 4.11.1982–21.05.1986							2	52.4	55.3	MW
Ruud Lubbers 14.07.19862.05.1989							2	52	54	MW
Ruud Lubbers 7.11.1989–3.05.1994							2	67.2	68.7	MW
Wim Kok I 22.08.1994–5.05.1998							2	43.9	47.3	MinC
Wim Kok II 3.08.1998–22.07.2002							2	53.7	49.3	MinC
Jan-Peter Balkenende I 22.07.2002–27.05.2003							3	50	62	MW
Jan-Peter Balkenende II 27.05.2003–7.07. 2006							3	50.6	52	MW
Jan-Peter Balkenende III 7.07.2006–22.03.2007							2	46.5	48	INT
Jan Peter Balkende IV 22.02.2007–14.10.2010							2	51.7	49.3	MW
Mark Rutte I 14.10.2010–5.11.2012						Parliamentary support of PVV	2	37.2	34.7	MINC
Mark Rutte II 5.11.2012–							2	51.3	52.7	MW

162   *Patterns of government in democracies*

In Luxembourg, electoral responsiveness was quite strong until 1989, but subsequently it became less influential (Dumont and De Winter 2000: 430). One important case was when Gaston Thorn from the Democratic Party became prime minister, because CSV lost the elections (losing about 8 per cent of the vote) and the LSAP became the strongest party. Clearly this showed a high level of responsiveness to electoral results. This respect for winners has made the Luxembourg system successful in integrating the three main parties, also known as the 'triagonal government cartel' (see Table 6.3). According to Michael Schroen, this is the reason why parties do not commit themselves to any coalition constellation before elections (Schroen 2009b: 106, 111). The first step towards coalition formation in these three countries is the appointment of an informateur by the King. After some time this actor reports back, recommending a possible government constellation; the King then appoints a formateur in charge of forming a government – potentially, this may be the next prime minister. In some cases there are several rounds of negotiations with potential parties. In Luxembourg, where the pivotal role of the Christian Democrats generally leads to a two-party coalition either with the Social Democrats or the Liberals (or, exceptionally, between the latter two), informateurs may be used, but the coalition negotiations are normally conducted by the largest party, in most cases the Christian Democrats (CSV). On average, less than one round of negotiations is required to determine a coalition; failed attempts are rare. Moreover, it takes less than a month on average to come to a conclusion (Dumont and De Winter 2000: 406–407, 411). Prior to 1990, this period was 25 days; afterwards it was 37 days, and, since the turn of the millennium, 40 days. This extension of the negotiation period is related to increasing discussion on European issues (Dumont *et al.* 2015).

The government formed by the liberal Democratic Party (DP) and the Social Democrats (LSAP) that emerged from the 2013 legislative elections took about 45 days to be formed. In this case, Grand Duke Henri (since 2000) was more involved than usual, appointing an informateur who genuinely explored the positions of the different parties. This informateur was George Ravarani, the president of the Administrative Court, who was non-political and therefore a neutral and honest broker. Xavier Bettel from the Democratic Party was appointed formateur, and he formed a coalition with the Social Democrats and the Greens. The previous coalition government between the CSV and the LSAP (2009–2013) took one day longer to form than the new government (Dumont and Kies 2014: 214). This contrasts somewhat with the more fast-track approach taken by the Grand Duke following the elections in June 2004, in which the incumbent prime minister Jean-Claude Juncker of the Christian Democratic Party was directly appointed formateur. Negotiations were undertaken only with the Social Democrats, and after 34 days the government was formed. Overall, the period of government formation has been increasing over time.

Austria is the least formalised system in terms of coalition government. The main reason for this is that until the end of the 1970s the two main political parties – the Socialists (SPÖ) and the People's Party (ÖVP) – were capable of

Table 6.3 Coalition government in Luxembourg

Prime Minister Start date–end date	CSV	LSAP	DP	Greens	Number of parties	Percentage elections total	Percentage of seats Lower Chamber (180 seats)	Coalition type
Pierre Werner 16.07.1979–20.07.1984					2	53.6	65.0	OC
Jacques Santer 20.07.1984–14.07.1989					2	68.5	76.7	GC
Jacques Santer 14.07.1989–13.07.1994					2	58.9	66.7	GC
Jacques Santer 13.07.1994–26.01.1995					2	56.2	63.3	GC
Jean-Claude Juncker 26.01.1995–7.08.1998					2	56.2	63.3	GC
Jean-Claude Juncker 7.08.1999–31.07.2004					2	52.5	56.7	MW
Jean-Claude Juncker 31.07.2004–23.07.2009					2	59.5	63.3	GC
Jean-Claude Juncker 23.07.2009–4.12.2013					2	59.6	65	GC
Xavier Bettel 4.12.2013–					3	48.7	53.3	MWC

164 *Patterns of government in democracies*

mobilising their encapsulated electoral constituencies or subcultures in order to achieve absolute majorities; however, this became more difficult after 1983 (see Table 6.4). The emergence of new political parties and the rise of the FPÖ as a major challenger led to a new context in terms of electoral competition. In the new system, no party can achieve absolute majorities, considerably constraining the possibility to govern alone. Minority governments can create significant political instability, so grand coalition governments would seem to be the best way to neutralise the competition between the two main parties. Although coalition governments have been in place for 44 of the 71 years of the Austrian Second Republic, government formation is still characterised by a freestyle pattern, as seen in Luxembourg. It means that no intermediary (e.g. informateur or formateur) is involved in the process, the largest party negotiates directly with other parties, and, if it does not come to a coalition government, this is left to the other parties. However, in comparison to Luxembourg, the negotiations tend to take much longer: more than 50 days on average during the period between 1945 and 2000. In the new millennium, the controversial ÖVP–FPÖ coalition (2000–2007) was preceded by the longest period of negotiations to date. More than 123 days were required to conclude the negotiations, and only after 129 days was the government sworn in (Fallend 2000: 243).

Following the elections of 2006/2007, the government formation negotiations took a considerable amount of time to reach a conclusion, in part due to the attempts of incumbent Chancellor Wolfgang Schüssel to remain in power despite having lost the election. He became the chief negotiator for the ÖVP but employed delay tactics to extend his hold on power. It took 102 days to form a new government – without Schüssel (*Der Spiegel*, 10 January 2007).

Although Chancellor Werner Faymann and his SPÖ party lost the elections in 2009, the Socialists remained in first place, and so they had to start negotiations with the other parties. Exploratory talks were conducted with Heinz-Christian Strache, leader of the FPÖ, but in reality the SPÖ wanted to continue its coalition with the ÖVP. In this case the negotiations took about two months, slightly above the average (Jenny 2014: 34).

The main reason behind the relatively long negotiations in all four countries is the drafting of a coalition agreement that may be signed by all the parties. This entails discussion of policy and procedural issues until the coalition agreement is acceptable to all. All four countries use working groups in which potential candidates for the respective positions are integrated. Over time, the length of coalition agreements has been increasing. These documents detail policy agreements and coalition governance procedures, creating a manual for a four- or five-year legislature period. Up until the 1960s, coalition agreements were undertaken in secrecy, but later it became common practice to publish them. Only in Luxembourg were coalition agreements kept secret until 1999, with ministers and the party archives in receipt of the only copies (Dumont *et al*. 2015). Moreover, the coalition agreement in Luxembourg seems to be more of a policy programme then a procedural document, a distinction that may have been internalised by the actors over time. The length of these agreements has varied between 130 and

Table 6.4 Coalition government in Austria, 1983 to 2016

Prime Minister Start date–end date	SPÖ	ÖVP	FPÖ	Number of parties	Percentage elections total	Percentage of seats Lower Chamber (180 seats)	Coalition type
Fred Sinowatz 24.05.1983–16.06.1986				2	90.9	93.4	MW
Franz Vranitzky I 16.06.1986–25.11.1986				2	90.9	93.4	MW
Franz Vranitzky II 21.01.1987–9.10.1990				2	84.4	85.8	GC
Franz Vranitzky III 17.12.1990–11.10.1994				2	74.9	76.5	GC
Franz Vranitzky IV 19.11.1994–12.03.1996				2	62.6	63.9	GC
Franz Vranitzky V 12.03.1996–20.01.1997				2	66.4	68.9	GC
Viktor Klima 28.01.1997–4.02.2000				2	66.4	68.9	GC
Wolfgang Schüssel I 4.02.2000–28.02.2003				2	53.8	56.8	MW
Wolfgang Schüssel II 28.02.2003–11.01.2007				2	52.3	53	MW
Alfred Gusenbauer 11.01.2007–2.12.2008				2	55.3	59	GC
Werner Faymann I 2.12.2008–16.12.2013				2	55.3	59	GC
Werner Faymann II 16.12.2013–9.05.2016				2	50.7	54.1	GC

166   *Patterns of government in democracies*

200 pages (Dumont and De Winter 2000: 412–415). In the cases of the Netherlands and Belgium, coalition agreements are even more important; they are referred to as the 'bible' of the coalition government (De Winter, Timmermans and Dumont 2000: 382; Dumont and De Winter 2000: 322). In these two countries, both policy and procedures are important. Especially in Belgium, the coalition agreement is an important instrument to build and maintain confidence among partners that may come from different socio-linguistic communities. The size of coalition agreements has varied. Probably the most extensive was for the Martens VII government in 1988, at over 100 (500-word) pages; interestingly, this administration lasted for just two years. Over 90 percent of the agreement is dedicated to policy, with about 10–14 percent covering general or specific procedures (De Winter *et al.* 2000: 330–331). In the Netherlands, written coalition agreements have existed since 1963. Their length has increased over time: from seven (500-word) pages, to over 90 pages in 1998. About 48 per cent of the first written agreement covered general and specific rules, but subsequently most agreements were over 90 per cent dominated by policy (Timmermans and Andeweg 2000: 374). Also in Austria, coalition agreements facilitate the cohesion of the coalition government. Austrian agreements are quite sophisticated; up until 1983 they were rather small documents of seven to nine pages, but afterwards their length increased to 30 pages, and to almost 50 pages in 1990. Up until 1983, agreements defined general and specific procedures within the coalition, the portfolio allocation and the planned policies. After 1983, the SPÖ–FPÖ coalition did not specify procedures, concentrating primarily on policy. This was emulated by the subsequent coalition governments between the SPÖ and the ÖVP. However, there was an interruption of this trend with the controversial coalition government between the ÖVP and the FPÖ. In order to keep the leader of the FPÖ out of government, a complex set of procedures was devised to ensure the efficient functioning of the coalition. However, internal party disagreements and even conflict within the FPÖ undermined coalition discipline significantly (Luther 2005: 28–29; Wineroither 2009: 282). The subsequent SPÖ–ÖVP governments returned to the previous pattern of coalition agreements. According to Marcelo Jenny, the Faymann II coalition government (2013–2016) was based on a 144-page coalition agreement (Jenny 2014: 34).

The final part of negotiations deal with the allocation of portfolios. This is the most important aspect of the process: party leaders engaged in negotiations want to obtain the best deal for their constituencies. In practice, in these four countries, the proportional distribution principle based on electoral processes determines the allocation of portfolios among the political parties. Each party is allocated a number of minister and state secretary (junior minister) posts and is sovereign over them. The prime minister cannot overrule decisions by the other party leaders, with very few exceptions, and he or she only has control over the ministers allocated to his or her party. According to Wolfgang C. Müller, this was referred to by Bruno Pittermann, the Social Democratic vice-chancellor between 1963 and 1966, as the 'chimpanzee principle'. If a coalition partner wants a chimpanze to be a minister, the prime minister and the other coalition

Patterns of government in democracies 167

partners have to allow it (Müller 2000: 108). A rule of thumb for all four countries is that Christian Democrats usually prefer the portfolios of family, finance, agriculture, defence and foreign affairs, whereas Social Democrats tend to manage social and labour affairs – and, in the case of Austria, finance and transport and infrastructure. The Liberals generally control economy, trade and justice. This may vary according to the coalition formation and country, but it can be regarded as a general pattern (Müller 2000: 112; De Winter *et al.* 2000: 335; Timmermans and Andeweg 2000: 377; Dumont and De Winter 2000: 424).

Once the negotiation process has been concluded, the political parties must agree to abide by the result. Usually, an extraordinary party conference is held to endorse the coalition agreement. Thus far, no coalition agreement has been rejected by the party conferences in any of the countries. This demonstrates that the negotiation process strives to include all the different constituencies within each party.

Following party investiture there is also a parliamentary investiture. In the case of the Netherlands and Austria, one can speak of a 'negative'majority (Bergman 1993), meaning that as long as there is not a majority against the particular government the investiture is successful (Timmermans and Andeweg 2000: 363). In contrast, in Belgium and Luxembourg, there is a formal investiture process; however, due to the negotiated working majority, it is very difficult to reject a new government (Dumont and De Winter 2000: 324). Moreover, in Belgium, a constructive motion of censure was introduced in the new constitution of 1993; this motion not only requires a majority against the new government, but also demands that an alternative candidate be presented within three days. This constructive motion of censure, which is used in Germany, Spain and Poland, strengthens the position of the government in relation to Parliament (De Winter *et al.* 2000: 324; De Winter and Dumont 2005: 961).

In Switzerland, there are no coalition negotiations or agreements. The members of the Federal Council are elected by the Federal Assembly, comprising both Houses of Parliament (the National Council and the Council of States). Each candidate is elected separately according to seniority, with the councillors that have more experience subject to election first. It is difficult to unseat federal councillors who have done their job well, resulting in an unusually high level of personnel stability. Renewal rates remain low.

The various members of the Federal Council are elected according to the 'magic formula' (*Zauberformel*) defined in 1959. This formula was established over time due to the emergence of new political parties in the mass democracy system. Originally, the Federal Council was dominated by the Liberals, who were the main founders of the new Swiss state. At the turn of the century, the Christian Democrats managed to win one seat, and later two seats. The Social Democrats won their first seat in 1943 and a second seat in 1959. The predecessor of the Swiss People's Party, the Citizens, Small Trade and Farmers' Party (*Bürger-Gewerbe und Bauernpartei*, BGB) was allocated one seat in 1929 (see Figure 6.7).

Due to the fact that the SVP has become the largest party in the country in recent decades, the magic formula had to be revised in 2003, with the Christian

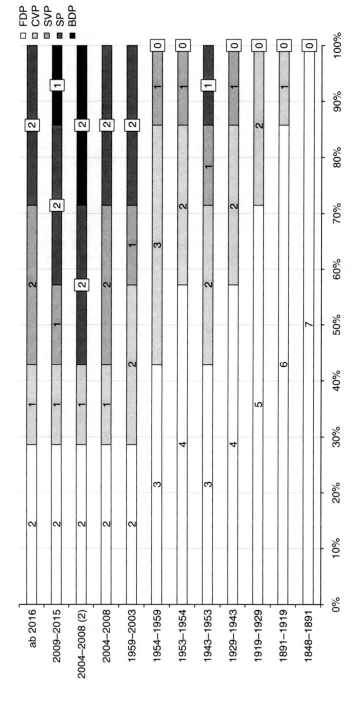

Figure 6.7 Composition of the federal council, 1848 to 2016.

Source: author's graph based on Bundesamt für Statistik (2016d).

Patterns of government in democracies 169

Democrats losing one of their two seats and the SVP receiving two seats. The current formula allocates two seats to the Liberals, Social Democrats and Swiss People's Party, and one seat to the Christian Democrats. In 2003, despite considerable resistance in the Federal Assembly, Christoph Blocher, the former leader of the SVP, became a federal councillor. Blocher's populism fomented disagreements within the Federal Council. Instead of following the informal rules of collegiality and collective responsibility, Blocher employed a double strategy by mobilising his electorate through direct democracy instruments. In this sense, he worked for the government within the Federal Council and against it in the extra-parliamentary arena. Consequently, despite his party becoming even stronger in terms of its share of the votes, the Federal Assembly did not re-elect him to the Federal Council in 2007 – a rare snub. Blocher was replaced by Eveline Widmer-Schlumpf; when he demanded that she resign, she refused and was expelled from the party. Along with others who were unhappy with the populist tendencies of the SVP, Widmer-Schlumpf created a new political party called the Citizens' Democratic Party (*Bürgerlich-Demokratische Partei*, BDP). In 2008, the other councillor of the SVP, Samuel Schmid, joined the new party, but at the end of 2008 he resigned and was replaced by Ueli Maurer from the SVP (Milic 2009: 1124). As a result of these machinations the magic formula was effectively suspended: the BDP is not one of the largest parties, but the Federal Assembly re-elected Widmer-Schlumpf in 2011. The SVP thus held only one seat, with the other seat taken by the BDP. The SVP argued that it should be allocated an additional seat, as the party is the largest in the country, but candidates from the SVP were unsuccessful, mainly due to the fact that Widmer-Schlumpf occupied their actual second seat. Widmer-Schlumpf was widely accepted among parliamentarians of other parties and the Federal Council, due in large part to the fact that she comes from political royalty in the BGB/SVP. Her father Leon Schlumpf, who belonged to the generation before Blocher, was a federal councillor between 1979 and 1987 (Interview CH). Following the retirement of Widmer-Schlumpf at the end of the legislature period, Guy Parmelin from the SVP was elected federal councillor by the Federal Assembly on 24 November 2015, thereby restoring the magical formula. Parmelin comes from the western part of Switzerland and has had a lengthy career in both the cantonal Parliament in Waadt and in the National Council of the Federal Parliament. He is regarded as moderate and collegial, very important qualities in a federal councillor (*Neue Zürcher Zeitung*, 25 November 2015).

Various criteria are used for the selection of potential candidates for the Federal Council. Potential candidates must come from different linguistic regions: the unwritten rule is that at least two candidates should come from the Francophone part of Switzerland (Romandie) and one from the Italian-speaking region. Throughout the twentieth century, the Federal Council consisted of four German-speaking, two French-speaking and one Italian-speaking councillor. This is also enshrined in the constitution in Article 170.2. A broader criterion of selection also takes into account the rotation of cantons in the highest executive. In reality, there is a certain dominance on the part of the larger cantons. Representatives of Zürich,

170 Patterns of government in democracies

Bern and Waadt are almost always on the Federal Council; Schwyz, Schaffhausen, Jura, Uri and Nidwalden never had a representative until October 2015 (Klötli 2002: 167; Klötli *et al.* 2014: 199–200). Religion was originally important, but it has lost significance as a selection criterion over time, although it was relatively important in the early twentieth century. There is no specific training in the Federal Council for new councillors; they have to learn their job by doing it (Interview CH).

Cabinet governance: internal and external coordination

As mentioned above, all five countries have sophisticated formal and informal rules of Cabinet governance. These rules have been developed over decades, becoming an *acquis consensuel* for the countries. Here again, Switzerland is an exception; however, many of the rules used in the Swiss federal council are similar to those found in the other four coalition governments.

In Austria, Belgium, Luxembourg and the Netherlands, the coalition agreement is the most important instrument for maintaining Cabinet governance among the political parties. All four countries have mechanisms in place to resolve conflicts and uphold the strategic positions of the coalition government. In Austria, there is a committee in which parliamentary and government party leaders regularly meet in order to resolve conflict, but at its core there is an inner Cabinet of just the party leaders who take informal decisions on unsolved problems. This body was important for the coalitions between 1987 and 2000 (Müller 2000: 105). According to Wineroither, in the Wolfgang Schüssel governments the nature of the coalition committee, which met 10 to 15 times per year, changed from a conflict-resolving to a coordinating and controlling unit. Up until 2002, Jörg Haider took part in the regular meetings, but subsequently he stopped attending. The informal meetings took place in the residence of one of the ministers (Khol 2006: 149, cited in Wineroither 2009: 297). Coalition discipline is quite strong in both the government and Parliament, meaning that most legislation is approved without proper consultation of Parliament. In the end, the pre-parliamentary negotiated legislation is accepted in Parliament without any major incidents. In the view of opposition parties such as the Greens and the Freedom Party, the dominance of the grand coalition over so many decades has contributed to the decline in parliamentarianism.

According to Andreas Khol, between 1994 and 2007 the chancellor controlled the agenda for the Council of Ministers, and there was a notable tendency to sideline important proposals of the junior coalition partner. The political parties may submit their proposals on the Thursdays before meetings. The political parties then send their amendments and comments by Monday, to be reviewed and discussed on Monday morning. This contributes to the formulation of the agenda of the meeting of the Council of Ministers later that week (Khol 2006: 153, cited in Wineroither 2009: 301). The Vranitzky governments followed this pattern closely, but the Viktor Klima and Wolfgang Schüssel governments institutionalised a wide range of about 12 policy coalition committees that included

Patterns of government in democracies 171

the presidents of the parliamentary groups of the two parties who also participated in the top-level coordination meetings. If there were still problems, a break-
fast meeting between the chancellor and vice-chancellor would take place on the
Friday before the Council of Ministers met (Wineroither 2009: 299).

As Wineroither asserts, it seems that Chancellor Wolfgang Schüssel was a
rather hands-off *primus inter pares* who pursued a collegial and cooperative
leadership style. He was extremely supportive of all ministers and tended to
avoid inner Cabinets consisting of only the grandees of the two parties (Wineroither 2009: 295).

Although it was highly controversial, the ÖVP–FPÖ coalition government
clearly contributed to the decline in social partnership as a power structure; it
also dismantled parts of the patronage and *Proporzdemokratie* regime of the two
large parties. At the same time, there was a tendency to replace the old system
with more FPÖ-friendly appointments (Karlhofer 2006).

Some FPÖ ministers had difficulties in establishing themselves due to an
allegedly antagonistic ministerial environment. Many civil servants in the ministries of Social Affairs and Infrastructure had been hired by Social Democratic
governments, and therefore FPÖ ministers (such as Infrastructure Minister
Monika Forstinger (2000–2002)) tried to bypass them with political advisers.
These two ministries were characterised by a high level of ministerial instability.
Acccording to Zellhofer, the Schüssel government spent between €40 and €60
million on political advisers, reportedly a record sum at that point (Wineroither
2009: 283, 304–305; Zellhofer 2005: 107, 111–113). After 2007, the old system
of grand coalitions was restored; thus, the role of coalition governance in maintaining strong party discipline in the decision-making process has been
reinforced.

At the centre of the Belgian system of Cabinet governance is the Core Cabinet
(*Kerncabinet*) consisting of the party leaders, usually the prime minister and the
vice-prime ministers from the various parties. This Core Cabinet meets quite
often, sometimes more than once a week, and takes decisions on conflictual
issues that are later ratified by the full Cabinet (De Winter and Dumont 2005:
962). Informal regular party meetings ensure that there is strong party discipline
so that the coalition agreement can be transposed into legislation. Until 1992
there were Cabinet committees, but major reforms led to their elimination (De
Winter and Dumont 2005: 962). In this sense, the role of the *Kerncabinet* in
dealing with conflictual issues gained importance. The members of the government belonging to the same party hold preparatory meetings one day before
Cabinet meetings (Moury 2013: 59). However, quite considerable preparations
are necessary before the *Kerncabinet* meets. A very important structure is the
Intercabinet Workgroup in which staff members from the different ministerial
Cabinets within government meet and achieve consensus of over 95 to 99 per
cent on all issues; this is followed by a meeting of Cabinet chiefs one day before
the Council of Ministers to sort out any difficult issues. There is a more or less
high level of isomorphism in terms of the processes at central and regional levels
(Interviews B). According to Catherine Moury, the Socialist members of the

172 Patterns of government in democracies

Cabinet are more disciplined and obedient in relation to party orders, whereas the Liberals tend to be more autonomous; the Christian Democrats and Greens fall somewhere in between (Moury 2013: 61–62).

In Parliament, the government parties tend to endorse the positions of the parties. Members of Parliament belonging to a government party generally do not amend legislation; the Greens and Christian Democrats may amend some of the bills, but this is regarded as almost an act of disloyalty (Moury 2013: 62). According to Catherine Moury, the Jean Luc Dehaene I (1991–1995) and the Guy Verhofstadt I (1999–2003) coalition governments achieved a relatively high level of transposition of the coalition agreement into legislation: Dehaene I transposed 78.2 per cent of pledges into Cabinet decisions, but Verhofstadt I was not far behind, with 76.8 per cent. This shows that Cabinet governance is geared towards the disciplined implementation of the coalition agreement (Moury 2013: 66). Additional new issues outside the coalition agreement are usually not domestic in nature, but are generally related to European and international policy issues; this dimension has the strongest impact on coalition governance (Moury 2013: 67). However, it should be emphasised that apart from the more Eurosceptic *Vlaamse Belang*, Belgian mainstream parties are strongly pro-European and internationalist, clearly facilitating decision-making in this area.

Cabinet governance in the Netherlands and Luxembourg is not very different from that in Belgium. However, in terms of the level of decision-making complexity, the Netherlands is closest to the Belgian pattern. At the core of Cabinet governance is the inner Cabinet consisting of the party leaders represented in the coalition, which is known as an informal institution (Timmermans and Andeweg 2000: 383). This is the most important body for conflict resolution. However, the standing orders of the Cabinet also foresee Cabinet committees that are organised by the prime minister's office. Up until 2000 it seems that these Cabinet committees met irregularly, but they have gained significance in the new millennium and now convene weekly on the eve of the Cabinet meeting. Some Cabinet committees are more important, requiring the inclusion of various departments. This is the case for the socio-economic policy committee, which includes the prime minister and the ministers of finance, social affairs and the economy. Moreover, the directors-general of the respective departments take part in the meetings (Timmermans and Andeweg 2000: 381; Moury 2013: 78). An important role is played by the subcouncils of civil servants and directors-general who discuss and decide on many difficult issues (Moury 2013: 80). According to Catherine Moury, there are six arenas in which a mutual veto can be activated if parties are unhappy: Parliament, followed by the Cabinet, the Cabinet committees, the coalition committee, the inter-party meetings and the budgetary process. The coalition committee consists of the prime minister, his or her deputy, the other party leaders in government and the parliamentary leaders; this body is central to the coalition governance as a whole (Moury 2013: 79–80). According to Moury, who used the Lubbers III (1989–1994) and Kok II (1998–2002) coalition governments as case studies, about 70 per cent of the coalition agreement pledges were transposed into legislation (Moury 2013: 86).

Patterns of government in democracies 173

European and international issues must be decided on outside the coalition agreement; however, similar to Belgium, the political elites are relatively pro-European and internationalist.

The small size of Luxembourg facilitates the cohesive functioning of coalition governments. There are no formal or informal structures coordinating the progress of the coalition agreement within the government. However, the prime minister and the vice-prime minister meet regularly to sort out any problems. Ministers or MPs in the coalition do not vote against the government, since this could significantly impact upon their careers. There are monthly meetings between the parliamentary groups of the coalition partners. These inter-parliamentary group meetings (*Inter-fraktionale Treffen*) include the prime minister, the vice-prime minister, the party leaders and the most active MPs. This is also the forum in which progress in implementing the coalition agreement is made (Dumont and De Winter 2000: 417–418; Schroen 2009b: 110). In the Juncker II (1999–2004) government, implementation of legislation cited in the coalition agreement reached a respectable 67 per cent (Dumont *et al.* 2015).

The deviant case, Switzerland, does not greatly differ from countries with a normal parliamentary democracy. It is expected that elected members of the Federal Council will cooperate in good faith and agree consensually in all decisions. This tradition came to the fore when the SVP leader Christoph Blocher, who was elected to the Federal Council in 2003, used his position of power to mobilise the population against decisions that he disagreed with through direct democracy instruments. It seems that some decisions had to be taken by a 6:1 vote, which went against the ingrained informal rule that votes should be unanimous (Vatter 2014: 225; Hempel 2010: 297–299). This behaviour was punished following the 2007 elections, when Blocher was unable to muster the number of votes required for nomination. This was only the fourth time that a federal councillor has not been re-elected (other cases occurred in 1854, 1872 and 2003 (Ruth Metzler)). Federal councillors may stay in office until they resign or retire, providing the government with strong continuity. In this sense, consensualism and consultation of all relevant groups are fairly important aspects of Swiss democracy (Hempel 2010: 290). Between 1991 and 1995, over 90 per cent of bills came from the government, and more recent figures (see Chapter 7) seem to suggest a similar pattern (Hempel 2010: 292).

Government longevity

The survival of the government over the full legislature period is enhanced in Switzerland due to the nature of its collegial structure; the Swiss are followed by Luxembourg and Austria in this regard. The Netherlands and Belgium represent the opposite extreme, which may be related to the complexity of government formation.

However, Belgium and the Netherlands have been improving in terms of the longevity of governments. The Ruud Lubbers and Wim Kok governments definitely contributed to improvements in terms of stability. The Jan Peter

174   *Patterns of government in democracies*

Table 6.5 Longevity of government

Period		Austria I:1945–1983 II:1983–2013	Belgium I:1945–1980 II:1980–2014	Luxembourg I:1945–1979 II:1979–2003	Netherlands I:1945–1981 II:1981–2013
First period 1945–1980s	**Number of governments**	11	23	11	16
	Average duration in years	2.4	1.4	3	2.1
Second period 1980s–2014	**Number of governments**	12	17	14	12
	Average Duration in years	2.6	1,7	2.4	2.4

Source: author's own calculations.

Notes
 I: First period
 II: Second period

Balkenende II and III administrations were relatively stable, although Balkenende I and IV were less stable. Balkenende I included the populist Pim Fortuyn List; without their leader, party members ended up fighting one another, and the government had to be abruptly terminated after one year. New elections led to the more stable Balkenende II government. Comparing government longevity between 1945 and 1982 and afterwards, the average increased from 2.1 to 2.4 years. Belgium also improved slightly, from 1.4 to 1.7 years' duration. In this context, one must highlight the stable governments of Jean-Luc Dehaene and Guy Verhofstadt. Following these administrations, instability has increased again; only the government of Elio di Rupio has been able to interrupt this pattern. However, one qualification must be made with regard to these figures. As discussed above, coalition negotiations are lengthy, and in some cases a short interim government is established to bridge the period – Verhofstadt III (2008) and Balkenende IV (2010), for example. This has happened quite often since 1945. In the case of the Netherlands, there has been an increase in instability at the beginning of the new millennium. While during the period between 1982 and 2002 the government lasted 893 (2.4 years), between 2002 and 2012 it decreased to 626 (1.7 years). Moreover, the lack of majorities in one or both houses has made governments more prone to instability (Thomassen *et al*. 2014: 192). Indeed, the veto activity in the *Eerste Kamer* has increased considerably since 1952 (Thomassen *et al*. 2014: 194).

Both Austria and Luxembourg have relatively stable governments, which is definitely related to their tendency towards grand coalitions. Austria has even increased its average longevity between the two periods, from 2.4 to 2.6 per cent. The Franz Vranitzky governments in the 1980s and 1990s played an important role in this regard. However, following Vranitzky's resignation, instability became more pronounced. Finally, Luxembourg is also a country with a high level of stability due to a cohesive political elite governing in grand coalitions. The longevity of leaders in power such as Jacques Santer and Jean-Claude Juncker provides a further explanation. Despite these factors, longevity has declined from 3 to 2.4 years on average. Overall, it may be argued that Belgium is the country with the highest level of instability, exhibiting similarities to the Italian pattern of government.

However, one characteristic common to all four countries is that despite the increasing instability in government formation, the political personnel has remained quite stable, and any less experienced politicians or parties in coalition governments are found in combination with a majority of more experienced individuals and organisations.

If we compare these figures from consensus democracies with those of traditionally majoritarian democracies, it is apparent that the former have much shorter governments. The major exception is France, due to the change of regime. British governments have had a much longer duration on average than any of these countries; however, the antagonistic competitive behaviour of the British system is not found in these consensus democracies. Thus, the higher instability notwithstanding, the constant cooperation between the political parties in the government and/or Parliament strengthens the policy continuity in these countries.

Conclusions: the art of sharing power

Government in consensus democracies is founded on the art of sharing power. As a result, coalition government is the most likely outcome in terms of the executive. The rules of the game are designed to achieve stable governments over time. Although Switzerland deviates from the other countries, the Swiss have also developed a more formalised process of coalition government. Due to the lack of single-party absolute majorities and aversion to unstable single-party majorities, coalition government is the only game in town. Instead of the 'winner-takes-all' mentality found in majoritarian democracies, a 'no-winners-or-losers' perspective dominates the negotiation process and governance of coalitions. This highly complex technology of coalition government is a specialty if not a science of advanced consensus democracies.

7 The institutional performance of parliaments in consensus democracies

Introduction: parliaments in consensus democracies

Parliamentarianism in all European countries has come under considerable pressure since the 1970s. The growing complexity of policy-making has further increased dependency on the information provided by governments. The European integration process has also been an important factor leading to major transformations of parliaments. Parliaments are an important arena for the integration of new political parties into the overall political culture of consensual politics. In this sense, the institutional performance of such inclusive legislatures is of the utmost importance.

The purpose of this chapter is to compare the performance of our five parliaments. The next section discusses the various parliaments in the context of their political systems. Subsequently, we delve deeper to analyse the performance of each of the legislatures before drawing some conclusions.

A contextualisation of parliamentarianism

All of our five parliaments still act in a political culture of consociationalism and consensus. However, they operate in different environments. Whereas the Swiss, Belgian and Austrian parliaments are embedded within a federal structure, the parliaments in the Netherlands and Luxembourg operate in unitary decentralised systems; yet there are major differences even among the legislatures in similar circumstances.

The structure of parliaments

Except for Luxembourg, all the countries in this study have bicameral parliaments. Switzerland is now characterised by symmetrical bicameralism, whereas Belgium, the Netherlands and Austria follow an asymmetrical model.

In Switzerland, the two chambers are balanced. The National Council (*Nationalrat*) consists of 200 MPs elected based on proportional representation in the 26 cantonal constituencies; the Council of States (*Ständerat*) includes two members from each canton and one from each half canton: a total of 46. The

Council of States is elected by a majoritarian system and thus plays a different role in the political system: it is effectively a reflection chamber populated by more senior, well-established politicians from the cantons. The approach is less conflictive than that of the National Council. Originally it was not directly elected, but appointed by the cantonal parliaments, and therefore the lower house felt that they were the most important chamber due to their legitimacy as the only directly elected chamber. However, since 1979, the Council of States is also directly elected, changing the balance between the two (Interview CH). Over recent decades, the parliamentary groups have been streamlined. In the past two legislatures (2011–2015 and the current term, 2015–2019), there have been only seven parliamentary groups. Some of the smaller party representations such as the Lega Ticinese and the Evangelical People's Party have joined the larger parliamentary groups with which they have some ideological affinity. Switzerland has a militia Parliament, or rather, a half-professional Parliament; this means that MPs receive no salary but only generous travel and per-diem expenses, paid as an agreed-upon lump sum. They are also granted CHF18,000 for an assistant, which seems like a very miserly salary, but MPs can use the money as they like, even for their own living costs or research. Officially, there are just four sessions of three weeks each per year. During these sessions, MPs come to Bern to deliberate on the legislative acts negotiated in the committees. Many committees work outside these four sessions.

The constitutional reforms undertaken starting in the 1970s have changed the nature of the Belgian national Parliament. Although it is still a bicameral Parliament, it is no longer symmetrical (as it was until 1995). The Senate has become the chamber of representation for the federalised units. At first, the body was partially elected, partially nominated by the federalised units; however, following the sixth state reform it became a non-elected chamber. Senators are nominated according to the strength of parties in the most recent election in each federalised unit (see below). As a result of these reforms, the Chamber of Representatives (*la chambre des representants*), the lower house, has increased in relevance. The number of MPs in the lower house was reduced from 212 to 150 in 1995, and now there are only 60 nominated and co-opted senators in the upper house.

In the case of Belgium there are six main party families, three of which are core to the Belgian party system: the Christian Democrats, the Social Democrats and the Liberals. The other three families, the Greens, the regionalists and the extreme right-wing parties, emerged in the 1980s and may be regarded as new parties (see Table 7.2). The complexity of Belgium is exacerbated by the fact that there are two party systems with the same party families in Flanders and Wallonia, and thus ten parties are regularly represented in Parliament. As in Switzerland, the Flemish party system is being challenged by a populist right-wing party, in this case the *Vlaams Belang* ('Flemish Interest', VB). There is a general institutional boycott of cooperation with the VB, also called a *cordon sanitaire*, due to its xenophobic discourse against the Muslim population and active endorsement of Flemish independence. An additional party

Table 7.1 Parliamentary groups in Swiss Parliament in 49th legislature period (2011–2015) and 50th legislature period (2015–)

| | 49th legislature period (2011–2015) | | | 50th legislature period (2015–) | | |
| | National council | | Council of states | National council | | Council of states |
	%	Seats	Seats	%	Seats	Seats
SVP	26.6	56	6	29.4	68	6
Geneva Citizens' Movement	0.4			0.3		
Lega dei Ticinesi	0.8			1.0		
SPS	18.7	46	11	18.8	43	12
FDP	15.1	30	11	16.4	32	13
CVP	12.3	31	13	11.6	30	13
EVP	2.0			1.9		
Christian–Social Party Obwalden	0.4			0.4		
Greens	8.4	15	2	7.1	13	1
Green liberals	5.4	12	2	4.6	7	0
BDP	5.4	9	1	4.1	7	1
Without affiliation		1	0		0	0
TOTAL		**200**	**46**		**200**	**46**

Source: author's compilation, based on Parliament of Switzerland (2016a) website.

Performance of parliaments in democracies   179

Table 7.2 Parliamentary groups in the Belgian House of Representatives in 2014

Parliamentary group	Ideological tendency	Chamber of Representatives		Senate*
		%	Seats	Seats
N-VA	Flemish Independents	20.3	33	12
PS	Francophone Socialists	11.7	23	9
MR	Francophone Liberals	9.6	20	9
CD&V	Flemish Christian Democrats	11.6	18	8
Open VLD	Flemish Liberals	9.8	14	5
SP.A	Flemish Socialists	8.8	13	5
GROEN	Flemish Greens	5.3		
ECOLO	Francophone Greens	3.3	12	6
CDH	Francophone Christian Democrats	5	9	4
VB	Far-right Flemish Independents	3.7	3	2
PTB	Communists	3.7	2	0
FDF	Francophone interests (Brussels)	1.8	2	0
PP	Conservative Liberals	1.5	1	0
			150	60

Source: author's compilation.

family is the regionalists, a group with roots in the Flemish *Volksunie* and the *Rassemblement Wallon* that were established in the 1950s and 1960s. More recently, in 2001, the regionalist Flemish party N-VA emerged, becoming a major force after the 2010 elections. Like the VB, they advocate independence for Flanders.

The Dutch Parliament consists of two houses: the *Eerste Kammer* (upper house, also known as the Senate) and the *Tweede Kamer* (lower house). The Senate consists of 75 MPs elected at the same time as provincial elections by a proportional representation formula according to the results and populations in each province. The centre of power is in the *Tweede Kamer* of 150 MPs, also elected by proportional representation in one constituency (divided into 19 subconstituencies; see Chapter 5). The bicameral system in the Netherlands is asymmetrical, although the veto of the Senate is definitive. Consequently, the bills passed in the *Tweede Kamer* should accommodate any changes informally proposed by the upper house. Usually, there is a government majority in both houses; however, in recent years it has been difficult to achieve such a majority. The fragmentation of the vote and divergent results in legislative and provincial elections also lead to varying compositions in the two houses.

Similar to the Belgian case, the Dutch party system is dominated by three core party families: the Christian Democrats (CDA), the Social Democrats (PvdA) and the Liberals (VVD). Starting in the late 1960s, splinter parties have joined these core party families. The emergence of the more left-wing and radical Socialist Party (SP), the reform-friendly liberals of the D66 and the environmentally focused Green Left (*Groenlinks*) reflects new social movements and

180   *Performance of parliaments in democracies*

represents a challenge to the traditional parties. In addition, the Calvinist-confessional Christian Union (CU) and the Reformed Political Party (SGP) are two small groups that have survived the erosion of religious–political cleavages. The volatility of the electorate remains a major issue impacting upon instability in the party system. The rise of the populist Party of Freedom (PVV) led by the charismatic Geert Wilders, with its xenophobic anti-Islam and anti-EU rhetoric, has become highly problematic for Parliament. However, the country's political culture based on consultation, consensus and compromise will doubtless be an important factor in reducing the appeal of populism over time (Pennings 2005) (see Table 7.3).

The Austrian Parliament is also bicameral, consisting of an upper house, the Federal Council (*Bundesrat*), and a lower house, the National Council (*Nationalrat*). The centre of power is the lower house; as in the other countries, the Federal Council serves as a chamber of reflection. The 183 members of the lower house are elected by proportional representation, whereas the 61 members of the upper house are nominated by the provincial parliaments (*Landtage*) following elections in each respective province according to the strength of the political parties. The allocation of seats to each province is based on population.

The Austrian Parliament is characterised by an asymmetrical bicameralism. The dominance of the lower house becomes more problematic when there are

Table 7.3 Parliamentary groups in the lower house (*Tweede Kamer*) and upper house (*Eerste Kamer*), 2015

		Tweede Kamer *(lower house)*		Eerste Kamer *(Senate)**
		%	Seats	Seats
VVD	Liberals	26.5	41	13
PvdA	Social Democrats	24.7	38	8
PVV	Far right	10.1	15	9
SP	Radical left	9.6	15	9
CDA	Christian Democrats	8.5	13	12
D66	Reform Liberals	8	12	10
CU	Christians	3.1	5	3
Groenlinks	Greens	2.3	4	4
SGP	Reformed Christians	2.1	3	2
50+	Pensioners	1.9	2	2
PvdD	Animal and Nature Welfare	1.9	2	2
Independent	Independents	–	–	1
			150	75

Sources: parties and elections in Europe (2016); websites of the Tweede Kamer and Eerste Kamer.

Note

* Following the provincial elections of March 2015.

Performance of parliaments in democracies 181

grand coalitions. During such periods, it is very difficult for the upper house to fulfil a checks-and-balances function (see below).

The Austrian party system has been undergoing major changes. Today, it is essentially a three-party system. The Social Democrats (SPÖ) have roots in the strong Austrian labour movement and close ties to the trade union tradition. In contrast, the Austrian People's Party (ÖVP) represents the bourgeois *Lager*, including farmers and the old middle classes. The Liberals also have a long tradition dating from the nineteenth century, but the post-1945 Freedom Party (FPÖ) consisted of at least of two main groups. One contained elements of what Austrians call the national German (*national deutscher*) *Lager*, a mindset that was influential in the nineteenth century, and on the other hand traditional liberals. The FPÖ emerged as a right-wing populist party in 1986, and, since then, it has sought to challenge the established consensus democracy. Traditional and new liberals unite under the banner of New Austria (*Neues Österreich*-NEOS), which, together with the Liberal Forum, emerged as a new pro-European liberal party in 2013. The Greens-Green Alternative (GA), established in the 1980s, has become an important small party in the political system. In 2013, the Austro-Canadian billionaire Frank Stronach founded a business-friendly party called Team Stronach, which focused on reducing the role of the state in the economy and enhancing freedom within the democratic setting. One criticism of the opposition parties is that due to the grand coalition government structure, parliamentarianism often involves only the rubber-stamping (*durchwinken*) of decisions taken in the executive branch or in the informal social partnership (Interviews A; see also Table 7.4).

In contrast to the other four consensus democracies, Luxembourg's Parliament is unicameral. The Chamber of Deputies (*Chambre des Députés*) consists of 60 members elected by a proportional system that allows voters to express

Table 7.4 Parliamentary groups in Lower (*Nationalrat*) and Upper (*Bundesrat*) Chambers in legislature period, 2016

Parliamentary groups	Ideological tendency	Nationalrat		Bundesrat*
		%	Seats	Seats
SPÖ	Social Democratic	26.8	52	22
ÖVP	Christian Democratic	24	47	20
FPÖ	New Right	20.5	40	13
Greens	Greens	12.4	24	4
Team Frank Stronach	Economic Liberalism	5.7	11	1
NEOS	Liberalism	5	9	0
Independent		0	0	1
		94.4	183	61

Sources: author's compilation based on Parties and elections in Europe (2016); Parliament of Austria (2016a, b).

Note
* changes composition according to regional elections in each *Bundesland*, stand of May 2016.

182   *Performance of parliaments in democracies*

their preferences (also across parties) through panachage (see Chapter 5). Although there is no upper chamber, the Council of State (*conseil d'état*), the advisory body of the government, also works indirectly for Parliament by evaluating the constitutionality of laws. In this sense, it serves as an informal second chamber.

In the previous chapter on government in consensus democracies, we saw that Luxembourg shares many similarities with Austria. In Luxembourg, the grand coalition between the Christian Democrats (CSV) and the Socialists (LSAP) has dominated parliamentarism since 1945. At times, the liberals (DP) have come to power in a coalition with the CSV or the LSAP. The CSV's longevity in power and the growing number of scandals resulted in an alternative coalition among the DP, the LSAP and, for the first time, the Greens (*Dei Gréng*) following the 2013 general elections. The conservative Alternative Democratic Reform (ADR) and the Left Party (*Dei Lénk*) are thus far the only parties that have not been integrated into the coalition government game. A parliamentary group consists of at least five MPs; however, the standing orders also allow smaller groups (e.g. the ADR and the Left Party) to form so-called 'politically sensitive groupings' (see Table 7.5).

The upper chamber: a chamber of reflection

In Switzerland, the upper house, the Council of States (*Ständerat*), represents the 20 cantons and six half cantons. The two representatives of each canton and one representative of each half canton are elected by a simple majority system and serve as a counterweight to the 200-strong National Council (*Nationalrat*), which is directly elected by proportional representation. Switzerland is the only country in our study that has a symmetrical bicameral system. Bills can be initiated by either house; government bills may be allocated to one chamber or the other according to topic. This allocation is determined by the speakers of both houses, although sometimes it is accomplished by a simple raffle system (Interview CH).

Table 7.5 Parliamentary groups in Luxembourg Chamber of Deputies in the legislature period since 2013

Parliamentary group	Ideological tendency	%	Seats
CSV	Christian Democrats	33.7	23
LSAP	Social Democrats	20.3	13
DP	Liberals	18.3	13
Greens	Ecology	10.1	6
Politically sensitive groupings			
ADR	National Conservatives	6.6	3
The Left	Radical Left	4.9	2
		93.9	60

Sources: author's compilation based on website Parties and Elections in Europe (2016) and Chambre des Deputés (2016a).

Performance of parliaments in democracies 183

In Switzerland, the central government has gained more powers over time because of the complexity of modern life; in contrast, the Belgian case after 1993 exemplifies the devolution of powers to the subnational units. This also reflects the difficult formula required to accommodate all the different subunits in the upper house, the Senate. Reforming the Belgian Senate has been a difficult undertaking. Its role has been watered down in recent decades through various state reforms. Following the sixth state reform in 2014, the Senate composition has been considerably simplified, and members are no longer elected.

Today, the Senate consists primarily of representatives of the country's federated units whose interests it protects. The chamber includes two kinds of senators:

1 Senators appointed by the federated assemblies in the communities and regions according to the share of the vote in the most recent elections; of these 50 senators there are 29 representatives of the Flemish Parliament, eight representatives of the Walloon Parliament, ten representatives of the French community Parliament, two representatives of the French linguistic group in Brussels' regional Parliament and one representative of the German-speaking Parliament.
2 Ten senators co-opted by the respective language groups in the Senate: six Flemish senators and four Francophone senators (Senat de Belgique 2016a).

The children of the King no longer sit in the Senate, as this category was abolished.

This type of institution naturally constrains national parliamentarianism in both Belgium and Switzerland. The primary difference between these two countries is that in the case of Switzerland, the centre has gained power over time, although the cantons and half cantons continue to be relatively autonomous, whereas in Belgium, the national executive has lost power to the subnational units in an attempt to accommodate the tensions resulting from the linguistic–ethnic conflict. For example, starting in 2007, Belgium was overwhelmed by a major crisis of institutional reordering that triggered the sixth state reform since the 1970s (see Chapter 3; Matagne *et al.* 2014: 7), in which the design of the Senate became an important issue. Flemish parties such as the N-VA and the VB wanted the Senate to be abolished, whereas the Walloon parties wanted to keep it. The ultimate compromise was a Senate with severely limited powers that holds plenary sessions only eight times a year. The asymmetry of the Belgian system of bicameralism thereby increased in favour of the elected Chamber of Representatives, which now oversees an enhanced second reading procedure (Goossens and Cannoot 2015: 38–41).

Following the sixth state reform, which came into force at the beginning of 2014, the Belgian Chamber of Representatives has 11 standing committees, whereas the Senate has only three (institutional, community and regional affairs). However, there are three additional committees formed jointly between the two chambers: the joint committee on EU affairs, which includes a delegation of the

184 *Performance of parliaments in democracies*

European Parliament, the joint committee on the monitoring of legislation and the concertation committee. Both chambers are committed to a process of concertation through the committee of concertation; in addition, the Senate can issue recommendations on the resolution of a particular question, but these are not binding. The Senate also has the power of reconciliation among the legislatures of the federal state. Overall, the Belgian Senate may be characterised as a chamber of reflection on legislation with extremely limited powers; most of the actual work takes place in the lower house. Notably, it is an important integrative element between the subnational and federal levels. Constitutionally, it operates at the same level as the Chamber of Representatives but in reality it has lost considerable power. There have even been calls for the complete elimination of the Senate by Flemish parties such as the New Flemish Alliance (N-VA). Most of the issues related to the regions and communities are addressed by the subnational assemblies. A further confusing aspect is the fact that the new Senate represents the federated units in the federal system, although, according to Article 42 of the constitution, senators should represent the entire country (Goossens and Cannoot 2015: 38–41).

Both Austria and the Netherlands are situated at the other end of the spectrum. Although Austria is a federal state with nine *Bundesländer*, Vienna as the centre of the national administration has always shown a tendency towards concentration; as a result, Austrian federalism may be described as 'executive federalism'. Decision-making processes are concentrated at the national level, with implementation delegated to various subnational executives and legislatures (Pelinka and Rosenberger 2003: 223–224). The provincial parliaments (*Landtage*) of the *Bundesländer* nominate a total of 61 representatives to the upper house based on the respective populations. The subnational delegation is appointed according to the results of the most recent regional elections. Thus, the composition of the chamber is always changing due to elections for regional parliaments. Upper chamber members also sit in the respective provincial parliaments. Many of them are part-time politicians working in their respective professions.

One interviewee asserted that the *Bundesrat* is rather a 'chamber without teeth' (*zahnloser Bundesrat*). In Germany the *Bundesrat* consists of representatives of the regional governments (*Länderregierungen*), but in Austria these representatives come from the regional parliaments (*Landtage*). An additional difference is that in the German case the seating order in the chamber is based on the *Länder* delegations, whereas in Austria representatives are grouped by political party. This further reduces the influence of the interests of the Austrian *Bundesländer* in relation to the federal government. In reality, the upper chamber just confirms what was agreed in the lower house. The second chamber of Parliament is much weaker than the first, making Austria a case of asymmetrical bicameralism (Interview A).

Both the Netherlands and Luxembourg are unitary states, but they are extremely decentralised. This is especially true in the Dutch case, as the size of Luxembourg does not necessitate a high degree of decentralisation. Consequently the latter country has no second chamber, but merely a unicameral

Parliament. The Netherlands consists of 12 provinces whose provincial assemblies are elected every four years, and based on these electoral results the political parties appoint 75 members to the upper house (*Eerste Kamer*, the Senate). There is a formula for the allocation of seats to each party, and there is preferential voting; however, in reality the ranking of the party list dominates the election process. Senate positions are part-time, and senators are poorly paid and not supplied with offices or human and material resources. In general, they are people with established careers who have been active in politics and their respective political parties for a long time. The influence of the parties results in the over-representation or under-representation of certain provinces in relation to one another (Interviews NL). After the 2015 provincial elections North and South Holland and Utrecht are significantly over-represented, whereas North Brabant, Overijssel and Groningen are under-represented. This does not matter very much, because senators do not represent their constituencies but the country as a whole. It is the party that decides which kinds of constituencies with which MPs should keep a strong link: the larger the party, the better they can accommodate this representative task (Interview NL).

The institutional performance of parliaments

There are necessarily limits to any comparative study of parliamentary performance. The differences in parliamentary cultures and especially the position of parliaments in their respective political systems make comparisons difficult. However, there is some merit in attempting to determine how functions common to all parliaments are performed by each of the legislatures of these consensus democracies. To this end, we will concentrate on five specific indicators of modern European parliamentarianism. The first aspect is the time spent in plenary sessions, which may provide a general idea of how important Parliament is in the political system. The second indicator is the role of committees in the parliamentary system: are we dealing with a '*Redeparlament*' (debate Parliament) or an '*Arbeitsparlament*' (working Parliament)? This naturally leads to questions about the human and financial resources that are allocated to the respective parliaments. The third factor is the role of Parliament in the legislative process. The increasing prevalence of government legislative proposals is an important aspect in this regard. When possible, the potential for influence or even legislative initiative are discussed in this context. The fourth aspect involves how successful the instruments of parliamentary control have been in these parliaments. Finally, we address the growing importance of the Europeanisation of national parliaments and how the European supranational level is constraining nationally inspired legislation, as a large proportion of current legislation is merely the transposition of EU laws.

186   *Performance of parliaments in democracies*

Parliamentary workload

As noted above, four of the national parliaments have two chambers, but the distribution of legislative power is different in each case. Only Switzerland has a symmetrical chamber structure, whereas Austria, Belgium and the Netherlands have asymmetrical chambers. In order to achieve a comparative figure, we concentrated on the hours worked in each Parliament per legislature period (four years for Austria, Netherlands and Switzerland, and five years for Belgium and Luxembourg) and per legislative session (each year of the legislature period).

In the Swiss case, the two chambers must approve legislative initiatives by the government. Although both chambers are equal in theory, they play different roles: the *Nationalrat* is an important arena of debate and conflict resolution, while the *Ständerat* serves as a reflection chamber. In addition to the fact that the lower house has more members, its levels of institutionalisation and professionalisation are higher. One indicator of the difference between the two chambers is the amount of time spent in plenary sessions: MPs in the National Council (*Nationalrat*) spend more time in session than those in the Council of States (*Ständerat*). However, there has been a definite increase in activity in the Council of States since the turn of the millennium. Up until 1991, the time spent by councillors in the upper house on parliamentary work was about half of that of the lower house; this ratio is now a stable 60 per cent. On average, between 1971 and 2011, MPs in the lower house spent 1171 hours over 223 days in Parliament per legislature, whereas the upper house spent only 600 hours over the same number of days, and in terms of legislative session 56 days and 293 hours in the National Council and about 150 hours in the Council of States, respectively. Thus, the workload of the Council of States is about half (51%) that of the National Council (calculations based on a database from Parliament of Switzerland 2016a). The two chambers are ostensibly of equal importance, and they have almost the same number of committees: 12 in the lower house and 11 in the upper house in 2016. Nine of these committees are related to the government's policy areas. Although the Swiss Parliament meets only four times a year for three weeks at a time, it may be regarded as an *Arbeitsparlament* (Lüthi 2003: 136; 2014: 174, 178–179).

In Belgium, the increasing importance of the federated subnational parliaments has resulted in the hollowing-out of the federal level. Although the Chamber of Representatives (lower house) gained a certain degree of power through the introduction of the constructive motion of censure and a third reading procedure, there is some disdain of the national Parliament among political parties from the Flemish region; consequently, the new federal architecture has lost influence. In terms of the division of labour, a picture similar to Switzerland emerges in the Belgian case. Between 1988 and 2014, the Chamber of Representatives spent 201 days and 831 hours working in plenary sessions per legislature period, whereas the Senate spent only 150 days and 645 hours, representing just 73.5 per cent of the workload of the lower house. Per legislative session, these figures are 43/190 and 33/104, respectively (Chambre des Représentants de Belgique 2016; Senat de Belgique 2015).

Performance of parliaments in democracies 187

In Austria, the *Bundesrat* has a suspensive veto, in contrast to the Netherlands, where the veto of the *Eerste Kamer* is final. In the case of Austria, the *Nationalrat* can overcome the suspensive veto of the *Bundesrat* by a simple majority if more than half of its MPs are present (Austrian constitution, Art. 42.4). However, it seems that informal discussions and other means have precluded any such objections on the part of the *Bundesrat* since 1994. The last legislature in which there was significant conflict between the two houses was during the coalition government of the SPÖ and the FPÖ between 1983 and 1986. During this period there were 47 objections to legislative proposals, of which 44 were upheld by the lower house (Schefbeck 2006: 154). If the government parties have a majority in the upper house there are usually no objections to legislation; however, if there is a shift in the majority towards the opposition parties due to regional elections in a particular *Bundesland*, more conflict may result. The ÖVP–FPÖ coalition government (2002–2006) saw 24 objections to legislation in the upper chamber, reflecting the clashes between the government and opposition parties. The opposition parties held a majority in the *Bundesrat* following the regional elections in Styria in 2005, increasing the pressure on the government parties (Parliament of Austria 2016a: 17). The *Bundesrat* has an absolute veto right on bills related to constitutional law and those that may considerably alter the competences of the *Bundesländer* (Parliament of Austria 2016a: 17–18).

This means that the *Nationalrat* effectively dominates the legislative process. There are 28 standing committees in the lower house and only 19 in the upper house, reflecting this power imbalance. In addition, the meetings of the upper house are relatively short due to the fact that most of the decision-making and deliberation takes place in the lower house (Schefbeck 2006: 153). An overview of the time spent in plenary sessions in the *Nationalrat* and the *Bundesrat* clearly demonstrates the dominance of the lower house. In quantitative terms, in comparison to Switzerland, the Austrian Parliament has a lesser workload; the upper house in particular is not very busy. In the past three legislature periods (2002–2013), the average number of plenary sessions in the *Bundesrat* was slightly more than a quarter of those in the *Nationalrat*. Between 2002 and 2015, MPs in the National Council worked 297 hours per legislative session on average, whereas members of the Federal Council worked about 90 hours, corresponding to about 30 per cent (author's compilation based on data from several reports posted on Parliament of Austria 2016c). This also has to do with the fact that the appointed members in the upper house additionally sit in their respective *Landtage* and are therefore only part-time MPs.

The Dutch Parliament gives final veto rights to the Senate, also known as the *Eerste Kamer*. The veto right is used sparingly, reflecting the Dutch parliamentary culture of consensual politics. In general, informal signs at the committee stage in the Senate lead to the withdrawal of the unacceptable proposed legislation for reconsideration by the *Tweede Kamer*, the lower house, which adjusts the bill according to the changes indicated by the Senate committee. The constitution also demands that the government and Parliament work together in the legislative process. This process starts in the Council of State, which reviews

188   *Performance of parliaments in democracies*

legislative proposals before they are sent to the *Tweede Kamer*. This double-check of legislative proposals before they reach the parliamentary agenda increases the quality of legislation. In this context, the position of the *Tweede Kamer* is more advantageous than that of the *Eerste Kamer*: the lower house, which is more stable in terms of composition, is the centre of decision-making, whereas the *Eerste Kamer* is more of a deliberative chamber (Lepszy and Wilp 2009). A brief glance at the number of plenary sessions in the two houses reveals the imbalance between the *Tweede Kamer* and the *Eerste Kamer*. On average, between 2000 and 2013, the *Tweede Kamer* had 111 meetings over the course of 1034 hours during a legislative session. In contrast, the Senate held about 38 meetings, but spent just 33.9 hours on legislative affairs (2014: 3; *Eerste Kamer* 2015). This lopsidedness is reinforced by considerable differences in resource allocation. Senators have no individual research assistants or any associated funding. The part-time nature of Senate positions also results in a more relaxed atmosphere in terms of the relationships among its members: they all are well established in their political and professional careers and can therefore adopt a more abstract distanced view towards legislation. Among some MPs, it is a matter of pride that their buildings and traditions are much older than the British Palace of Westminster, which was rebuilt following a fire in the nineteenth century (Interview NL). The Dutch Parliament works more hours than the Austrian, Belgian, Luxembourg and Swiss parliaments – on average, over 1000 hours per year in the lower house.

One Dutch interviewee explained the normal workload throughout the four-year legislature:

> If you have to divide in percentage of time spent basically on each task, I would say it is hard to say because in a four-year term each year has its own dynamics, the first year Parliament is relatively easy, because legislation is being made within the ministries, in order to execute the agreement on which we govern.
>
> The second year, that legislation comes to Parliament, first to the *Tweede Kamer*, and then to *Eerste Kamer* so that year we are extremely busy on passing legislation.
>
> The third year of such a term is more focused on implementing legislation, and therefore in a more controlling task of the Parliament to oversee if the implementation is done correctly.
>
> The fourth year is traditionally gearing up to next elections, so each year division between different types of work will be different.
>
> For instance, this previous year, this is the second year of this Parliament the focus was on passing legislation, I would say 60 per cent of my time was spent on committees, 20 per cent on plenary sessions, and 20 per cent on the rest of it, preparing, etc.
>
> (Interview NL)

Luxembourg's unicameral Parliament adheres closely to the Benelux model of legislative procedure, which assigns a relatively strong role to the Council of State,

Performance of parliaments in democracies 189

an advisory body for government policy and legislation. Due to the lack of a second deliberative chamber, Luxembourg basically uses the Council of State as an informal second chamber in which both government and parliamentary legislation is reviewed and commented on before being finally adopted and approved (see Chapter 6). Compared to other consensus democracies the workload is heavy, especially considering the small number of MPs. It should be noted that about two-thirds of MPs also work at the local level, a large number of them as mayors, which only increases the time pressures on them (see Chapter 8).

Luxembourg MPs work hard and must be specialists in a variety of fields. This is the case for government ministers as well (Schroen 2009b: 109). Between 1974 and 2013, Luxembourg MPs held 327 meetings and spent 1225 hours working per legislature session, amounting to about 65 meetings and 245 hours per legislative session (Chambre des Deputés 2013: 19).

Table 7.6 summarises the workload in plenary sessions for our five countries. The Netherlands emerges as the most industrious Parliament, followed by Switzerland and Luxembourg (especially taking into account their low levels of human and financial resources), whereas Austria and Belgium are underperforming, mainly due to the fact that their coalition governments have contributed to the erosion of parliamentarianism to a mere rubber-stamping exercise (Magnette 2004: 98–99; Interviews A).

Parliamentary committee work in consensus democracies

At the centre of the legislative process are the committees. The amount of time spent in committee is a good indicator of the nature of the Parliament. Specifically, we assume that parliaments whose members spend a great deal of time in committee may be regarded as working parliaments. It is also important to determine how much support is provided for individual MPs, committees and parliamentary groups. This section will attempt to analyse the importance of committee work for the various parliaments in consensus democracies.

In Switzerland, committee work is quite important. A study by Annina Jegher and Wolf Linder on the legislative process of 162 bills during the period 1995 to 1997 indicates that the committees for Foreign Policy and Economy and Taxation are the busiest groups in the Swiss National Council. Overall, Foreign Policy (20%), Economy and Taxation (21%) and Finance (9%) account for 50 per cent of all business. The committees for Public Buildings and Transport and Communication, in contrast, require less commitment from MPs (Jegher and Linder 1998: 38).

Table 7.6 Average time spent by MPs in plenary sessions per year, lower house

Austria	Belgium	Luxembourg	Netherlands	Switzerland
Time spent in hours in plenary sessions during a legislative period on average				
297	221	245	1034	292

Source: author's calculations based on activity reports of the five parliaments.

190   *Performance of parliaments in democracies*

The vast majority of bills are decided by unanimity in the committees, and this sets the tone for the rest of the legislative process (61 per cent by unanimous vote, 25 per cent close to unanimous for a total of 86 per cent). Only a minority of bills lead to disagreement (4 per cent disagreement, 10 per cent close to disagreement). The highest level of unanimity may be found in the committees for Foreign Policy and Environment, Planning and Energy. The lowest levels of unanimity are exhibited by the Finance Committee, the Economy and Taxation Committee and the Legal Affairs Committee (Jegher and Linder 1998: 41). Consensus is much higher in the Council of States (78 per cent by unanimous vote, 18 per cent close to unanimous vote for a total of 96 per cent); interestingly, the higher levels of disagreement are found in the same committees (Jegher and Linder 1998: 42). Following the national elections of 2003, stronger polarisation between the SVP and the other parties in the lower house may be observed. However, in the upper house the SVP has a small representation, and a more moderate approach tends to prevail. This leads to even greater cohesion among the parties represented in the Federal Council (Schwarz and Linder 2006: 17–19; see also Schwarz and Linder 2007; Interviews CH).

Although, for Lijphart, Switzerland has the strongest Parliament in relation to both the distribution of legislative power and executive–legislative relations, an excellent study by Heidi Z'Graggen and Wolf Linder on the level of professionalisation and institutionalisation concludes that the Swiss Parliament is one of the weakest in the OECD countries. This claim is borne out by the number of hours spent in committee work per MP. Z'Graggen and Linder note that despite the hard work of the Swiss MPs, they are the second weakest professionalised and institutionalised Parliament; only the Spanish Parliament is weaker. Remuneration for Swiss MPs is the lowest in the OECD, and they have the least support in terms of human and financial resources; even though they spend more time on legistative work than do MPs in Portugal and Belgium, the Swiss Parliament remains among the weakest in the developed world (Z'Graggen and Linder 2004: 18; see also Z'Graggen 2009).

These findings notwithstanding, Switzerland has a working Parliament, due more to the engagement of its members than to its working conditions. A reform of the system has been discussed for decades, but no major changes in regime have been undertaken. About one-third of MPs are new to the job, and the turnover rate is considerably higher in the upper house (Z'Graggen and Linder 2004: 36; Z'Graggen 2009). A standard complaint is that a large number of MPs are also presidents or chairmen of interest groups, raising questions about potential conflicts of interest, although this aspect of the Swiss system is sometimes even praised as positive for democracy. Committees are well resourced and, depending on the importance of the committee there are three to five research assistants and two to three logistics assistants. Moreover, pragmatically, committees can request experts from the close by ministries or universities. In the latter case, experts from outside Switzerland may also be allocated to committees, but this depends if it really fits the issues that are being raised. Switzerland being a small country tends to look for synergies in terms of human and financial resources

(Interviews CH). The major problem for Switzerland is really the growing importance of representatives of lobby groups or interest groups that are elected to the two chambers, influencing processes from within. This leads to a relatively asymmetrical relationship among MPs. One interviewee identified three groups: the militia parliamentarians, in the majority lawyers, enterpreneurs and some rich farmers; the part-time politicians who are mainly presidents of national interest groups or at least employed by it; and third, the professional politicians that are dedicated full-time to the office. The part-time politicians are probably the ones that may considerably damage the reputation of the Swiss Parliament, due to their conflict of interest. Allegedly, the reform of the pensions bill has been a major target for such part-time politicians. There is a real danger that the Swiss Parliament could become a chamber of corporatist interests, if the transparency threshold is not upgraded considerably (*Schweiz am Sonntag*, 23 May 2015; Angeli 2016; Interviews CH).

In the Netherlands, the constitutional framework makes it imperative for the government and Parliament to cooperate in the creation of legislation. The committee stage is the most important part of the process, and it is here that the opposition can have the most success in changes and amendments to bills, although this is constrained by the power of the *Eerste Kamer* to reject legislation. Parliament is also constrained by pre-parliamentary informal negotiations that structure the legislative process before it even begins. According to Kenneth Gladdish, there has been a substantial increase in amendments and requests for changes since the late 1980s (Gladdish 1991: 115). Rudy Andeweg and Galen Irwin find that there is a more conflictive approach between government and Parliament at the committee stage, but that in general terms the vast majority of MPs regard the relationship as cooperative. The amendments introduced by the opposition are considered by the incumbent coalition government, and a significant proportion is ultimately added to bills. In the end, about half of the bills take into consideration amendments by the opposition parties and the parliamentary parties supporting the government. Consequently, over 90 per cent of government bills are also supported by the opposition parties before they are approved (Andeweg and Irwin 2014: 180–181). Similar processes of pre-parliamentary informal negotiation are also found in Switzerland, Austria, Luxembourg and Belgium. Negotiations start within the coalition governments before being extended to include the opposition parties.

It seems that there is a high degree of acceptance of governmental bills, with many even winning the support of opposition parties. The underlying reason for this cooperation is the highly developed dialogue culture in the Dutch Parliament. Legislation is discussed at length, as well as in informal roundtables, in order to ensure the highest level of consent. The results are bills with a considerable number of amendments. In 2013, none of the proposed bills was rejected in the *Tweede Kamer*. The low number of private bills is an interesting consequence of this constructive approach to legislation (Tweede Kamer 2014: 8).

Many amendments are not even submitted for consideration because they are unable to pass the standards of the Law Office (*Bureau wetgeving*, BW) or the

192 *Performance of parliaments in democracies*

Office for Research and Government Expenditure (*Bureau OnderzoekenRijksuit-gaven*, BOR), both of which are parts of the *Tweede Kamer*. In the official report for 2013, some criticism is expressed by the authors that many amendments are submitted at the last minute, at times immediately before the plenary sessions, preventing them from being properly assessed by the two scrutinising bodies (Tweede Kamer 2014: 9).

Nonetheless, the rise of the extreme right has taken away votes from the main parties, so that the upper house has become more fragmented and politicised due to the fact that the Rutte governments were unable to have an absolute majority in the upper house. Therefore, governments had to negotiate bills with all the parties to get them passed in the upper house, which has no right of amendment but absolute veto right. One interviewee explains the new situation due the fragmentation of both houses:

> One addition with the regard to the amendments, as the government knows that it is only the first hurdle now the lower house, it already takes opinions in [the upper] house, because [there] it has to pass the final hurdle and that means that nowadays, those amendments that are proposed in the lower house have their origin [there], because [there] for example our CU is a small party and has two votes, and the other party SGP have one vote, but these three votes are of imminent importance for the government majority, so that they give signals 'listen if you do not change [the bill], then you will have problems here'. So that you see it is amendments proposed by the lower house, but also amemdments proposed by the lower house inspired in the upper house. We are the chamber of the second thought, but sometimes we become the chamber of the first thought, that inspires the lower house. This is done in a quite open way and we see parties of the lower house negotiating with those parties in the upper house that they need for a majority. This makes them rather complex, because officially the upper house does not deal with the lower house, but in practice everybody sees you are proposing this, because you want a majority in the other side, in the upper house.
>
> (Interview NL)

The Austrian case showcases the influential input of committees in the transformation of bills. Subcommittees are used extensively to discuss details of certain bills. However, over time, subcommittees have become less important, as informal extra-parliamentary fora have been tasked with negotiating changes. A general phenomenon of acceleration of the legislative process may be observed, thanks to the bypassing of tedious subcommittees (Schefbeck 2006: 153). The negotiation of legislation at different stages of the process leads to relatively high levels of the unanimous approval of laws. However, this pattern of unanimity has been severely compromised over the past three decades, and therefore committees, subcommittees and especially informal fora are even more essential in achieving high levels of support for bills.

Performance of parliaments in democracies 193

Committees are also central to the Belgian Parliament. The role of the Senate as an equal chamber makes it imperative that legislation be negotiated before it goes through the parliamentary procedure. There are three procedures overall: the monocameral procedure, the compulsory bicameral procedure and the facultative bicameral procedure. For bicameral issues, the two chambers have a committee of concertation designed to achieve compromises on legislation. This means that some legislation may be adopted by the lower chamber. However, coalition governments are a major framing factor in the Belgian consensual style of politics. Strong party discipline among the government parties bound by the coalition agreement does not permit very much leeway in terms of developing autonomous initiatives. On the contrary, according to a major study conducted by Catherine Moury, Parliament has almost become a rubber stamp for the government. Amendments or initiatives by the parliamentary groups of the government parties are avoided. Among the political parties that have served in government, only the Christian Democrats and Greens have attempted to amend legislation; however, this was regarded by their peers as disloyal (Moury 2013: 62). According to Paul Magnette, partyocracy tends to bypass Parliament through informal package deals agreed upon in extra-parliamentary committees controlled by the main parties (Magnette 2004: 98–99). As a result, quantitative figures are rather misleading. Between 1999 and 2014, the average time spent by permanent committees on legislative work was 692 meetings over 171 days, comprising 1025 hours per legislative session. Committee work therefore represented 41 per cent of all parliamentary work (*Chambre des Représentants de Belgique* 2016). The figures compiled by Z'Graggen and Linder (2004: 50) indicate that the Belgian Chamber of Deputies had the fewest hours of committee work, but the data for the past 15 years seem to suggest that work in legislative committees has doubled.

As mentioned above, the small size of the Luxembourg Chamber of Deputies forces MPs to be specialists in several topics. This clearly represents a major constraint on the work of the Luxembourg Parliament. In 2012/2013 there were 636 committee meetings, although this figure also includes the conference of presidents and meetings of working groups (Chambre des Deputés 2013: 18). One should bear in mind that many MPs are also local councillors or even mayors, limiting their time available for legislative work.

In terms of human resources, there were 146 civil servants working for the Swiss Parliament in 2001, a figure that increased to 183 in 2007 (Lüthi 2003: 137; Parliament of Switzerland 2016a). On 1 January 2016, there were 311 staff (211 full-time employees in total) working for Parliament services. Just 32.2 per cent were full-time employees; the rest of the positions were part-time, with 15.4 per cent less than half-time (Parliament of Switzerland 2016b). A major study commissioned by the Swiss Parliament in 2001 determined that MPs were struggling in terms of obtaining independent scientific advice. The parliamentary administrative services are under-resourced in their task of supporting committee work (Krüger *et al.* 2001: 3–4). Several interviewees pointed out this deficit, noting that there are not enough resources to fund independent studies. However,

194 *Performance of parliaments in democracies*

parliamentary services can take advantage of the government's human and financial resources. Indeed, the government and Parliament are situated in close proximity, and the civil servants of the two core public administrations know one another well. In spite of all the criticisms, central parliamentary services have improved quite considerably in the past two decades (Interviews CH). However, even today, Swiss MPs have no personal offices and receive a lump sum of CHF18,000 (€16,500) for research work which may also be used for oneself as additional funding; remedying this deficit would represent a significant improvement. Parliamentary groups receive about CHF6.2 million (€5.7 million) funding from Parliament which allows them to hire a pool of experts; however, this is clearly an advantage for the larger parties but less so for the smaller ones. Based on the data provided on the website, on average an MP is able to earn between CHF100,000 to CHF150,000 (€92,000 to €138,000) if he or she attends all four sessions, and takes part in one or two committees. The more hard-working, the more funding one may be able to collect through the system of compensation payments. A young MP may also still be able to work in his normal job outside Parliament, but professionalisation leads to more responsibility and participation in more committees, leading to more funding (Interviews CH).

The Dutch *Tweede Kamer* has about 367.5 people working for the parliamentary groups and 615 civil servants supporting the work of the lower house, among them 222 part-time workers. Each MP is entitled to an office in Parliament and a personal assistant. Parliamentary groups are generously funded from Parliament's budget, allowing them to hire quite a considerable number of policy specialists, which is a great help to MPs. However, it seems that there is a high level of rotation among these policy advisers and research assistants, preventing access to a stable pool of expertise in Parliament (Interview NL). Due to a major savings programme, these numbers have remained relatively stable. The overall budget for 2016 was €136.25 million, of which 71.9 per cent was allocated for the whole support apparatus of MPs, and one-fifth directly to fund the parliamentary groups. It is intended to reduce this figure to €130.2 million by 2020 (Tweede Kamer 2015b). One Interviewee spoke of a continuing pressure to save money in the performance of their duties, which in the end weakens the possibility for parlamentarians to make proper checks on government (Interview NL).

In Belgium in 2009, there were 651 civil servants supporting the chamber of representatives plus additional personnel attached to the parliamentary groups. About 24 per cent of staff members were involved in legislative work. This group represented 42 per cent of all the high-ranking civil servants, as well as 73 per cent of the members of staff tasked with legislative duties (Chambre des Representants de Belgique 2016).

Instead of providing direct party subsidies, the Belgian model encourages generous support for MPs. In 2009, each recognised parliamentary group had the right to one secretary, 1.05 university research assistants per member of the parliamentary group, one secretary each for the offices of president, vice-president, quastors and the presidents of the permanent commissions, assistants for the president of the chamber and one administrative assistant per member of

Performance of parliaments in democracies 195

the chamber (Chambre des Representants de Belgique 2016). This is clearly a major outlet for party patronage. The research institutes of the political parties can use these positions for patronage and clientelism, similar to the use of ministerial cabinets in the government. The economic and financial crisis since 2008 led to drastic measures to considerably reduce the budget deficit and public debt, and the Belgian Parliament also had to do their part. As a result, there was no increase in personnel, and many benefits were cut in order to reduce the budget. It seems that these measures were successful, with a saving of €5 million in 2013/2014 (Chambre des Representants de Belgique 2016).

A similar system of support for MPs and parliamentary groups was also implemented in Luxembourg. In the legislative session of 2010/2011, €10.2 million (€170,000 per MP) and €2.4 million were allocated to individual MPs and to the parliamentary groups, respectively. This represents about 47 per cent of the annual parliamentary budget (Chambre des Deputés 2013: 3). Overall, the Chamber of Deputies employs 87 people, the majority of whom deal with protocol (19.5%) and committee work (17.2%; Chambre de Deputés 2016b).

In 2016, due to the renovation of its facilities, the budget of the Austrian Parliament increased from €165.56 million to €196.15 million. This budget also includes an increase of staff from 416 to 430. The additional staff will be primarily assigned to support committees and the IT area. Each MP is entitled to an assistant, and the parliamentary group also receives funding. For 2016, parliamentary groups (*parlamentarische Klubs*, combining MPs across the two houses) will receive a total subsidy of €22.6 million distributed to the political parties according to the share of the vote (Parliament of Austria 2015c). This funding is used to hire a considerable pool of experts, so-called political secretaries (*politische Sekretäre*). These are generally highly qualified experts but are also very close to the respective parties. Some of them may work only part-time, and be politicians in other contexts (e.g. the *Landtag* (provincial Parliament) of Vienna). One interviewee regards as a major deficit the lack of support of parliamentary services for creating templates for bills, obtaining legal reports on specific bills, or getting legislative-legal advice on laws. He mentioned the case of the bill on a reform of the law for a committee of enquiries which has strengthened the rights of the opposition in Parliament approved in 2014, which led to the unusual step of a holiday ban for in-house lawyers and jurists until after the law had been completed (Interview A).

Conflict and consensus in the legislative process

The above analysis shows that all five parliaments have both formal and informal structures designed to maximise cooperation between the government and Parliament. This combination of formal and informal structures is certainly an indication of a mature and strong parliamentarianism that keeps the interests of the population at heart. It also reinforces the cooperative consensual nature of the political system. The best way to determine this cooperative consensual politics is to analyse how the legislative process is undertaken in practice – in

196   *Performance of parliaments in democracies*

particular, whether the government imposes or negotiates legislative bills, as well as the success of bills coming from committees or members of the house.

As in most other countries, the Swiss government dominates the legislative process (Table 7.7). However, the government is challenged by a very active Parliament. According to an excellent study by Wolf Linder, 39.1 per cent of legislative initiatives are undertaken by the government, whereas 60 per cent are proposed by Parliament, mainly through motions (27.3%) or legislative initiatives (20.7%; Schwarz and Linder 2006: 27). Another finding of Linder's study is that the economy, finance and law dominate both the deliberations and the voting in the National Council. Together, these issues represent 40 per cent of all votes. In contrast, European Union-related issues only account for 2.5 per cent. This indicates that the budgetary process and other financial issues are central to the work in the National Council (Schwarz and Linder 2006: 29). One of the characteristics of the legislative process is that it is relatively consensual. The parties represented in the Federal Council may have different preferences, but there is a strong tendency to support legislative acts in Parliament consensually. The only parties that have voted outside this consensual framework thus far have been the Swiss People's Party and, to a lesser extent, the Social Democrats. A total of 67 per cent of all legislative acts presented by the SVP and 56.6 per cent of those presented by the Social Democrats are successful; this increases to 90.1 per cent in the case of the Christian Democrats and 81.4 per cent for the Liberals.

These differences notwithstanding, it may reasonably be argued that the institutional performance in the legislative process in Switzerland reflects a significant level of consensus. Even the SVP has a high rate of success. Naturally, most legislation is supported by coalitions of the parliamentary groups. It appears that the Christian Democratic parliamentary group is an important pivotal actor in sustaining this consensual style of politics. According to Linder, there are two kinds of coalitions, and both include the Christian Democrats. On the one hand, there is the right–centre coalition formation (CVP–FDP–SVP), which generally applies to voting on traditional issues such as the economy, finance, immigration policy and agriculture. On the other hand, there is the

Table 7.7 Adopted governmental and parliamentary bills in Switzerland, 2003 to 2015

	Government bills			*Private members' bills*			*Total of adopted bills*
	Submitted	*Adopted*	*%*	*Submitted*	*Adopted*	*%*	
47 (2003–2007)	569	425	74.6	373	61	16.4	486
48 (2007–2011)	602	529	87.8	502	69	13.8	598
49 (2011–2015)	599	490	81.8	374	21	5.6	511
50 (2015–2016)*	154	49	31.8	42	0	0	49

Source: information provided by Boris Burri, parliamentary services, via email on 7 June 2016.

Note
* Just first legislative period.

Performance of parliaments in democracies 197

left–centre coalition formation (CVP–Greens–SP), which is found more often for bills dealing with education, international politics and also European Union policy (Schwarz and Linder 2006: 52). Due to the fact that bills must be approved by both of the chambers, there are sometimes different versions that must be reconciled. For this purpose, the Swiss Parliament has a consensus committee (*Einigungsausschuss*), although this body is used sparingly. Since 1991, there have been about 17 meetings of this committee per legislature period on average: about four per legislative session. This figure has been relatively constant over the years, except in the 43rd legislature period (1991–1999), when there were seven such meetings (Parliament of Switzerland 2016a). It is regarded as rather negative if a compromise is not reached. Politicians are elected to find pragmatic solutions. As one interviewee put it, 'It is better to achieve a bad compromise than no compromise' (Interview CH).

Coalition government in Belgium is a serious business. Once the coalition agreement is established it becomes something resembling a bible, as discussed in Chapter 6. This has considerable repercussions for parliamentary work. The MPs of the coalition parties are severely constrained by party discipline, explaining the high success rate of government bills in the lower house. On average, over 93 per cent of government bills are adopted, many of them without any major amendments introduced by MPs of the coalition parties. Private bills, primarily a privilege of the opposition parties, have a very low rate of success. According to the figures in Table 7.8, this success rate has been declining since the turn of the millennium. Only rarely does the Senate discuss legislation adopted by the Chamber of Representatives. Exceptions mainly concern laws referring to the division of competences between the central and the subnational units, as well as European and international legislation that may substantially affect national law. Since 1995, legislation discussed in the Senate has represented an average of 6.2 per cent of all bills per legislature period (Chambre des Representants 2014: 30). This pattern is also reflected in the almost non-existent

Table 7.8 Success rate of government and private bills in Belgium Chamber of Representatives, 1991 to 2014

	Government bills			Private bills		
	Submitted	*Adopted*	*Percentage of adopted bills*	*Submitted*	*Adopted*	*Percentage of adopted bills*
1991–1995	384	338	88	1157	157	13.6
1995–1999	726	692	95.3	1297	195	15
1999–2003	742	671	90.4	1483	218	14.7
2003–2007	830	789	95.1	2048	169	8.3
2007–2010	366	337	91.8	1929	107	5.5
2010–2014	713	708	99.3	2421	233	9.6
Average	627	589	93.3	1723	180	10.4

Source: Chambre de Representants (2014: 30).

198 *Performance of parliaments in democracies*

reference of legislation to the Committee of Concertation. Most legislation seems to be uncontroversial in terms of affecting or changing the institutional balance between the centre and the subnational units.

According to data from the *Tweede Kamer*, the Dutch Parliament works more than the Belgian and Swiss parliaments. Moreover, a great deal of parliamentary work is accomplished in committees and informal roundtables, arenas that allow the opposition to amend and change proposed government bills. As in Belgium, there are a limited number of private members' bills, and their rate of success is much lower than that of government bills. As noted above, the government and Parliament are supposed to work together (Andeweg and Irwin 2014: 168). Due to the 'coalition machinery', as Arco Timmermans describes the Dutch method of politics, government bills have an extremely high success rate – almost 90 per cent (Timmermans and Andeweg 2000: 382–383; see Table 7.8). The extensive investment by all political parties in improving government bills through amendments, changes and other mechanisms (such as roundtables and informal circles, and even private conversations with individual members) results in a very low number of private bills submitted to Parliament (see Table 7.9).

Moreover, peer pressure seems to suggest that politicians have to learn to be quite patient and look for compromises. One of the most important skills is to remain loyal to your goal and celebrate every small gain on the way towards it. One interviewee explained:

> In the first year I knew that things worked slowly, you have to have a strategy, and if you are a new member, of course takes some time before you know how it works, and to get to the position when you have more decisive power, I am not disappointed, my expectations are realistic, you have just to be patient. And I think in every political system, except a few in

Table 7.9 Submitted government and private bills in Dutch *Tweede Kamer*, 2001 to 2013

	Government bills	*Private members' bills*
	Submitted	*Submitted*
2009	297	6
2010	257	8
2011	295	15
2012	267	18
2013	235	10
2014	264	15
2015	226	13

Source: author's compilation based on Tweede Kamer (2014: 7; 2016a: 4).

Note
Unfortunately, the annual statistical reports do not give the figure of adoption of governmental and private bills. As a rule of thumb about 90 per cent of government bills are adopted after a lengthy process of amendments. Private bills have less chance of being adopted.

Performance of parliaments in democracies 199

the revolution in which you are able to overthrow everything overnight, in democracy you need to be patient.

(Interview NL)

Another interviewee said:

You have to have the ability to have long-term goals based on your beliefs and belief system, at the same time not disappointed or demoralised if you can only achieve part or parts of it, because of our consensus system you cannot have it exactly your way, and if you have strong opinions on how you want to have it and the only way is either your way or the highway, then you will not function in Dutch politics, so the trick is to have your eye on the prize in the future, the way you want to do it, the way you want to change society, and at the same time, appreciate the small steps you can make towards that bigger goal.

(Interview NL)

As discussed above, there are very few private members' bills in the total numbers shown in Table 7.9, indicating that the main work of the Dutch Parliament is done in the committees where amendments to legislation are proposed and crafted.

Finally, the Austrian Parliament is also characterised by the dominance of government legislation, and here again, the input of Parliament at the committee stage seems to matter the most. The figures from Austria basically confirm the thesis that legislation is changed and transformed in order to achieve a broader consensus. In terms of work, the Austrian National Council resembles Swiss and Belgian institutions more than its counterpart in the Netherlands.

The data suggest that the *Bundesrat* has thus far been a rather low-key second chamber. In terms of legislation, the government dominates the entire process, a pattern reinforced by the very strict discipline of the parliamentary groups. As seen in the Dutch parliamentary culture, the opposition tends to concentrate on work in the committees, wielding its influence there to amend legislation. There is also a growing tendency towards informal agreements outside the formal structures of the *Nationalrat* and the *Bundesrat* (Schefbeck 2006: 153).

One interesting measure of consensus is the percentage of laws that were approved unanimously. In the 1970s, during the Social Democratic absolute majority of Chancellor Bruno Kreisky, the level of unanimously approved bills was between 75 and 86 per cent. However, between 1986 and 1996, during the grand coalition government under Chancellor Franz Vranitzky and later Viktor Klima, figures declined quite considerably. In the grand coalition period between 1986 and 1999 unanimity sank to an all-time low of 25.67 per cent. Interestingly, the ÖVP–FPÖ and BZÖ coalitions between 2000 and 2006 have seen an increase in unanimously approved legislation, although far from the consensus culture of the 1970s. This confirms that in Austria, consensus democracy has become more polarised between the left and the right. In addition, since 2007, the pattern of consensus has been steadily eroding (Table 7.10).

Table 7.10 Bills adopted in *Nationalrat* (lower house) of the Austrian Parliament, 1971 to 2013

	Governmental bills		Adopted unanimously (%)	Private bills		Other bills		Total bills adopted
	Submitted	*Adopted (%)*		*Submitted*	*Adopted*	*Submitted*	*Adopted (%)*	
XIII (1971–1975)	475	83	85	52	9	46	8	573
XIV (1975–1979)	318	78	79.2	70	17	22	5	410
XV (1979–1983)	351	76	75.1	89	19	22	5	462
XVI (1983–1986)	228	65	78.9	99	28	25	7	352
XVII (1986–1990)	361	67	40.7	134	25	40	7	535
XVIII (1990–1994)	436	69	27.4	165	26	31	5	632
XIX (1994–1996)	76	62	34.4	35	29	11	9	122
XX (1996–1999)	423	71	25.7	116	19	57	10	596
XXI (1999–2002)	257	66	41.9	85	22	49	13	391
XXII (2002–2006)	365	70	50.8	115	22	44	8	524
XXIII (2006–2008)	161	69	37.1	49	21	22	9	232
XXIV (2008–2013)	478	74	37.4	120	19	49	8	647
XXV (2013–)	167	74	26.5	46	20	13	6	226

Source: figures kindly supplied by Günther Schefbeck from the Austrian Parliamentary Archives upon request.

Performance of parliaments in democracies 201

An analysis of the Werner Faymann I period, which was characterised by the dominance of the grand coalition between the SPÖ and ÖVP between 2008 and 2013, suggests that despite the significant decline in unanimous voting, there is still cooperation between the government parties and the opposition. It demonstrates just how pragmatic the Faymann government was in its search for strong majorities for the adoption of legislation.

The grand coalition had a strong, constructive relationship with the Greens: about 28 per cent of all legislation was approved with the support of the Greens, either along with other parties or as the sole third party. Ideological differences notwithstanding, the grand coalition also received support from the right-wing FPÖ and BZÖ for 19 per cent of legislation. The lowest level of cooperation was with the anti-establishment party Team Stronach, which supported only 9.3 per cent of legislation.

Thus far, the Luxembourg Parliament has also been primarily dominated by grand coalition governments with strong party discipline. The use of inter-parliamentary group meetings ensures that legislation is approved successfully with the votes of the main parties.

Moreover, the small size of the Luxembourg Parliament allows for more direct contacts between the various political parties, such that legislation can be negotiated informally in order to achieve the highest possible level of consensus. Similar to the Netherlands, the number of private bills is quite low, suggesting strong investment on the part of MPs in changing and amending legislation proposed by the government parties (Table 7.11).

In sum, consensus seems to still prevail in all five countries; however, it is eroding or at least evolving rapidly in Austria in comparison to the other four countries. Switzerland also shows signs of increased polarisation due to the conflictive role of the SVP. In the Netherlands, Luxembourg and Belgium, consensus in parliamentary work remains a central feature.

Controlling instruments

The fourth aspect that we will briefly address is the use of control and oversight in relation to the government. It is quite difficult to discuss the use of such

Table 7.11 Government bills and private bills submitted and adopted in the Chamber of Deputies in Luxembourg, 2009 to 2013

	Government bills			Private bills		
	Submitted	_Adopted_	_Percentage_	_Submitted_	_Adopted_	_Percentage_
2009–2010	101	92	91	5	1	20
2010–2011	106	102	96	4	1	25
2011–2012	110	80	72.7	4	2	50
2012–2013	108	93	86.1	13	0	0

Sources: Chambre des Deputés (2010: 18; 2011: 22; 2012: 18; 2013: 18).

202 *Performance of parliaments in democracies*

instruments in terms of qualitative input. However, a quantitative comparison may provide an indication of how often the instruments are used. Among these instruments are interpellations, oral and written questions, motions and ultimately the use of committees of enquiry. In all five parliaments, written questions are the most important method of controlling the government. The Austrian, Belgian and Dutch parliaments exhibit a high level of questioning. Oral questions are used less frequently in all parliaments, but Belgium stands out as a very active chamber in this respect. The Swiss Parliament is much less active, and there is a significant difference between the National Council and the Council of States, with the Council of States using these forms of control less. This indicates that the institution is not only a chamber of reflection, but also a guardian of the consensus culture (Parliament of Switzerland 2016a).

Overall, the lower houses of the Dutch and Belgian parliaments are the most active in terms of the use of control instruments. In the Netherlands, Tuesday question time is an important controlling instrument; however, oral and written questions may also be submitted. Interpellations and urgent debates can easily be initiated in order to scrutinise the government. Urgent debates have become more common over the past decade. According to Rudy Andeweg and Galen Irwin, one can observe an overall increase in the use of the available controlling instruments. According to these scholars, some MPs refer to this as 'motion inflation' in comparison to previous decades. There has certainly been a change in the attitude of MPs towards the government over the past decade (Andeweg and Irwin 2014: 173; Wilp 2012: 102; Tweede Kamer 2014: 11).

Due to the lack of opportunities to challenge the government in the legislative process, Belgian MPs are quite active in the use of controlling instruments. The number of interpellations is relatively high in comparison to the other countries, as is also the case for oral and written questions. Prior to 2003, according to Paul Magnette, these instruments were used most by the populist VB (and previously by the *Volksunie*). Since then, the number of interpellations has been declining, whereas the numbers of oral and written questions have increased considerably. The number of oral questions increased from 9692 in the 1999 to 2003 legislature, to 16,153 in 2010 to 2014; written questions increased from 8163 to 18,391 during the same period (Magnette 2004: 101; Chambre des Representants 2014: 33).

In Belgium, committees of enquiry were highly important during the period of scandals in the late 1990s, when the legitimacy of partyocracy was significantly undermined. In the new millennium, committees of enquiry were established to investigate the murder of Patrick Lumumba in the Democratic Republic of Congo (2000–2002), a former colony of Belgium, and the bankruptcy of Sabena (2001–2002), among other cases (Chambre des Representants 2003: 14).

In the *Fragestunde* (question time) in Austria, time is allocated according to the strength of the parliamentary group, and questions are frequently used by the opposition as an instrument of control. This is especially interesting because the government generally responds to all questions, and thus the feedback loop is complete. In the period 2008 to 2013, there were 16,166 written questions, of

Performance of parliaments in democracies 203

which the opposition parties, the FPÖ and the Greens, submitted 48.8 per cent and 15.7 per cent, respectively. If we add in the questions submitted by the BZÖ and Team Stronach (founded in 2012 with four defectors from other parties), this figure increases to a total of 69 per cent (Parliament of Austria 2013: 71).

In Austria, there were 16 committees of enquiry between 1945 and 2006. As in most countries, the requirement of a relative majority for the establishment of such committees represents a major obstacle to their approval. The rationale behind this requirement involves the risk that the opposition may abuse the instrument and unnecessarily destabilise the political system (Fallend 2000: 182–184). After the end of the ÖVP–FPÖ coalition government following the 2006 elections, several enquiry committees were set up to address scandals in the previous government, in particular the abuse of power in the Interior Ministry, the untransparent acquisition of military aircraft and several intransparent financial transactions in which either central or regional governments were involved, such as the Hypo Alpe Adria Bank in Carinthia. Significant financial and human resources are invested in these committees. For example, the committee of enquiry on the abuse of power in the Interior Ministry, which took place between March and June 2008, cost about half a million euro (Parliament of Austria 2007: 13; 2008: 14–15). The Hypo Alpe Adria Bank committee of enquiry has thus far cost €2.6 million, and an additional €1 million for IT and infrastructure has been invested in the committee room (Parliament of Austria 2015c).

In the case of Luxembourg, debates with the government are common; however, the conference of presidents of Parliament has recognised that the system of parliamentary questions is not working properly, since a high number of questions have remained unanswered for a long time. The volume of written questions is considerably lower than in the other parliaments (Chambre des Deputés 2013: 2). For example, in the legislative session of 2011/2012, just 613 out of 650 questions were answered (Chambre des Deputés 2012: 18).

In sum, the control instruments are used in different ways across the consensus democracies. It seems that the Netherlands is most active in controlling the government. Belgium and Austria are moderately active, whereas Luxembourg and Switzerland give the impression of being weaker in controlling the executive.

European integration and national parliaments

Although many European Union member-states had some provision to scrutinise European legislation in the 1980s, it was only with the Treaty of the European Union (adopted in 1993) that this role of national parliaments was enshrined in protocol. Since then, the integration of national parliaments into the European Union political framework has been steadily growing. Both the Treaty of Amsterdam and the Treaty of Lisbon enhanced the role of national parliaments in scrutinising EU legislation. The principle of subsidiarity adopted in the Treaty of the European Union has been an important factor in strengthening the position

204 *Performance of parliaments in democracies*

of national parliaments. Subsidiarity means that decision-making should occur at the appropriate level in the European Union's system of multi-level governance; governments are therefore entitled to take decisions on policies that do not fall under the competences of the supranational level. Although the process is still relatively new, the Treaty of Lisbon allows national parliaments to join together and present a 'yellow card' on new legislative proposals by the European Commission that may considerably affect national competences. A yellow card may only be triggered by a vote of one-third of the member-state parliaments; a quarter of the parliaments are required to express reservations in the areas of freedom, security and justice. Beyond that, there is also an 'orange card', which requires half of all the votes of national parliaments. When presented with an orange card, the Commission must provide a better justification for the legislation at the supranational level or withdraw the proposal. National parliaments are entitled to be informed about internal security issues and measures of mutual recognition, and legislative proposals may be reviewed over a six-month period (European Commission 2016; Verdun 2013b: 1133; Sprungk 2013). Thus far, the European Commission has withdrawn legislative proposals on the right of collective action within the context of the freedom of establishment and the freedom to provide services (Monti II Proposal-COM (2012) 130) and a Council regulation on the European Public Prosecutor Office (EPPO-Proposal COM (2013) 534; European Commission 2016).

The national parliaments of Austria, Belgium, Luxembourg and the Netherlands have created bodies to deal with the increasing Europeanisation of national legislation (see Table 7.12). In Belgium, the first committee of European affairs was created in 1962 and eliminated in 1979, meeting only 100 times (De Winter and Laurent 1996: 76–79). In 1985, an Advice Committee in Charge of European Matters was established in the House of Representatives. This new body includes equal numbers of MPs and MEPs, at ten each. Its main competence is to advise on the EU legislation that other committees are dealing with. The inclusion of MEPs has facilitated this parliamentary work immensely. The Advice Committee has also been proactive in obtaining information from external actors (De Winter 1996: 80–84). In 1990, an Advice Committee was also created in the Senate, consisting of 22 senators. In the case of joint meetings of the two committees, ten representatives from each of the three groups (MPs, MEPs and senators) atttend. However, most of the output of these committees has been the post-facto rubber-stamping of government decisions (Vandevivere 2001: 85–86). Neither the Amsterdam nor the Lisbon Treaty has altered the weak position of the Belgian Parliament. Moreover, the highly pro-European political culture of the Belgian political elite limits critical questioning of certain aspects of European integration (Delreux and Randour 2015: 161–162). The recent reduction in the power of the Senate further undermines the importance of the scrutiny of EU legislation (Vanden Bosch 2014: 7–8). Furthermore, there is also pressure from the subnational parliaments to enhance their role in the scrutiny of EU legislation, due to the widespread decentralisation of competences to regions and communities. Indeed, any of the federations – even the

Table 7.12 Committees of EU affairs in consensus democracies, 2015

	Responsible committee	Number of members	Involvement of standing committees	Scope of scrutiny/binding character/scrutiny reserve
Austria	*Nationalrat:* Main Committee on European Affairs;	26 members	No systematic involvement	Mainly EU documents Binding position No scrutiny reserve
	Standing Subcommittee on European affairs	16 members		
	Bundesrat: Committee of European Affairs	14 members		
Belgium	*Chambre des Representants*: Federal Advisory Committee on European Affairs	10 MPs and 10 MEPs	Advisory involvement	Mainly EU documents Position non-binding No scrutiniy reserve
	With Senate: Joint Committee on European Affairs	10 MPs, 10 MEPs and 10 Senators		
Luxembourg	*Chambre des Deputés:* Comitttee of Foreign and European Affairs, for Defence, for Cooperation and for Immigration	12 members	Full involvement	Mainly EU documents Position is politically binding, government has to justify deviation
Netherlands	*Tweede Kamer:* Committee of European Affairs	24 members	Full involvement	Both documents and government position
	Eerste Kamer: Committee on European Affairs	25 members		Formally, position is non-binding, but government will usually justify deviation Scrutiny reserve

Source: adapted and extended by the author from Auel (2015: 370–371).

206 *Performance of parliaments in democracies*

small German community of 80,000 inhabitants – can veto a Treaty ratification (Vanden Bosch 2014: 3). This forces the federated units and the central government and Parliament to work together. However, it must be noted that the Belgian 'parliamentary system' in relation to European affairs is still in the making (Vanden Bosch 2014).

Also in the Netherlands, a strong pro-European political culture has prevented 'Europe' from becoming a salient issue. A standing Committee of European Affairs was only created in 1986, tasked with the legislative workload related to the Single European Market programme. This committee was intended to coordinate the work of other committees related to EU matters; however, as Rinus Van Schendelen asserts, the 'commtttee, designed to coordinate the Second Chamber on EU affairs, in fact hardly achieved any substantial parliamentary co-ordination' (Van Schendelen 1996: 66). It seems that the Dutch EC presidency of 1991 marked a turning point in the relationship between the country and Europe. According to Van Schendelen, the failure of this presidency was the first time that the Dutch elite felt that the Netherlands, as a small country, was unable to influence politics and policy in the supranational organisation (Van Schendelen 1996: 69–70). Most of the adopted treaties related to the European Union have been ratified through statutory laws that clearly establish the involvement of Parliament. Parliament has a particularly strong say in justice and home affairs, the third pillar of the Treaty of the European Union (Högenauer 2015: 253).

In 1993, a General Committee of European Affairs was established, but it was not very efficient (Hoetjes 2001: 349–351). In this context, the role of a highly disciplined coalition government constrains MPs in the *Tweede Kamer*, and it is very difficult for the opposition to influence policy. The agenda-setting powers are strongly dominated by the government parties, but the tradition of consensus encourages cooperation on EU matters (Holzhacker 2005: 438, 440–441). The referendum on 1 June 2005 was a major shock for the political establishment: the 'no' to the constitutional treaty revealed a growing gap between the political elites and the population (Högenauer 2015: 253). This led to a reinforcement of the mechanisms of scrutity of EU legislation and issues by the *Tweede Kamer*. Since 2006, the EU scrutiny mechanism has been highly decentralised. There is extensive sharing of information and workload between the General Committee of European Affairs and the other sectoral committees. According to Anna Lena Högenauer, the number of technical briefings with the staff of the permanent representation in Brussels and other important officials in the EU policy-coordination machinery has increased substantially. Prior to 2006, only one-third of White and Green papers were analysed; currently, all are scrutinised. In addition, ministers attend hearing committee meetings before scheduled Council meetings. The prime minister is required to appear more regularly before Parliament to report on EU affairs. This indicates that the *Tweede Kamer* has increased its 'soft' ex-ante powers (Högenauer 2015: 255). One important aspect of the work of Parliament is the proper and timely transposition of directives and EU legislation. This work has been decentralised to the respective sectoral committees

Performance of parliaments in democracies 207

(Högenauer 2015: 255–256), although some committees are more active than others. The committees on economic and financial affairs, agriculture and foreign affairs are among the busiest in relation to EU issues (Högenauer 2015: 256). This qualitative change has been confirmed by other studies, such as those by Thomas König and his team. In their analysis of the impact of European legislation on the work of national parliaments, the Finnish Parliament emerges as the most active, followed by its Austrian counterpart. Nevertheless, the Dutch Parliament has substantially increased its activity since 2005. Some increased activity may be found in Belgium, but Luxembourg's involvement remains limited (König *et al.* 2012: 32). The *Eerste Kamer* mirrors the procedures of the *Tweede Kamer*, but meets less frequently (Högenauer 2015: 256–257). A report commissioned by the *Tweede Kamer* seems to suggest that better management of EU issues is still required, especially with regard to the selection of the most salient issues rather than intense scrutiny of everything. Furthermore, the report suggests that the Dutch Parliament should not waste too much time with counterparts that exhibit little interest in EU scrutiny; instead, it should increase its collective action endeavours with more proactive legislatures. Finally, the report proposes that during the Dutch presidency of 2016, the Dutch Parliament should be proactive in introducing major management reforms of the Committee of Bodies of European Affairs of the EU (*Comité des Organs Specialisés en Affaires Communautaires, COSAC*). Rather than long plenary sessions, additional side sessions are proposed (Mastenbroek *et al.* 2014: 31–35). At the moment, the major problem seems to be one of coordination between the two chambers. In order to speed up the process of opinion formation, EU legislation and material is sent to both chambers at the same time which then have to work on the material independently and give a positive opinion independently of each other at the same time. This leads sometimes to contradictory opinions, clearly leading in turn to a lack of influence in the process. Moreover, it is the *Tweede Kamer* that has all the resources in order to undertake detailed scrutiny, something that the *Eerste Kamer* lacks. Due to this escalating problem between the two houses, including the lack of congruent majorities, Prime Minister Mark Rutte announced in 2015 that a state reform commission will be set up to look at all of these questions (Interview NL).

The small size of the Luxembourg Parliament and the country's very pro-European political culture has resulted in a low profile for European affairs. The dominance of government and the almost part-time nature of Luxembourg's Parliament further reduce the importance of Europe. Another factor is that European affairs fall under the competence of a larger committee, the Committee for Foreign and European Affairs, Defence, Cooperation and Immigration. The scrutiny of EU legislation is rather informal due to the size of the Luxembourg Parliament (Bossaert 2001: 303). Opposition from the AdR and the Greens, which are sceptical about policies at the European level and the position of the government, has been intensifying (Spreitzer 2015: 246). The referendum on the constitutional treaty in 2005 led to a very narrow victory for its supporters. In many ways, the Luxembourg Parliament is constrained in terms of human

208   *Performance of parliaments in democracies*

resources, putting MPs under considerable pressure in light of the huge amount of material produced by the European institutions. This is somewhat compensated by a stronger consensual constructive cooperation between the government and Parliament. However, meetings of the committee are held behind closed doors, it fails to be a proper governmental watchdog, it is not a public forum and it has no relevant expertise (Spreitzer 2015: 248; Interview LU).

The Benelux countries are founding members of the EC/EU, but Austria only joined in 1995, meaning that it had to rapidly adapt its parliamentary structures to the European integration process. As in Belgium, one main issue was how to deal with European issues in a federal setting. The *Bundesländer* are clearly the major losers in this process of European integration. The subnational legislative assemblies (*Landtage*) have the right to establish committees of European affairs, but not all of them have done so. Some rely on the intergovernmental integration conference of the *Länder*, others on good informal relationships between the regional government and the legislative assembly (Blümel and Neuhold 2001: 315–317; Fallend 2002; Interview A). The federal Parliament, through its committee system in the *Nationalrat* (lower house), dominates the scrutiny of EU legislation. Nevertheless, as in the Benelux countries, the Austrian lower house is severely overwhelmed by the numbers of documents that accumulate every month in the respective committees in charge of European affairs. The Austrian case exemplifies the problems found across the national parliaments. In the *Nationalrat*, there is a EU main committee that primarily handles the scrutiny of EU affairs. Since 1999, a subcommittee on EU affairs was created in order to reduce the workload of the main committee. In addition, a so-called 'fire brigade' committee can be created ad hoc in order to deal with specific urgent issues such as the negotiation of treaties. The *Bundesrat*, the upper house in which the interests of the regions are represented, there is also a committee of European affairs. Since 1996, committees in both houses can issue binding opinions with which the government must comply (Blümel and Neuhold 2001: 324). As already mentioned, the *Bundesrat* is extremely important to disseminating information at a subnational level, because it focuses its attention on subsidiarity questions affecting the competences of the provinces (Interview A).

Despite the increasing workload and number of meetings of the subcommittee of European affairs, the government dominates the entire process. An assessment by Eric Miklin seems to suggest that the Austrian national Parliament is merely a policy-shaper, and certainly not a watchdog of the government. In addition, it is not a public forum, nor does it have much expertise. Although the Austrian Parliament has been implementing the new provisions of the Lisbon Treaty by using the Early Warning System and the Political Dialogue with the European Commission, its usage is still moderate and does not indicate a qualitative step towards becoming a European player (Miklin 2015: 404, 396–398). The majority of MPs are not very knowledgeable about or conscious of the impact of EU legislation, and the Parliament's insufficient human resources preclude a more active role (Miklin 2015: 403).

Performance of parliaments in democracies 209

In 2001, Andreas Maurer and Wolfgang Wessels developed a typology of how different national parliaments deal with European Union issues, creating a matrix based on ideal types of actors in a two-level game: participation in the Brussels/Strasbourg arena, and participation in the national arena. Four types emerge: multi-level players, European players, national players and slow adapters (see Table 7.13). Multi-level players are able to fulfil a role at all levels and to considerably influence the policy outcome of both their governments and the EU. They have access to adequate resources to play this proactive role (Denmark, Finland, possibly Estonia, Germany). Among our consensus democracies, the Dutch *Tweede Kamer* comes closest to being a multi-level player. European players tend to have a strong relationship with the European Parliament and the Brussels/Strasbourg arena (Belgium and the UK prior to the Treaty of Lisbon). National players are quite strong nationally, but do not intervene in the subsequent phases in the multi-level governance system. They have enough resources to play a role nationally and challenge the government, but they are poorly equipped to play a more proactive role at all levels (Austria, the UK and France). Finally, slow adapters are countries that are struggling to create and maintain a robust system of scrutiny of EU affairs. In this context, both Belgium and Luxembourg seem to be good examples of slow adapters (Maurer 2001: 34; Maurer and Wessels 2001: 463; typology also based on Auel *et al.* 2015; Auel 2015: 373–374).

Between 2010 and 2012, the financial, Euro and sovereign debt crises put most national parliaments under considerable pressure, in particular because the

Table 7.13 Strength of consensus democracies parliaments in EU multi-level governance before and after Lisbon, 2001 and 2014

Participation in the Brussels/Strasbourg arena		*Participation in the national arena*	
		Strong	*Weak*
	Strong	**Multi-level players** Denmark 2001/2014 (2) Finland 2001/2014 (1) Estonia 2014 (3) Germany 2014 (3) *Netherlands 2014 (5)* Germany 2001	**European players** European Parliament 2001/2014 Medium
	Weak	**National players** *Netherlands 2001* *Austria 2001/2014 (6)* France 2014 (7) UK 2001/2014	**Slow adapters** *Luxembourg 2001/ 2014 (10),* *Belgium 2001/2014 (11)*

Sources: Maurer, Wessels (2001): 463) and own calculations based on ranking data on strength of national parliaments on EU affairs based on 12 point-scale: (1) strongest, 12 weakest; see Auel and Höing (2014) quoted in Auel (2015: 373).

210 *Performance of parliaments in democracies*

time frames for parliamentary consideration of the huge bailouts were quite short. Apart from EU non-member Switzerland, all the other countries in this study are part of the Eurozone and are net payers, and they all felt this pressure. Governments in Austria and the Netherlands confronted strong opposition from their populist parties, the FPÖ and the PVV, respectively. In contrast to Euro-enthusiastic Benelux, Austria had to deal with Eurosceptic caveats presented by the FPÖ and the BZÖ up until 2013. However, unlike weaker national parliaments, the four West Central European parliaments fared quite well overall (Auel and Höing 2014; Maatsch 2014).

Conclusions: Parliament as the centre of consensus democracies

The five consensus democracies analysed in this volume all have a robust parliamentary tradition. Their performance is respectable; however, there are certain major differences. In this regard, we can draw three conclusions.

First, the most industrious Parliament with the most resources is the Dutch Parliament, especially the lower chamber. The parliaments in Luxembourg and Switzerland are quite hard-working in light of the limited resources at their disposal, whereas Austria and Belgium are probably underperforming if their resources are taken into account.

Second, the Dutch and Belgian parliaments seem to be the most proactive in controlling the government; the other parliaments are weaker in this respect.

Finally, also in terms of the scrutiny of EU legislation, the Dutch Parliament has reacted better by more proactively adjusting to the steadily growing mountain of documentation. Austria is overwhelmed by the number of documents that require scrutiny, but it has relatively adequate instruments in place. Belgium and Luxembourg, two traditionally Euro-enthusiast countries, may be categorised as slow adapters to the challenges of European integration. As a EU non-member, the Swiss have no mechanisms to deal with European integration at this point. For Switzerland, this is still foreign policy and is thus a matter for the Federal Council. The majority of Swiss interviewees do not regard European integration as an important aspect of their work (Interviews CH).

8 Regional and local patterns in consensus democracies

Introduction: the expansion of consensus democracies

For consensus democracies, one important source of strength is the fact that their national patterns of behaviour have been extended to the subnational level over the past 200 years. All of our five cases have developed similar power-sharing cultures based on proportional representation and compromise. However, this expansion of the consensus democracy is expressed differently in different countries. There is also the strong possibility that divergent patterns of regional and local democracy will emerge within the same country.

This chapter first analyses the simpler multi-level unitary systems of the Netherlands and Luxembourg, and then turns to the more complex federal systems of Austria, Switzerland and (more recently) Belgium. Finally, some conclusions will be drawn.

Patterns of subnational democracy in unitary states: the Netherlands and Luxembourg

Although the Netherlands and Luxembourg are unitary states, they are both relatively decentralised at the local level. The three-tier model of the Netherlands dates back to the reforms initiated by Johan Rudolf Thorbecke following the adoption of a democratic constitution in 1848. This three-tier model is widely referred to as a 'decentralised unitary state', although, in reality, the decentralisation emerged over time. The municipality, the most important unit in this administrative structure, and the principle of municipal autonomy evolved over the course of several legislative acts, including the Local Government Act and the Provincial Government Act of 1851. In theory, municipal autonomy is the concrete embodiment of citizens' sovereignty, protecting and promoting the freedom of action. However, already in Thorbecke's time, the dangers of unconstrained municipal autonomy were recognised – namely its potential to jeopardise the functioning of the other tiers of the Dutch administrative system. In this regard, provincial governments are an important supervising and controlling tier of local government intended to prevent such unconstrained and detrimental behaviour. The provincial government is a tier of rationalisation that provides

212   *Regional and local patterns in democracies*

structure to municipal autonomy. It is thus a tier of 'negative power' that acts against the 'positive power' of municipal autonomy (Toonen 1990: 287).

Theo Toonen refers to an additional important aspect of the 'decentralised unitary state' developed by Thorbecke: the consensual system of conflict regulation that was created as an intrinsic element within the public administrative system (Toonen 1990: 285–286). However, at the same time he emphasises the interdependence between the tiers, the so-called 'flexible co-governance' model (Toonen 1990: 286–288). The societal complexity of the twentieth century pushed this model towards a hierarchised unitary state; ultimately, a crisis in the 1960s and 1970s prompted Dutch politicians to undertake major reforms (Toonen 1990: 288–289; Kickert 2004: 8). These reforms were based on new public management (NPM), a philosophy seeking to put the citizen at the centre of local public administration, but also to make administrations more efficient and results-oriented. NPM aims to create a model of co-responsibility among civil society actors (VNG 2008: 32–33; for a review of the reforms see Kickert 2000; Hendriks and Schaap 2011).

The Ruud Lubbers (1982–1994) and Wim Kok (1994–2002) governments played major roles in promoting this reform of local public administration as part of the wider restructuring of the Polder model. The result became known as the Tillburg model, a system geared towards improving the organisation of local financing. This reform led to considerable improvements in financial governance as well as the reduction of budget deficits. By the mid-1980s, the Tillburg model had become the dominant paradigm. Provincial governments were granted stronger financial supervisory rights. In the case of financial difficulties, municipalities could request extra funding from the provincial government; however, this would involve strong conditionality. Today, local governments remain relatively autonomous in terms of their expenditures, although so many tasks have been decentralised to the local level that most of the funding is earmarked from the outset. Nevertheless, there is a general provision that municipal autonomy will remain central to the Dutch system, and that municipalities are not merely extensions of the central administration. Indeed, the high level of decentralisation has increased municipal autonomy, but it has also made national ministries and departments dependent on the efficient implementation of policies at the local level (Hendriks and Schaap 2011: 103–104; Interview NL).

A turning point was reached with the local elections of 1990 and 1994, in which participation decreased and extreme-right parties increased their share of the vote considerably; this was perceived by the national political elite as a crisis of democracy. This led to a major reorientation, moving from the customer-oriented internal organisation of local public administration based on New Public Management reforms to a citizen-friendly organisation oriented on the external environment (Kickert 2000: 55; Hendriks and Tops 2003: 311). Today, citizens have several instruments at their disposal that can shape the decision-making process in local politics: the local referendum, which has more of an advisory nature, consumer panels and audit offices that sometimes include citizens (VNG 2008: 31–32).

Regional and local patterns in democracies 213

This qualitative democratisation of local government has had significant implications for the political system. Thorbecke's model envisaged a monistic system of government for the local level; the mayor and aldermen would be part of both the local legislative assembly and the local executive council. The sweeping reforms undertaken in 2002 and 2003 (Act of 7 March 2002 for municipalities and Act of 12 March 2003 for provinces) sought to gradually transform the monistic model into a dualist one (OECD 2014a: 203). The primary result is the strict separation of powers: the appointed aldermen are no longer members of the local assembly but merely participate in the local executive council. A leftover from the earlier monistic system is the figure of the appointed mayor, who is still chairman of both the local assembly and the local executive council.

The mayor is chosen by a confidential selection committee at the local level. Originally, mayors were appointed by the monarch through the Interior Ministry, but now there is a more direct connection to the local level. There is also the possibility to organise a referendum to determine the profile for the position preferred by the population. Based on this profile, potential candidates can apply for the position to the King's Commissioner at the provincial level. The confidential committee at the provincial level draws up a shortlist of two candidates, and the local council makes a recommendation to the interior minister. Finally, the interior minister confirms the new mayor, almost always following the recommendation of the local council. In order to avoid party-political congruence with local elections, the mayor is appointed for a period of six years (VNG 2008: 29–30). The position of mayor is political only to a limited extent; mayors are referred to as managers who head both the local police and local fire brigades, assisted by a local council secretary (VNG 2008: 33–34).

The executive council generally consists of two to seven aldermen. Smaller municipalities have a lower number, and they may only be part-time positions; in larger cities like Amsterdam, the maximum number of seven full-time aldermen may be required. In municipalities with more than 18,000 inhabitants, all aldermen work full-time. Ideal candidates for the position are politicians with strong executive abilities. As seen at the national and provincial levels, coalition governments dominate the executive branch in the Netherlands. A study on coalition agreements in six municipalities – Amsterdam, Rotterdam, Enschede, Arnhem, Helmond and Franekeradael – between 1986 and 2010 demonstrates that a large number of local governments are grand coalitions; however, there are also occasionally right–centre or left–centre governments. Out of the 42 cases studied, 29 (69%) were mixed grand coalitions, including Christian Democratic, Social Democratic, Liberal, Green and other local parties, ten (24%) only consisted of parties on the left side of the spectrum, and three (7%) on the right side (Breeman *et al.* 2015: 31). Another finding was that despite a degree of institutional isomorphism between the levels, the local level is relatively constrained by co-governance (*medebewind*; Breeman *et al.* 2015). According to the authors, between 70 per cent and 80 per cent of local agendas involve co-governance issues shared with other levels (Breeman *et al.* 2015: 34). Another interesting conclusion is that the introduction of dualism in subnational governments in

214 *Regional and local patterns in democracies*

2002/2003 has resulted in more carefully constructed coalition agreements. The form of coalition agreements has become more similar across municipalities, and their length has been reduced significantly (Breeman *et al*. 2015: 29–30). Therefore, the study seems to indicate that coalition agreements have converged in terms of content towards a single pattern, suggesting that national priorities dominate at the municipality level (Breeman *et al*. 2015: 33–35).

In terms of public administration, the municipality level is the most important one. In 2012, over 163,115 civil servants worked at the municipality level, in comparison to 116,997 civil servants at the central level in the ministries. In between the two, there are 12,000 civil servants in the provincial governments (Table 8.1; OECD 2014a: 211). Overall, the civil service comprises about 2.9 per cent of the population, a remarkable figure for such a large population (*Dutch News*, 22 November 2011).

However, the reality is rather different. There are at least half a million civil servants employed in non-profit quasi-governmental organisations (so-called 'quangos') that do government work. The process of agencification has been widespread and is relatively decentralised at the municipality level. These organisations are known as self-administrative bodies (*Zelf-bestuursorganisatie*, ZBOs). Moreover, education and security are not included in these figures. The Dutch education system features both public and private schools, with many faith-based institutions. Overall, however, the Netherlands has one of the most decentralised civil services of the unitary states, topped only by Denmark. In terms of government expenditure, one-third of spending is done at the local level – a high figure, but still below levels in the Nordic countries and Switzerland. Statistically, the amount allocated to the provincial government is negligible, with most of the funding going directly to the local level (see Table 8.2).

The Dutch state system reflects an 'hourglass' model in which the central and the municipal levels receive the bulk of the funding, whereas the provincial level has much more modest human and financial resources. Table 8.1 summarises public expenditures according to the subnational structures of government in the Netherlands.

As noted above, local government has gained considerable importance as the central arena for consensus democracy. Power-sharing and consensual decision-making prevail at local and provincial levels; in addition, new instruments for enhancing democracy have been created. Significantly, in 2006, 23.7 per cent of

Table 8.1 Number of civil servants at different government levels, 2003 and 2012

	2003		*2012*	
	Numbers	*Percentage*	*Numbers*	*Percentage*
Municipality	191,727	57.9	163,115	55.8
Province	14,019	4.2	12,179	4.2
Central government	125,393	37.9	116,997	40.1

Source: OECD (2014a : 211).

Table 8.2 Expenditure at different levels of government in selected OECD countries, 1995 to 2013

	1995			2005			2013		
	Central	Regional	Local	Central	Regional	Local	Central	Regional	Local
Austria	**69.0**	**13.4**	**17.6**	**69.4**	**16.1**	**14.5**	**68.7**	**16.3**	**15.1**
Belgium	**66.7**	**21.0**	**12.3**	**63.8**	**23.1**	**13.1**	**62.1**	**24.5**	**13.4**
Denmark	46.5		53.5	38.3		61.7	38.0		62.0
Finland	70.0		30.0	62.0		38.0	59.3		40.7
France	82.8		17.2	80.5		19.5	79.5		20.5
Germany	67.1	18.9	14.0	62.6	22.3	15.1	60.8	22.6	16.6
Greece							94.2		5.8
Luxembourg	**86.7**		13.3	88.0		12.0	89.3		10.7
Netherlands	60.6		39.4	65.4		34.6	69.6		**30.4**
Poland				70.7		29.3	69.3		30.7
Portugal	88.4		11.6	86.3		13.7	86.9		13.2
Spain	67.3	21.5	11.1	51.6	35.7	12.7	57.5	31.8	10.8
Sweden	63.3		36.7	56.0		44.0	52.2		47.8
Switzerland	**45.3**	**33.0**	**21.7**	**45**	**35.4**	**19.5**	**42.4**	**38.5**	**19.1**
UK	73.6		26.3	71.6		28.5	74.7		25.3

Source: based on OECD (2015b).

216 *Regional and local patterns in democracies*

Table 8.3 Public expenditure according to subnational structures, 2005 and 2011

	2005		2011	
	Bn €	%	Bn €	%
Regional water authorities	3.2	5.3	3.6	4.8
Provinces	4.5	7.5	8.5	11.3
Joint arrangements (mainly municipal)	8.6	14.3	9.3	12.4
Municipalities	43.5	72.7	53.6	71.5

Source: OECD (2014a: 213), taken from Central Bureau of Statistics.

the vote was won by local parties or parties challenging the partyocratic structures at the local level. In Noord Brabant and Limburg, these figures were as high as 37.2 and 33.5 per cent, respectively (Boogers and Voerman 2010: 79). This surge in support for diminutive local parties (about 100 members on average, of which 15 to 25 are highly active) is creating major problems for the national established parties, in particular for the CDA, the VVD and the D66 (Boogers and Voerman 2010: 81). The reasons underlying the emergence of local independent parties vary widely; three primary causes have been identified by Boogers and Voerman. The first is that citizens may be mobilised by a local issue and desire to shape the decision-making process. The local level requires pragmatic solutions that only local actors can truly deliver. The second reason is dissatisfaction with established politics: independent local parties offer a grassroots platform to express protest and present alternatives to the status quo. Here, the Pim Fortuyn revolt is cited as an important example. Before Pim Fortuyn created his national party, similar movements such as Leefbar ('liveable') existed at the local level. The third reason is based on the idea that local politics is independent from national politics, and that traditional political parties are not a good fit in this context. Some national political parties form coalitions with independent local parties under a different name as a response to this reality. Civil society is strong at the local level and is consequently capable of playing a constructive role in shaping local decision-making.

The provincial level is merely a bureaucratic supervisory structure without a strong identity, but the local level is a key arena for lively consensus democracy. The Netherlands has been a leader in the move towards a model of governance based on networks that include not only government structures but also civil society actors and local economic actors. To this end, a genuine effort is being made by local councillors to experiment with new forms of citizen participation (Denters and Klok 2013: 663, 669). Nevertheless, informal local power structures remain an important factor (Boogers 2014: 348–349).

Municipalities are active in spatial planning (16 per cent of expenditures), the provision of social benefits and services (26%), police, traffic issues (3%), and transportation and public works (8%; OECD 2014b: 214). In terms of funding, the largest item across municipalities is a general grant from the central government; municipalities have some degree of leeway and autonomy in the allocation

Regional and local patterns in democracies 217

of these funds. In 2011, the general grant represented 36 per cent of funding. In addition, municipalities receive specific earmarked grants for concrete policies (18%); these offer little or no leeway for local decision-making. Both types of grants come from the 'municipality fund' (*Gemeentenfonds*). The second largest source of revenue is the municipality's own resources derived from market and property activities. This represents 31 per cent of funding on average. The third major source of revenue is local taxes, which accounted for 15 per cent of funding in 2011 (OECD 2014b: 220–221).

At the provincial level, expenditures are focused on policies that are important for the entire province: traffic and the road system (25 per cent of expenditures) are regulated and organised, the main guidelines for spatial planning are determined (3%) and certain social benefits are disbursed (19%). In a country in which water is always encroaching on the land, there is a preoccupation with not wasting space for misguided purposes. This gives the provinces a crucial strategic role in spatial planning (OECD 2014b: 414).

In 2011, a significant proportion of provincial budgets came from a general central government grant (12%) from the 'provinces fund' (*provinciesfond*). Earmarked central government funding accounted for 22 per cent, but provincial resources related to dividends from utility companies made up almost half of all revenues (49%). An additional 17 per cent came from provincial taxes and levies (OECD 2014a: 222).

The Netherlands spends about 65.8 per cent of direct public investment at the subnational level, which is high, but below the EU27 average of 72.2 per cent in 2012. In comparison to our cluster of consensus democracies, Belgium (almost 90%), Switzerland (over 80%) and Austria (over 70%) spend much more than the Netherlands; only Luxembourg (about 40%) spends less (OECD 2014a: 214–215).

Although the provincial level was an essential part of Thorbecke's conceptualisation of the 'hourglass'-shaped three-tier state, it remains largely underresearched and in some ways neglected. Up until the 1980s, provincial officials had almost no funding support to fulfil their duties. This changed when the public authorities underwent a shift from a type of governance capable of influencing all areas of politics, society, the economy and culture, to governance in which they were merely *primus inter pares*. The supervisory role of the provinces became central to the rescaling of the relationship between the two subnational levels. In particular, the fiscal squeeze following the two oil crises and the socio-economic reforms of the Lubbers and Kok governments in the 1980s and 1990s led to the rediscovery of the province as an important instrument to discipline debtor municipalities. Provinces could provide financial support from a special fund to deal with emergency debt problems; however, the price was strong conditionality and the implementation of stringent austerity measures (Interview NL). The strategic role of provinces in the continuing decentralisation and democratisation of the subnational government has been recently acknowledged (OECD 2014a: 208–209). Currently, there is an ongoing general debate over granting more powers and resources to the provinces in order to ensure the

218 *Regional and local patterns in democracies*

equalisation of living conditions across the territory; there have even been proposals to eliminate and merge provinces (OECD 2014a: 27). This strategic process is scheduled to last until 2025.

Provincial officials are directly elected, and government structures at the provincial level are similar to those at the local level. Specifically, there is a dualist structure with a provincial assembly and a provincial government. Like mayors at the local level, a King's (or Queen's) Commissioner is appointed by the interior minister after a similar process of application, selection and nomination. Also similar to the local level, the political parties elect their government representatives (*Gedeputeerde*); numbers of representatives reflect a party's share of the vote. Members of the executive are not allowed to be members of the provincial assembly as well. Again, the exception is the King's Commissioner, who chairs both institutions. Similar to the national and local levels, the programme of the government is based on a coalition agreement (*regeerakkord*), which is strongly influenced by the priorities set at the national level.

In addition to these formal political structures, Dutch subnational governments have experimented extensively with New Public Management and various governance arrangements. This has led to some 700 inter-municipal arrangements in a variety of policy areas, including attempts to increase efficiency in social welfare policies (46 percent of arrangements), traffic and transport (21%) as well as health and the environment (17%). One particularly important development is the emergence of eight city-regions (*stadregios*) in Amsterdam, Twente, Utrecht, Haaglanden, Rotterdam, Nijmegen, Eindhoven and Limburg. These are all large cities with close ties to smaller urban areas in their periphery, creating sizeable areas of cooperation (Schaap 2003; OECD 2014b: 225–226).

Our discussion of the Dutch subnational government system would not be complete without a mention of the traditional and vital role of the 23 water boards managing the complex network of dykes and channels that aid the Netherlands in its quest to keep water out of the country. These water boards are the origin of the Polder model based on consensus democracy. Due to the difficulty of controlling the water, communities had to cooperate with one another; the result was the *waterschappen* (water boards) that seek to prevent catastrophic flooding. The structure of these systems is similar to local governments, with a directly elected assembly and an executive appointed by the interior minister. The only difference is that non-elected stakeholders are also allowed to sit in the assembly. About €2.79 billion is spent annually on water management, with most of the funding directly collected through water-use taxes and levies. There are 10,500 people currently working for the water boards (OECD 2014a: 203–204). However, a merger between the water boards and the provinces is being contemplated in the discussion on increasing efficiency in the decentralised governments.

Keeping out the water is an essential and preferred principle of Dutch politics. Interviewees are aware of the struggle of Dutch people against flooding. One interviewee explained Dutch politics as going back to the management of the channels:

Regional and local patterns in democracies   219

This was always a country of compromise, we were always small, we were always wet, to keep the country free from overflooding, we needed to compromise with the neighbour and you always wanted that neighbour paid for the dykes, as the neighbour had the same idea about you, you had to find a compromise to pay together for the dykes, so on on the 18th of March [2015, provincial and *waterschappen* elections] we did not only elect our provinces, so that we also elect a system of those that in charge of the dykes and the waters, nobody knows that is still there, but we also elect, from ages that we learned being small and being on a place on the earth that the Lord which meant not to be a country but part of the North Sea, this is I think it is in our culture.

(Interview NL)

Another interviewee regards this as a continuing priority for the future of the Netherlands. He asserts as follows:

It is of people's importance, however it is completely under the radar among the electorate. The reason we elect these bodies democratically, because they can charge tax. We rule that if you can tax, you have to be democratically elected, so you can be checked and controlled by the electorate, the problem is for years now that that has been very few interest in these elections. People take for granted that the water supply, drink water, also the channels, the rivers are being run correctly. So we now have the *waterschappen* elections similar, paralleled to the provincial elections, see if we can get like more voters out, but these bodies have important work to do, and still again we take it for granted, well we are lucky that we can take for granted, but it is up to us politicians to also to explain that is important to people that pay attention to them and also are aware of the fact that they have to be checked to see if they do what they have to do, this is of existential importance for the Netherlands, because these are the bodies to keep our feet dry.

(Interview NL)

In comparison to the Netherlands, Luxembourg's unitary structure is quite simple. The diminutive size of the country obviates substantial decentralisation. In fact, the country's municipalities are relatively weak in comparison with those in other states due to their limited financial resources and lack of professionalised civil servants (in relation to the national civil service). The French and Dutch influence of the eighteenth and nineteenth centuries is reflected in the organisation of the unitary state. In 2011 there were 116 municipalities, of which 60 per cent had fewer than 2500 inhabitants, and 80 per cent fewer than 5000 (Dumont *et al.* 2011: 129). Since 2012, the number of communities has been reduced to 105, as the government is paying an extra subsidy of €2500 per inhabitant to motivate municipalities to merge voluntarily (*Tageblatt*, 10 May 2011). By 2017, the number of municipalities will be cut to 71, and at the end of the process only 40 larger communities should remain (*Tageblatt*, 10 May 2011; Müller 2009: 148, 153).

220   *Regional and local patterns in democracies*

In contrast to the Netherlands, Luxembourg adheres to the French model of *cumul des mandats*, meaning the accumulation of local and national offices. The small size of the country facilitates this strong link between the two levels. However, this has repercussions for the quality of the national Parliament, as local bigwigs tend to invest in their own strongholds. In the first decade of the millennium, 75 per cent of national MPs held a local office position, and there are basically no rules against drawing multiple salaries. Forty-two per cent of MPs hold a local executive position, and two-thirds of these are mayors (Dumont *et al.* 2011: 133). In 2013, 20 MPs (one-third of the chamber) were mayors and 13 were local councillors (almost one-quarter of the chamber); in addition, there were seven executive councillors. In total, 40 MPs out of 60 (66.6%) worked both at the local as well as the national level, combining their MP salaries of €6500 per month with those of their local jobs – mayor (€5900 per month) or councillor (€3900 per month). Former Prime Minister Jean-Claude Juncker presented plans for a significant reform of this system, which was supported by the Green Party; however, resistance on the part of parliamentary and local elites has been strong (*L'essentiel*, 24 September 2013). Following the legislative elections of 2013, the new coalition government between the Liberals (DP), Socialists (LSAP) and Greens (Dei Greng) included such a reform in the coalition agreement, and they intend to prohibit the accumulation of positions (i.e. mayor and MP). The main reason cited is that mayors should concentrate fully on their role as leader of their municipality. Nevertheless, at present, it is still possible to hold a local office and be an MP. It is expected that a reform will be announced closer to the local and legislative elections in 2017 (*Luxemburger Wort*, 9 December 2013). The size of the country means that the office of mayor is a powerful position. Especially when mayors are also national MPs, they can rely on an extensive network that reaches deep into the government. They are also seen as potential future ministers. In this regard, one neglected area of research is the nature and influence of informal power networks in Luxembourg (Müller 2009: 144).

The governmental structure of local authorities involves a legislative assembly (council) and an executive council chaired by a mayor. The mayor and the members of the executive council are appointed by the monarch and the interior minister, respectively. Currently, most appointments are made in line with recommendations. Above this structure, there are 12 non-elected administrative cantons supervised by three larger non-elected districts. These officials are appointed by the central government. The districts in particular are highly relevant due to the small size of the municipalities. These units, which are headed by appointed district commissioners, contribute to inter-municipal cooperation and serve an important role in the supervision of municipalities (OECD 2009: 151). Many small municipalities have developed inter-municipal syndicates in order to manage major responsibilities such as hospitals, retirement homes and swimming pools. The central state would like to modernise this complex web of relationships through new spatial and regional planning (Müller 2009: 148). Although the constitution in Article 107 and the Law on Municipalities of 1988 grant formal autonomy to the municipalities, the reality on the ground is the

Regional and local patterns in democracies 221

gradual reduction of powers, with the implementation of policies decided at the centre. Dependency on funding from the central government despite several local taxes characterises the revenue structure of Luxembourg's communities.

One major strategic project for the country is the cross-border Grande Region (SaarLorLux), which seeks to unify certain Belgian and German regions and Luxembourg. This concept dates back to a document drafted by the Ministry of the Interior in 2005 entitled 'Integrated Concept of Territorial and Administrative Reform in the Grand-Duchy of Luxembourg', which led to the establishment of a special parliamentary committee on the 'Territorial Restructuring of Luxembourg'. A report by this committee was published on 1 July 2008 (OECD 2009a: 147; Chambre de Deputés 2008; Müller 2009: 152–154; on the Grande Region see Moll and Niedermeyer 2009). Since then, successive Luxembourg governments have been engaged in this long-term plan of restructuring.

The national political parties dominate local politics; however, there are limits to party political organisation in the municipalities with fewer than 2000 inhabitants. As a result, majority electoral systems frequently prevail in these smaller municipalities. The representatives of larger municipalities are elected by proportional representation. Political parties are well established; nevertheless, there are differences in terms of electoral strength depending on the size of the municipality. The Christian Social People's Party (CSV) tends to be stronger in the smaller communities in which elections operate by a majority system, whereas the Socialists have more support in the cities. Overall, the Socialists are generally stronger at the local level than the Christian Socials (Dumont *et al.* 2011: 132). Local elections actually have higher turnouts than national elections, proving that this is an important level of politics in Luxembourg – although one of the main reasons behind this high level of participation is the fact that there is compulsory voting also at the local level (Müller 2009: 149; see alsoTable 8.6).

In comparison to other European countries, Luxembourg is probably under the greatest pressure to integrate its foreign population. Foreigners who have lived in the country for at least five years have the right to vote and stand for election. However, only those candidates who speak Luxembourgish (*Letzebergisch*) are entitled to become mayors or councillors in the executive branch; there is no such requirement for positions in the legislative council. In 2011, about 18 per cent of voters were foreigners, and they represented 7 per cent of candidates. Luxembourg City is quite an interesting capital, as almost two-thirds (65.22%) of residents are foreigners; 34.78 per cent are Luxembourg nationals. However, only a small number of foreigners are registered in the electoral lists, making strong integration policies imperative. In addition, the number of women elected has been steadily increasing, with about 32.1 per cent in 2011 (CDSP 2011: 7; Besch *et al.* 2011).

Over the past 20 years, local governments have been introducing direct democracy instruments such as local referendums, the consultation of citizens before new projects are implemented and also the possibility of preferential voting in local elections. This final element is found more often in larger cities and municipalities than in smaller ones. Consultative immigrants' committees have also

222 *Regional and local patterns in democracies*

been established; however, they are chaired by Luxembourg citizens (Dumont *et al.* 2011: 134–137). This democratisation of local government notwithstanding, the level of practice still lags behind Dutch, Belgian, Austrian and Swiss municipalities. In fact, Luxembourg's local government is the weakest of the five consensus democracies, and is dominated by informal networks spanning the national and local levels.

Patterns of subnational democracy in federal systems: Austria, Switzerland and Belgium

In comparison to unitary systems, federal systems are designed to devolve as much power to subnational governments as possible. The federalised parts become an important element in the conceptualisation of policy-making. Local government may or may not profit from this decentralisation. In some cases, decentralisation leads to a new centralisation at the regional level to the detriment of the local authorities. There are certainly differences in the ways in which federal systems are structured. Switzerland is possibly the most devolved federal system in Europe and worldwide. The structure of the Swiss government focuses much more on the local municipality and canton levels than on the national level. As mentioned in previous chapters, the nation-building process in Switzerland occurred quite late and was characterised by resistance by some cantons. One important additional veto instrument in Switzerland is the direct democratic referendum, which is used quite frequently at the cantonal level, and more often than at the national level.

In comparison to the Netherlands and Luxembourg, the subnational system of Switzerland is extremely fragmented. There are 26 cantons and about 2596 municipalities with a high level of autonomy, making it problematic to merge municipalities. The Swiss have a system of symmetric federalism, meaning that all federalised parts are equal in terms of rights. The cantons are represented at the national level in the upper chamber of the bicameral parliamentary system, the Council of States (*Ständerat*). The Council consists of 46 members: two for each canton and one each for the half cantons (see Table 8.4).

One major problem in Switzerland is that some cantons are better represented than others in the Chamber of States. Some cantons are quite small, with barely 100,000 inhabitants (Appenzell Innerrhoden, Obwalden, Uri, Glarus, Nidwalden, Appenzell Aussenrhoden, Jura and Schaffhausen) and only four have more than 500,000 inhabitants (Zurich, Berne, Waadt and Aargau). The others have intermediate populations. Over 90 per cent of the population live in municipalities with fewer than 1000 inhabitants (Ladner 2011: 201).

Subsidiarity and fiscal autonomy are two important pillars of the Swiss political system. The historically evolved political structures remain more or less intact today, despite pressures for modernisation and improving the efficiency of decision-making. This is particularly relevant for cantons and municipalities that still hold popular meetings in which most decisions are taken. This is a particularly old form of government that is still practised in some locations in Switzerland. In a

Table 8.4 The 26 cantons in Switzerland, 2015

Cantons	Year of membership	Population	Number of cantonal executive members	Number in cantonal Parliament	Number of municipalities
Uri (UR)	1291	36,023	7	64	20
Schwyz (SZ)	1291	152,775	7	100	30
Obwalden (OW)	1291	36,837	7	55	7
Nidwalden (NW)	1291	42,082	7	62	11
Luzern (LU)	1332	394,571	5	120	83
Zürich (ZH)	1351	1,446,093	7	180	170
Glarus (GL)	1352	39,794	5	60	29
Zug (ZG)	1352	120,071	7	80	11
Bern (BE)	1353	1,009,204	7	160	356
Fribourg (FR)	1481	303,343	7	110	163
Solothurn (SO)	1481	263,665	5	100	109
Basel-City (BS)	1501	190,597	7	110	3
Basel-Land (BL)	1501	281,266	5	87	86
Schaffhausen	1501	79,420	6	60	26
Appenzell-Ausserrhoden (AR)	1513	54,061	5	65	20
Appenzell-Innenrhoden (AI)	1513	15,853	7	50	6
St Gallen (SG)	1803	495,756	7	120	77
Graubünden (GR)	1803	195,916	5	120	125
Aargau (AG)	1803	645,251	5	140	213
Thurgau (TG)	1803	263,703	5	130	80
Ticino (TI)	1803	350,399	5	90	135
Vaud (VD)	1803	761,157	7	150	318
Valais (VS)	1815	331,794	5	130	14
Neuchâtel (NE)	1815	177,303	5	115	37
Geneva (GE)	1815	477,321	7	100	45
Jura (JU)	1979	72,396	5	60	57

Sources: author's compilation based on websites of the cantons in 2015; Vatter (2014); Bundesamt für Statistik (2016f).

224 *Regional and local patterns in democracies*

seminal study by Adrian Vatter, the author identifies five types of government found among the cantons and municipalities in Switzerland.

The first type, typical of Basel and Geneva, is labelled the *centralised direct democratic* group; here, the party system is fragmented and political structures are relatively centralised. There is a strong use of direct democratic structures. The second type is called the *decentralised direct democratic* system, of which Zurich and Bern are the best examples. These governments show many similarities to the first type, but the political structures are more decentralised, meaning that municipalities enjoy more financial and political autonomy. The third type is referred to as the *representative democratic* system, which is common in Ticino, Lucerne and Solothurn; it is characterised by stable party systems with few parties and large coalition governments. The fourth type, the *formal participative* system, often found in Aaargau and Jura, features many parties and easy access to the institutions of direct democracy. It also has a decentralised political system, allowing for a high level of political and fiscal autonomy in municipalities. The fifth type, common in Glarus, Zug and Uri, is called the *executive power-sharing* system; it features few parties and a low level of direct democracy, although instruments are easily accessible. These cantons of the fifth type may be regarded as the core of historical Switzerland, reflecting the country's popular assembly tradition that was eroded over the course of the twentieth century. This tradition still exists, but it has a largely symbolic character (Vatter 2007: 157–161).

With regard to the municipality level, in a survey conducted by Andreas Ladner and Julien Fiechtner in 2009, about 81.9 per cent of municipalities have a popular assembly that meets regularly two or three times a year, mainly to approve the budget and review expenditure at the end of the year. In contrast, just 18.1 per cent have a Parliament, a system found primarily in the larger cities and municipalities. The popular assembly is more widespread in the German-speaking region (94.5%) than in the Romandie (62.3%) or in Italian Switzerland (23.7%; Ladner and Fiechter 2012: 439).

In spite of all these differences, Switzerland has one of the highest levels of fiscal autonomy at the subnational level. According to the OECD database on public expenditures in the various levels of government, in 2013 Switzerland spent about 42.9 per cent of public expenditure at the central level, but 37.8 per cent at the cantonal level and 19.4 per cent at the municipal level (a total of 57.2 per cent at the subnational level). These proportions have been fairly constant over recent decades. Cantonal and municipal autonomy also means that the subnational level wields wide-ranging taxation rights. According to Andreas Ladner, about 70 per cent of taxation is undertaken at the subnational level (see Table 8.2; also Ladner 2011: 201).

At the cantonal level, the executive comprises between five and seven members; in the municipalities this number may vary from three to 30, but the average size is six. Higher numbers are generally found in the larger cities. Mayors are directly elected, a major difference from the national level (Vatter 2002: 31). At the cantonal level, members of the executive have full-time positions with sufficient

Regional and local patterns in democracies 225

remuneration, whereas smaller communities may have to rely on voluntary office-holders, which have been increasingly difficult to find. As a result, some municipalities have had the same leader for long periods of time, as nobody else is willing to take on the unpaid burden. In addition, many local leaders are elected merely because there are no other candidates. In 14 per cent of cases, they are actually elected by the legislative assembly (Ladner 2011: 202; Horber-Papazian and Jacot-Descombes 2014: 238–239). This is another peculiar aspect of Swiss government, which still relies on the militia voluntary system at all levels, including the national Parliament. This means that most cantonal and municipal parliaments are fairly weak and suffer from a low level of professionalisation; in fact, they consist primarily of part-timers who dabble in politics as a side job. According to a survey conducted in 2009, 94 per cent of the 15,000 local councillors serve in government as an additional part-time job, which in most cases represents about 50 per cent of their working time. The remuneration for these militia voluntary local elites is still not completely regulated; they tend to receive compensation payments rather than a monthly wage. The majority of professionalised local elites serve in the executives of large municipalities, especially in the cities; however, even city parliaments lack financial and human resources (Vatter 2002: 32–33; Horber-Papazian and Jacot-Descombes 2014: 280).

The case of Berne may illustrate how cantons work. Although the Berne government is accountable to Parliament (*Grosser Rat*), it occupies a very strong position within the cantonal political system. A professional public administration is at the government's disposal. One of the main reasons is that the government controls most of the administrative resources in relation to Parliament. The cantonal Parliament has a small staff with few resources that are used very efficiently, one of the trademarks of Swiss government. Therefore, the top administrative position in Parliament (the secretary-general) is carefully appointed and is quite important in public administration terms. As in the national Parliament, the Berne Parliament consists of militia MPs who are part-time. More than at the national level, these parliamentarians have to reconcile their professional and political lives, and eventually family. As at national level, top positions in Parliament are characterised by rotation. Consensualism and cooperation among MPs is the norm. One of the main reasons is that cantonal parliamentarianism is less targeted by the media than the national Parliament. Therefore, cooperation between government and Parliament is the norm; however, clashes may emerge depending on the ideological composition both of government and Parliament. In terms of the collegial structure of government and its relationship to Parliament there is isomorphism between the national and cantonal political systems across the country (Interviews CH).

In addition to the direct election of the leader of the cantonal executive and the weak parliamentarianism, Adrian Vatter also discusses the fact that the party system is less complex at the subnational level. At the subnational level, there are on average three relevant parties, not four. Moreover, parties wield more power due to the lack of influential interest groups, which generally concentrate their efforts at the national level through the institutionalised structures in the

226   *Regional and local patterns in democracies*

pre-legislative process. Furthermore, the weakness of local and cantonal parliaments strengthens the position of the parties in the executive (Vatter 2002: 33–35). The role of political parties in municipalities is fairly constrained, as about 40 per cent of local executives are not members of political parties: instead, they regard their role as neutral and professional. This is particularly the case in smaller communities; party politics is stronger in the larger cities (Horber-Papazian and Jacot-Descombes 2014: 287).

Direct democracy is the most distinctive aspect of Swiss democracy. According to Wolf Linder and Rolf Wirz, Switzerland is the only country that puts the referendum above the constitution. This gives direct democratic instruments a prominent place in the Swiss political system (Linder and Wirz 2014: 160). The same holds true at cantonal and municipality levels, where direct democratic instruments are used even more often. According to a study by David Altman, there are about 103 direct democratic initiatives per year on average. However, Altman points out that only 33 of these are actually initiatives launched by citizens; the rest are top-down projects. Moreover, on average only 45 per cent of the electorate take part in these initiatives, although this figure can be as high as 65 per cent and as low as 23 per cent (Altman 2013: 744). Referendums are more common in the larger municipalities, mainly in the major cities; in the small, rural cantons of Obwalden, Graubünden, Thurgau, Valais and Neuchâtel, very few democratic initiatives take place, in part due to the institution of the popular assembly (Linder and Wirz 2014: 150). The lack of legislation controlling campaign funding is highly problematic and there has been a tendency towards populism in the campaigns over the past decade. The populist, anti-immigrant posters of the SVP are a good example of this excess (Lindner and Wirz 2014: 152–154).

As discussed above, the municipalities have extensive autonomy in the implementation of their policies. However, similar to the cases of Austria and Belgium, the cantons are clearly the dominant subnational structure. Apart from the fact that they are the larger unit, historical developments have made cantons the equivalent of (almost) sovereign states within the federation. Although some competences of the municipalities are delegated from the federal level, most of the others are established by cantonal law. The municipalities have a wide variety of responsibilities, including schooling, social security, transportation and communication, protecting the environment and spatial planning, policies concerning local identity (such as sports, cultural, religious and leisure activities), security, public order and defence (linked to the militia system). Municipalities now seek out cooperation with their counterparts in order to manage issues such as security policies and education. The cantons have gradually taken on an active role in creating these economies of scale. One important development has been the cantonalisation of the health policy, which includes the management of hospitals (Steiner and Kaiser 2013: 149). This becomes even more important if we examine the highly fragmented map of municipalities in Switzerland – in 2013, there were 2408 such entities. In terms of public administration, Bauen in the canton of Uri, with 178 inhabitants, has just one administrator,

Regional and local patterns in democracies 227

whereas Haiden in Appenzell-Outer Rhoden, with 4030 inhabitants, has a staff of 34; in contrast, in Bern, which has over 125,000 inhabitants, there are 3557 administrators (Steiner and Kaiser 2013: 153–154).

The reforms currently taking place represent an attempt to improve the efficiency and professionalism of services across Switzerland. NPM will help to ensure better value for money and establish a more customer-friendly public administration. In 2008, a major multi-level agreement including the federal, cantonal and municipal levels was signed for the first time. This document envisages the modernisation of the financial equalisation mechanism among municipalities through improved economies-of-scale management via the cantons, which have more professionalised administrations. This process is linked to the redistribution of tasks and competences in order to reduce the burden on the smaller municipalities in particular. About 75 per cent of municipalities are enmeshed in inter-communal arrangements involving one or more tasks (Horber-Papazian and Jacot-Descombes 2014: 292–297; Steiner and Kaiser 2013: 156). The continuing investment in the merging of municipalities is also crucial. For a long time, mergers were exceedingly rare, but over the past two decades municipalities have come to recognise the advantages of creating economies of scale. This has been an asymmetrical process – intensive in Glarus, Thurgau, Ticino, Fribourg and Jura, and more moderate in Berne, Solothurn, St Gallen and Aargau (Horber-Papazian and Jacot-Descombes 2014: 298).

Switzerland is also characterised by a highly sophisticated system of horizontal and vertical coordination and co-decision between the centre and the cantons. Critical in this regard are the Director's Conferences (DK) for the individual policy areas; a national conference in which the representatives from various DKs meet with federal-level officials is regularly held. Such cooperation leads to common policies based on majority voting. According to Nicole Bolleyer, DKs are a long-standing instrument of coordination that dates back to 1897. However, the growing pressures of the European Union have made coordination and cooperation even more complex, and so a Conference of the Cantons (*Konferenz der Kantone*, KdK) was established on 8 October 1993 to increase horizontal coordination between cantons in EU policy, constitutional matters and improvement of cooperation between the federal and cantonal level. Since 2008, a House of the Cantons (*Haus der Kantone*) in Bern has overseen the complex system of intergovernmental conferences. One has to differentiate between the high-ranking KdK and the myriad directors' conferences (*Direktorenkonferenzen*) at civil service level. The KdK is based on an agreement signed in 1993, and renewed and improved over the years at least up until 2006 (KdK 2006). This group, which meets twice a year, has become an important forum for conflict resolution. The dominance of coalition or power-sharing governments at the canton level based on consensus and compromise facilitates this co-decision-making process. Resolutions and decisions are taken when 18 cantons support it. The KdK's main addressee is the central public administration attached to the *Bundesrat*, but it also acts as a lobby in the pre-parliamentary and parliamentary phase. In 2014, the core machinery comprised 29 members of staff, mainly

228   *Regional and local patterns in democracies*

seconded by public administration, and it has an overall budget of CHF3.2 million (about €2.9 million). The House of the Cantons comprises a total of 200 members of staff and holds over 1600 meetings a year. The budget has led to surpluses over the years (Interview CH; Maissen 2016; KdK 2015; Bolleyer 2006: 400–401). The overall intergovernmental decision-making model is replicated at the cantonal level in relation to the municipalities. It is estimated that over 500 such cantonal conferences exist (Bolleyer 2006: 400; Interview CH).

At the municipality level, the Federation of Swiss Municipalities (*Verband der Schweizer Gemeinden/Association des Communes Suisses*, SGV/ACS), founded in 1953, represents 71 per cent of all municipalities and serves as an important interlocutor for the cantonal and federal governments.

Austria: a centralised federal system

Austria is known for its strongly centralised form of federalism, which presents a stark contrast to the highly decentralised Swiss federal system. This is historically related to the important role which Vienna played in the Austro-Hungarian Empire and later in the First and Second Republics. As a result, Austrian federalism is often referred to as 'executive federalism' (*exekutiver Föderalismus*), meaning that the subnational government primarily implements delegated policies determined at the centre (Pelinka and Rosenberger 2003: 223–232). Jan Erk argues that this dominance of the centre over the provinces was present from the outset (Erk 2004: 2). Federalism was a compromise between the Social Democrats (SPÖ) and the Christian Socials during the constitutional settlement. Due to the large working-class population in Vienna, the Social Democrats dominated the capital; they advocated more of a unitary, centralised structure for the country. The Christian Socials, who were stronger in the western regions such as Tyrol and Vorarlberg, proposed federalism as a way of accommodating their concerns regarding centralistic Socialist dominance. There were calls for independence in Tyrol and Vorarlberg; however, the constitutional settlement was instrumental in preventing these movements from getting off the ground (Erk 2004: 4–6; see also Table 8.5).

In comparison to Switzerland, municipal autonomy is constrained by the tendencies towards centralisation in the provincial governments. In this sense, Austria's federalism is characterised by a double centralisation at both federal and provincial levels. This is clearly visible in terms of public expenditures: 68.9 per cent of the overall budget is spent at the federal level, and just 31.1 per cent is spent at the subnational level (16 per cent at the provincial level and 15 per cent at the municipal level; see Table 8.2). However, about half of expenditures at the municipal level involve the capital city of Vienna. Provincial and local governments are evidently limited in their ability to pursue autonomous policies.

As in Switzerland, the municipal level is still relatively fragmented. Mergers between municipalities have been taking place at an accelerated rate in recent decades; however, in 2015, there were still 2100 municipalities, 74 per cent of which had fewer than 3000 inhabitants. Several *Bundesländer* have introduced

Table 8.5 The nine provinces (*Bundesländer*) of Austria

	Area (square kilometres)	Population in 1,000s	Number of people sitting in Landtage	Number of people on executive	Number of municipalities
Burgenland	3962	288.4	36	7	171
Kärnten (Carinthia)	9538	557.6	40	7	132
Niederösterreich (Lower Austria)	19,186	1637.3	56	9	573
Oberösterreich (Upper Austria)	11,980	1436.8	56	9	442
Salzburg	7156	538.6	47	7	119
Steiermark (Styria)	16,401	1221.6	48	8	287
Tyrol (Tirol)	12,640	728.8	36	8	279
Vorarlberg	2601	378.5	45	7	96
Wien (Vienna)	415	1797.3	129	13	1
	83,879	8584.9			2100

Sources: Statistik Austria (2015); websites of provincial governments and parliaments.

230   *Regional and local patterns in democracies*

programmes for mergers, as seen in Steiermark. Upper Austria (*Oberösterreich*) and Lower Austria (*Niederösterreich*) have the highest numbers of municipalities; Vienna, in contrast, has only one: the capital itself (Statistik Austria 2015).

Austria's federal system is still governed by the principles of *Proporzdemokratie*, meaning that the *Bundesländer* are part of the overall pool of the distribution of spoils. The partyocratic dominance of Austrian subnational democracy results in the territorial distribution of power based on the strength of the respective *Bundesland*. This is also one of the reasons behind the high level of political stability in Austria. Right-wing populist parties are also constrained by this reality. Moreover, in the past, a majority of provincial governments (*Landesregierungen*) were 'concentration governments' (*Konzentrationsregierungen*) consisting of all the relevant parties in Parliament and the rest were coalition governments. This has been changing over time, so that today only Lower Austria, Upper Austria and Carinthia are all-party governments. Therefore, in Carinthia, a stronghold of the FPÖ, cooperation and consensual politics with other parties is crucial in order to achieve political stability and successful decision-making and implementation of policy.Vienna was an all-party government up until 1973, but since then it has followed a majoritarian system, leading in the past decade to coalition government (Table 8.6).

In the most recent Upper Austrian provincial elections of 27 September 2015, the nine seats in the government were distributed based on a D'Hondt proportional representation system as follows: four ÖVP, three FPÖ, one SPÖ and one Grüne. Following this allocation, a coalition agreement is forged for the subsequent legislative period. The FPÖ is an active participant in this process, exhibiting respect for compromise and government responsibility at local and regional levels, as seen with the SVP in Switzerland. The 'concentration government model' allows the FPÖ to contribute to pragmatic consensual politics with the other parties. Even when former FPÖ leader Jörg Haider was the *Landeshauptmann* (president) of Carinthia, he still had to work within a proportional representation government. This demonstrates that the FPÖ is far more integrated in the Austrian political system and political culture than outsiders might think; they represent the 'Alpine populism' ingrained in the country, again similar to the SVP in Switzerland. The vast majority of FPÖ politicians tend to cooperate with their peers in the search for pragmatic, down-to-earth solutions. Table 8.6 shows that the overwhelming majority of provincial governments between 1945 and 2015 have been grand coalition governments (49.2%) and concentration governments (33.9%). Taking into account the minimum winning coalition type (52.6%), power-sharing arrangements impact upon almost 95 per cent of governments at the provincial level. In addition to this fairly stable and long-term power-sharing approach to provincial government, provincial presidents generally stay in power for a long time – for example, Leopold Gratz (1973–1984), Helmut Zilk (1984–1994) and Michael Häuptl (1994–) in Vienna, the 'dynasty' of Josef Krainer Sr. (1948–1971) and Jr. in Steiermark (1981–1996), and Wilfried Haslauer (1977–1989) Sr. in Salzburg and his son with the same name since 2013, a potential dynasty in the making. Probably the

Table 8.6 Type of provincial government in Austria, 1945 to 2015

	Number of governments	Single party absolute majority		Single party minority		Minimum winning coalition		Grand coalition		Concentration government	
		N	%	N	%	N	%	N	%	N	%
Burgenland	19							19	100		
Carinthia	21									21	100
Lower Austria	16									16	100
Upper Austria	20									20	100
Salzburg	19					1	5.3	3	15.8	15	78.9
Steiermark	21							13	62	8	38
Tyrol	19					1	5.3	13	68.4	5	26.3
Vienna	22	10	45.5			1	4.5	10	45.5	1	4.5
Vorarlberg	18	1	5.6			10	55.6	1	5.6	6	33.2
	175	**11**	**6.3**	**0**	**0**	**13**	**7.4**	**59**	**33.7**	**92**	**52.6**

Source: author's compilation based on Austrian Provinces website.

232 Regional and local patterns in democracies

most charismatic *Landesvater* ('father of the province') was Eduard Wallnöfer (1963–1987) in Tyrol, an archetype of the strong autonomy found in western Austria. The role of provincial presidents in rallying the troops but also in protecting the (limited) regional autonomy in relation to the centre cannot be underestimated (Fallend 2006a: 979–981). However, charismatic leadership may also have negative consequences. Longevity in power can lead to the establishment of resilient informal networks, patronage, clientelism and even political corruption that bypasses the state. Former president of Carinthia Jörg Haider may be a good example in light of the Hypo Alpe Adria Bank affair. It took decades for the Austrian government to discover all the implications of his networks of power.

Party politics at subnational and local levels does not differ significantly from that in the centre, due to the isomorphism of the structure of opportunities (the electoral system, electoral threshold and parties are almost identical). In addition, political changes in government have been more limited at the provincial level than at the federal level. According to Laurenz Ennser-Jedenastik and Martin Ejnar Hansen, in 131 statewide elections between 1945 and 2010, there were only five major changes in the governor's partisan identification, and four of these occurred in the past 25 years (since 1985; Ennser-Jedenastik and Hansen 2013: 781). The rise of the FPÖ after 1985 is certainly a major factor in this moderate but growing instability, which may represent an important element in the renewal of Austrian democracy.

The structure of the provincial political system consists mainly of a provincial assembly (*Landtag*) and a provincial government (*Landesregierung*). Electoral results influence the process of government formation, which is much simpler in 'concentration government' provinces. In the vast majority of cases, as Table 8.5 shows, the alternative is a grand coalition between the two main parties. In contrast to the parallel institution at the federal level, the *Landtag* is relatively limited in its powers due to a much lower level of professionalisation, but also due to the dominance of party discipline. In many ways, the introduction of the FPÖ, the Greens, Team Stronach and, most recently, the NEOS has been crucial to the revival of parliamentary arenas in the nine provinces. *Landtage* can influence policy through their representatives at the *Bundesrat*, but in reality they lack the resources to play a decisive role. Many provincial MPs have a *cumul des mandats* with positions in their municipalities (for an overview see Aigner 2006; Wolfgruber 1997).

The strong majorities upon which provincial executives base their incumbencies make it difficult for the *Landtage* to be truly effective, especially when Austria's system of executive federalism is taken into account. The provincial office (*Landesamt*) is the joint administrative machinery for all provincial executive councillors. The number of executive councillors varies across provinces, but generally there are between seven and nine councillors. Vienna, the exception, has 13, some of whom are non-executive, which is controversial but constitutional. The political parties dominate the selection procedure, which is a fairly partyocratic process. Among our five countries, Austria has the second lowest

Regional and local patterns in democracies   233

level of regional autonomy after Luxembourg. One interviewee clearly criticised the concentration governments, because many of the officeholders were non-executive as in Vienna, thereby doubling the bureaucratic structures and making the system of government more expensive (Interview A).

Austria's system of *Verwaltungsföderalismus* (executive federalism) grants a number of powers to the provinces. According to Franz Fallend, the provinces have the following responsibilities: nature conservation, construction law, regional planning, hunting and fishing, youth and child welfare, and tourism – a lengthy but highly restrictive list of autonomous competences. Most of the other important policies are delegated by the centre through executive federalism. Judicial matters are handled at the federal level as well, and provincial taxation powers are very limited. Provincial governments are extremely dependent on grants coming from the centre (Fallend 2011: 178).

The Austrian *Bundesländer* have developed a complex system of inter-governmental cooperation similar to the Swiss one, in which they coordinate their positions in relation to the central government. The Conference of Provincial Presidents (*Konferenz der Landshauptleute*, KLH) meets regularly. The first liaison structure of coordination for provincial governments was established in 1951 in the central administration of the government of Lower Austria. The first conference took place in 1966, extending the already dense network of relationships among and between provinces and the central government. Representatives of the government are always invited to take part in these meetings (Fallend 2006b: 1035). In many cases, this prevents the emergence of the infamous joint decision-making trap (*Politikverflechtungsfalle*) described by Fritz Scharpf. The restricted autonomy of the Austrian *Bundesländer* generally results in close cooperation with the central government. Franz Fallend estimates that this conference of provincial ministers and presidents holds over 600 meetings per year when all policy areas are taken into account. This includes the Conferences of the Provincial Directors of Administration (*Landesamtdirektoren Konferenzen*), which prepare the groundwork for the meetings of higher ranking ministers and presidents (Fallend 2006b).

The main powers of municipalities are as follows: local police (3 per cent of total expenditures), traffic-related services (8%), land-use planning, social services (11%), education (16%) and services such as water treatment and waste management, markets, and sport and leisure facilities (29%; Fallend 2011: 178; Österreichischer Gemeindebund 2015b).

Here again, financial resources are limited. The majority of budgets are provided by provincial and local taxes; however, there is an annual financial equalisation in order to prevent excessive inequalities. At the provincial level, half of revenues come from taxes, and the other half from taxes shared with the federal level; in the municipalities, this ratio is 28.9 per cent to 71.1 per cent (Fallend 2011: 179).

Austrian municipalities are relatively disciplined. According to figures from the Austrian Association of Municipalities, local finances are in excellent shape overall, achieving a surplus since 2012. This has permitted more investment in

234 *Regional and local patterns in democracies*

and improvement of the population's quality of life. The financial equalisation system seems to be working quite well. In total, local communities (excluding the special case of Vienna) have revenues of €18 billion but spend just €17.1 billion (Österreichischer Gemeindebund 2015a, 2015b).

Mayors play crucial roles in local political systems, and therefore legislation was introduced to enable their direct election. According to Barbara Steininger quoting Manfred Welan's study on the office in Lower Austria, the mayoral position is a multi-hat job. He or she is simultaneously the representative of the state, the head of government, the president of the local assembly, the director of the administration, the economic chief and the party leader (Steininger 2006: 996, quoting Welan 1999: 20). Local councils (*Gemeinderat*) and local executives (*Gemeindevorstand*) work closely together under the leadership of the mayor, who is also the president of the council. The local political system is based on power-sharing and consensual politics, facilitating long-term planning (Steininger 2006: 998–999). Mayors of municipalities are the most trusted political figures in Austria. As in Switzerland, Luxembourg and the Netherlands, NPM tools have been introduced in recent decades to enhance the quality of services, but also to increase the participation of the population in the political system. The use of direct democratic instruments such as local referendums and initiatives have increased over time, and informal consultation meetings have become more common in local decision-making (Steininger 2006: 999). However, local leaders are overwhelmingly men; there are very few female mayors. According to data from the Austrian Association of Municipalities, at the turn of the millennium there were 45 female mayors and 2314 male mayors (Österreichischer Gemeindebund 2015b).

There is an unelected (appointed) coordination structure that provides some economies of scale for specific tasks such as the fire department: the districts (*Bezirkshauptmannschaften*). There are 99 such districts, each chaired by a district director (*Bezirkshauptmann*). This is an integral part of the provincial administration. In addition, several inter-municipal cooperation associations have been established to manage common policy areas such as social security, education and health (Steininger 2006: 1002).

Two major interest groups shape the role of municipalities and cities in the multi-level Austrian federalist system. One is the Austrian Association of Cities (*Österreichischer Städtebund*), consisting of 249 cities and representing 65 per cent of the population. According to its website, 71 per cent of all workplaces are located in these cities. The association is celebrating its centenary this year (Österreichischer Städtebund 2015). The other interest group that influences the multi-level federalism debate on behalf of the municipalities is the Austrian Association of Municipalities (*Österreichischer Gemeindebund*), founded in 1947, which currently represents 1089 municipalities out of 2100, or 70 per cent of the population (Österreichischer Gemeindebund 2015c). Cities can have overlapping memberships in the two organisations.

Regional and local patterns in democracies 235

Belgium: the emergence of a confederation

Probably the most difficult case to analyse is Belgium. In previous chapters, we have discussed the growing tensions between the two main linguistic groups: Dutch- and French-speaking. Since 1970, a peaceful devolution process has been taking place, effectively hollowing-out the centre and upgrading the federalised units, and in 1993 a new constitution was adopted. Meanwhile, six state reforms have completely changed the territorial structure of Belgium (see Chapters 2 and 3). There are now four tiers: the central government, regional and community governments, provincial governments and local governments. Belgium has three regions (Flanders, Wallonia and Brussels-Capital) and three communities (Dutch- , French- and German-speaking). The Flemish- and Dutch-speaking communities have merged, so now there are only five federalised units rather than six. There are also ten elected provincial authorities, five in each region.

The old provinces have a very long tradition, going back to the Middle Ages. The provinces have a more coordinating role involving economies of scale in the newly restructured Belgian state; they take on all tasks that are not covered by other levels. The provinces play an important role in social and education policy, but also in roads, traffic and spatial planning. There are five Dutch-speaking provinces (West Flanders, East Flanders, Antwerpen, Limburg and Flemish Brabant) and five French-speaking provinces (Hainaut, Namur, Brabant-Wallon, Liége and Luxembourg). Brussels is led by the capital governor.

The interesting thing about the provinces is that although they are a relic of the old system, they are still quite useful for supporting inter-municipal cooperation in policies that exceed the competences of the municipalities. Provincial governments are elected every six years, providing a certain stability in terms of policy-making at this level. The directly elected provincial assembly approves provincial legislation proposed by the Permanent Deputation. This is reminiscent of the Dutch model, as the Permanent Deputation is headed by a governor appointed by the King; in reality, the governor is an appointee agreed upon by the regional government and the national government and then formally appointed by the monarch. He or she (thus far, the vast majority of provincial governors have been men) is appointed for an undefined period and heads a government of between seven and four provincial MPs who are appointed by the provincial council according to a system of proportional representation. It is crucial that these leaders be experienced, well versed in the Belgian political system and masters of the art of consensus, power-sharing and cooperation, as they have no voting rights in the deputation; nevertheless, they play an important integrating role. Ideal candidates would have extensive experience in institutions at all levels of the complex Belgian political system.

As Table 8.7 shows, all provinces have provincial governments. The most recent elections in 2012 catapulted the N-VA to the leadership of the province of Antwerpen. The success of the moderately nationalist N-VA has weakened the more extreme VB, which is suffering not only from this new competition but also from a general internal party crisis: they lost almost two-thirds of their

236 Regional and local patterns in democracies

Table 8.7 Ten provinces in Belgium in 2016

Provinces	Number of provincial MPs	Number of members of deputation	Coalition government 2012–2018
Flanders			
West Flanders	72	9	CD&V-Open VLD-SP.a
East Flanders	72	8	CD&V-Open VLD-SP.a
Antwerpen	72	8	N-VA-CD&V-SP.a
Limburg	63	8	C&DV-SP.a/Groen-Open VLD
Flemish Brabant	72	8	CD&V-Open VLD-SP.a-Groen
Wallonia			
Francophone Brabant	37	5	MR-PS
Hainaut	56	5	PS-MR
Namur	37	6	MR-CdH
Liége	56	6	PS-MR
Luxembourg	37	5	CdH-PS

Source: author's compilation based on websites of provinces.

support in Flanders, their stronghold (Dandoy 2013: 248). The separate party systems notwithstanding, Régis Dandoy has determined that there are now four equal party families, each of which carries about 19 to 20 per cent of the total vote. The traditional party families of the Socialists, Christian Democrats and Liberals are either stagnating or declining while the regionalists are on the rise, especially in Flanders with the emergence of the N-VA. Results at the provincial level seem to be a good indicator of national trends in the country. In Wallonia, a four-party system is emerging in which the Socialists and Liberals dominate and two smaller parties, the Christian Democrats (CdH) and the Greens (Ecolo), participate in coalitions. In Flanders, the regionalists (N-VA) and the Christian Democrats are the main groups; the smaller Liberals and Socialists are potential coalition partners (Dandoy 2013: 252).

The crucial subnational tier is the region and the community. Research on Belgian subnational political systems thus far has been biased towards the Flemish region, which exhibits a high level of compactness and governs with a long-term perspective. Research on the Wallonian region has lagged behind, and work on the other subnational units and the politics of the respective political systems has been rather scarce (Table 8.8).

There is a clear division of labour between regions and communities. Regions cover all policies related to economics, infrastructure, innovation, industrial issues and policies governing small and medium-sized enterprises. Communities are primarily responsible for all social and cultural policy areas, specifically education, social policy, cultural policy and also health policy. Whereas regions deal with 'hard' technical policies, communities focus more on 'soft' identity policies. This means that regions and communities must work closely together in

Table 8.8 The regions and communities of the Belgium Federation

Subnational unit	Area (square kilometres)	Population		Subnational Parliament		Subnational government		Number of municipalities
		N	%	N	Location	N	Location	
Flemish region and community	13,522	6,444,127	57.5	124	Brussels	9	Brussels	308
Walloon region	16,844	3,312,888	32.7	75	Namur	8	Namur	
Federation Wallonia-Brussels (Francophone community)	17,000	[4,300,000 (est.)]	[38.6]	90	Brussels	7	Brussels	262
German community	875	[68,961]	[0.7]	25	Eupen	4	Eupen	
Brussels-Capital Region	161,38	951,580	9.4	89	Brussels	5	Brussels	19

Sources: author's compilation based on websites of subnational governments and parliaments; Statistics Belgium (2015: 6).

238 *Regional and local patterns in democracies*

order to ensure a level playing field. All of these subunits follow the dominant Belgium institutional model of parliamentary democracy with a unicameral Parliament and a regional government. The highly fragmented party systems in all regions and communities always result in coalition governments that are sometimes oversized in order to maximise the levels of consensus and power-sharing. For a long time, political parties tried to create governments at federal and regional levels with the same ideological party composition, under the assumption that these governments should be similar in order to facilitate policy-making in the regions and communities. However, governmental instability at the federal level and the refusal of the New Flemish Alliance (*Nieuw-Vlaamse Allianz-* N-VA) to participate in the Elio Di Rupio government in 2010 has led to the current diversity of government composition at the various levels (Pilet and Fiers 2014: 126).

Consequently, coalition agreements represent an important integrating element that strengthens the cohesion of the government. When regional elections were introduced in 1995, there was a tendency to create congruent coalitions at federal and regional/community levels; however, this became more difficult over time due to the difficulty of forming a stable government at the national level. Moreover, the collapse of governments at the federal level before the end of the legislative term created additional divergence between the two levels (Deschouwer 2009b). Today, the idea of congruence remains an important orientation for political parties at both levels, but now they view it more pragmatically.

Federal and regional elections take place every five years. There is a super-election day that is generally the same day as European Parliament elections. Four subnational regional and community elections are held in Flanders, Wallonia, the Brussels capital region and the German-speaking community. Only the Parliament of the federation of Wallonia-Brussels is indirectly appointed, consisting of 75 MPs from the Walloon regional Parliament and 19 francophone MPs from the Brussels capital regional Parliament.

In Wallonia and Brussels the Socialists and the Liberals are the leading parties, with the Christian Democrats in third place, whereas in Flanders the Christian Democrats, the Liberals and the independence-seeking New Flemish Alliance (N-VA) dominate coalition governments. There is a strong ideological affinity between the CD&V and the NV-A. Both are moderate parties; however, the NV-A emphasises independence as a major priority for Flanders. Governments in the regions and communities are relatively well endowed with resources. They feature sizeable ministerial cabinets that are exploited for patronage for party functionaries, similar to the central government.

A quick glance at the federal, regional and community budgets shows that the vast majority of funds are spent at the subnational level. In this context, Flanders accounts for 53.5 per cent of all subnational expenditures, followed at a distance by Wallonia (17.9%) and the Federation of Wallonia-Brussels (the name of the francophone community; 13.9%). These two budgets together represent 32.2 per cent of funding. As we compare Flanders to the other subnational units, it is

Regional and local patterns in democracies 239

apparent that it is extremely efficient at keeping its budget within existing revenues. In contrast, both the region of Wallonia and the Federation of Wallonia-Brussels have incurred budget deficits year after year; Brussels capital is facing the same dilemma. In 2015, this led to tensions between the president of the region of Wallonia, Paul Magnette, and Prime Minister Charles Michel, and the issue of budget planning has become quite salient. The region of Wallonia has a considerable deficit, and the centre is asking the region to reduce its expenditures, prompting Magnette to regard the central government as constraining the region too much (Table 8.9; *Le Soir*, 1 April 2015).

Strategically, the Flemish government has made clever decisions. In addition to mergers of institutions, it has used consensual politics to adopt long-term policies that are paying off, such as its education policies (De Rynck 2005). Despite extensive public programmes in Wallonia such as the Marshall Plan for Wallonia, now in its fourth iteration (2015–2020), Flanders has been socio-economically more successful. Even today, the region of Wallonia is struggling with the decline of its industrial sector, particularly the coal industry; this region and Brussels are hotspots for 'welfare without employment'. Originally the idea of former Regional President Elio di Rupio in 1999, the Marshall Plan for Wallonia was first implemented in 2005 for a period of four years. Strategically, it forms part of the Di Rupio government's 'contract of the future' (*contrat d'avenir*; Accaputo *et al.* 2006). Since then, there has been a Marshall Plan dedicated to green energy (2009–2014), and the latest Marshall Plan 4.0 focuses on vocational training and new technologies. Internationally and in European terms Wallonia is not doing so badly; even in comparison to Flanders, it is only lagging slightly behind. The Marshall Plan investments are also designed to shift the region's economic culture towards innovation, the green economy and new technologies (Interviews BE; *La Libre Belgique*, 8 April 2015, 3 September 2015; *Le Soir*, 29 May 2015). Similar plans are now being devised for Brussels, an extremely wealthy city that has major problems in terms of location issues for

Table 8.9 Budgets of federal, regions and communities in Belgium, 2015

Unit of government	Revenues (bn €)	Expenditure	
		Bn €	% of subnational budgets
Federal government	56.7	64.1	
Flanders	38.3	38.2	53.5
Region of Wallonia	12.2	12.8	17.9
Federation Wallonia-Brussels (Community)	9.6	9.9	13.9
Brussels-Capital region	3.9	4.9	6.9
German community		5.6	7.8

Sources: Government of Belgium (2015); Government of Flanders (2015); Parliament of Wallonia (2015); Government of Federation Wallonia-Brussels (2015); Parliament of Brussels-Capital region (2015); Government of German community (2015).

240 *Regional and local patterns in democracies*

enterprises and the relatively high level of unemployment in comparison to other Belgian cities (*La Libre Belgique*, 16–17 June 2015; on the dynamics of regional elections see Coffé 2006). There has been a general discussion on the cost of transfers from Flanders to Wallonia. According to interviewees and scientific research, the sum may be about €5 to €6 billion (OECD 2009b: 71). However, inter-regional disparities in Belgium are normally exaggerated. If we use European indicators from the European Commission for the year 2014, taking the EU regional GDP average of 100, then we come to 136 for Flanders and 90 for Wallonia. It is particularly the rich region of Brabant-Wallon that leads to this result for Wallonia. The four Walloon provinces are still considerably below, at 75 to 85 of the EU average. If compared to the year 2004, the gap between the two parts of the country has been widening, while Wallonia seems to stagnate; in spite of all considerable efforts with the Marshall Plan, Flanders increased their GDP in relation to the EU average from 116.5 to 136. Even the quite rich Brussels region GDP average decreased from 237 to 207, showing considerable problems (Eurostat 2016m).

The German-speaking part of the country is economically peripheral in Belgium. The integration of German speakers with the rest of the country is still highly problematic, and the major railway line to the German-speaking capital, Eupen, is underdeveloped. There have been calls to create a new region to address these issues. The German-speaking part is heavily involved in cross-border cooperation, especially with the Netherlands and Germany in the EU Region Maas-Rhine, but also in the Grande Region. Although it may be peripheral in Belgium, it is located at the very centre of Europe, an ideal space for the development of a sophisticated economic structure with numerous small and medium-sized enterprises. However, cross-border migration has had a negative impact on the German-speaking community, as the flow of people is in the direction of neighbouring countries rather than towards the German-speaking community, unlike the case of Luxembourg (Palm *et al.* 2010). The intense cooperation between political parties will be an important factor in strengthening the position of this community in the Belgian federation. The Christian Democrat Bruno Maraite was a long-standing contributor to institution-building in the community through its council (Brüll 2010: 34–40). Between 1999 and 2014, the Socialist Karl Heinz Lambertz put the German-speaking community on the map during his tenure as regional president. His government was a strong supporter of the community region model for that part of the country; this resulted in significant tensions with the region of Wallonia, which regarded them as German-speaking Walloons (Brüll 2010: 40–43; Milquet 2013: 8). The visibility of the German-speaking community is particularly important in the wider German-speaking Europe, encompassing Germany, Austria, Liechtenstein, Luxembourg, Switzerland and South Tyrol. Lambertz is a great communicator and networker who managed to enhance the region's political and economic standing over the past two decades. He has recently been elected president of the regional Parliament. A new generation of young politicians is taking over, revitalising the community's ambitions (Interviews B).

Regional and local patterns in democracies 241

In terms of the lowest tier of local government, the municipality, the political structures are basically the local assembly (five to 77 members based on the size of the municipality) and the executive. Flanders is more advanced in restructuring the space between regions, provinces and local authorities, a process that started in the 1980s. New laws on local government enacted in Flanders (2005) and Wallonia (2006) led to similar structures in the two parts of the country (Verhelst *et al.* 2013: 279). In Flemish municipalities, a municipal clerk (*chief executive officer*) manages the administrative part of the system. In contrast, in Wallonia, there are still notaries or first civil servants, following a more legalistic and Weberian tradition (Wayenberg *et al.* 2011: 83).

Brussels remains the main challenge for Belgian federalism. Due to the clash between the two linguistic groups in the Brussels capital region, the restructuring of the local government has been rather slow. Despite the centrifugal tendencies in Belgian federalism, the Brussels issue (a capital city claimed by both parts) has thus far been the main factor holding the federation together, apart from the European Union (Van Wynsberghe 2014).

Although attempts have been made to implement directly election of the mayor, the office is pro forma still an appointee of the King. This is a Dutch legacy that is inadequate for the twenty-first century. In reality, mayors are selected primarily on the basis of preferential voting. In the 2006 local elections, 83 per cent of voters used preferential voting, 82 per cent of mayors were elected by preferential voting and 95 per cent were among the top three candidates (Wayenberg *et al.* 2011: 85). Another aspect of this Dutch legacy is the monism of local government. The municipal assembly is the centre of local government; however, the mayor is head of both the executive and the local assembly, such that the local assembly ultimately degenerates into a rubber-stamping institution. A reform towards dualism would certainly enhance democratic structures at the local level (Verhelst *et al.* 2013: 279). As with the other consensus democracies analysed in this book, a major challenge for the future of Belgium will be to find a balance between local councillors as lay participants in democratic politics and the growing need for professionalisation. The vast majority of Belgian councillors are laymen; on average, they are male, middle-aged (about 40 years old) and have strong roots in their municipality (Verhelst *et al.* 2013: 282). It is estimated that one-third of councillors are professionalised, attached to parties, and perceive their work as part of a long-term career (Verhelst *et al.* 2013: 282). One factor that impedes professionalisation is the inadequate salary for councillors, who only have their expenses reimbursed for ten meetings a year. In contrast, mayors and executive councillors (aldermen) are entitled to a part-time or full-time salary depending on the size of the municipality (Verhelst *et al.* 2013: 278).

The main vehicle of coordination between the levels is the committee of concertation (*comité de concertation*), which is coordinated by the prime minister's office; however, each subnational unit also undertakes bilateral relations with its counterparts. This committee is also in charge of coordinating the devolution process from the centre to the regions. The 18 inter-ministerial conferences that allow comparison of notes and the extension of common policies are also vital,

242 *Regional and local patterns in democracies*

as is the principle of 'good faith' that governs how politicians should act: above all, they should be loyal to the constitution (Chancellerie du Premier Ministre 2014: 26–27; Chancellerie du Premier Ministre 2015: 16). The Constitutional Court, which adjudicates issues of competences and legal disputes between the central and subnational governments, has a more formalised structure (Poirier 2002: 30–35; Interview B).

The small size of Belgium permits smooth and continuous cooperative dialogue that results in consensual solutions to practical problems. This is most evident in the coordination of EU policy, which sometimes requires quick answers that emerge from informal meetings between the representatives of the federalised units and the central government in the cafés and restaurants of Brussels. This is facilitated by the long-term relationships between the relevant actors, which have fostered a common culture of cooperation within the Belgian government at all its levels (Van den Brande 2012; Interview B).

Conclusions: subnational government in an age of Europeanisation and globalisation

Over the past 40 years, subnational governments in consensus democracies have undergone radical change. Democratisation pressures within countries, the expansion of the welfare state and the need for improved services have led to major shifts in local government. In this respect, the Netherlands and Switzerland seem to be at the forefront, whereas Belgium, Austria and Luxembourg are lagging behind.

9 The changing political economy of consensus democracies

Introduction

The success of consensus democracies in West Central Europe and the Scandinavian countries cannot be fully understood without consideration of their supporting social market economies. These liberal democracies decided at an early stage to identify mechanisms to tame the worst effects of capitalism (also known as 'Manchester capitalism'). The crisis of the 1930s was an important traumatic experience and turning point for small consensus democracies, as their political steering capabilities were revealed to be very limited in a turbulent world.

In this chapter we focus on various aspects of the changing political economy of consensus democracies. We start with a discussion of the varieties of capitalism in the context of European integration and globalisation. This is followed by a section on the differences between the coordinated market economies in our five consensus democracies, concentrating primarily on the systems of industrial relations in these countries. The chapter ends by drawing a number of conclusions.

Varieties of coordinated capitalism in the context of Europeanisation and globalisation

Peter Hall and David Soskice developed the seminal typology of 'varieties of capitalism', differentiating between liberal and coordinated market economies (LMEs vs. CMEs). This typology is a highly useful tool for understanding the changing nature of the political economies of our five consensus democracies. The authors propose the USA and Germany as the two main types: LME and CME, respectively. The main difference between the two is that LMEs are embedded in cultures of competitiveness and hierarchies, with market mechanisms supplying the coordination needed for enterprises. The formal contract is an important element of this type of capitalism. In contrast, CMEs are embedded in cultures of cooperation and non-market relationships characterised by greater exchange of information within networks. Whereas competition tends to create the necessary equilibrium in interactions in LMEs, such equilibria are achieved in CMEs through strategic interactions among firms and actors (Hall and Soskice

244 Changing political economy of democracies

2001: 8). At the centre of the typology are the relations between enterprises and the various socio-economic institutions of the respective types of capitalism. The four main institutions in this regard are the corporate governance system (including financing), the system of inter-company relations, industrial relations and the education system. First, LMEs feature a very competitive corporate governance system in which the stock market plays a key role and financing is competitive; in contrast, in CMEs, corporate governance is less dominated by the stock market, and companies tend to avoid being listed in the stock exchange. Moreover, enterprises in CMEs generally have longer relationships with banks, the *Hausbank* ('house bank') in the case of Germany. This allows for long-term and nearly constant cooperation between companies and their banks. Second, as noted above, LMEs operate in inter-company systems that are quite competitive, whereas the relations between companies in CMEs are more cooperative, encouraging the exchange of information within well-established stable networks. Third, LMEs feature weak systems of industrial relations (or none at all) for representatives of labour and capital to negotiate bargaining agreements; in CMEs, industrial relations are central to the national political economy. Finally, LMEs have very general systems of education, whereas CMEs enjoy both general but also vocational training systems in the enterprises that are funded by employers as well as by the state. This dual system is a major characteristic of CMEs (Hall and Soskice 2001: 27–33). The literature on the varieties of capitalism has expanded considerably since the publication of this typology, which positively contributed to the scholarly debate (among the prolific literature see Streeck 2010; Amable 2003: 202–207). Despite many criticisms, the simplicity of the typology developed by Hall and Soskice is certainly its most attractive element, and it offers an excellent way to analyse our five consensus democracies. All five countries definitely belong more to the coordinated type, at least during the *trente glorieuses*; however, globalisation and Europeanisation since the 1980s have radically changed their capitalist outlooks. Although coordinated elements are still visible, the nations are all involved in a process of transition from a national capitalist paradigm to a Europeanised and globalised system. The problem with typologies is that it is often difficult to integrate the dynamics of socio-economic change. Indeed, the Bretton Woods system that was established after 1945 and remained in effect until 1973 contributed to a stable global political economy that was still dominated by the Western world. When the Bretton Woods system broke down, currency and economic instability did not allow for a new equilibrium to be established. Since then, such equilibria have been difficult to achieve, particularly after the fall of the Berlin Wall. The one world of capitalism with the USA at its centre remains in place, but there are also new centres emerging, such as Europe and Asia (see Castells 1998). Since 1985, the EC/EU has been engaged in building a strong single market with a common currency in order to enhance its importance within world capitalism. The rules of this single market that stretches from Rejkjavik to Nicosia and from Riga to Santa Cruz de Tenerife in the Canary Islands have eroded national protective approaches to capitalism. However, this Europeanisation has been uneven

Changing political economy of democracies 245

and has sometimes been resisted by member-states. It is a difficult process in which member-states must sacrifice their sacred cows in the public sector to privatisation, particularly in the utilities, transportation and communications sectors. One major problem is that people still think in the frame of national markets, not in a European frame (McCann 2010: ch. 3; see also Schmidt 2011; Hall 2014).

According to Martin Schneider and Mihai Paunescu, who conducted the most complete quantitative study on the evolution of capitalism in 26 OECD countries, there are major differences in the way in which different consensus democracies have responded to globalisation pressures. According to these authors, between 1995 and 2005, Austria, Belgium and Germany remained CMEs, but the Netherlands became more LME-like, and Switzerland fell into the category of full LME (Schneider and Paunescu 2012: 740).

Two institutional features of coordinated market economies, namely corporate governance and vocational training systems, may be used to illustrate the hybridisation of CMEs towards the liberal model. Although the process of change in corporate governance started quite slowly, it has been accelerating since the 1990s. The European Commission has been using soft governance approaches to achieve institutional isomorphism in terms of corporate governance across the EU. These soft governance methods, which include the open method of coordination (OMC), benchmarking and good practices, are based on voluntarism and exposure through naming and shaming (Héritier 2002).

All this is taking place in the context of transforming national capitalism into a European and global capitalism. In this regard, the directives related to the European company statute (*Societas Europea*, SE) of 2001/2004 are highly significant. These directives required a long time for approval, and even today they permit companies considerable leeway, such as the choice between 28 different models, and after Brexit 27 ones (for more details see Nicolopoulos *et al.* 2009); nevertheless, some streamlining has been achieved. The statute allows companies to act based on one version of European company law across the entire territory. The majority of enterprises that have shifted from national rules to the European company statute are German. One advantage of the European statute is that enterprises can choose an American-style monistic system (with only an executive board) instead of the dual-board system (executive and supervisory boards, as found in Germany, Austria, the Netherlands and Switzerland), thereby eliminating or reducing the power of employee representatives. On 18 May 2016, there were 2547 established SEs. In March 2014, out of 2125 SEs, 13.7 per cent were German companies, followed by the UK (3.1%), the Netherlands (1.6%), Luxembourg (1.3%), Austria (0.9%) and Belgium (0.5%; ETUI 2016). These figures are still small; however, this system may well become more important due to the pressures of Europeanisation and the promises of greater efficiency in the European context (ETUI 2016).

An analysis of corporate governance produces related results. Over the past two decades, a process of convergence across corporate governance codes has been taking place. Each of our consensus democracies has adopted corporate

246 *Changing political economy of democracies*

governance codes based on the recommendation on quality of reporting for corporate governance ('comply or explain'; 2014/208/EU, 9 April 2014). Companies can depart from the provisions of the recommendation, but they must then present a clear and qualitative explanation. Central to this code are transparency and the accountability of the executive board to shareholders. As a result, national company laws are gradually being superseded by a European and global code based on Shareholder Value Orientation (SVO). In the Netherlands, several corruption scandals involving Dutch enterprises such as Royal Dutch Shell and Ahold have led to greater transparency in corporate governance. The Tabaksblatt Committee, which was established in 2003 to examine corporate governance practices in the Netherlands and create common rules, was reinforced by a compromise reached in the Economic and Social Committee (SER) that also took workers' rights into consideration (Goodijk 2010: 13–17). The Netherlands is among the EU countries with the highest levels of non-EU shareholder ownership, with 58 per cent in 2011; in contrast, for Germany the figure is 28 per cent, but that of the UK is about 70 per cent (OEE 2013: 38). Nevertheless, ownership concentration in the 100 listed companies in the Netherlands remained at 20.8 per cent in 2009, in comparison to a European average of 35 per cent (Van Bekkum *et al.* 2010: 15–18; Goodijk 2010: 1). Many have claimed that SVO may not be compatible with the socio-economic context of the Netherlands, as it tends to create international isomorphism rather than taking into account the specific national model of the Netherlands (see Bezemer *et al.* 2015 for more on legal aspects of corporate governance).

In the other four countries we find similar convergence processes in corporate governance. In Belgium, a corporate governance code was adopted in 2009, and in Luxembourg, such a code has been revised several times, most recently in 2013. The monistic executive board tends to prevail among companies in Luxembourg. In Austria, the dual board remains central to the Austrian corporate governance code; however, shareholders have become important players in the dynamics.

With regard to criticism of this trend, the study by Konrad Lachmayer on the situation in Austria is a case in point, and the author's comments clearly apply to all the other countries in the European Union. First, the working group that drafted and supervises the code is highly informal, and the selection of its members was accomplished in a non-transparent fashion, although a claim of inclusiveness has been made. Trade union confederations are not represented – only business leaders, financial institutions and the government. Second, the code relies on voluntary compliance by enterprises, but there are no sanction mechanisms. Third, control consists of regular surveys filled out by the enterprises, but this may lead to an attitude of 'just playing the game'. An independent institution enforcing the code would be necessary in order to achieve actual compliance. Fourth, the code relies heavily on the ethical and moral responsibility of top management (Lachmayer 2013). According to the newspapers *Kurier* and *Die Presse*, only three listed enterprises – DO&CO, VoestAlpine and Wienerberger – abided by all the corporate governance prin-

Changing political economy of democracies 247

ciples in 2011 (*Kurier*, 29 October 2013; *Die Presse*, 13 November 2013). Switzerland has also been under considerable pressure to adopt the new European corporate governance guidelines; there is widespread fear that national enterprises will be at a disadvantage if Swiss company laws and codes of practices are not updated to the European level. Legislation to this effect has been discussed in and adopted by the Swiss Parliament; notably, the main business organisation, *Economiesuisse*, was the primary actor in this drafting process. The Swiss code of best practice for corporate governance was adopted in 2015, adhering closely to the European guidelines. The role of shareholders in companies was strengthened. Another positive note is the fact that 30 per cent of board members must now be women. The next step will be to reform the shareholder law (*Aktienrecht*; Schmid 2014; *Neue Zürcher Zeitung*, 11 December 2014; Kunz 2015: 258–262). This will mean the erosion or end of many protectionist measures designed to prevent takeovers of Swiss enterprises, such as *Vinkulierung* (the right of enterprises to block the sale or transmission of shares to others) and *Partizipationsscheine* (non-voting right shares; Schneyder and Widmer 2011: 412–413).

According to Hall and Soskice, dual education based on vocational training in enterprises is a major characteristic of coordinated market economies. Of our five consensus democracies, only Austria and Switzerland have robust permanent programmes of vocational training funded by the public and private sectors in partnership. However, both of these dual education systems are under pressure in terms of places offered by firms (Switzerland) and the number of apprentices (Austria). The number of Swiss enterprises offering places has declined in recent decades, placing the national system in jeopardy. In 1985, 24 per cent of Swiss enterprises offered vocational training places, but by 2001 this figure had declined to 17.4 per cent. The lowest number of places was registered in 1995, with 15.5 per cent (Rohrer and Trampusch 2011: 153). In Switzerland, in 2013 44.3 per cent of young people in secondary education opted for a vocational training involving apprenticeship in an enterprise and schooling (*duale Berufsbildung*) a further 12.4 per cent enrolled in professional schools, a total of 56.7 per cent; in Austria, the figures are 37.5 per cent and 39 per cent, respectively, a total of 76.5 per cent (BMWFW 2014: 4; SBFI 2016: 11). These two countries feature the highest levels of apprentices taking part in dual education. In a distant second tier, in 2011/2012 we find the Netherlands with 69.5 per cent, Luxembourg 60.7 per cent and Belgium 72.5 per cent; however, the vast majority are students in professional schools, and not direct in the enterprises as apprentices. The figures for the Netherlands, Luxembourg and Belgium are 26.4, 23.5 and 4.3 per cent, respectively. Luxembourg and Belgium fall below the OECD average of 26.5 per cent (CEDEFOP 2016). Among the Benelux countries, the Netherlands has the most sophisticated vocational training system while Luxembourg and Belgium lag behind. However, Luxembourg is making a major effort in this regard, despite the fact that many of its enterprises are small or medium-sized and have only limited human and financial resources.

248 *Changing political economy of democracies*

Industrial relations as coordination: from interventionism to light neo-corporatism

In a simplified fashion, we could equate coordinated market economies with the neo-corporatism concept developed by Gerhard Lehmbruch and Philippe Schmitter in the late 1970s and early 1980s. Lehmbruch and Schmitter describe neo-corporatism as based on key centralised organisations (in certain countries something very close to political parties) that are integrated into fora in which important socio-economic policies are discussed and agreed upon with the social partners (Schmitter and Lehmbruch 1979; Lehmbruch and Schmitter 1982). Schmitter goes even further in creating a continuum showing how interest groups are integrated into the polity. The Anglo-Saxon (mainly American) style, pluralism, and its opposite pole, neo-corporatism, may be found in continental Western Europe, particularly in the small consensus democracies, but also in Germany and France (Schmitter 1982: 263–264; Lehmbruch 1982: 4–5). Due to the wide variety of approaches, agreement on the definition of neo-corporatism has been difficult. In a review of the neo-corporatism literature, Lehmbruch demonstrates the dimensions that different authors have included in describing the concept. By the time Lehmbruch and Schmitter conducted their studies, neo-corporatism was being challenged by globalisation and, subsequently, by Europeanisation. Probably the best summary on neo-corporatism is provided by Alan Siaroff, who attempted to gather all the different definitions and develop a more encompassing concept. Siaroff defines 'liberal' corporatism as a system of interest intermediation:

> [W]ithin an advanced industrial society and democratic polity, the coordinated, co-operative and systematic management of the national economy by the state, centralised unions, and employers (these latter co-operating directly in industry) presumably to the relative benefit of all three actors.
>
> (Siaroff 1999: 177)

Siaroff also proposed an interesting ranking based on a number of studies on neo-corporatism that is highly valuable for our analysis by ranking countries on the basis of five categories on a continuum between strong neo-corporatism and pluralism.

Siaroff differentiates between integrated and pluralist economies. The more neo-corporatist elements found in an economy, the more integrated it is; the fewer neo-corporatist elements in the economy, the more pluralist it is. The integrated vs. pluralistic economy is very close to what Hall and Soskice described as CMEs vs. LMEs. Siaroff computes several factors in determining his classification. His ranking consists of five levels: (1) pluralism, (2) weak corporatism, (3) moderate corporatism, (4) moderate to strong corporatism, and (5) strong corporatism. Among our five consensus democracies, only Austria is ranked as a strong corporatist in all three decades between 1970 and 1999. Luxembourg and Switzerland are ranked as strong to moderate corporatist, whereas

Changing political economy of democracies 249

the Netherlands and Belgium tend more towards the moderate type (Siaroff 1999: 170–172).

Among the most easily identifiable elements of coordination in consensus democracies are their sophisticated systems of industrial relations. Peter Katzenstein's analysis of social and liberal democratic corporatism describes the two main types of coordinated economies found at least until the 1980s. He defines democratic corporatism as follows:

1 The ideology of social partnership: instead of class conflict, consensus and cooperation between representatives of labour and capital are emphasised.
2 The centralised and concentrated system of industrial relations allows for national deals; conflict between key organisations is a possible outcome, although consensus and cooperation tend to prevail. There is also a strong linkage to political parties.
3 Voluntary informal continuous coordination of conflicting objectives between interest groups, state bureaucracies and political parties (Katzenstein 1984: 27).

The primary difference between social and liberal democratic corporatism is that the ideologies of social partnership in the two systems promote diverging market economies, one emphasising social democracy and the other liberalism. The two prototypes of social and liberal democratic corporatism are Austria and Switzerland. In the Austrian case, the Social Democratic party and the main trade union confederation (Austrian Trade Union confederation, ÖGB) are quite strong and have achieved a balance of interests between labour and capital, whereas in Switzerland there is traditionally an imbalance towards capital, as Swiss trade unions are relatively weak (Katzenstein 1984: 30–32). Nevertheless, the consensual approach has allowed a considerable share of workers to be covered by collective agreements: collective agreement coverage has been about 50 per cent. The trade-off was that the economy was kept fairly open, permitting the use of a foreign workforce, but in times of recession, unemployment was exported by the selective firing of such workers (Katzenstein 1984: 23). In a more expansive work, Katzenstein used the same typology to include additional countries. Austria, Denmark and Norway were grouped under the category of social democratic corporatism; Switzerland, the Netherlands and Belgium fell under the liberal category. Sweden was regarded as a mixture of the two systems (Katzenstein 1985: 104–105). Although Luxembourg was not included in Katzenstein's study due to its open economy, it would be assigned to the liberal democratic corporatism group. In 2003, Katzenstein wrote a review of his two books which demonstrated that his main thesis regarding the flexible adjustment of small states with open economies was still valid. His comments centre on the concept of the ability of countries to 'learn' through deliberation in informal or informalised structures how to develop new adaptation strategies to overcome crises and rebalance their political economies. This is possible because citizens exhibit a high level of trust in their country's political structures. Small states tend to

250   Changing political economy of democracies

avoid past mistakes and concentrate on creating external and internal alliances to overcome imminent threats (Katzenstein 2003: 17–19). Katzenstein also refers to the study by Philippe Schmitter and Jürgen Grote called *The Corporatist Sisyphus*, whose main thesis is that corporatism reinvents itself every 20 to 25 years to adjust to the new reality (Schmitter and Grote 1997). All of our five small consensus democracies have certainly adjusted their corporatist structures in order to adapt to the new reality of European integration and globalisation. They no longer feature the interventionist neo-corporatism of the 1970s, but instead a more liberal, light neo-corporatism designed to regulate and provide order to policy-making processes in an increasingly European setting. The Treaty of the European Union in 1993 and the introduction of Economic and Monetary Union (EMU) in 1999 is transforming member-states' socio-economic framing from methodological nationalism to methodological Europeanism. In this sense, member-states no longer operate in a context of national sovereignty but of shared sovereignty, particularly those countries that are part of the Eurozone. Even before the global financial crisis, national governments had to adhere to stability and growth pacts (SGPs) requiring national budgets to remain balanced with low deficits and low levels of public debt (on shared sovereignty see Wallace 1999, 2005). The US financial crisis and the Eurocrisis proved that more mechanisms at the central EU level were necessary; this prompted new legislation such as the two-pack and six-pack that will force governments to assume their share of responsibility for sound finance in the Eurozone. The European semester starting in September compels member-states to submit their budgets to the European Commission before they are sent to national parliaments for approval in order to identify and prevent imbalances (Schweiger 2014). In this sense, governments in the member-states need the support of their main social partners in order to maintain a high level of stability and favourable conditions for economic growth. Between 1980 and 2006, there were 110 social pacts covering 145 issues related to welfare, the labour market and wage reform issued in 16 West European countries. In total, there were 157 pact offers, of which 47 were rejected (Hamann and Kelly 2010: 1). Europeanisation means that the incorporation of social partners in socio-economic policy-making has become even more important. Even Switzerland decided on its own to adjust to the policies of the EU, despite not being a member. According to Wolf Linder, 'Europeanisation without membership' is taking place in Switzerland: at quite an early stage, the Swiss government decided to implement the almost automatic autonomous adaptation (*autonomer Nachvollzug*) of Swiss law to European law. Although a referendum in 1992 rejected membership in the European Economic Area (EEA), the Swiss population accepted seven bilateral agreements with the EU in a referendum in 2000. Before EEA membership was rejected, the Swiss administration had already adopted a package of laws related to the *acquis communautaire* called *Eurolex*, which had to be relabelled *Swisslex* following the 1992 referendum (Linder 2011: 46). According to Linder, the asymmetrical power relationship between Switzerland and the EU will definitely lead to full membership; all other options can only be transitional. However, this depends

Changing political economy of democracies 251

on how the EU will evolve and whether it will accept quasi-membership arrangements or membership *á la carte* (Linder 2011: 55–57; Interview CH). One interviewee even believes that the autonomous adaptation allows Switzerland to 'be the most integrated country in the European Union' (Interview CH).

Switzerland: changing Schweiz AG

Among our five countries of interest, Switzerland probably comes closest to a liberal market economy; however, many of its coordination elements are not visible and are above all informal. The Swiss political economy, despite being highly competitive, is a dualist economy featuring strong machine, watch, pharmaceutical and chemical industries that are export-oriented. This sector employs about 25 per cent of the working population and represents 50 per cent of GDP. Another important sector is the banking industry, which has obviously been suffering considerably from globalisation due to the increasing number of international regulations constraining its activities, among them the fight against corruption and the abolition of bank secrecy. The rest of the economy is more protected and consists primarily of the agricultural sector and industries for domestic consumption (Mach and Trampusch 2011: 19–20). The stability of the Swiss economy is characterised by long-standing cooperation among the business associations representing different interests. A so-called 'bourgeois bloc' has been able to preserve a system that balances export-oriented and domestic-oriented interests. Labour organisations have always been in a subordinate position in this liberal corporatist system. Before we delve deeper into the changes in liberal democratic corporatism in Switzerland, it is important to provide a brief overview of the main socio-economic interest groups and how they have evolved.

As noted above, employers' and business organisations have changed significantly. Keen to avoid reliance on the pre-parliamentary phase of policy-making, they have sought to directly influence legislation through lobbying, including the colonisation of political parties. There has also been major restructuring among the Business Interest Associations (BIAs). An attempt to create a united business association failed due to differences among interests. Historically, business organisations played an important role in supporting the emerging Swiss nation-state in the nineteenth century. One of the main reasons for this is that state structures were quite weak, and therefore business organisations (and later trade union organisations) were allowed to take over certain state tasks, with the state subsidising many of these activities. Wolfgang Streeck and Philip Schmitter have referred to this as 'private interests government/governance', which is embedded in overarching national policy-making structures (an excellent historical reconstruction may be found in Gruner 1964; Eichenberger and Mach 2011: 64–66; Streeck and Schmitter 1986). Today, the vast majority of businesses in Switzerland are represented by *Economiesuisse*, which was founded in Lausanne in 2000 as a fusion of the traditional Association of Swiss Industry and Trade (*Verein der Schweizerische Industrie und Handel*, also known as 'Vorort') and

252 Changing political economy of democracies

the Society for the Promotion of the Swiss Economy (*Gesellschaft zur Förderung der Schweizerischen Wirtschaft*). *Economiesuisse* represents over 100,000 enterprises with two million employees and consists of 100 sectoral associations and 20 cantonal chambers of commerce (Economiesuisse 2016). This organisation is paralleled by the Swiss Confederation of Employers (*Schweizerischer Arbeitgeberverband*, SAV-USP) founded in 1908, which is involved in the collective bargaining process. The Banking Association (*Bankenvereinigung*) has always worked closely with Vorort, and in 2000 it became part of *Economiesuisse*. The Farmers' Association (*Bauernverband*, SBV-USP) founded in 1897 remains the primary association representing the interests of the farming industry. Finally, the Association of Artisans (*Schweizerischer Gewerbeverband*, SGV-USAM) represents the majority of small and medium-sized enterprises, covering the more protected sectors of the Swiss economy. Employers' organisations generally have a high level of membership: up to 80 to 90 per cent.

A major restructuring of the traditional interest groups including the power relationship between business organisations and trade union confederations has taken place in recent decades, significantly affecting Swiss liberal democratic corporatism. This entailed a move towards liberalism.

Trade unionism has had to adjust to a new reality due to a variety of causes. First, the recession of the 1990s led to a loss of workplaces in the construction and manufacturing sectors. Simultaneously, the neo-liberal agenda of employers' organisations pushed for deregulation and the flexibilisation of the labour market. In addition, the European integration process and autonomous adaptation were reshaping opportunities for the working population (Oesch 2011: 83).

As mentioned above, the uneven relations between labour and capital organisations continue to facilitate increasingly liberal corporatism in Switzerland. Trade union confederations have had to develop new strategies in order to protect the interests of their constituencies. Their main weapon has been the potential threat of calling for a referendum on key issues involving the flexibilisation of the labour market or forging alliances with like-minded groups. The actions of Operation Libero in the referendum on the deportation of foreigners that have committed crimes in February 2016 is a good example (see Chapter 4). This strategy has been quite successful for trade union groups. Moreover, like business organisations, trade unions have a strong influence on the Social and Christian Democratic parties. The trade union movement in Switzerland is fragmented; there are two major confederations, one closer to the Social Democrats and the other closer to the Christian Democrats. In 2014, the former (*Schweizerischer Gewerkschaftsbund*, SGB) is more important, featuring 363,341 (49 per cent of the total); the pro-Christian Democratic *Travail.Suisse* is the second-largest group with 151,960 (20.5%), having emerged in 2002 as a merger between Christian Democratic trade unions and the Association of Swiss Employee Federations (*Angestellten Schweiz-Employés Suisse*). There are also a large number of people who are organised in trade unions, but not as part of the larger confederations which comprise 226,010 members (30.5 per cent of the

Changing political economy of democracies 253

total) (Ackermann 2014: 5, 8, 9). Since the 1990s, a major restructuring has been taking place. In 2014, the unionisation level had declined to 19.9 per cent (Ackermann 2014: 9; Oesch 2011: 83).

There is something like a 'Schweiz AG' similar to 'Deutschland AG' in which very dense networks are intertwined with national actors providing medium- and long-term national strategic guidance (on the decline of 'Deutschland AG', see Streeck and Höpner 2003; Höpner and Krempel 2012). Here, the studies by Hans Peter Kriesi using reputational analysis can serve as a guide to identify coordination. In his seminal study in the 1970s, Kriesi identified 27 people with overlapping memberships in business associations, three political parties (FDP, CVP, SVP) and the government which were able to coordinate most socio-economic activities in Switzerland through compromise, consensus and cooperation. The business associations were actually the central actors in this dense reputational network. Although, informally, business associations had a major influence in Switzerland in the interwar period, it was only in 1947 that their input into policy-making became formalised through what is known as the *Vernehmlassungsphase*, or the 'pre-parliamentary phase' (Steiner 1971; Kriesi 1980, 1982; Sciarini 2014b: 117–118). These negotiations took a considerable amount of time, as the federal council wanted to ensure that business associations would not abuse their veto by organising referendums or popular votes to override decisions counter to their interests. The system involved a highly formalised government process featuring a long period of internal hearings and reports within and between the ministries before interest groups could officially participate (Klöti 2003: 177; Sciarini 2014a: 531–541).

As one interviewee emphasised, social partnership is not formalised through one particular major institution as is the case in the Netherlands, Belgium, Luxembourg or Austria, but more of a sectoral type embedded in all possible industries. Moreover, social partners are part of tripartite committees in central and cantonal public administration shaping socio-economic legislation. It means that at first sight social partnership does not exist in Switzerland, but at the second sight one realises that they are considerably involved behind the scenes. In 2016, in total there are 28 administrative committees (*Verwaltungskommissionen*) and 91 agency committees (*Behördenkommissionen*). Most of them are before or after the official pre-parliamentary process. The level of transparency in terms of conflict of interests is quite high and posted on the internet (Interview CH).

However, over the past three decades, this so-called 'Schweiz AG' has been eroding, and conflicts among interest groups between export-oriented and domestic-oriented enterprises have increased considerably. Moreover, European integration is creating new pressures on the Swiss political and economic system. The growing importance of the SVP in the political system has also led to more polarisation and conflict. Pascal Sciarini, in basically replicating Kriesi's study for the first decade of the new millennium, identified a major shift from the previous pattern of pre-parliamentary consultation to a more liberal logic of influence during the parliamentary phase. The deals between business associations and political parties have now become crucial across the entire process.

254 *Changing political economy of democracies*

Significantly, business organisations have virtually captured the political parties, with a number of MPs also sitting on the boards of business enterprises. In addition, Parliament has obtained more resources since the 1990s, such that committees have become more relevant. An even more direct impact stems from the fact that many presidents of interest groups actually stand in general elections backed by their organisations and are successful. This is possible because the Swiss Parliament is a semi-professional militia Parliament with no rules governing conflicts of interest. The number of presidents of interest groups in Parliament has been on the increase according to some interviewees. There is even an informal threat of some interest groups to cut funding to political parties if they do not implement certain legislative acts (Interviews CH).

Among the reasons for the decline in the traditional Schweiz AG cited by Sciarini are the following:

1   There are more conflicts between social partners, particularly due to the imbalance between business and labour. European integration has contributed to further liberalisation and re-regulation, which changed the rules of the game in many policy areas. One difficult task has been the regulation of cheap labour coming from new EU member-states in Central and Eastern Europe.
2   The pre-parliamentary phase has become less attractive for interest groups and social partners. The possibility of achieving greater gains by directly influencing Parliament and political parties has contributed to the decline of the postwar system.
3   The previous corporatist system was unable to accommodate new political issues.
4   Crucial sectors such as social policy and agriculture are being challenged by developments at global and European levels, and the old corporatist networks are no longer regarded as central to the Swiss model (Sciarini 2014b: 119).

According to Sciarini, there has been a strong decline in the perceived importance of the pre-parliamentary phase since the 1970s. However, the parliamentary phase is only important when domestic issues are at stake; it does not extend to European matters. Indeed, Sciarini believes that Europeanisation has led to the 'de-parliamentarisation' of the Swiss Parliament (Sciarini 2014b: 122).

A major issue for the economy of Switzerland is the Transatlantic Trade and Investment Partnership (TTIP) negotiations between the EU and the USA which are viewed with apprehension, due to the fact that this would mean a complete liberalisation of the highly protected Swiss agricultural market (Interview CH).

In spite of all this, Switzerland remains more of a hybrid or LME-like economy than a pure LME. The Schweiz AG still exists, although it is being eroded by new cultural traits of business elites and the internationalisation of firms. Support for social partnerships remains high among policy-makers (Interviews CH).

Changing political economy of democracies 255

The Netherlands: continuity and flexibility in the Polder model

The Netherlands has always been something of a hybrid between the liberal type exemplified by the United Kingdom and the more coordinated type of Germany. Historically, the *trente glorieuses* were just an intermediate period; at the beginning and the end of the twentieth century, the liberal market prevailed. Being an open economy in a globalised world is part of the culture of the Netherlands (Sluyterman 2015: 9–12). Nevertheless, the *trente glorieuses* created a highly sophisticated system of coordination based on new private and public law institutions.

Membership in trade unions has been declining; in parallel, there has been a major restructuring event in the formal fusion of the Social Democratic National Confederation of Trade Union Associations (*Nationaal Verbond Vakvereinigingen*, NVV) and the National Catholic Trade Union Confederation (*Nationaal Katholieke Verbond*, NKV) in 1982. Although the Christian National Trade Union Confederation (*Christenlijk Nationaal Vakverbond*, CNV) founded in 1909 was involved at first, it later decided not to join this merger. The first secretary-general of the new National Trade Union Confederation (*Federatie Nationaal van Vakverbond*, FNV) was Wim Kok, who contributed to the success of the Wassenaar agreement and the revival of the Polder model based on consensus, negotiation and compromise (Kleinfeld 2012: 495). While the FNV has 1.13 million members, the CNV remains the second largest trade union confederation with 287,000 members. Another relevant confederation is the Central Trade Union for Professionals (*Vakcentrale voor Professionals*, VCP), which was founded in 1973 and reinvented itself in 2013, and which represents 54,100 mid- and high-ranking executives. There is also the Union (*De Unie*), primarily representing civil servants (Van Het Kaar 2016; CBS 2015).

Trade union confederations have evolved into providers of professional services. The continuing decline in membership is a major problem, reinforced by the high rates of membership among the retired: about one-third of union members are retired people (Kleinfeld 2012: 495). The level of unionisation declined from 34 per cent in 1980 to 20 per cent in 2012 (Ter Steege *et al.* 2012: 23).

In contrast, business groups are relatively well organised, with 80 to 90 per cent coverage of enterprises (Van Het Kaar 2016). The most important is the Federation of Dutch Entrepreneurs-Christian Employers' Organisation of the Netherlands (*Federatie Nederlandse Ondernemer-Nederlandse Christelijk Werkgeversverbond*, FNO-NCW), representing over 120,000 enterprises. This group mainly consists of larger enterprises, but also a large number of medium-sized and small enterprises. The merger of the FNO and the NCW was quite arduous due to considerable resistance among parts of the NCW; however, it was finally accomplished in 1996. The main argument for the fusion of the two groups was that there was a need to join forces in order to defend Dutch interests in the European Union (Kleinfeld 2012: 497). Small and medium-sized enterprises are represented by the Royal Association of Small and Medium-sized Enterprises of

256   Changing political economy of democracies

the Netherlands (*Koninglijke Vereiniging Midden en Kleinbedrijfen Nederland*, MKB Nederland), which comprises over 150,000 firms. The main representative of the farming industry is the Farming and Gardening Organisation (*Land en Tuibouworganisation*, LTO), which claims to represent 50,000 agrarian enterprises (LTO 2016). Similar to Switzerland, there is also a General Employers' Association of the Netherlands (*Algemene Werkgevers Vereiniging Nederlands*, AWVN), which is actively involved in collective agreements and negotiations with trade unions. This association has participated in about half of the 1000 collective agreements in the Netherlands and therefore represents an important advisory resource. AWVN acts closely with the FNO-NCW but is independent from it; there was an attempt to integrate AWVN into FNO-NCW, but disagreement over finances led to the abrupt end of the merger process (Kleinfeld 2012: 498). All three main confederations work together in the Council of Central Business Organisations (*Raad van de Centrale Ondernemensorganisationen*, RCO), which facilitates the coordination of positions and exchanges of opinions among these major social partners.

The above-mentioned main business confederations and labour organisations joined together to create a new Dutch Polder model that led to the establishment of institutions to promote socio-economic dialogue. Indeed, this socio-economic dialogue is internalised among social partners; this is simply part of the way they do things in the Netherlands. Over the decades, there have been conventions and the development of a dense network of groups that sustains the Dutch model of social market economy based on mutual trust and goodwill (Houwing and Vandaele 2011: 133; Hendriks 2011). The postwar period saw the rise of the Foundation of Labour (*Stichting van de Arbeid*, STAR), comprising the social partners that must be consulted on major economic and social matters. The origins of this institution can be traced back to the need to reconstruct the country following the Second World War: on 19 May 1945, employees' and employers' organisations as well as representatives from industry, agriculture and trade unions united to issue a joint declaration emphasising the need to work together to rebuild the nation (SER 2014a: 11). The STAR still remains central to Dutch policy-making and contributes to long-term strategic thinking, and the group is always involved in the spring and autumn government consultations on policies, thereby shaping the country's medium- and long-term socio-economic policies.

Even more interesting is the Social and Economic Committee (*Sociaal en Economische Raad*, SER). Founded in 1950 and enshrined in the Industrial Organisation Law (*Wet op de bedrijfsorganisatie*), the SER consists of representatives from trade unions and business associations as well as experts appointed by the government. The SER is less involved in collective bargaining; it is foremost a permanent advisory body to the Dutch government. An independent body established by the social partners, it is funded by all businesses in the Netherlands and has an annual budget of €16 million. The secretary-general is appointed through a competitive selection process so that government will have no power over the organisation; this clearly strengthens the position of the

Changing political economy of democracies 257

secretary-general within the SER. Indeed, it may be said that the SER represents the idea of Dutch democracy based on consultation (*overleg*; SER 2014b: 7, 10).

Members of the SER are to always keep three objectives in mind:

1 Balanced economic growth and sustainable development.
2 The highest possible employment rate.
3 A fair distribution of income (SER 2014b: 9).

The SER consists of 33 members: 11 from employers' and business organisations (VNO-NCW 7, MKB-Nederland 3, LTO 1), 11 from employees' organisations (FNV 8, CNV 2, VCP 1) and 11 experts (SER 2014b: 13).

According to one interviewee, the SER has now expanded its activities to long-term policy-making pacts. The Energy Agreement for Sustainable Growth (the energy pact) follows the lead of Germany in moving from fossil fuel to renewable energy (the so-called *Energiewende*). The deal was signed by the social partners, the big players of Dutch industry and the government. In total, 47 signatories are committed to this transition to renewable energies. Overall, over 100 objectives were set out that are now being monitored by the SER in the form of a traffic-light system. Since then, other policy area actors have asked for similar processes. One of the reasons for this success is that the 100 staff members of the SER are extremely well trained in consensus-building techniques and in overcoming deadlocks. This decision-making process takes a lot of time, but then the implementation is quite easy because there are virtually no conflicts. It means that the SER has expanded its expertise from a bipartite model to a multi-stakeholder one dealing with complex policy issues. Even more astonishing is that there is a strong ambition to achieve unanimous decisions. This means a process of taking and giving, until the package deal is done, preventing a cherry-picking attitude. Once agreed, signatories have to show a common position towards politics and other arenas. As one Interviewee stresses:

> If you come to an agreement, in a consensus sense, you have a package of things you have negotiated about, there are always some points you win, and some points you lose, it is give and take, some points you like and some points you do not like, you do not walk out of the door, and mention to politics I like this, I did not like this, this is a package as whole, and we stick together as a whole, take as a whole, do not take some parts out of it, because then you do not have anything more.
>
> (Interview NL)

Up until 2014, the SER also had the administrative task of supervising the vast number of industry consultative boards (*Publiekrechtlike Bedrijfsorganisatie*, PBOs) for employers' and employees' organisations throughout the Netherlands. Over the decades, the number of such boards got out of hand. In 1977, there were about 407 boards; a reduction policy decreased this number to about 200 in 2010. In addition, a major push towards modernisation led to the redefinition of

258   *Changing political economy of democracies*

the conditions under which PBOs may be founded. The SER was in charge of reviewing the existing PBOs and determining whether they should continue to exist according to the new governmental regulations (see Andeweg and Irwin 2014: 192; SER 2014b: 8). Any recommendations prepared by the SER must be achieved through consensus and unanimity, such that deliberation and negotiation are essential aspects in winning a compromise.

At the end of the *trente glorieuses* these postwar institutions lost importance, as there was more conflict and instability in the economy, society and politics. However, after 1982, the Lubbers and Kok governments revived the role of these institutions. Particularly important was the revival of the social partnership through the Wassenaar Agreement of 1982, which led to compromises in restoring the balance between labour and capital, with a shift towards the latter. The stagnating economy, a growing government deficit and a welfare state that was becoming expensive resulted in major liberalisation reforms. This system, based on a culture of consultation, compromise and consensus, became known as the Polder model: the cooperative spirit of the polder and dyke system established centuries ago in the Netherlands in order to keep the water out and gain new land was used as a metaphor for the new Dutch model (Hendriks and Toonen 2001: 4). It seems that the Netherlands has a tendency towards a viscous discourse of stagnation and delayed response. This leads to slow processes, complex structures and the lack of anyone with overarching responsibility. Events in the 1970s demonstrated the country's inability to implement a flexible response to changing world markets (Hendriks and Toonen 2001: 9–10). The Lubbers governments from 1982 and 1994 used the viscosity argument to make the Dutch economy more competitive. In 1992, a major document entitled 'Convergence and Consultation Economy' produced by the SER set out a new model of decentralised wage bargaining, with the government seeking to restrain economic and social policies (Hendriks 2001). This entailed a great deal of flexibility for the previously rigid institutions (for example, the welfare state that was created during the *trente glorieuses*). The dynamics of the Polder model prevailed, and today the pragmatic, flexible approach to the economy remains a major feature of the Dutch coordination system.

Belgium: multi-level neo-corporatism

In Belgium, neo-corporatism was more of a process towards the institutionalisation of conflict and resolution. The federalisation process since the 1970s has represented a peaceful strategy to cope with the growing conflict between the two main linguistic groups. Although it was relatively easy to federalise the country politically, it has been more difficult to accomplish this in social and economic terms. The largest business organisation in Belgium is the Belgian Federation of Enterprises (*Fédération des Entreprises de Belgique/Verbond van Belgische Ondernemingen*, FEB/VBO), which consists mainly of large enterprises, but also small and medium-sized enterprises. The FEB/VBO has thus far resisted attempts at federalisation and remains a national organisation. The focus

Changing political economy of democracies 259

of the business organisation is maintaining a united national market, avoiding a split into smaller Flemish and Wallonian markets. There are regular conflicts between the FEB/VBO and all the other regional business organisations. In particular, the Flemish business organisations want to move towards a regional market economy that would be able to take decisions on wage agreements and welfare policies that are still centralised (Houwing and Vandaele 2011: 128). The main Flemish business organisation is the Union of Independent Enterprises (*Unie van Zelfstandige Ondernemers*, UNIZO); the main francophone organisation is the Union of Middle Classes (*Union des Classes Moyennes*, UCM). These three groups are the recognised business organisations at the national level and participate in the various institutions of social dialogue and social concertation. In addition, on the employers' side, there are the two regionally separate organisations of the Wallon Federation of Agriculture (*Fédération Wallone Agriculture*, FWA) and the Flemish *Boerenbond* (BB), as well as the Confederation of Social Profit Enterprises (UNISOC).

Belgian trade unions are a result of the three pillars, and they represent important organisational structures of the three subcultures. The two largest trade union confederations are the Christian Democratic Confederation of Christian Trade Unions (*Confédération des Syndicats Chrétiens/Algemeen Christelijk Vakverbond*, CSC/ACV) and the Socialist General Federation of Labour of Belgium (*Federation General de Travail de Belgique-Algemeen Belgische Vakverbond*, FGTB/ABVV). The third largest group, the Federation of Liberal Trade Unions of Belgium (*Centrale Générale des Syndicats Libéraux de Belgique/Algemene Centrale der Liberale Vakbonden van België*, CGSLB/ACLVB), is much smaller, less ideological and more professional. Although trade union confederations are still confederally united at the national level, federalisation has been eroding centralising tendencies, and over recent decades one can observe a strong trend towards regionalisation. However, trade unions, like the main business organisations, still resist a complete split into two political economic systems. Trade union representation remains quite high: in 2013, there were over 3.8 million members, amounting to 55.1 per cent of the workforce (Visser 2016). There are two main reasons for this high level of union density, which is only matched by the Scandinavian countries. First, trade unions are involved in providing unemployment benefits. According to figures from a study in 2008, about 1.2 million people receive some kind of unemployment benefit, representing about 25 per cent of the workforce. This does not mean that all of these people are unemployed; however, they are receiving benefits from the state to stay in the labour market (Van Rie *et al*. 2011: 128–129). This funding comes from the central government through the national office of employment (*Office national d'emploi/Rijksdienst voor Arbeidsvorziening*, ONEM/RSA) founded in 1961, but it is allocated by the trade unions to their constituencies. In order to receive unemployment benefits, workers or employees must apply through the trade union system; this is the so-called 'Ghent system' in which trade unions cooperate with state organisations in order to provide services to their members. However, since 1944, unemployment insurance has been compulsory, such that

260　*Changing political economy of democracies*

Belgian is regarded as having a partial Ghent system, in contrast to the Nordic countries of Finland and Sweden where unemployment insurance is voluntary (Hooghe 2012: 61; Van Rie 2011: 137). The insurance system follows a traditional Bismarckian conservative welfare state based on contributions by employers and employees, although over time the state has heavily subsidised the system, contributing to its problems by controlling the budget deficit. The social partners sit on the relevant committees and commissions and co-manage these funds with the state institutions.

Second, if we examine the evolution of the employment rate of the population aged between 15 and 64 between 2004 and 2014, Belgium has experienced a relative stagnation, with employment increasing from 60.3 to 61.9 per cent; this is below the EU average of 64.9 per cent. In comparison, the employment rate in the Netherlands is much higher, at 73.1 per cent, although it has declined somewhat from a peak of 77.2 per cent prior to the Euro and the financial crisis in 2008. Austrian employment increased from 66.5 per cent to 71.1 per cent despite the crisis, and the same is true for Luxembourg, whose rate increased from 62.5 per cent to 66.6 per cent. The employment rates of these EU member-states are lagging in comparison to Switzerland, where employment saw an increase from 77.4 to 79.8 per cent during the same period (Eurostat 2016k). Unemployment represents a major problem in Belgium, particularly in Wallonia; there is a definite gap between the more successful Flemish labour market and the more problematic Wallonian market (Houwing and Vandaele 2011: 135). The lower rate of employment is statistically correlated with a higher level of unionisation.

As noted in Chapter 2, like the Netherlands, the social partnership in Belgium was basically built following the Second World War. After the war, planning was fashionable, and the integration of social partners thus became an important element in the new political economy. In comparison to all the other consensus democracies studied here, Belgium has the highest number of bipartite and tripartite institutions at the central, regional and language community levels. It is evident that Belgium has a multi-level governance system for socio-economic reasons.

At the national level, there are two important bodies, one of which is the Central Economic Council (*Conseil central de l'économie/Centrale Raad voor het bedrijfsleven*, CCL/CRB), which is the key strategic forum for the entire Belgian economy. Parallel to the CCL/CRB and responsible for social issues is the National Labour Council (*Conseil national du travail/National Arbeids Raad*, CNT/NAR). Whereas the CCL/CRB is more of an advisory model in which important decisions are taken, the CNT/NAR serves as an advisory and concertation council. The CNT/NAR is where most central collective agreements are agreed. In this sense, it plays a major role in the economy. In spite of all socio-economic devolution processes, social partners are very keen to think in Belgian terms. This is also important due to the growing impact of European integration through macro-economic policies (Interview B).

The new economic and social committees in the regions and concertation institutions are still under-researched. In addition, there are economic and social

Changing political economy of democracies 261

committees in the communities. There are thus myriad committees at all levels of the Belgian federation with networks of mutual influence. Regional socio-economic concertation is more developed in Wallonia and Flanders. Many of the other institutions were founded over the past decade, specifically after 2007/2008; as a result, interest groups must act within a dynamic multi-level governance system. However, the diminuitive size of the country and its dense networks of cooperation permit considerable influence on the policy process (Vandaele and Hooghe 2014: 157; Hooghe 2012: 68). Multi-level meetings between the national and the subnational committees did not exist formally until 2012, but since then there has been a tendency to meet at least once a year. One advantage of Belgium is that it is a small country and many of the issues can be discussed and coordinated between the institutions by phone (Interview B).

One important body is the semi-institutionalised high-level committee referred to as the 'Group of Ten', which deals with inter-professional agreements and thus has a definite macro-economic impact on government decisions. The new European governance framework established following the Euro and the financial crises has constrained governments significantly in terms of macro-economic policy. National government representatives have therefore participated in the meetings of this committee in order to achieve moderate wage bargaining deals or reforms. In reality, the Group of Ten is actually a group of 11, as it is chaired by the president of the VEB/FBO (*Rtbf*, 17 December 2014). In December 2015, the social partners agreed to develop measures to prevent the abuse of temporary unemployment by enterprises. Moreover, measures were enacted to reintegrate workers who were ill or handicapped (*Le Soir*, 9 December 2015). Meetings can last a long time; for example, the session addressing the issue of complementary occupational pensions lasted for over ten hours (*Le Vif*, 15 October 2015). This is the forum in which indicative wage bargaining takes place, a process that still occurs at the national level despite growing conflict between the Flemish business organisations that seek decentralisation and the VEB/FBO, which wants a level playing field across Belgium. In 2002, the Flemish social partners and the Flemish Parliament attempted to regionalise the wage-bargaining agreements that had only regional implications; however, this move was contested by the key social partners, in particular the VEB/FBO and the socialist trade union confederation the FGTB, the Wallonian government and the central government. The latter two parties decided to appeal to the Court of Arbitration (founded in 1984 but since 2007 called the Constitutional Court), which ruled that labour policy is a national matter, not a regional one. This meant that the legislation approved by the Flemish Parliament was overruled (Vanachter 2004: 41–44; Vandaele and Hooghe 2014: 159).

Due to the growing conflict between the social partners in the multi-level governance setting, the government has increased its involvement in negotiating the indicative wage agreements (Houwing and Vandaele 2011: 147–148). This so-called 'statism' is undertaken with great care, using a sophisticated research methodology to determine a competitive figure. Indeed, a law on competitiveness was adopted in 1996 to ensure that wage moderation and competitiveness would be

262 *Changing political economy of democracies*

central in establishing wage agreements. The average wage agreements of the neighbouring countries of Germany, the Netherlands and France are used as a reference to calculate the indicative figure. These calculations are done by an expert committee in the Central Council of the Economy; however, if the social partners are unable to agree, statism comes into effect. In this context, the Federal Bureau of Planning (*Bureau federal du Plan-Federal Planbureau*, BFP/FPB) is responsible for offering indicative figures for wage bargaining (Houwing and Vandaele 2011: 136). At the European level, the European semester has further increased the role of government in constraining wage agreements in Belgium. In 2013, legislation taking into account the European dimension of wage coordination was adopted.

One major factor is Belgium's high level of public debt – 106 per cent of GDP in 2015, well above the 60 per cent threshold set out in the Maastricht criteria (Eurostat 2016a) – and the public deficit which has increased considerably during and after the financial crisis. In comparison, in the same year, public debt in the Netherlands reached 65.1 per cent, Austria's debt level was 86.2 per cent and Luxembourg's 24.1 per cent (Eurostat 2016a; see Figure 9.1). In 2015, the government deficit was 2.6 per cent of GDP, slightly below the Maastricht threshold of 3 per cent (Eurostat 2016b). During the same year, the Netherlands had a deficit of 1.8 per cent, Austria 1.2 per cent and Luxembourg actually had a surplus of 1.2 per cent (see Figure 9.2). The tiny country of Luxembourg must maintain sound finances, as its margin of error is relatively restricted. Even low public debt figures can increase very quickly if not strictly controlled.

The socio-economic strategy for the Belgian economy is well summarised by one interviewee, who set three main priorities for the future. First of all, the Belgian economy should remain competitive within the European Union, avoiding a mainly macro-economic path. Second, both the national and the European internal market have to be stimulated for economic reasons (e.g. the Juncker package, or the Wallonian Marshall Plan). Third, Belgium needs to find a balance between micro-economic competitiveness and social affairs, due to the fact that Belgian wages are quite high because of taxes and social security costs and therefore they need to improve continuously on their productivity as is the case in Germany. This means that the Belgian market is extremely hard for business, and only the most competitive are able to survive. In order to keep its competitiveness, Belgium has been paying a high price in terms of taxes, social costs and 15 per cent structural unemployment for over 30 years (Interview B).

Belgium has traditionally been a partyocratic state with a very expensive public administration and coordination system; this clearly creates problems in terms of public debt and deficit, but at the same time it ensures political and social peace. Nevertheless, the potential of a fragmentation into two markets may weaken the competitiveness of the country in the long run.

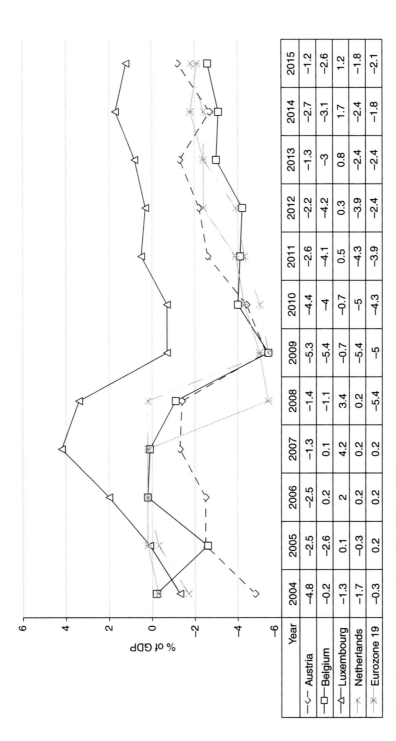

Figure 9.1 Government budget deficit, 2004 to 2015.
Source: Eurostat (2016a).

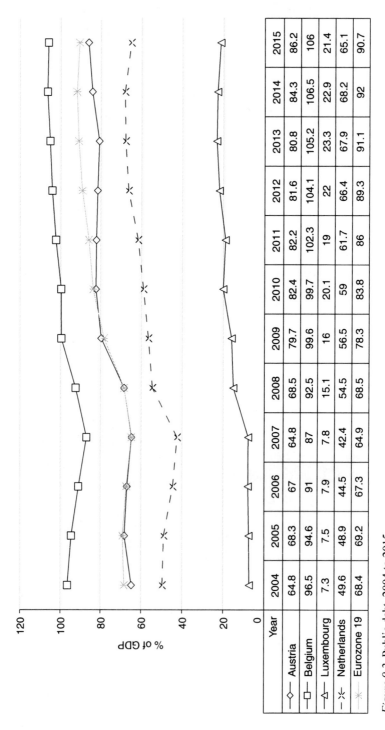

Figure 9.2 Public debt, 2004 to 2015.
Source: Eurostat (2016b).

Changing political economy of democracies 265

Luxembourg; cooperation and coordination in the Luxembourg social model

The Benelux model of cooperation and coordination may also be found in Luxembourg. Following the *trente glorieuses*, the Luxembourg steel industry faced a major crisis due to growing competition from the Asian countries. During this period, the labour–liberal government that came into power introduced a tripartite committee on the steel industry in order to prevent layoffs and provide workers with a smooth transition to new jobs or early retirement. This tripartite approach comprising government, trade union confederations and business organisations became known as the 'Luxembourg social model'. Since then, the existing systems of coordination have been reinforced, and additional institutions have emerged (Hirsch 2010a, 2010b, 2012). The small size of the country allows for dense networks among government officials and social partners; all actors know one another and are confident in their ability to find solutions to problems. The vulnerability of a small country in a globalised world is a powerful incentive to work together and pragmatically develop short- , medium- and long-term strategies.

Along with Austria, Luxembourg is the country with the most highly developed system of chambers. The six compulsory chambers (*associations imposés*) that were created in the nineteenth and early twentieth centuries structure the economic life of the Grand Dukedom. In 1841, a Chamber of Commerce (*Handelskammer*) was established, following the examples of many other countries (Schroen 2012: 434). In order to exercise control over the working class and the development of a trade union movement, a Labour Chamber (*Arbeiterkammer*) was created on 28 June 1920. The right to strike was only enshrined after the constitutional reform of 1948 (Schroen 2012: 418). A subsequent law enacted on 4 April 1924 allowed for the creation of additional chambers: the Chamber of Employees (*Angestelltenkammer*), the Chamber of Agriculture (*Landwirtschaftskammer*), the Chamber of Artisans (*Handwerkskammer*) and the Chamber of Civil Servants (*Beamtenkammer*), which was established in 1964/1965. These organisations are all involved in the legislative process through various advisory and decision-making committees attached to the different departments. They all have a democratic constitution and hold regular elections in order to elect their main bodies. In 2006, the labour and employees' chambers merged to create the Chamber of Wage-earners (*chambre des salariés*). These two chambers had previously worked closely together, and the merger allowed them to better defend the interests of dependent workers and employees.

Parallel to the compulsory chamber system, Luxembourg also has voluntary interest groups (*associations spontanées*) which represent the social partners, among other areas. On the employers' side, the main organisation is the Union of Luxembourg's Enterprises (*Union des Enterprises Luxembourgeois*, UEL), established in 2000; the UEL consists of some 85,000 companies that represent 80 per cent of employment in the country. This is complemented by several

266 Changing political economy of democracies

sectoral business organisations: the industrial sector is represented by the Federation of Industrialists of Luxembourg (*Federation des Industriels de Luxembourg*, FEDIL), the banking sector is represented by the Association of Banks and Bankers of Luxembourg (*Association des Banques et Banquiers de Luxembourg*, ABBL), the vast retail sector is represented by the Luxembourgish Confederation of Trade (*Confederation Luxembourgeois du Commerce*, CLC), the hotel and gastronomy sector is represented by the National Federation of Hotel, Restaurant and Coffee-shop Owners (*Federation Nationale des Hoteliers, Restaurateurs et Cafetiers*, Horesca) and the artisan sector is represented by the Federation of Artisans (*Fédération des Artisans*, FDA), which was founded in 1905 and consists of 51 member organisations. In addition, farmers are represented by the Confederation of Farmers (*Central Paysanne Luxembourgeois*, CPL), as well as the Free Luxembourger Farmers' Association (*Fräie Lëtzebuerger Bauernverband*, FLB) and the Farmers' Alliance (*Bauernallianz*). As in Germany, Austria and other European countries, agriculture in Luxembourg has a problem with overproduction in certain highly efficient sectors. In particular, the price of milk has been declining in recent years. According to calculations by the Farmers' Alliance, in 2015, farmers lost about €25 million due to the reduction in the milk price (*5 minutes*, 1 February 2016). Representing the country's vintners, the Federation of Wine Producers (*Federation des associations viticoles de la Moselle Luxembourgeois-Wenzerverband*) celebrated its centenary in 2011; it is also one of the social partners participating in the multitude of bipartite and tripartite bodies of socio-economic concertation and consultation. The level of organisation density among employers is quite high, reaching 80 per cent among active employees and 61 per cent in private sector establishments (Etienne-Robert *et al.* 2015).

On the employees' side, similar to Belgium, Luxembourg has three trade union confederations that were once central pillars of the country's society. Today, two major trade union confederations dominate – the Socialist Independent Trade Union Confederation of Luxembourg (*Onofhängege Gewerkschaftsbond Lëtzebuerg*, OGB-L) and the Christian Democratic Confederation of Christian Unions in Luxembourg (*Lëtzebuerger Chrëschtleche Gewerkschafts-Bond*, LCGB) – and are recognised as social partners. More specialised employee representatives include the General Public Sector Confederation (*Confédération Générale de la Fonction Publique*, CGFB), the Luxembourg Association of Bank and Insurance Employees (*Association Luxembourgeoise des Employés de Banque et Assurance*, ALEBA), the General Federation of the Municipal Administration (*Fédération générale de la fonction communale*, FGFC) and the National Federation of Railroad Workers, Transport Workers, Civil Servants and Employees (*Fédération nationale des cheminots, travailleurs du transport, fonctionnaires et employés, Luxembourg*, commonly known as the FNCTTFEL-Landesverband). This variety of organisations demonstrates that the Luxembourg social model is both inclusive and broad in terms of coverage across sectors. Chamber representatives as well as representatives of interest groups officially participate in the various bipartite bodies.

The stricter economic governance of the European Union following the Euro and financial crises is putting Luxembourg under considerable pressure. Apart from the country's reputation as a tax haven for large corporations (Luxleaks), the generous Luxembourg welfare state, featuring some of the highest levels of support, has increasingly come under scrutiny. Debates over much-needed reforms took place during the recent crises, which affected Luxembourg significantly. The Socialist trade union confederation OGB-L blocked all proposed reforms of the pension system and the welfare state in 2010 (Hirsch 2010a: 2). However, it seems that in recent years, not only did the Luxembourg economy rebound, but the government is also taking proactive steps to ensure the sustainability of public finances. The International Monetary Fund (IMF) regularly assesses the situation in Luxembourg and attests to the government's strong fiscal policy; nonetheless, the situation could deteriorate by 2019 if expenditures are not reduced (IMF 2014).

The conflict between OGB-L and the government notwithstanding, Luxembourg's myriad consultation and concertation institutions facilitate the continuation of the social dialogue. The tripartite committee of coordination is the best example of a structure that has a strategic impact on the government's decision-making process. The committee's monthly meetings permit consultations and the exchange of information between government and social partners, and most long-term and structural decisions concerning the labour market, wage policy and the reform of the pension system are taken in this setting. The high level of support for tripartite arrangements is particularly intriguing. The social partners seem to appreciate the risks that the state is taking; this is especially evident with regard to the welfare system, which is now predominantly funded and administered by the state. Since the Second World War, the state has steered a process basically unifying the dispersed insurance systems, thereby transitioning from a system based on Bismarckian German-style contributions to a generous and universal Beveridge-style welfare state. This is quite expensive for the country, but it is clearly critical for the sustainability of the Luxembourg social model (Klenk 2012: 270–277).

Crucial socio-economic issues have been depoliticised over the years; because the state is strongly involved, it acts as a security net for social partners, creating an environment of consensus and cooperation. Lack of cooperation in the tripartite institutions would mean loss of influence in other fora, in particular with regard to consultations on new socio-economic legislation. As a result, the corporatist system of Luxembourg is all-inclusive, but at the same time it is closed to new actors. It consists of a community of policy-makers, parliamentarians and social partners who know one another quite well; consequently, there are some personal connections in terms of political, chamber and interest group positions. The end result is a dense network of cooperation that prioritises the well-being of the country above individual interests (Klenk 2012: 254).

One focal point of this culture of consensus and cooperation is the economic and social committee, a highly inclusive body. The chambers also participate in the economic and social committee, making it easy for the group to take broad

268   *Changing political economy of democracies*

decisions. Interestingly, the economic committee is a legacy of the steel industry crisis of the 1970s; the group was intended to be active only until the 1990s. A representative of the main steel company ArcelorMittal continues to sit on the economic and social committee, demonstrating the importance still attributed to the sector. This economic committee was quite relevant during the finance crisis, taking decisions about the short-term work (*Kurzarbeit*) programme for companies facing the recession. Its actions allowed many companies to keep their staff by moving them to part-time positions; the rest of the workers' salaries were funded by the state. Similar programmes were set up in Germany, Belgium, the Netherlands and Austria (Arpaia *et al.* 2010).

Austria: the reinvention of social corporatism

Austrian neo-corporatism, which was heavily influenced by social democracy, is a coordination system that tends to emphasise equality and social justice. This was the model that Katzenstein characterised as social corporatism in contrast to Switzerland's liberal corporatism (Katzenstein 1984: 32).

With regard to the scores in the corporatism index, Austria has always been at the top, indicating the continuing importance of the social partnership in the country's policy-making. Despite major transformations over the past 40 years, this social partnership has been able to reinvent itself (see Karlhofer and Talos 1999). This has been possible because the two main parties, namely the Social Democrats (SPÖ) and the People's Party (ÖVP), governed most of the postwar period together. The main interest groups comprising the social partners are also very closely linked to the two main political parties. As in all consensus democracies, overlapping positions and personal connections are still common. The role of the main trade union organisation, the Austrian Trade Union Confederation (*Österreichischer Gewerkschaftsbund*, ÖGB) in the Socialist Party, remains important; the subcultural traits of a *Lager* (camps) perspective are still visible, although they are eroding with time. The ÖGB is an umbrella organisation of many federations, but by law it is the only recognised trade union. The group works closely with the Industrial Federation (*Industrielle Vereinigung*, IV). The Austrian chamber system, which was the model copied by Luxembourg, is well established in the political culture of the country. These chambers are compulsory and hold regular elections; here again, the power of the political parties cannot be neglected. There are four chambers that represent constituencies or entire economic sectors: the Federal Economic Chamber (*Wirtschaftskammer Österreichs*, WKÖ) and the Federal Chamber of Agriculture (*Landwirtschaftskammer Österreichs*, BLK) have close ties to the ÖVP, with minority representation of the other parties, whereas the Federal Labour Chamber (*Arbeiterkammer Österreichs*, AK) is dominated by the SPÖ. However, the other political parties also have their minority stakeholder status confirmed in regular elections (Fink 2006: 452–454; Karlhofer 2006: 470–471). These direct links to political parties are paralleled by a strong connection between interest groups and the chambers. The personnel of the industrial federation dominate the WKÖ,

Changing political economy of democracies 269

and the ÖGB's personnel are heavily involved in the AK (Fink 2006: 454–455; Karlhofer 2006: 471–473). This results in a dense triangular interaction network of political parties, interest groups and chambers. At the centre of this neo-corporatist system of intermediation are the chambers. They enjoy a relatively high level of social autonomy and are involved in private interest governance through the regulation of specific sectors; they also award certificates for certain professions and shape vocational training programmes. The compulsory membership is definitely a major negative aspect of the chambers system in Austria. All members must pay membership fees, and the WKÖ in particular profits from many of the larger enterprises in this regard.

The history of the chambers dates back to the nineteenth century, although they were refounded after 1945. Both the WKÖ and the AK were re-established in 1946, and through their compulsory membership the two organisations wield considerable power in the political system: the WKÖ represents over 480,000 enterprises, whereas the AK represents three million workers and employees. The ÖGB, founded in 1946, represented about 1.2 million workers and employees in 2014 (ÖGB 2015). The unionisation density in Austria was estimated at 27.4 per cent in 2014 (Krenn *et al.* 2015).

In terms of centralisation, the major exceptions are the nine provincial territorial chambers of agriculture, which are (like the other chambers) regulated by public law with the right to self-administration and autonomy. Again, membership is compulsory. However, the centralised key organisation is actually a private law association, the Conference of Presidents of the Agricultural Chambers of Austria (*Konferenz der Präsidenten der Landwirtschaftskammern Österreichs*), which refers to itself as the Austrian Chamber of Agriculture (*Landwirtschaftskamer Österreichs*, LKÖ). The Conference was founded in 1923 and reinstated in 1946 after the Second World War. The largest political faction in elections is the Austrian Farmers' Federation (*Österreichischer Bauernbund*), which wins 80 per cent of the votes on average and is strongly linked to the ÖVP. The weakest support for the *Österreichischer Bauernbund* is in Burgenland, a stronghold of the SPÖ, and in Carinthia, which is dominated by the FPÖ (Krammer and Hovorka 2006: 481, 489; Karlhofer 2012: 435).

The roots of the Austrian social partnership can be traced to the difficult period of reconstruction after the Second World War. The need to take decisions on prices and wages led to the creation of an economic commission (*Wirtschaftskommission*) in 1947. Between 1947 and 1951, this commission achieved several agreements on prices and wages. In 1957, an informal parity commission for wages and prices was established. Three subcommittees of the parity commission were later set up: in 1958 and 1962 two subcommittees on wages and prices, and in 1963 the advisory committee for social and economic questions. Members of the parity commission and the subcommittees included the four recognised social partners (WKÖ, AK, LKÖ and ÖGB). The parity commission enabled the peaceful settlement of issues between the government and social partners, and thus it became a central institution in the *trentes glorieuses*. It also formed part of what has been discussed as *Proporzdemokratie*, which encouraged personal connections and

270 *Changing political economy of democracies*

strong relationships among political and interest groups. The parity commission was chaired by the chancellor such that the body was, in fact, tripartite. Most socio-economic legislation went first to the parity commission to be negotiated by the social partners and the government. Only then would the government send it to Parliament to be rubber-stamped thanks to its grand coalition majority (Gerlich 1992: 135). Central figures in this era of success in the social partnership were ÖGB Secretary-General Anton Benya and WKÖ President Rudolf Sallinger, both of whom shaped the social partnership over a period of 25 years (Gerlich 1992: 136). A major study has analysed the various positions of well-known politicians ('political stars') in relation to the political class between 1945 and 1995. The researchers determined that political stars had lengthy political careers of 22.7 years on average and held an average of 10.9 positions over the years; in addition, they managed to accumulate on average up to 5.5 top positions. This interlocking network of political stars and elite positions was and remains a specific feature of this social partnership of the postwar era and a key element of *Proporzdemokratie* (see Treib 2012).

In the 1980s, Austrokeynesianism, a policy involving frequent government interference, underwent a major crisis. The large public sector of state enterprises, one of the strategic assets of Austrokeynesianism, became a burden, and the modernisation of and innovation in the public sector were recognised as important priorities. During this period, it became clear that Austria was losing its competitiveness internationally (Lauber 1992; Unger 1999). The social partnership was an inadequate instrument to open up the system, and by the end of the 1980s there was already talk of a crisis in the partnership (Gerlich 1992: 141). The original set-up of the parity commission was antiquated, and reforms were needed. In 1992, the price subcommittee, which had lost influence, was transformed into a subcommittee on competition. Moreover, a new subcommittee on international issues was established. The debate and progress towards EU membership in 1995 led to a major revival of the social partners, which were Euro-enthusiastic. The social partners campaigned on the side of the grand coalition government led by Chancellor Franz Vranitzky to join the European Union. This is regarded as a key event for both political and socio-economic actors (Gehler 2009, 2012). However, Europeanisation further undermined the position of the social partners. It took a long time for the country to shift from a nationally oriented approach to a European perspective. At the end of the 1990s, the social partnership was a mere shadow of its previous self. The integration process had put the Austrian government under considerable pressure. Although the social partners have offices in the Permanent Representation in Brussels and are involved in many committees attached to the ministries, they must also lobby as part of the Eurogroups (Kittel and Talós 1999: 113–115; Karlhofer and Talós 2002; Falkner 1999; Interviews A). The stability and growth pact required the support of the social partners, but apart from this there was a loss of competences: the number of areas of influence was reduced to issues such as competition and the labour market. In other areas, the government established specialised policy networks that are less closely linked to these social partners (e.g. education and environmental policy; Kittel, andTalós 1999: 116–119).

Changing political economy of democracies 271

Probably the strongest factor leading to the decline of the social partnership was the impact of the ÖVP–FPÖ government between 2000 and 2006. Chancellor Wolfgang Schüssel, who had been part of previous grand coalitions, now sought to implement a major programme of liberalisation of the economy. This was supported by the FPÖ which wanted to dismantle the negative aspects of *Proporzdemokratie*, of which the social partnership was the most obvious example. Many of the policy-making networks in which the social partners were involved were challenged by the new approaches adopted by the ÖVP–FPÖ government (Karlhofer and Tálos 2006).

Following the general elections of 2006, the new grand coalition government between the SPÖ and the ÖVP restored the role of the social partners. The absolute majority of the grand coalition has been eroding ever since, but this turn of events allowed the social partners to reinvent themselves. In 2006, following the issuance of the Bad Ischl declaration, they have again became an important part of policy-making in the grand coalition. However, the role of the social partners has changed in relation to the heyday of the *trente glorieuses*. They found a new European identity with other, similar committees (i.e. through the network of economic and social councils) across Europe, and they now regard themselves as part of the wider European social model. Their role as advisers to the government's socio-economic legislation has remained the same; however, they now concentrate on achieving a more balanced approach to high employment and the enhancement of competitiveness. According to a long-standing expert on what is now the advisory committee on social and economic issues, Austria remains a highly competitive country supported by a strong social partnership; nonetheless, it needs to think hard about the future of its political economy. Compared to Switzerland, Austria must reduce its level of government spending and encourage greater competitiveness (Aiginger 2014).

The advisory council on social and economic issues is now the central focus of the parity commission. There are still other subcommittees for wages, prices and competition and international questions, but they are barely mentioned by the social partners; it is the advisory committee that runs the show. This committee consists of 25 members who take decisions by unanimity but behind closed doors. There are no public protocols of the sessions.

The process of negotiation is similar to that of the SER and STAR in the Netherlands. Normally, package deals in which the social partners take and give are the rule. The long-standing experience over many generations strengthens this collective spirit of cooperation. As interviewees put it, 'We are damned to succeed, otherwise we lose our legitimacy.' They regard themselves as having 'total economic responsibility' and therefore do not want to become victims of globalisation, but 'managers or even designers of change'. This clearly fits into a future-oriented ambition to keep both economic competitiveness and the Austrian social model in the context of deeper European integration (Interviews A).

Although the social partnership is well established throughout the administrative system of the social state, such as in the management labour market service (*Arbeitsmarktservice*, AMS) and the social insurance coordinating body

272 *Changing political economy of democracies*

(*Österreichischer Sozialversicherung*), criticisms about the overall set-up have been voiced over recent decades. First, compulsory membership of the chambers allows them considerable funding, but at the cost to society. These membership fees are collected by the state. In 2012 this amounted to €1.2 billion for the three social partners (AK, WKÖ and LKÖ) alone, while a further €300 million went to the other 11 chambers (e.g. notaries, medical doctors, lawyers). Second, the generous funding allows the chambers to sustain a large bureaucratic structure of 10,000 employees with excellent social and pension benefits, in part above the population's average (*Neue Zürcher Zeitung*, 6 September 2012; Interview A). Third, the grand coalition consults the social partners on every new legislative act before it goes to Parliament, reducing the role of the legislature to a rubber-stamping institution, at least on socio-economic issues (Interviews A). Fourth, the majority of the grand coalition has been diminishing from election to election, and the share won by the FPÖ has been increasing. The FPÖ is very keen to dismantle *Proporzdemokratie*, or at least to alter it in order to integrate its own partisans. The previous ÖVP–FPÖ government showed less interest in maintaining a strong relationship with social partners. As a result, the social partnership is heavily dependent on the highly problematic grand coalition, which clearly has implications for the quality of democracy in Austria.

Conclusions: coordination and flexibility in a European setting

The five consensus democracies have developed similar but not identical political economies. The methods of coordination among the government, interest groups and political parties are all different. Europeanisation and globalisation are eroding the old foundations of national capitalism and further Europeanising industrial relations and national enterprises. This has major implications for the old systems of coordination, and new ones are still in the making. In any case, the powerful impact of European integration is significantly constraining national socio-economic solutions; nevertheless, strategic coordinating management still plays an important role in this process of deeper European integration and accelerating globalisation.

10 Consensus democracies as the model for European and global governance

The statecraft of consensus democracies in West Central Europe

Consensus democracies did not emerge out of nowhere but through a lengthy process of giving and taking without winners, but also without losers. This is the essence of the consensus model: advanced rationalised and mature democratic behaviour moulded by a storehouse of collective experiences of trial, error and learning, as exemplified by the five democracies of West Central Europe. Four of them – Belgium, Luxembourg, the Netherlands and Switzerland – were shaped by a long-term continuous process of democratisation. Belgium, Luxembourg and the Netherlands have had only two brief interruptions in their political systems, namely during German occupation in the First and Second World Wars. Switzerland was able to maintain its neutrality during these periods, whereas Austria emerged from the Second World War only to be annexed by the Third Reich in 1938. Prior to 1918, Austria was part of the Austro-Hungarian Empire, which significantly influenced its later development. In this context, Austria is an excellent example of a true shift from a conflictive political culture in the First Republic (1918–1934) to a consensual culture after the Second World War. Although historicism should be avoided – and it must be noted that these West Central European consensus democracies emerged out of contingent situations – the stability of political elites and subcultural patterns allowed sufficient time for learning and consolidating the practices of consensus, consultation, cooperation, concertation and compromise. This process took place in parallel with and surrounded by key European developments that led to industrialisation and the modern state, namely the triangle of the 'big three': France, the United Kingdom and Germany.

The primacy of political stability: coalition governments and parliamentary majorities

The political systems of these countries were devised in the nineteenth or early twentieth century. As such, they are clearly historical products that have stood the test of time, evolving according to the circumstances. Total constitutional

274   *European and global models of democracies*

revisions have taken place in Switzerland and Belgium; Luxembourg is currently modernising its constitution, and the Netherlands did so in 1983. In Austria, a so-called 'convent' attempted to generate the impetus to reform in 2006, but without success (Pollack and Slominski 2005).

Coalition governments prevail in all five countries, thereby preventing majoritarian or presidential tendencies in the political system. In three of the countries the monarch has only formal powers; however, he or she also plays a role as a force of moderation, particularly in negotiations over the formation of a new coalition government. This process is quite sophisticated in the Netherlands and Belgium, and less complicated in Luxembourg. In Austria, the political arena is relatively polarised between the left and the right – or rather, between the right-wing populist FPÖ and the established parties (the ÖVP and SPÖ) – but the difficulty of winning absolute majorities results in coalition governments. The fact that the FPÖ is getting stronger is problematic; at times, the ÖVP and the SPÖ struggle to achieve even a 50 per cent share of the vote together. It is likely that the Greens will soon join the two in a three-party coalition in order to create a *cordon sanitaire* against the FPÖ.

The best example of the current Austrian situation is the presidential election of April/May 2016, in which a Green candidate, the renowned 72-year-old professor and former leader of the Green Party, Alexander Van der Bellen, managed to beat the FPÖ candidate Norbert Hofer, the third president of the Lower Chamber of Parliament, in a thrilling second round. This election illustrated just how divided the country has become, with anti-immigration and Eurosceptic discourses increasingly viewed as mainstream. Sloppy electoral management led to the Federal Constitutional Court declaring the election null and void, so that it had to be repeated. In spite of many criticisms, the FPÖ is securely integrated into a variety of provincial governments, including Carinthia, Burgenland, Upper Austria and Vienna. FPÖ politicians take part in the standard process, and exhibit moderation and restraint when serving in these provincial governments and in Parliament. In my view, the FPÖ is a populist new-right party that should not be described as extreme right. It is part of the Austrian tradition, the so-called 'third *Lager*', and therefore does not represent a new phenomenon. Moreover, although German nationalist sentiments are still strong among some party members, the vast majority have accepted Austria as their homeland. The presidential elections made it clear that there is a growing cleavage emerging between the rural and urban populations, who voted for Norbert Hofer and Alexander Van der Bellen, respectively. This is complemented by a cleavage in which the less educated and less internationalised segments of the population voted for Hofer, whereas better educated and more open-minded individuals voted for Van der Bellen. Moreover, men and older people voted for Norbert Hofer, and women and the younger generation for Van der Bellen (*Der Spiegel*, 22 May 2016).

In Switzerland, the Federal Council is a permanent coalition government between the four main parties: the Swiss People's Party, the Socialists, the Liberals and the Christian Democrats – the so-called 'magic formula' (*Zauberformel*). Although there is no such thing as a coalition agreement in Switzerland,

European and global models of democracies 275

a kind of legislative programme is proposed by the core public administration (as seen in the European Commission for the European Union), and in the other countries a technology of coalition-building has developed over time, based on previous experiences. The core element of coalition formation is the coalition agreement, the bible of the (four-year, or five-year in Luxembourg and Belgium) legislative term. Coalition governments condition Parliament; that is, coalition parties impose discipline when voting on issues related to the coalition agreement, and opposition parties must cooperate in order to introduce some of their programme as bills. For the Netherlands and Belgium, coalition governments have become more difficult due to the fragmentation of the party system. In the case of Belgium, the regionalisation of the party system means that each ideological family has two parties, one in Flanders and one in Wallonia; this leads to coalition governments that need five parties in order to maintain a stable majority. In the Netherlands, it has become evident that the volatility of the electorate results in different majorities in the lower house (*Tweede Kamer*) and the upper house (*Eerste Kamer*). Consequently, more time is required for the government to push its bills through. In Luxembourg the party system is fairly stable, even when the Christian Social Party (CSV) lose. The inclusion of the Greens in a coalition government with the Liberals and Social Democrats has been a positive development, extending the responsibility of government to an additional party. As noted above, the same coalition expansion may soon happen in Austria.

Switzerland is definitely the major exception with regard to coalitions. The only factor of instability of its permanent coalition government is the double strategy of government participation and populism in the public space of the SVP. However, there is some hope for the future following the defeat of the referendum on the implementation of expulsion laws for foreigners on 28 February 2016; it may be the case that we are experiencing a turning point. Following three decades of rising support for the SVP, a new, more open-minded generation is spearheading a movement against the imagined 'heartland' of a Swiss world of domestic peace and stability – as they call it, an open-air museum – that must be protected against the winds of globalisation and Europeanisation (*Die Zeit*, 28 February 2016).

The changing architecture of politics: from welfare states to competition states

Consensus itself has become a strategy for political stability. All five of our countries are now characterised by a fragmented party system, more so in Belgium, the Netherlands and Switzerland, and less so in Austria and Luxembourg. None of the parties is able to achieve an absolute majority on its own. Even the FPÖ and the SVP seem to have reached peak support of about 30 per cent. In Belgium, the Flemish separatists represent no more than 20 to 30 per cent of the population. This means that coalition government will remain the main form of government for the foreseeable future. In this sense, shared executives should not be viewed negatively, but rather as a positive

276   *European and global models of democracies*

phenomenon that facilitates more diverse and extensive legislative work. Politicians in these countries have inculcated the rules of the game for coalition government and regard them as essential for maintaining domestic political stability. Why is political stability so important? Stability helps safeguard the steering or strategic management of the country over time; without it, the country may experience significant losses in the global economy consisting mainly of competition states.

The competition state emerged in the 1980s, when Thatcherism and Reaganomics contributed to a change in the political-economic ideology of global markets towards neo-liberalism. This led to a decline in the organised capitalism of the *trente glorieuses* and a move to a *desorganised* system. Since the 1980s, our five small consensus democracies have struggled to preserve their political and economic systems. As a result, they are restructuring their administrations and political economies to resemble competition states in order to be more compatible with the demands of the global economy.

Consensus democracies are undergoing the painful transition from 'organised capitalism' based on a generous welfare state and a large industrial sector, to 'competition capitalism' reorganised more or less at the European Union level. This shift is marked by a constant search for new markets and innovation that will help maintain the countries' high standards of living (Cerny 1997, 1990: ch. 8; Jessop 2002).

This development has significant consequences for the welfare state, which is no longer regarded as a decommodification instrument for the redistribution of national wealth, but instead as an instrument of social investment in the context of an increasingly competitive global economy. The European Union concepts of social investment and flexicurity are euphemisms for the 'workfare' state, in which achieving the highest possible level of participation in the labour market has become an imperative in order to optimise a country's human resources. Demographic changes have placed European countries in general and the small consensus democracies of West Central Europe in particular under considerable pressure to put these European strategies into practice. The Netherlands seems to be the most advanced of the five nations in terms of the adoption of this new employment strategy, followed by Switzerland; activation policies have traditionally been much weaker in Austria and Luxembourg, and Belgium, especially Wallonia, lags far behind.

The hybridisation of coordinated market economies and the welfare state

Unfortunately, many studies on consensus democracies, including those of Arend Lijphart, tend to take the political economy of capitalism in consensus democracies for granted. One of the main theses of this study is that politics and the political economy go hand-in-hand. It is a bicycle built for two, not just for politics or just for the political economy. Although politics may dominate, the political economy plays a substantial role in keeping the political system stable.

European and global models of democracies 277

What makes consensus democracies different from most other democracies is that capitalism was tamed in the interwar period, allowing everyone to profit from the wealth produced in the country. In some ways, this attitude towards the economy has created even more stability and productivity. Happy people will work harder and smarter for companies. These social market economies were established over more than a century as a consequence of considerable struggles on the part of the working class and their political and socio-economic organisations, particularly in Social-Democratic and Christian Democratic subcultures. The neo-corporatist era of the *trente glorieuses* represented the peak of this shift towards tamed social capitalism. These concepts still persist and remain essential parts of the coordinating mechanisms of the political economy.

This leads us to the type of political economy that consensus democracies require. In the *trente glorieuses*, our five consensus democracies could rely on 'organised capitalism' to ensure a high level of political and economic stability. According to the typology developed by Peter Hall and David Soskice, they were coordinated market economies similar to Germany, in contrast to pure liberal market economies like the USA (Hall and Soskice 2001). This national 'organised' capitalism allowed for some intervention of the state in order to coordinate or protect the less competitive sectors, such as agriculture (still the case for Switzerland and most European economies, now via the Common Agricultural Policy (CAP)). Since the 1980s, organised capitalism has been eroding, replaced by a more 'liberal' system. The acceleration of the European integration process since 1985 under the leadership of Jacques Delors has contributed to the dismantling of highly nationalised economies. The restructuring of welfare states into competition states under 'reorganised capitalism' at the European Union level has resulted in the hybridisation of coordinated market economies. All five consensus democracies have become much more liberal and Europeanised over the past 40 years, limiting the options of the governments of these 'social market economies'. The competition state is now the new model in the context of a single European market. This process of the national liberalisation of markets has as its ultimate objective the creation of a European market. National policies will remain important, but they will have to be shared and constrained by European policies. This is the greatest challenge that consensus democracies will face in the future: as more powers are transferred to the European Union, it becomes more difficult to act as they did during the *trente glorieuses*. Full economic integration into a single market also means that labour markets and economies will become more Europeanised. Right-wing and left-wing populism represent reactions to the emergence of a capitalist single European market that may or may not create strong political institutions to the detriment of the member-states. Nonetheless, the dynamics of European and global capitalism will definitely set the agenda for these consensus democracies (Schmidt 2011; Hall 2014; McCann 2010).

278   *European and global models of democracies*

Big democracy and small democracy: the importance of civil society

Another conclusion of this book is that the political principles of consensus, consultation, cooperation, concertation and compromise were disseminated across societies over time, including within enterprises. Democracy has become the way of life in these five consensus democracies, and thus the 'big democracy' of the political institutions may also be found at the level of civil society. The myriad interest groups, non-governmental organisations and voluntary associations represent an important critical mass with regard to national politics. The 'small democracy' exercised in civil society associations does not always have to be political, but it does use political principles similar to those in 'big' politics. All five democracies have vibrant civic cultures with a high number of civil society associations. Although this civic activity does not match the level found in the Nordic countries, it comes very close (Van Deth and Maloney 2015). This is a factor that has been neglected by many scholars. Democracy is more than just a nation's political institutions; it also includes the wider civil society.

In this study, we have highlighted the persistence of the old civil society organisations of pillarisation and their adaptation to change, identifying significant differences between the five countries. Austria and Belgium are still influenced by the old pillarised civil society, whereas on the other side of the spectrum the Netherlands and Switzerland are characterised by a high level of erosion; Luxembourg falls in between these two extremes. More research is needed to analyse civil society in consensus democracies in greater depth.

The necessity of European Union governance

The European Union is the best thing that could happen to the small consensus democracies of West Central Europe. The policies of the European Union (and, before it, the European Community) have contributed to the internal political stability of the consensus democracies. This political and economic stability has been expressed in a variety of ways. In particular, European Union governance has tamed our countries' three major neighbours – Germany, France and Italy – and has facilitated and fostered relationships of trust and cooperation.

Consensus democracies as co-founders and rule-makers in the EC/EU

The Benelux countries were at the forefront of the process of European integration after the Second World War. The political structure of the EC/EU was shaped by these smaller nations, which feared that Germany and France would dominate the new organisation. The Commission (High Authority in the European Community for Steel and Coal, ECSC) and the Council of Ministers are collective bodies based on shared government, consensus, cooperation, consultation and compromise (Wallace 1999, 2005). This was essential for the small consensus democracies, as they were afraid of the power of their larger neighbours.

European and global models of democracies 279

Unfortunately, the history of European integration has focused on the large countries; in reality, the European Union was a major achievement of the small countries. The West Central European countries between France and Germany were keen to build a system of collective security that would control the ambitions of the large states (Nasra and Segers 2012). The weakness of West Germany following its defeat in the Second World War and its subsequent pariah status due to the Holocaust represented an unique opportunity to shape a new European order on the Continent. This was also possible because the USA supported the creation of a single European market that would allow American industry to sell its products more efficiently. In the early 1950s, the Organisation for European Economic Cooperation (OEEC), in combination with the Marshall Plan, was intended to be the instrument to create such a single European market, but it was met with resistance from the small countries like Belgium that sought to protect their markets. A second, more successful attempt was made with the introduction of the Schuman Plan (9 May 1951), proposed by the French Foreign Minister Robert Schuman, whose efforts were strongly supported by the American administration. In many ways, without the USA, the European Union would not exist today (Milward 1984: 168–169, 192, 210; Clemens *et al.* 2008: 95–108). For the Benelux countries, the guarantee of collective security through the North Atlantic Treaty Organisation (NATO) was crucial. The USA could count on the support of the political elites and populations in the Benelux countries, due in particular to the American role in liberating the countries from German occupation. The inclusion of West Germany in NATO in a divided Europe was a further positive step in the creation of peace and stability in Europe.

The Messina Conference of 1955 led to the establishment of the European Economic Community (EEC), a project that was largely engineered by the Dutch, Belgians and Luxemburgers. Its successor, the European Union (established in 1993), was originally approved in Maastricht in 1992 with what is generally known as the Maastricht Treaty. In this context, the role of Luxembourg in achieving a compromise on the three pillars model (EC, Common Foreign and Security Policy, Justice and Home Affairs) cannot be underestimated (see Loth 2013: 77–78, 81–82; Ludlow 2013). In 1999, the Amsterdam Treaty was ratified; this document addressed the 'leftovers' from the Maastricht Treaty. All of these events showcase the vital input of Dutch and Luxembourg diplomacy.

In the November 2014 Eurobarometer, 51.3 per cent of Belgians and 72.2 per cent of Luxembourgers described themselves as very or fairly attached to the European Union. Belgium and Luxembourg are regarded as among the most pro-European countries; being European is part of their national identities. The Netherlands (31.7%) tends to have lower attachment levels, and only 40.8 per cent of Austrians are very or fairly attached to the European Union. This discrepancy notwithstanding, citizens of the three Benelux countries generally believe that they have benefited from European integration: Belgium (68.6%), Luxembourg (72.5%) and the Netherlands (67.3%) all had relatively high scores with regard to the appreciation of the benefits of membership (data from May 2011).

280 *European and global models of democracies*

In contrast, the Austrian population is split in the evaluation of such benefits (Eurobarometer 2016).

In 2013, a study by the Bertelsmann Foundation determined that two decades after the establishment of the single European market, the four West Central European consensus democracies in the EU have profited considerably from it. In Western Europe, the big winners have been Denmark, Germany, Austria, Finland, Sweden, Belgium and the Netherlands. All of these countries are consensus democracies that are geographically situated close to Germany, the motor of the European economy. Countries including Portugal, Greece and the United Kingdom have not profited very much (Bertelsmann Foundation 2014: 27). These figures demonstrate that European integration has been relatively positive for the countries located at the core of the European Union. Their strategic position between Germany and France represents a great political and socio-economic advantage.

Consensus democracies as models for other small states

Although the EU has been enlarged to 28 members, the co-founders Benelux and Austria remain at the organisation's centre. They are all net contributors to the EU budget and therefore play an important role in the financial decisions of the supranational organisation. Moreover, they are important Eurozone members due to their (more or less) excellent budgetary discipline. The Dutch Finance Minister Jeroen Dijsselbloem has been president of the Eurogroup over the past three years, and he was re-elected by the Eurogroup in 2015. He succeeded former Luxembourg Prime Minister Jean-Claude Juncker in the job; Juncker became president of the European Commission in early 2015. Before him, other Luxembourg prime ministers – Gaston Thorn (1981–1985) and Jacques Santer (1994–1999) – were also presidents of the European Commission. This engagement by representatives of small democracies is essential to their role in shaping the discourse on the European Union (on the importance of EMU for the Benelux see Maes and Verdun 2005).

In this sense, they are role models for other small democracies, particularly the Baltic States, which are also in the Eurozone and may evolve towards consensus democracy in the long run. Slovakia, Slovenia, Malta and Cyprus could also be natural allies of this group of small democracies. In addition, certain influence may be exerted over Eurozone members Greece and Portugal, which need a more consensual form of domestic politics in light of their poor financial situation and the important decisions that must soon be taken (e.g. reforms of the pension system, educational system and health sector).

This concept of serving as a role model represents an approach that might counter the current negative perceptions of the EU among the Dutch population. Instead of being reactive, Benelux and Austria could be proactive, contributing to the construction of consensus democracies in other small countries. The Nordic member-states are like-minded countries in terms of both policies and the democratic model. Benelux and Austria have very good reputations in the

European Union, and their support is not seen as negative, unlike that of the larger countries. Germany is also a consensus democracy; ultimately, this fact could strengthen this bloc of countries. In total, the 21 small member-states (those with a population of not more than 20 million) have about 150.7 million inhabitants. If Germany is added to this group, this alliance would represent 232 million people, or 45.9 per cent of the EU (based on Eurostat 2016g). This would be a highly effective bloc – a majority of member-states (22) and almost half of the European population.

Why would such an alliance be necessary? An alliance led by consensus democracies could contribute to the resolution of many problems in the transition from nationally oriented competition states to a system of EU multi-level governance that is proactive in the global arena.

All four consensus democracies in the European Union are keen on preserving their egalitarian societies; they have emphasised the need for the European social model to be safeguarded in the establishment of the single European market. The social market economy model is enshrined in the Lisbon Treaty, bolstering the expansion of the model of consensus democracy to the European level. This also means that these four consensus democracies must engage with the other small countries with weaker systems of social protection, helping them improve the efficiency of their governments and their economies. Such intensive cooperation would probably lead to joint ventures and economies of scale that would profit the European Union in general and the small countries in particular. More like-minded member-states in terms of internal and external consensual politics would translate into better prospects for the European Union's endeavours.

It will be quite difficult for Switzerland to maintain a special status in relation to the European Union. As a capitalist country, it is important for it to be fully integrated into the larger European economy. Alternatively, it would have to work even harder to retain its current political economy. More than 60 per cent of Switzerland's exports go to the country's immediate neighbours, all of which are in the European Union. The anti-EU referendums organised by the SVP with the support of AUNS have certainly damaged Switzerland's reputation. In addition, the decision of the National Bank to allow the Swiss Franc to free-float led to a revaluation that is creating major problems for the economy (*Handelsblatt*, 28 February 2016; Interview CH). Switzerland could become a very expensive enclave if it does not join the European Union at some stage. It would be much cheaper and more efficient for the Swiss to participate in decision-making and to cooperate with the other small consensus democracies in order to achieve its aims. Moreover, the European Union could learn a great deal from many aspects of the Swiss hybridised economy. Although largely unknown, the Swiss central public administration is engaged in pushing further integration of Switzerland in the European Union. The cases of Austria, Sweden and Finland have shown that neutrality is not necessarily affected by joining the European Union, even if the dominance of NATO members in the European Union is sometimes putting neutral countries under considerable naming-and-shaming pressure (Interview A).

282 *European and global models of democracies*

Therefore, it would be desirable for the European Union to be more independent militarily from the USA, and to concentrate on building their own capabilities. The small consensus democracies can make a considerable contribution in this respect.

Controlling turbulence through global governance

The role of the European Union in promoting the pax democratica

The principles of the EU with regard to human rights, the abolition of the death penalty, democracy, freedom, equality and solidarity may be summarised in the concept of *pax democratica* (democratic peace). These principles are constantly violated; nevertheless, they have definitely increased in salience over the past 60 years. Karen Sikkink's book *The Justice Cascade* (2011) describes how human rights prosecutions have gained in prominence since the 1970s. New institutions such as the International Criminal Court have socialised several generations of lawyers into new kinds of behaviour in international law. The world is undergoing a major transition, from an international society of states based on power relations to a potential International of global governance and democratic peace (see Magone 2006). As transparency and justice proliferate, dictators have fewer and fewer places to flee to when overthrown.

Consensus democracies are at the core of this quest for global governance and democratic peace, in part because these values are in their interest. The European Union may be regarded as a megaphone for the principles and ideas of consensus democracies framed in the concepts of global governance and democratic peace. The EU itself is an example of democratic peace: it is a region of democratic states that solves conflicts and issues through consultation, cooperation, consensus and ultimately compromise (Whitehead 2001). The process takes time and can be arduous, but it results in solutions agreed upon by all. For small consensus democracies the EU is a value-added structure, a means of achieving greater influence by disseminating their values across the world.

The technology of consensual politics is central to international cooperation, and it also contributes to international collective security. Consensus democracies are essential elements in the strengthening of the Common Foreign and Security Policy (CFSP), although military power remains important in this transition to global governance and democratic peace. Austria, Finland and Sweden have demonstrated that neutral countries can play a role in the CFSP without participating in military action. There are many peacekeeping operations that require humanitarian support from civilians. It should not be overlooked that the EU is the closest ally of the United Nations in terms of the level of funding and contributions from the supranational organisation and its member-states. Indeed, the EU and the UN are like-minded organisations in terms of an emerging regime of democratic peace.

Changing global capitalism: expanding the European social model

In addition to shaping politics, consensus democracies need to use the EU as a political-economic structure to change the nature of capitalism in the world. The EU has the unique potential to upgrade the quality of capitalism in environmental and social terms (see Telò 2006: ch. 4). Its member-states have strong political economies with vibrant welfare states that have been created over the past two centuries. It is important that lessons are learned from this process in a way that will contribute to changes in the hegemonic design of neo-liberalism. The principles of the social market economy should be expanded globally, using the European Union as a force for good. In this quest, consensus democracies could alter the structure of opportunities in global markets to their advantage. New welfare states across the world based on consensus democracies would certainly represent a major victory for the West Central European democracies. Welfare states are emerging in China and other countries, and this could be a great opportunity for consensus democracies: the competition state could be replaced by a cooperative state. With the help of the European Union, global governance could become a force for taming global neo-liberal capitalism. To this end, the European Union must either become the dominant economy in the world or influence the USA and China to move towards a more social model.

Conclusions: consensus democracies as a way of life

Consensus democracies are highly sophisticated systems of governance. The European Union is very fortunate to have many of the most advanced consensus democracies among its member-states. Their like-mindedness means that they have the potential to influence the evolution of the EU in terms of the type of polity it becomes. However, consensus democracies are dynamic entities: because they change over time, the socialisation of their principles in schools, workplaces, political parties, civil society associations and other contexts is critical for their survival. Strong consensus democracies encourage democratic practices to be a way of life. Ultimately, it is the quality and strategic skills of political leaders capable of upholding the principles of consensus democracies that will ensure the survival of these unique laboratories of horizontal cooperation. Exercising the statecraft required to preserve and further develop consensus democracies is thus one of the most challenging and exciting undertakings in the turbulent world of the present and the future.

List of interviews and written testimonies

Austria

Alexander Balthasar, Chancellery of Austria, Institute for Administrative Innovation, Vienna, 10 March 2015.

Dieter Brosz, Member of Parliament, Nationalrat, Green Party, Vienna, 11 March 2015.

Rudolf Lichtmannegger, Economy Chamber of Austria (WKÖ), Department of Economic Policy, Vienna, 11 March 2015.

Christian Mandl, Economy Chamber of Austria (WKÖ), Department of EU Affairs Coordination, Vienna, 11 March 2015.

Christa Peutl, Chancellery of Austria, Director of Department of European Affairs, Vienna, 11 March 2015.

Nikolai Soukup, Workers' Chamber of Austria (AK), Vice-coordinator of Social Partnership, Vienna, 11 March 2015.

Kurt Stürzenbecher, Member of Regional Parliament Vienna (Landtag, Stadtrat), Secretary of SPÖ parliamentary group, Nationalrat, Vienna, 10 March 2015.

Nurten Yilmaz, Member of Parliament, Nationalrat, Vienna, 9 March 2015.

Gerald Zelina, Member of Parliament, Bundesrat and Regional Parliament of Lower Austria, Team Stronach, Vienna, 9 March 2016.

Thomas Zotter, Workers' Chamber of Austria (AK), Coordinator Social Partnership, Vienna, 11 March 2016.

Email responses

Karl Heinz Kopf, President, second president of Nationalrat, Austrian People's Party (ÖVP), 23 March 2015.

Sonja Zwazl, President of Bundesrat 2014 to 2015, 2 March 2015.

Belgium

Gerolf Annemans, Member of Parliament, Chamber of Deputies, political group of Vlaams Belang, Brussels, 15 May 2012.

Michael Balter, Member of Parliament of German-speaking Parliament, Chairman of political group Vivant, Eupen, 24 May 2012.

Geert Bourgeois, Minister of Foreign Affairs, Flemish government, Brussels, 23 May 2012.

Emil Dannemark, Member of Parliament of German-speaking Community, Chairman of Party for Freedom and Progress (PFF), Eupen, 24 May 2012.

Rudy Demotte, President of the Government of the Federation Wallonia-Brussel, Brussels, 16 May 2012.

Sam de Smets, Chief of Cabinet of Minister Joke Schauvliege, Flemish government, Brussels, 16 May 2012.

Dimitri Hoegaerts, Political Secretary of parliamentary group chairman Gerolf Annemans, House of Representatives in Parliament of Belgium, 15 May 2012.

Jan Jambon, Member of Parliament, Chamber of Representatives, political group of the Nieuw-Vlaamse Alliantie, Brussels, 15 May 2012.

Karl Heinz Lambertz, President of the government of the German-speaking Community, Eupen, 24 May 2012.

Laurent Louis, Member of Parliament, Chamber of Representatives, Movement of Freedom and Democracy, Brussels, 15 May 2012.

Anne Peeters, Cabinet Office of Vice-president Jean-Claude Marcourt, Government of Federation Wallonia-Brussel, Namur, 9 May 2012.

Jan Peumans, President of the Flemish Parliament, political group of the Nieuw Vlaamse Alliantie, Brussels, 15 May 2012.

Raf Suys, Chef de Cabinet of First Minister Kris Peeters, Flemish government, Brussels, 25 May 2012.

Willem van der Voorde, Joint Director of Cabinet of Vice-president Didier Reynders of national government in Belgium, Brussels, 16 May 2012.

Paul Windey, President of the National Council of Labour (CNT), Brussels, 16 May 2012.

Written response

Jean Charles Lupert, President of the Parliament of Federation Wallonia-Brussels, Namur, 9 May 2012.

Luxembourg

Claude Meisch, Member of Luxembourg Parliament, Democratic Party (DP), 31 May 2012.

Laurent Mosar, President of Luxembourg Parliament, Christian Social People's Party (CSV) Luxembourg, 11 May 2012.

Jacques Santer, Prime Minister of Luxembourg (1984–1994), President of the European Commission (1994–1999), Luxembourg, 31 May 2012.

Netherlands

Michael Berkhout, provincial government of The Hague, public administration, The Hague, 24 February 2015.

Tiny Cox, Senator of Eerste Kamer, The Hague, 24 February 2015.

Ruard van Ganzevoort, Senator, Eerste Kamer, and professor at University of Amsterdam, The Hague, 23 February 2015.

Hans van Heijningen, Party Secretary of the Socialist Party (SP), Tweede Kamer, 24 February 2015.

Johannes Hers, Department of Public Finances, Centraal Planbureau, The Hague, 26 February 2015.

286 *Interviews and testimonies*

Godelieve van Heteren, Member of Parliament, Tweede Kamer, The Hague, 7 September 2005.

Josje den Ridder, researcher, Sociaal en Cultuurbureau (SCB), The Hague, 25 February 2015.

Wim Suyker, Department Public Finances, Centraal Planbureau, The Hague, 26 February 2015.

Joost Taverne, Member of Parliament, Tweede Kamer, The Hague, 26 February 2015.

Véronique Timmerhuis, Secretary-general, Economic and Social Council (SER), The Hague, SER Building, 25 February 2015.

Mei Li Vos, Member of Parliament, Tweede Kamer, The Hague, 26 February 2015.

Switzerland

Interviews

Peter Briner, Member of Parliament, Ständerat, Berne, 20 June 2005.

Boris Burri, Secretary of Committees and National Council, Parliament of Switzerland, Berne, 15 March 2016.

Luca Cirigliano, Swiss Trade Union Confederation (SGB), Central Secretary, Labour Law, Berne, 16 March 2016.

Marc Jost, President of the Berne Parliament 2015 to 2016, Berne, 16 March 2016.

Sandra Maissen, Secretary-general, Conference of the Cantons (KdK), Berne, 15 March 2016.

Thomas Moser, Department of Communication, responsible for foreign affairs, Government of Canton Berne, 16 March 2016.

Alois Ochser, Department of European Affairs, Ministry of Foreign Affairs, Berne, 16 March 2016.

Käthy Rifkin, Member of Parliament, Nationalrat, 15 March 2016.

Stephan Schmid, former Integration Bureau, now Department of European Affairs, Ministry of Foreign Affairs, Berne, 24 June 2005.

Barbara Schmid-Federer, Member of Parliament, Nationalrat, Berne, 14 March 2016.

Philip Schwab, Secretary-general of Swiss Parliament, Berne, 15 March 2016.

Patrick Trees, Secretary-general of Berne Parliament, Berne, 15 March 2016.

Email response

Maja Ingold, Member of Parliament, Nationalrat, Evangelical People's Party (EVP), 26 February 2016.

References

Accaputo, Laurelien, Benoît Bayenet and Giuseppe Pagano (2006) 'Le Plan Marshall pour la Wallonie'. *Courrier hebdomadaire du CRISP* 2006/14 no. 1919/1920, pp. 5–73.

Ackermann, Ewald (2014) *Zur Mitgliederzahl der Gewerkschaften 2014. Dossier 112.* Schweizerischer Gewerkschaftsbund (SGB). Posted at www.sgb.ch/fileadmin/user_upload/Bilder/Symbolbilder_Artikel/112d_EA_Mitgliederentw2014.pdf (accessed 15 February 2016).

Àgh, Attila (2001) 'Early Consolidation and Performance Crisis: The Majoritarian–Consensus Democracy Debate in Hungary'. *West European Politics* 24(3): 89–112.

Agnew, John (1993) 'The United States and American Hegemony'. In Peter J. Taylor (ed.) *Political Geography of the Twentieth Century. A Global Analysis.* London: Belhaven, pp. 207–233.

Ahrne, Göran (1990) *Agency and Organization. Towards an Organizational Theory of Society.* London: Sage.

Aiginger, Karl (2014) 'Korporatismus und Wirtschaftliche Leistungsfähigkeit' 2, April. Fiftieth anniversary of Advisory Committee for Social and Economic Issues. Powerpoint presentation posted at www.sozialpartner.at/wp-content/uploads/2015/08/Karl-Aiginger-1-april-2014.pdf (accessed 24 February 2016).

Aigner, Dagmar (2006) 'Die Landtage'. In Herbert Dachs, Peter Gerlich, Herbert Gottweis, Helmut Kramer, Volkmar Lauber, Wolfgang C. Müller and Emmerich Tálos (eds) *Politik in Österreich. Das Handbuch.* Vienna: Manzsche Verlags- und Universitätsbuchhandlung, pp. 959–973.

Aktion für eine Unabhängige und Neutrale Schweiz (AUNS) (2015) 30. Geschäftsbericht der AUNS. Berne: AUNS. Posted at http://auns.ch/content/uploads/2016/03/AUNS_Geschaeftsbericht_2015.pdf (accessed 20 April 2016).

Algemen Rekenkamer (2011) *Party Funding. Tweede Kamer.* The Hague: Algemen Rekenkamer. Posted at www.rekenkamer.nl/dsresource?objectid=16720&type=org. (accessed 8 June 2016).

Almond, Gabriel A. (1970) *Political Development. Essays in Heuristic Theory.* Boston, MA: Little Brown & Co.

Almond, Gabriel A. and Sidney Verba (1963, 1989) *The Civic Culture. Political Attitudes and Democracy in Five Nations.* London: Sage.

Altman, David (2013) 'Does an Active Use of Mechanisms of Direct Democracy Impact Electoral Participation? Evidence from the U.S. States and the Swiss Cantons'. *Local Government Studies* 39(6): 739–755.

Amable, Bruno (2003) *The Diversity of Modern Capitalism.* Oxford: Oxford University Press.

288 *References*

Andersen, Torben M., Nicole Bosch, Anja Deelen and Rob Euwals (2011) 'The Danish Flexicurity System in the Great Depression'. Website of VOX-Centre for Economic Policy Research-Aarhus posted at http://voxeu.org/article/flexicurity-danish-labour-market-model-great-recession (accessed 20 April 2016).

Anderson, Benedict (1991) *Imagined Communities. Reflections on the Origin and Spread of Nationalism.* London: Verso.

Andeweg, Rudy B. (1988) 'The Netherlands'. In Jean Blondel and Ferdinand Müller-Rommel (eds) *Cabinets in Western Europe.* Basingstoke: Macmillan, pp. 47–67.

Andeweg, Rudy B. (2008) 'The Netherlands: The Sanctity of Proportionality'. In Michael Gallagher and Paul Mitchell (eds) *The Politics of Electoral Systems.* Oxford: Oxford University Press, pp. 491–510.

Andeweg, Rudy B. and Galen A. Irwin (2014) *Governance and Politics in the Netherlands* (4th edn). Basingstoke: Palgrave.

Andrey, Georges (2004) 'Auf der Suche nach dem neuen Staat (1798–1848)'. In Ulrich Im Hof, Pierre Ducrey, Guy P. Marchal, Nicolas Morard, Martin Körner, François de Capitani, Georges Andrey, Roland Ruffieux, Hans Ulrich Jost, Peter Gilg and Peter Hablützel, *Geschichte der Schweiz und der Schweizer.* Basel: Schwabe Verlag, pp. 527–638.

Angeli, Thomas (2016) 'Ach wie weit ist Kasachstan'. Lobbywatch, 13 June. Plattform für transparente Politik. Posted at http://lobbywatch.ch/de/artikel/ach-wie-weit-kasachstan (accessed 3 July 2016).

Annemans, Gerolf and Steven Utsi (2011) *After Belgium: The Orderly Split-up.* Brussels: Uitgeverij Egmont.

Antoniades, Andreas (2008) 'Social Europe and/or Global Europe? Globalisation and Flexicurity as Debates on the Future of Europe'. *Cambridge Review of International Affairs* 21(3): 327–346.

Armingeon, Klaus (2002) 'The Effects of Negotiation Democracy: A Comparative Analysis'. *European Journal of Political Research* 41(2): 81–105.

Armingeon, Klaus (2011) 'A Prematurely Announced Death? Swiss Corporatism in (Comparative) *Switzerland* Perspective'. In Christine Trampusch and André Mach (eds) *In Europe. Continuity and Change in the Swiss Political Economy.* London: Routledge, pp. 165–185.

Armingeon, Klaus and Sarah Engler (2015) 'Polarisierung als Strategie. Die Polarisierung des Schweizer Parteiensystems im internationalen Vergleich'. In Markus Freitag and Adrian Vatter (eds) *Wahlen und Wählerschaft in der Schweiz.* Zürich: Verlag Neue Zürcher Zeitung, pp. 355–381.

Armingeon, Klaus, Fabio Bertozzi and Giuliano Bonoli (2004) 'Swiss Worlds of Welfare'. *West European Politics* 27(1): 20–44.

Arpaia, A., N. Curci, E. Meyermans, J. Peschner and F. Pierini (2010) 'Short Time Working Arrangements as a Response to Working Cycle Fluctuations'. *European Economy,* Occasional Paper 64, June. Brussels: European Commission.

Atlas of European Values Survey (Atlas of EVS) (2016) Database posted at www.atlasofeuropeanvalues.eu/kaartenoverlay.php?lang=de (accessed 20 April 2016).

Attinà, Fulvio (2003) *La Sicurezza degli Stati nell'Era dell'Egemonia Americana.* Milan: Giuffrè Editore.

Attinà, Fulvio (2011) *The Global Political System.* Basingstoke: Palgrave.

Auel, Katrin (2015) 'The Europeanization of National Parliaments'. In José M. Magone (ed.) *Routledge Handbook of European Politics.* London: Routledge, pp. 366–385.

References 289

Auel, Katrin and Oliver Höing (2014) 'Scrutiny in Challenging Times: National Parliaments in the Eurozone Crisis'. *European Policy Analysis*, 1 January. Swedish Institute of European Policy Studies.

Auel, Katrin, Olivier Rozenberg and Angela Tacea (2015) 'Fighting Back? And, If So, How? Measuring Parliamentary Strength and Activity in EU Affairs'. In Claudia Hefftler, Christine Neuhold, Olivier Rozenberg and Julie Smith (eds) *Palgrave Handbook on National Parliament and the European Union*. Basingstoke: Palgrave, pp. 60–94.

Bågenholm, Andreas, Kevin Deegan-Krause and R. Murray (2014) 'Political Data 2013'. In Andreas Bågenholm, Kevin Deegan-Krause and R. Murray (eds) *European Data Yearbook 2013*. A special issue of *European Journal of Poltitical Research* 53(1): 1–14.

Bartolini, Stefano (2005) *Restructuring Europe: Centre Formation, System Building, and Political Structuring between the Nation State and the European Union*. Oxford: Oxford University Press.

Becker, Frans and René Cuperus (2010) 'Innovating Social Democracy – Houdini-style: A Perspective from Dutch Labor Party (PvdA)'. *Internationale Politik and Gesellschaft* 4: 100–114. Posted at http://library.fes.de/pdf-files/ipg/ipg-2010-4/becker_cuperus.pdf (accessed 20 January 2016).

Behnke, Natalie (2009) *Towards a New Organization of Federal States? Lessons from the Processes of Constitutional Reform in Germany, Austria and Switzerland*. Polis no. 66/2009. Hagen: Fernuniversität Hagen.

Behrendt, Christian (2013) 'The Process of Constitutional Amendment in Belgium'. In Xenophon Contiades (ed.) *Engineering Constitutional Change. A Comparative Perspective on Europe, Canada and USA*. London: Routledge, pp. 35–50.

Beke, Wouter (2004) 'Living Apart Together: Christian Democracy in Belgium'. In Steven van Hecke and Emmanuel Gerard (eds) *Christian Democratic Parties in Europe since the End of the Cold War*. Leuven: Leuven University Press, pp. 133–158.

Benz, Arthur (2009) *Politik in Mehrebeben Systemen. Lehrbuch*. Opladen: Verlag Sozialwissenschaften.

Berger, Peter and Thomas Luckmann (1966, 1991) *The Social Construction of Reality. A Treatise in the Sociology of Knowledge*. London: Penguin Books.

Bergman, Torbjörn (1993) 'Constitutional Design and Government Formation: The Expected Consequences of Negative Parliamentarianism'. *Scandinavian Political Studies* 16(4): 285–305.

Bernauer, Julian and Sean Mueller (2015) 'Einheit in der Vielfalt? Ausmass und Gründe der Nationalisierung von Schweizer Parteien'. In Markus Freitag and Adrian Vatter (eds) *Wahlen und Wählerschaft in der Schweiz*. Zürich: Verlag Neue Zürcher Zeitung, pp. 325–353.

Bertelsmann Foundation (2014) '20 Jahre Binnenmarkt. Wachstumseffekte der zunehmenden europäischen Integration'. Bertelsmann Foundation. Posted at www.ged-project.de/uploads/tx_uandiproducts/files/20JBinnenmarkt_2014_final.pdf (accessed 23 December 2014).

Bertelsmann Foundation (2015) 'Policy Performance and Governance Capacities in the OECD and EU Sustainable Governance Indicators 2015'. Gütersloh: Bertelsmann Stiftung. Posted at www.sgi-network.org/docs/2015/basics/SGI2015_Overview.pdf (accessed 10 June 2016).

Besch, Sylvain, Nenad Dubajic, Altay Manço and Monika Schmidt (2011) *Les elections communales d'octobre 2011*. RED serie 17. Luxembourg: CEFIS. Posted at www.olai.public.lu/fr/publications/etude/RED17.pdf (accessed 21 November 2015).

290 References

Besselink, Leonard F.M. (2008) 'Fundamental Structures of the Constitution of the Netherlands'. Posted at http://dspace.library.uu.nl/handle/1874/25731 (accessed 2 September 2015).

Bezemer, Pieter-Jan, Edward J. Zajac, Ivana Naumovska, Frans A.J. Vanden Bosch and Henk W. Volberda (2015) 'Power and Paradigms: The Dutch Response to Pressures for Shareholder Value'. *Corporate Governance* 23(1): 60–75.

Billiet, Jaak, Bart Maddens and André-Paul Frognier (2006) 'Does Belgium (Still) Exist? Differences in Political Culture between Flemings and Walloons'. *West European Politics* 29(5): 912–932.

Bitsch, Marie-Thérèse (2004) *Histoire de la Belgique*. Brussels: Editions Complexe.

Blockmans, W.P. (2014) 'De vorming van een politieke unie'. In J.C.H. Bloom and E. Lamberts (eds) *Geschiedenis van de Nederlanden*. Amsterdam: Prometheus. Bert Bakke, pp. 63–144.

Blom, J.C.H. (2014) 'Nederlands sinds 1830'. In J.C.H. Blom and E. Lamberts (eds) *Geschiedenis van de Nederlanden*. Amsterdam: Prometheus. Bert Bakker, pp. 381–452.

Blom, J.C.H. and E. Lamberts (eds) (2014) *Geschiedenis van de Nederlanden*. Amsterdam: Prometheus. Bert Bakker.

Blümel, Barbara and Christine Neuhold (2001) 'The Parliament of Austria: A Large Potential with Little Implications'. In Andreas Maurer and Wolfgang Wessels (eds) *National Parliaments on their Ways to Europe: Losers and Latecomers?* Baden-Baden: Nomos Verlagsgesellschaft, pp. 313–336.

Bolleyer, Nicole (2006) 'Intergovernmental Arrangements in Spanish and Swiss Federalism: The Impact of Power-concentrating and Power-sharing Executives on Intergovernmental Institutionalization'. *Regional and Federal Studies* 16(4): 385–408.

Bonoli, Giuliano and Silja Häusermann (2011) 'Swiss Welfare Reforms in a Comparative European Perspective. Between Retrenchment and Activation'. In Christine Trampusch and André Mach (eds) *Switzerland in Europe. Continuity and Change in the Swiss Political Economy*. London: Routledge, pp. 186–204.

Boogers, Marcel (2014) 'Pulling the Strings: An Analysis of Informal Local Power Structures in Three Dutch Cities'. *Local Government Studies* 40(3): 339–355.

Boogers, Marcel and Gerrit Voerman (2010) 'Independent Local Political Parties in the Netherlands'. *Local Government Studies* 36(1): 75–90.

Bormann, Nils-Christian (2010) 'Patterns of Democracy and Its Critics'. In *Living Reviews in Democracy*, Vol. 2. Posted at www.ethz.ch/content/dam/ethz/special-interest/gess/cis/cis-dam/CIS_DAM_2015/WorkingPapers/Living_Reviews_Democracy/Bormann.pdf (accessed 27 April 2016).

Bossaert, Danielle (2001) 'The Luxembourg Chamber of Deputies: From a Toothless Tiger to a Critical Watchdog?' In Andreas Maurer and Wolfgang Wessels (eds) *National Parliaments on their Ways to Europe: Losers and Latecomers?* Baden-Baden: Nomos Verlagsgesellschaft, pp. 301–311.

Bovens, M. and Wille, A. (2008) 'Deciphering the Dutch Drop. Ten Explanations for Decreasing Political Trust in The Netherlands'. *International Review of Administrative Sciences* 74(2): S. 283–30.

Braudel, Fernand (1979) *Civilisation matérielle, économie et capitalisme (XVe-XVIIIe)*. Paris: Armand Colin.

Braudel, Fernand (1993) *A History of Civilizations*. London: Penguin Books.

Breeman, Gerard, Peter Scholten and Arco Timmermans (2015) 'Analysing Local Policy Agendas: How Dutch Municipal Executive Coalitions Allocate Attention'. *Local Government Studies* 41(1): 20–43.

References 291

Brooks, Robert C. (1920) *Government and Politics of Switzerland*. New York: World Book Company.

Brühl-Moser, Denise (2007) *Die schweizerische Staatsleitung im Spannungsfeld von nationaler Konsensfindung, Europäisierung und Internationalisierung. Mit Bezüge zu Belgien, Deutschland, Frankreich, Grossbritannien und Österreich*. Berne: Stämpfli Verlag AG.

Brüll, Christoph (2010) '"Hilft dir selbst, dann hilft der Gott"? Eine politische Geschichte der deutschsprachigen Gemeinschaft Belgiens'. In Anne-Begenat Neuschäffer (ed.) *Die Deutschsprachige Gemeinschaft Belgiens. Ein Bestandsaufnahme*. Part of the series Belgien in Fokus. Geschichte-Sprachen-Kulturen, edited by Anne-Begenat Neuschäffer. Berne: Peter Lang, pp. 27–46.

Bühlmann, Marc and Mariène Gerber (2015) 'Von der Unterschichtspartei zur Partei des gehobenen Mittelstands? Stabilität und Wandel der Wählerschaften der Sozialdemokraten und anderer grosser Schweizer Parteien zwischn 1971 und 2011'. In Markus Freitag and Adrian Vatter (eds) *Wahlen und Wählerschaft in der Schweiz*. Zürich: Verlag Neue Zürcher Zeitung, pp. 71–94.

Bulsara, Hament and Bill Kissane (2009) 'Arend Lijphart and the Transformation of Irish Democracy'. *West European Politics* 32(1): 172–195.

Bumb, Christoph (2011) *Luxemburgs Weg zur parlamentarischen Demokratie*. Berlin: Wissenschaftlicher Verlag.

Bundesamt für Statistik (2015) 'Wahlen-Detaillierte Daten. Pro Kanton: nationale/kantonale'. Wahlen database for each canton posted at www.bfs.admin.ch/bfs/portal/de/index/themen/17/02/blank/data/06.html (accessed 12 December 2015).

Bundesamt für Statistik (2016a) 'Bevölkerungsstand und – struktur-Indikatoren 2014'. Posted at www.bfs.admin.ch/bfs/portal/de/index/themen/01/02/blank/key/alter/gesamt.html (accessed 10 April 2016).

Bundesamt für Statistik (2016b) 'Indikatoren der Bevölkerungsstruktur-Database 1970–2014'. Posted at www.bfs.admin.ch/bfs/portal/de/index/themen/01/02/blank/key/alter/gesamt.html (accessed 10 April 2016).

Bundesamt für Statistik (2016c) 'Lebensstandard, soziale Situation und Armut – Daten, Indikatoren.Wohlbefinden in Europa'. Posted at www.bfs.admin.ch/bfs/portal/de/index/themen/20/03/blank/key/09/08.html#parsys_26449 (accessed 20 April 2016).

Bundesamt für Statistik (2016d) 'Zusamensetzung und Mitglieder des Bundesrats 1848–2016'. Posted at www.bfs.admin.ch/bfs/portal/de/index/themen/17/02/blank/key/bundesrat.html (accessed 13 May 2016).

Bundesamt für Statistik (2016e) 'Statistical Data on Switzerland'. Excerpt from *Statistical Yearbook*. Posted at www.bfs.admin.ch (accessed 13 April 2016).

Bundesamt für Statistik (2016f) 'Ausgewählte Indikatoren im regionalen Vergleich (Kantone)'. Posted at www.bfs.admin.ch/bfs/portal/de/index/regionen/kantone/daten.html (accessed 10 June 2016).

Bundeskanzleramt (2016a) 'Bundesgesetz über die Finanzierung politischer Parteien (Parteiengesetz 2012 – PartG) StF: BGBl. I No. 56/2012'. Posted at Rechtsinformationssystem (RIS) at www.ris.bka.gv.at/GeltendeFassung.wxe?Abfrage=Bundesnormen&Gesetzesnummer=20007889 (accessed 14 January 2016).

Bundeskanzleramt (2016b) 'Bundesgesetz über Förderungen des Bundes für politische Parteien (Parteien-Förderungsgesetz 2012 – PartFörG) StF: BGBl. I No. 57/2012'. Posted at Rechtsinformationssystem (RIS) at www.ris.bka.gv.at/GeltendeFassung.wxe?Abfrage=Bundesnormen&Gesetzesnummer=20007891 (accessed 14 January 2016).

Bundeskanzleramt (2016c) 'Bundesgesetz über die Förderung politischer Bildungsarbeit und Publizistik 1984 (Publizistikförderungsgesetz 1984 – PubFG) StF: BGBl.

292 References

No. 369/1984'. Posted at Rechtsinformationssystem at www.ris.bka.gv.at/Geltende-Fassung.wxe?Abfrage=Bundesnormen&Gesetzesnummer=10000784 (accessed 14 January 2016).

Bundeskanzleramt (2016d) 'Parteienförderung 2005–2015'. Posted at www.bundeskanz leramt.at/Docs/2015/7/7/Parteienf%C3%B6rderung_2005_2015.pdf (accessed 14 January 2016).

Bundeskanzleramt (2016e) 'Förderung der Parteienakademien 2005–15'. Posted at www. bundeskanzleramt.at/Docs/2015/7/7/Parteiakademief%C3%B6rderung_2005_2015.pdf (accessed 14 January 2016).

Bundeskanzleramt (2016f) 'Geschäftseinteilung des Bundeskanzleramts-BKA Organigramm'. Posted at www.bundeskanzleramt.at/gfe/Visio-Organigramm.pdf (accessed 11 May 2016).

Bundesministerium für Wissenschaft, Forschung und Wirtschaft (BMWFW) (2014) 'Die Lehre. Duale Berufsausbildung in Österreich. Moderne Ausbildung mit Zukunft'. Vienna: BMWFW. Posted at www.wko.at/Content.Node/Service/Bildung-und-Lehre/ Lehre/Lehrlingsausbildung-in-Oesterreich/HP_Kern_Die-Lehre_2014_311.pdf (accessed 30 June 2016).

Bunse, Simone (2009) *Small States and EU Governance. Leadership through Council Presidency*. Basinstroke: Palgrave.

Burroni, Luigi and Maarten Keune (2011) 'Flexicurity: A Conceptual Critique'. *European Journal of Industrial Relations* 17(1): 75–91.

Callaghan, Helen (2010) 'Beyond Methodological Nationalism: How Multilevel Governance Affects the Clash of Capitalisms'. *Journal of European Public Policy* 17(4): 564–580.

Cantillon, Bea, Veerle de Maesschalck, Stijn Rottiers and Gerlinde Verbist (2006) 'Social Redistribution in Federalised Belgium'. *West European Politics* 29(5): 1034–1056.

Caramani, Daniele (2004) *The Nationalization of Politics. The Formation of National Electorates and Party Systems in Western Europe*. Cambridge: Cambridge University Press.

Caramani, Daniele and Yves Meny (2005) 'Introduction. The Alpine Challenge to Identity, Consensus, and European Integration'. In Daniele Caramani and Yves Meny (eds) *Challenges to Consensual Politics: Democracy, Identity and Popular Protest in the Alpine Region*. Berne, Brussels: Peter Lang-Presses Interuniversitaires Européennes, pp. 21–49.

Castells, Manuel (1996) *The Rise of the Network Society. The Information Age: Economy, Society and Culture*. London: Blackwell.

Castells, Manuel (1997) *The Power of Identity: The Information Age: Economy, Society, and Culture Volume II*. London: Blackwell.

Castells, Manuel (1998) *End of Millennium: The Information Age: Economy, Society, and Culture Volume III*. London: Blackwell.

Centraal Bureau voor Statistiek (CBS) (2015) 'Leden van vakverenigingen; geslacht en leeftijd', 27 October 2015. Posted at http://statline.cbs.nl/StatWeb/publication/? VW=T &DM=SLNL&PA=80598NED&D1=a&D2=a&D3=0&D4=a&D5=0,8-11&HD=140304-1019&HDR=T,G2,G1&STB=G3,G4 (accessed 15 February 2016).

Centre des Données Socio-Politiques-Science Po (CDSP) (2009) 'Local Elections in Luxembourg'. Posted at https://cdsp.sciences-po.fr/fichiers_elections25_FR/Luxembourg. pdf (accessed 13 December 2015).

Centre des Données Socio-Politiques Science Po (CDSP) (2011) 'Luxembourg'. Posted at http://cdsp.sciences-po.fr/fichiers_elections25_FR/Luxembourg.pdf (accessed 21 November 2015).

Cerny, Philip G. (1990) *The Changing Architecture of Politics. Structure, Agency and the Future of the State*. London: Sage.

References   293

Cerny, Philip G. (1997) 'The Paradoxes of the Competition State. The Dynamics of Political Globalization'. *Government and Opposition* 32(2): 251–274.

Chambre des Deputés (2007) *Rapport de l'Activité de la session parlamentaire de 2006–7.* Posted at www.chd.lu/wps/wcm/connect/4fddbc804e2961e4b709f7010df100b c/Rapport_annuel2008.pdf?MOD=AJPERES&CACHEID=4fddbc804e2961e4b709f70 10df100bc (accessed 30 May 2016).

Chambre des Deputés (2008) *Rapport De La Commission Speciale 'Reorganisation Territoriale Du Luxembourg'*, 19 June. Debat d'Orientation sur la reorganisation territoriale de Luxembourg, No. 5890. Session ordinaire de 2007–2008, 1 July 2008. Posted at pdf at www.schengen.lu/fr-FR/notre-commune/Rapport_Reorg_ territoriale.pdf?FileID= fusion%2Frapport_reorg_territoriale.pdf (accessed 13 December 2015).

Chambre des Deputés (2010) *Rapport de l'Activité de la session parlamentaire de 2009–2010.* Posted at 2d4e004513d31899b5bb20a29bcc2c/Chamber_Rapport_2009–2010_ Internet.pdf?MOD=AJPERES&CACHEID=f32d4e004513d31899b5bb20a29bcc2c (accessed 30 May 2016).

Chambre des Deputés (2011) *Rapport de l'Activité de la session parlamentaire de 2010–2011.* Posted at www.chd.lu/wps/wcm/connect/9987110049a90a578f4aff41d8fa 1b85/Rapport_2010-2011_internet.pdf?MOD=AJPERES&CACHEID=9987110049a9 0a578f4aff41d8fa1b85 (accessed 30 May 2016).

Chambre des Deputés (2012) *Rapport de l'Activité de la session parlamentaire de 2011–2012.* Posted at www.chd.lu/wps/wcm/connect/52a1cd37-a281-4352-8e4e-536727b4aaf0/Chamber_Rapport_2011-2012_Internet.pdf?MOD=AJPERES& CACHEID=52a1cd37-a281-4352-8e4e-536727b4aaf0 (accessed 30 May 2016).

Chambre des Deputés (2013) *Rapport de l'Activité de la session parlamentaire de 2012–2013.* Posted at www.chd.lu/wps/wcm/connect/ba007e0e-5993-4957-adf8-6590d 9c6ed2c/Rapport_2012-2013_internet.pdf?MOD=AJPERES&CACHEID=ba007e0e-5993-4957-adf8-6590d9c6ed2c (accessed 29 May 2016).

Chambre des Deputés (2015a) *Revisiounspropositioun Iwwer D'aféierung Vun Enger Neier Verfassung.* Posted at www.referendum.lu/De/Nouvelle-Constitution/ (accessed 4 May 2016).

Chambre des Deputés (2015b) *Financement des partis politiques.* Posted at www.chd.lu/ wps/portal/public/!ut/p/b1/rZLRboIwFIafZQ-w9FDQlktKSy1CJ5SqcGMw GoNDX-TIzJ08_trhkMZnuYudcneT__v_k5KAK1Q7FQDzqux6ao2pfvzWb-tgc9nX-7OVfDRY75NFceBgDPByXURPtSuCGDXlD2AkypyWWQCt-3DBSEjhEZw6D-wPX6GSnYxgV8qgC8T_m0iSeYBjkVMrNEu5cMLf0Nwg5cj95qnod-vLrNkHDoD-kJT87Qg3Au7wZS8gP_ITRgHrlDBkpFzgA1SgOXgLsz2_qO65y7dwgjSx8Fp-k2OG2S-12pgvRFatIFzx1wTpxIVptuihJ4fSe-svJappbFoTcrL3jdaBMFAEcwRMbOx-mAdP49MEbVpj0s-4-ahUiPDrs121Vtcm6a5rHue3l6-ABqQqnE/dl4/d5/ L2dJQSEvUUt3QS80SmtFL1o2X1IyRFZSSTQyMDAwNDkwSUVJUE45R0Uz-Q0Iw/ (accessed 14 January 2016).

Chambre des Deputés (2016a) 'Groupes politiques et sensibilités politiques'. Posted at www.chd.lu/wps/portal/public/!ut/p/b1/04_SjzQ0Nza2MDGzMDfSj9CPykssy0xPLM-nMz0vMAfGjzOJdjFzCgjxNjAzczQNNDIy8XL3MQ4P9jN09jIEKIoEKDHAAR-wNU_f6uwWYGRsYBxo5BwUZAeROofiMLi-Agd0dfV0vLUCcDTwNnw2DXQC-cjA08j4uzHYwEB_X4e-bmp-rlROW5uFo6KAA7m4uA!/dl4/d5/L2dJQSEvUUt3 QS80SmtFL1o2X0QyRFZSSTQyMDEc3UTQwMkpFSjdVU04zR0o2/ (accessed 13 May 2016).

294   References

Chambre des Deputés (2016b) Organigramme. Posted at www.chd.lu/wps/wcm/connect/ adb48a004d7aa000beeebebf9dfc74d4/organigramme+Trombinoscope+2016%282% 29.pdf?MOD=AJPERES (accessed 14 September 2016).

Chambre des Représentants de Belgique (2003) *Releve Statistique de l'Activité Parlamentaire 1999–2003*. Brussels: Chambres de Représentants. Doc 50 007/002, 11 April 2003. Posted at www.lachambre.be/kvvcr/pdf_sections/statistics/50K0007002.pdf (accessed 24 October 2015).

Chambre des Représentants de Belgique (2014) *Rapport des Activités. Session Ordinaire 2013–4*. Brussels: Chambre des Représentants de Belgique.

Chambre des Representants de Belgique (2016) Legislatures and legislative reports website. Posted at www.lachambre.be/kvvcr/showpage.cfm?section=/publications/ann ualreport&language=fr&story=2014-2015.xml (accessed 13 May 2016).

Chancellerie du Premier Ministre (2014) *Rapport d'Activités 2013*. Brussels: SPF Chancellerie du Premier Minister. Posted at http://kanselarij.belgium.be/sites/default/files/ Rapport_Activites_2013_0.pdf (accessed 9 December 2015).

Chancellerie du Premier Ministre (2015) *Rapport d'Activités 2014*. Brussels: SPF Chancellerie Premier Minister. Posted at http://kanselarij.belgium.be/sites/default/files/ rapport_GRI_2014_FR.pdf (accessed 9 December 2015).

Chancellerie du Premier Ministre (2016) 'Organigramme'. Posted at http://kanselarij. belgium.be/fr/org (accessed 10 June 2016).

Chorherr, Thomas (2005) *Eine kurze Geschichte der ÖVP*. Vienna: Ueberreuter.

Chrëschtlech-Sozial Volekspartei (CSV) (2014) *Aktivitéitsrapport. Nationalkongress 2013–2014*. Luxemburg: CSV. Posted at https://csv.lu/files/2014/02/Aktivit%C3%A9it srapport-2013_2014.pdf (accessed 14 January 2016).

Christiansen, Thomas and Christine Reh (2009) *Constitutionalizing the European Union*. Basingstoke: Palgrave.

Church, Clive H. (2004) *The Politics and Government of Switzerland*. Basingstoke: Palgrave.

Clemens, G., A. Reinfeldt and G. Wille (2008) *Geschichte der europäischen Integration*. Paderborn: Ferdinand Schöningh-UTB.

Coffé, Hilde (2006) '"The Vulnerable Institutional Complexity": The 2004 Regional Elections in Brussels'. *Regional and Federal Studies* 16(1): 99–107.

Comité de liaison des associations d'étrangers (CLAE) (2016) Presentation. Posted at www.clae.lu/clae/ (accessed 26 May 2016).

Conseil national d'étrangers (CNE) (2016) 'Conseil national d'étrangers'. Posted at www. olai.public.lu/fr/relations-nationales/organismes_consultation/conseil-nat-etrangers/ (accessed 28 May 2016).

Costa, Olivier and Paul Magnette (2003) 'The European Union as a Consociation? A Methodological Assessment'. *West European Politics* 26(3): 1–18.

Crespy, Amandine and Vivien Schmidt (2014) 'The Clash of Titans: France, Germany and the Discursive Double Game of EMU Reform'. *Journal of European Public Policy* 21(8): 1085–1101.

Daalder, Hans (1987) 'The Dutch Party System: From Segmentation to Polarization –And Then?' In Hans Daalder (ed.) *Party Systems in Denmark, Austria, Switzerland, The Netherlands and Belgium*. London: Frances Pinter, pp. 193–284.

Daalder, Hans (2011) *State Formation, Parties and Democracy. Studies in Comparative European Politics*. Colchester: European Consortium for Political Research.

Dachs, Herbert (2006a) 'Parteiensysteme in den Bundesländern'. In Herbert Dachs, Peter Gerlich, Herbert Gottweis, Helmut Kramer, Volkmar Lauber, Wolfgang C. Müller and Emmerich Tálos (eds) *Politik in Österreich. Das Handbuch*. Vienna: Manzsche Verlags- und Universitätsbuchhandlung, pp. 1008–1023.

Dachs, Herbert (2006b) 'Die Grünalternative'. In Herbert Dachs, Peter Gerlich, Herbert Gottweis, Helmut Kramer, Volkmar Lauber, Wolfgang C. Müller and Emmerich Tálos (eds) *Politik in Österreich. Das Handbuch.* Vienna: Manzsche Verlags- und Universitätsbuchhandlung, pp. 389–401.

Dandoy, Régis (2011a) 'Le SP.a (Socialistische Partij anders)'. In Pascal Delwit, Benoit Pilet and Emilie van Haute (eds) *Les Partis Politiques en Belgique*. Brussels: Edition de l'Université de Bruxelles, pp. 83–105.

Dandoy, Régis (2011b) 'Groen!' In Pascal Delwit, Benoit Pilet and Emilie van Haute (eds) *Les Partis Politiques en Belgique*. Brussels: Edition de l'Université de Bruxelles, pp. 163–177.

Dandoy, Régis (2011c) 'La formation des gouvernements en Belgique'. In Pascal Delwit, Benoit Pilet and Emilie van Haute (eds) *Les Partis Politiques en Belgique*. Brussels: Edition de l'Université de Bruxelles, pp. 299–317.

Dandoy, Régis (2013) 'The Mid-term Provincial Elections as a Springboard for the Flemish Nationalists'. *Regional and Federal Studies* 23(2): 243–253.

Dandoy, Régis, Caroline Van Wynsberghe and Geoffroy Matagne (2014) 'L'Avenir du Fédéralisme Belge: Une Analyse des Programmes Electoraux et des Accords de Gourvenement'. In Régis Dandoy, Geoffroy Matagne and Caroline Van Wynsberghe (eds) *Le Féderalisme Belge. Enjeux institutionels, acteurs socio-politiques et opinions publiques*. Louvain- La-Neuve: Academia-L'Harmattan, pp. 87–109.

Dassoneville, Ruth (2015) *Net Volatility in Western Europe: 1950–2014*. Dataset. KU Leuven: Centre for Citizenship and Democracy. Posted at http://soc.kuleuven.be/web/staticpage/11/95/eng/1197 (accessed 21 January 2016).

De Capitani, François (2004) 'Beharren und Umsturz (1648–1815)'. In Ulrich Im Hof, Pierre Ducrey, Guy P. Marchal, Nicolas Morard, Martin Körner, François de Capitani, Georges Andrey, Roland Ruffieux, Hans Ulrich Jost, Peter Gilg and Peter Hablützel, *Geschichte der Schweiz und der Schweizer*. Basel: Schwabe Verlag, pp. 447–526.

Dedecker, Nicolás (2011a) 'Le open VLD'. In Pascal Delwit, Benoit Pilet and Emilie van Haute (eds) *Les Partis Politiques en Belgique*. Brussels: Edition de l'Université de Bruxelles, pp. 129–144.

Dedecker, Nicolás (2011b) 'Le Mouvement reformateur (MR)'. In Pascal Delwit, Benoit Pilet and Emilie van Haute (eds) *Les Partis Politiques en Belgique*. Brussels: Edition de l'Université de Bruxelles, pp. 145–162.

Delreux, Tom and François Randour (2015) 'Belgium: Institutional and Administrative Adaptation but Limited Political Interest'. In Claudia Hefftler, Christine Neuhold, Olivier Rozenberg and Julie Smith (eds) *Palgrave Handbook on National Parliament and the European Union*. Basingstoke: Palgrave, pp. 153–169.

Delsen, Lei (2012) 'From Welfare State to Participation Society. Welfare State Reform in the Netherlands 2003–2010'. Nijmegen Centre for Economics (NiCE) Working Paper 12–103, May. Posted at www.ru.nl/publish/pages/516298/nice_12103.pdf (accessed 19 April 2016).

Delwit, Pascal (1999a) 'The Belgian Socialist Party'. In Robert Ladrech and Philippe Marliére (eds) *History, Organization, Policies*. Basingstoke: Palgrave, pp. 30–42.

Delwit, Pascal (2002) 'Du parti liberal à la fédération PRL-FDF-MCC'. In Pascal Delwit (ed.) *Liberalisme et partis liberaux en Europe*. Brussels: Editions de l'Université de Bruxelles, pp. 179–198.

Delwit, Pascal (2003) *Composition, Décomposition et Recomposition du paysage politique en Belgique*. Brussels: Editions Labor.

296 References

Delwit, Pascal (2011a) 'Partis et systemes de partis en Belgique en perspective'. In Pascal Delwit, Benoit Pilet and Emilie van Haute (eds) *Les Partis Politiques en Belgique*. Brussels: Edition de l'Université de Bruxelles, pp. 6–33.

Delwit, Pascal (2011b) 'Le Parti Socialiste'. In Pascal Delwit, Benoit Pilet and Emilie van Haute (eds) *Les Partis Politiques en Belgique*. Brussels: Edition de l'Université de Bruxelles, pp. 108–127.

Delwit, Pascal and Jean Michel Waele (eds) (1999) *Les Partis Verts*. Brussels: Editions Complexe.

Delwit, Pascal, Benoit Pilet and Emilie van Haute (eds) (2011) *Les Partis Politiques en Belgique*. Brussels: Edition de l'Université de Bruxelles.

Demokratesch Partei (2015) DP en bref. Posted at www.dp.lu/docs/dl/371_dp_en_bref. pdf (accessed 14 January 2016).

Denters, Bas and Pieter-Jan Klok (2013) 'Citizen Democracy and the Responsiveness of Councillors: The Effects of Democratic Institutionalisation on the Role Orientations and Role Behaviour of Councillors'. *Local Government Studies* 39(5): 661–680.

De Rooy, Piet (2014) *Ons stipje op de waereldkaart. De politieke cultuur van Nederland in de negentiende en twintigste eeuw*. Amsterdam: Wereldbibliotheek.

De Rynck, Stefaan (2005) 'Regional Autonomy and Education Policy in Belgium'. *Regional and Federal Studies* 15(4): 485–500.

Deschouwer, Kris (2004) 'Political Parties and their Reactions to the Erosion of Voter Loyalty in Belgium: Caught in a Trap'. In Peter Mair, Wolfgang C. Müller and Fritz Plasser (eds) *Political Parties and Electoral Change: Party Responses to Electoral Markets*. London: Sage, pp. 179–206.

Deschouwer, Kris (2009a) *The Politics of Belgium. Governing a Divided Society*. Basingstoke: Palgrave.

Deschouwer, Kris (2009b) 'Coalition Formation and Congruence in a Multi-layered Setting: Belgium 1995–2008'. *Regional and Federal Studies* 19(1): 13–35.

Deschouwer, Kris (2015) 'The Rise and Fall of Belgian Regionalist Parties'. In Eve Hepburn (ed.) *New Challenges for Stateless Nationalist and Regionalist Parties*. London: Routledge, pp. 80–98.

Deutsche Gemeinschaft in Belgien (2015) Posted at www.dg.be/desktopdefault.aspx/tabid-2794/5382_read-45665/ (accessed 3 June 2016).

Dewaechter, Wilfried (1987) 'Changes in a Particratie: The Belgian Party System from 1944 to 1986'. In Hans Daalder (ed.) *Party Systems in Denmark, Austria, Switzerland, The Netherlands and Belgium*. London: Frances Pinter, pp. 285–363.

De Wijk, Rob (2006) 'The Multiple Crises of Dutch Parallel Societies'. In Rob De Wijk, Samir Amghar, Amel Boubekeur and Alexei Maleshenko, *Between Suicide Bombings and Burning Banlieues: The Multiple Crises of Europe's Parallel Societies*. Centre for European Policy Studies (CEPS) Working Paper 12, pp. 7–13. Posted at www.isn.ethz.ch/Digital-Library/Publications/Detail/?ots591=0c54e3b3-1e9c-be1e-2c24-a6a8c7060233&lng=en&id=22628 (accessed 13 April 2016).

De Winter, Lieven (1992a) 'Christian Democratic Parties in Belgium'. In Mario Caciagli, Lieven de Winter, Albrecht Mintzel, Joan B. Culla and Alain de Brouwer, *Christian Democracy in Europe*. Barcelona: Institut des Ciencies Politiques i Socials.

De Winter, Lieven (1996) 'Party Encroachment on the Executive and Legislative Branch in the Belgian Polity'. *Res Publica* 38(2): 325–351.

De Winter, Lieven (2000) 'Liberal Parties in Belgium: From Freemasons to Free Citizens'. In Lieven de Winter (ed.) *Liberalism and Liberal Parties in the European Union*. Barcelona: Institut de Ciéncies Politiques i Socials, pp. 141–182.

De Winter, Lieven (2008) 'Belgium: Empowering Voters or Party Elites?' In Michael Gallagher and Paul Mitchell (eds) *The Politics of Electoral Systems*. Oxford: Oxford University Press, pp. 417–432.

De Winter, Lieven and Patrick Dumont (1999) 'Belgium: Party System(s) on the Eve of Desintegration'. In David Broughton and Mark Donovan (eds) *Changing Party Systems in Western Europe*. London: Pinter, pp. 183–206.

De Winter, Lieven and Patrick Dumont (2006) 'Do Belgian Parties Undermine the Democratic Chain of Delegation?' *West European Politics* 29(5): 957–976.

De Winter, Lieven and Thierry Laurent (1996) 'The Belgium Parliament and European Integration'. In Philip Norton (ed.) *National Parliaments and the European Union*. London: Frank Cass, pp. 75–91.

De Winter, Lieven, Arco Timmermans and Patrick Dumont (2000) 'Belgium: On Government Agreements, Evangelists, Followers, and Heretics'. In Wolfgang C. Müller and Kaare Strøm (eds) *Coalition Governments in Western Europe*. Oxford: Oxford University Press, pp. 300–355.

Dimmel, Nikolaus and Josef Schmee (eds) (2005) *Politische Kultur in Österreich 2000–2005*. Vienna: ProMedia.

Di Palma, Giuseppe (1990) *To Craft Democracies. An Essay on Democratic Transitions*. Berkeley and Los Angeles: University of California Press.

Dirkx, Paul (2012) *La concurrence ethnique. La Belgique, l'Europe et le neoliberalisme*. Bellecombe-en-Bauges: éditions du croquant.

Dumont, Patrick and Raphäel Kies (2014) 'Luxembourg'. In Andreas Bågenholm, Kevin Deegan-Krause and Rainbow Murray (eds) *European Political Data Yearbook 2013*. Special issue of *European Journal of Political Research* 53(1): 211–222.

Dumont, Patrick and Lieven de Winter (2000) 'Luxembourg: Stable Coalitions in a Pivotal Party System'. In Wolfgang C. Müller and Kaare Strøm (eds) *Coalition Governments in Western Europe*. Oxford: Oxford University Press, pp. 399–432.

Dumont, Patrick, Fernand Fehlen and Philippe Poirier (2009) 'Politisches System, politische Parteien und Wahlen'. In Wolfgang H. Lorig and Mario Hirsch (eds) *Das politische System Luxemburgs*. Wiesbaden: Verlag für Sozialwissenschaften, pp. 155–159.

Dumont, Patrick, Raphaël Kies and Philip Poirier (2011) 'Luxembourg: The Challenge of Inclusive Democracy in a Local State'. In John Loughlin, Frank Hendriks and Anders Lindström (eds) *Oxford Handbook on Subnational Democracy in Europe*. Oxford: Oxford University Press, pp.123–145.

Dumont, Patrick, Arco Timmermans and Catherine Moury (2015) 'Coping with Domestic and European Complexity. How Consensus Democracy is Maintained in the Low Countries' Government'. In Hans Vollard, Jan Beyers and Patrick Dumont (eds) *European Integration and Consensus Politics in the Low Countries*. London: Routledge, pp. 24–47.

Dumont, Patrick, Raphaël Kies, Astrid Spreitzer, Maria Bozinis and Philippe Poirier (eds) (2010) *Les elections législatives et européennes de 2009 du Grand Duché de Luxembourg*. Rapport elaboré pour la Chambre de Deputés. Programme Gouvernance européenne. Ètudes parlementaires et politiques. Luxembourg: Université du Luxembourg.

EconomieSuisse (2016) 'Mitglieder'. Posted at www.economiesuisse.ch/de/content/mitglieder (accessed 24 February 2016).

Eerste Kamer (2016) Website posted at https://www.eerstekamer.nl/home (accessed 10 June 2016).

Eichenberger, Pierre and André Mach (2011) 'Organized Capital and Coordinated Market Economy. Swiss Business Interest Associations between Socio-economic Regulation

298 References

and Political Influence'. In Christine Trampusch and André Mach (eds) *Switzerland in Europe. Continuity and Change in the Swiss Political Economy*. London: Routledge pp. 63–81.

Emanuele, V. (2015) *Dataset of Electoral Volatility and its Internal Components in Western Europe (1945–2015)*. Rome: Italian Center for Electoral Studies. Posted at http://cise.luiss.it/cise/dataset-of-electoral-volatility-and-its-internal-components-in-western-europe-1945-2015/ (accessed 21 January 2016).

Ennser-Jedenastik, Laurenz and Martin Ejnar Hansen (2013) 'The Contingent Nature of Local Party System Nationalisation: The Case of Austria 1985–2009'. *Local Government Studies* 39(6): 777–791.

Erk, Jan (2004) 'Austria: Federation without Federalism'. *Publius* 54(1): 1–20.

Ertmann, Thomas (2000) 'Liberalization and Democratization and the Origins of a "Pillarized" Civil Society in Nineteenth Century Belgium and Netherlands'. In Philip Nord and Nancy Bermeo (eds) *Civil Society before Democracy. Lessons from Nineteenth-century Europe*. Lanham, MD, and London: Rowman and Littlefield, pp. 155–178.

Esping-Andersen, Gösta (1985) *Politics against Markets: The Social Democratic Road to Power*. Princeton, NJ: Princeton University Press.

Esping-Andersen, Gösta (1990) *The Three Worlds of Welfare Capitalism*. Cambridge: Polity Press.

Etienne-Robert, Fanny, Nicole Kerschen, Vassil Kirov, Patrick Thill, Adrien Thomas and Frédéric Turlan (2015) 'Belgium: Country Working Life Profile'. Posted at www.eurofound.europa.eu/observatories/eurwork/comparative-information/national-contributions/luxembourg/luxembourg-working-life-country-profile (accessed 23 February 2016).

Euractiv (2011) 'Burka Verbot in Belgien', 11 July. Posted at www.euractiv.de/section/soziales-europa/news/burka-verbot-in-belgien/ (accessed 13 April 2016).

Eurobarometer (2005) *Social Capital. Eurobarometer Special Survey no. 223*. Luxembourg: Office of the Official Publications of the European Communities. Posted at http://ec.europa.eu/public_opinion/archives/ebs/ebs_223_en.pdf (accessed 8 June 2016).

Eurobarometer Interactive (2016) Database. Posted at http://ec.europa.eu/COMMFrontOffice/PublicOpinion/index.cfm/Chart/index (accessed 20 April 2016).

European Centre for the Development of Vocational Training (CEDEFOP) (2016) Statistical Overviews on Vocational Education and Training (VET). Posted at www.cedefop.europa.eu/en/publications-and-resources/country-reports/statistical-overviews-on-vet (accessed 30 June 2016).

European Commission (2005) *Flash Eurobarometer. The European Constitution: Post-referendum Survey in the Netherlands*, 2–4 June.

European Commission (2013) *European Union Employment and Social Situation – Quarterly Review – March 2013 – Special Supplement on Demographic Trends*. Luxembourg: Publications Office of the European Union.

European Commission (2016a) National Parliament Opinions and Commission Replies. Posted at http://ec.europa.eu/dgs/secretariat_general/relations/relations_other/npo/index_en.htm (accessed 30 May 2016).

European Commission (2016b) *Employment and Social Development in Europe 2015*. Luxembourg: Office of the Official Publications of the European Communities. Posted at http://ec.europa.eu/social/main.jsp?catId=738&langId=en&pubId=7859&furtherPubs=yes (accessed 10 April 2016).

European Institute of Gender Equality (EIGE) (2015) *Gender Equality Index 2015. Measuring Gender Equality in the European Union 2005–2012*. Report. Brussels: EIGE.

References 299

posted at http://eige.europa.eu/sites/default/files/documents/mh0215616enn.pdf (accessed 20 April 2016).

European Social Survey (2004) European Social Survey Round 2 Data. Data file edition 3.4. Norwegian Social Science Data Services. Norway – Data archive and distributor of ESS data for ESS ERIC.

European Social Survey (2010) European Social Survey Round 5 Data. Data file edition 3.2. Norwegian Social Science Data Services. Norway – Data archive and distributor of ESS data for ESS ERIC.

European Social Survey (2012) European Social Survey Round 6 Data. Data file edition 2.2. Norwegian Social Science Data Services. Norway – Data archive and distributor of ESS data for ESS ERIC.

European Social Survey (2014) European Social Survey Round 2 Data. Data file edition 1.0. Norwegian Social Science Data Services. Norway – Data archive and distributor of ESS data for ESS ERIC.

European Trade Union Institute (ETUI) (2016) 'European Company (SE) Database-ECDB'. Posted at http://ecdb.worker-participation.eu/ (accessed 18 May 2016).

Eurostat (2016a) 'General Government Gross Debt – Annual Data'. Posted at http://ec.europa.eu/eurostat/tgm/table.do?tab=table&init=1&language=en&pcode=teina225&plugin=1 (accessed 18 February 2016).

Eurostat (2016b) 'General Government Deficit (–) and Surplus (+) – Annual Data'. posted at http://ec.europa.eu/eurostat/tgm/table.do?tab=table&plugin=1&language=en&pcode=teina200 (accessed 18 February 2016).

Eurostat (2016c) 'Tables by Functions, Aggregated Benefits and Grouped Schemes – In PPS per Head' (last update: 6 April). Posted at http://appsso.eurostat.ec.europa.eu/nui/show.do (accessed 7 April 2016).

Eurostat (2016d) 'Fertility Rates By Age'. Posted at http://appsso.eurostat.ec.europa.eu/nui/show.do (accessed 10 April 2016).

Eurostat (2016e) 'Income Quintile Share Ratio (S80/S20) (Source: SILC)'. Posted at http://ec.europa.eu/eurostat/tgm/table.do?tab=table&init=1&language=en&pcode=tessi180&plugin=1 (accessed 13 April 2016).

Eurostat (2016f) 'Gini Coefficient of Equivalised Disposable Income (Source: SILC)'. Posted at http://ec.europa.eu/eurostat/tgm/table.do?tab=table&language=en&pcode=tessi190 (accessed 13 April 2016).

Eurostat (2016g) 'Percentage of the Population Rating their Satisfaction as High, Medium or Low by Domain, Sex, Age and Educational Attainment Level [ilc_pw05]. Posted at http://appsso.eurostat.ec.europa.eu/nui/submitViewTableAction.do (accessed 20 April 2016).

Eurostat (2016h) 'BIP und Hauptkomponenten – Jeweilige Preise [nama_gdp_c]Letzte Aktualisierung: 05–04–2016'. Posted at http://appsso.eurostat.ec.europa.eu/nui/submitViewTableAction.do (accessed 28 April 2016).

Eurostat (2016i) 'Arbeitslosenquote, insgesamt in %'. Posted at http://ec.europa.eu/eurostat/tgm/table.do?tab=table&init=1&language=de&pcode=tsdec450&plugin=1 (accessed 28 April 2016).

Eurostat (2016j) 'Reales BIP pro Kopf, Wachstumsrate und insgesamt'. Posted at http://ec.europa.eu/eurostat/tgm/refreshTableAction.do?tab=table&plugin=1&pcode=tsdec100&language=de (accessed 31 May 2016).

Eurostat (2016k) 'Employment Rate, Age Group 15–64, 2004–14'. Posted at http://ec.europa.eu/eurostat/statistics-explained/index.php/File: Employment_rate,_age_group_15%E2%80%9364,_2004%E2%80%9314_ (%25)_YB16.png (accessed 31 May 2016).

300   References

Eurostat (2016l) 'Bevölkerung am 1. Januar nach Alter und Geschlecht' (22 April). Posted at http://appsso.eurostat.ec.europa.eu/nui/show.do (accessed 31 May 2016).

Eurostat (2016m) 'Regional GDP: GDP per capita in the EU in 2013: seven capital regions among the ten most prosperous'. In Eurostat, news release 90/2015, 21 May 2015. Posted at http://ec.europa.eu/eurostat/documents/2995521/6839731/1-21052015-AP-EN.pdf/c3f5f43b-397c-40fd-a0a4-7e68e3bea8cd (accessed 15 September 2016).

Falkner, Gerda (1999) 'Korporatismus auf österreichischer und europäischer Ebene: Verflechtung ohne Osmose?' In Ferdinand Karlhofer and Emmerich Talós (eds) *Zukunft der Sozialpartnerschaft. Veränderungsdynamik und Reformbedarf*. Vienna: Zentrum für angewandte Forschung, pp. 215–240.

Falkner, Gerda (2005) 'Österreich als EU-Mitglied: Kontroversen auf internationaler und nationaler Ebene'. In Emmerich Talós (ed.) *Schwarz-Blau. Eine Bilanz des 'Neu-Regierens'*. Vienna: LIT, pp. 86–101.

Falkner, Gerda (2006) 'Zur "Europäisierung" des österreichischen politischen Systems'. In Herbert Dachs, Peter Gerlich, Herbert Gottweis, Helmut Kramer, Volkmar Lauber, Wolfgang C. Müller and Emmerich Talós (eds) *Politik in Österreich. Das Handbuch*. Vienna: Manzsche Verlags- und Universitätsbuchhandlung, pp. 95–102.

Fallend, Franz (2000) 'Demokratische Kontrolle oder Inquisition. Eine empirische Analyse der parlamentarischen Untersuchungsausschüsse des Nationalrats nach 1945'. *Österreichische Zeitschrift für Politikwissenschaft* 29(2): 177–209.

Fallend, Franz (2002) 'Europäisierung, Föderalismus und Regionalismus: Die Auswirkungen der EU-Mitgliedschaft auf bundesstaatliche Strukturen und regionale Politik'. In Heinrich Neisser and Sonja Puntscher Riekmann (eds) *Europäisierung der österreichischen Politik. Konsequenzen der EU Mitgliedschaft*. Vienna: WUV-Universitätsverlag, pp. 201–230.

Fallend, Franz (2004) 'The Rejuvenation of an Old Party'? Christian Democracy in Austria'. In Steven van Hecker and Emmanuel Gerard (eds) *Christian Democratic Parties in Europe since the End of the Cold War*. Leuven: Leuven University Press, pp. 79–104.

Fallend, Franz (2005) 'Die ÖVP'. In Emmerich Talós (ed.) *Schwarz-Blau. Eine Bilanz des 'Neu-Regierens'*. Vienna: LIT, pp. 3–18.

Fallend, Franz (2006a) 'Landesregierung and Landesverwaltung'. In Herbert Dachs, Peter Gerlich, Herbert Gottweis, Helmut Kramer, Volkmar Lauber, Wolfgang C. Müller and Emmerich Talós (eds) *Politik in Österreich. Das Handbuch*. Vienna: Manzsche Verlags- und Universitätsbuchhandlung, pp. 974–989.

Fallend, Franz (2006b) 'Bund-Länder Beziehungen'. In Herbert Dachs, Peter Gerlich, Herbert Gottweis, Helmut Kramer, Volkmar Lauber, Wolfgang C. Müller and Emmerich Talós (eds) *Politik in Österreich. Das Handbuch*. Vienna: Manzsche Verlags- und Universitätsbuchhandlung, pp. 1024–1049.

Fallend, Franz (2011) 'Austria: From Consensus to Competition to Participation?' In John Loughlin, Frank Hendriks and Anders Lindström (eds) *Oxford Handbook on Subnational Democracy in Europe*. Oxford: Oxford University Press, pp, 173–195.

Federal Chancellery of Switzerland (2015) *The Swiss Confederation. A Brief Guide 2015*. Zurich: Swiss Federal Chancellery.

Federal Chancellery of Switzerland (2016a) 'Politische Volksrechte-Chronologie Volksabstimmungen'. Posted at www.admin.ch/ch/d/pore/va/vab_2_2_4_1.html (accessed 27 May 2016).

Federal Chancellery of Switzerland (2016b) 'Die Bundeskanzlei'. Posted at www.bk.admin.ch/org/index.html?lang=de (accessed 11 May 2016).

References   301

Fiers, Stefaan and André Krouwel (2005) 'The Low Countries: From "Prime Minister" to President-Minister'. In Thomas Poguntke and Paul Webb (eds) *The Presidentialization of Politics. A Comparative Study of Modern Democracies.* Oxford: Oxford University Press, pp. 128–158.

Fink, Marceh (2006) 'Unternehmerverbände'. In Herbert Dachs, Peter Gerlich, Herbert Gottweis, Volker Lauber, Wolfgang C. Müller and Emmerich Tálos (eds) *Politik in Österreich. Das Handbuch.* Vienna: Manzsche Buchhandlung, pp. 443–461.

Fischer, Manuel, Pascal Sciarini and Denise Traber (2010) 'The Silent Reform of Swiss Federalism: The New Constitutional Articles on Education'. *Swiss Political Science Review* 16(4): 747–771.

Fitzmaurice, John (1999) 'The Luxembourg Socialist Workers Party'. In Robert Ladrech and Philippe Marliére (eds) *History, Organization, Policies.* Basingstoke: Palgrave, pp. 148–154.

Fleiner, Thomas (2013) 'Constitutional Revision: The Case of Switzerland'. In Xenophon Contiades (ed.) *Engineering Constitutional Change. A Comparative Perspective on Europe, Canada and USA.* London: Routledge, pp. 337–358.

Forum (2012) 'Mehrsprachigkeit in der Schule. Statistik zur Sprachenvielfalt'. Posted at www.forum.lu/wp-content/uploads/2015/11/7532_324_forum_Redaktion.pdf (accessed 20 April 2016).

Forum (2015) 'Die Verfassungsreform. Informationen, Analysen, Meinungen. Eine Initiative der Zeitschrift Forum'. Posted at www.forum.lu/constitution/ (accessed 2 September 2015).

Freedman, Lawrence (2013) *Strategy. A History.* Oxford: Oxford University Press.

Freiheitliche Partei Österreichs (2011) *Österreich zuerst. Parteiprogramm der Freiheitlichen Partei Österreichs (FPÖ) Beschlossen vom Bundesparteitag der Freiheitlichen Partei Österreichs am 18 Juni 2011 in Graz.* Pdf document. Posted at www.fpoe.at/fileadmin/user_upload/www.fpoe.at/dokumente/2015/2011_graz_parteiprogramm_web.pdf (accessed 2 January 2016).

Freitag, Markus (2014) 'Politische Kultur'. In Peter Knoepfel, Yannis Papadopoulos, Pascal Sciarini, Adrian Vatter and Silja Häusermann (eds) *Handbuch der Schweizer Politik.* Zürich: Verlag Neue Zürcher Zeitung, pp. 71–94.

Frey, Deya (18 August 2015) 'Die Parteienfinanzierung in der Schweiz'. *Vimentis*, 18 August. Posted at www.vimentis.ch/d/publikation/463/Die+Parteienfinanzierung+in+der+Schweiz.html (accessed 3 January 2016).

Friedman, Thomas (2007) *The World is Flat. The Globalized World in the Twenty-first Century. Expanded Version.* London: Penguin Books.

Friesl, Christian, Regina Polak and Ursula Hamachers-Zuba (Hg.) (2008) *Die Österreicher innen. Wertewandel 1990–2008.* Vienna: Czernin Verlag.

Frognier, André Paul (1988) 'Belgium'. In Jean Blondel and Ferdinand Müller-Rommel (eds) *Cabinets in Western Europe.* Basingstoke: Macmillan, pp. 68–85.

Fröhlich-Steffen, Susanne (2003) *Die österreichische Identität im Wandel.* Vienna: Braumüller.

Fukuyama, Francis (1992) *The End of History and the Last Man.* New York: Avon Books.

Fukuyama, Francis (2006) *After the Neocons. America at the Crossroads.* New York: Profile.

Garland, Jess and Chris Terry (2015) *The 2015 General Election. A Voting System in Crisis.* London: Electoral Reform Society. Posted at file: ///C: /Users/Jos%C3%A9/Downloads/2015%20General%20Election%20Report%20web.pdf (accessed 26 April 2016).

Gehler, Michael (2009) *Österreichs Weg in die Europäische Union.* Vienna: Studien Verlag.

302   *References*

Gehler, Michael (2012) 'Paving Austria's Way to Brussels: Chancellor Franz Vranitzky (1986–1997): A Banker, Social Democrat, and a Pragmatic European Leader'. *Journal of European Integration History* 18(2): 159–182.

Gerkrath, Jörg (2013a) 'Some Remarks on the Pending Constitutional Change in the Grand Duchy of Luxembourg'. *European Public Law* 19(3): 449–460.

Gerkrath, Jörg (2013b) 'Constitutional Amendment in Luxembourg'. In Xenophon I. Kontiades (ed.) *Engineering Constitutional Change. A Comparative Perspective on Europe, Canada, and the USA.* London: Routledge, pp. 229–256.

Gerlich, Peter (1987) 'Consociationalism to Competition: The Austrian Party System since 1945'. In Hans Daalder (ed.) *Party Systems in Denmark, Austria, Switzerland, The Netherlands and Belgium.* London: Frances Pinter, pp. 61–106.

Gerlich, Peter (1992) 'A Farewell to Corporatism'. In Kurt Richard Luther and Wolfgang C. Müller (eds) *Politics in Austria. Still a Case of Consociationalism?* Special Issue of *West European Politics* 15(1): 132–146.

Gerlich, Peter and Wolfgang C. Müller (1988) 'Austria'. In Jean Blondel and Ferdinand Müller-Rommel (eds) *Cabinets in Western Europe.* Basingstoke: Macmillan, pp. 138–150.

Giddens, Anthony (1984) *The Constitution of Society.* Cambridge: Polity Press.

Giddens, Anthony (1985) *The Nation-state and Violence.* Cambridge: Polity Press.

Giddens, Anthony (1998) *The Third Way: The Renewal of Social Democracy.* Cambridge: Polity Press.

Gindin, Sam and Leo Panitch (2013) *The Making of Global Capitalism. The Political Economy of American Empire.* London: Verso.

Gladdish, Kenneth (1991) *Governing from the Centre. Politics and Policy-making in the Netherlands.* London: Hurst & Co.

Goodijk, Rienk (2010) 'Corporate Governance and Works Council: A Dutch Perspective'. Paper presented at the International Industrial Relations Association (IIRA). Posted at http://faos.ku.dk/pdf/iirakongres2010/track4/76.pdf/ (accessed 23 February 2016).

Goossens, Jurgen and Pieter Cannoot (2015) 'Belgian Federalism after the Sixth State Reform'. *Perspectives on Federalism* 7(2): 29–55. Posted at www.on-federalism.eu/attachments/213_download.pdf (accessed 8 October 2015).

Gottweis, Herbert (1983) 'Zur Entwicklung der ÖVP: Zwischen Interessenpolitik und Massenintegration'. In Peter Gerlich and Wolfgang C. Müller (eds) *Zwischen Koalition und Konkurrenz. Österreichs Parteien seit 1945.* Vienna: Braumüller, pp. 53–68.

Government of Austria (2013) Federal Constitutional Law (B-VG) of Austria. Posted at www.ris.bka.gv.at/Dokumente/Erv/ERV_1930_1/ERV_1930_1.pdf (accessed 2 July 2016).

Government of Belgium (2014) Elections on 24 May 2014. Posted at http://polling2014. belgium.be/en/ (accessed 2 July 2016).

Government of Belgium (2015a) 'Historical Outline of the Federalisation of Belgium'. Posted at www.belgium.be/en/about_belgium/country/history/belgium_from_1830/formation_federal_state/ (accessed 4 September 2015).

Government of Belgium (2015b) 'Budget of the Belgium Government 2015'. Posted at www.begroting.be/FR/figures/Documents/chiffres%202015.pdf (accessed 7 December 2015).

Government of Federation of Wallonia-Brussels (2015) *La Féderation Wallonie-Brussels en chiffres.* Brussels: Ministére de la Federation Wallonie-Bruxelles.

Government of Flanders (2015) 'De Vlaamse begroting in cijfers'. Posted at www.vlaanderen.be/nl/vlaamse-overheid/werking-van-de-vlaamse-overheid/de-vlaamse-begroting-cijfers (accessed 7 December 2015).

References   303

Government of Luxembourg (2013a) 'Population and Demographics'. Posted at www. luxembourg.public.lu/en/luxembourg-glance/population-languages/population-demographics/index.html (accessed 30 August 2015).

Government of Luxembourg (2013b) *La Constitution du Grand-Duché du Luxembourg.* Posted at www.legilux.public.lu/leg/textescoordonnes/recueils/Constitution/constitution_gdl.pdf (accessed 7 September 2015).

Government of Luxembourg (2014) *Rapport d'Activité 2013. Service central de Legislation. Ministére d'État.* Luxembourg: Ministére d'État. Posted at www.gouvernement. lu/3544926/2013-rapport-activite-scl.pdf (accessed 29 September 2015).

Government of Luxembourg (2016a) 'Présidence du Gouvernement, Ministére d'État'. Posted at www.annuaire.public.lu/index.php?idMin=2453 (accessed 11 May 2016).

Government of Luxembourg (2016b) 'Ministére d'État'. Posted at www.gouvernement. lu/3313499/minist-etat (accessed 11 May 2016).

Government of the Netherlands (1992) Gemeentenwet 14 February 1992. Posted at http:// wetten.overheid.nl/BWBR0005416/volledig/geldigheidsdatum_13-12-2015 (accessed 13 December 2015).

Government of the Netherlands (2008) *The Constitution of the Kingdom of the Netherlands.* Posted at www.government.nl/topics/constitution/documents/regulations/ 2012/10/18/the-constitution-of-the-kingdom-of-the-netherlands-2008 (accessed 2 September 2015).

Government of the Netherlands (2015) 'Ministry of General Affairs. Organisational Structure'. Posted at www.government.nl/ministries/ministry-of-general-affairs/contents/ organisational-structure (accessed 17 September 2015).

Government of Switzerland (2015) *Federal Constitution of the Swiss Confederation of 18 April 1999 (Status as of 14 June 2015).* Posted at www.admin.ch/opc/en/classified-compilation/19995395/201506140000/101.pdf (accessed 7 September 2015).

Group of States against Corruption (GRECO) (2011) *Evaluation Report on Switzerland Transparency of Political Party Funding (Theme II). Third Evaluation Round.* Public Greco Eval. III Rep. (2011) 4E Theme II. Posted at www.coe.int/t/dghl/monitoring/ greco/evaluations/round3/GrecoEval3 (2011)4_Switzerland_Two_EN.pdf (accessed 3 January 2016).

Group of States against Corruption (GRECO) (2015) *Zweiter Zwischenbericht über die Konformität der Schweiz 'Strafbestimmungen' (SEV 173 und 191, GPC 2). Transparenz der Parteienfinanzierung. Dritte Evaluationsrunde.* Veröffentlicht. Greco RC-III (2015) 6. Zwischenbericht, 17 August. Posted at www.bj.admin.ch/dam/data/bj/ sicherheit/kriminalitaet/korruption/grecoberichte/ber-iii-2015-6f-d.pdf (accessed 3 January 2016).

Gruner, Erich (1964) '100 Jahre Wirtschaftspolitik. Etappen des Interventionismus in der Schweiz'. *Schweizerische Zeitscrift für Volkswirtschaft und Statistik* 100(1–2): 35–70.

Gruner, Erich (1969) *Die Parteien in der Schweiz.* Berne: Francke Verlag.

Gruner, Erich (1981) 'Die Schweiz'. In Frank Wende (ed.) *Lexikon zur Geschichte der Parteien in Europa.* Stuttgart: Kroner Verlag, pp. 599–625.

Gruppe Schweiz ohne eine Armee (GsOA) (2016) 'Geschichte'. Posted at www.gsoa.ch/ gsoa/geschichte/ (accessed 20 April 2016).

Gustavsson, Gina (2015) 'Contemporary European Liberalism: Exclusionary, Enlightened or Romantic?' In José M. Magone (ed.) *Routledge Handbook of European Politics.* London: Routledge, pp. 75–96.

Hall, Peter A. (2014) 'Varieties of Capitalism and the Euro Crisis'. *West European Politics* 37(6): 1223–1243.

304 *References*

Hall, Peter A. and David Soskice (eds) (2001) 'An Introduction to Varieties of Capitalism'. In Peter A. Hall and David Soskice (eds) *Varieties of Capitalism. The Institutional Advantages of Comparative Advantage*. Oxford: Oxford University Press, pp. 1–68.

Hamann, Kerstin and John Kelly (2011) *Parties, Elections And Policy Reforms in Western Europe. Voting For Social Pacts*. London: Routledge.

Hanisch, Ernst (2005) *Der lange Schatten des Staates. Österreichische Gesellschaftsgeschichte im 20. Jahrhundert*. Österreichische Geschichte 1890–1990, edited by Herwig Wolfram. Vienna: Ueberreuter.

Harmsen, Robert (2005) 'The Dutch Referendum on the Ratification of the European Constitutional Treaty, 1 June'. European Parties, Elections and Referendums Network (EPERN), EPERN Briefing Paper no. 13. Posted at www.sussex.ac.uk/webteam/gateway/file.php?name=epern-ref-no-13.pdf&site=266 (accessed 21 July 2015).

Haslinger, Josef (1987, 2001) *Politik der Gefühle. Ein Essay über Österreich*. Frankfurt am Main: Fischer Verlag.

Hecking, Claus (2003) *Das politische System Belgiens*. Opladen: Leske+Budrich.

Hecking, Claus (2006) 'Das Parteiensystem Belgiens'. In Oskar Niedermayer, Richard Stöss and Melanie Haas (eds) *Die Parteiensysteme Westeuropas*. Wiesbaden: Verlag Sozialwissenschaften, pp. 41–65.

Helliwell, John, Richard Layard and Jeffrey Sachs (2016) *World Happiness Report I. Update*. New York: Sustainable Development Solutions Network.

Hemerijck, Anton C. (1995) 'Corporatist Immobility in the Netherlands'. In Colin Crouch and Franz Traxler (eds) *Organized Industrial Relations in Europe: What Future?* Aldershot: Avebury, pp. 189–216.

Hemerijck, Anton C. (2013) *Changing Welfare States*. Oxford: Oxford University Press.

Hempel, Yvonne (2010) 'Politische Führung im Direktorialsystem: Die Schweiz'. In Martin Sebaldt and Henrik Gast (eds) *Politische Führung in westlichen Regierungssystemen: Theorie und Praxis im internationalen Vergleich*. Wiesbaden: Verlag Sozialwissenschaften, pp. 281–303.

Hendriks, Corina (2011) *The Story behind the Dutch Model. Consensual Politics of Wage Restraint*. Amsterdam: University of Amsterdam-academisch proefschrift.

Hendriks, Frank (2001) 'Polder Politics in the Netherlands: The "Viscous State" Revisited'. In Frank Hendriks and Theo A.J. Toonen (eds) *Polder Politics. The Re-invention of Consensus Democracy in the Netherlands*. Aldershot: Ashgate, pp. 21–40.

Hendriks, Frank (2010) *Vital Democracy. Democracy in Action*. Oxford: Oxford University Press.

Hendriks, Frank (2012) *Democratie onder druk. Over de uitdaging van de stemmingendemocratie*. Amsterdam: Van Gennep.

Hendriks, Frank and Linze Schaap (2011) 'The Netherlands. Subnational Democracy and the Reinvention of Democracy'. In John Loughlin, Frank Hendriks and Anders Lindström (eds) *Oxford Handbook on Subnational Democracy in Europe*. Oxford: Oxford University Press, pp. 96–122.

Hendriks, Frank and Th.A.J. Toonen (2001) 'Introduction: Towards an Institutional Analysis of the Dutch Consensualism'. In Frank Hendriks and Theo A.J. Toonen (eds) *Polder Politics. The Re-invention of Consensus Democracy in the Netherlands*. Aldershot: Ashgate, pp. 3–19.

Hendriks, Frank and Pieter Tops (2003) 'Local Public Management Reform in the Netherlands: Fads, Fashions and Windows of Change'. *Public Administration* 81(2): 301–323.

References 305

Héritier, Adrienne (2002) 'New Modes of Governance in Europe: Policy-making without Legislating?' In Adrienne Héritier (ed.) *Common Goods. Reinventing European and International Governance.* Lanham, MD: Rowman and Littlefield, pp. 185–206.

Hermann, Michael and Heiri Leuthold (2004) 'Ein Graben der Werte trennt Stadt und Land'. *Tagesanzeiger*, 2 December, p. 12. Posted at http://sotomo.ch/media/publis/mh_hl_2004_graben.pdf (accessed 2 January 2016).

Hermann, Michael and Heiri Leuthold (2005) 'Der doppelte Gegensatz von Stadt und Land. Wirtschaftliche und gesellschaftliche Dimension einer politischen Konfliktlinie'. *Neue Zürcher Zeitung*, Staatspolitisches Forum, 14 September. Posted at http://sotomo.ch/media/publis/mh_hl_2005_doppeltegegensatz.pdf (accessed 2 January 2016).

Hirsch, Mario (2010a) 'Luxembourg. La coordination tripartite à l'épreuve'. *Grande Europe* 21, June – La Documentation française. Posted at www.ladocumentationfrancaise.fr/pages-europe/d000515-luxembourg.-la-coordination-tripartite-a-l-epreuve-par-mario-hirsch/article (accessed 10 July 2015).

Hirsch, Mario (2010b) 'The Luxembourg Model Has Reached its Limits. Sozialpartnership and Tripartite Arrangements Work Only Under Fair Weather Conditions'. Paper presented at the Politocologenetmaal 2010 (Workshop 1B: European integration and consensus making in the Low Countries. KULeuven 28 May). Posted at https://soc.kuleuven.be/web/files/11/72/W1B-122.pdf (accessed 24 February 2016).

Hirsch, Mario (2012) 'Sind Konkordanz-, Konsens und Drei-Partnermodelle Schönwetter-Veranstaltungen? Der Fall Luxemburg'. In Stefan,Köppl and Uwe Krannenpohl (eds) *Konkordanzdemokratie. Ein Demokratietyp der Vergangenheit.* Baden-Baden: Nomos Verlagsgesellschaft, pp. 177–132.

Hix, Simon and Bjorn Hoyland (2011) *The Political System of the European Union* (3rd edn). Basingstoke: Palgrave.

Höbelt, Lothar (1998) *1848. Österreich und die deutsche Revolution.* Vienna, Munich.

Hobsbawn, Eric J. (1990, 2000) *Nations and Nationalism since 1780. Programme, Myth, Reality.* London: Canto.

Hoetjes, Ben J.S. (2001) 'The Parliament of the Netherlands and the European Union: Early Starter, Slow Mover'. In Andreas Maurer and Wolfgang Wessels (eds) *National Parliaments on their Ways to Europe: Losers and Latecomers?* Baden-Baden: Nomos Verlagsgesellschaft, pp. 337–358.

Hofer, Thomas (2005) *Spin Doktoren in Österreich. Die Praxis amerikanischer Wahlkampfberater. Was Sie können, was sie beraten, wie sie arbeiten.* Vienna: LIT.

Högenauer, Anna-Lena (2015) 'The Dutch Parliament and EU Affairs: Decentralizing Scrutiny'. In Claudia Hefftler, Christine Neuhold, Olivier Rozenberg and Julie Smith (eds) *Palgrave Handbook on National Parliament and the European Union.* Basingstoke: Palgrave, pp. 252–272.

Holzhacker, Ronald (2005) 'The Power of Opposition Parliamentary Party Groups in European Scrutiny'. *The Journal of Legislative Studies* 11(3): 428–445.

Hooghe, Marc (1999) 'Selectieve uitsluiting in het Belgisch politiek systeem. Innovatie en protest door nieuwe sociale bewegingen'. *Res Publica* 41(1): 41–69.

Hooghe, Marc (2012) 'Belgien: Die langsamer Erosion neokorporatistischer Interessenvermittlung'. In W. Reutter (Hrsg.) *Verbände und Interessengruppen in den Ländern der Europäischen Union.* Wiesbaden: Springer Verlag, pp. 55–74.

Höpner, Martin and Lothar Krempel (2012) 'Deutschland AG in Auflösung. Die Entflechtung der deutschen Unternehmensbeteiligungen hält an/Ende eines langen Kapitels deutscher Energiepolitik'. MPIfG Themen. Posted at www.mpifg.de/aktuelles/themen/d-ag.asp (accessed 16 May 2016).

306 *References*

Horber-Papazian, Katia and Caroline Jacot-Descombes (2014) 'Communes'. In Peter Knoepfel, Yannis Papadopoulos, Pascal Sciarini, Adrian Vatter and Silja Häusermann (eds) *Handbuch der Schweizer Politik*. Zürich: Verlag Neue Zürcher Zeitung, pp. 275–305.

Houwing, Hester and Kurt Vandaele (2011) 'Liberal Convergence, Growing Outcome Divergence? Institutional Continuity and Changing Trajectories in the Low Countries'. In Uwe Becker, *The Changing Political Economies of Small West European Countries*. Chicago, IL: Chicago University Press, pp. 125–148.

Inglehart, Ronald and Christian Welzel (2005) *Modernization, Cultural Change and Democracy. The Human Development Sequence*. Cambridge: Cambridge University Press.

International Monetary Fund (IMF) (2014) Luxembourg. 2014 Article IV Consultation – Staff Report; Press Release; Statement by the Executive Director for Luxembourg, May. Posted at www.imf.org/external/pubs/ft/scr/2014/cr14118.pdf (accessed 24 February 2016).

Interparliamentary Union (2016) 'Women in National Parliaments'. Posted at www.ipu. org/wmn-e/arc/classif011215.htm (accessed 21 January 2016).

Israel, Jonathan (1998) *The Dutch Republic. Its Rise, Greatness, and Fall 1477–1806*. Oxford: Oxford University Press.

Jalali, Carlos and Patricia Silva (2015) 'Party Patronage: An Old Solution for New Problems?' In José M. Magone (ed.) *Handbook of European Politics*. London: Routledge, pp. 560–575.

Janssen, Siebo H. (2006) 'Das Parteiensystem Luxemburgs'. In Oskar Niedermayer, Richard Stöss and Melanie Haas (eds) *Die Parteiensysteme Westeuropas*. Wiesbaden: Verlag Sozialwissenschaften, pp. 321–329.

Jegher, Annina and Wolf Linder (1998) *Schweizerische Bundesversammlung. Ein actives Gesetzgebungsorgan. Eine empirische Untersuchung des Gesetzgebungsprozesses 1995–97*. Berne: Dokumentationszentrale der Bundesversammlung. Posted at www. parlament.ch/d/dokumentation/berichte/weitere-berichte-und-studien/documents/ed-pa-gesetzgebungsprozess.pdf (accessed 17 October 2015).

Jenny, Marcelo (2014) 'Austria'. In Andreas Bågenholm, Kevin Deegan-Krause and Rainbow Murray (eds) *European Political Data Yearbook. A special issue of European Journal of Political Research* 53(1): 16–26.

Jessop, Bob (2002) *The Future of the Capitalist State*. Cambridge: Polity Press.

Jones, Erik (2008) *Economic Adjustment and Political Transformation in Small States*. Oxford: Oxford University Press.

Jost, Hans-Ulrich (2004) 'Bedrohung und Enge (1914–1945)'. In Ulrich Im Hof, Pierre Ducrey, Guy P. Marchal, Nicolas Morard, Martin Körner, François de Capitani, Georges Andrey, Roland Ruffieux, Hans Ulrich Jost, Peter Gilg and Peter Hablützel, *Geschichte der Schweiz und der Schweizer*. Basel: Schwabe Verlag, pp. 731–819.

Kalina, Ondrej (2012) 'Europa in Prokrustes' Bett? Die Europäische Union als Konkordanzsystem im Demokratiedilemma'. In Stefan Köppl and Uwe Krannenpohl (eds) *Konkordanzdemokratie. Ein Demokratietyp der Vergangenheit*. Baden-Baden: Nomos Verlagsgesellschaft, pp. 189–217.

Karlhofer, Ferdinand (2006) 'Arbeitnehmerorganisationen'. In Herbert Dachs, Peter Gerlich, Herbert Gottweis, Volker Lauber, Wolfgang C. Müller and Emmerich Tálos (eds) *Politik in Österreich. Das Handbuch*. Vienna: Manzsche Buchhandlung, pp. 462–479.

Karlhofer, Ferdinand (2012) 'Österreich zwischen Korporatismus und Zivilgesellschaft'. In W. Reutter (Hrsg.) *Verbände und Interessengruppen in den Ländern der Europäischen Union*. Wiesbaden: Springer Verlag, pp. 521–550.

References 307

Karlhofer, Ferdinand and Emmerich Tálos (eds) (1999) *Die Zukunft der Sozialpartnerschaft. Veränderungsdynamik und Reformbedarf.* Vienna: Signum Verlag-Zentrum für angewandte Politikforschung.

Karlhofer, Ferdinand and Emmerich Tálos (2002) 'Österreich und EU: Gegenläufige Entwicklungen in der Interessenvermittlung und Interessenpolitik'. In Heinrich Neisser and Sonja Puntscher Riekmann (eds) *Europäisierung der österreichischen Politik. Konsequenzen der EU Mitgliedschaft.* Vienna: WUV-Universitätsverlag, pp. 231–246.

Karlhofer, Ferdinand and Emmerich Talós (2005) 'Sozialpartnerschaft am Abstieg'. In Emmerich Tálos (ed.) *Schwarz-Blau. Eine Bilanz des 'Neu-Regierens'.* Vienna: LIT, pp. 102–117.

Katz, Richard S. and Peter Mair (1995) 'Changing Models of Party Organization and Party Democracy'. *Party Politics* 1(1): 5–28.

Katzenstein, Peter (1984) *Corporatism and Change: Austria, Switzerland and the Politics of Industry.* Ithaca, NY: Cornell University Press.

Katzenstein, Peter (1985) *Small States in World Markets. Industrial Policy in Europe.* Ithaca, NY: Cornell University Press.

Katzenstein, Peter (2003) '*Small States* and Small States Revisited'. *New Political Economy* 8(1): 9–30.

Kayser, Martin and Dagmar Richter (1999) 'Die neue schweizerische Bundesverfassung'. *Zeitschrift für ausländisches öffentliches Recht und Völkerrecht* 59(4): 985–1106. Posted at www.zaoerv.de/59_1999/59_1999_4_a_985_1106.pdf (accessed 7 September 2015).

Keane, J. (2010) 'Civil Society, Definitions and Approaches'. In Helmut K. Anheier and Stefan Toepler (eds) *International Encyclopedia of Civil Society.* New York: Springer, pp. 461–464.

Kennedy, Paul, Dirk Messner and Franz Nuscheler (eds) (2002) *Global Trends and Global Governance.* London: Pluto Press.

Kerr, Henry H. (1987) 'The Swiss Party System: Steadfast and Changing'. In Hans Daalder (ed.) *Party Systems in Denmark, Austria, Switzerland, The Netherlands and Belgium.* London: Frances Pinter, pp. 107–192.

Kerschen, Nicole (2009) 'The Welfare System of Luxembourg: From Path Dependency to the European Approach'. In Klaus Schubert, Simon Hegelich and Ursula Bazant (eds) *Handbook of European Welfare Systems.* London: Routledge, pp. 310–327.

Khol, Andreas, Reinhold Lopatka and Wilhelm Molterer (eds) (2005) *Zukunftsfest. 60 Jahre Österreichische Volkspartei.* Vienna: Molden Verlag.

Kickert, Walter J.M. (2000) *Public Management Reforms in the Netherlands. Social Reconstruction of Reform Ideas and Underlying Frames of Reference.* Delft: Uitgeverij Eburon.

Kickert, Walter J.M. (2004) *History of Governance in the Netherlands.* The Hague: Elsevier.

King, Tim (2015) 'Belgium is a Failed State: Brussels' Nest of Radicalism is Just of the Failings of a Divided, Dysfunctional Country'. Posted at www.politico.eu/article/belgium-failed-state-security-services-molenbeek-terrorism/ (accessed 16 April 2016).

Kirchheimer, Otto (1965) 'Der Wandel des westeuropäischen Parteiensystems'. *Politische Vierteljahresschrift* 6(1): 20–41.

Kittel, Bernhard and Emmerich Talós (1999) 'Interessenvermittlung und politischer Entscheidungsprozeß: Sozialpartnerschaft in den 1990er Jahren'. In Ferdinand Karlhofer and Emmerich Talós (eds) *Zukunft der Sozialpartnerschaft. Veränderungsdynamik und Reformbedarf.* Vienna: Zentrum für angewandte Forschung, pp. 95–136.

Kleinfeld, Ralf (2001a) 'Der niederländische Sozialstaat auf dem Weg zum postindustriellen Wohlfahrtsstaat'. In Katrin Kraus and Thomas Geisen (Hrsg.) *Sozialstaat. Geschichte. Entwicklung. Perspektiven.* Wiesbaden: Westdeutscher Verlag, pp. 117–141.

308 References

Kleinfeld, Ralf (2012) 'Niederlande: Verbände und Verbändesystem'. In W. Reutter (Hrsg.) *Verbände und Interessengruppen in den Ländern der Europäischen Union.* Wiesbaden: Springer Verlag, pp. 477–520.

Klenk, Tanja (2012) 'Luxemburg: Etatisierung des Selbstverwaltungsmechanismus'. In Tanja Klenk, Philine Weyrauch, Alexander Haarmann and Frank Nullmeyer (eds) *Abkhehr vom Korporatismus? Der Wandel der Sozialversicherungen im europäischen Vergleich.* Frankfurt am Main: Campus, pp. 241–286.

Klöti, Ulrich (2002) 'Regierung'. In Ulrich Klöti, Peter Knoepfel, Hanspeter Kriesi, Wolf Linder and Yannis Papadopoulos (eds) *Handbuch der Schweizer Politik. Manuel de la politique suisse.* Zürich: Neue Zürcher Zeitung, pp. 159–185.

Klöti, Ulrich, Yannis Papadopoulos and Fritz Sager (2014) 'Regierung'. In Peter Knoepfel, Yannis Papadopoulos, Pascal Sciarini, Adrian Vatter and Silja Häusermann (eds) *Handbuch der Schweizer Politik.* Zürich: Verlag Neue Zürcher Zeitung, pp. 193–218.

Konferenz der Kantonsregierungen (2006) *Vereinbarung über die Konferenz der Kantonsregierungen vom 8. Oktober 1993.* Document kindly supplied by Dr Sandra Maissen, Director-general of KdK.

Konferenz der Kantonsregierungen (2015) *Jahresbericht 2014.* KdK. Berne: KdK.

König, Thomas, Tanja Dannwolf and Brooke Luetgert, 'EU Legislative Activities and Domestic Politics'. In Sylvain Brouard, Olivier Costa and Thomas König (eds) *The Europeanization of Domestic Legislatures. The Empirical Implications of the Delors' Myth in Nine Countries.* New York: Springer, pp. 21–37.

Koole, Ruud (2000) 'Fukuyama's Paradise? Liberal Parties in the Netherlands'. In Lieven de Winter (ed.) *Liberalism and Liberal Parties in the European Union.* Barcelona: Institut de Ciencies Politiques i Socials, pp. 141–182.

Kopécky, Petr and Peter Mair (2012) 'Conclusion: Party Patronage in Contemporary Europe'. In Petr Kopécky, Peter Mair and Maria Spirova (eds) *Party Patronage and Party Government in European Democracies.* Oxford: Oxford University Press, pp. 357–374.

Kopeinig, Margaretha and Christoph Kotanko (2000) *Eine europäische Affäre. Der Weisen-Bericht und die Sanktionen gegen Österreich.* Vienna: Czernin Verlag.

Köppl, Stefan (2012) 'Die besondere Form der Konsensdemokratie in Italien. Entwicklung von consociativismo zum Konkurrenzmodell?' In Stefan Köppl and Uwe Krannenpohl (eds) *Konkordanzdemokratie. Ein Demokratietyp der Vergangenheit.* Baden-Baden: Nomos Verlagsgesellschaft, pp. 147–168.

Körner, Martin (2004) 'Glaubensspaltung und Wirtschaftssolidarität (1515–1648)'. In Ulrich Im Hof, Pierre Ducrey, Guy P. Marchal, Nicolas Morard, Martin Körner, François de Capitani, Georges Andrey, Roland Ruffieux, Hans Ulrich Jost, Peter Gilg and Peter Hablützel, *Geschichte der Schweiz und der Schweizer.* Basel: Schwabe Verlag, pp. 357–446.

Krammer, Josef and Gerhard Hovorka (2006) 'Interessenorganisation der Landwirtschaft: Landwirtschaftskammern, Präsidentenkonferenz und Raiffeisenverband'. In Herbert Dachs, Peter Gerlich, Herbert Gottweis, Volker Lauber, Wolfgang C. Müller and Emmerich Tálos (eds) *Politik in Österreich. Das Handbuch.* Vienna: Manzsche Buchhalung, pp. 480–492.

Krannenpohl, Uwe (2012) 'Konkordanzdemokratie, Konsensdemokratie, Verhandlungsdemokratie. Versuch einer terminologischen und typologischen Strukturierung'. In Stefan Köppl and Uwe Krannenpohl (eds) *Konkordanzdemokratie. Ein Demokratietyp der Vergangenheit.* Baden-Baden: Nomos Verlagsgesellschaft, pp. 13–32.

Kreis, Georg (ed.) (2015) *Städtische versus ländliche Schweiz? Siedlungsstrukturen und ihre politischen Determinanten.* Zürich: Verlag Neue Zürcher Zeitung.

Kreis, Georg (ed.) (2016) *Reformbedürftige Volksinitiative. Verbesserungsvorschläge und Gegenargumente.* Zürich: Neue Zürcher Zeitung.

Krenn, M., C. Hermann and G. Adam (2015) 'Austria: Country Working Life Profile'. Posted at www.eurofound.europa.eu/observatories/eurwork/comparative-information/national-contributions/austria/austria-working-life-country-profile (accessed 23 February 2016).

Kriechbaumer, Robert (2004) *Die Ära Kreisky. Österreich 1970–1983.* Vienna: Böhlau.

Kriesi, Hans-Peter (1980) *Entscheidungsstrukturen und Entscheidungsprozesse in der Schweizer Politik.* Frankfurt am Main: Campus Verlag.

Kriesi, Hans-Peter (1982) 'The Structure of the Swiss Political System'. In Gerhard Lehmbruch and Philippe Schmitter (eds) *Patterns of Corporatist Policy Making.* London: Sage, pp. 133–162.

Kriesi, Hans-Peter (1998) *Le Systéme Politique Suisse.* Paris: Economica.

Kriesi, Hans-Peter and Alexander H. Trechsel (2008) *The Politics of Switzerland. Continuity and Change in a Consensus Democracy.* Cambridge: Cambridge University Press.

Krüger, Paul, Alain M. Schoenberger, Michael Derrer and Claudio Bologna (2001) *Entschädigung und Infrastruktur der Parlamentsarbeit. Analytisches Profil über den Wert der parlamentarischen Arbeit. Beurteilung der heutigen Entschädigung in Bezug auf ihre Kongruenz zur Leistung. Lösungsvorschläge für die Verbesserung der Arbeitsbedingungen. Gutachten.* Geneva: Eco Diagnostic-Analyses et Etudes Economiques. Posted at www.parlament.ch/d/dokumentation/berichte/weitere-berichte-und-studien/Documents/ed-pa-entschaedigung-infrastruktur.pdf (accessed 18 October 2015).

Kruis, Tobias (2011) 'Primacy of European Law – From Theory to Practice'. *Ritsumeikan Law Review* 28: 269–279.

Kunz, Peter V. (2015) 'Swiss Corporate Law – Past, Present and Future: Reflections on European Influences'. *Zeitschrift für vergleichende Rechtswissenschaften* 114(2): 241–266.

Laakso, Markku and Rein Taagepera (1979) '"Effective" Number of Parties: A Measure with Application to Western Europe'. *Comparative Political Studies* 12(1): 3–27.

Lachmayer, Konrad (2013) *Demokratierechtliche Analyse des Österreichischen Corporate Governance Kodex.* Vienna: Arbeiterkammer. Posted at https://media.arbeiterkammer.at/PDF/Analyse_des_Corporate_Governance_Kodex.pdf (accessed 23 February 2016).

Ladner, Andreas (2001) 'Swiss Political Parties: Between Persistence and Change' *West European Politics* 24(1): 123–144.

Ladner, Andreas (2004) *Stabilität und Wandel von Parteien und Parteiensystemen.* Wiesbaden: Verlag Sozialwissenschaften.

Ladner, Andreas (2006) 'Das Parteiensystem der Schweiz'. In Oskar Niedermayer, Richard Stöss and Melanie Haas (eds) *Die Parteiensysteme Westeuropas.* Wiesbaden: Verlag Sozialwissenschaften, pp. 397–419.

Ladner, Andreas (2011) 'Switzerland: Subsidiarity, Power-sharing and Direct Democracy'. In John Loughlin, Frank Hendriks and Anders Lindström (eds) *Oxford Handbook on Subnational Democracy in Europe.* Oxford: Oxford University Press, pp. 196–217.

Ladner, Andreas (2014) 'Politische Parteien'. In Peter Knoepfel, Yannis Papadopoulos, Pascal Sciarini, Adrian Vatter and Silja Häusermann (eds) *Handbuch der Schweizer Politik.* Zürich: Verlag Neue Zürcher Zeitung, pp. 361–389.

Ladner, Andreas und Michael Brändle (2001) *Die Schweizer Parteien im Wandel. Von Mitgliederparteien zu professionalisierten Wählerorganisationen?* Zürich: Seismo Verlag.

Ladner, Andreas and Marc Bühlmann (2007) *Demokratie in den Gemeinden. Der Einfluss der Gemeindegrösse und anderer Faktoren auf die Qualität der lokalen Demokratie.* Zürich: Rüegger Verlag.

310 References

Ladner, Andreas and Julien Fiechter (2012) 'The Influence of Direct Democracy on Political Interest, Electoral Turnout and Other Forms of Citizens' Participation in Swiss Municipalities'. *Local Government Studies* 38(4): 437–459.

Ladrech, Robert (1994) 'Europeanization of Domestic Politics and Institutions: The Case of France'. *Journal of Common Market Studies* 32(1): 69–88.

Ladrech, Robert (2010) *The Europeanization of National Politics*. Basingstoke: Palgrave.

Laffan, Brigid (2014) 'Framing the Crisis, Defining the Problems: Decoding the Euro Area Crisis'. In Christian Schweiger and José M. Magone (eds) *The Effects of the Eurozone Sovereign Debt Crisis: Differentiated Integration between the Centre and the New Peripheries of the EU*. Special issue of *Perspectives on European Politics and Society* 45(3): 266–281.

Laffan, Brigid (2016) 'Core–Periphery Dynamics in the Euroarea: From Conflict to Cleavage?' In José M. Magone, Brigid Laffan and Christian Schweiger (eds) *Core–Periphery Relations in the European Union. Power and Conflict in a Dualist Political Economy*. London: Routledge, pp. 35–55.

Lane, David (2009) 'Russia's Transition to Capitalism: The Rise to World Power?' In Andrew Gamble and David Lane (eds) *The European Union and World Politics. Consensus and Division*. Basingstoke: Palgrave pp. 58–78.

Lane, Jan Erik (2009) *State Management. An Enquiry into Models of Public Administration and Management*. London: Routledge.

Lauber, Volkmar (1992) 'Changing Priorities in Austrian Economic Policy'. In Kurt Richard Luther and Wolfgang C. Müller (eds) *Politics in Austria. Still a Case of Consociationalism?* Special Issue of *West European Politics* 15(1): 147–172.

Laws, David (2016) *Coalition: The Inside Story of the Conservative–Liberal Democrat Coalition Government*. London: Biteback Publishers.

Lefévre, Catherine (2014) 'Understanding Belgian Politics and its Growing Separatist Movement'. Website of Global Public Policy Watch, 9 February. Posted at https://globalpublicpolicywatch.org/2014/02/09/understanding-belgian-politics-and-its-growing-separatist-movement/ (accessed 20 April 2016).

Lehmbruch, Gerhard (1967) *Proporzdemokratie. Politisches System und politische Kultur in der Schweiz und Österreich*. Recht und Staat in Geschichte und Gegenwart. Eine Sammlung von Vorträgen und Schriften aus dem Gebiet der Gesamten Staatswissenschaften. Tübingen: J.C.B. Mohr (Paul Siebeck).

Lehmbruch, Gerhard (1982) 'Introduction: Neo-corporatism in Comparative Perspective'. In Gerhard Lehmbruch and Philippe Schmitter (eds) *Patterns of Corporatist Policy Making*. London: Sage, pp. 1–28.

Lehmbruch, Gerhard (1991) 'Das konkordanzdemokratische Modell in der vergleichenden Analyse politischer Systemen'. In Helga Michalsky (ed.) *Politischer Wandel in konkordanzdemokratischen Systemen*. Vaduz: Verlag der Liechtensteinischen Akademischen Gesellschaft: 13–24. Original contribution before print posted at http://geser.net/gesleh/hs11par/lehmbruch.pdf (accessed 26 April 2016).

Lehmbruch, Gerhard (1996) 'Die korporative Verhandlungsdemokratie in Westmitteleuropa'. *Swiss Political Science Review* 2(4): 1–41.

Lehmbruch, Gerhard (2002) 'Quasi-consociationalism in German Politics. Negotiated Democracy and the Legacy of the Westphalian Peace'. In Jürg Steiner and Thomas Ertman (eds) *Still the Politics of Accommodation? Consociationalism and Corporatism in the Western World*. Special issue of *Acta Politica* 37(3–4): 175–194.

Lehmbruch, Gerhard (2012) 'Die Entwicklung der vergleichenden Politikforschung und die Entdeckung der Konkordanzdemokratie-eine historisch-institutionelle Perspektive'. In

Stefan Köppl and Uwe Krannenpohl (eds) *Konkordanzdemokratie. Ein Demokratietyp der Vergangenheit.* Baden-Baden: Nomos Verlagsgesellschaft, pp. 33–49.

Lehmbruch, Gerhard and Philippe Schmitter (eds) (1982) *Patterns of Corporatist Policy Making.* London: Sage.

Leibfried, Stefan and Michael Zürn (eds) (2005) *Transformations of the State.* Cambridge: Cambridge University Press.

Lepszy, Norbert und Markus Wilp (2009) 'Das politische System der Niederlande'. In Wolfgang Ismayr (ed.) *Die politischen Systeme Westeuropas. 4.aktualisierte und überarbeite Ausgabe.* Wiesbaden: Verlag für Sozialwissenschaften, pp. 405–450.

Leschke, Janine, Andrew Watt and Mairead Finn (2012) *Job Quality in the Crisis – An Update on the Job Quality Index.* European Trade Union Institute Working Paper 2012.07. Posted at www.etui.org/Publications2/Working-Papers/Job-quality-in-the-crisis-an-update-of-the-Job-Quality-Index-JQI (accessed 20 April 2016).

Léton, André and André Miroir (1999) *Les conflits communautaires en Belgique.* Paris: Presses Universitaires de France.

Lëtzebuerger Sozialistesch Aarbechterpartei (LSAP) (2015) 'Le LSAP aujourd'hui'. Posted at www.lsap.lu/lsap_Lsap-aujourdhui.124-2.html (accessed 14 January 2016).

Liegl, Barbara (2005) 'SPÖ'. In Emmerich Tálos (ed.) *Schwarz-blau. Eine Bilanz des 'Neu-Regierens'.* Vienna: LIT, pp. 38–52.

Lijphart, Arend (1971) 'Comparative Politics and the Comparative Method'. *The American Political Science Review* 65(3): 682–693.

Lijphart, Arend (1975) *The Politics of Accommodation. Pluralism and Democracy in the Netherlands.* Berkeley: University of California Press.

Lijphart, Arend (1977) *Democracy in Plural Societies. A Comparative Exploration.* New Haven, CT: Yale University Press.

Lijphart, Arend (1984) *Democracies: Patterns of Majoritarian and Consensus Government in Twenty One Countries.* New Haven, CT: Yale University Press.

Lijphart, Arend (1989) 'From the Politics of Accommodation to Adversarial Politics: A Reappraisal'. In Hans Daalder and Galen Irwin (eds) *The Politics in the Netherlands. How Much Change?* London: Frank Cass, pp. 139–152.

Lijphart, Arend (1999) *Patterns of Democracies. Government Forms and Performance in Thirty-six Countries.* New Haven, CT: Yale University Press.

Lijphart, Arend (2000) 'Varieties of Non-majoritarian Democracy'. In Markus L. Crepaz, Thomas A. Koelble and David Wilsford (eds) *Democracy and Institutions: The Life Work of Arend Lijphart.* Ann Arbor: University of Michigan Press, pp. 225–246.

Lijphart, Arend (2002a) 'The Evolution of Consociational Theory and Consociational Practices 1965–2000'. In Jurg Steiner and Thomas Ertman (eds) *Consociationalism and Corporatism in Western Europe. Still the Politics of Accommodation?* Special issue of *Acta Politica* 37(2–3): 11–22.

Lijphart, Arend (2002b) 'Negotiation Democracy Versus Consensus Democracy: Parallel Conclusions and Recommendations'. *European Journal of Political Research* 41(2): 107–113.

Lijphart, Arend (2008) *Thinking about Democracy. Power-sharing and Majority Rule in Theory and Practice.* London: Routledge.

Lijphart, Arend (2012) *Patterns of Democracy: Government Forms and Performance in Thirty-six Countries.* New Haven, CT: Yale University Press.

Linder, Wolf (2003) 'Politische Kultur'. In Ulrich Klöti, Peter A. Knoepfel, Hanspeter Kriesi, Wolf Linder and Yannis Papadopoulos (eds) *Handbuch der Schweizer Politik.* Zürich: Verlag Neue Zürcher Zeitung, pp. 15–34.

312 References

Linder, Wolf (2005) *Schweizerische Demokratie. Institutionen, Prozesse, Perspektiven*. 2. Auflage. Berne: Haupt.

Linder, Wolf (2011) 'Europe and Switzerland: Europeanization without EU Membership'. In Christine Trampusch and André Mach (eds) *Switzerland in Europe. Continuity and Exchange in the Swiss Political Economy*. London: Routledge, pp. 43–59.

Linder, Wolf and Rolf Wirz (2014) 'Direkte Demokratie'. In Peter Knoepfel, Yannis Papadopoulos, Pascal Sciarini, Adrian Vatter and Silja Häusermann (eds) *Handbuch der Schweizer Politik*. Zürich: Verlag Neue Zürcher Zeitung, pp. 145–167.

Linz, Juan J. and Alfred Stepan (1978) *The Breakdown of Democratic Regimes. Crisis, Breakdown and Reequilibration*. Baltimore, MD: Johns Hopkins University Press.

Lipset, Seymour Martin and Stein Rokkan (1967) 'Cleavage Structures, Party Systems and Voter Alignments: An Introduction'. In Seymour Martin Lipset and Stein Rokkan (eds) *Party Systems and Voter Alignments. Cross National Perspectives*. New York: The Free Press, pp. 1–64.

Lorig, Wolfgang H. (2009) 'Politische Kultur'. In Mario Hirsch and Wolfgang H. Lorig (eds) *Das politische System Luxemburgs*. Wiesbaden: Verlag Sozialwissenschaften, pp. 30–44.

Loth, Wilfried (2013) 'Negotiating the Maastricht Treaty'. *Journal of European Integration History* 19(1): 67–84.

Lucardie, Paul J. (2004) 'Paradise Lost, Paradise Regained? Christian Democracy in the Netherlands'. In Steven van Hecke and Emmanuel Gerard (eds) *Christian Democratic Parties in Europe since the End of the Cold War'*. Leuven: Leuven University Press, pp. 159–78.

Lucardie, Paul (2006) 'Das Parteiensystem der Niederlande'. In Oskar Niedermayer, Richard Stöss and Melanie Haas (eds) *Die Parteiensysteme Westeuropas*. Wiesbaden: Verlag Sozialwissenschaften, pp. 331–350.

Ludlow, N. Piers (2013) 'European Integration in the 1980s: On the Way to Maastricht?' *Journal of European Integration History* 19(1): 11–22.

Luther, Kurt Richard (1992) 'Consociationalism, Parties and Party System'. In Kurt Richard Luther and Wolfgang C. Müller (eds) *Politics in Austria. Still a Case of Consociationalism?* Special Issue of *West European Politics* 15(1): 45–98.

Luther, Kurt Richard (1999) 'Austria: From Moderate to Polarized Pluralism?' In David Broughton and Mark Donovan (eds) *Changing Party Systems in Western Europe*. London: Pinter, pp. 118–142.

Luther, Kurt-Richard (2005) 'Strategien und "Fehl"-Verhalten: Die Freiheitlichen und die Regierungen Schüssel I und II'. In Emmerich Talós (ed.) *Schwarz-Blau. Eine Bilanz des 'Neu-Regierens'*. Vienna: LIT, pp. 19–37.

Lüthi, Ruth (2002) 'Das Parlament'. In Ulrich Kloeti, Peter Knoepfel, Hanspeter Kriesi, Wolf Linder and Yannis Papadopoulos (eds) *Handbuch der Schweizer Politik*. Zurich: Verlag NZZ, pp. 131–158.

Lüthi, Ruth (2014) 'Parlament'. In Peter Knoepfel, Yannis Papadopoulos, Pascal Sciarini, Adrian Vatter and Silja Häusermann (eds) *Handbuch der Schweizer Politik*. Zürich: Verlag Neue Zürcher Zeitung, pp. 169–192.

Lutz, Georg, Peter Selb (2014) 'Wahlen'. In Peter Knoepfel, Yannis Papadopoulos, Pascal Sciarini, Adrian Vatter and Silja Häusermann (eds) *Handbuch der Schweizer Politik*. Zürich: Verlag Neue Zürcher Zeitung, pp. 465–496.

Maatsch, Aleksandra (2014) 'Are We All Austerians Now? An Analysis of National Parliamentary Parties' Positioning on Anti-crisis Measures in the Eurozone'. *Journal of European Public Policy* 21(1): 96–115.

References   313

Mabille, Xavier (1997) *Histoire politique de la Belgique*. Brussels: Centre de recherché et d'information socio-politiques (CRISP).

Mach, André and Christine Trampusch (2011) 'The Swiss Political Economy in Comparative Perspective'. In Christine Trampusch and André Mach (eds) *Switzerland in Europe. Continuity and Exchange in the Swiss Political Economy*. London: Routledge, pp. 11–26.

Maddens, Bart and Jaak Billiet (2002) 'The Monarchy as a Factor of Political Support. The Impact of the 1999 Royal Wedding in Flanders'. *Acta Politica* 37(2): 347–379.

Maderthaner, Wolfgang (1996) 'Die Entstehung einer demokratischen Massenpartei. Sozialdemokratische Organisation von 1899 bis 1918'. In Wolfgang Maderthaner and C. Müller (eds) *Die Organisation der österreichischen Sozialdemokratie 1889–1995*. Vienna: Löcker Verlag, pp. 21–92.

Maes, Ivo and Amy Verdun (2005) 'Small States and the Creation of EMU: Belgium and the Netherlands, Pace-setters and Gate-keepers'. *Journal of Common Market Studies* 43(2): 327–348.

Magnette, Paul (2004) 'Parlementarisme dans une democratie de compromise. Refléxions sur le cas belge'. In Olivier Costa, Eric Kerrouche and Paul Magnette (eds) *Vers un renouveau du parlementarisme en Europe?* Brussels: Editions Université de Bruxelles, pp. 92–106.

Magone, José M. (2006) *The New World Architecture. The Contribution of the European Union in the Making of Global Governance*. New Brunswick, NJ: Transaction.

Magone, José M. (2011) *Contemporary European Politics. A Comparative Introduction*. London: Routledge.

Magone, José M. (2014) 'Por uma cultura de consenso em Portugal. Algumas observações comparativas com as democracias de consenso na Europa'. In Presidência da República (ed.) *Portugal. Rotas de Abril. Democracia, Compromisso e Desenvolvimento*. Lisbon: A Presidência da República, pp. 71–108.

Magone, José M. (2015) 'Introduction: The "Great Transformation" of European Politics: A Holistic View'. In José M. Magone (ed.) *Routledge Handbook of European Politics*. London: Routledge, pp. 1–37.

Magone, José M., Brigid Laffan and Christian Schweiger (eds) (2016a) *Core–Periphery Relations in the European Union. Power and Conflict in a Dualist Political Economy*. London: Routledge.

Magone, José M., Brigid Laffan and Christian Schweiger (2016b) 'The European Union as a Dualist Political Economy: Understanding Core–Periphery Relations'. In José M. Magone, Brigid Laffan and Christian Schweiger (eds) *Core–Periphery Relations in the European Union. Power and Conflict in a Dualist Political Economy*. London: Routledge, pp. 1–16.

Mair, Peter (1997) *Party System Change. Approaches and Interpretations*. Oxford: Oxford University Press.

Mair, Peter (2008a) 'Electoral Volatility and the Dutch Party System: A Comparative Perspective'. *Acta Politica* 43(1): 235–253.

Mair, Peter (2008b) 'The Challenge to Party Government'. *West European Politics* 31(1): 211–234.

Mair, Peter, Fritz Plasser and Wolfgang C. Müller (2004) 'Party Responses to Electoral Challenges'. In Peter Mair, Fritz Plasser and Wolfgang C. Müller (eds) *Political Parties and Electoral Challenge. Party Responses to Electoral Markets*. London: Sage, pp. 1–16.

Maissen, Sandra (2016) 'Konferenz der Kantonsregierungen und Haus der Kantone'. Stand 15, March. Powerpoint slides kindly provided by Secretary-general Dr Sandra Maissen on 15 March.

314   *References*

Manatschal, Anita und Carolin Rapp (2015) 'Welche Schweizer wählen die SVP und warum?' In Markus Freitag and Adrian Vatter (eds) *Wahlen und Wählerschaft in der Schweiz.* Zürich: Verlag Neue Zürcher Zeitung, pp. 187–215.

Manoschek, Walter and Thomas Geldmacher (2006) 'Vergangenheitspolitik'. In Herbert Dachs, Peter Gerlich, Herbert Gottweis, Helmut Kramer, Volkmar Lauber, Wolfgang C. Müller and Emmerich Talós (eds) *Politik in Österreich. Das Handbuch.* Vienna: Manz Verlag, pp. 577–593.

Marchal, Guy P. (2004) 'Die Ursprünge der Unabhängigkeit (401–1394)'. In Ulrich Im Hof, Pierre Ducrey, Guy P. Marchal, Nicolas Morard, Martin Körner, François de Capitani, Georges Andrey, Roland Ruffieux, Hans Ulrich Jost, Peter Gilg and Peter Hablützel, *Geschichte der Schweiz und der Schweizer.* Basel: Schwabe Verlag, pp. 109–214.

Marx, Ive (2009) 'Belgium: The Quest for Sustainability, Legitimacy and a Way Out of "Welfare without Work"'. In Klaus Schubert, Simon Hegelich and Ursula Bazant (eds) *Handbook of European Welfare Systems.* London: Routledge, pp. 49–64.

Mastenbroek, Ellen, Pieter Zwaan, Afke Groen, Wim van Meurs, Hilde Heiding, Nora Dörrenbächer and Christine Neuhold (2014) *Engaging with Europe. Evaluating National Parliamentary Control of EU Decision Making after the Lisbon Treaty.* Management Report Part II. Nijmegen: Institute for Management Research. Posted at www.tweedekamer.nl/sites/default/files/atoms/files/engaging_with_europe_management_report_2nd_edition.pdf (accessed 31 October 2015).

Matagne, Geoffreoy, Régis Dandoy and Caroline Wynsberghe (2014) 'Les dynamiques du fédéralisme belge'. In Dandoy, Régis, Geoffroy Matagne and Caroline Van Wynsberghe (eds) *Le Féderalisme Belge. Enjeux institutionels, acteurs socio-politiques et opinions publiques.* Louvain- La-Neuve: Academia-L'Harmattan, pp. 5–26.

Maurer, Andreas (2001) 'National Parliaments in the European Architecture: From Latecomers' Adaptation towards Permanent Institutional Change?' In Andreas Maurer and Wolfgang Wessels (eds) *National Parliaments on their Ways to Europe: Losers and Latecomers?* Baden-Baden: Nomos Verlagsgesellschaft, pp. 27–76.

Maurer, Andreas and Wolfgang Wessels (2001) 'National Parliaments after Amsterdam: From Slow Adapters to National Players?' In Andreas Maurer and Wolfgang Wessels (eds) *National Parliaments on their Ways to Europe: Losers and Latecomers?* Baden-Baden: Nomos Verlagsgesellschaft, pp. 425–470.

McCann, Dermot (2010) *The Political Economy of the European Union.* Cambridge: Polity Press.

McNally, Christopher A. (2013) 'Refurbishing State Capitalism: A Policy Analysis of Efforts to Rebalance China's Political Economy'. *Journal of Current Chinese Affairs* 42(4): 45–71.

Merlingen, Michael, Cas Mudde and Ulrich Sedelmeier (2001) 'The Right and the Righteous? European Norms, Domestic Politics and the Sanctions against Austria'. *Journal of Common Market Studies* 39(1): 59–77.

Michel, Bastiaan (2012) 'Wet financiering politieke partijen: einde in zicht-maar wat en gaten!' Posted at www.montesquieu-instituut.nl/id/vj5fc9te8y1c/wet_financiering_politieke_partijen?utm_campaign=1212&utm_source=nbrief&utm_medium=email (accessed 3 January 2016).

Miklin, Eric (2015) 'The Austrian Parliament and EU Affairs: Gradually Living Up to its Legal Potential'. In Claudia Hefftler, Christine Neuhold, Olivier Rozenberg and Julie Smith (eds) *Palgrave Handbook on National Parliament and the European Union.* Basingstoke: Palgrave, pp. 389–405.

Milic, Thomas (2009) 'Schweiz'. In *Political Data Yearbook 2008.* Special issue of *European Journal of Political Research* 48(7–8): 1124–1129.

References 315

Milquet, Julien (2013) *La communauté germanophone peut-elle devenir une Région? Présentation, historique et avenir.* Collection 'Au quotidien'. Brussels: Centre permanente pour la Citoyenneté et la Participation. Posted at www.cpcp.be/medias/pdfs/publications/region_germanophone.pdf (accessed 16 May 2016).

Milward, Alan S. (1984) *The Reconstruction of Western Europe 1949–51.* Berkeley, Los Angeles: University of California Press.

Ministry of the Interior of the Netherlands (2016) 'Overzichten financiering politieke partijen 2014'. Posted at www.rijksoverheid.nl/onderwerpen/democratie/documenten/publicaties/2015/09/21/overzichten-financiering-politieke-partijen-2014 (accessed 15 September 2016).

Mintzberg, Henry Bruce Ahlstrand and Joseph Lampel (2009) *Strategy Safari. Your Complete Guide through the Wilds of Strategic Management.* Harlow: Prentice Gate.

Modelski, George (2000) 'World System Evolution'. In Robert A. Denemark, Jonathan Friedman, Barry K. Gills and George Modelski (eds) *World Systems History. The Social Science of Long-term Change.* London, New York: Routledge, pp. 24–53.

Molitor, André (1980) 'The Reform of the Belgian Constitution'. In Arend Lijphart (ed.) *Conflict and Consensus in Belgium. The Dynamics of Culturally Divided Societies.* Berkeley: University of California-Institute of International Studies, pp. 139–153.

Moll, Peter and Martin Niedermeyer (2009) '"Das Zukunftsbild 2020": Leitlinien und Perspektiven der grenzüberschreitenden Kooperation in der Großregion SaarLorLux'. In Wolfgang H. Lorig and Mario Hirsch (eds) *Das politische System Luxembourgs.* Wiesbaden: Verlag Sozialwissenschaften, pp. 344–364.

Moury, Catherine (2013) *Coalition Government and Party Mandate. How Coalition Agreements Constrain Ministerial Action.* London: Routledge.

Mudde, Cas (2004) 'The Populist Zeitgeist'. *Government and Opposition* 39(4): 542–563.

Müller, Rudolf (2009) 'Die politischen Kommunen'. In Wolfgang H. Lorig and Mario Hirsch (eds) *Das politische System Luxembourgs.* Wiesbaden: Verlag der Sozialwissenschaften, pp. 143–154.

Müller, Wolfgang C. (1996) 'Die Organisation der SPÖ, 1945–1995'. In Wolfgang Maderthaner and C. Müller (eds) *Die Organisation der österreichischen Sozialdemokratie 1889–1995.* Vienna: Löcker Verlag, pp. 195–356.

Müller, Wolfgang C. (2000) 'Austria: Tight Coalitions and Stable Government'. In Wolfgang C. Müller and Kaare Strøm (eds) *Coalition Governments in Western Europe.* Oxford: Oxford University Press, pp. 86–125.

Müller, Wolfgang C. (2001) 'Amtsverständnis und Tätigkeit der Abgeordneten- ein erster Überblick'. In Wolfgang C. Müller, Marcelo Jenny, Barbara Steininger, Martin Dolezal, Wilfried Philip and Sabine Preisl-Westphal (eds) *Die österreichischen Abgeordneten. Individuelle Präferenzen und politisches Verhalten.* Vienna: Zentrum für Angewandte Politik- Wiener Universitätsverlag, pp. 65–87.

Müller, Wolfgang C. (2004) 'Party Responses to the Erosion of Voter Loyalties in Austria: Weakness as an Advantage and Strength as a Handicap'. In Peter Mair, Wolfgang C. Müller and Friz Plasser (eds) *Political Parties and Electoral Change. Party Responses to Electoral Markets.* London: Sage, pp. 145–178.

Müller, Wolfgang C. (2006a) 'Das Regierungssystem'. In Herbert Dachs, Peter Gerlich, Herbert Gottweis, Helmut Kramer, Volkmar Lauber, Wolfgang C. Müller and Emmerich Tálos (eds) *Politik in Österreich. Das Handbuch.* Vienna: Manzsche Verlags- und Universitätsbuchhandlung, pp. 105–118.

316   References

Müller, Wolfgang C. (2006b) 'Regierung und Kabinettsystem'. In Herbert Dachs, Peter Gerlich, Herbert Gottweis, Helmut Kramer, Volkmar Lauber, Wolfgang C. Müller and Emmerich Tálos (eds) *Politik in Österreich. Das Handbuch*. Vienna: Manzsche Verlags- und Universitätsbuchhandlung, pp. 168–187.

Müller, Wolfgang C. (2006c) 'Der Bundespräsident'. In Herbert Dachs, Peter Gerlich, Herbert Gottweis, Helmut Kramer, Volkmar Lauber, Wolfgang C. Müller and Emmerich Tálos (eds) *Politik in Österreich. Das Handbuch*. Vienna: Manzsche Verlags- und Universitätsbuchhandlung, pp. 188–200.

Müller, Wolfgang C. (2006d) 'Party Patronage and Party Colonization of the State'. In Richard S. Katz and William Crotty (eds) *Handbook of Party Politics*. London: Sage, pp. 189–195.

Müller, Wolfgang C. (2008) 'Austria: A Complex Electoral System with Subtle Effects'. In Michael Gallagher and Paul Mitchell (eds) *The Politics of Electoral Systems*. Oxford: Oxford University Press, pp. 397–416.

Müller, Wolfgang C. and Kaare Strøm (eds) (2000) *Coalition Governments in Western Europe*. Oxford: Oxford University Press.

Müller, Wolfgang C., M. Wilfried Philipp and Barbara Steininger (1995) ' "Politische Klasse", Politische Positionselite, Politische "Stars" '. In Herbert Dachs, Peter Gerlich and Wolfgang C. Müller (eds) *Die Politiker. Karrieren und Wirken bedeutender Repräsentanten der Zweiten Republik*. Vienna: Manz-Wirtschaft, pp. 27–32.

Münch, Richard (2011) *Das Regime des liberalen Kapitalismus. Inklusion und Exklusion im neuen Wohlfahrtstaat*. Frankfurt am Main: Campus.

Naim, Moisés (2013) *The End of Power. From Boardrooms to Battlefields and Churches to States, Why being in Charge isn't What it Used to Be*. New York: Basic Books.

Nasra, Skander and Mathieu Segers (2012) 'Between Charlemagne and Atlantis: Belgium and the Netherlands during the First Stages of European Integration (1950–1966)'. *Journal of European Integration History* 18(2): 183–205.

Neumann, Peter R. (2015) *Die Neuen Dschihadisten. IS, Europa und die nächste Welle des Terrorismus*. Berlin: Econ.

Nicklauss, Karlheinz (2014) *Kanzlerdemokratie: Regierungsführung von Konrad Adenauer bis Angela Merkel*. Wiesbaden: Springer VS.

Nicolopoulos, Andreas, Michael Gold and Alexander Kluge (eds) (2009) *The European Company Statute. A New Governance Approach*. Oxford, Berne: Peter Lang.

Norris, Pippa (2001) 'The Twilight of Westminster? Electoral Reform and its Consequences'. *Political Studies* 49(5): 877–900.

North, Michael (2003) *Geschichte der Niederlande*. Munich: Verlag C.H. Beck.

Observatoire d' epargne européenne (OEE), INSEAD OEE Dataservices (IODS) (2013) 'Who Owns the European Economy. Evolution of the Ownership of EU-listed Companies between 1970 and 2012. Posted at http://ec.europa.eu/finance/finservices-retail/docs/fsug/papers/1308-report-who-owns-european-economy_en.pdf (accessed 23 February 2016).

Oesch, David (2011) 'Swiss Trade Unions amd Industrial Relations after 1990. A History of Decline and Renewal'. In Christine Trampusch and André Mach (eds) *Switzerland in Europe. Continuity and Change in the Swiss Political Economy*. London: Routledge pp. 82–102.

Öhlinger, Theo (2002) 'Die Europäisierung der österreichischen Verfassung'. In Heinrich Neisser and Sonja Puntscher Riekmann (eds) (2002) *Europäisierung der österreichischen Politik. Konsequenzen der EU Mitgliedschaft*. Vienna: WUV-Universitätsverlag, pp. 81–100.

References 317

Oorschot, Wim (2009) 'The Dutch Welfare System: From Collective Responsibility to Individual Responsibility'. In Klaus Schubert, Simon Hegelich and Ursula Bazant (eds) *Handbook of European Welfare Systems*. London: Routledge, pp. 363–377.

Operation Libero (2016) 'Chancenland statt Freilicht Museum. Ein Appel für die Zukunft'. Posted at www.operation-libero.ch/de/appell (accessed 18 April 2016).

Organisation for Economic Cooperation and Development (OECD) (2009a) *OECD Territorial Reviews: Luxembourg 2009*. Paris: OECD. Posted at www.keepeek.com/Digital-Asset-Management/oecd/urban-rural-and-regional-development/oecd-territorial-reviews-luxembourg-2007_9789264038585-en#page1 (accessed 13 December 2015).

Organisation for Economic Cooperation and Development (OECD) (2009b) *OECD Economic Survey Belgium 2009*. Paris: OECD.

Organisation for Economic Cooperation and Development (OECD) (2014a) *OECD Territorial Reviews: Netherlands 2014*. Paris: OECD. Posted at www.keepeek.com/Digital-Asset-Management/oecd/urban-rural-and-regional-development/oecd-territorial-reviews-netherlands-2014_9789264209527-en#page1 (accessed 13 December 2015).

Organisation for Economic Cooperation and Development (OECD) (2014b) 'Social Expenditure Update: Social Spending is Falling in Some Countries, but in Many Others it Remains at Historically High Levels'. Insights from OECD Social Expenditure Database (SOCX), November. Posted at www.oecd.org/els/soc/OECD2014-Social-Expenditure-Update-Nov2014-8pages.pdf (accessed 19 April 2016).

Organisation for Economic Cooperation and Development (OECD) (2015a) 'Youth Not in Education or Employment (NEET) (Indicator)'. doi: 10.1787/72d1033a-en. Posted at https://data.oecd.org/youthinac/youth-not-in-education-or-employment-neet.htm (accessed 13 April 2016).

Organisation for Economic Cooperation and Development (OECD) (2015b) *Consolidated Government Expenditure as Percentage of Total General Government Expenditure (Consolidated)* (Table 5: 1970–2013). Posted at www.oecd.org/tax/federalism/oecdfis-caldecentralisationdatabase.htm#C_3 (accessed 19 November 2015).

Organisation for Economic Cooperation and Development (OECD) (2016a) 'Social Expenditure Database (SOCX)'. Posted at www.oecd.org/social/expenditure.htm (accessed 7 April 2016).

Organisation for Economic Cooperation and Development (OECD) (2016b) 'Employment Protection Indicators'. Posted at www.oecd.org/els/emp/oecdindicatorsofemploymentprotection.htm (accessed 12 April 2016).

Organisation for Economic Cooperation and Development (OECD) (2016c) 'How Good Is Your Job? Measuring and Assessing Job Quality'. Posted at www.oecd.org/std/labour-stats/Job-quality-OECD.pdf (accessed 12 April 2016).

Organisation for Economic Cooperation and Development (OECD) (2016d) 'Employment Database'. OECD database. Posted at https://data.oecd.org/emp/labour-force.htm#indicator-chart (accessed 13 April 2016).

Organisation for Economic Cooperation and Development (OECD) (2016e) 'Migration Database'. OECD database. Posted at https://data.oecd.org/migration/foreign-born-employment.htm (accessed 17 April 2016).

Organisation for Economic Cooperation and Development (OECD) (2016f) 'Trade Union Density'. OECD database. Posted at https://stats.oecd.org/Index.aspx?DataSetCode=UN_DEN (accessed 17 April 2016).

318 *References*

Organisation for Economic Cooperation and Development (OECD) (2016g) 'Real GDP Forecast'. OECD database. Posted at https://data.oecd.org/gdp/real-gdp-forecast.htm (accessed 28 April 2016).

Organisation for Economic Cooperation and Development (OECD) (2016h) 'Unemployment Rate. Yearly 2009–2015'. OECD database. Posted at https://data.oecd.org/unemp/unemployment-rate.htm (accessed 28 April 2016).

Österle, August and Karin Heitzmann (2009) 'Welfare State Development in Austria: Strong Traditions Meet New Challenges'. In Klaus Schubert, Simon Hegelich and Ursula Bazant (eds) *Handbook of European Welfare Systems*. London: Routledge, pp. 31–48.

Österreichischer Gemeindebund (2015a) 'Wofür die Gemeinden Geld ausgeben'. Posted at http://gemeindebund.at//wofuer-die-gemeinden-geld-ausgeben (accessed 5 December 2015).

Österreichischer Gemeindebund (2015b) 'Genderatlas'. Posted at http://genderatlas.at/articles/buergermeisterinnen.html (accessed 5 December 2015).

Österreichischer Gemeindebund (2015c) 'Über den österreichischen Gemeindebund'. Posted at http://gemeindebund.at//ueber-den-oesterreichischen-gemeindebund (accessed 5 December 2015).

Österreichischer Gewerkschaftsbund (2016) 'ÖGB Mitgliederstatistik gesamt nach Gewerkschaften'. Membership 1 January 2013 and 1 January 2014. Posted at www.oegb.at/cs/Satellite?blobcol=urldata&blobheadername1=content-type&blobheadername2=content-disposition&blobheadervalue1=application%2Fpdf&blobheadervalue2=inline%3B+filename%3D%22Mitglieder_nach_Gewerkschaft_2014.pdf%22&blobkey=id&blobnocache=false&blobtable=MungoBlobs&blobwhere=1342601116069&ssbinary=true&site=S06 (accessed 24 February 2016).

Österreichischer Städtebund (2015) 'Woher kommt das geld das die Gemeinden brauchen'. Posted at http://gemeindebund.at//woher-kommt-das-geld-das-die-gemeinden-brauchen (accessed 5 December 2015).

Otjes, Simon and Gerrit Voerman (2013) 'The Netherlands'. In Andreas Bågenholm, Kevin Deegan-Krause and Liam Weeks (eds) *European Political Data Yearbook 2012*. Special issue of *European Journal of Political Research* 52(1): 162–169.

Otjes, Simon and Gerrit Voerman (2014) 'The Netherlands'. In Andreas Bågenholm, Kevin Deegan-Krause and Rainbow Murray (eds) *European Political Data Yearbook 2013*. Special issue of *European Journal of Political Research* 53(1): 229–234.

Palm, Franz (2010) 'Wirtschaftsstandort und Wirtschaftsgeographie DG'. In Anne-Begenat Neuschäffer (ed.) *Die Deutschsprachige Gemeinschaft Belgiens. Ein Bestandsaufnahme*. Part of series Belgien in Fokus. Geschichte-Sprachen-Kulturen, edited by Anne-Begenat-Neuschäffer. Berne: Peter Lang, pp. 171–199.

Parliament of Austria (2007) *Tagung des Nationalrates 30.Oktober 2006–10.Juli 2007. Bilanz*. Vienna: Parlamentsdirektion, Springer Verlag. Posted at www.parlament.gv.at/ZUSD/PDF/OeP_Bilanz_2006-2007_WEB.pdf (accessed 11 October 2015).

Parliament of Austria (2008) *Tagung des Nationalrat. 2007/2008. XXIII Gesetzgebungsperiode. Bilanz*. Vienna: Parlamentsdirektion, Springer Verlag. Posted at www.parlament.gv.at/ZUSD/PDF/OeP_Bilanz_2007-2008_WEB.pdf (accessed 11 October 2011).

Parliament of Austria (2013) *XXIV Gesetzgebungsperiode des Nationalrates 28 Oktober 2008 bis 28 Oktober 2013. Bilanz*. Vienna: Parlamentsdirektion, Springer Verlag. Posted at www.parlament.gv.at/ZUSD/PDF/Nationalrat_BilanzGPXXIV.pdf (accessed 11 October 2015).

Parliament of Austria (2015a) *Jahresbericht 2014. Nationalrat*. Vienna: Parlamentsdirektion, Springer Verlag. Posted at www.parlament.gv.at/ZUSD/PDF/OeP_Bilanz_2014_FINAL_WEB.pdf (accessed 11 October 2015).

References 319

Parliament of Austria (2015b) Übersicht über die Einsprüche des Bundesrates in der II. Republik. Posted at www.parlament.gv.at/ZUSD/PDF/Einsprueche_d_BR_II_Rep.pdf (accessed 11 October 2015).

Parliament of Austria (2015c) 'Parlamentsbudget steigt durch Kosten für Parlamentssanierung'. *Parlamentskorrespondenz* 1254, 17 November. Posted at www.parlament.gv. at/PAKT/PR/JAHR_2015/PK1254/index.shtml (accessed 13 May 2016).

Parliament of Austria (2016a) 'Abgeordnete zum Nationalrat, die derzeit ein Mandat innehaben'. Posted at www.parlament.gv.at/WWER/NR/ (accessed 13 May 2016).

Parliament of Austria (2016b) 'Mitglieder des Bundesrates, die derzeit ein Mandat innehaben'. Posted at www.parlament.gv.at/WWER/BR/ (accessed 12 May 2016).

Parliament of Austria (2016c) 'Legislature and Legislative Reports of Nationalrat and Bundesrat'. Posted at www.parlament.gv.at/SERV/STAT/index.shtml (accessed 11 July 2016).

Parliament of Brussels-Capital Region (2014) 'Budget des recettes et depénses pour l'année budgetaire 2015. Exposé General. Session Ordinaire 2014–15. 30 October 2014. A 51/1–2014/2015'. Posted at http://be.brussels/files-fr/a-propos-de-la-region/finances/budget-regional/2015/expose-general-du-budget-2015 (accessed 7 December 2015).

Parliament of Switzerland (2016a) 'Statistical Database'. Posted at www.parlament.ch/de/%C3%BCber-das-parlament/fakten-und-zahlen (accessed 10 June 2016).

Parliament of Switzerland (2016b) 'Personalstatistik'. Posted at www.parlament.ch/centers/documents/de/personalstatistik-d.pdf (accessed 15 May 2016).

Parliament of Wallonia (2014) 'Budgets des recettes et des dépenses de la Région Wallone Pour L'Année budgetaire 2015'. Exposé General 13 November. Session 2014–15. Doc 59–60, Annexe 1. Posted at http://spw.wallonie.be/budget/expose/expgen-synth.pdf (accessed 7 December 2015).

Parties and Elections in Europe (2016) Database on European elections. Posted at www. parties-and-elections.eu/ (accessed 10 June 2016).

Partij voor de Vrijheid (PVV) (2012) 'Hún Brussel, ons Nederland. Verkiezings programma 2012–2017'. Posted at www.pvv.nl/images/stories/verkiezingen2012/VerkiezingsProgramma-PVV-2012-final-web.pdf (accessed 2 January 2016).

Pauly, Michel (2011) *Geschichte Luxemburgs*. Munich: C.H. Beck.

Pauwels, Teun (2011) 'Le Vlaams Belang'. In Pascal Delwit, Benoit Pilet and Emilie van Haute (eds) *Les Partis Politiques en Belgique*. Brussels: Edition de l'Université de Bruxelles, pp. 219–234.

Pauwels, Teun (2014) *Populism in Western Europe: Comparing Belgium, Gemany and the Netherlands*. London: Routledge.

Pedersen, Mogens N. (1979) 'The Dynamics of European Party System Systems: Changing Patterns of Electoral Volatility'. *European Journal of Political Research* 7(1): 1–26.

Pelinka, Anton and Sieglinde Rosenberger (2003) *Österreichische Politik. Grundlagen, Strukturen, Trends*. Vienna: WUV.

Peñalver Garcia, Nereo and Julian Priestley (2015) *The Making of a European President*. Basingstoke: Palgrave.

Pennings, Paul (2005) 'Parties, Voters and Policy Priorities in the Netherlands 1971–2002'. *Party Politics* 11(1): 29–45.

Pennings, Paul and Hans Keman (2003) 'The Dutch Parliamentary Elections in 2002 and 2003: The Rise of the Fortuyn Movement'. *Acta Politica* 38(1): 51–68.

320 References

Perchinig, Bernhard (1983) 'National oder liberal: Die Freiheitliche Partei Österreichs'. In Peter Gerlich and Wolfgang C. Müller (eds) *Zwischen Koalition und Konkurrenz. Österreichs Parteien seit 1945.* Vienna: Braumüller, pp. 69–90.

Perin, Emanuelle and Michel Ajzen (2015) 'Belgium: Working Life Profile'. European Observatory of Working Life (EURWORK). Posted at www.eurofound.europa.eu/ observatories/eurwork/comparative-information/national-contributions/belgium/ belgium-working-life-country-profile (accessed 19 February 2016).

Pernice, Ingolf (2015) 'The EU as a Citizens' Joint Venture: Multilevel Constitutionalism and Open Democracy in Europe'. In José M. Magone (ed.) *Handbook of European Politics.* London: Routledge, pp. 184–201.

Pierson, Paul (1998) 'The Path to European Integration: A Historical-institutionalist Analysis'. In Wayne Sandholtz and Alec Stone Sweet (eds) *European Integration and Supranational Governance.* Oxford: Oxford University Press, pp. 27–58.

Pilet, Jean-Benoit (2011) 'Le Centre Démocrate Humaniste (CdH)'. In Pascal Delwit, Benoit Pilet and Emilie van Haute (eds) *Les Partis Politiques en Belgique.* Brussels: Edition de l'Université de Bruxelles, pp. 62–82.

Pilet, Jean-Benoit and Stefaan Fiers (2014) 'Vers la constitution d'Elites politiques séparées? Carriéres des Parlementaires et Représentation Territoriale dans la Belgique Fédérale'. In Régis Dandoy, Geoffroy Matagne and Caroline Van Wynsberghe (eds) *Le Féderalisme Belge. Enjeux institutionels, acteurs socio-politiques et opinions publiques.* Louvain-La-Neuve: Academia-L'Harmattan, pp. 111–138.

Pilet, Jean Benoit and Marie Helene Schrobiltgen (2011) 'Ecolo'. In Pascal Delwit, Benoit Pilet and Emilie van Haute (eds) *Les Partis Politiques en Belgique.* Brussels: Edition de l'Université de Bruxelles, pp. 79–199.

Plasser, Fritz and Günther Lengauer (2009) 'Wie "amerikanisch" sind europäische Wahlkämpfe'. In Hanna Kaspar, Harald Schoen, Siegfried Schumann and Jürgen R. Winkler (eds) *Politik-Wissenschaft-Medien. Festschrift für Jürgen W. Falter zum 65. Geburtstag.* Wiesbaden: Verlag der Sozialwissenschaften, pp. 323–346.

Plasser, Fritz and Peter A. Ulram (1995) 'Konstanz und Wandel im österreichischen Wählerverhalten'. In Wolfgang C. Müller, Fritz Plasser and Peter A. Ulram (eds) *Wählerverhalten und Parteienwettbewerb. Analysen zur Nationalratswahl 1994.* Vienna: Signum Verlag, pp. 341–406.

Plasser, Fritz and Peter A. Ulram (2006) 'Das Parteiensystem Österreichs'. In Oskar Niedermayer, Richard Stöss and Melanie Haas (eds) *Die Parteiensysteme Westeuropas.* Wiesbaden: Verlag Sozialwissenschaften, pp. 351–372.

Poguntke, Thomas and Paul Webb (2005) 'The Presidentialization of Politics in Democratic Societies: A Framework of Analysis'. In Thomas Poguntke and Paul Webb (eds.) *The Presidentialization of Politics. A Comparative Study of Modern Democracies.* Oxford: Oxford University Press, pp. 1–25.

Poirier, Johanne (2002) 'Formal Mechanisms of Intergovernmental Relations in Belgium'. *Regional and Federal Studies* 12(3): 24–54.

Poirier, Philippe (2002) 'Quelle(s) identité(s) politique(s) pour le parti démocratique luxembourgeois?' In Pascal Delwit (ed.) *Libéralismes et partis libéraux en Europe.* Brussels: Editions de l'Université de Bruxelles, pp. 247–262.

Poirier, Philippe (2004) 'At the Centre of the State. Christian Democracy in Luxembourg'. In Steven van Hecke and Emmanuel Gerard (eds) *Christian Democratic Parties in Europe since the End of the Cold War.* Leuven: Leuven University Press, pp. 179–196.

Polanyi, Karl (1944, 1953) *The Great Transformation. The Political and Economic Origins of Our Time.* Boston, MA: Beacon Press.

References 321

Pollack, Johannes and Peter Slominski (2005) ' "Konstitutioneller Moment" und Verfassungsreform: eine Einschätzung des Österreich-Konvents'. *Österreichische Zeitschrift für Politikwissenschaft* 34(3): 337–349.

Pollack, Mark (1994) 'Creeping Competence: The Expanding Agenda of the European Community'. *Journal of Public Policy* 14(2): 95–140.

Pollack, Mark (2000) 'The End of Creeping Competence? EU Policy Making Since Maastricht'. *Journal of Common Market Studies* 38(3): 519–538.

Quesel, Carsten (2012) 'Konkordanz, föderale Verflechtung und direktdemokratische Mobilisierung. Eine Fallstudie zur Bildungspolitik in der Schweiz'. In Stefan Köppl and Uwe Krannenpohl (eds) *Konkordanzdemokratie. Ein Demokratietyp der Vergangenheit*. Baden-Baden: Nomos Verlagsgesellschaft, pp. 293–316.

Radaelli, Claudio M. (2003) 'The Europeanization of Public Policy'. In Kevin Featherstone and Claudio M. Radaelli (eds) *The Politics of Europeanization*. Oxford: Oxford University Press, pp. 27–56.

Radio et television belge francophone (RTBF) (2014) 'Syndicats et patronat: le groupe des 10, c'est quoi?', 17 December. Posted at www.rtbf.be/info/belgique/detail_syndicats-et-patronat-le-groupe-des-10-c-est-quoi?id=8594495 (accessed 15 September 2016).

Raschke, Joachim and Ralf Tils (2007) *Politische Strategie. Eine Grundlegung*. Wiesbaden: Verlag der Sozialwissenschaften.

Rathkolb, Oliver (2005) *Die paradoxe Republik. Österreich 1945 bis 2005*. Vienna: Paul Zsolnay.

Reinhardt, Volker (2006) *Geschichte der Schweiz*. Munich: C.H. Beck.

Reitan, Claus (2014) *Gesellschaft im Wandel. Perspektiven für Österreich*. Vienna: Edition Steinbauer.

Reiterer, Albert F. (2003) *Gesellschaft in Österreich. Struktur und Sozialer Wandel im globalen Vergleich*. Vienna: WUV.

Reuchamps, Min (2014) 'Structures Institutionelles du Fédéralisme Belge'. In Régis Dandoy, Geoffroy Matagne and Caroline Van Wynsberghe (eds) *Le Féderalisme Belge. Enjeux institutionels, acteurs socio-politiques et opinions publiques*. Louvain-La-Neuve: Academia-L'Harmattan, pp. 29–61.

Rietbergen, P.J. (2014) *A Short History of the Netherlands. From Pre-history to the Present Day*. Amersfort: Bekking en Blitz.

Rimé, Bernard, Pierre Bouchat, Olivier Klein and Laurent Licata (2005) 'When Collective Memories of Victimhood Fade: Generational Evolution of Intergroup Attitudes and Political Aspirations in Belgium'. *European Journal of Political Research* 45(4): 515–532.

Robertson, R. (1992) *Globalization: Social Theory and Global Culture*. London: Sage.

Rohrer, Linda and Christine Trampusch (2011) 'Continuity and Change in the Swiss Cocational Training System'. In Christine Trampusch and André Mach (eds) *Switzerland in Europe. Continuity and Change in the Swiss Political Economy*. London: Routledge pp. 144–161.

Rosenau, James N. (1990) *Turbulence in World Politics. A Theory of Change and Continuity*. Princeton, NJ: Princeton University Press.

Rosenau, James N. and Ernst-Otto Czempiel (eds) (2000) *Governance Without Government: Order and Change in World Politics*. Cambridge: Cambridge University Press.

Ross, George (1995) *Jacques Delors and European Integration*. Cambridge: Oxford University Press.

Rothmayr Allison, Cristine and Frédéric Varone (2014) 'Justiz'. In Peter Knoepfel, Yannis Papadopoulos, Pascal Sciarini, Adrian Vatter and Silja Häusermann (eds) *Handbuch der Schweizer Politik*. Zürich: Verlag Neue Zürcher Zeitung, pp. 219–242.

322 References

Ruffieux, Roland (2004) 'Die Schweiz des Freisinns (1848–1914)'. In Ulrich Im Hof, Pierre Ducrey, Guy P. Marchal, Nicolas Morard, Martin Körner, François de Capitani, Georges Andrey, Roland Ruffieux, Hans Ulrich Jost, Peter Gilg and Peter Hablützel, *Geschichte der Schweiz und der Schweizer*. Basel: Schwabe Verlag, pp. 639–730.

Rüger, Carolin (2016) 'From Core to Periphery? The Impact of the Crisis on the EU's Role in the World'. In José M. Magone, Brigid Laffan and Christian Schweiger (eds) *Core–Periphery Relations in the European Union*. London: Routledge, pp. 269–282.

SAFEGE Baltija (2015) *Report on Centres of Government in the EU Member States*, 14 July. Posted at www.eupan.eu/files/repository/20150918145544_SB-ES_ZINOJ_ENG_SAFEGE.pdf (accessed 11 May 2016).

Schaap, Linze (2003) 'Government or Governance in the Rotterdam Region'. In José M. Magone (ed.) *Regional Institutions and Governance in the European Union*. Westport, CT: Praeger, pp. 153–172.

Scharpf, Fritz (1988) 'The Joint Decision Making Trap. Lessons from German Federalism and European Integration'. *Public Administration* 66(3): 239–278.

Schefbeck, Günther (2006) 'Das Parlament'. In Herbert Dachs, Peter Gerlich, Herbert Gottweis, Helmut Kramer, Volkmar Lauber, Wolfgang C. Müller and Emmerich Tálos (eds) *Politik in Österreich. Das Handbuch*. Vienna: Manzsche Verlags- und Universitätsbuchhandlung, pp. 139–167.

Schellenbauer, Patrik and Gerhard Schwarz (eds) (2015) *Bilateralismus-Was Sonst. Eigenständigkeit trotz Abhängigkeit*. Zürich: Avenir Suisse und Neue Zürcher Zeitung.

Schmid, Stefan (2014) 'Neuer Swiss Code of Best Practice for Corporate Governance'. AccountingundControlling.ch Blogsite. Posted at www.accountingundcontrolling.ch/accounting/neuer-swiss-code-of-best-practice-for-corporate-governance/ (accessed 18 May 2016).

Schmidt, Manfred G. (2002) 'The Consociational State. Hypotheses Regarding the Political Structure and Potential for Democratization in the European Union'. In Jurg Steiner and Thomas Ertman (eds) *Consociationalism and Corporatism in Western Europe. Still the Politics of Accommodation?* Special issue of *Acta Politica* 37(2–3): 213–227.

Schmidt, Manfred G. (2013) 'Vier Welten der Demokratie. Ein Kommentar zu Arend Lijpharts Neubearbeitung von Patterns of Democracy (2012)'. For 'Varieties, Crises, and Innovations of Democracy': An International Symposium to honour Gerhard Lehmbruch on the occasion of his 85th birthday, Berlin, 3 May 2013. Posted at www.uni-heidelberg.de/md/politik/personal/schmidt/2013_4_welten_der_demokratie_-_kommentar_zu_lijphart_2012.pdf (accessed 26 April 2016).

Schmidt, Vivien A. (2011) 'Small Countries, Big Countries under Conditions of Europeanisation and Globalisation' In Uwe Becker, *The Changing Political Economies of Small West European Countries*. Chicago, IL: Chicago University Press, pp. 149–172.

Schmitter, Philippe (1982) 'Reflections on Where the Theory of Neo-corporatism Has Gone and Where the Praxis May Be Going'. In Gerhard Lehmbruch and Philippe Schmitter (eds) *Patterns of Corporatist Policy Making*. London: Sage, pp. 259–279.

Schmitter, Philippe C. and Jürgen R. Grote (1997) *The Corporatist Sisyphus: Past, Present and Future*. European University Institute (EUI) Working Paper SPS no. 97/4. Posted at http://cadmus.eui.eu/bitstream/id/986/97_4.pdf/1997 (accessed 24 February 2016).

Schmitter, Philippe C. and Gerhard Lehmbruch (eds) (1979) *Trends Toward Corporatist Intermediation*. London: Sage.

References 323

Schneider, Martin R. and Mihail Paunescu (2012) 'Changing Varieties of Capitalism and Revealed Comparative Advantages from 1990 to 2005: A Test of the Hall and Soskice Claims'. *Socio-economic Review* 10(4): 731–753.

Schneyder, Gerhard and Frédéric Widmer (2011) 'Swiss Corporate Governance. Institutional Change in the Law and Corporate Practices'. In Christine Trampusch and André Mach (eds) *Switzerland in Europe. Continuity and Change in the Swiss Political Economy.* London: Routledge, pp. 105–123.

Schroen, Michael (2009a) 'Das politische System Luxemburgs'. In Wolfgang Ismayr (ed.) *Die politischen Systeme Westeuropas. 4. aktualisierte und überarbeite Ausgabe.* Wiesbaden: Verlag für Sozialwissenschaften, pp. 483–514.

Schroen, Michael (2009b) 'Parlament, Regierung und Gesetzgebung'. In Wolfgang H. Lorig and Mario Hirsch (eds) *Das politische System Luxemburgs. Eine Einführung.* Wiesbaden: Verlag Sozialwissenschaften, pp. 106–129.

Schroen, Michael (2012) 'Interessenvermittlung in einem Kleinstaat'. In W. Reutter (Hrsg.) *Verbände und Interessengruppen in den Ländern der Europäischen Union.* Wiesbaden: Springer Verlag, pp. 417–444.

Schütz, Alfred (1932) *Der sinnhafte Aufbau der sozialen Welt. Eine Einleitung in die vergleichende.* Vienna: Verlag Julius Springer.

Schwarz, Daniel and Wolf Linder (2006) *Mehrheits- und Koalitionsbildung im schweizerischen Nationalrat 1996–2005. Studie im Auftrag der Parlamentsdienste der schweizerischen Bundesversammlung.* Berne: Universität Berne. Posted at www.parlament.ch/d/dokumentation/berichte/weitere-berichte-und-studien/Documents/ed-pa-mehrheit-koalition-nr-vollst.pdf (accessed 18 October 2015).

Schwarz, Daniel and Wolf Linder (2007) *Fraktionsgeschlossenheit im schweizerischen Nationalrat 1996–2005. Studie im Auftrage der Parlamentsdienste der schweizerischen Bundesversammlung.* Berne: Universität Berne. Posted at www.parlament.ch/d/dokumentation/berichte/weitere-berichte-und-studien/Documents/unibe-fraktionsgeschlossenheit-2007-09-de.pdf (accessed 18 October 2015).

Schweiger, Christian (2014) *The EU and the Global Financial Crisis. New Varieties of Capitalism.* Cheltenham: Edward Elgar.

Schweizerische Bundeskanzlei (2016) 'Die Bundeskanzlei'. Posted at www.bk.admin.ch/org/index.html?lang=de (accessed 11 May 2016).

Schweizerische Gewerkschaftsbund (SGB-USS) (2008) *Streiken wirkt. Arbeitskämpfe in der Schweiz. 90 Jahre Generalstreik.* Berne: SGB-USS.

Schweizerische Volkspartei (SVP) (2007) *Wahlplattform 2007–2011. Mein Zuhause-Unsere Schweiz.* Berne: SVP. Posted at www.svpkreispartei-rorschach.ch/Dokumente/Wahlplattform.pdf (accessed 1 January 2016).

Schweizerische Volkspartei (2015) 'SVP – The Party of Switzerland'. Party Programme 2011–2015. Posted at www.svp.ch/de/assets/File/positionen/parteiprogramm/svp_parteiprogramm_e.pdf (accessed 2 January 2016).

Schweizerisches Bundesgericht (2016) 'Geschichtliches'. Posted at www.bger.ch/index/federal/federal-inherit-template/federal-status.htm (accessed 25 May 2016).

Schweizerisches Bundesverwaltungsgericht (2016) 'Das Gericht'. Posted at www.bvger.ch/gericht/index.html?lang=de (accessed 25 May 2016).

Sciarini, Pascal (2014a) 'Processus legislative'. In Peter Knoepfel, Yannis Papadopoulos, Pascal Sciarini, Adrian Vatter and Silja Häusermann (eds) *Handbuch der Schweizer Politik.* Zürich: Verlag Neue Zürcher Zeitung, pp. 527–561.

Sciarini, Pascal (2014b) 'Eppure si muove: The Changing Nature of the Swiss Consensus Democracy'. *Journal of European Public Policy* 21(1): 116–132.

324   References

Secker, Ineke (2000) 'Representatives of the Dutch People: The Smooth Transformation of the Parliamentary Elite in a Consociational Democracy 1849–1998'. In Heinrich Best and Maurizio Cotta (eds) *Parliamentary Representatives in Europe 1848–2000. Legislative Recruitment and Careers in Eleven European Countries.* Oxford: Oxford University Press, pp. 270–309.

Senat de Belgique (2015) 'Statistics'. Posted at www.senate.be/www/?MIval=/index_senate&MENUID=14170&LANG=fr (accessed 16 October 2015).

Senat de Belgique (2016a) 'Composition du Sénat, Situation a partir de 25 May 2014'. Posted at www.senaat.be/www/?MIval=/index_senate&MENUID=24200&LANG=fr (accessed 13 May 2016).

Senat de Belgique (2016b) 'La Constitution Belge'. Posted at www.senate.be/doc/const_fr.html (accessed 25 May 2016).

Seyd, Ben (2004) *Coalition Government in Scotland and Wales.* London: The Constitutional Unit – Nuffield College. Posted at https://kar.kent.ac.uk/34623/1/Coalition-governance.pdf (accessed 24 April 2016).

Siaroff, Alan (1999) 'Corporatism in 24 Industrial Democracies: Meaning and Measurement'. *European Journal of Political Research* 36(2): 175–205.

Sickinger, Hubert (2005) 'Parlamentarismus'. In Emmerich Tálos (ed.) *Schwarz-Blau. Eine Bilanz des 'Neu-Regierens'.* Vienna: LIT, pp. 70–85.

Sickinger, Hubert (2009) *Politikfinanzierung in Österreich.* Vienna: Czernin.

Sikkink, Kathryn (2011) *The Justice Cascade: How Human Rights Prosecutions are Changing World Politics.* New York: W.W. Norton.

Simon, Walter B. (1978, 1994) 'Democracy in the Shadow of Imposed Sovereignty: The First Republic of Austria'. In Juan J. Linz and Alfred Stepan (eds) *The Breakdown of Democratic Regimes. Europe.* Baltimore, MD: Johns Hopkins University Press, pp. 80–121.

Sluyterman, Keetie (2015) 'Introduction: Varieties of Capitalism and Business History: The Dutch Case'. In Keetie Sluyterman (ed.) *Varieties of Capitalism and Business History: The Dutch Case.* London: Routledge, pp. 1–21.

Smulders, Jef (2014a) *Le Financement et la compatibilité des partis politiques (2008–2013). I. Bases juridiques et partis francophones.* Brussels: CRISP, Courrier Hebdomadaire du CRISP 2014/no. 33–34.

Smulders, Jef (2014b) *Le Financement et la compatibilité des partis politiques (2008–2013). II. Partis flammandes et analyse transversale.* Brussels: CRISP, Courrier Hebdomadaire du CRISP 2014/no. 33–34.

Smulders, Jef and Bart Maddens (2014a) 'De financiële gevolgen voor de politieke partijen na de hervorming van de Senaat'. Leuven Catholic University – Institute of Government. Posted at https://lirias.kuleuven.be/handle/123456789/443566 (accessed 10 January 2016).

Smulders, Jef and Bart Maddens (2014b) *De financiële gevolgen van de verkiezingsuitlag van 25 mei 2014 voor de Vlaamse politieke partijen.* KU Leuven – Institute of Government, 26 May. Posted at https://lirias.kuleuven.be/handle/123456789/454328 (accessed 10 January 2016).

Sociaal-Economische Raad (SER) (2014a) *The Power of Consultation. The Dutch Consultative Economy Explained.* The Hague: SER.

Sociaal-Economische Raad (SER) (2014b) *The Social and Economic Council of the Netherlands (SER).* The Hague: SER.

Sociaal-Economische Raad (SER) (2015) 'The Dutch Consultation Economy in Perspective'. Powerpoint slides. Document provided by SER.

References 325

Sociaal en Cultureel Planbureau (SCP) (2014) *Buergerperspectieven*, 4. The Hague: Sociaal en Cultureel Planbureau.

Spreitzer, Astrid (2015) 'Luxembourg's Chamber of Deputies and EU Affairs'. In Claudia Hefftler, Christine Neuhold, Olivier Rozenberg and Julie Smith (eds) *Palgrave Handbook on National Parliament and the European Union*. Basingstoke: Palgrave, pp. 232–251.

Spreitzer, Astrid and Arco Timmermans (2015) 'European Integration and the Flexibility of Consensus Democracies in the Low Countries'. In Hans Vollard, Jan Beyers and Patrick Dumont (eds) *European Integration and Consensus Politics in the Low Countries*. London: Routledge, pp. 48–68.

Sprungk, Carina (2013) 'A New Type of Representative Democracy? Reconsidering the Role of National Parliaments in the European Union'. *Journal of European Integration* 35(5): 547–556.

Staatssekretariat für Bildung, Forschung und Innovation (SBFI) (2016) *Berufsbildung in der Schweiz. Fakten und Zahlen 2016*. Berne: SBFI. Posted at www.sbfi.admin.ch/berufsbildung/01606/index.html?lang=de (acccessed 30 June 2016).

Stadelmann-Steffen, Isabelle and Karin Ingold (2015) 'Ist der Name schon Programm? Die GLP-Wählerschaft und ihre grünen freisinnigen Wurzeln'. In Markus Freitag and Adrian Vatter (eds) *Wahlen und Wählerschaft in der Schweiz*. Zürich: Verlag Neue Zürcher Zeitung, pp. 217–243.

Statista (2015) 'Ausgaben für Wahlwerbung in der Schweiz nach Parteien im Zeitraum April bis Oktober 2011 bzw. 2015 (in Millionen CHF)'. Posted at http://de.statista.com/statistik/daten/studie/463518/umfrage/wahlwerbeausgaben-in-der-schweiz-nach-parteien/ (accessed 3 January 2016).

Statista (2016a) 'Mitgliederzahlen der politischen Parteien in der Schweiz Stand Februar 2015*'. Posted at http://ezproxy.hwr-berlin.de: 2097/statistik/daten/studie/288709/umfrage/mitgliederzahlen-der-politischen-parteien-in-der-schweiz/ (accessed 14 January 2016).

Statista (2016b) 'Mitgliederzahlen der politischen Parteien in Österreich Stand September 2014'. Posted at http://ezproxy.hwr-berlin.de: 2097/statistik/daten/studie/288668/umfrage/mitgliederzahlen-der-politischen-parteien-in-oesterreich/ (accessed 14 January 2016).

Statistics Belgium (2015) *Chiffres Clés 2015. Aperçu Statistique de Belgique*. Brussels: Direction Général dStatistique.

Statistik Austria (2015) 'Gemeindegrößenklassen mit Einwohnerzahl 2015'. Posted at ///C:/Users/Jos%C3%A9/Downloads/gemeindegroessenklassen_mit_der_einwohnerzahl_2015.pdf (accessed 29 November 2015).

Statistik Austria (2016) *Statistisches Jahrbuch Österreichs*. Vienna: Statistik Austria.

Steiner, Jürg (1971) *Amicable Agreement versus Majority Rule. Conflict Resolution in Switzerland. Revised and Enlarged Edition*. Chapel Hill: The University of North Carolina Press.

Steiner, Jürg and Thomas Ertman (eds) (2002) *Still the Politics of Accommodation? Consociationalism and Corporatism in the Western World*. Special issue of *Acta Politica* 37(3–4).

Steiner, Reto and Claire Kaiser (2013) 'Administration communale'. In Andreas Adner, Jean-Loup Chappelet, Yves Emery, Peter Knoepfel, Luzius Mader, Nils Soguel and Frédéric Varone (Hrsg.) *Handbuch der öffentlichen Verwaltung in der Schweiz*. Zürich: NZZ libro, pp. 143–160.

Steininger, Barbara (2006) 'Gemeinden'. In Herbert Dachs, Peter Gerlich, Herbert Gottweis, Helmut Kramer, Volkmar Lauber, Wolfgang C. Müller and Emmerich Tálos

326 References

(eds) *Politik in Österreich. Das Handbuch.* Vienna: Manzsche Verlags- und Universitätsbuchhandlung, pp. 880–1077.

Steinmo, Sven, Kathleen Thelen and Frank Longstreth (eds) (1992) *Structuring Politics. Historical Institutionalism in Comparative Analysis.* Cambridge: Cambridge University Press.

Stelzer, Manfred (2013) 'Constitutional Change in Austria'. In Xenophon Contiades (ed.), *Engineering Constitutional Change. A Comparative Perspective on Europe, Canada and USA.* London: Routledge, pp. 7–34.

Stone Sweet, Alec (2000) *Governing with Judges. Constitutional Politics in Europe.* Oxford: Oxford University Press.

Streeck, Wolfgang C. (2010) *E Pluribus Unum? Varieties and Commonalities of Capitalism.* Max Planck Institut für Gesellschaftsforschung Discussion Paper 10/12. Cologne: MPIfG.

Streeck, Wolfgang and Martin Höpner (eds) (2003) *Alle Macht dem Markt? Fallstudien zur Abwicklung der Deutschland AG.* Frankfurt am Main: Campus.

Streeck, Wolfgang C. and Philippe Schmitter (eds) (1985) *Private Interest Government. Beyond the Market and the State.* London: Sage.

Studer, Brigitte (1996) ' "L'Etat c'est l'Homme": politique, citoyenneté et genre dans le débat autour du suffrage féminin après 1945'. *Schweizerische Zeitschrift für Geschichte* 46(3): 356–382.

Swenden, Winfried (2002) 'Asymmetric Federalism and Coalition Making in Belgium'. *Journal of Federalism* 32(2): 67–87.

Swiss Banks Settlement Fund (2014) 'Holocaust Victim Asset Litigation (Swiss Banks)'. Posted at www.swissbankclaims.com/ (accessed 18 July 2015).

Swyngedouw, Marc, Koen Abts, Sharon Haute, Jolien Galle and Bart Meuleman (2015) 'Het Communautaire In De Verkiezingen Van 25 Mei 2014Analyse Op Basis Van De Postelectorale Verkiezingsonderzoeken 1991–2014'. Onderzoeksverslag Centrum voor Sociologisch Onderzoek (CeSO) Instituut voor Sociaal en Politiek Opinieonderzoek (ISPO) CeSO/ISPO/2015–1. Posted at https://soc.kuleuven.be/ceso/ispo/downloads/Het%20communautaire%20in%20de%20verkiezingen%20van%202014.pdf (accessed 6 May 2016).

Taggart, Paul (2000) *Populism.* Buckingham: Open University Press.

Taggart, Paul (2004) 'Populism and Representative Democracy in Contemporary Europe'. *Journal of Political Ideologies* 9(3): 269–388.

Tálos, Emmerich (2006) 'Politik in Schwarz-Blau/Orange. Eine Bilanz'. In Emmerich Tálos (ed.) *Schwarz-Blau. Eine Bilanz des 'Neu-Regierens'.* Vienna: LIT, pp. 326–343.

Teffer, Peter (2014) 'Deal Reached on Centre–Right Government in Belgium'. EUObserver, 8 October. Posted at https://euobserver.com/news/125950 (accessed 25 July 2015).

Teggelbekkers, Friedrich (1974) *Das Politische System Belgiens.* Inaugural Dissertation zur Erlangung des Doktorgrades der Wirtschafts- und Sozialwissenschaftliche Fakultät der Universität zu Köln.

Telò, Mario (2006) *Europe: A Civilian Power? European Union, Global Governance and World Order.* Basingstoke: Palgrave.

Ten Napel, Hans-Martien (1999) 'The Netherlands: Resilience Amidst Change'. In David Broughton and Mark Donovan (eds) *Changing Party Systems in Western Europe.* London: Pinter, pp. 163–182.

Ter Steege, Dick, Esther van Groeningen, Rob Kujpers and Jo van Cruchten (2012) 'Vakbeweging en organisationsgrad van werknemers'. *Sociaaleconomische Trends,* 4e kvaartal, pp. 9–25.

References 327

The Flemish Republic (2008) 'Senator Karim Van Meire: Belgium Will Be Easier to Divide than Czechoslovakia', February/March. Posted at www.flemishrepublic.org/files/flemishrepublic_2008-21.pdf (accessed 2 January 2016).

Thelen, Kathleen and Sven Steinmo (1992) 'Historical Institutionalism in Comparative Politics'. In Sven Steinmo, Kathleen Thelen and Frank Longstreth (eds) *Structuring Politics. Historical Institutionalism in Comparative Analysis.* Cambridge: Cambridge University Press, pp. 1–32.

Therborn, Göran (1995) *European Modernity and Beyond. The Trajectory of European Societies 1945–2000.* London: Sage.

The Soufan Group (2015) *Foreign Fighters. An Updated Assessment of the Flow of Foreign Fighters into Syria and Irak.* New York: Soufan Group. Posted at http://soufangroup.com/wp-content/uploads/2015/12/TSG_ForeignFightersUpdate3.pdf (accessed 20 April 2016).

Thewes, Guy (2011a) *Les gouvernements du Grand-Duché de Luxembourg depuis 1848.* Luxembourg: Information and Press Service of the Luxembourg Government.

Thewes, Guy (2011b) *About ... History of Grand-Duchy of Luxembourg.* Luxembourg: Information and Press Service of the Luxembourg Government.

Thewes, Marc and Marc Glesener (2015) 'Perspektiven für eine moderne und lebendige Volkspartei. Reformpisten für die CSV'. Luxemburg: CSV. Posted at https://csv.lu/files/2015/01/PERSPEKTIVEN1.pdf (accessed 14 January 2016).

Thijs, Nick (2008) 'Modernising the Belgian Federal Administration'. In Centro di Formazione di Studi (Formez) (ed.) *Innovazione amministrativa e crescita. Volume 9.* Rome: Formez, pp. 379–417. Posted at http://biblioteca.formez.it/webif/media/Giannini_2/pdf/vol. 0911.pdf (accessed 9 May 2016).

Thomassen, J.J.A., van Ham, Carolien and Andeweg, R.B. (2014) *De wankele democratie. Heeft de democratie haar beste tijd gehad?* Amsterdam: Prometheus Bert Bakker.

Timmermans, Arco and Rudy B. Andeweg (2000) 'The Netherlands: Still the Politics of Accommodation'. In Wolfgang C. Müller and Kaare Strøm (eds) *Coalition Governments in Western Europe.* Oxford: Oxford University Press, pp. 356–398.

Toonen, Theo J. (1990) 'The Unitary State as a System of Co-governance: The Case of the Netherlands'. *Public Administration* 68(3): 281–286.

Tóth, Barbara and Hubertus Czernin (eds) (2006) *1986. Das Jahr, das Österreich veränderte.* Vienna: Czernin Verlag.

Touwen, Jerome K. (2008) 'How Does a Coordinated Market Economy Evolve? Effects of Policy Learning in the Netherlands in the 1980s'. *Labour History* 49(4): 439–464.

Touwen, Jerome K. (2014) *Coordination in Transition: The Netherlands and the World Economy 1950–2010.* Leiden: Brill.

Transparency International (TI) (2016) Corruption Perception Index 2015. Full ranking table at bottom of webpage. Posted at www.transparency.org/cpi2015 (accessed 28 April 2016).

Trausch, Gérard (2006) Le Conseil Economique et Social et la Societé Luxembourgeoise. Luxembourg: Conseil Economique et Social. Posted at www.ces.public.lu/fr/publications/trausch-gerard.pdf (accessed 14 September 2016).

Trausch, Gilbert (1981) 'Luxemburg'. In Frank Wende (ed.) *Lexikon zur Geshichte der Parteien in Europa.* Stuttgart: Kröner Verlag, pp. 387–393.

Trausch, Gilbert (2003) *Histoire du Luxembourg. Le destin européen d'un 'petit pays'.* Toulouse: Privat.

Treib, Oliver (2012) 'Party Patronage in Austria: From Reward to Control'. In Petr Kopécky, Peter Mair and Maria Spirova (eds) *Party Patronage and Party Government in European Democracies.* Oxford: Oxford University Press, pp. 31–53.

328   References

Tresch, Tibor Szvircsev, Andreas Wenger, Thomas Ferst, Sabina Pfister and Andreas Rinaldo (2015) *Sicherheit 2015. Aussen-, Sicherheits- und Verteidigungspolitische Meinungsbildung im Trend.* Zürich: Centre for Security Studies-Eidgenössische Technische Hochschule.

Tweede Kamer (2014) *De staat van de Tweede Kamer (2013).* Tweede Kamer de Staten-Generaal 2. Vergadejaar 2013–2014. Statistical overview provided by the library of the Tweede Kamer.

Tweede Kamer (2015a) *De staat van de Tweede Kamer (2014).* Tweede Kamer de Staaten Generaal. Vergadejaar 2014–2015. Posted at ///C: /Users/Jos%C3%A9/Downloads/De_ Staat_van_de_Tweede_kamer_ (2014)_%20 (1).pdf (accessed 30 May 2016).

Tweede Kamer (2015b) *Raming der voor de Tweede Kamer in 2016 benodigde uitgaven, alsmede aanwijzing en raming van den ontvangsten (34 183).* Vergaderjaar 2014–2015. Posted at www.tweedekamer.nl/kamerstukken/verslagen/detail?id=2015Z05869&did= 2015D29796 (accessed 3 July 2016).

Tweede Kamer (2016a) *De staat van de Tweede Kamer (2015).* Tweede Kamer de Staten Generaal. Vergadejaar 2015–2016. Posted at https://zoek.officielebekendmakingen.nl/ kst-34444-4.html (accessed 9 May 2016).

Tweede Kamer (2016b) Website posted at https://www.tweedekamer.nl/ (accessed 10 June 2016).

Ucakar, Karl (1985) *Demokratie und Wahlrecht in Österreich. Zur Entwicklung von politischer Partizipation und staatlicher Legitimationspolitik.* Vienna: Verlag für Gesellschaftskritik.

Ucakar, Karl (2006) 'Die Verfassung: Geschichte und Prinzipien'. In Herbert Dachs, Peter Gerlich, Herbert Gottweis, Helmut Kramer, Volker Lauber, Wolfgang C. Müller and Emmerich Tálos (eds) *Politik in Österreich. Ein Handbuch.* Vienna: Manz, pp. 119–138.

Ucakar, Karl and Stefan Geschiegl (2014) *Das politische System Österreichs und die EU.* Vienna: Facultas-WUV.

Uhl, Heidemarie (1992) *Zwischen Versöhnung und Verstörung: eine Kontroverse um Österreichs historische Identität fünfzig Jahre nach dem Anschluss.* Vienna: Böhlau.

Ulram, Peter A. (2006) 'Politische Kultur in der Bevölkerung'. In Herbert Dachs, Peter Gerlich, Herbert Gottweis, Helmut Kramer, Volkmar Lauber, Wolfgang C. Müller and Emmerich Talós (eds) *Politik in Österreich. Das Handbuch.* Vienna: Manz Verlag, pp. 512–525.

Unger, Brigitte (1999) 'Österreichs Wirtschaftspolitik: Vom Austro-keynesianismus zum Austro-Neoliberalismus?' In Ferdinand Karlhofer and Emmerich Talós (eds) *Zukunft der Sozialpartnerschaft. Veränderungsdynamik und Reformbedarf.* Vienna: Zentrum für angewandte Forschung, pp. 165–191.

Vanachter, Othmar (2004) 'Labour Law and the Division of Power between the Federal Level, the Communities and the Regions in Belgium'. In Othmar Vanachter and Martin Vranken (eds) *Federalism and Labour Law. Comparative Perspectives.* Antwerpen: Intesentia, pp. 21–48.

Van Bekkum, J., J.B.S. Hijink, M.C. Schouten and J.W. Winter (2010) 'Corporate Governance in the Netherlands'. *Electronic Journal of Comparative Law* 14(3): 1–35.

Vancoppenolle, Diederik and Marleen Brans (2010) 'Kabinetten als spil en het begijnhof voor de ambtenaren? Een vergelijkende analyse van de beleidsinteracties van kabinetsmedewerkers en ambtenaren in de Vlaamse beleibsvorming'. *Res Publica* 52(4): 483–512.

Vandaele, Kurt and Marc Hooghe (2014) 'L´appel de la voie communautaire: syndicats, organisations patronales et nouveaux movements sociaux dans une Belgique redimensionée'. In Régis Dandoy, Geoffroy Matagne and Caroline Van Wynsberghe (eds) *Le Féderalisme Belge. Enjeux institutionels, acteurs socio-politiques et opinions publiques.* Louvain-La-Neuve: Academia-L'Harmattan, pp. 139–176.

Van Dam, Peter (2012) 'Polarisierung und Poldermodell. Versäulung und Entsäulung in den Niederlanden seit 1945'. In Stefan Köppl and Uwe Krannenpohl (eds) *Konkordanzdemokratie. Ein Demokratietyp der Vergangenheit.* Baden-Baden: Nomos: Verlagsgesellschaft, pp. 99–116.

Van den Brande, Karoline (2012) 'Intergovernmental Co-operation for International Decision making in Federal States: The Case of Sustainable Development in Belgium'. *Regional and Federal Studies* 22(4): 407–433.

Vanden Bosch, Xavier (2014) 'The Belgian Parliament and EU Affairs: Reasons behind their Limited Involvement'. *European Policy Brief* no. 28, Egmont Institute. Posted at www.egmontinstitute.be/wp-content/uploads/2014/03/EPB-28-ENG-Parliaments.pdf (accessed 31 October 2015).

Van Den Wijngaert, Mark (2011) 'D'une Belgique unitaire à une Belgique fédérale'. In Mark Van Den Wijngaert (ed.) *D'une Belgique unitaire à une Belgique fédérale. 40 ans d'évolution politique des communautés et des regions (1971–2011).* Brussels: Academic and Scientific Publishers (ASP), pp. 19–38.

Van der Brug, Wouter (2003) 'How the LPF Fuelled Discontent: Empirical Tests of Explanations of LPF Support'. *Acta Politica* 38(1): 89–106.

Vander Linden, H. (1920) *Belgium. The Making of a Nation.* Oxford: Clarendon Press.

Van Deth, Jan and William Maloney (2015) 'Associations and Associational Involvement in Europe'. In José M. Magone (ed.) *Routledge Handbook of European Politics.* London: Routledge, p. 826–842.

Vandevivere, Claire (2001) 'The Federal Parliament of Belgium: Between Wishes, Rules and Practice'. In Andreas Maurer and Wolfgang Wessels (eds) *National Parliaments on their Ways to Europe: Losers and Latecomers?* Baden-Baden: Nomos Verlagsgesellschaft, pp. 77–97.

Van Dooren, Ron (2000) *Traditie en Transformatie. Politiek en staastsinrichting in Nederland.* Amsterdam: Instituut voor Publiek en Politiek.

Van Dyk, Silke (2006) 'The Polder Model and its Order of Consensus. A Foucauldian Perspective of Power and Discourse within the Process of Consensus Creation'. *Acta Politica* 41(4): 408–429.

Van Haute, Emilie (2011a) 'Le C&DV (Christen-Democratisch en Vlaams)'. In Pascal Delwit, Benoit Pilet and Emilie van Haute (eds) *Les Partis Politiques en Belgique.* Brussels: Edition de l'Université de Bruxelles, pp. 35–61.

Van Haute, Emilie (2011b) 'Volksunie, Nieuw-Vlaams Alliantie, Vlaams-Progressief et Spirit'. In Pascal Delwit, Benoit Pilet and Emilie van Haute (eds) *Les Partis Politiques en Belgique.* Brussels: Edition de l'Université de Bruxelles, pp. 201–218.

Van Haute, Emilie, Anissa Amjahad, Arthur Borriello, Caroline Close and Giulia Sandri (2013) 'Party Members in a Pillarised Partitocracy. An Empirical Overview of Party Membership Figures and Profiles in Belgium'. *Acta Politica* 48(1): 68–91.

Van Het Kaar, Robbert (2016) 'Netherlands: Working Life Country Profile', 25 November. Posted on European Observatory on Working Life (EurWork) website at www.eurofound.europa.eu/observatories/eurwork/comparative-information/national-contributions/netherlands/netherlands-working-life-country-profile (accessed 15 February 2016).

Van Holsteyn, Joop, Galen A. Irwin and Josje M. den Ridder (2003) 'In the Eye of the Beholder: The Perception of the List Pim Fortuyn and the Parliamentary Elections of May 2002'. *Acta Politica* 38(1): 69–87.

330   References

Van Holsteyn, Joop, J.M. Galen and A. Irwin (2004) 'The Dutch Parliamentary Elections of 2003'. *West European Politics* 27(1): 157–164.

Van Kersbergen, Kees (1999) 'The Dutch Labour Party'. In Robert Ladrech and Philippe Marliére (eds) *History, Organization, Policies*. Basingstoke: Palgrave, pp. 155–165.

Van Kessel, Stijn (2015) *Populist Parties in Europe: Agents of Discontent?* Basingstoke: Palgrave.

Van Leeuwen, Karin (2012) 'On Democratic Concerns and Legal Traditions: The Dutch 1953 and 1956 Constitutional Reforms "Towards" Europe'. *Contemporary European History* 21(3): 357–374.

Van Rie, Tim, Ive Marx and Jeroen Horemans (2011) 'The Ghent System Revisited: Unemployment Insurance and Union Membership in Belgium and the Nordic Countries'. *European Journal of Industrial Relations* 17(2): 125–139.

Van Schendelen, M.P.C.M. (1996) 'The Netherlands: From Founding Father to Mounding Baby'. In Philip Norton (ed.) *National Parliaments and the European Union*. London: Frank Cass, pp. 60–74.

Van Wynsberghe, Caroline (2014) 'Bruxelles, Sa Périphérie et l'Europe'. In Régis Dandoy, Geoffroy Matagne and Caroline Van Wynsberghe (eds) *Le Féderalisme Belge. Enjeux institutionels, acteurs socio-politiques et opinions publiques*. Louvain-La-Neuve: Academia-L'Harmattan, pp. 63–84.

Vatter, Adrian (2002) *Kantonale Demokratien im Vergleich. Entstehungsgruende, Interaktionen und Wirkungen politischer Institutionen in den Schweizer Kantonen*. Opladen: Leske+Budrich.

Vatter, Adrian (2007) 'Lijphart Goes Regional: Different Patterns of Consensus in Swiss Democracies'. *West European Politics* 30(1): 148–171.

Vatter, Adrian (2012) 'Vom Prototyp zum Normalfall? Die schweizerische Konsensdemokratie im Wandel'. In Stefan Köppl and Uwe Krannenpohl (eds) *Konkordanzdemokratie. Ein Demokratietyp der Vergangenheit*. Baden-Baden: Nomos Verlagsgesellschaft, pp. 51–72.

Vatter, Adrian (2014) *Das politische System der Schweiz*. Baden-Baden: Nomos-UTB.

Vauchez, Antoine (2015) 'Methodological Europeanism at the Cradle: Eur-lex, the *Acquis* and the Making of Europe's Cognitive Equipment'. *Journal of European Public Policy* 37(2): 193–210.

Verdun, Amy (2013a) 'Decision-making Before and After Lisbon: The Impact of Changes in Decision-making Rules'. *West European Politics* 36(6): 1128–1142.

Verdun, Amy (2013b) 'The Building of Economic Governance in the European Union'. *Transfer: European Review of Labour and Research* 19(1): 23–35.

Vereiniging van Nederlandse Gemeenden (VNG) (2008) *Local Government in the Netherlands*. The Hague: VNG.

Verhelst, Tom, Herwig Reynaert and Kristof Steyvers (2013) 'Necessary Asymmetry or Undemocratic Imbalance? Professionalisation in the Recruitment and Career of Belgian Local Councillors'. *Local Government Studies* 39(2): 273–297.

Verkiezingensraad (2015b) Official database on elections in the Netherlands (Local, provincial, Waterboards, Senate and Tweede Kamer). Posted at www.verkiezingsuitslagen.nl/Na1918/Verkiezingsuitslagen.aspx?VerkiezingsTypeId=4 (accessed 13 December 2015).

Visser, Jelle (2016) ICTWSS database, version 5.0. Amsterdam: Amsterdam Institute for Advanced Labour Studies AIAS, November 2015. Posted at www.uva-aias.net/208 (accessed 24 February 2016).

Vlaamse Belang Magazine (January 2007a) 'SOS Democratie-Des te populairder het Vlaams Belang wordt, des te harder slaat het Belgische regime terug met ondemocratische maatregelen van allerlei slag, p. 15. Posted at www.vlaamsbelang.org/files/vbm_200701.pdf (accessed 1 January 2016).

References 331

Vlaamse Belang Magazine (February 2007b) 'SOS Democratie-Het Vlaams Belang kan met plezier en niet zonder enige fierheid terugkijken op de stembusslag van 8 oktober 2006', pp. 10–11. Posted at www.vlaamsbelang.org/files/vbm_200702.pdf (accessed 1 January 2016).

Vocelka, Karl (2003) *Geschichte Österreichs. Kultur-Gesellschaft-Politik.* Munich: Heyne.

Voegelin, Eric (1938) *Politische Religionen.* Vienna: Bermann-Fischer.

Voermans, Wim J.M. (2013) 'The Constitutional Revision Process in the Netherlands: Sensible Security Valve or Cause of Constitutional Paralysis'. In Xenophon Contiades (ed.) *Engineering Constitutional Change. A Comparative Perspective on Europe, Canada and USA.* London: Routledge, pp. 257–273.

Vrooman, Cok, Mérove Gijsberts and Jeroen Boelhouwer (eds) (2014) *De hoofdzaken van het Sociaal en Cultureel Rapport 2014.* The Hague: Sociaal en Cultureel Planbureaun.

Wallace, William (1999) 'The Sharing of Sovereignty: The European Paradox'. *Political Studies* 47(3): 503–521.

Wallace, William (2005) 'Post-sovereign Governance: The EU as a Partial Polity'. In Helen Wallace, William Wallace and Mark A. Pollack (eds) *Policy-making in the European Union.* Oxford: Oxford University Press, pp. 483–503.

Wayenberg, Ellen, Filip de Rynck, Kristof Steyvers and Jean Benoit Pilet (2011) 'Belgium: A Tale of Regional Divergence?' In John Loughlin, Frank Hendriks and Anders Lindström (eds) *Oxford Handbook on Subnational Democracy in Europe.* Oxford: Oxford University Press, pp. 71–95.

Welan, Manfred (1999) *Der Bürgermeister in Niederösterreich.* Vienna: LexisNevis.

Wende, Frank (1981) 'Niederlande'. In Frank Wende (ed.) *Lexikon zur Geschicte der Parteien in Europa.* Stuttgart: Kröner Verlag, pp. 9–28.

Wernli, Boris (2002) 'Les élections fédérales helvétiques'. In Ulrich Klöti, Peter Knoepfler, Hanspeter Kriesi, Wolf Linder and Yannis Papadopoulos (eds) *Handbuch der Schweizer Politik.* 3. überarbeitete Auflage. Zürich: Neue Zürcher Zeitung, pp. 509–555.

Wessels, Wolfgang (2008) *Das politische System der Europäischen Union.* Wiesbaden: Verlag Sozialwissenschaften.

Weyrauch, Philine (2012) 'Belgien: Auf dem Weg zu einer tripartitischen Selbstverwaltung'. In Tanja Klenk, Philine Weyrauch, Alexander Haarmann and Frank Nullmeyer (eds) *Abkhehr vom Korporatismus? Der Wandel der Sozialversicherungen im europäischen Vergleich.* Frankfurt am Main: Campus, pp. 179–240.

Whitehead, Laurence (2001) 'Democratic Regions, Ostracism, and Pariahs'. In Laurence Whitehead (ed.) *The International Dimension of Democratization. Europe and the Americas. Expanded Version.* Oxford: Oxford University Press, pp. 395–412.

Wicki, Martin (2001) 'Sozialsicherung in der Schweiz: ein europäischer Sonderfall?' In Katrin Kraus and Thomas Geisen (Hrsg.) *Sozialstaat in Europa. Geschichte. Entwicklung. Perspektiven.* Wiesbaden: Westdeutscher Verlag, pp. 249–272.

Wiesli, Reto (2003) 'The Militia Myth: And Incomplete Professionalization'. In Jens Borchert and Jürgen Zeiss (eds) *The Political Class in Advanced Democracies. A Comparative Handbook.* Oxford: Oxford University Press, pp. 374–392.

Williams, E.N. (1999) *The Ancien Regime in Europe. Government and Society in the Major States 1648–1789.* London: Pimlico.

Wilp, Markus (2012) *Das politische System der Niederlande. Eine Einführung.* Wiesbaden: Springer Verlag.

Wimmer, Andreas and Nina Glicker Schiller (2002) 'Methodological Nationalism and Beyond: The Nation State Building, Migration and Social Sciences'. *Global Networks* 2(4): 301–334.

332 References

Wineroither, David (2009) *Kanzlermacht, Machtkanzler. Die Regierung Schüssel im historischen und internationalen Vergleich.* Vienna: LIT.

Wineroither, David (2012) 'Windstille oder Fahrtwind? Wandel und Zukunftsfähigkeit österreichischer Konkordanz'. In Stefan Köppl and Uwe Krannenpohl (eds) *Konkordanzdemokratie. Ein Demokratietyp der Vergangenheit.* Baden-Baden: Nomos Verlagsgesellschaft, pp. 73–98.

Witte, Els, Jan Crayeybeckx and Alain Meynen (2009) *Political History of Belgium. From 1830 Onwards.* Brussels: Academic Scientific Publishers.

Wolfgruber, Elisabeth (1997) 'Politische Repräsentation auf Länderebene: Die Landtage und ihre Abgeordneten'. In Herbert Dachs, Franz Fallend and Elizabeth Wolfgruber (eds) *Länderpolitik. Politische Strukturen und Entscheidungsprozesse in den österreichischen Bundesländern.* Schriftreihe des Zentrums für angewandte Politikforschung. Bd.14. Vienna: Signum Verlag, pp. 73–229.

Wolinetz, Steven B. (1989) 'Socio-economic Bargaining in the Netherlands: Re-defining the Post-war Policy Coalition'. In Hans Daalder and Galen Irwin (eds) *The Politics in the Netherlands. How Much Change?* London: Frank Cass, pp. 90–97.

Wood, Robert W. (2014) 100 Swiss Banks get US Ultimatum: Hand over Americans or Face Prosecution'. Forbes, 13 October. Posted at www.forbes.com/sites/robertwood/2014/10/13/100-swiss-banks-get-us-ultimatum-hand-over-americans-or-face-u-s-prosecution/ (accessed 18 July 2015).

World Economic Forum (WEF) (2015) *Global Competitiveness Report 2015–16.* Geneva: WEF.

World Economic Forum (WEF) (2016a) *The Global Gender Gap Report 2015.* Geneva: WEF. Posted at www3.weforum.org/docs/GGGR2015/cover.pdf (accessed 13 April 2016).

Zahlen, Paul (2016) 'Sur la confiance institutionelle et sociale'. *Regards 06*, March. Luxembourg: STATEC-Institut National de la statistique et des études economiques.

Zellhofer, Klaus (2005) 'Die Stunde der Berater'. In Nikolaus Dimmel and Josef Schmee (eds) *Politische Kultur in Österreich 2000–2005.* Vienna: ProMedia, pp. 107–115.

Z'graggen, Heidi (2009) 'Die Professionalisierung von von Parlamenten und Parlamentsmitglieder'. In Adrian Vatter, Fréderic Varone and Fritz Sager (eds) *Demokratie als Leidenschaft. Planung, Entscheidung und Vollzug in der schweizerischen Demokratie. Festschrift für Prof. Dr. Wolf Linder zum 65. Geburtstag.* Berne: Haupt, pp. 139–156.

Z'graggen, Heidi and Wolf Linder (2004) *Professionalisierung der Parlamente in internationalen Vergleich.* Studie im Auftrag der Parlamentsdienste der Schweizerischen Bundesversammlung. Posted at www.parlament.ch/d/dokumentation/berichte/weitere-berichte-und-studien/documents/ed-pa-prof-parl-int.pdf (accessed 16 October 2015).

Ziegler, Béatrice (1996) 'Frauenstimmrechtskampf in der Schweiz: zum Verhältnis von Frau und Staat'. *Schweizerische Zeitschrift für Geschichte* 46(3): 297–305.

Zirnig, Dieter (2014) 'Entwicklung und Überblick: Parteienmitglieder in Österreich', 23 November. Posted at https://neuwal.com/2014/11/23/entwicklung-und-ueberblick-parteimitglieder-in-oesterreich/ (accessed 14 January 2014).

Zürn, Michael (1998) *Das Regieren jenseits des Nationalstaats. Globalisierung und Nationalisierung als Chance.* Frankfurt am Main: Suhrkamp.

Index

Page numbers in *italics* denote tables, those in **bold** denote figures.

Aargau 35, 222–4
American Revolution 1776 35, 38
Amsterdam 92, 203–4, 213, 218, 279
Anseele, Paul 45
Appenzell-Innerrhoden 35, 122, 222–3
Aruba 65
associationism 100
Austria 2–3, 6–7, 9, 11–12, 14, 15–16, 18, 26–7, **29**, 31, 33–4, 36, 38–40, 42, 47–9, 54–6, 66, 69–71, 79, **80**, 81–5, 88, **89**, 90–3, **94–5**, 87–103, 107, **108**, 109, 112, 114–15, 117–21, 124, 127, **128**, 129, **134**, 136, **138**, 139–40, 142, 145, 147, 149, 150–1, 154–5, **158**, 159, 162, 164, **165**, 166–7, 170, 173, *174*, 175, 176, 180, **181**, 182, 184, 186–7, 188, **189**, 191–2, 195, 199, **200**, 201–5, 207–8, **209**, 210–11, **215**, 217, 222, 226, 228, **229**, 230, **231**, 232–4, 240, 242, 245–9, 253, 260, 262, **263–4**, 265–6, 268–71, 273, 274–5, 280–2; accession of European Union 1995 54; Alliance for the Future of Austria (BZÖ) 118, **128**, 132, **134**, 139, 199, 201, 203, 210, 55; Anschluss to Nazi Germany 1938 40; Austro-Hungarian monarchy 34, 39, 69, 228, 273; Austro-Marxism 39; Bundesländer *see* subnational government; Bundesrat *see* Parliament; Carinthia (Kärnten) *see* Carinthia (Kärnten) 55, 118, 203, **229**, 230, **231**, 232, 269, 274; Christian Socials (Christlich-Soziale) 39–40, 47, 112, 221, 228; Constitutional Court (Verfassungsgerichtshof) 69, 80, 83, 147, 154, 274; Constitutional information office (Verfassungsdienst) 155; executive

federalism (Vollzugsföderalismus) 47, 70–1, 184, 228, 232–3; First Republic (1918–1934) 40, 112, 120, 273; Freedom Party (FPÖ) 48, 54–5, 70, 79, 97, 102, **108**, 114, 117–19, 121, **128**, **131**, 132, **134**, 139, 142, 147, 151, 164, 166, 170–1, **181**, 187, 199, 201, 203, 210, 230, 232, 269, 271–2, 274–5; German nationals (Deutschnationalen) 39, 40; Habsburg monarchy 33–4, 36–9, 70; Hainburger Au Protests 102; Hypo Alpe Adria bank scandal 55, 203, 232; ideological camps (Lager) 47, 102, 268, 274; Kurt Waldheim affair *see* Waldheim, Kurt; Lagerstrasse 47; Landtage *see* subnational government; parity commission (*paritätische Kommission*) 48, 269–71; Parlament *see* Parliament; People's Party of Austria (ÖVP) 47–8, 55, 69, 97, **108**, 112, 118, 121, 127, **128**, 132, **134**, 139, 142, 151, 162, 164, **165**, 171, **181**, 187, 199, 201, 203, 230, 268–9, 271–2, 274; pillarisation and de-pillarisation *see* civil society; politics of memory (Vergangenheitspolitik) 54–6, 98; president 54–5, 69, 79, **80**, 81, 109, 139, 147, 151, 274; *Proporzdemokratie* 9, 47, 49, 55, 69–70, 97, 101, 114–15, 127, 151, 171, 230, 269–72; Raab-Kamnitz Kurs 48; referendum on Zwentendorf 1978 70, 102; Social Democratic Party of Austria (SPÖ) 97, 109, 112, 114, 118, 121, 127, 128, 132, 134, 139, 142, 162, 164, 165, 166, 181, 187, 201–2, 230; State Treaty of 25 May 1955 47–8; Voest conglomerate 48

334 Index

Balkenende, Jan Peter 58, 59, 130, 140, 149, **161**, 174
Basel 35, 223–4
Baudouin, King of Belgium 51
Beatrix, Queen of the Netherlands 51
Bech, Joseph 46, 53
Beerenbrouck, Charles Ruijs 43
Belgium 2–3, **6**, *7*, 9, 11, *12*, **14**, *15*, 16, 18, 21, 26–7, 31, 36–7, 38, 42–5, 51–2, 59–61, 66–7, *68*, 74, **75**, 79, 81–4, **87**, 88, **89**, 90–1, *92*, *93*, **94**, **95**, **96**, 99–101, 103, *108*, 109–11, 113–15, 117, 118, 120, 124, *126*, 127, 129, 132, **133**, 136, **138**, 139, 140, **141**, 142, 145, 148–9, 151–2, **157–8**, 159, *160*, 166, 170, 172–3, *174*, 175–7, 183, 186, *189*, 190–1, 194, *197*, 198, 201, 203, *204*, 207–8, *209*, 210–11, *215*, 217, 222, 226, 235, *236*, *237*, *239*, 240–2, 245–7, 249, 253, 258–62, **263**, **264**, 266, 268, 273–4; Brussels Islamic terrorist attacks 22 March 2016 61; Brussels-Capital *see* subnational government; Brussels-Halle-Vilvorde *see* Brussels-Halle-Vilvorde; Central Council of Economy (CCE/CRB) 52, 260; Christian Democrats and Flemish (CD&V) *108*, 115, *126*, 132, **133**, 160, *179*, *236*, 238; constitution of 1994 74, 82; constitution 1831 43, 67; Copernicus reform 136, 151; cordon sanitaire 60, 118, 177, 274; de-industrialisation 102; Democratic Humanist Centre (CDH) *108*, 111–12, 124, *126*, **133**, 160, 179, *236*; Dutch-speaking university in Ghent 45; federalisation process 61, 67, *68*, 69, 72, 82, 124, 159, 177, 183, 235, 258; Flemish Block/Flemish Interest (VB) 60, *108*, 115, 117–18, *126*, **133**, 139, 177, *179*, 183, 202, 235; Flemish Greens (Groen!) *108*, 114, *126*, 133, *160*, 179, *236*; Flemish Liberals and Democrats (VLD) *108*, 113, *126*, **133**, 160, *179*, *236*; Flemish National Association (VNV) 45; insurance companies (mutualités) 101; inter-war period 1918–1940 45; labour market 88, 91, 261–2; Loppem reform compromise November 1918 44; Louvain, La Neuve *see* Louvain, La Neuve; Marc Dutroux affair *see* Marc Dutroux Affair; Marshall Plan 4.0 (Wallonia) 8, 47, 50, 91, 239–40, 262, 279; Molenbeek *see* Molenbeek; National Council of Labour

(CNT/NAR) *see* interest intermediation systems; New Flemish Alliance (N-VA) 61, *108*, 111, 115, 118, 124, *126*, 132, **133**, 139, 159, *160*, *179*, 183–4, 235, *236*, 238; People's Union (VU) 115, *160*; pillarisation *see* civil society; political culture *see* political culture; Reform movement (MR) 20, 61, *108*, 113, 124, *126*, **133**, *160*, *179*, *236*; revolution of independence 1830 39; Rex Party 45; role of monarchy 51, 95–6; Sabena 60; School Pact of 1958 51–2, 68; Social Catholic Party (PSC) 51, 111, *160*; Socialist Party (PS) 109–10, *126*, **133**, 160; Socialist Party Different/Social Progressive Alternative (sp.a) 110, *126*, **133**, 160; state models 96; state reforms 67, *68*, 183, 235; Wallonia *see* Wallonia; Wallonian Greens (Ecolo) *108*, 114, 124, *126*, **133**, *160*, *179*, 236; welfare state 88, 91; 'welfare without work' 91; White March/White movement 60; Workers' Party of Belgium (POB) 60
Benelux (Belgium, Netherlands, Luxembourg) 16, 27, 33, 36, 38, 42, 47, 50–1, 66–7, 70, 72, 74, 79, 83, 87, 154, 156, 188, 208, 210, 247, 265, 278–80
Benya, Anton 270
Berlin Wall 1, 53–4, 112, 244
Bern 34–5, 41, 122, 170, 177, 222–7, 228
Bettel, Xavier 62, 67, 113, 143, 153, 162, **163**
Beyen, Johan 50
Blochhausen, Baron de 46
Bonaire 65
Bonaparte, Napoleon 32–3, 35
Braudel, Fernand 1, 24; *la longue durée* 24
Brazil 25
Bretton Woods system 244
Bruges 36
Brussels 37, 51, 61, 71, **75**, 84, 88, 92, 95, 113, 117, 120, 124, 132, 183, 206, 209, 235, *237*, 238, *239*, 240–2, 270
Brussels-Halle-Vilvorde (BHV) 68, 159
Bulgaria 57, **89**, **6**, *7*, *13*
Burgundy 33, 36–7; Duchy of Burgundy 33, 36–7; Order of Golden Vlies 36; Pragmatic Sanction 37; States-General 1477 36
Business Interest Association (BIAs) 251–2, 255–6, 258–9, 265–6, 268–9; Austria 268–9; Belgium 258–9; Luxembourg 265–6; Netherlands 255–6; Switzerland 251–2

Index   335

capitalism 1, 20, 23–4, 29, 32, 43–4, 47, 86, 243, 272, 276–7, 283; Chinese state capitalism 23; coordinated market economy 243; disorganised 28; liberal market economy 243; Manchester capitalism 243; organised 28; reorganised 28, 29; US-style capitalism 28; varieties of capitalism 243–7
Catholicism 37–8, 102
Central Planning Bureau (CPB) *see* Netherlands
Chambers 252, 265, 269–70; Austria 269–70; Luxembourg 265–6; Switzerland (cantonal) 252
Charles V, Emperor of the Habsburg Empire 33, 36
Charles VI King and Emperor of Austria 38
Charlotte, Grand Duchess of Luxembourg 46
China 23, 25, 53, 283
civil society 10–11, 13, 18, 21, 22, 26, 100–6, 212, 216, 278, 283
Coljin, Hendrikus 43
communism 20
consociationalism 3, 149, 176
constitution 63–85; flexible 4, 5, 63; rigid 5
corporate governance 244–7; Austria 246; Belgium 246; 'comply and explain' 2014/208/EU, 9 April 2014 246; Luxembourg 246; Netherlands 245–6; Shareholder Value Orientation (SVO) 246; Switzerland 247
corruption, political 48, 122–3, 232, 246, 251; Austria 48, 232; Belgium 60; Corruption Perception Index (CPI) 15; Group of of States Against Corruption (GRECO) 122–3; Luxembourg 62; Netherlands 246
Council of Europe 62–3, 122, 124
counter-reformation 33
Croatia **6**, *32*, **14**, 55, **89**
Curaçao 65
Cyprus **6**, *7*, *13*, **89**, 150, 280
Czech Republic *7*, *12*, 26, **89**, 117

De Man, Henri 45
decision-making trap (*Politikverflechtungsfalle*) 9, 148, 233
Dehaene, Jean Luc 59–60, 111, 149, *160*, 172, 174
Delors, Jacques 25, 277
democracy 1–32, 39–43, 47, 50, 56, 59, 70, 72, 85, 92–3, 95–6, 98, 100, 103–5, 110–12, 116, 118, 148, 151, 167, 169,

173, 181, 190, 199, 211–12, 214, 216, 218, 221–2, 224, 226, 230, 232, 238, 249, 257, 268, 272, 278, 280, 281, 282; concordance (*Konkordanzdemokratie*) 9; consensus 1–4, *5*, **6**, 7, *8*, 9–21, 23, 27, **28**, 29–31, 33, 38, 47, 50, 53, 59, 62–3, 67, 74, 85–6, **87**, 90–3, 96–7, 99–100, 105, 107, 109, 119, 122, 124, 127, 129, 136, **138**, 140, 143–9, 151, 156, **158**, 175–6, 181–2, 185, 188–9, 199, *205*, *209*, 210–11, 214, 216–18, 222, 241–5, 247–50, 260, 268, 272–3, 276–8, 280–3; consociational 2, 3, 9–10, 16, 40, 42, 149, 176; consultation democracy (*overleg democratie*) 3, 103, 257; liberal 20, 31; majoritarian 1, 3–4, *5*, **6**, *7*, 11, *12–13*, 82, 144–5, 148, 175; negotiated democracy (*Verhandlungsdemokratie*) 9, 32; power-sharing 5, 10, 230, 238; procedural 11, *12–13*; substantive 11, 18, 31; Westminster model *see* Westminster model
democratic peace 282
Den Uyl, Joop 51
Denmark **6**, *7*, 9, *12*, **14**, 89–90, 93, 101, *209*, 214, *215*, 249, 280
D'Hondt, Victor 44, 120, 230; D'Hondt electoral method 120, 230
Di Rupio, Elio 60–1, 149, *160*, 174, 238–9
Dijsselbloem, Jeroen 280
Dollfuss, Engelbert 40
Drees, Willem 50
Dupong, Pierre 46, 53
Dutroux, Marc 60, 94, 101

Economic Monetary Union (EMU) 26, 55, 60, 250, 280
economy 1–4, 10–11, 17–18, 20–31, 38, 41, 47–8, 50, 52–3, 58–60, 62, 90, 95, 98, 109, 113, 115, 119, 127, 167, 172, 181, 189, 190, 196, 217, 239, 243–72, 276–7, 281–3
Egmont, Count 37
electoral system 120–2; Austria 12; Belgium 120; Luxembourg 121; Netherlands 120; Switzerland 121–2
Estonia **6**, 7, 11, *12*, **89**, *209*
European Alliance of Liberals and Democrats (ALDE) 8
European Community for Steel and Coal (ECSC) 278
European Economic Area (EEA) **29**, 56, 114, 119

336 *Index*

European Economic Community (EEC) 279
European Free Trade Area (EFTA) 29, 56
European Greens 8
European Parliament 8, 61, 82, 127, 132, 184–5, *209*, 210, 238; European Union governance 278–82; intergovernmental conferences 8; Laeken declaration 2001 60
European People's Party (EPP) 8, 19
European Recovery Programme (ERP, also known as Marshall Plan) 8
European Socialist Party (ESP) 8
European Stability Mechanism (ESM) 25
European Union (EU) 55–7, 59, 64, 70–1, 117–19, 150, 196–7, 203–4, 206, 209, 227, 241, 246, 250–1, 255, 262, 267, 270, 275–82; College of Commissioners 8; Common Agricultural Policy (CAP) 277; Common Foreign and Security Policy (CFSP) 71, 282; Constitutional Treaty referendum June 2005 59, 64, 97, 206–7; Council of the European Union 8; European Commission 8, 25, 28, 61, 90, 150, 204, 208, 240, 245, 250, 275, 280; European Company Statute (societas europea) 245; European Council 8, 62, 150; European Court of Justice Costa/ENEL 1964 ruling 63
Europeanisation 63–4, 72, 116, 119, 185, 204, 242–5, 248, 250, 254, 270, 272, 275
Eurozone 26–7, **29**, 150, 210, 250, **263**, **264**, 280
Eyschen, Paul 46

Fascism 20, 40, 71
Faymann, Werner 55, 109, 164, *168*, 166, 201
federalism 4, 47, 70, 89, 71, 73, 88, 98, 111, 184, 222, 228, 232, 234, 241
Figl, Leopold 48
Finland **6**, *7*, 9, *12*, 54, **89**, *93*, *209*, *215*, 260, 280–2
Flanders 36, 44, 51, 110–11, 114–15, 117, 132, 177, 179, 235–6, *237*, 238, 239, 240–1, 261, 275
flexicurity *see* welfare state
Fordism *22*
foreign-born population *92*
France 6, *7*, 10–11, *12*, 14, 25, 34–5, 36, 38, 46, 54, 64, 66, 89, 92, *93*, 98, 145, 175, *209*, *215*, 248, 262, 273, 278–9, 280; French Revolution 1789 32, 35–6, 38, 72, 81, 147

Fribourg/Freiburg 34–5
Frieden, Luc 62

Geer, Dirk Jan 43
Geneva 104, 122–3, 178, *223*, 224
Germany **6**, *7*, 9, *12*, **14**, 16, 25, 34, 36–7, 39–40, 45–8, 51, 54, 83, **89**, 91–2, *93*, 98–101, 117, 118, 148, 167, 184, *209*, *215*, 240, 243–6, 248, 255, 257, 262, 266, 268, 272, 277–81; Customs union (Zollverein) 46; fall of Berlin Wall 1989 1, 53–4, 112, 244
Ghent 38, 45, 259–60
Glarus 35, 119, 122, 222, *223*, 224, 227
Global competitiveness index 15, 27
global governance 10, 17, **20**, 23, 25, 28, 149, 273, 283
globalisation 1–2, 18, **20**, 23–7, 29, 116, 242, 243–5, 248, 250–1, 271–2, 273, 275
glocalisation 24
golden thirty years (*trentes glorieuses*) 16, 269
Gorbach, Alfons 48
Gorbachev, Mikhail 54; glasnost' 54; perestroika 54
government 4, 8, 17–18, 21, *22*, 24, 28, 30, 34–5, 37, 41–55, 57–62, 64–5, 66, 67, *68*, 70–1, 73–4, **75–8**, 79, **80**, 81–5, 88, 91, 94, **95**, 97, 99–103, 107, 109, 111–18, 130, 132, 139–40, 142–3, 144–76, 179, 181–9, 191–204, *205*, 206–13, *214*, *215*, 246, 250–1, 253, 256–9, 261–2, **263**, 265, 267, 269–78, 281; Austria 54–5, **80**, 147, 150–1, 154, **155**, **158**, 164, *165*, 166–7, 170–1, *174*, 175; Belgium 149, 151, **152**, 154, 157, **158**, 159, *160*, 166–7, 171–2, *174*; cabinet governance 170–3; cabinet 145–8; government formation 146–70; government longevity 173–5; Luxembourg 150, 153, **154**, **158**, 162, *163*, 173, *174*, 175; Netherlands 149, **153**, 154, 157, **158**, 159, *161*, 166–7, 172, *174*; prime minister 148–56; Switzerland 147, 156, **157–8**, **168**, 169, 173
government, subnational 211–42; Austria 228–35; Belgium 228–42; Luxembourg 219–22; Netherlands 211–19; Switzerland 222–8
Grande Region (SaarLorLux) 221, 240
Gratz, Leopold 230
Graubünden 119, 122, 223, 226

Greece 5, **6**, **89**, *7*, *13*, 101, 150, *215*, 280
Group of States Against Corruption
(GRECO) *see* corruption, political
Gusenbauer, Alfred 55, 151, *165*

Haider, Jörg 54–5, 118, 170, 230, 232
Haslauer, Wilfried, Senior and Junior
230–1
Häuptl, Michael 230
Henri Grand Duke of Luxembourg 66
Hofer, Norbert 79, 136, 274
Hong Kong 53
Horn 37
Hungary 5, **6**, *7*, 10, *13*, **14**, 33, 66, **89**, 145

Iceland **6**, *7*, 9, *12*, 29, **89**, 145
income distribution *15*, *92–3*
India 25
industrial age 17, *22*
industrial relations *see* interest
intermediation
information age *22*, 29
interest intermediation 248–72; Austria
268–72; Belgium 258–62; Luxembourg
265–8; neocorporatism 248–51;
Netherlands 255–8; social partnership
18, 28, 48, 102, 171, 181, 249, 253–4,
258, 260, 268–71; Switzerland 251–14
Internet Corporation for Assigned Names
and Numbers (ICANN) 17
Iran 1
Iraq 92
Ireland **6**, *7*, 8, *12*, 23, **89**, 150; 'Celtic
Tiger' 8; northern Ireland 4
Islam 59, 102, 116, 119, 180; anti-Islam
parties 59; anti-Islamic sentiment 104;
Islamic State of Iraq and Syria (ISIS/
Daesh) *see* Islamic State of Iraq and Syria
(ISIS/Daesh); Islamic way of life 92;
Islamisation 119; Islamophobia 116, 117
Islamic State of Iraq and Syria (ISIS)/
Daesh) 92
Italy 5, **6**, *7*, *12*, **14**, 34, *93*, 97, 278, **108**

Japan 53
Jaspar, Henri 45
Judaism 102
Juncker, Jean-Claude 8, 61–2, 66, 150,
162, *163*, 173, 175, 220, 262, 280

Kamnitz, Reinhard 48
Kelsen, Hans 39, 69
Kirchheimer, Otto 107; People's Party
(*Volkspartei*) *see* political parties

Klaus, Josef 48, 151
Klestil, Thomas 55, 151
Klima, Viktor 55, 151, *165*, 170, 199
Kohl, Helmut 54
Kok, Wim 58, 149, *161*, 172–3, 212, 217,
255, 258
Konkordanzdemokratie *see* democracy
Krainer, Joseph, Senior and Junior 230
Kreisky, Bruno 48, 54, 147, 150–1, *165*,
170, 199
Kuypers, Abraham 42

La longue durée *see* Braudel, Fernand
Latvia **6**, *7*, *12*, **89**
Leopold III, King of Belgium 45, 51
Leterme, Yves 60, 111, 159, *160*
Lisbon Strategy (2000–2010) 24, 90;
Europe 2020 Strategy (2010–2020) 24,
90
Lotharingia 36
Louvain, la Neuve 52
Lubbers, Ruud 58, 149, 161, 172–3, 212,
217, 258
Lueger, Karl 39, 58, 149, *161*, 172–3, 212,
217, 255, 258
Luxembourg 3, 6, 7, 9–10, 12, 14, 15, 16,
18, 26, 27, 29, 30–1, 36–8, 42, 45–6,
51–3, 61–2, 65–7, 74, 76, 79, 81–2,
84–5, 87–91, 92, 93, 94, 95, 97, 99–103,
107, 108, 109–10, 112–14, 118, 121,
127, 129, 135, 136, 138, 139, 140, 141,
142, 145–6, 149–50, 153, 154, 158, 159,
162, 163, 164, 167, 170, 172–3, 174,
175–6, 182, 184, 186, 188, 189, 191,
193, 195, 201, 203–4, 205, 207, 209,
210–11, 215, 217, 219–22, 233–5, 240,
242, 245–9, 253, 260, 262, 263, 264,
265–8, 273–6, 278–9; Association for
the Support of Foreign Workers (ASTI)
103; Central Office of Legislation
(Service Central de Legislation) 154;
Christian Social People's Party (CSP)
52–3, 112, 127, *108*, *129*, **135**, 136, 143,
162, *163*, 182, 221, 275; Committee of
Liaison of Foreigners' Associations
(CLAE) 103; Committee of tripartite
coordination 53; constitution 1868 45,
74, 79, 81, 83, 85; constitutional revision
1919 46; Democratic Party (DP) 46, 53,
57, 109, 112–14, 135, 163, 182, 220;
Economic and Social Council (CES) 53,
267–8; Economic Union of Luxembourg
and Belgium (UELB) 46; Luxembourg
social model 53, 109, 265–7;

338 Index

Luxembourg *continued*
   Luxembourg Socialist Workers' Party
     (LSAP) 46, 53, 108, 109, 114, 127, 129,
     135, 136, 143, 162, 163, 182; Luxleaks
     62, 267; Monarchy referendum on 28
     September 1919 46; National Council of
     Foreigners (CNE) 103; Party of the
     Right (PdR) 46; Tripartite Steel Industry
     Conference 53

Malta **6**, *7*, *13*, **89**, 280
Margarethe of Flanders, Countess of
   Burgundy 36
Maria Theresia of Austria, Queen and
   Empress of Austria 33, 38
Marie Adelaide, Grand Duchess of
   Luxembourg 46
Marshall Plan *see* European Recovery
   Programme
Martens, Wilfried 59–60, 111, 149, *160*,
   166
Merkel, Angela 25
Metternich, Prince 34
Michel, Charles 61, 160, 239

National Socialism 20, 40, 43, 97
neocorporatism *see* interest intermediation
neo-institutionalism 21, 144; historical 21,
   144; sociological 21
neo-medievalism 20
Netherlands 2, 3, **6**, *7*, 9, 11, *12*, **14**, *15*, 16,
   18, 26–7, **29**, *31*, 36–8, 42–6, 50–2, 54,
   58–9, 61, 64–6, 74, 77, 79, 82–5, 87–8,
   89, 90–6, 99–101, 108, 110, 112,
   114–16, 120, 123–5, 127, 130–1, 136,
   138–42, 145–6, 148–50, 153, 157–9,
   161, 166, 170, 172–4, 176, 179, 184–7,
   189, 191, 199, 201, 201–6, 209–11,
   213–20, 222, 234, 240, 242, 245–7, 249,
   253, 256–8, 260, 262, **263**, **264**, 268,
   271, 274–6, 278–80; Anti-Revolutionary
   Party (ARP) 42, 111; Catholic People's
   Party (KVP) 50; Central Planning
   Bureau (CPB) 3, 50, 58; Charter for the
   United Kingdom of Netherlands (*Statuut*
   voor het Koninkrijk der Nederlanden)
   64–5; Christian Democratic Appeal
   (CDA) 108, 111, 116, 123, *125*, **131**,
   140, 161, 179–80, 216; Christian
   Historical Union (CHU) 111, 130;
   constitution/Basic Law (Grondwet) 65,
   74, 79, 81–3, 85; Dutch referendum on
   free trade agreement of EU with
   Ukraine 2016 59, 97; Dutch republic

   (1581–1795) 37–8; Freedom Party
   (PVV) *108*, 113, 116–17, 130, 140, 142,
   160, *161*, *180*, 210; Grand Pensionary
   (*Raadspensioneer*) 37; Groenlinks *108*,
   114, *125*, 140, 142, 179, *180*; High
   Court (*Hooge Raad*) 77; Industrial
   Organisation Law (*Wet op*
   bedrijfsorganisatie) 256; Labour
   Foundation (STAR) 103, 256, 271;
   Labour Party (PvdA) 50, 109, *125*, **131**,
   133, *161*, 180; Lockheed scandal 51;
   National Socialist Movement (NSB) 43;
   Old Age Law (*Algemene Ouderdomset*)
   1957 50; pacification (*pacificatie*) 42–3;
   Party of the Animals (PvdD) 55, 115,
   125, *180*; People's Party for Freedom
   and Democracy (VVD) *108*, 112, 116,
   123, *125*, **131**, 159, *161*, 179, 180, 216;
   Pillarisation *see* civil society; Pim
   Fortuyn List (LPF) 58–9, 116, *161*;
   political/civic culture *see* political/civic
   culture; privatisation programme
   (Lubbers governments) 58; Roman
   Catholic State Party (RKSP) 42;
   Scientific Council for Government
   Policy (WRR) 3; self-administrative
   bodies (ZBOs) 214; Social and
   Economic Council (SER) 51, 58, 256–8;
   Social democratic Workers' Party
   (SDAP) 42; Socialistische Partij *108*,
   110, *125*, *180*; Stadtholder (Stadhouder)
   37; State Council (Raad van de Staate)
   37; Union 50+ 115; Wassenaar
   Agreement 58, 255, 258
new public management 70, 73, 151, 171,
   212, 218
Nidwalden 34, 170, 222, *223*
non-governmental organisation (NGO) 17,
   100, 278
North Korea 1
Norway 6, *6*, 9, *12*, **29**, 54, **89**, 249

Obwalden 35, *178*, 222, *223*, 226
oil crisis of 1973 19
open method of coordination (OMC) 245;
   Petersberger Tasks 71; Treaty of
   Amsterdam 203; Treaty of the European
   Union (Maastricht) 1993 203, 206, 250;
   Treaty of Lisbon 203–4, 209
Organisation of Economic Cooperation
   and Development (OECD) 8–9, 11, 47,
   62, **87**, 190, 213–14, 224, 245, 247
Organisation of European Economic
   Cooperation (OEEC) 8, 279

Index

Organisation of Petroleum Exporting Countries (OPEC) 51
Ostend 38

Parliament 176–210; Austria 71, 180–1, 187, 199, *200, 205*, 208; Belgium 177, 186, 193–5, *197*, 202, *205*; Committee work 189–95; Controlling functions 201–3; European integration 203–10; Legislative process 195–201; Luxembourg 67, *129*, 181–2, 189, 193, 195, 197, 201, *205*, 203; Netherlands **97**, 179, *180*, 187–8, 191–2, 194, *198*, 202, *205*, 209, 275; parliamentary workload 186–9; Switzerland 98, 176, 182, 186–7
party funding 122–9; Austria124, 127–8; Belgium 124, 128; Luxembourg 127, 129; Netherlands 123–5; Switzerland 122–3
party patronage index *see* political parties
party system 130–43; decline of established parties 130–40; Effective number of Electoral Parties (ENEP) **141–2**; Effective number of Parliamentary Parties (ENPP) **141–2**; fragmentation 140–3; volatility 136–40
party, political 1–5, *7*, 8–9, 11, 21, *22*, 26, 27, 30, 39–42, 44–5, 46, 52, 55, 56–61, 66, 69–70, 79, **80**, 81–2, 86–7, 99, 101–5, 106–46, 148–9, 151, 156–7, **158**, 159, *160*, 162, *163*, 164, *165*, 166–72, 176–7, 180, *181*, *182*, 184–5, 190–8, 201, 203, 206, 210, 212–13, 216, 218, 221, 224–6, 230, 232, 236, 238, 240–1, 248–9, 251–4, 261, 268–9, 272, 274–5, 283; cartel party 22, 107, 111, 129, 143; Christian democrats 110–11; Communists 110; Greens 114–15; Liberals 112–14; mass party 22, 39, 42, 111; party patronage index 101; People's Party (Volkspartei) 40, 41, 47, 107, 112, 119; Populist new right 115–19; Regionalists and other parties 115; Social democrats/Socialists 109–10
peace 2, 10, 31, 33–5, 36–7, 39, 41, 47, 50, 52, 99, 105, 115, 117–18, 235, 258, 269, 275, 279; democratic peace 282; first and second peace of Kappel 35; peace of Westphalia (1648) 33–4; social 41, 50, 262
Philip II of Spain 36–7
Philip, the Bold, Count of Burgundy 36

pillarisation and de-pillarisation 42, 50, 100–5
Pittermann, Bruno 166
Poland **6**, *7*, 10, *12*, **14**, 33, **89**, 93, 167, 215
political/civic culture 93–9, 278; political cynicism 99; trust in main institutions 94–9
pooled shared 20, 24–5, 64, 250
populism 26, 74, 106, 115–19, 169, 180, 226, 230, 275, 277; Alpine populism 119, 34, 230, 246
Portugal 5, **6**, *7*, *12*, **89**, 97, 150, 190, *215*, 280
post-Cold War *see* War
Proporzdemokratie see democracy
Protestantism 102
Prüm, Pierre 46

Raab, Julius 48
re-equilibration
Reuter, Emile 46
Robespierre, Maximilien 147
Roman Holy Empire 32
Romania **6**, *7*, *13*, 57, **89**, 99, 145
Rotterdam 92
Russia **6**, 25–6, 34, 71; Soviet Union 47, 117
Rutte, Mark 59, 130, 159, *161*, 192, 207

Saba 65
Sallinger, Rudolf 40
Santer, Jacques 61, 92, 150, *163*, 175, 280
Sarkozy, Nicolas 25
Schönerer, Georg 39
Schuschnigg, Kurt 40
Schütz, Alfred 21
Servais, Emmanuel 45
Singapore 53
Sinowatz, Fred 151, *165*
Slovakia **6**, *7*, *13*, **89**, 280
Slovenia **6**, *7*, *12*, **89**, 280
Social and Cultural Planning Bureau (SCP) *see* Netherlands
Scientific Council for Government Policy (WRR) *see* Netherlands
social constructivism *see* sociological neo-institutionalism
society 17–18, 20–1, *22*, 29–30, 34, 38, 43, 47, 51, 86–105, 111, 199, 212, 216–17, 248, 252, 258, 266, 272, 278
Solothurn 34–5, *223*, 224, 227
South Korea 53

340 *Index*

sovereignty 20, 24, 47, 64–5, 145, 211, 250; legal sovereignty 65
Soviet Union *see* Russia
Spaak, Paul Henri 45, 50
Spain 5, *7*, 10–11, *12*, 33, 36, 66, **89**, *93*, 150, 167, *215*
St. Eustatius 65
St. Maarten 65
stagflation 28, 51
strategic management 2, 16–19, 24, 28, 276
sustainable governance indicators (SGI) 10–11, *12–13*
Sweden **6**, *7*, 9, *12*, 54, **89**, 91, 93, 123, *215*, 249, 260, 280–2
Switzerland 2, 3, **6**, *7*, 9, *12*, **14**, 15–16, 18, 26–7, 29, 31, 33–6, 40, 49, 54, 56–8, 69, 72–4, 78–9, 81, 82–4, **87**, **89**, 90–110, 112, 114, 119, 121–3, 127, 136–8, 141–2, 145, 147–9, 155–7, 167, 169–70, 173, 175–8, 182–3, 186–7, 189, 190–1, 193, 197, 201–2, 210–11, 214, 215, 217, 222–4, 226–8, 230, 234, 240, 242, 245, 247, 250–4, 260, 268, 271, 273–8, 281; Action for an Independent and Neutral Switzerland (AUNS) 56, 104–5, 281; amicable agreement 9, 49; autonomous adaptation (autonomer Nachvollzug) 250; Christian Democratic Party (CVP/ PSC) 98, 119, 123, 136, **137**, **168**, *178*, 196–7, 253; Citizens' Democratic Party (BDP) 41, 119, 124, 167, 169; civil war November 1847 36; constitution 1999 72–4, 79, 81, 84; economisation of politics (*Verwirtschaftlichung der Politik*) 41; EU bilateral agreements 29, 56–7, 250; Eurolex/Swisslex 56, 250; Eydgenossenschaft 1291 34; Farmers', Small Trade and Citizens' Party (BGB) 34, 41, 49, 167; Federal Administrative Court 83–4; Federal Administrative Court 83–4; Federal council (Bundesrat) 49, 90, 72, 78, 98, 105, 154; Federal Supreme Court 78, 83–4; Federal Supreme Court 78, 83–4; Helvetic Republic 35; Liberal Democratic Party (FDP/PLR) 40, *108*, 109, 114, 123, 136, **137**, 168, 178, 196, 253; magic formula 1959 49, 57, 81, **137**, 167, 169, 274; mental defence of the country (*geistige Landesverteidigung*) 56; National Council (Nationalrat) *see* Parliament; neutrality 35, 104, 119, 273, 281; Operation libero 105, 252; Parliament

see Parliament; Peace of Kappel in 1529 and 1531 *see* peace; people's rights (Volksrechte) 98; political culture *see* political/civic culture; referendums 57, 70, 73–4, 103–5, 226, 253, 281; Socialdemocratic Party of Switzerland (SPS) 41, *108*, 109, 119, 136, *178*; Swiss Bank Settlement Fund 57; Swiss People's Party (SVP) 41, 56–7, 98, 101, 104–5, *108*, 109, 112, 114, 119, 123, 136, 137, 139, 167–9, 173, *178*, 190, 196, 201, 226, 230, 253, 275, 281; Swisslex *see* Eurolex and autonomous adaptation; trade unions *see* trade unions; United Nations referendum 1986 104; welfare state *see* welfare state
Syria 92

Taiwan 53
Thorbecke, Rudolf 42, 211–13, 217
Thorn, Gaston 61, 162, 280
Ticino *223*, 224, 227
trade unions 252–3, 255–7; Austria 268–9, 271; Belgium 259–62; Luxembourg 265–8; Netherlands 255–7; Switzerland 252–3
Transatlantic Trade and Invest Partnership (TTIP) 254
trentes glorieuses see golden thirty years
Turkey **6**, *7*, *13*

Ukraine **6**, *7*; Dutch referendum on Ukraine 2016 *see* Netherlands
United Kingdom (UK) **6**, 11, *12*, **14**, 23, 64, 273, 280; New Labour government 4
United States of America (USA) 3, *7*, 8, 23, 25–6, 54, 57, 122, 145, 243–4, 254, 277, 279, 282–3
Uri 34, 122, 170, 222, *223*, 224, 226

Van Agt, Dries 51
Van der Bellen, Alexander 274
Van Gogh, Theo 59
Van Rompuy, Herman 60, 62, *160*
varieties of capitalism *see* capitalism
Verhandlungsdemokratie see democracy
Verhofstadt, Guy 60, 93, 95, 113–14, 149, *160*, 172, 174
Vienna Congress 1815 32–3, 35
vocational training (*duale Berufsbildung*) 247
Vranitzky, Franz 54–5, 147, 150–1, *165*, 170, 175, 199, 270
Waadt 108, 169–70

Waldheim, Kurt 54, 97, 151
Wales 4
war 113, 146, 151, 256, 260, 267, 269,
273, 278–9; Cold War 17, 23, 47; First
World War 273, 278; post-Cold War 17,
65; Second World War 113, 146, 151,
256, 260, 273, 278–9; Thirty Years'
War (1618–1648) 33
welfare state 1, 4, 11, 17, **20**, *22*, 28, 32,
48–50, 53–4, 58, 86–8, 90, 105, 112–13,
143, 242, 258, 260, 267, 275–7, 283;
de-commodification 276; flexicurity 30,
90, 276; social benefits per capita **89**;

social expenditure 86, **87**; social
investment 29–30, 86, 88, 276; workfare
20–1, 90, 276
Werner, Pierre 53, 61, 150, *163*
Westminster model *see* democracy
Wilders, Geert 59, 116, 117, 180
Wilhelmina, Queen of the Netherlands 43
William III, King of Netherlands 43, 45–6

Ypres 36

Zilk, Helmut 230
Zurich 34–5, 56, 122, 222, *223*, 224

Taylor & Francis eBooks

Helping you to choose the right eBooks for your Library

Add Routledge titles to your library's digital collection today. Taylor and Francis ebooks contains over 50,000 titles in the Humanities, Social Sciences, Behavioural Sciences, Built Environment and Law.

Choose from a range of subject packages or create your own!

Benefits for you
- Free MARC records
- COUNTER-compliant usage statistics
- Flexible purchase and pricing options
- All titles DRM-free.

Benefits for your user
- Off-site, anytime access via Athens or referring URL
- Print or copy pages or chapters
- Full content search
- Bookmark, highlight and annotate text
- Access to thousands of pages of quality research at the click of a button.

REQUEST YOUR FREE INSTITUTIONAL TRIAL TODAY

Free Trials Available
We offer free trials to qualifying academic, corporate and government customers.

eCollections – Choose from over 30 subject eCollections, including:

Archaeology	Language Learning
Architecture	Law
Asian Studies	Literature
Business & Management	Media & Communication
Classical Studies	Middle East Studies
Construction	Music
Creative & Media Arts	Philosophy
Criminology & Criminal Justice	Planning
Economics	Politics
Education	Psychology & Mental Health
Energy	Religion
Engineering	Security
English Language & Linguistics	Social Work
Environment & Sustainability	Sociology
Geography	Sport
Health Studies	Theatre & Performance
History	Tourism, Hospitality & Events

For more information, pricing enquiries or to order a free trial, please contact your local sales team:
www.tandfebooks.com/page/sales

Routledge
Taylor & Francis Group

The home of Routledge books

www.tandfebooks.com